D1565476

Studies in Music with Text

OXFORD STUDIES IN MUSIC THEORY

Series Editor Richard Cohn

Studies in Music with Text, David Lewin

Studies in Music with Text

DAVID LEWIN

2006

Oxford University Press, Inc., publishes works that further
Oxford University's objective of excellence
in research, scholarship, and education.

Oxford New York
Auckland Cape Town Dar es Salaam Hong Kong Karachi
Kuala Lumpur Madrid Melbourne Mexico City Nairobi
New Delhi Shanghai Taipei Toronto

With offices in
Argentina Austria Brazil Chile Czech Republic France Greece
Guatemala Hungary Italy Japan Poland Portugal Singapore
South Korea Switzerland Thailand Turkey Ukraine Vietnam

Published by Oxford University Press, Inc.
198 Madison Avenue, New York, New York 10016

www.oup.com

Library of Congress Cataloging-in-Publication Data
Lewin, David, 1933–
Studies in music with text / David Lewin.
p. cm.—(Oxford studies in music theory)
Includes bibliographical references and index.
ISBN-13 978-0-19-518208-8
ISBN 0-19-518208-1
1. Vocal music—History and criticism. 2. Musical analysis.
I. Title. II. Series.
ML1400.L48 2006
782—dc22 2005026738

This volume is published with generous support from the
Gustave Reese Publication Endowment Fund
of the American Musicological Society.

9 8 7 6 5 4 3 2 1

Printed in the United States of America
on acid-free paper

PREFACE

This book has been brought to completion with the collaboration of a small but dedicated group of people. Chief among them are Fred Lerdahl and Richard Cohn, both close personal friends and professional colleagues of my late husband, David Lewin. By early in 1998 David had essentially finished the manuscript, which was, in his words, "in not quite final form." For a variety of reasons, including deteriorating health, he set it aside. He intended perhaps to get back to it on his retirement from teaching at Harvard, which was imminent at the time of his death in May 2003. I was encouraged—urged, in fact—first by Fred Lerdahl and then by Rick Cohn, to make every attempt to bring the manuscript to publication. Fred in particular spent many hours facilitating this project.

Once Oxford University Press accepted the book, Edward Gollin joined our team. Ed had been David's Ph.D. student at Harvard and is now on the faculty of Williams College; he is intimately acquainted with David's work process, his written output, and his teaching methods. Ed was entrusted with preparing the manuscript for publication, reconciling inconsistencies, and putting it into "final form." All of the figures and examples, many of which had appeared in a variety of formats in previously published articles, were redrawn by Don Giller. My son, Alex Lewin, has advised me and helped with the creation of an electronic version of the text. Raphael Atlas, another of David's former students, generously offered his help with the final stages of preparation by indexing and proofreading the text.

I am particularly indebted to Jeanne Bamberger, Reinhold Brinkmann, Joseph Kerman, and Lewis Lockwood for their encouragement and support.

Special thanks to Kim Robinson and Suzanne Ryan, our editors at Oxford University Press, and to Eve Bachrach, Norman Hirschy, and the editorial staff at Oxford.

Finally, thanks are due to the Society for Music Theory and the American Musicological Society for their financial support of this project.

Our guiding principle throughout has been to present the text, as nearly as possible, exactly as David wrote it, respecting his intentions and avoiding the temptation to correct, update or "improve" it.

—June K. Lewin
Cambridge, Massachusetts

ACKNOWLEDGMENTS

My thanks to the following sources for permission to reprint material:

To *Current Musicology*, for permission to reprint "Figaro's Mistakes."

To Cambridge University Press, for permission to reprint "Music Analysis as Stage Direction."

To *Music Perception*, for permission to reprint "Music Theory, Phenomenology, and Modes of Perception."

To the University of Nebraska Press and to *19th Century Music*, for permission to reprint "*Auf dem Flusse*: Image and Background in a Schubert Song."

To *19th Century Music*, for permission to reprint "Amfortas's Prayer to Titurel, and the Role of D in *Parsifal*: The Tonal Spaces of the Drama and the Enharmonic C♭/B," and again for permission to reprint "Some Notes on Analyzing Wagner: *The Ring* and *Parsifal*."

To *The Journal of Musicology*, for permission to reprint "Women's Voices and the Fundamental Bass."

To *Perspectives of New Music*, for permission to reprint "Toward the Analysis of a Schoenberg Song," and again for permission to reprint "*Moses und Aron*: Some General Remarks, and Analytic Notes for Act I, Scene 1."

To Belmont Music Publishers, for permission to reprint Schoenberg's Opus 15, No. XI.

To *in theory only*, for permission to reprint "A Way into Schoenberg's Opus 15, Number VII" and "Vocal Meter in Schoenberg's Atonal Music, with a Note on a Serial Hauptstimme."

To the *Journal of Music Theory Pedagogy*, for permission to reprint "Some Problems and Resources of Music Theory."

I am very grateful to the Rockefeller Foundation for awarding me a residency at the Villa Serbelloni in Bellagio, Italy, during April 1997. There I accomplished a good deal by way of organizing previously published material, and also by way of writing up hitherto unpublished material. I owe special thanks to the staff at Bellagio for their amazing hospitality and unfailing courtesy, as well as for their formidable efficiency.

CONTENTS

INTRODUCTION

I have organized the book into sections determined mainly by the composers involved, in order of the times during which they flourished: Mozart, Schubert, Clara and Robert Schumann, Wagner, Brahms, Schoenberg (in his tonal, atonal, and twelve-tone phases), and Milton Babbitt (whom I count as following in the tradition). The arrangement is more than a mechanical convenience. Readers interested in music with text, but unfamiliar or uncomfortable with the music of Schoenberg and Babbitt, are likely to feel more at ease with the music of Mozart and Schubert, and—if drawn into the book through that port of entry and interested in continuing—will probably find the chronological arrangement a reasonable way to proceed through the material.

The essays do not fit completely within the historical containers assigned to them by the chronological arrangement of sections. Many of them touch on more general issues involving music with text. Two of the Mozart essays, for example, touch on Freudian slips made by characters in either text or music or both; another touches on relations between music analysis and stage direction. One of the Schubert essays is primarily about the phenomenology of listening; to illustrate its critical stance and technical apparatus it discusses a Schubert song in some depth. Two of the Schumann essays investigate a music-theoretical topic as they explore, within their respective songs, relations between minor tonality and Phrygian modality. Two of the Wagner essays discuss the nature, uses, and problems of an influential analytic system promulgated by Hugo Riemann at the end of the nineteenth century. One of them illustrates certain kinds of analytic observations, in such a context, that are facilitated by some theoretical concepts of my own devising. The Brahms essay brings to the fore ideas associated with Brechtian Epic acting style: it examines who the singers are in their social context, and what social roles they are fulfilling by performing the song. One of the Schoenberg essays explores that composer's attitude toward melody, rhythm, and meter in general, beyond the bounds of music with text; the sorts of observations made there resonate in an interesting way with some of Riemann's ideas about rhythm, though the essay does not explicitly engage those theories as such. Another Schoenberg essay brings to an operatic scene a method of large-scale analysis, pertinent to Schoenberg's hexachordal music in general, that sprang from my own theoretical work of the 1960s. Yet another essay, containing fairly extended analytic commentary on Schoenberg's second string quartet, primarily focuses on ways in which the traditional European musical canon uses women's voices; the essay interrelates that topic with aspects of fundamental bass theory from Rameau's *Traité* on.

As I review the essays, I find that most of them—one way or another, either explicitly or implicitly—involve a particular attitude toward texted European-American music of the nineteenth and twentieth centuries. I seem to be looking for ways in which music and text, in this repertory, *enact* each other. I like the term "enact" better than "read" or "allegorize," because the term emphasizes *gestural*—often even *bodily*—aspects of the interrelation.

I restrict myself to German tradition(s)—counting Babbitt in the line—partly in order to set reasonable boundaries on the work at hand, and partly because of my own familiarity with that tradition, as a matter of cultural background and musical training. I have done a certain amount of analytic work on scenes from Verdi, and I believe I could produce some interesting observations on vocal music with French text, by French composers, Debussy in particular.[1] I have as yet, however, published no analyses of texted works by Verdi, Debussy, or other composers outside my "German tradition," and—as just explained—I wanted to keep the subject matter of the present book reasonably bounded.

1. The curious reader will find various of my ideas about Debussy's music published in three places. "Some Instances of Parallel Voice-Leading in Debussy," *19th Century Music* 11.1 (1987), 59–72, explores the phenomenon of its title in various contexts, focusing on the *Violin Sonata*, *Le vent dans la plaine*, and *Canope*. *Generalized Musical Intervals and Transformations* (New Haven, Conn.: Yale University Press, 1987), 230–244, studies the first part of *Reflets dans l'eau*. Chapter 4 of *Musical Form and Transformation* (New Haven, Conn.: Yale University Press, 1993), 97–159, is an extended analytic study of *Feux d'artifice*.

Studies in Music with Text

PART I

Mozart

Each of the following three chapters engages an ensemble from *The Marriage of Figaro.* The restriction will allow us to concentrate on the composer's practice at one particular moment in his career. It will also enable us to observe variations in the behavior of certain characters as the drama develops through a variety of situations: Susanna appears in all three of the ensembles, and the Count in two.

The chapter entitled "Figaro's Mistakes" discusses the opening duet (*Cinque! Dieci!*). It transcribes a lecture I gave on January 28, 1993, for the Muriel Gardiner Program in Psychoanalysis and the Humanities of New Haven, Connecticut, a lecture that I subsequently repeated for the Symposium on Music and Psychoanalysis at Harvard University on October 16, 1993. I directed the lecture primarily at psychoanalysts educated in the traditional musical canon—they were my hosts in New Haven—and I had in mind as well a number of literary academics who attended the lecture there. I was concerned not to bore a number of musicians who attended the lectures, but I was not thinking of them primarily when I prepared the material. I subsequently published the lecture in *Current Musicology,* volume 57 (1995).

The chapter entitled "Musical Analysis as Stage Direction" was also composed as a lecture, given for the Conference on Music and the Verbal Arts at Dartmouth College, May 1988. It was subsequently published as a chapter in the proceedings of that conference, *Music and Text: Critical Inquiries,* edited by Steven Paul Scher (Cambridge, England: Cambridge University Press, 1992). The chapter puts forth some general ideas but focuses narrowly for its examples on the very opening of the first act trio, *Cosa sento!* The lecture had a twenty-minute time limit. When I wrote it up for the Dartmouth collection, I could have expanded it greatly, beyond the twenty-minute confines of the lecture. I could have gone on to address the rest of the number—which the present chapter does to some extent, but only fitfully and tangentially. Reprinting the essay here, I also could have expanded it by adding an appendix in response to some stimulating observations by Hayden White, who critiques the entire Dartmouth conference at the end of the Scher collection. But—after some thought and some sketching—I decided not to expand the essay at all, either while writing it up for its original publication or when reprinting it here. I like the way it makes its point and then gets offstage before becoming heavy or tiresome.

The chapter on the third act duet, *Crudel! perchè finora*, was written for this book; it has not appeared in public before, either as a lecture or in print.

A postscriptum for the Mozart section of the book reviews the different ways in which "tonics" and "dominants" enact drama, and are enacted by drama, in the three numbers studied. This leads to some thoughts about the uses and misuses of music-theoretical terminology in analyzing tonal music for the stage, and arguably in analyzing music more generally—whether traditionally tonal or not, whether for the stage or not.

CHAPTER One

Figaro's Mistakes

Freud, in the second of his *Introductory Lectures*, catalogues some common forms of erroneous performance, such as misspeaking, misreading, mishearing, and mislaying.[1] In that connection he analyzes various theatrical passages.[2] Today I propose to continue those lines of thought, analyzing the opening duet from Mozart's *The Marriage of Figaro*. There, as we shall see and hear, the musical aspect of the theater work lends special interest to Figaro's miscounting and mis-singing.

Example 1.1 Mozart/Da Ponte, *The Marriage of Figaro*, Act I, opening duet (from Robert Pack and Marjorie Lelash, *Three Mozart Libretti: Complete in Italian and English* [New York: Dover, 1993]; trans. David Lewin).

Camera quasi smobiliata. Figaro prende la misura d'un letto; Susanna prova il suo cappello di nozze.	A half-furnished room. Figaro is measuring a bed; Susanna is trying on her wedding hat.
Figaro: Cinque—dieci—venti—trenta— trenta sei—quarantatre.	F: Five—ten—twenty—thirty— thirty-six—forty-three.
Susanna: Ora sì, ch'io son contenta, Sembra fatto in ver per me.	S: Yes, now I'm happy. It really seems made for me.
F: Cinque—	F: Five—
S: Guarda un po', mio caro Figaro!	S: Just look, Figaro, dear!

(continued)

1. Sigmund Freud, *Vorlesungen zur Einführung in die Psychoanalyse* (Berlin: Gustav Kiepenheuer Verlag, 1955), 18–34. "Erroneous performances" translates *Fehlleistungen;* "misspeaking," "misreading," "mishearing," and "mislaying" translate *das Versprechen, das Verlesen, das Verhören,* and *das Verliegen,* respectively (18–19).
2. Freud, *Vorlesungen,* 18–34. Freud discusses passages from Schiller and Shakespeare on pages 32–34. In the third lecture, Freud also mentions a passage from Shaw (on page 51). It is curious that all three playwrights' names begin with the same phoneme. I have been unable to make a Freudian analysis of that, but I am sure that Freud himself would have found one, had we been able to ask him for free associations.

Example 1.1 cont.

F: Dieci—
S: Guarda un po', mio caro Figaro!
F: Venti—
S: Guarda un po',
F: Trenta—
S: Guarda un po', guarda adesso
il mio cappello,
F: Trenta sei—
S: Guarda adesso il mio cappello!
F: Quaranta tre.
S: Guarda un po' mio caro Figaro,
guarda adesso il mio cappello,
il mio cappello, il mio cappello!
F: Sì, mio core, or è più bello,
sembra fatto in ver per te,
sembra fatto in ver per te.
S: Guarda un po'!
F: Sì, mio core.
S: Guarda un po'!
F: Or è più bello.
S: Ora sì, ch'io son contenta,
Ora sì, ch'io son contenta,
sembra fatto in ver per me,
per me, per me!
F: Sì, mio core, or è più bello,
sembra fatto in ver per te,
per te, per te!
F & S: Ah! il mattino alle nozze
vicino, quant'è dolce al tuo (mio) tenero
sposo, questo bel cappellino vezzoso,
che Susanna ella stessa si fè.

F: Ten—
S: Just look, Figaro, dear!
F: Twenty—
S: Just look,
F: Thirty—
S: Just look, look at my hat now,
F: Thirty-six—
S: Look at my hat now!
F: Forty-three.
S: Just look, Figaro dear, look at my
hat now, my hat, my hat!
F: Yes, my love, it's prettier now, it really
seems made for you; it really seems
made for you.
S: Just look!
F: Yes, my love.
S: Just look!
F: It's prettier now.
S: Yes, now I am happy,
Yes, now I am happy,
it really seems made for me,
for me, for me!
F: Yes, my love, it's prettier now; it really
seems made for you, for you, for you!
F & S: Ah! with our wedding day so near,
how sweet for your (my) tender, tender
fiancé is this pretty, charming little hat,
that Susanna herself has made.

I shall first play the number. The text, with my translation, appears as Example 1.1. Before listening, you should know that Figaro and Susanna, about to marry, are servants in the employ of Count Almaviva, that the Count has been making harassing advances toward Susanna, that Figaro does not yet know of those advances, and that the bedroom that the Count is providing for the couple lies close to his own quarters. [Here I played a recording.]

One immediately notices tension and conflict in the opening of the scene. Susanna, anxious about the marriage and confronting a serious problem with the Count, is looking to Figaro for affection and support. Figaro is compulsively evading Susanna's appeals; he is clearly terrified by the bed he is measuring, in which he will have to measure up to what he imagines as Susanna's sexual expectations. Using the magic of his phallic measuring instrument, he is trying to avoid confronting such menacing female symbols as the bed and the flowery hat, not to mention the woman herself, and the imminent marriage. "Don't distract me," he is saying in effect, "I am trying to do serious and difficult male business." The ten-

Example 1.2 Beaumarchais, *Le marriage de Figaro* (from the nineteenth edition, Pierre Richard, ed. [Paris: Classiques Larouse, 1934], 45).

F: Dix-neuf pieds sur vingt-six.	F: Nineteen by twenty-six.
S: Tiens, Figaro, voilà mon petit chapeau: le trouves-tu mieux ainsi?	S: Well, Figaro, there's my little hat; do you like it better this way?
F: (lui prend les mains) Sans comparaison, ma charmante. Oh! que ce joli bouquet virginal, élevé sur la tête d'une belle fille, est doux le matin des noces, à l'oeil amoureux d'un époux!	F: (taking her hands) Incomparably, my charmer. Oh! how sweet, on the wedding morning, is this pretty bridal bouquet crowning the head of a beautiful girl to the amorous eye of a fiancé!

sions are particularly clear if one compares the opening of our scene to the opening of the Beaumarchais play (Example 1.2).

The French Figaro is not compulsively measuring and remeasuring; he has just finished measuring. He has measured the room, not the bed. Furthermore, when Susanna asks him for concern and reassurance, he is right there, understanding her emotion even though he is not yet aware of her problem with the Count; his flowery response immediately gives her everything she wants. Going back to the Italian libretto of Example 1.1, we can see that the drama of the operatic scene is constructed around Susanna's gradually winning Figaro's attention, allaying his anxieties sufficiently for him to allay hers. That process, as we shall see, is essentially musical rather than textual.

Example 1.3 Mozart/Da Ponte, *Marriage of Figaro*, I, opening duet, numerical series.

5 10 20 30	36	43
Multiples of 5; ruler or tape presumed so grouped	6 more; estimated final measurement?	7 more; nonsense.

Before proceeding to the music, though, let us review the numerical series 5, 10, 20, 30, 36, 43, provided by Mozart's librettist Da Ponte. Example 1.3 will help us out.

The idea, I think, is this. Figaro begins measuring 5, 10, 20, 30, and we infer that his measuring instrument is ruled in groups of five units. The measurement 36, 6 more than 30, then makes sense only as an estimated final measurement. But then the whole structure collapses with 43, which is 7 more than 36. The joke is one of the *lazzi* associated with stage business in the commedia dell'arte tradition; one imagines Figaro holding up his measuring tape or rod to the audience after each announcement. [I acted his doing so, while speaking the pertinent numbers.] The business is very thematic for the opera, which throughout contrasts the obsessive calculations of its men—calculations that always go haywire—with the appeals for recognition and love from its women.

Example l.4a shows aspects of Mozart's response to Da Ponte's joke. The music is the version of Figaro's measuring theme played by the violins in measures 1–6. Beneath the music is some commentary showing how the rhythm suggests measuring in groups of 5 units; this is a strong mimetic cue for the actor measuring the bed. [Here I sang the violin theme and acted measuring "1, 2, 3, 4, 'Cinque'" in

Example 1.4 Mozart, *Marriage of Figaro*, I, opening duet.

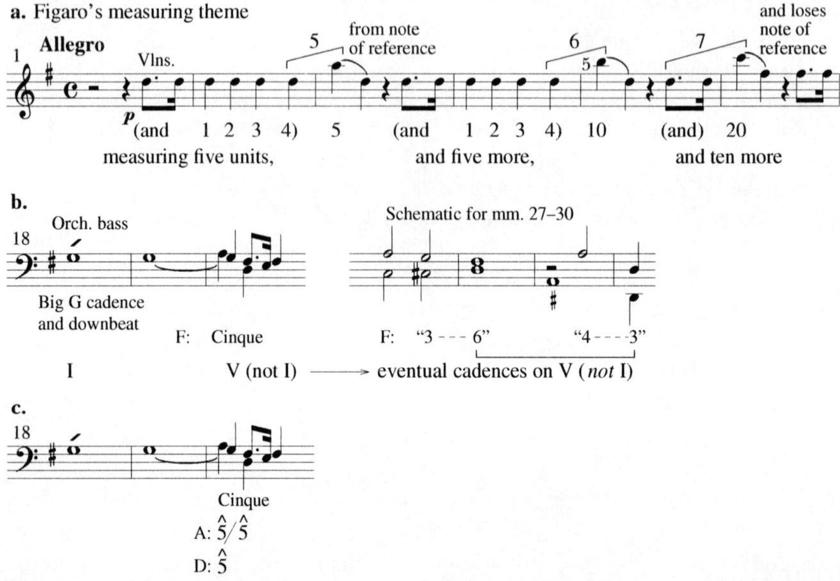

rhythm.] More commentary appears above the music; it shows how the theme first measures off the bracketed interval of a *fifth* from the melodic note of reference [here I played the bracketed fifth], then the interval of a *sixth* [simile], and then the interval of a *seventh* [simile], after which the note of reference is lost. The numerical scheme correlates perfectly with Example 1.3: An interval of 5 becomes an interval of 6, which becomes an interval of 7, after which the structure breaks down. In both text and music, the idea of the expanding intervals, followed by a deflating collapse, is suggestive in connection with the phallic aspect of Figaro's compulsive and unsuccessful measuring.[3]

Example 1.4b shows another "five-ish" aspect of Figaro's theme, now in the sung version. Measure 18, the cadence of the orchestral introduction, provides a big tonic downbeat in G major [I played into the cadence and remarked, "that's what I mean by 'tonic downbeat'"]; two measures later, when Figaro first sings, his vocal motive changes the harmony from tonic to dominant, that is, to the harmony on the *fifth* degree of the key. [I played I–V in G, then relevant G and D harmonies from the passage.] Harmonically, Figaro's entrance thus asserts both not-tonic and dominant. The theme as a whole cadences on a strong dominant, expanding this gesture. The right side of Example l.4b schematically shows the cadence. Note that there are actually two dominant cadences here: First the music cadences on the dominant at the sung number 36, following the model of the orchestral introduction. [I played the cadence, singing "trenta sei."] The number 36 is the estimated final measurement. But Figaro still has the "mistake" number 43 to sing; in order

3. The discussion around Examples 1.3 and 1.4a uses some material from my earlier article, "Some Musical Jokes in Mozart's *Le Nozze di Figaro*," *Studies in Music History: Essays for Oliver Strunk*, ed. Harold Powers (Princeton, N.J.: Princeton University Press, 1968), 443–447.

to get it in, he extends the music two more measures, to provide a new and confirming cadence on D. [I played the cadence, singing "quaranta tre."] The idea of *extending* the Figaro theme thus arises from the superfluous and ill-fitting mistaken measurement of 43.

Example 1.4c focuses in on the way in which "Cinque" changes the tonic harmony to dominant. Figaro's first sung note, the A of "Cin-," turns the tonic G into a suspension dissonance [I played the pertinent music, singing "Cin-"; then I sang "Cin-" while playing G]; the dissonant G then resolves into the dominant harmony, with the sung D of "-que" as its bass. [I did appropriate singing and playing here.] The fifth of "Cinque," A to D, is not $\hat{5}$ to $\hat{1}$ in G [playing D–G], but rather $\hat{5}$-of-$\hat{5}$ to $\hat{5}$ [playing A–D]. Figaro, that is, characteristically moves *to* the dominant, even elaborating it with its own dominant. The move from A to D will later expand into a large-scale tonal progression, when Figaro first sings Susanna's theme [I played and sang the beginning of "Sì, mio core"]; as sung at that time, in Figaro's key of D, the theme moves from A harmony to D harmony. [I played quickly through the "Sì, mio core" theme, emphasizing the D harmonies at its beginning and end. Then I played A–D, saying "Cinque."]

G as tonic key and harmony, of course, represents the proper state of affairs. Susanna's theme, as originally presented, moves from D to G, from dominant to tonic [I played its beginning and end in G]. Later on in the opera, the wedding ceremony begins in G major [I played its opening]; G major is also the key in which the final reconciliation of the Count with the Countess will occur [I played "Contessa, perdono!"]. Figaro's emphatic rejection of G harmony and G key, in Examples 1.4b and 1.4c, can thereby be associated with his compulsive evasion of Susanna's emotional appeals, at the opening of the scene.

Example 1.5 Mozart, *Marriage of Figaro*, I, opening duet.

	Pass 0:
Introduction:	*Figaro's theme:* rejects G, goes to D; rejects tonic, goes to dominant. *Susanna's theme:* from D to G, from dominant to tonic (Codetta: subdominant and cadence)
	Pass 1:
F: Cinque—dieci—venti—trenta— trenta sei—quarantatre S: Ora sì, ch'io son contenta, Sembra fatto in ver per me	*Figaro's theme:* rejects G, goes to D rejects tonic, goes to dominant *Susanna's theme:* from D to G from dominant to tonic
	Pass 2:
F: Cinque— S: Guarda un po', mio caro Figaro! F: Dieci— S: Guarda un po', mio caro Figaro! F: Venti— S: Guarda un po', F: Trenta—	*Figaro's theme:* because of Figaro's big mistake, Susanna can take control of his theme.

(continued)

Example 1.5 cont.

S: Guarda un po', guarda adesso il mio cappello,	
F: Trenta sei— S: Guarda adesso il mio cappello! F: Quaranta tre. S: Guarda un po' mio caro Figaro, guarda adesso il mio cappello, il mio cappello, il mio cappello!	After the first D cadence (36), she leads the theme's extension for "43" to an A cadence, and extends that extension, prolonging A harmony.
F: Sì, mio core, or è più bello, sembra fatto in ver per te, sembra fatto in ver per te.	*Susanna's theme, sung by Figaro!:* He can sing it because he is on A, the dominant of D. The theme goes from dominant to tonic, but now in D, so that he can move to D.
	Pass 3:
S: Guarda un po'! F: Sì, mio core. S: Guarda un po'! F: Or è più bello. S: Ora sì, ch'io son contenta, Ora sì, ch'io son contenta, sembra fatto in ver per me, per me, per me!	After four measures confirming the local D tonic, Susanna leads Figaro through rising notes of the D harmony, (somewhat in the manner of *Figaro's theme*). Introducing C natural, she changes the D from a local tonic back to a global dominant (seventh).
F: Sì, mio core, or è più bello, sembra fatto in ver per te, per te, per te!	And Figaro follows along.
F & S: Ah! il mattino alle nozze vicino, quant'è dolce al tuo (mio) tenero sposo, questo bel cappellino vezzoso, che Susanna ella stessa si fè!	Now it is time to sing *Susanna's theme;* Figaro obliges, singing together with her, *supporting her* as she goes from D to G, and from dominant to tonic.

The top sections of Example 1.5 summarize some features we have observed anent the metaphorical interplay of music and drama. Pass 0 (the orchestral introduction) and Pass 1 both present the Figaro theme as rejecting tonic and moving to dominant, rejecting G and moving to D, rejecting the real state of affairs and moving into his erroneous computing fantasy. Pass 0 and Pass 1 both present the Susanna theme as moving from Figaro's dominant back to tonic, moving from Figaro's D back to G, attempting to pull Figaro back from his fantasy to the exigencies of the dramatic reality. Pass 1 extends the Figaro theme, as already noted, to fit in the superfluous and mistaken number 43.

Example 1.6 shows how Figaro makes a crucial mis-singing mistake at the beginning of Pass 2. The G-major tonic downbeat that begins the music is now provided not by a purely orchestral introduction, but by the cadence of Susanna's actual sung theme, on the word "me!," Figaro is so distracted by her audible person that he starts his theme wrong when he tries it again. He starts singing a measure and a half too soon. In the previous versions of the Figaro theme, the "Cinque" motive came in exactly two measures after the tonic G downbeat, in a relatively strong metric position. [I played the pertinent music, emphasizing the downbeat.] But now

Example 1.6 Mozart, *Marriage of Figaro*, I, opening duet, mm. 36–40.

the motive appears only a half measure after the big G downbeat, in a very weak metric position. [I played the pertinent music, emphasizing the downbeat.]

Furthermore, Figaro mis-sings the characteristic fifth of "Cinque" [playing it], singing instead a fourth [playing it], so distracted is he by Susanna. Instead of contradicting the tonic note G, making it dissonant by singing A as in Example 1.4c [playing it], he now accepts, sings, and reverberates the tonic note G on which he has just heard Susanna cadence [playing Susanna's G and Figaro's subsequent "Cinque"]. We can imagine him thinking at Susanna, "Now look what you've made me do! I'll never get this measuring done properly if you keep disturbing me."

Example 1.6 shows Susanna's response to Figaro's blunder. She takes Figaro's mistaken sung G and moves it to the correct note A at the correct time, two measures after the G downbeat. [I played the music from Susanna's "me!" through her "Figaro!," putting a strong accent on the latter.] We may imagine the subtext sketched on Example 1.6: "Oh dear, let me help. You meant to sing on A at this moment, didn't you, Figaro dear?" And Figaro echoes her "correction" a half-measure later, with his "dieci" on A. [I played the A–D while singing "dieci."] The pitches are now correct, a half-measure late, but the number is now wrong, "dieci" instead of "cinque" on the sung fifth. Figaro continues echoing the note Susanna gives him, as he did two measures earlier with her G. This state of affairs continues through the theme; Example 1.6 shows the next stage, where Susanna leads Figaro by the nose to the note B at the right time, and Figaro echoes her "correct" pitch a half-measure later, using the number that belongs a measure and a half later, all of this in relatively weak metric positions. [I played and sang the pertinent music.]

One must admire the dramatic complexity of Susanna's musical behavior here; it is at once hypocritically helpful, manipulative, and truly helpful. It is hypocritically helpful because Susanna has no desire to help Figaro with his maniacal miscalculations, as her tune might suggest to him. In that sense she is being manipulative, seizing control of his theme and of the dramatic flow. There is indeed a Strindberg drama just under the surface of the opera, and it is important to recognize the Punch-and-Judy aspects of the farce. Peter Sellars's recent production showed how effective that directorial approach can be (though he did not apply it to this scene). The problem with the Sellars production, I feel, is not that the approach is false, but rather that it brings the Strindberg drama right up to the surface, as secondary elaboration, rather than leaving it lurking under the surface, as primary process. And that distorts other aspects of the classical comedy. Finally, Susanna is being really helpful here, because her manipulations are directed toward a loving and therapeutic end, to get Figaro back on track with reality, and with their relationship. As we shall see, she will allow him considerable space to work out his psychic problems on his own terms.

Example 1.7 Mozart, *Marriage of Figaro*, I, opening duet.

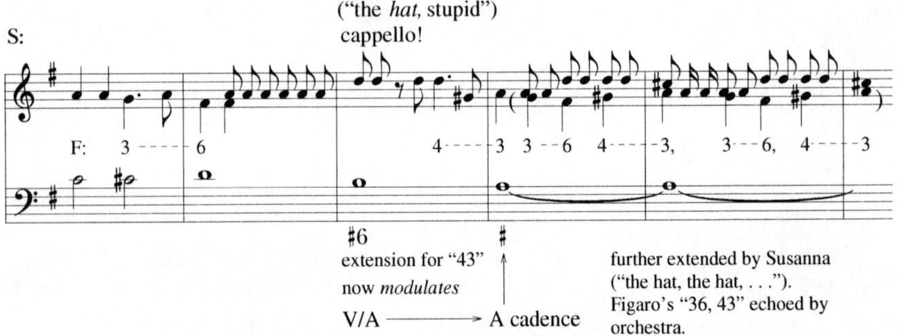

Example 1.7 shows that Susanna, in leading Figaro through his Pass 2 theme, finally gets him together with the correct number "36" at the correct time for the usual D cadence that has always set the text "36" (the estimated final measurement). [I played and sang the beginning of Example 1.7.] We shall explore later just how she does this. As before, the theme must now be extended so that Figaro may sing the superfluous number "43." Susanna continues to lead; now she controls the extension so that the music, instead of making another D cadence as before, modulates to A major, the dominant of D, and cadences there, followed by an extra extension prolonging A major. [I played and sang the pertinent music.] In modulating to A, Susanna actually lands on the dominant of A [playing the harmony at "capello!"], that is, the dominant of the dominant of the dominant in the main key. [I played E–A–D–G harmonies as I said "dominant," etc.] In presenting Figaro with a heap of piled-up dominants in this way, Susanna is further solicitously making amends for having caused him to sing her tonic harmony at the beginning of Example 1.6. Figaro, as we have heard, likes dominants; they are a way of manifesting his obsession with fives. When Susanna, on Example 1.7, presents him with the dominant of A, he is all too happy to sing "43," believing that he is now in control of the situation, in a very dominant position.

Among the other nice things about the A harmony, for Figaro, is that it can serve as the dominant of his favorite key D. We noticed that on a small scale in Example 1.4c; there the fifth of his first sung music, the fifth of his original "Cinque," was A to D [playing it]. Now that Figaro is on a big A harmony at the end of Example 1.7, he can proceed to his favorite key D via a big tonal expansion of the A-to-D motif.

And a theme lies conveniently at hand that will enable him to carry out that idea. It is Susanna's theme, which leads a local dominant to its local tonic. Accordingly, Figaro sings Susanna's theme in the key of D. [I played the pertinent phrase.]

In doing so, he must proceed from local dominant to local tonic, something he has not done before. On the other hand, by treating D as the local tonic, he can satisfy his urge to sing music that aims for D harmony, being consistent with his earlier behavior. Susanna's modulation to A has thus provided Figaro with an occasion to exult in his favorite harmony of D; he has only to acknowledge her presence by singing her theme. In this way, both characters give some to get some. As before, Susanna's behavior is at once hypocritically helpful, manipulative, and truly helpful. In particular, the helpful transaction between the couple, each giving and getting, could not have taken place without her initiative. (Example 1.5 summarily logs the musical analysis we have been making to the right of the text for Pass 2.)

At the end of Pass 2, Figaro believes himself satisfied. He has established D major as tonic, and Susanna has recognized his desire to do so, temporarily abandoning her distracting G major, even helping him by providing the occasion for him to establish the key. Susanna, however, is not yet satisfied. Figaro has noticed her hat, the ostensible subject of her nagging, but he has not yet acknowledged her real concerns, of which the hat is only a symbol—that is, her anxiety over the forthcoming wedding and her uncertainty over the extent to which he will support her in future complications involving the Count. D major is the key of Figaro's calculating, not the key of their love.

Accordingly, Susanna has yet to establish G major, to get Figaro to agree to G major, and to win from him the emotional acknowledgment she needs. These ideas are sketched on Example 1.5, to the right of the text for Pass 3. During this pass, as the commentary explains, Susanna leads Figaro through rising notes of the D harmony, somewhat in the manner of the Figaro theme [playing pertinent music]. Then she introduces C natural, the seventh of the D harmony [playing it]. (This is the interval "7" of Example 1.4a [playing it], the interval where the Figaro theme and the calculating numbers have always broken down before.) The seventh of the harmony changes D from a local tonic, back to a global dominant. Figaro is happy to follow Susanna along, since she has already obliged him by her earlier leading behavior, which allowed him to attain his favorite key. And after they linger on the dominant-seventh harmony [playing the "lingering" music], he is happy to accompany her as she sings her theme in G, from dominant to tonic, from D harmony to G harmony. [I played quickly through that music.] She has already given him what he wanted; now he reciprocates in kind. He is not just singing along with her, he is *supporting her* in counterpoint as she sings her theme. Her machinations-cum-therapy, that is, have served their purpose.

There follows a coda, prolonging G major with various cadences. Particularly amusing is the motive Susanna sings right after the big downbeat that begins the coda (shown on the right side of Example 1.8).

Here, Susanna's falling fifth, D to G, on her text "Susanna!" [playing it] is the G-major answer to Figaro's D-major falling fifth, A to D, on his opening "Cinque" [playing it]. Susanna's fifth is the "right" fifth for the tonality, and as the final text says, "Susanna herself made it."

Example 1.9 studies in further detail the vicissitudes of the Figaro theme in Passes 0, 1, and 2, where Susanna takes control of it. The three versions are aligned by their bass lines. That is a significant formatting, since alignment by consecutive

Example 1.8 Mozart, *Marriage of Figaro*, I, opening duet.

bar lines would give quite a different picture; so would alignment by the numbers of the series 5, 10, and so forth. In the formatting of Example 1.9, the beginnings of the three versions all align at the big G downbeats, and the D cadences at the number 36 all align.

Pass 0 is completely orchestral, so the numbers under the violin part on the example are bracketed; they correlate with the numbers Figaro sings in Pass 1. It takes two measures to get from the G downbeat to the number 5, two more measures to get from there to the number 10. Then Figaro's rate of measuring increases: It takes only one musical measure to get from 10 to 20, and only one measure to get from 20 to 30. After that Figaro's measuring calms down again, taking two measures again to get from 30 to the estimated final measurement, 36. The theme cadences there, and there is no music for the erroneous number 43 in this first version of the theme.

In the Pass 1 version, Figaro is singing, calling out the numbers, and not just silently measuring. Very audible from the example is the way in which he squares off the rhythm of the Pass 0 version. The numbers are called off at a regular rate, a number every two measures. [While acting the measuring, I tapped off the quarter-note beats with my foot, calling out the numbers at regular temporal intervals.] The calm and steady rate of Figaro's pronouncements makes a hilarious cognitive dissonance against the nonsense of his number series. We see at the end of the Pass 1 version how the embarrassing extra number 43 necessitates extending the theme beyond the Pass 0 version; here, as observed earlier, the thematic extension confirms the D cadence, thereby preserving Figaro's dignity to a certain extent.

In Pass 2, the measures underlie the measures of Pass 0 perfectly, up to the D-major cadence at the number 36. One hears thereby how Figaro's anxiety surfaces again, disturbing his "rational" every-two-measures rhythm of Pass 1. As discussed earlier, the number 5 of Pass 2 comes one and a half measures too early, compared to Pass 1, and its pitches are wrong. Alternatively, we could say that the pitches A–D of Pass 2 come a half-measure too late, with the wrong number. This state of affairs continues up to the measure marked "adesso"; that is where the word (meaning "now") first appears in the text. According to the pattern established so far, Figaro ought to sing "36" at the point marked "now." But Susanna activates her singing rhythm into eighth notes just here, to distract Figaro from that idea [playing her line]. She pauses only a measure later, enabling Figaro to get himself into phase with the tune so that he can sing "36" at just the proper moment, the D cadence [playing it yet once more]. In this way Susanna helps Figaro get back on track, after his initial blunder.

Example 1.9 Mozart, *Marriage of Figaro*, I, opening duet, Passes 0–2.

Example 1.10 Mozart, *Marriage of Figaro*, I, opening duet.

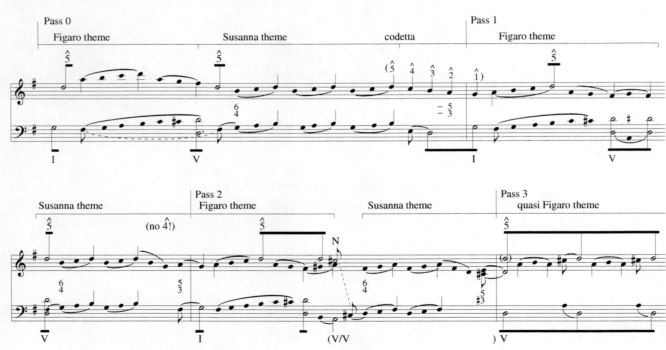

Pass 0
Figaro theme
Susanna theme
codetta
Pass 1
Figaro theme
$\hat{5}$ $\hat{5}$ ($\hat{5}$ $\hat{4}$ $\hat{3}$ $\hat{2}$ $\hat{1}$) $\hat{5}$
6 4
5 3
I V I V

Susanna theme
Pass 2
Figaro theme
Susanna theme
Pass 3
quasi Figaro theme
$\hat{5}$ (no $\hat{4}$!) $\hat{5}$ N $\hat{5}$
6 4
5 3
6 4
5 ♯3
V I (V/V) V

Example 1.10 cont.

Example 1.9 beautifully illustrates Mozart's virtuosity in projecting large-scale rhythmic complexities. There are three different time-systems on the example. In one system, we count the passing of time by the progress of the bass line; this is the system that controls the underlay format of the example. A second, different, system marks the passage of time by the Newtonian or Kantian time-flow of the measures; in this system, Passes 0 and 2 contract the longer time-flow of Pass 1, presumably reflecting Figaro's anxiety. A third and yet different time-system marks the passage of time by the numbers 5, 10, and so forth of Figaro's measuring series; this is the time-system in which Figaro's "Cinque" of Pass 2 is judged as one and a half measures too soon, rather than a half-measure too late. Mozart's compositional virtuosity here is much subtler than that in the notorious passage from *Don Giovanni,* where three different bands are playing three different dances at the same time, in different rhythms.

Example 1.10 is a Schenkerian analysis of the number, up to the end of Pass 3, omitting the coda. [I said that the best way for nonmusicians to get a sense of the symbols was to listen to a performance that projected them. Then I played Example 1.10, using sustaining, accenting, phrasing, and pedaling to project the assertions of the sketch.] The beamed tones with open noteheads on the treble clef constitute a Schenkerian *Urlinie;* they build a structural line that is supported by a bass using notes of the G harmony to form an *Ursatz.* The *Urlinie* descends from $\hat{5}$ of the G-major scale, stepwise down through $\hat{4}$, $\hat{3}$, $\hat{2}$, and $\hat{1}$. The descent from $\hat{5}$ to $\hat{1}$, step by step, is delightfully thematic here as a "Cinque." A lower-level structural descent from $\hat{5}$ to $\hat{1}$ in the melody takes place at the end of Pass 0, to foreshadow the larger structure.

Up until the beginning of Pass 3 the melodic D, the $\hat{5}$ of the *Urlinie*, is in force. In particular, Susanna's theme in Passes 0 and 1 puts structural weight on its D [playing the opening of the theme with weight on the D], rather than its B [playing the music with weight on the B]. It is only with Susanna's C natural of Pass 3, marked with a $\hat{4}$ and an exclamation point on the example, that the structural line can begin to descend from $\hat{5}$. In particular, after that $\hat{4}$, the line descends to $\hat{3}$ (with exclamation point), when Susanna's theme begins for the last time. The structural weight of the theme thus shifts here, to fall on the B [playing] rather than the D [playing]. At the end of the example, one hears how the little Susanna motif in the coda [playing it] summarizes the overall descent of the *Urlinie* [playing it].

Figaro's mistakes, as we have just seen, eventually lead him to reaffirm his commitment to Susanna, thanks to her insightful management of the situation. Figaro, in German, *verspricht sich* first in one sense (making slips of the tongue) and then in the other sense (promising himself to Susanna in marriage). Freud, I think, would have been pleased.

CHAPTER Two

Musical Analysis as Stage Direction

I propose here two linked ideas about Classical music theater. First, I suggest that each analytical observation about the music-cum-text intends (*inter alia*) a point of dramatic direction. Second and conversely, I suggest that each intuition we have about the behavior of characters on stage naturally seeks its validation (*inter alia*) through musical-textual analysis. To oversimplify the matter in a brief maxim: no analysis without direction; no directing without analysis. The maxim makes my ideas sound more like imperatives than they need be taken as here; for present purposes I will propose only that it is often fruitful to proceed according to the maxim. Meaning to demonstrate that method, rather than to promulgate my particular readings as such, I shall study fairly closely a short passage from Mozart's *Le Nozze di Figaro*. The passage, comprising a solo by the Count, and a subsequent solo by Basilio, opens the first act trio "Cosa sento!"

We shall consider the Count's solo first. In numerous analysis courses, I have found most people ready to articulate a directorial intuition that the Count is confused, uncomfortable, not in good control of himself or his situation. Most people will also articulate an analytic observation that the Count has trouble making a firm cadence on the tonic, that the cadence on "sento" is somehow unconvincing, that the Count must work hard—too hard—to achieve the eventual cadence at the end of his solo. These people readily accept the implications of the maxim here, that their directorial intuitions and their analytic observations about the music are bound together in a reciprocal relation. That is: one feels the Count is not in control because one observes a musical problem about his early attempt to assert a tonic cadence; conversely, one's attention is drawn to the feebleness of the cadence on "sento" because one has a directorial impression of the Count as unsure of himself, as not in command.

The idea of command will be a useful point of departure for the continuation and elaboration of our analysis-cum-direction. It will be helpful to inspect the text. Example 2.1 gives in its left column Da Ponte's text for the end of the recitative and the beginning of the trio; in the right column, the example aligns the corresponding French of Beaumarchais.[1]

1. The Italian text is taken from Robert Pack and Marjorie Lelash, *Mozart's Librettos* (Cleveland, 1961), 114–116. The French is taken from Beaumarchais, *Le Mariage de Figaro*, vol. 1, ed. Pierre Richard, in the series Classiques Larousse (Montrouge, 1934), 60.

Example 2.1 Italian and French text for the opening of the first act trio in *Figaro*.

(IL CONTE *si alza da dietro la poltrona.*)	LE COMTE *se lève.*
IL CONTE: Come! Che dicon tutti?	—Comment, tout le monde en parle!
DON BASILIO (*a parte*): Oh bella!	SUZANNE. —Ah ciel!
SUSANNA (*a parte*): O cielo!	BAZILE. —Ha, ha!
[The recitative ends; the trio begins]	
IL CONTE: Cosa sento! Tosto andate E scacciate il seduttor.	LE COMTE. —Courez, Bazile, et qu'on le chasse.
DON BASILIO: In mal punto son qui giunto; / Perdonate, o mio signor.	BAZILE: —Ah! que je suis fâché d'être entré!
SUSANNA: Che ruina! Me meschina! Son' oppressa dal terror!	SUZANNE, *troubleé.* —Mon Dieu! Mon Dieu!

The trio begins just where the Count, in the French, issues his first command of the play: "Courez, Bazile, et qu'on le chasse." The preceding scenes of the play, in which we have seen the Count behaving as a philanderer, not an overt authority figure, are set as recitative in the opera.[2] Da Ponte and Mozart thereby put emphasis on the Count as someone who is supposed to take charge of things; his command to Basilio is virtually the first thing he sings in the opera with full orchestral support.

But the qualification of "virtually" is critical. Da Ponte inserts into the text at the opening of the trio, before the Count's command, the exclamation "Cosa sento!" Da Ponte's Count begins the trio still in the grip of confusion and outrage, and only then pulls himself together to issue his command. In a play without music, the exclamation would be redundantly ineffective. Its point has already been made more effectively on the stage by the Count's rising from concealment at the beginning of Example 2.1, and by his text at that point. Da Ponte presumably inserted the text "Cosa sento!" so that Mozart could portray the Count's confusion and outrage by a big orchestral effect at the beginning of the trio. Da Ponte, specifically, might have anticipated something like Example 2.2.

Measures 1 through 3 of the example portray the confused outrage of "Cosa sento!" by a loud agitated tutti that elaborates a dominant-seventh harmony, demanding resolution. Measures 4 and 5 provide the resolution into a tonic cadence; here the hypothetical Count, with calm and quiet accompaniment takes command both of himself and of the situation; here he can appropriately issue the textual command "Tosto andate." The new motive of measures 6 and 7, which continues past the end of Example 2.2, is appropriate to the gesture of searching; it can easily take the text "e scacciate." The hypothetical setting of Example 2.2 is useful as a norm to keep in mind when analyzing Mozart's actual setting, shown in Example 2.3.

2. To be sure, Susanna has been made all too aware of the Count's political authority, while he has gone through the cruel pretence of approaching her as a simple lover. We share her awareness through her. Still, we have not seen his authority exercised on stage before this point.

Example 2.2 Hypothetical setting for mm. 1–7.

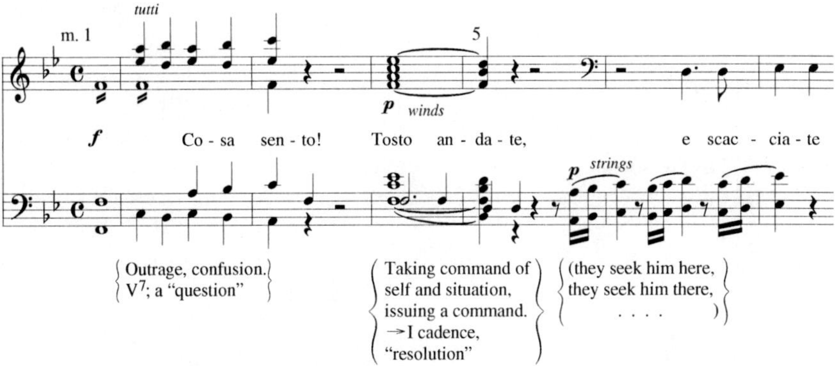

Mozart essentially sets the gestural profile of Da Ponte's text as per Example 2.2. But he consistently displaces the actual words forward in time; thus, in Example 2.3, the text for measures 4–5, "Cosa sento," goes gesturally with the music of measures 1–3, and the text for measures 6–7, "Tosto andate," goes gesturally with the music for measures 4–5. The text "e scacciate," which goes gesturally with the

Example 2.3 Actual setting for mm. 1–7.

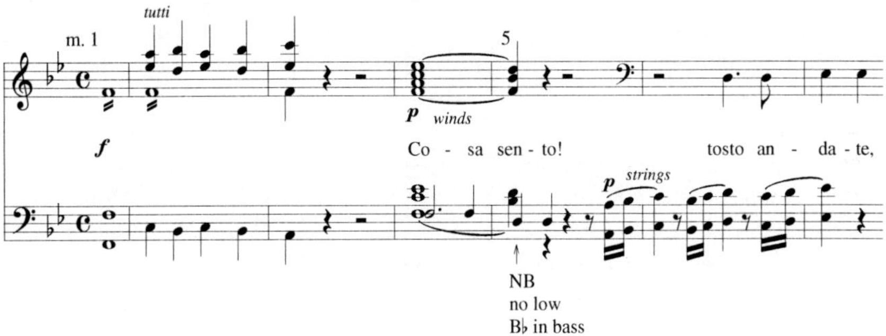

music of measures 6–7, has not yet appeared on Example 2.3; like the preceding text, it will also appear a couple of measures "too late."

This analysis of Mozart's setting gives pointed theatrical direction to the actor singing the Count. Mozart's Count does not give impetus to the music by his verbal utterances, as an effective authority figure should—as the hypothetical Count of Example 2.2 does. Rather, he consistently takes his verbal cues from whatever music he has just heard, and then reacts to his impressions. As a stage director, I am specifically suggesting, for example, that the actor should take the loud agitated music of measures 1–3, and not Basilio's earlier gossip, as a cue for the reaction "Cosa sento!" during measures 4–5. "What do I hear" in measures 1–3? Mozart thereby rehabilitates Da Ponte's theatrically redundant exclamation, providing a new, completely musical cue for the Count, a cue to which he can respond on the spot. The notion may seem farfetched to a scholar, but it will be very clear (and

Example 2.4 The Count takes cues for his text from the immediately preceding music.

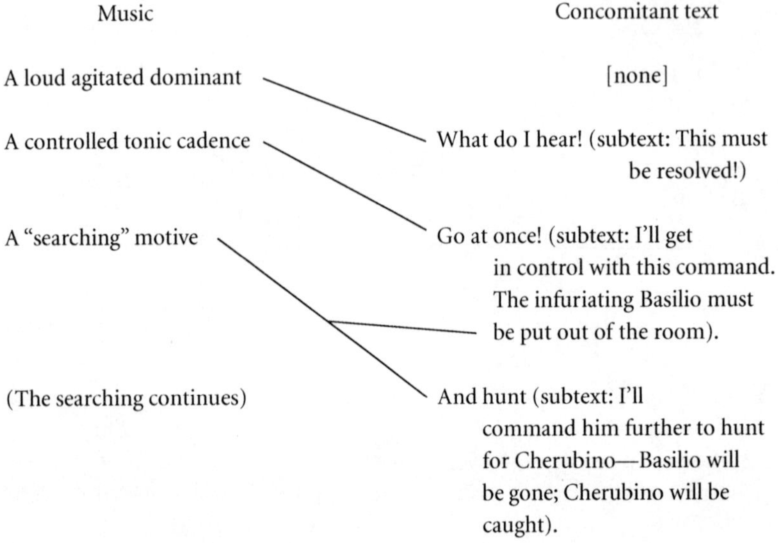
Music
Concomitant text
A loud agitated dominant
[none]
A controlled tonic cadence
What do I hear! (subtext: This must be resolved!)
A "searching" motive
Go at once! (subtext: I'll get in control with this command. The infuriating Basilio must be put out of the room).
(The searching continues)
And hunt (subtext: I'll command him further to hunt for Cherubino—Basilio will be gone; Cherubino will be caught).

welcome) to an actor. Mozart's setting proceeds through Example 2.3 in a similar vein, as suggested by Example 2.4.

Throughout the first big section of the trio, up to "Parta, parta . . . ," the Count continues to take his cues, both thematic and tonal, from preceding music. And throughout that section, Basilio and Susanna struggle to take control of those cues. They contend in initiating themes and harmonic moves to which the Count responds; each tries thereby to win the authority of the Count to use against the other.

It is primarily the observations we have been making, I believe, that make us feel the dominant-to-tonic cadence on "sento" is somehow weak and unconvincing. Specifically, there is a rhythmic dissonance in the syncopation between musical gesture and textual utterance, a rhythmic dissonance which makes us unable to accept the harmonic formula as authoritative and governing here. According to our maxim, we are thereby fleshing out our intuition that the Count is not authoritative and governing.

Once the maxim has turned our attention to the weakness of the cadence on "sento," we can make other interesting analytic observations. For instance, there is a particularly fine touch of orchestration in the bass under "sento!" The annotation on Example 2.3 points out that the Count's would-be cadence is not supported by a tonic note in the bass—the Count's third degree is the lowest note of the texture. To be sure, the ear supplies a low B♭ for a number of psychoacoustical reasons; still the effect, subtly unhinging the authority of the would-be cadence, is remarkable. One would expect the accompaniment of Example 2.2 for this cadence, an accompaniment that does provide the low B♭.

Example 2.5 gives the complete vocal line for the Count's opening phrase. After his search over measures 6–12, the Count finally manages at measure 13 to enun-

Example 2.5 Vocal line for the Count's opening phrase.

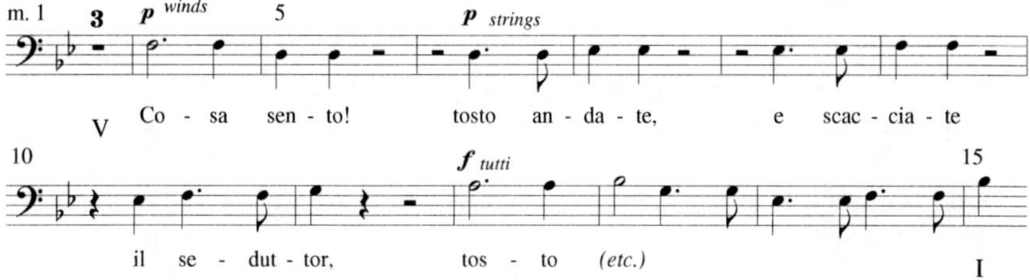

ciate an authoritative textual command, "Tosto andate," together with an effective tonic arrival in the music, on the high B♭. Characteristically, he does this only by recycling old text, text that did not work before. Characteristically, too, he does it only on the high B♭. Even at measure 15, where one strongly expects the low B♭, the Count is still unable to project the ground tone that should govern the number. He is still projecting the high B♭ on his later downbeat at "Parta, parta"; he will not project the low B♭ effectively until "Onestissima signora," after he discovers Cherubino. These analytic observations all arise, via our maxim, from a directorial intuition noted earlier, "that the Count must work hard—too hard—to achieve the eventual cadence at the end of his solo." At the beginning and the end of Example 2.5 are displayed the respective Roman numerals V and I. These symbolize the overall progression of the pertinent music, from dominant to tonic. Indeed, the convincing projection of a dominant-to-tonic cadence is as it were the essence of the Count's problem.

Example 2.6 Vocal line of Basilio's solo.

Example 2.6 displays the vocal line of Basilio's following solo, which reverses the Count's progression: it departs from the tonic and arrives at the dominant.

The reversal leaps to our analytic attention. The Count has labored mightily to construct a commanding move from dominant to tonic; Basilio's solo wipes out the Count's labors, abandoning the Count's hard-earned tonic command and leading back to the dominant whence the Count started out in rage and confusion. According to our maxim, we should look for directorial correlates to go with the musical analysis. I have sketched some of my own intuitions in Example 2.7; the example will be fleshed out by later commentary.

In these features, Mozart's Basilio goes far beyond Beaumarchais's and Da Ponte's. To see how much Mozart's music has contributed, it will be useful to consult the texts of Example 2.1 again.

We know that Beaumarchais's Basilio is enjoying himself, but we know this only because of his earlier laughter at the end of what has become Mozart's recita-

Example 2.7 Correlation of musical analysis and stage direction, as regards Basilio's harmonic plan.

Analysis	Direction
1. Basilio does not confirm the Count's tonic cadence.	1. Basilio has no intention of leaving the scene, as commanded by the Count in that cadence.
2. Basilio moves back to the dominant harmony, whence the Count began the number.	2a. Basilio is specifically undoing the Count's previous labors; he is thwarting him, not just defying his command to leave. 2b. Basilio is manipulating the Count. 2c. Basilio expects to enjoy the Count's rage and confusion some more. 2d. Not only is Basilio unwilling to leave, he attempts specifically to prolong the delightful situation at the beginning of the number.

tive. We know, therefore, that the Beaumarchais character enjoys witnessing the scandal at hand. But we do not find in his "je suis fâché" line any overt irony or taunting, let alone disobedience, defiance, or manipulation. In the French scene, a director could consistently have Basilio here on the verge of obeying the Count's command to leave, when Susanna distracts both men by her fainting spell, already "troublée" as she begins her text.

Da Ponte's Basilio goes farther: he speaks with irony, and he taunts his superior. The Count has been discovered by a notorious gossipmonger in a highly compromising situation, and Da Ponte's Basilio enjoys rubbing that in. The Italian text draws attention to the Count himself as a seducer; the irony is especially nice because the Count himself has introduced the word "seducer," which was not in the French. To point all this, Da Ponte introduces a strong parody relation between the sounds of Basilio's text and the Count's preceding text. The parody structure is sketched in Example 2.8.

Example 2.8 Basilio's Italian text parodies the Count's.

C. Cosa Sento! Tos - to an-date, e scacciate il seduttor.
B. In mal punto
son qui giunto;
Per - do - n - ate, o mio si - gnor.

Still, Da Ponte's Basilio does not go beyond ironic impertinence to outright disobedience, let alone manipulative defiance of the Count's authority. In Da Ponte's text, as in Beaumarchais's, we can still imagine Basilio preparing to leave, obeying the Count's direct command to do so. Example 2.9 shows how Da Ponte's text could be set in that manner. Here, Basilio's solo would not move to the dominant; rather it would append itself to the Count's solo as a confirming tonic coda. One hears how the musical initiative would pass at once to Susanna; we shall return to that observation very soon.

Example 2.9 Hypothetical music, if Basilio did confirm the Count's tonic cadence.

To Example 2.9 we can compare Example 2.10, which expresses in an imagined musical setting some of the directorial notions listed in Example 2.7 above, notions implicit in Mozart's overall harmonic progression for Basilio. Example 2.10 gives the end of Basilio's actual music, and follows it with a hypothetical response from the Count that Basilio would be delighted to provoke.

Example 2.10 Hypothetical music, if the Count reacted to Basilio's cadential dominant as the Count had reacted to the orchestral dominant at the opening of the number.

The example emphasizes how Basilio's solo closes a musical loop involving himself and the Count: the Count can go on all day attempting to resolve Basilio's discombobulating dominant to an effective tonic cadence; Basilio can likewise go on all day returning the Count's would-be tonic command back to another dominant. In this infinite tennis game Susanna has no place whatsoever. (One contrasts Example 2.9, where the initiative passes automatically to Susanna.) The game is a struggle for power and control between the two males, a struggle that Basilio is delighted to initiate, feeling himself the stronger, for the befuddled Count—obsessed by thoughts of Cherubino and the Countess—scarcely apprehends what is going on.[3]

3. Susanna, however, quite understands Basilio's game, and she is quite aware that she must break up the game before it continues any further; she must win the Count's attention herself, to secure his authority for her interests against Basilio's. That is why she proceeds immediately, in the music that follows, to attack Basilio's dominant in the most forceful way possible: she moves from Basilio's F major harmony toward a cadence in F minor, destroying the dominant function of F major by denying the leading tone A natural. Her F minor key will not press towards a tonic cadence in the key of B♭ major. Unfortunately, just as she faints (or "faints") away in F minor, Basilio hastens with feigned solicitude to "console" her in F major, thus restoring the harmony he wants, the harmony she was trying to escape. There is not space in this study to analyze adequately the fantastic tonal duel that ensues between Susanna and Basilio, as they compete with each other for control of the Count during the farcical stage events which follow; I shall content myself with sporadic observations in later text and notes.

Like Iago, Mozart's Basilio is playing a dangerous game, trying to manipulate and defy a superior who wields absolute authority, a superior who is not in good control of himself. Because of that, Basilio's unctuous hypocrisy, only a flat character trait in the texts, becomes a dynamic and purposeful tool for the Mozartean actor. Mozart's Basilio *uses* his unctuousness to keep the Count duped and mollified; the unction becomes purposeful and tension-laden, rather than merely incidental and amusing. The Count, if not sufficiently distracted, could at any moment focus his indignant rage on the insubordinate Basilio, who remains about as a potential target for that rage.[4]

We hear Basilio's hypocritical fawning in Mozart's music as well as in Da Ponte's text. Very audible, for instance, is the false solicitude with which Basilio's repetitive four-note rhythmic motive smooths out the jagged contours of the Count's four-note rhythms. The motivic transformation is displayed in Example 2.11.

Example 2.11 Basilio smooths out the Count's rhythmic motive.

Ostensibly calming the Count down, Basilio is actually duping him. Mozart uses to good effect here the ironic parody in Da Ponte's text, discussed earlier (Example 2.8). The ostensible calming makes the musical impetus relax: the tonic has already been reached and now the rhythmic motives lose their drive as well. In order to maintain a suitable level of dramatic tension, it is useful for the actor play-

4. I think that Susanna is fully aware of Basilio's danger. I believe she attempts precisely to focus the Count's rage against Basilio during her rape accusation later in the scene. Specifically, I believe she means not so much to cry rape against both men, as to cry rape to the Count against Basilio. Useful in this connection is the split in the two men's texts after the rape cry: the Count says, "Do not be upset, darling," while Basilio at the same moment assures Susanna, "Your honor is secure." I would therefore stage a pertinent part of her earlier faint (or "faint") as follows: the two men together sing "O God how her heart is beating"; the Count feels her left breast with genuine concern—or so he persuades himself—or at least so he pretends; Basilio, taking advantage of the situation (and quite possibly realizing or believing that Susanna is fully conscious) symmetrically feels her right breast.

This interpretation of Susanna's rape cry makes sense of her seizing the dominant harmony herself thereafter, when she urges the Count not to believe the "impostor" Basilio. One understands: "Take and resolve my dominant, not his, with your authority. Look how impertinent he is being."

The way in which the men treat Susanna during the trio, both musically and theatrically, would be intolerable to an audience of any sensibility, were that treatment not disguised by the heavily farcical mode that supervenes from time to time within the comedy for just that purpose. Mozart and Da Ponte are expert at moving along the edge of this line. (They do so throughout *Don Giovanni.*) In the French text, Basilio leaves Susanna completely alone and is completely silent during her fainting spell. There is no mention of Susanna's heartbeat; it is the Count's idea to put her in the chair; furthermore, it is the Count, not Basilio, who reassures her after her indignant outcry that "il n'y a plus le moindre danger!"

ing Basilio to sense and project the danger underlying his Iago-like behavior, and his own Iago-like delight at his mastery over that danger. Among other things, as he leads the wandering harmonies of the solo along he must savor at all times his intention to arrive at the dominant when he closes.

Example 2.12 Basilio's harmonic progression compared to the harmonies of the Count's final cadence.

m. 13				m. 15
Tosto andate, e		scacciate il	sedut - - - - - - -	tor.
B♭	g	E♭	(F	B♭)

m. 16				
In	mal punto son qui giunto;		Perdonate, o mio signor.	
B♭	g	E♭	(c	F)

The wandering harmonies themselves constitute another aspect of Basilio's hypocrisy. Example 2.12 shows how the first three of Basilio's local tonics, B♭, G minor, and E♭, replicate and expand the harmonies of the Count's final cadence, just heard during measures 13–15. Basilio's solo thereby seems, up to its very end, to be confirming and extending the Count's final tonic cadence—as if Basilio were about to obey the Count's command.

Only at the end of Basilio's solo, as indicated by the parenthesized harmonies in Example 2.12, does Basilio reveal his true intention: instead of confirming the Count's final harmonies, F-to-B♭, Basilio substitutes C minor-to-F. He thereby sneaks in his insubordinate cadence on the dominant only after lulling the Count into supposing that he is about to confirm the Count's tonic cadence. The tactic is designed to keep the Count off-balance so that Basilio can get away with his game.

In Example 2.12, B♭, G minor, and E♭ build a segment from a chain of falling thirds, heard in the harmonic structure of both the Count's solo and Basilio's solo. Example 2.13 shows how chains of falling thirds are also manifest in the melodic structure of both men's vocal lines.

Example 2.13 Chains of falling thirds in the melodic structure of the two men's solos.

F	D	(scalewise ascent . . . to) B♭	G	E♭	(F	B♭)
Cosa	sento!	Tosto andate . . . , tosto andate	e scacciate		il seduttor.	

F	D	B♭	G	E♭	C
In mal punto		son qui giunto;	Perdonate,		
				o mio signor.	

As in the harmonic structure of Example 2.12, so in the melodic structure of Example 2.13 we hear how Basilio apes his master's model right up to the final cadence, as if he were about to confirm the Count's tonic closure. Instead, just where the Count breaks off his chain of thirds to form the melodic cadence F-to-B♭, Basilio extends his chain of thirds one link farther, arriving at a melodic cadence on the note C, the second degree of the scale, utterly incompatible with any possibility of tonic closure. One notes here the sudden vivification of Basilio's hitherto "unctuous" four-note rhythmic motive.

The manipulative mastery we have observed so far in Basilio's solo remains much in evidence during the remainder of the number. In particular, Basilio consistently manages to outwit and foil Susanna during their tonal dueling for the Count's authority. As a director, one wonders if our Iago-like Basilio would not be paying close attention to Susanna, as well as to the Count, during the solo we have been examining. Applying our maxim, we are thereby led to analyze the music of the solo even further, to find some relation between Basilio and Susanna therein. The desired relation is indeed forthcoming. For Basilio's music does not refer alone to the Count's solo that immediately precedes it. It refers as well to Cherubino's famous aria, *Non so più*, the preceding number in the opera. Example 2.14 shows the relationship, which binds because it fits so clearly the repetitive motivic doggerel of each tune. In the example, Cherubino's tune has been transposed to the same key as Basilio's solo; this facilitates the comparison.

Example 2.14 Basilio's solo compared to Cherubino's *Non so più*.

Now, applying our maxim again, let us see what we can infer in the way of stage direction from the musical analysis of Example 2.14. We can begin by inferring that Basilio has heard Cherubino's tune. (Basilio, we must remember, is a music master.)[5] Since Basilio has heard the tune, he must have heard its only performance. That is, Basilio must have been lurking about outside Susanna's door, listening to Cherubino, just before the Count went into the room.

5. I cannot entertain the possibility that Basilio's quotation is only Mozartean irony, like Wagner's irony when he makes Siegmund sing the Renunciation of Love motive in *Die Walküre*. That sort of irony seems to me not only pointless here but utterly foreign to the dramatic mode of *Figaro*. In any case, why reject a resource for deepening Basilio's character and his interactions with the others on stage?

For some time I believed that Basilio might not have heard the performance of *Non so piú*; I thought that he might instead be looking at the score, which Cherubino or Susanna could have dropped in the scramble to conceal the boy. But this reading does not hold water: the score which Cherubino has brought to Susanna is *Voi che sapete*. Just before Cherubino will sing that song later on, Susanna will refer to it as "the song you gave me this morning." I am grateful to Edward T. Cone for the clarification.

Basilio, therefore, knowing or strongly suspecting that Cherubino is presently hiding somewhere in the room, is now making sure that Susanna knows his suspicion and suspects his certain knowledge. Thus, while Basilio's solo is manipulating the Count in all sorts of ways, it is also keeping a tight grip on Susanna. This aspect of Basilio's solo will be very useful to the actress singing Susanna, as she responds with the punning text "Che ruina!" [= "Cherubino!"].

Since Basilio knows or suspects that Cherubino is in the room, a further delicious irony emerges: in defying the Count's first command—to leave the room—Basilio is deliberately and infuriatingly obeying the Count's second command—to hunt out Cherubino.

I assure those who are not musicians that I could go on exploring the two men's solos considerably farther in this vein, and I could go on for several times as long on Susanna's subsequent solo. But I think I have made the points I wanted to make; to continue would make little sense unless I were to analyze the entire number through in equal detail and also in its global musical structure—a worthy project but one so extensive as to be out of place in the context of the present volume. I should rather like now to stand back and comment on what I think I have been doing.

First, I hope to have indicated the depth and thickness with which it is possible to explore Mozart's dramaturgy using my maxim. In one sense, I am only very belatedly attempting to show that one can perform as well for Mozart the traditional sort of close character analysis that A. C. Bradley and Harley Granville-Barker performed for Shakespeare some sixty to ninety years ago. I hope thereby to render less ephemeral the intuitions of critics who have ranked Mozart and Shakespeare together on the summit of theatrical art.[6]

Beyond that, I hope to have shown the utility of the maxim as such. I think it is useful for opera at least from Mozart through Verdi, given some adjustments for a variety of musical styles and theatrical conventions over the period. I believe furthermore that the maxim is also useful for other vocal genres so far as the notion of "drama" pertains to them in some extended sense. I would put many Lieder into this category.[7]

Going farther still, I think the maxim might be useful for investigating the technical basis underlying the aesthetics of program music and programmatic criticism in nineteenth-century Europe. The urge to supply a program for an instrumental piece, either to help compose it or to help criticize it, might fruitfully be viewed as an urge to supply a theatrical dimension for the music at hand, enabling the composer or critic to move freely back and forth between musical analysis and dramatic direction, as I have been moving here. That sort of motion might well have been felt especially natural and constructive in the years following Mozart's theatrical achievements. Scott Burnham has recently approached one of A. B. Marx's

6. For example: "Up to this winter I owed my most enjoyable evenings in the theater to Shakespeare and Mozart," Eric Bentley, "God's Plenty in Paris" (1949), *In Search of Theater* (New York, 1954), 55.
7. The reader will find the notion developed at some length in "*Auf dem Flusse*: Image and Background in a Schubert Song," Chapter 5 in the present volume.

programmatic analyses in this spirit, yielding results that seem to me very promising.[8] Thomas Grey's critique of another Marxian analysis is suggestive in the same way.[9] I sense that there are crucial distinctions to be made between drama and "narrative" in these contexts, but I do not have the expertise to formulate my impressions in a literary mode.

8. "A. B. Marx and Beethoven's *Eroica:* Drama, Analysis and the *Idee*," lecture delivered to the meeting of the New England Conference of Music Theorists, Brown University, Providence, April 4, 1987. Mr. Burnham's lecture is largely incorporated within his Ph.D. dissertation, "Aesthetics, Theory and History in the Works of Adolph Bernhard Marx" (Ph.D. diss., Brandeis University, 1988).
9. Thomas Grey, "Metaphorical Modes in Nineteenth-Century Music Criticism: Image, Narrative and Idea," in Steven Paul Scher, ed., *Music and Text: Critical Inquiries*, Cambridge and New York: Cambridge University Press (1992), 93–117.

CHAPTER Three

Crudel! perchè finora . . .

Da Ponte's text takes Beaumarchais's Act III, Scene IX, as its point of departure:

C. Pourquoi donc, cruelle fille, ne me l'avoir pas dit plus tôt?	Crudel! perchè finora far mi languir così?
S. Est-il jamais trop tard pour dire la vérité?	Signor, la donna ognore tempo ha di dir sì.
C. Tu te rendrais sur la brune [at twilight] au jardin?	Dunque in giardin verrai?
S. Est-ce que je ne m'y promène pas tous les soirs?	Se piace a voi, verrò.
	C. E non mi mancherai?
	S. No, non vi mancherò.
	C&S. Verrai?/ Sì!/Non mancherai?/ No!/Non mancherai?/Non mancherò, no, non vi mancherò.
C. Tu m'as traité ce matin si sévèrement! (etc. at some length. . .; finally)	
C. [*veut l'embrasser*] Délicieuse créature!	
S. [*s'échappe*] Voilà du monde.	
C. [*à part*] Elle est à moi. [*Il s'enfuit.*]	Mi sento dal contento, pieno di gioia il cor.
S. Allons vite rendre compte à Madame.	[*a parte*] Scusate mi se mento! Voi che intendete amor.

The first four lines of Beaumarchais's text are all questions, exchanged alternately by the Count and Susanna. The two characters then review earlier events of the day with various reproaches, explanations, asides, and more questions (from both characters). Finally, the Count is convinced of Susanna's sincerity. He tries to kiss her; she avoids this on the pretext that people are coming; he announces that she is his (as he believes)—but only in an aside—and departs.

Da Ponte modifies the opening of the scene so that the Count has all the questions and Susanna none—she gives explicit answers, partial, evasive, or unsatisfying as they may be. Da Ponte adds to Beaumarchais's text an extra question for the Count, "E non mi mancherai?" together with Susanna's answer, "No, non vi mancherò." The extra question portrays the Italian Count as even more suspicious of Susanna than is the French Count.

Da Ponte and Mozart then insert into Beaumarchais's scene an intensive stichomythy, which I shall call "the question-and-answer review session." This comprises a brisk abbreviated reprise of already-posed questions from the Count and already-given answers from Susanna: "Verrai? Sì! Non mancherai? No! Non mancherai? Non mancherò, no, non vi mancherò."

Throughout all of this, the Italian Count continues asking questions, and the Italian Susanna continues giving declarative answers. Only in the Count's last line of Da Ponte's text does the would-be lover make a declarative statement himself, rather than posing a question. Satisfied that Susanna is (as he now believes) in earnest, the Count expresses his joy. He announces this to Susanna as well as to the audience (unlike "Elle est à moi," which is strictly an aside to the audience), and it is Susanna, not the Count, who has the aside ("Scusatemi se mento! . . ."). Susanna's last remark in the French—that she will hasten to report the proceedings to the Countess—is omitted from the Italian text, which substitutes Susanna's apology, aside to the audience.

The rest of Mozart's setting recapitulates—now in the major key—all of the Italian text from "Dunque in giardin" to the end. The major-key question-and-answer review session appears with some variations in its text and is then immediately repeated with some other variations in its text. We shall later have things to say about those variations.

∾

At the beginning of the number, Mozart enacts the Count's initial questioning by musical phrases that end with half-cadences on the dominant of a minor. The first of these half-cadences comes in measure 2, to conclude the orchestral introduction. The next half-cadence comes at "così?" in measure 6; the dominant harmony is then extended (alternating with six-four harmonies) through the next "così?" at measure 10, which finishes the Count's opening solo.

These musical questions on the dominant demand a resolving musical answer on a tonic harmony—at least the tonic of a minor if not the tonic of A major. Throughout the number, though, Susanna's music never provides the Count with such an answer.[1] Eventually the Count provides the indicated musical answer *him-*

1. Susanna's first "No, non vi mancherò" (mm. 21–22), which cadences in a minor, does not provide the Count's opening dominant questioning with such an answer, because the Count has already modulated back to a minor and arrived on its tonic during the question ("E non mi mancherai?") that precedes her answer here. "E non mi mancherai?" is a tonic a-minor musical antecedent (mm. 19–20) to her tonic a-minor musical consequent (mm. 21–22).

Susanna's first "Scusatemi se mento! voi che intendete amor" (mm. 32–35), in the A major section, might seem somewhat more of a tonic answer to the Count's original dominant questioning, but that reading does not hold water very well. First, she sings this material as an aside to the audi-

self with his big A major tonic downbeat at "Mi sento," where he finally stops asking questions and makes a declarative statement. This curious musical behavior, which engages the single largest musical articulation within the piece, will receive a good deal of our attention.

The key to the apparent paradox is to observe that the tonic A major downbeat, while *sung* by the Count, actually enacts a dramatic arrival that belongs to *Susanna*, not to him. The big downbeat specifically signals Susanna's attainment of her main dramatic goal in the scene, which is to convince the Count that she is in earnest about keeping their appointment. The Count's "Mi sento," which he sings not only to himself, and not just as an aside to the audience (like the French Count's "Elle est à moi") but also to *her*, lets us know that she has succeeded, and lets *her* know that she has succeeded.

The tonic major downbeat is a particular relief for Susanna to hear, because throughout the minor section of the number she has been playing a dangerous and tricky game. The game has been tricky because, up until this number in the opera, she has been assiduously fending off the Count's advances. If she should now suddenly express a strong interest in them, seeming to accommodate herself too willingly, too quickly, he would become suspicious and the women's plot would fail. She must seem intrigued by the sexual bargain being discussed but not too intrigued too soon.

Then, too, the Count does not simply want a straight business transaction—Susanna's body for the dowry—he wants to believe that she finds him attractive, perhaps even irresistible, as a lover. Such reassurance will not only satisfy a personal sexual vanity, it will also satisfy a *political* vanity, helping him to maintain his view of himself as an enlightened "liberal" master: he has ostentatiously abolished the medieval *droit du seigneur*, and he can hardly afford politically—if only for his self-image—to reinstate that privilege on the first occasion that tempts him. So Susanna does well to flirt with him during the *minore* of the number, humoring his vanity by allowing him to "woo" her and "win" her.

The flirtation, on the other hand, is full of danger for her. Should she seem *too* eager, the Count might not be content to wait until evening to satisfy his desires. And should she seem either too eager or not eager enough, at any point during the number, the Count might become aware that she is toying with him—as indeed he seems to suspect, with his "E non mi mancherai?" That could lead to her quick and summary dismissal from the Count's employ, and/or Figaro's dismissal; it could also lead to the Count's summarily enforcing the threatened marriage of Figaro with Marcellina.

ence, not directly to the Count. Second, the Count is no longer questioning her on the dominant of a minor or A major but has just himself provided the big A major downbeat musical "answer" of the scene, with his big A major downbeat at measure 29 and his entire ensuing solo phrase ("Mi sento . . . cor"). True, his four-measure solo phrase does end on the dominant of A major, but the tonic answer to this dominant is not really provided by Susanna's aside to the audience. The answer is rather provided by the Count himself, who continues through the musical consequent (mm. 33–36, repeating the text "mi sento . . . cor"), and cadences firmly on the tonic of A, without taking any input from Susanna. Her "Scusatemi . . . amor" thus does not accomplish any tonal work on its own initiative; it is, rather, a musical descant to the Count's cadencing phrase.

Susanna's flirtation begins immediately following the Count's last insistent half-cadence on the dominant of a minor, at "così" in measure 10. She does not answer the Count's musical questions with an immediately subsequent full cadence in A major; such an answer might seem too obliging too suddenly. Rather she slips away from his tonic key and answers him with a cadence in C major. Thus her musical flirting accommodates him to some degree—cadencing in a major key related to his languishing a minor—but the flirting also frustrates him to some degree—slipping away from the specific major key in which he wants to be answered.

Example 3.1

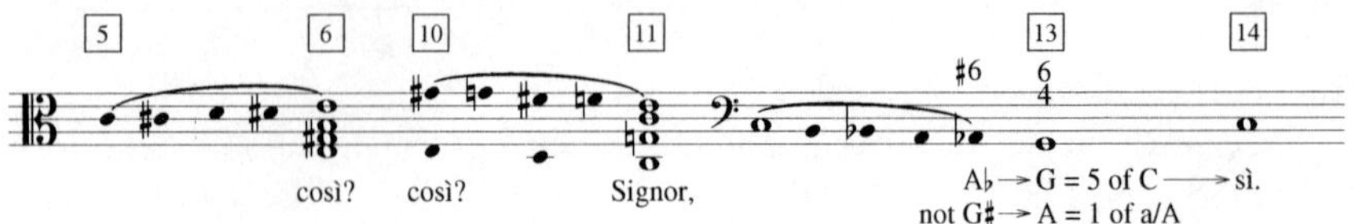

Her evasion is nicely portrayed by Mozart's play with chromatic scale-segments that fill major thirds. Example 3.1 portrays pertinent such segments. In measures 5 and 6, the Count's half-cadence is supported by a chromatic scale segment in the second violins that rises insistently through a major third from C to E. Then, after the Count's next half-cadence at measure 10, Susanna's evasion of his question is portrayed by a chromatic scale segment in the second violins and flute, a figure that descends deflatingly through a major third from G♯ to E (mm. 10–11). Underneath that descent, cellos and basses move E–D–C, retrograding the earlier rise from C to E in measures 5–6, and thus further deflating the Count's earlier importunate insistence. The celli-basses, having arrived at C in measure 11, then continue chromatically downward, filling out the major third from C to A♭ (mm. 11–12). Thus there have so far been chromatic scale segments that fill the major thirds C–E, G♯–E, and C–A♭. The segments arrange themselves neatly, abstractly filling out the augmented triad {C, E, G♯ = A♭}. The G♯ of measure 6, the questioning leading-tone of a minor (and A major), has enharmonically become A♭, the lowered sixth degree of C. Rather than G♯, insistently demanding an answering rise to a tonic A for its resolution, the enharmonically reinterpreted note has become a deflating A♭, wanting to sink down for its resolution, to relax into G natural, the fifth degree of C. And indeed the A♭ does just that at measure 13, leading into the C major cadence in which the flirting Susanna both engages and evades the Count's insistent questions. The augmented-sixth chord over the bass A♭ makes a nice point, as it recalls the Count's earlier augmented-sixth chords (m. 1 and m. 5). Unlike the earlier augmented-sixths, which push insistently toward cadences in a minor, the new augmented-sixth chord relaxes into Susanna's C major cadence. It is interesting that the various augmented-sixth chords are all ficta forms of F–A–C–D: the Count's chords are F–A–D♯–C, and Susanna's chord is A♭–D–F♯–C.[2]

I have not been able to resist putting a few bits of the text beneath the musical symbols of Example 3.1, to show how the syllable "sì" of the Count's half-cadencing

2. Edward Gollin pointed this out in class discussion.

"così?" on V-of-a (at m. 6 and again at m. 10), is both answered and evaded by Susanna's "Si" of "Signor," on $\hat{5}$ of C at the pickup to measure 11, and then her final "sì" at measure 14, where she sings the tonic note of the C major cadence, *singing the word "sì" at the biggest cadence so far* just as her text speaks of women *finally saying "sì."* Alas, the English pun on Susanna's "sì" and the note C does not hold water. But there might be something to the observation that the *Count* sings "sì?" on the leading tone of A—that is, the solfège note SI of *his* key.

Example 3.2

The left side of Example 3.2 shows how the harmonic and tonal matters just discussed are reflected in the large-scale melodic-and-metric structure of the characters' vocal lines during measures 3–14. The Count's melody is sketched with stems down, an octave above his vocal register, and Susanna's melody is sketched with stems up. After the Count's initial vocal downbeat on A at measure 3, all the metrically and/or agogically accented notes of his vocal part up to measure 10 are Cs or G♯s or Es, engaging the "augmented triad" discussed earlier. Susanna's answering vocal phrase, measures 10–14, then hangs on Es and Cs and G naturals. She maintains the Count's Es and Cs but treats his earlier G sharps *as if* they had been A♭s, so far as the vocal lines themselves are concerned, "resolving" the would-be A♭s into her G♮s by way of answer. This aspect of the melodic question/answer relation in the vocal lines is, to my ear, even stronger than the diatonic transposition of the Count's vocal hexachord on E–A–C, into Susanna's vocal hexachord on G–C–E, a more traditional aspect of the relationship.

The right side of Example 3.2 continues sketching the vocal lines through the rest of the *minore*, providing as well a bass sketch for measures 15–28. This music sets the tighter question-and-answer pair, "Dunque in giardin verrai? Se piace a voi, verrò," (mm. 15–18), which extends to a balanced textual quatrain through the new question-and-answer that Da Ponte added to the French, "E non mi mancherai? No, non vi mancherò," (mm. 19–22). On the right side of Example 3.2, the question marks at measures 16 and 20 articulate the Count's question marks in the text, and the symbols "ans" at measures 18 and 22 articulate the completion of Susanna's textual answers.

There follows the yet tighter part of the Italian text that I referred to earlier as the question-and-answer review session: "Verrai? Sì! Non mancherai? No! Non mancherai? Non mancherò, no, non vi mancherò." (The reader will recall that this material in the Italian text was inserted by Da Ponte and/or Mozart into Beaumarchais's French scene.) The stretto of questions-and-answers goes by too swiftly to be captured adequately at the rhythmic level of Example 3.2. We shall explore it soon at a more detailed rhythmic level. On Example 3.2, all that is captured of this fast stichomythy is the Count's last question at measure 25, marked with a question mark on the example, and Susanna's answer at measure 26, marked "ans!" The exclamation point will be discussed soon.

On Example 3.2, some curious musical phenomena are manifest, which we shall note at first only synoptically, and then explore in more detail. The Count's questions at measures 16 and 20—unlike his questions during measures 1–10—are not set to any dominant harmonies, whether dominant of a minor or dominant of C major. Rather, the Count's questions cadence melodically both times on the pitch C, which is the third degree (not the fifth or raised seventh degree) of a minor, and that is, even more curiously, the local tonic that Susanna has just established—both harmonically and melodically—at measure 14. Musically, the Count is not questioning Susanna's vocal C at all. He has completely abandoned his questioning dominants-of-a from measures 1–10. Measures 15–16, in particular, do not question Susanna's cadence at measure 14 in the slightest. Nay, far from challenging Susanna, the music for the Count's supposed "question" at measures 15–16 actually *confirms* the music for Susanna's earlier answer in measure 14—confirming both the melodic cadence on the note C and the local status of that C as harmonic tonic.

And while the Count's question of measure 25 does get away from his earlier melodic and harmonic Cs, he does not land on a melodic fifth degree or leading tone in the local key (of a minor), nor is his melodic second degree of a minor supported here by dominant harmony. It is *Susanna* whose *answering* text, at measure 26, arrives on the leading tone of a, recalling precisely the Count's *questioning* G♯ from measures 6 and 8. And this *answering* leading tone of hers is supported (mm. 26–28) by a very extended dominant harmony of a minor, precisely the Count's *questioning* dominant from measures 6 and 8. To emphasize this apparent paradox, the symbol "ans" over Susanna's melodic G♯ at measure 26 on Example 3.2 is emphasized by an exclamation point. The extended bass E of the dominant harmony that supports her is also annotated by the symbol "ans!?"

The bass line of Example 3.2 reinforces very powerfully the association of Susanna's "answering" G♯-over-V-of-a, at measure 26, with the Count's questioning during measures 1–10. From measure 19 up to measure 26, the bass line of the sketch diminutes an arpeggiation of the pitches A-C-E, elaborating the arpeggiation with neighboring and passing tones. The arpeggiation composes out, on a higher structural level, the arpeggiated metrically accented apex tones A–C–E in the melody of the orchestral introduction during measures 1–2. Both the bass E of measure 26–28 and the melodic E of measure 2 are set by emphatic dominant-of-a harmony—indeed, the E harmony of measure 2 is "the" paradigmatic questioning-dominant harmony of the number. In the bass line for measures 22–26 on Example 3.2, the structural arpeggiation from C to E is filled in by passing tones D and D♯. The almost-chromatic gesture recalls the little rising chromatic figure C–C♯–D–D♯–E from measures 5–6, a figure portrayed at the left of Example 3.1 and discussed earlier in that connection. On Example 3.1, the E of the chromatic figure was the "paradigmatic" E that coincided both melodically and harmonically with the Count's first sung textual "question mark" of the number. Finally, the last harmony of measure 25, immediately preceding the big cadential dominant of measure 26, is the diminished seventh chord D♯–F♯–A–C. (The harmony, occupying the fourth quarter of measure 25, does not appear on the sketch of Example 3.2, where it yields to the more salient dominant-of-E harmony on the third quarter of the measure.) The diminished-seventh harmony, as a ficta form of D–F–A–C, associates powerfully with the earlier "paradigmatic" pre-dominant forms D♯–F–A–C (m. 1, immediately preceding the big V-of-a in m. 2) and D–F♯–A♭–C (m. 12, immediately preceding the big V-of-C in m. 13).

Example 3.3

Example 3.3 continues the exploration begun by Example 3.2. It shows the vocal melody and rhythm in the foreground of the question-and-answer review session, measures 23–28. The musical behavior of both characters in Example 3.3 reinforces the behaviors we observed in Example 3.2. The Count's textual questions in measure 23 and measure 24 begin on, inflect, and cadence on the stable tonic note A, while Susanna's textual answers there hammer on the "questioning" leading-tone G♯.[3] The example focuses one's ear very strongly on the way in which Susanna's G♯s and Bs set up the big tonic downbeat at the beginning of the *maggiore*, where the Count responds to her prompting—one might almost say prodding—with an enormous harmonic and melodic A.

Example 3.4

Susanna's melodic and rhythmic material during measures 25–28, as seen on Example 3.3, sounds familiar. Example 3.4 displays derivations for this material. Example 3.4a gives the melody for Susanna's "non mancherò" at measures 25–26. On the example, (b) and (c) show how her melodic half-cadence, on the G♯ leading tone, is derived from the Count's earlier "paradigmatic" questioning cadences on G♯, at measures 5–6 ("[lan]guir così?") and measures 6–8 ("perchè? crudel!").

Susanna's cadence motive going into measure 26, C–A–G♯ with rhythm dotted-eighth, sixteenth, quarter, acquires a descant motive, E–C–B with the same rhythm,

3. Particularly neat is the text "Sì!" for Susanna's first answer here, on her G♯ in m. 23. Her syllable echoes the "-sì?" of the Count's text in measure 6, setting the paradigmatic first sung question mark of the scene on his G♯ there. As we noted earlier, Mozart may be punning on the solfège syllable SI for the leading tone G♯.

during her extension of the cadence through measure 28. Example 3.4d gives Susanna's extension melody during measures 26–28; the notes of her part are displayed with stems up. The other melodic line of Example 3.4d, the line with stems down, transcribes exactly the material from the Count's opening solo, measures 3–10, as it appeared on Example 3.2 in melodic-rhythmic reduction. One thus hears how Susanna's foreground line, on Example 3.4d, works as a descant to the Count's earlier middleground line. The musical relationship (which I find startlingly ingenious) prepares her later musical relationship with the Count when, in measures 32–36, she sings "Scusatemi se mento" as a descant to his "mi sento dal contento."

In all the ways just surveyed, Susanna *expropriates*, during measures 23–28, the role of musical questioner from the Count, who had asserted that role forcefully during measures 1–10. Since her musical questions set textual answers, her behavior requires interpretation. The actress—and the actor, too (who is about to sing the big "answering" tonic downbeat of "Mi sento" on the tonic of A major)—will need to feel some dramatic point in her musical behavior, to execute their assigned theatrical roles with conviction.

The interpretation I shall propose takes its point of departure from two considerations. First, Susanna's musical questioning (even prodding), during measures 23–28, leads up to the Count's big musical "answer" at measure 29. Second, Susanna is able to take over the role of musical questioner after measure 23 partly because the Count has already relinquished that role during measures 15–23. The two considerations will be examined in turn.

Earlier, we noted that "the tonic A major downbeat [of m. 29], while *sung* by the Count, actually enacts a dramatic arrival that belongs to *Susanna*, not to him. The big downbeat specifically signals Susanna's attainment of her main goal in the piece, which is to convince the Count that she is in earnest about keeping their appointment." Susanna's role as musical questioner, during measures 23–28, fits very well with the earlier observation. Musically, Susanna is asking, "Do you believe me *now*? Don't you trust me *yet*?" And so forth, over and over until the Count yields to this insistent prodding and gives her the answer for which she is looking—the big A major downbeat.

Susanna is able to assume such an aggressive musical role during measures 23–28 because the Count, during measures 15–23, has abandoned his earlier aggressive musical position. Example 3.2 is a helpful aid for exploring this phenomenon. After Susanna's C major cadence at measure 14, the Count seems to be lured into the flirtation game, which is an essential feature of Susanna's strategy in the number. Suave lover that he fancies himself, he ingratiatingly echoes and confirms her C major melodic and harmonic cadence (mm. 15–16), whereupon she ingratiatingly echoes and confirms his echoing confirmation (mm. 17–18). He then echoes and confirms the essential melodic B–C gesture yet once more (Example 3.2, mm. 19–20), while the harmony slyly leads away from C major (the key of her flirtatiously evasive answer during mm. 11–14) back to a minor (his original key, in which he had originally demanded an answer from her). He seems to feel that he is gently wooing her back from her modest C major, to bring her back to the tonic key of the number where—as he seems to fantasize—she will finally yield to his solicitous wooing and his irresistible charms as she sings a tonic A downbeat.

And indeed measures 21–22 might encourage him to believe that he has succeeded. Susanna actually sings an essential melodic G♯–A (on Example 3.2), supported harmonically by a dominant-tonic progression in a minor. But the harmonies are in inversion, and her essential melodic B–C is not yet gone—it recurs yet once again at measures 21–22, now in the bass line, which is already getting into motion—through that C—toward its eventual arrival on the E of measure 26. We have already observed (in note 1) that the force of her phrase here is also weakened by its rhetorical relation as consequent to the Count's antecedent of measures 19–20—her phrase is more an echo of his local tonic than a resolution of his earlier large-scale dominants. The echo relation, with the exchange of outer voices from measures 19–20 to measures 21–22 of Example 3.2, varies and develops Susanna's echoing musical relation to the Count during measures 15–18. Her echoing is a musical equivalent to the text "Se piace a voi, verrò [e non vi mancherò]." The crux of the relation is the passivity of "Se piace a voi," with its rhetorical analog in the musical echoing. The Count can hardly believe that she has yielded so easily at measures 21–22, singing G♯–A over dominant-tonic harmony in a minor with so little resistance. As suggested earlier, he becomes suspicious of such an easy victory, given her past history of resistance to his importunings. Hence, his textual questions become even more peremptory, and his insistent suspicion is projected by the tightened rhythm of the musical setting for the question-and-answer review session. Example 3.3 is a useful aid to follow at this point. The subtext I am reading goes somewhat as follows. "Do you *really* mean A?" the Count asks (A–B♭–A, m. 23 with pickup, "Verrai?"). "Yes!" says Susanna, "Don't you believe me?" (questioning G♯ in m. 23, "Si!"). "*Really* A; this isn't just some trick?" (A–B♭–A, m. 24 with pickup, "non mancherai?"). "No, it's no trick; don't you trust me?" (questioning G♯ in m. 24, "No!").

The Count's lunge at B natural in measure 25 is not completely clear in this connection. I have yet to work out an interpretation with which I feel completely comfortable. Such an interpretation would, I believe, address two aspects of his musical behavior there. First, he abandons his tonic question mark A of measure 23 and measure 24, varying his melodic motive of measures 23–24 so as to set the question mark of measure 25 with a melodic B natural instead. The B natural, incompatible with tonic harmony, is a highly significant change in the Count's musical behavior, all the more so because his textual question repeats absolutely literally his text for measures 23–24 ("non mancherai?"). Second, his variation at measures 24–25 of the rhythmic motive for measures 23–24 is also significantly not quite exact: the melodic C–B at the end of the motive is set as a pair of eighths, not a pair of quarters. (That is why I referred to it as a "lunge.") The rhythmic variation certainly seems to portray a certain impatience on the Count's part here—perhaps he is tiring of his effort to maintain a solicitous and courtly facade in the flirtatious wooing game. Impatience also seems portrayed by the melodic variation in the motive: rather than coming to rest yet again on the melodic tonic A, the Count seems to be prodding the music, and hence Susanna, to move. Just what does he expect Susanna to do musically, in her answer? Or what does he hope she will do? This is not completely clear to me—and I think that I should ideally have a clear and viable interpretation (if only intuitively), were I performing in the scene.[4]

Beneath the Count's B in measure 25 I find the harmony suggestive. While the melodic B is clearly nontonic, it does *not* appear over dominant harmony. That enables Susanna's subsequent melodic Bs in measures 27–28, which *do* appear over dominant harmony, to set her textual answer to the Count's B, which was a B over a dominant-*preparation* harmony. (Susanna's diminished-seventh chord on the last beat of measure 25, bringing the Count's bass D up to D♯, has already been noted in this context.)

∾

The Count's harmonic turn to dominant-preparation B-root harmony, mentioned just above in connection with his "lunge at B" in measure 25, is picked up and amplified strongly in the subsequent music for the two question-and-answer review sessions of the *maggiore*—measures 42–47 and then measures 48–53. In the latter passages, the Count asks all his questions over harmony that functions as V-of-E, a dominant-preparation B-root harmony, and Susanna gives her immediate answers to those questions on the E harmony that the Count's B-roots are preparing. The local tonic is E major, but on a slightly higher middleground level the tonicized E harmonies are clear as V-of-A. The Count takes an evident pleasure in this activity—his vocal line is marked "dolce" both at measure 42 and again at measure 48. I think the idea is that *he has now, at last, found a questioning dominant harmony to which Susanna will respond with "tonic" answers.* True, the pertinent "dominants" and "tonics" are only local; on a slightly higher level they are dominant-preparations and dominants. Still, the Count certainly seems to enjoy the progressions at the local level. Measures 25–28, in the *minore*, have already given him the clue—as discussed earlier—that Susanna would respond to B-root questioning with E-root answers, to that extent fulfilling the harmonic role proper to question-and-answer text.

Susanna's E-root harmonies during the *maggiore*, when heard as dominants on the middleground level, continue to enact her role as subtextual questioner: "Don't you believe me *yet*?" The subtextual question becomes more pointed during the *maggiore*, where the Count has already provided the big A-major-downbeat answer by having already sung "Mi sento." The idea, I think, is that even after the first "Mi sento" the Count is still insecure and suspicious; that is why Mozart and Da

4. A performer involved in the scene—the Count, Susanna, or the conductor—does not really have an option to "avoid" interpretation while performing. If the Count stares with panic-stricken eyes at the conductor, the audience will take that as an interpretation. Likewise, if he stands stiffly with arms and hands symmetrically arranged about his torso. Likewise, if the director invents some self-styled "postmodern" bit of business at measure 25—for example, if the Count pulls forth a cheese sandwich and munches on it while Susanna is singing during measures 25–28, swallowing ostentatiously at the fermata in measure 28, and rubbing his stomach as he continues with "Mi sento dal contento" at measure 29. (This is only "self-styled" postmodernism; I have no quarrel with informed and performatively sensitive postmodern approaches to theater as such.)

Ponte have him go through two more question-and-answer review sessions after the first "Mi sento," before singing "Mi sento" a second time, at measure 54, now with the full orchestra behind him (winds as well as strings).

The Count's insecurities and suspicions in this connection were already noted in earlier commentary: the question "E non mi mancherai?" was added to the Italian text, and then Mozart had the Count *repeat* that extra question during the question-and-answer session of the *minore*. Indeed, that very place (mm. 24–25) was the original source for the Count's "lunge at B," the questioning lunge that generated Susanna's E-answering cadences over measures 25–28. The *repetition* of "E non mi mancherai?" at measures 24–25 thus comports very plausibly with the *repetition* of an entire (varied) textual question-and-answer session at measures 42–47, and then of yet another such session at measures 48–53 (again textually varied). All these repetitions are tied up with the Count's singing questions on B-root harmonies, for Susanna to answer on E-root harmonies.

Example 3.5

Example 3.5a transcribes, from the music for measures 42–44, pertinent aspects of the Count–Susanna exchanges. The singers' lines appear at concert pitch. Example 3.5b shows a source for this music in the introductory motto at the very beginning of the number, measures 1–2. The E harmony at the beginning of measure 2 is a "paradigmatic" E harmony for the piece; here of course it sounds as a dominant in the foreground as well as the middleground. A subtle touch on Example 3.5ab as a whole is the absence of any explicit note B during the second half of any measure. In Example 3.5b, the C of the main melody in the violins definitely denies any possible sense of a B root for the augmented-sixth chord—if forced to hear a root, we will likely choose "altered D," in conformity with the spelling D♯–F–A–C discussed earlier. In Example 3.5a, though, where no C is present, we will be quite ready to assign a B root (function) to the F♯–A–D♯ harmony—the Count has by now discovered the usefulness of the B-root sensation.

Let us now devote some attention to the variations in the texts for the question-and-answer review sessions of the *maggiore*. The question-and-answer table on the next page provides a convenient format in which to synopsize the variations. The left-hand column of the table, reading downwards, presents in Roman type the Count's three consecutive questions during the first question-and-answer review (Q&AR1). Susanna's answers appear in italics to the right of the Count's respective questions. All her answers here are "correct"—meaning that they are what the Count wants to hear. (Of course, these "correct" answers are in fact all false.)

Q&AR1 (mm. 23–25)		*Q&AR2 (mm. 42–47)*		*Q&AR3 (mm. 48–53)*	
Verrai?	*Sì!*	Verrai?	*Sì*	Non mancherai?	*No*
Non mancherai?	*No!*	Non mancherai?	*No*	Dunque verrai?	*Sì!*
Non mancherai?	*No!* etc.	Dunque verrai?	***No!***	Non mancherai?	***Sì!***
		NO!?	***Sì!*** etc.	**SÌ!?**	***No!*** etc.

The second column of the table arranges the text for the second question-and-answer review session—the first one of the *maggiore*—in a similar format. The Count has varied the order and content of his questions. Susanna's third answer, which is "incorrect" (i.e., in fact the truth) appears in boldface, as does the Count's subsequent enraged exclamation-question, and as does her subsequently revised answer, amended so as to become "correct" (i.e., in fact false). The third column of the table follows the format of the second column.

The structuring of the table requires interpretations (if only intuitive) from both the actors. I think that a number of interpretations are viable for the Count, who takes the initiative in the variation process by varying the order of his questions. Which interpretation an actor finds comfortable would depend on a larger conception of the role. Certainly, under any interpretation the Count's textual variations arise from his suspicions and insecurities, the same characteristics that made him repeat "Non mancherai?" during Q&A review session 1. At one extreme, an actor could conceive a very forceful Count introducing all his subsequent text variations quite deliberately in a conscious effort to trap Susanna. This Count, despite the first "Mi sento," would still be virtually convinced that the whole affair is some sort of plot. Since the Count takes evident pleasure in his *dolce* major questions, the forceful Count would be quite a masochistic person, taking pleasure in catching Susanna out in her "incorrect" answers, humiliating though they be to him. On the flip side of this pathology, he might well take a sadistic pleasure in making her squirm and labor to give the "correct" answers, playing cat-and-mouse with her. "Since she is toying with me, I'll toy with her." Significant, in this interpretation, is the word "Crudel!" that begins the text of the number, and the music immediately preceding "Crudel!"—as we saw on Example 3.5, the music of measures 1–2 has a decided influence on the music for Q&A review sessions 2 and 3. In general, too, there is a decidedly sadistic component to the Count's treatment of Susanna through the entire opera.

At another extreme, another actor might conceive the Count to be so discombobulated by his new situation vis-à-vis Susanna, that he asks his questions over and over virtually in a random fashion, unable to cope emotionally or intellectually with his sudden apparent good fortune. While this conception seems to me viable (particularly on the stage as opposed to the page), it also seems to me to weaken the character too much by turning him into a virtual clown. This releases too much dramatic tension during the *maggiore*, at the expense of the scene. To be sure, there is a substantial release of tension after the big downbeat of the first "Mi sento," but the number does have to hold the stage for some time thereafter.

Besides, on the page (as opposed to the stage) the order of the Count's questions is hardly so random. If we cast away the repeated "Non mancherai?" of Q&A review session 1, then there is a very organized, even "logical" structure to the

Count's series of questions. Specifically, discounting the third question "glitch" of Q&AR1 as suggested, we will observe that the Count simply alternates his two basic questions quite methodically and mechanically: (Q&AR1) Verrai? Non mancherai? (Q&AR2) Verrai? Non mancherai? Dunque verrai? (Q&AR3) Non mancherai? Dunque verrai? Non mancherai? Completely consistent with this strict pattern of alternations (always omitting the third question/answer of Q&AR1) is the ordering of the Count's questions during the two "regular" (i.e., nonreview) question-and-answer quatrains, in the *minore* at measures 15–22 and again in the *maggiore* at measures 37–42: "Dunque in giardin verrai? (*Se piace a voi, verrò.*) E non mi mancherai? (*No, non vi mancherò.*)"

The duple rhythm of this formalistic structure is concealed by the "hemiola" of the three Q&A sessions, each containing three questions. The structure is of course also concealed by the necessity of reading an "extra" question within Q&A review session 1, and by the temporal distance of Q&AR1 from the two *maggiore* Q&AR sessions. A less presumptuous formalism might simply consider Q&AR2 and Q&AR3 by themselves: the two musical passages are reasonably proximate, and within them the alternation of questions is strict (though still somewhat concealed by the large rhythmic hemiola, and also by the shock of the characters' expostulations after Susanna's "incorrect" answers).

The Count who mechanically asks alternate questions is stupid and discombobulated, but not so out-of-control and clownish as a Count who asks questions at random. In some sense, he can still view himself as authoritative, "in control" of the proceedings. If acting the part, I would find this aspect of the formalism useful. The formalism by itself, though, does not address adequately what seems to me a certain sexual character in the music for Q&A review sessions 2 and 3. The Count, singing his questions *dolce*, seems to get a sensuous enjoyment out of the rocking undulations in the accompaniment figuration. He seems as well to enjoy prompting Susanna's climaxes on her high F♯s, when she "corrects" her "incorrect" answers—as if she were responding to him sexually, rather than venting intolerable exasperation and/or panic. These enjoyments seem to go better with the sadomasochistic Count than with the mechanical question-alternating one. But perhaps the Count, under any interpretation, might plausibly be indulging himself in a pleasurable sexual fantasy during these passages, whatever the species of his sexuality. Under any interpretation, the Count is certainly enjoying Susanna's local-tonic responses to his local-dominant questions.

Now let us examine the Q&AR table from Susanna's point of view. When we do, another formalism leaps to the eye: in each Q&AR session, Susanna's second answer is the opposite to her first, and her initial third answer is the same as her second. The formalism is plausible because the pattern makes sense in light of the very first Q&AR session, where the Count's third question repeated his second. There, Susanna did not make a "mistake" in answering the third question the same as the second. Susanna thus reads the repeated question of Q&AR1 not as an inadvertent "glitch," but as [if it were] an *essential aspect* of the Count's modus interrogandi. This provides a solid cognitive basis for her mistakes in answering the third questions of Q&A review sessions 2 and 3. And she is in fact a good psychologist—we observed on several earlier occasions how the Count's third question of Q&A

review session 1, repeating his second question, was a highly characteristic aspect of his psychology during the scene, particularly in connection with his "lunge at B" when he sings the question. The cognitive analysis is especially useful because Susanna does not give "incorrect" answers at *other* plausible moments in the text—for instance, at the beginning of Q&AR session 3, where she has to answer a first question "No" instead of "Sì."

So she is cognitively prepared to make her "incorrect" answers to the third questions for Q&AR sessions 2 and 3, where she "ought" to give answers opposite to those for the second questions of the sessions. But what, then, triggers her *actually* making the "incorrect" answers? In particular, having made one mistake during Q&AR2, why does she not take special care, when alerted in this fashion, to get the third answer of Q&AR3 "correct"?

A Freudian view of her psychology is I think helpful for the actor here. In Susanna's "Scusatemi" phrase, she has just announced that she is lying. And of course she is in fact actually lying, when she gives "correct" answers to the Count's questions. She is also aware (or at least considers it possible) that the Count continues to suspect her of lying. Under those conditions, her "wrong" answers amount to the subtext "I am lying," as that subtext breaks through into her verbal discourse. Or perhaps the subtext, directed as if aside to the audience, is "I am *not* really a liar after all; you see how unaccustomed I am to lying,"—as she gives truthful (rather than "correct") answers. The subtext might not have broken through, were she not already primed to answer the third question of each Q&AR session the same as the second. This behavior fits very well with Freud's theoretical explanations for slips of the tongue.[5] In particular, his theory explains quite well why people often make slips of the tongue exactly when they are concentrating on correcting earlier slips of the tongue—an idea that responds to our query above as to why Susanna makes a mistake in answering the third question of Q&AR3, even forearmed with the realization that she made a mistake answering the third question of Q&AR2.[6]

A bit earlier I spoke of the Count's "prompting Susanna's climaxes on her high F♯s, when she 'corrects' her 'incorrect' answers" (toward the end of Q&AR sessions 2 and 3, m. 45 and m. 51). His prompting has a strong harmonic component. Each of those Q&AR sessions begins by oscillating three times between dominant-of-E harmony (Count's questions) and E harmony (Susanna's answers). Then, on Susanna's giving her "incorrect" answer to question 3 (still and again on E harmony), the Count indignantly challenges her "incorrect" answer with a shift to D harmony, singing the melodic tone D. Immediately after, Susanna "corrects" her answer, singing a melodically climactic F♯ over the D harmony still persisting from the Count's challenge.

The Count thus asserts a strong musical initiative when he challenges Susanna's "incorrect" answers. He introduces a harmonic function (subdominant of

5. Sigmund Freud, *Vorlesungen zur Einführung in die Psychoanalyse* (Berlin: Gustav Kiepenheuer Verlag, 1955), 18–34.

6. Freud, *Vorlesungen zur Einführung*, 25. Freud gives as an example a Social-Democratic newspaper that reported the presence, at a certain ceremony, of "his majesty the Grain Prince" [*Kornprinz* for *Kronprinz* (Crown Prince)]. The next day, the newspaper published an apology, explaining that they had naturally meant the "Gnarl Prince" [*Knorprinz*].

A) antithetic to the middleground dominant function of E harmony here. Indeed, as he does so, he sings the root tone of the subdominant harmony. Furthermore, dynamics accent his gesture very powerfully—he sings *forte*, with *forte* accompaniment, in a context surrounded by piano dynamics both before and after.[7]

The pure subdominant side of the Count is something we did not hear in the *minore*. Although the *minore* contained a number of significant harmonies with "4th-degree roots" on paper, none of them asserted an unambiguous subdominant function with an unambiguous D root.[8] The Count's challenging subdominants, at measures 45 and 51, are thus characteristic aspects of his behavior during the *maggiore*, of his behavior *after* he has once sung "Mi sento."

Putting the matter that way, we can hear at once how characteristic a feature the unambiguous D-root subdominant function is, within the Count's "Mi sento" theme itself. The Count expresses this harmonic side of his character, with a I–IV progression setting a full verse of text ("Mi sento dal contento"), only after he is (provisionally) satisfied (contento) that Susanna is not deceiving him. Once he has expressed this subdominant, he can then compose out the *double emploi* idea with his ii harmony in the next verse, using the B root (NB) to approach once more a cadential dominant-of-A at "pieno di gioia il cor," the first phrase in which the Count cadences on dominant-of-A-or-a since measure 10 in the *minore*. I read the following subtext: "Now that you (Susanna) have convinced me you are in earnest about our assignation, you will of course have no further hesitation in taking my dominant and leading it to a tonic cadence in A major."

And in fact Susanna's following phrase ("Scusate mi . . . amor") executes exactly the harmonic move, V–I in A, for which the Count is asking. Only—as mentioned on several earlier occasions—the Count does not hear her text. He is himself singing a V–I phrase at the same time (just as he provided his own major tonic at the first "Mi sento"); Susanna's phrase is a descant to his, and she sings it to the

7. A keen touch of orchestration further emphasizes these features of the Count's musical challenge. The string basses drop out and the celli, doubling the Count's sung D at the unison, play *sf*. The *sf* puts a harsh color on the Count's sung note, rendering his challenge all the more peremptory; the absence of string basses makes the Count's sung D the acoustic bass of the entire texture at the moment of his challenge, appropriately emphasizing the harmonic significance of his D as a fresh fundamental bass, with its fresh subdominant function.

8. Most of these harmonies are augmented-sixth chords or diminished-seventh chords: D♯–F–A–C in measure 1, D♯–F–A in measure 5, D–F♯–A♭–C in measure 12 (heard, beyond that, as a local second-degree harmony in C), D♯–F♯–A–C in measure 25. All of the chords on this list have their Ds altered to D♯s, except for the augmented-sixth chord in measure 12, heard not in a minor but as ii of a local C major. All of the chords function as dominant-preparations, not subdominants. The B♭–D–F harmonies of measures 23 and 24 might be argued as having "subdominant function," but they would have to be analyzed as Riemannian transformations (*Leittonwechselklänge*) of fourth-degree harmony in that event, not as D-root fourth-degree harmony per se. The root function of the B♭ triads is highly attenuated at best in any case, because of the fauxbourdon. The D–F–A–C harmony in the middle of measure 5 looks like a "fourth-degree harmony of a minor" on paper, but in its context it sounds far more like an added-sixth harmony based on the F triad that begins measure 5. The chord at the beginning of measure 25, where the Count "lunges at B" in his vocal line, does indeed have a strong cadential subdominant function, but the sense of a D root is ambiguous because of the *double emploi*—the sense of B root here, as we have noted earlier, sets up the "dominant of E" function for the Count's questions during the *maggiore*.

audience. Still, she does sing V-I in A major, and that is something for which she feels an urge to apologize—to the audience, and presumably to herself. In for a penny, in for a pound—she is not going to be able to avoid singing some sort of V–I, if she is to succeed in convincing the Count of her sincerity. Perhaps the Count is vaguely aware that she is doing so, in that he might hear that her descant melody is concordant with his own vocal phrase here, even if he doesn't hear exactly what she is singing.

A few brief remarks should suffice to get interested readers started, should they wish to continue exploring the rest of the number on their own. During the regular question period in the *maggiore* (mm. 36–42), the Count proposes IV–I antecedent half-phrases, which Susanna answers with V–I consequents. Significantly, the dominants are hers (beginning the consequent subphrases). She does not answer any dominants propounded by the Count's antecedents, but rather confirms and prolongs the tonic harmonies on which he ends. The little antecedent-consequent model happens three times in the music of measures 36–42, making a hemiola against the duple rhythm of the text, which projects two questions-and-answers. At the reprise of "Mi sento" (mm. 54ff.), Susanna interjects, at the subdominant, an imitation of the Count's opening motive, taking his "contento" harmony as her point of departure. (She sings by herself in measure 55, and the Count hears her.) Transformations of motivic material from the *minore* into the *maggiore* constitute a fascinating if tricky area for further analysis.

Postscript: A Methodological Note

A review of "tonics" and "dominants" in the three foregoing analyses provides some interesting thoughts about the applications and misapplications of music-theoretical terminology. In *Cinque, Dieci*, the dominant, and its root D, mark places where Figaro likes to be and to go, avoiding adequate responsibility for his relations with Susanna. The tonic and its root G mark places where Susanna feels secure about her marriage, and in her relation with Figaro more generally. In *Cosa sento!*, the initial dominant, with its F (major) root sense, marks the Count's rage, confusion, and loss of control; Basilio taunts the Count by returning to F major harmony to conclude his initial "apology"; he also taunts Susanna, later on, by "consoling" her in F major after she tries to evade the uncomfortable situation by fainting (or "fainting") in f minor. The tonic B♭, in this number, is a place where the Count can exercise (tries to exercise, hopes to exercise) the control and authority proper to his socio-political role. In *Crudel!*, the forceful dominants of the opening measures, with their E roots, mark the Count's persistent questioning of Susanna; the overall A major tonic of the number marks a place where his doubts and suspicions will be resolved.

The foregoing review brings to our attention the Protean nature of the roles played by "dominants" and "tonics" in Mozart's overall dramaturgy. Their nature is even more Protean, considering the ways in which those roles develop and transform over the course of any one number. For example, in *Cinque, Dieci,* Susanna at one point helpfully (and/or "helpfully") provides Figaro with a dominant of a dominant of his dominant, thus enabling him to make an eventual forceful arrival and cadence on his favorite D major harmony—at the expense of treating it as a local tonic and singing her theme. During *Crudel!*, the Count executes a musically similar maneuver during the question-and-answer review sessions of the *maggiore*: he feeds Susanna dominants-of-the-dominant, so that her dominant replies will provide the local impression of her answering his dominants with tonics, even though her local tonics are global dominants. She has already expropriated the Count's initial questioning dominants, to enact her own subtextual questioning—"Don't you believe me?"

In a certain sense, then, there is no abstract Platonic meaning to "a dominant" as such in Mozart's dramaturgy, nor to "a tonic." Dramatic significance always resides in this dominant, and in this tonic, of which there are as many different species as there are different readings of different scenes. The point will bear a certain amount of generalization—various readers will decide for themselves to what extent. The observation could be generalized so as to apply to tonal compositions for the stage, to tonal compositions with text, to tonal compositions in general so far as they can be heard to enact "drama." The observation could also be generalized so as to apply to theoretical terminology in general, beyond tonal theory as such. To paraphrase Schenker: *semper aliter, sed eisdem vocabulis.*[1] Our jargon appears "Protean" because we insist on retaining it as we discuss many different phenomenological experiences; each individual experience is itself highly focused. To be sure, if we did not retain, over a wide variety of experiential contexts, jargon terms such as "tonic," "dominant," "strong beat," "cadence," "accent," and the like (arguably including "up," "down," "before," "after," "motion," "repose," and the like), there would be little point in using the terms at all for critical discourse—more useful would then be such indexical expressions as "what the Count is singing here," "what the violins are playing here," and the like—accompanying each expression with a suitable acoustic stimulus. I am not in the slightest discounting the value of such productions for critical discourse—if anything, I wish we could use them more, and to better effect, in public discourse about music. On the other hand, I do not feel that the virtues of those productions obviate the usefulness of standard jargon, when that jargon can be used to produce observations that stimulate hearing and thought.

1. Heinrich Schenker, *Free Composition* (*Der freie Satz*), trans. and ed. Ernst Oster (New York: Longman, 1979). Schenker's epigraph, on the title page, reads "*Semper idem sed non eodem modo.*" ("*sed non,*" instead of the more elegant Ciceronian "*nec,*" is curious. Perhaps Schenker was playing with the sonorous effects of *sem-/sed, idem/eodem,* and *non/eo-/modo.*) In my variation I intend both to agree with him and to offer a strong antithesis, playing fox and hedgehog to his hedgehog and fox.

These are suggestive matters for music theorists to ponder, contemplating the (often revealing) methodological uses and (difficult to avoid) misuses of music-theoretical terminology in various species of discourse (verbal or symbolic) about music.

PART II

Schubert

This section comprises three chapters, each focusing in one way or another on some Schubert song.

"Music Theory, Phenomenology, and Modes of Perception," although quite extensive and broad in theoretical scope, draws heavily for examples on the middle section of *Morgengruß*. It was published in *Music Perception,* vol. 3, no. 4 (1986).

The chapter on *Auf dem Flusse* first appeared in *19th Century Music,* vol. 6, no. 1 (1982). Revised and extended, it was reprinted in *Schubert: Critical and Analytical Studies*, ed. Walter Frisch (Lincoln: University of Nebraska Press, 1986). The later version is reproduced here.

The chapter on *Ihr Bild* was written for this book. It is designed to lead on into the next section of the book: there, I shall discuss a different setting of the same poem by Clara Schumann.

CHAPTER Four

Music Theory, Phenomenology, and Modes of Perception

Part I: Phenomenological Preface

Overtly phenomenological study of music in Husserl's sense begins with the man himself, who made central to his theories of perception a famous analysis for perceiving a sustained tone.[1] That analysis is highlighted by Izchak Miller in a recent philosophical commentary, which the interested reader will find especially clear.[2] Miller puts the heart of the matter as follows:

> Whereas it does seem true that I am hearing that tone throughout a certain interval of time, it does not seem it can be true that I am hearing all of it (or an extended part of it) at any given instant of that interval. Yet . . . throughout that interval I continuously experience the endurance, or the continuity, of that tone, and this requires (contrary to the previous hypothesis) that I experience at any given instant . . . more than a mere instantaneous phase of the tone. How, then, is an instantaneous perceptual experience of the temporal continuity, or the temporal passage, of a tone possible?
>
> Answering this and other related questions about our temporal awareness is of crucial importance to Husserl for reasons which go beyond the mere desire to provide an adequate, or a complete, account of perception. The subject matter of Husserlian phenomenology is our conscious experience, and Husserl presupposes our ability to reflect on our various experiences and discern their structures. However, our conscious experiences, or—as Husserl calls them—our *acts* of consciousness, are themselves processes, albeit mental processes. How do we, then, succeed in being reflectively aware at any given moment of the continuity, or the passage, of our mental acts? How does one, in other words, succeed in reflecting at any given moment on anything more than the corresponding momentary phase of the act reflected upon?

1. Edmund Husserl, *The Phenomenology of Internal Time Consciousness*, trans. J. S. Churchill (Bloomington: Indiana University Press, 1964), 43.
2. Izchak Miller, *Husserl, Perception, and Temporal Awareness* (Cambridge, Mass.: The MIT Press, 1984).

> According to Husserl, the structure of our temporal awareness which makes the continuous perception of the temporal passage of a tone possible is the very same structure which makes a continuous reflection on the temporal passage of our mental acts possible. Accounting for the possibility of the first is, thus, accounting for the possibility of the second.[3]

Miller also devotes much attention to "Husserl's Account of Perceiving a Melody."[4] This discussion, which includes an account of listening to the opening theme from Mozart's Clarinet Concerto, does not itself invoke sophisticated music-theoretical apparatus; still, any theorist interested in Schenker, or Kurth, or Leonard Meyer, or Narmour—or serialism for that matter—is sure to find the commentary, in the context of Miller's book, resonating with familiar mental/aural experiences.

Among explicitly phenomenological writers who do invoke sophisticated music-theoretical concepts, Judith Lochhead is especially noteworthy. Her dissertation in particular projects an avowedly phenomenological view of Western art music from many periods; it comments very suggestively on temporal issues that have to do with our finding much recent music recalcitrant to received analytic approaches, a problem that she finds phenomenological in nature.[5]

Thomas Clifton also proclaimed a phenomenological approach to music theory, although of a quite different sort. The title of his recently published book reflects his stance.[6] Taylor Greer's perceptive critique of Clifton's earlier work does not extend to this book, but Greer is well worth reading for anyone interested in the methodological issues raised by applying phenomenology to music theory.[7] The book itself has recently been reviewed concisely and perceptively by Nicholas Cook and by James Tenney.[8]

Few professional music theorists have proclaimed so explicitly phenomenological a program or approach as have those just mentioned. However, phenomenological thinking is implicitly manifest in the work of others as well. Jonathan Kramer's temporal studies (e.g., Kramer, 1981) engage such modes of thought.[9] So

3. Miller, *Husserl*, 2–3.

4. Miller, *Husserl*, 118–144.

5. Judith Lochhead, "The Temporal Structure of Recent Music: A Phenomenological Investigation" (Ph.D. diss., State University of New York at Stony Brook, 1982). Lochhead worked extensively with the philosopher Don Ihde, who authored an important work on the phenomenology of hearing, *Listening and Voice: A Phenomenology of Sound* (Athens: Ohio University Press, 1976).

6. Thomas Clifton, *Music as Heard: A Study in Applied Phenomenology* (New Haven, Conn.: Yale University Press, 1983). Unfortunately, further development of Clifton's thought was cut short by his untimely death.

7. Taylor A. Greer, "Listening as Intuiting: A Critique of Clifton's Theory of Intuitive Description" *In Theory Only* 7.8 (1984), 3–21.

8. Nicholas Cook, "Review of Clifton, *Music as Heard*," *Music Analysis* 2.3 (1983), 291–294; James Tenney, "Review of Clifton, *Music as Heard*," *Journal of Music Theory* 29.1 (1985), 197–213.

9. See, for example, Jonathan Kramer, "New Temporalities in Music," *Critical Inquiry* 7.3 (1981), 539–556. Kramer was a consulting editor for *Music Theory Spectrum*, vol. 7 (1985), an issue devoted entirely to time and rhythm in music. The volume contains much material of relevance to this article. Its editor is Lewis Rowell, who has himself done extensive work on temporality in music. Of phenomenological interest (and of wider interest too) is his article "The Subconscious Language of Musical Time," *Music Theory Spectrum* 1 (1979), 96–106. Rowell notes in particular that "the terms for temporality

do Christopher Hasty's.[10] So, in a less obvious way, does a recent study of my own.[11] The article builds a numerical model that counts, at each "now"-time t, the number of time-spans I recall from the pertinent recent past that have (had) duration d.[12] In this way I construct a function W(d,t) that gives me an "unfolding durational-interval vector" as the "now"-cursor t advances. The concept underlying my construction engages a Husserlian two-dimensional model of perceptual time, a model that allows both for Husserl's "primal impressions," impressions that follow the now-cursor t, and also for Husserl's "retentions," projections of remembered past times (and past durations) into my present consciousness. Later in my article, I even become involved with something much like Husserl's "protensions," projections of future expectations into present consciousness.[13] Since writing the article, I have found the idea of an "unfolding rhythmic interval vector" highly suggestive in connection with a great variety of other rhythmic formalisms.[14]

Marvin Minsky—like myself I suppose—is not popularly considered a phenomenologically oriented thinker. And yet the following quotation would find itself very much at home in Husserl's *Time-Consciousness*: "to really understand how memory and process merge in 'listening' we will simply have to use much more 'procedural' descriptions—that is, the kinds that can describe *how processes proceed*."[15] Minsky makes his statement in connection with a critique of "'generative' and 'transformational' methods of syntactic analysis." He means neo-Schenkerian methods. The same species of criticism is voiced by Eugene Narmour when, protesting what he calls the "schemata" and "archetypal patterns" of Schenkerian theory, he writes that "the true 'genetic' basis in musical process is to be found by discovering what patterns imply in prospect . . . in relation to what they realize in retrospect."[16] This sort of discourse jibes well with Husserl's vocabulary: primal impressions are patterns doing Narmour's work of presently-implying-and-realizing; retentions are retrospective contexts brought into present perception; protensions are prospective contexts brought into present perception.

The works of the nonphenomenologists just cited suggest but do not formulate and examine very adequately the idiosyncratically *recursive* aspects of Husserl's

in music . . . denote physical gesture as well as the more abstract thing that is measured by the gesture" (102–103); his elaboration of this idea ties in suggestively with remarks I shall make much later concerning performance as a mode of perception.

10. See, for example, Christopher Hasty, "Rhythm in Post-tonal Music: Preliminary Questions of Duration and Motion," *Journal of Music Theory* 25.2 (1981), 183–216.

11. David Lewin, "Some Investigations into Foreground Rhythmic and Metric Patterning," *Music Theory: Special Topics*, ed. Richmond Browne (New York: Academic Press, 1981), 101–136.

12. For the model, it is perfectly workable to replace the exact number "*d*" by the idea, "more-or-less-*d*, as distinguishable from other durations I retain in my awareness at time *t*."

13. Husserl's terms and pertinent diagrams are explained in Miller, *Husserl*, 120ff.

14. I explore this in my book, *Generalized Musical Intervals and Transformations* (New Haven, Conn.: Yale University Press, 1987). [See, for example, sections 3.3.1 and 5.4.2 therein.]

15. Marvin Minsky, "Music, Mind, and Meaning," in *Music, Mind, and Brain*, ed. M. Clynes (New York: Plenum, Press, 1982), 1–19. The quotation appears on page 6. Compare this excerpt from Miller, cited earlier in this article: "our conscious experiences, or—as Husserl calls them—our *acts* of consciousness, are themselves processes, albeit mental processes. How do we, then, succeed in being reflectively aware at any given moment of the continuity, or the passage, of our mental acts?"

16. Eugene Narmour, *Beyond Schenkerism* (Chicago: University of Chicago Press, 1977), 40.

perception-structures. By the italicized term I mean to suggest the way in which such structures characteristically involve themselves in loops with other perception-structures that are among their objects or arguments. The other perception-structures are typically in characteristic *relationships* to the given structure (e.g. of retention, protension, implication, realization, denial), and those relationships, as well as other sorts of relations between perceptions, can also enter into recursive configurations as objects or arguments of perception-structures.

Let me illustrate the sort of loop I mean by a simple example using English text. Consider a thing we might call a perception, that is p = Siegmund's watching Sieglinde's watching Siegmund's watching Sieglinde's watching . . . (etc.). We can study the infinitely recursive aspect of p by using a pair of finite perceptions SGM and SGL, defined in a mutually recursive relationship. SGM = Siegmund's watching SGL, and SGL = Sieglinde's watching SGM. The pair SGM and SGL can also generate another infinite perception q; q is Sieglinde's watching Siegmund's watching . . . (etc.). A computer could generate p by sending SGM to some evaluation routine (let us call it EVAL); the machine would generate q by EVALuating SGL. There is of course a small difficulty: in either case, the EVALuation would go on forever, trapped in an infinite loop. I can think of two ways to avoid this difficulty that make sense to me both in their eventual musical implications and in light of the small knowledge I possess of computer science. One would be to have an overriding external call from a more global part of the system interrupt the endless tryst of the sibling lovers. Another would be to have some sort of preliminary higher-level parsing applied to the environment before anything gets sent to the EVALuator. The parser could spot the endless loop; it would then arrange for the eventual EVALuation to be terminated (by a special symbol, jump instruction, or what you will) after a certain number of rides around the loop. This, after all, is what we ourselves do in writing out p, when we terminate with the special symbols ". . ." and/or "(etc.)", or something of the sort, once the loop structure has been made clear to the reader.[17] The two methods of avoiding the infinite loop could be combined, producing EVALuated output like "Siegmund's watching Sieglinde's watching Siegmund's watching . . . Sieglinde's suddenly noticing Hunding." (Four Wagner tubas make an excellent external interrupt.)

Having explored the abstract textual example to help the reader get a feeling for the kinds of recursive systems in which I am interested, I shall now examine an abstract musical example (Example 4.1).

I shall be especially interested first in musical perceptions as objects of musical perceptions; this corresponds to SGL-as-an-object-of-SGM, or SGM-as-an-object-of-SGL, in the English example. Then I shall be interested in the specifically recursive aspect of certain musical perception structures; this corresponds to the recursive aspect of SGM-and-SGL when considered together as a perception-structure.

Imagine a string ensemble playing the score shown by Example 4.1a, produc-

17. If the parser applies itself only to a restricted family of formal strings called "perceptions," and the perceptions do not engage the parsing language itself, then certain technical "Church-Turing" problems should not arise. Computer buffs will know what I mean (although they may not agree). For other readers, one might put the matter this way in intuitive discourse: if parsing is to be applied, then musical perceptions should not form a "language," and/or the parsing itself should be "imperceptible."

Example 4.1

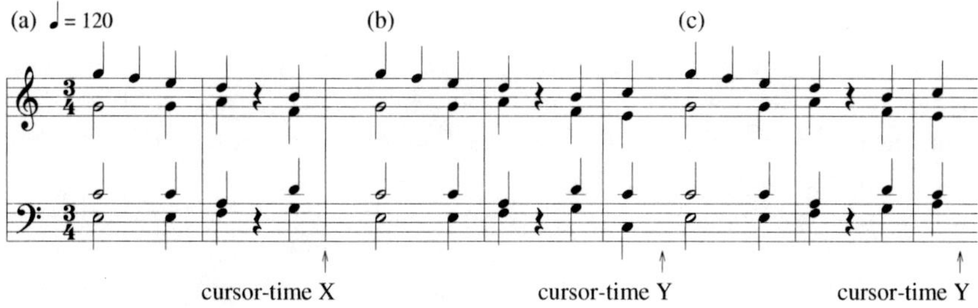

ing an acoustic signal that we shall call Signal(a). We ask, just *what* am I "perceiving" as I listen musically to that signal at the now-time corresponding to cursor-time X on the score? According to Husserl's theory, what I am perceiving—let us call it Perception(a)—is a hugely complex network of things, things including other perceptions, their relations among themselves, and their relations to Perception(a) itself. I have, for example, perceptions (a1), "V^7 harmony over the last beat," (a2), "5th degree in the bass over the last beat," and (a3), "7th degree in the melody over the last beat." I perceive how the perceptions (al), (a2), and (a3) are interrelating among themselves. I perceive how each of them is relating to my overall Perception(a) at cursor-time X. And I am retaining perceptions of how (a1), (a2), and (a3) each relate to yet earlier perceptions. For instance, "5th degree in the bass over the last beat" at cursor-time X involves among *its* objects retained perceptions of "5th degree in the bass since the attack of the last beat" at *every* perceptually functional moment during the half-second of clock time preceding X; this is Husserl's analysis of the sustained tone. "Dominant-seventh harmony over the last beat" at cursor-time X involves an analogous family of objects; it also has other objects that engage clock-time well behind the G^7 chord itself, time within which other perceptions built musical contexts of the piece that can render significant my mental acts of "perceiving a dominant" and "perceiving a beat" at now-time X. To the extent that "dominant" and "beat" involve acculturated theoretical ideas and language, their contexts here are even partly outside the time of the entire musical performance.

Particularly interesting as an object of Perception(a) is a perception corresponding to the score of Example 4.1b. Let us call this object Perception(b). Perception(a) does not notice Perception(b) in a vacuum; it perceives Perception(b) *in certain relations* to Perception(a), relations that include at least "protension" (if not "implication"). The difference between this view of affairs and the traditional view needs considerable emphasis. In the traditional view, Perception(b) "has not yet happened" at cursor-time X, but we "expect" it, perhaps with a certain probability or entropy value. In the Husserlian view, Perception(b) *does actually happen at cursor-time X*: I perceive *at time X* the structure symbolized by the score of Example 4.1b, and that perception—along with certain of its relationships—is one object of Perception(a) *at cursor-time X*. Among the relationships are protension ("coming up"), mensurated protension ("coming up in one beat's time"), likelihood ("very likely in the pertinent Markoff chain"), and others.

"The C eight-three chord" is *not* an object of my perception at time X, at least not directly. The chord is perceived only indirectly, as an object of Perception(b), which is as yet perceived only as an object of Perception(a). It is not "the C chord" that is "very likely coming up in one beat's time"; rather it is "the confirmation-time for Perception(b)" that is "very likely coming up in one beat's time," as I perceive things at X. Listening at that time to Signal(a), I do not form the idea of a disembodied C major chord coming up over the next beat as a context-free phenomenon; I do have a mental construct of a C major chord coming up over the next beat, but *only* in the context of a broader mental construct that is Perception(b).

We are now in a position to explore what I have called the recursive aspects of musical perception-structure. We can approach our study by inquiring after the objects of Perception(b). Among them we shall find Perception(a) itself, in a particular relationship to (b). Using Narmour's terminology, we could describe the relationship by saying that what-we-perceive in Perception(b) includes Perception(a) in a relation of implication-realized. Here we encounter a branch of the recursion, for if we inquire what we perceive that is implied by (a), we find that it is just Perception(b) in a relation of realization-implied. We can isolate the recursive aspect of the situation by formulating expressions IMP and RLZ in the earlier manner of SGM and SGL: IMP = (a)'s implication of RLZ; RLZ = (b)'s realization of IMP.

For a more general model of perception, though, we shall not want to isolate recursive relationships in this way from their parent perceptions; our primary focus must be on the perceptions themselves as totalities. Here is how the model I shall soon propose will address the recursive loop above: Perceptions (a) and (b) will each be defined by a formal list of a certain sort; in the list for Perception(a), we might place a formal subargument consisting of the pair [Perception (b), implication], while in the list for Perception(b) we should then place a formal subargument consisting of the pair [Perception(a),realization]. One can imagine the recursive potentialities of the situation to lie within two symbolic computer statements: (DEFINE Perception(a) . . . (. . . (Perception(b),implication) . . .)); (DEFINE Perception(b) . . . (. . . (. . . (Perception(a),realization) . . .)).[18] By casting my discourse into symbolic computer language of this sort, I mean to suggest the possible utility of Artificial Intelligence (actor language, frames, et al.) in studying these matters. Thereby I mean specifically to make points of contact with Minsky, and with certain features of Miller's presentation as well.[19] Minsky ("Music, mind and meaning") devotes a lot of attention to programming strategies. Miller (*Husserl*, pp. 93–97) uses at times a formalism involving argument lists that suggests an AI environment. Soon I shall develop my own model in more detail.

18. Within the DEFINE list for Perception(a), the formal term "implication" could be suitably qualified by a formal probability value or entropy value, modeling an intuitive level of expectation or predictability associated with the "implication" of Perception(b), or of something-(b)-like in some well-stipulated sense. Alternatively, one could build refinements like these into a formal definition of "implication."

19. My stance here is not particularly new or original. Points of contact between Husserl's phenomenology and the worlds of Artificial Intelligence are the primary subject, for instance, of a recent publication edited by H. L. Dreyfus and H. Hall, *Husserl, Intentionality, and Cognitive Science* (Cambridge, Mass.: The MIT Press, 1982), that assembles fifteen related essays. The editors' introduction contains sections headed "*Husserl's Anticipation of Artificial Intelligence*" (17–19) and "*Husserl's (and AI's) Problems*" (19–27); the former section characterizes Minsky's frame construct of 1973 as "a new data structure remarkably similar to Husserl's for representing everyday knowledge" (19). Particularly important work in this area has been done by Otto Laske. In "Toward an Explicit Cognitive

Before I get to that, though, let me dwell on something that may have slipped the reader's attention by now: while we have been freely discussing Perception(b) as part of what-(a)-perceives (at cursor-time X), and Perception(a) as part of what-(b)-perceives, nowhere in our discussion have we supposed that our imaginary quartet actually *plays* the score of Example 4.1b, producing an acoustic stimulus we might call Signal(b). The point deserves some exploration.

First let us suppose that the quartet does *not* continue their performance of Example 4.1a to produce a performance of Example 4.1b; suppose they instead perform Example 4.1c, producing acoustic Signal(c) and triggering an appropriate Perception(c). In this case, all the things we have so far said about Perception(b) and its relations, at now-time X, to Perception(a) remain exactly as we have already said them; the acoustic production of Signal(c) at now-time Y changes nothing of all that. Perception(b) as already discussed continues to "exist," and it retains in retrospect at time Y all the functions it had at time X. Indeed it acquires a new function as well, in connection with Perception(c); one characteristic thing that (c) "perceives" is precisely *that (b) is not being confirmed* by the event of time Y. We imagine a computer statement: (DEFINE Perception(c) . . . (. . . (Perception(b), denial) . . .) . . .). In order for (b) to be "denied" by (c) at time Y, (b) must be at hand at that time, in a phenomenological location different from that of (c). One must not think of (b) as "disappearing" and of (c) as "replacing" (b).

Let us consider next the trickier case in which the quartet *does* play Example 4.1b, producing acoustic Signal(b). The tricky thing is to realize that we now have at hand a *new* Perception (b-yes), a new perception that is *different* from our old acquaintance Perception(b). (b), as something (a) expects, defined at cursor-time X, continues to "exist" as in the previous case; now it additionally becomes at cursor-time Y an object of the new perception (b-yes). We might say that (b-yes) "confirms" (b), in the sense that (c) in the previous case "denied" (b). Symbolically, we could write (DEFINE Perception(b-yes) . . . (Perception(b),confirmation) . . .) . . .).

Part II: A General Model[20]

> If one were to sequester the notion of "good" continuation as a descriptor . . . in tonal music, one would have to introduce . . . powerful concepts of relation—including those of contradiction, opposition, and paradox—as natural to the process, even necessary to it.[21]

Theory of Musical Listening," *Computer Music Journal* 4.2 (1980), Laske develops an AI model that addresses recursive aspects of perception very explicitly and clearly. The article, along with a hefty body of other work by Laske, is also available in the Computer Music Association Report *Music and Mind, An Artificial Intelligence Perspective* (San Francisco: Computer Music Association, 1981).

20. I must express very heartfelt gratitude to Fred Lerdahl and Diana Deutsch who, by inviting me to give a lecture about musical perception, started me thinking along the lines of this present chapter, and in particular along the lines of the model here proposed. The lecture, "Changing Perceptions over a Passage in Schubert," was given at the Fourth Workshop on Physical and Neuropsychological Foundations of Music, Ossiach, Austria, in August of 1983.

21. Richmond Browne, "The Dialectic of Good Continuation in Tonal Music," *Music Analysis* 4.1/2 (1985), 5–13.

To help us entertain the ideas discussed in Part I, and others of their ilk, I propose as a provisional model for "a musical perception" this basic formula:

$$p = (EV,CXT,P\text{-}R\text{-}LIST,ST\text{-}LIST).$$

Here the musical perception p is defined as a formal list containing four arguments. The argument EV specifies a sonic *event* or family of *events* being "perceived." The argument CXT specifies a musical *context* in which the perception occurs. The argument P-R-LIST is a list of pairs (p_i,r_i); each pair specifies a *perception* p_i and a *relation* r_i which p bears to p_i. The argument ST-LIST is a list of *statements* $s_1, \ldots s_K$ made in some stipulated *language* L.

As an example, we can construct one formal musical perception pertinent to our intuition of "what we hear" when a quartet plays the last quarter-note of Example 4.1c to finish a performance of Example 4.1c. For the formal perception, EV is "this thing that happens on the last beat." CXT is all-of-Example 4.1c, and also a culturally conditioned theoretical component that makes us responsive to categories we call beats, keys, tonics, dominants, et al. The P-R-LIST includes a pair (Perception(b),denial). The ST-LIST might include, in a suitable language L, a statement, "deceptive cadence."

One might wonder why we need an argument EV at all, in the specific example or in the general model. In the example, we describe EV as "this thing that happens on the last beat." Now "on the last beat" is a perceptual statement that might very easily be added to our ST-LIST. Generalizing that observation, we can plausibly wonder what words we could possibly use, in pointing to an EV, that could not be excised from the phrase "this thing that . . . " and placed among the statements on a ST-LIST. The language L could be expanded as necessary. Clearly we cannot describe EV or CXT, for any specific example, without using *some* language L′; then why not simply meld L and L′ into one superlanguage? In that case our first argument EV is only a syntactic dummy, and we could reduce our model to a list of only three arguments: a context CXT, a P-R-LIST of perceptions-cum-relations, and a ST-LIST of statements we are making at the moment, possibly including certain statements that focus our attention on this or that particular "event" in the given ConteXT.

I go over this possibility so that the reader will know I have considered it and rejected it, even though I admit its plausibility. I admit, too, the appeal to Occam's Razor, and yet I would not be comfortable with a model that implicitly denied the existence of any "real event" apart from the various statements about it that could be articulated by various interested parties. The social and political history of the last fifty years certainly contributes to my discomfort, and I freely admit my bourgeois-liberal class bias, my susceptibility to the Will-to-Truth, and all the rest of my predilections in this position. I prefer to believe that the statements we make in connection with a perception are *about* something, which is to say about some *thing*. The thing EV will have at the very least a lexical function, enabling us to mark, collect, and compare a certain ensemble of formal perceptions, that is, perceptions-about-EV. The role of EV in my model corresponds in this respect with Miller's analysis of Husserl's "determinable-X." Miller writes that there must be "a feature . . . of the perceptual act which determines the (purported) object of the act *in abstraction from its (purported) properties,* a feature which provides us with an intentional 'fix' on that (purported) object through a course of experience along which the attribute-meanings of our act may shift and change radically. That feature of the perceptual noematic *Sinn* is what Husserl refers to by 'the determinable-X.' It seems that what Husserl has in mind is that the determinable-X of the perceptual act is a 'purely referring' element of meaning, something like a meaning of an indexical, probably (at least part of) the meaning of the word 'this.'"[22] I share the urge to suppose such a demonstrable-X, my EV, although I am not persuaded of its logical necessity for perceptual discourse about music.

The necessity for a musical context CXT in such discourse is much clearer. For example, when perceiving the event of the a-minor chord in Example 4.1c, I have one set of impressions perceiving it in its own context, as an isolated harmonic structure, and quite another set of impressions perceiving it in the context of Example 4.1c as a whole. In the former context, I could not make statements involving a "deceptive cadence," or a "cadence" of any sort, or indeed a "key" or a "beat." Perceiving the isolated chord might involve further problems, in that I might not be able to *locate* its sound within the pertinent music: there might be more than one such sound in that music.

To illustrate the problem of locatability more thoroughly, let me suppose I have before me, poised and ready, a classical orchestra. I bring down my hand, cuing them in, and they produce a chord, forte and staccato, that lasts about one-third of a second; then they rest for about two-thirds of a second; then I cut them off. This "this," this EVent, this determinable-X of the situation, is produced by these instruments on these notes: flutes on E♭6 and B♭5; oboes on G5 and E♭5; clarinets on E♭5 and G4; bassoons on E♭4 and E♭3; horns on E♭4 and G3; trumpets on E♭5 and E♭4; kettledrum on E♭3; first violins on G5, B♭4, E♭4, and G3; second violins on E♭5, E♭4, and G3; violas on E♭4 and G3; cellibass on E♭2 and E♭1. I turn to you and ask, "What was that?" You reply, "It must be the opening of the *Eroica* Symphony." "No," I respond, "it was actually measure 2 of the symphony." "Unfair!" you exclaim. But *why* is it unfair? I had indeed instructed the players to play measure 2 when I cued them; they were in fact all looking at measure 2 in their parts as they played. In any conceivable sense you might imagine, they did play measure 2. Only you did not *perceive* measure 2! Your sense of unfairness arises here precisely because there is a crucial phenomenological sense in which *measure 2 is not a well-formed ConteXT*. Measures 1-and-2-together *are* a well-formed ConteXT; you would be able to locate measure 2 in *that* context. Measure 1 by itself, or rather measure 1 preceded by a certain amount of sound typical of "orchestra-not-playing," is *also* a well-formed musical ConteXT. That is why you immediately *perceived* measure 1. According to my model, you were quite correct in that perception; indeed it would have been impossible, in the formal sense of the model, for you to have perceived anything else in the context at hand.

22. Miller, *Husserl*, 70–71. We shall explore just such shifts and changes of attribute-meanings for fixed musical EVents, in the Schubert analysis that will occupy Part III of this chapter.

Example 4.2

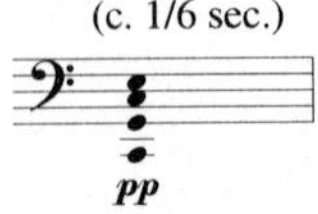

Let us study another example. Suppose I refer to the place in the *Waldstein* Sonata "where it goes like *this*," playing or pointing to Example 4.2. Although the event is perfectly well defined as an acoustic stimulus, even as an *auditory* perception, there is no *musical* perception at hand, since you have only the vaguest idea of what I might be referring to, so far as the *music* under discussion is concerned. This is because the EVent, the thing that "goes like *this*," has not been located in an adequate ConteXT. Failing such a CXT, you can not have a musical perception, although you have a perfectly clear auditory perception. If I refer to the EVent of Example 4.2 as "the third eighth of measure 2," I have placed it in an adequate musical ConteXT. Event-and-context are suggested by Example 4.3.

Example 4.3

If, on the other hand, I refer to the EVent of Example 4.2 as "the sixth eighth-note of the reprise measure," I have implicitly specified another ConteXT, one that is suggested by Example 4.4.

Example 4.4

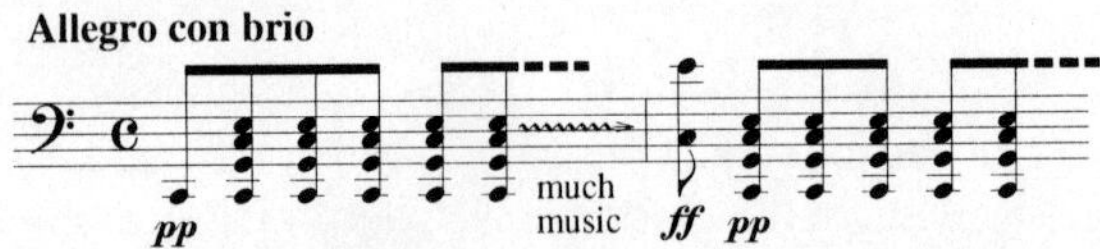

I am claiming, in as radical a sense as you please, that "the sixth eighth of the reprise measure" does NOT sound like Example 4.2. It sounds like Example-4.4-focused-on-the-pertinent-event, so far as we are talking about musical perception. We are usually so talking when we speak of how a certain *musical* event "sounds." In contrast, one could say that the acoustic signal delimited by the specific event gives rise to an auditory perception which "sounds" like Example 4.2. But that is a very different kind of statement.

The problem of locatability deserves much further study in its own right. Here, I shall indicate only one possible direction such study might take. Suppose that my orchestra is assembled here, and that they have not yet played anything for you. I bring down my hand, cuing them in, and they produce a chord, fortissimo and staccato, that lasts about one-third of a second; then they rest for about two-thirds of a second; then I cut them off. The chord is as follows: flutes on G6 and B♭5; oboes on E♭5; clarinets on E♭5 and G4; bassoons on E♭4 and E♭3; horns on G4 and E♭4; trumpets on E♭5 and E♭4; kettledrum on E♭3; first violins on G5, B♭4, E♭4, and G3; second violins on G5, B♭4, E♭4, and G3; violas on E♭5, E♭4, and G3; cellibass on E♭3 and E♭2. I turn to you and ask, "What was that?" If you are Beethoven, or a responsible conductor, or a first-flute player, or an alert orchestral cellist, and so on, you *might* answer, "It was the penultimate measure from the first movement of the *Eroica*," and you would be right. More likely, though, you will answer, "It was the opening of the *Eroica*." "No," I respond, "it was actually the penultimate measure of the first movement, measure 690." "Unfair!" you exclaim. But now the unfairness is of a very different type. For the chord under discussion is locatable, "technically speaking." You are protesting only because the demands that I am making on your ear, and on your knowledge of the symphony, seem unreasonable to you. You will nevertheless admit that a musician with an excellent ear and a thorough knowledge of the piece could "in theory" locate the chord. You will further admit that a student in an advanced conducting class, or an advanced orchestration class, might reasonably be asked to hear such subtle differences between sounds as are at issue here; you will admit that a student in an advanced analysis class might reasonably be asked to ponder why Beethoven comes so close to the sound of measure 1 in measure 690, but does not reproduce it exactly; you will admit in these connections the propriety, if not the sufficiency, of studying how measure 690 sounds in and of itself. That is, you will admit "in theory," specifically in the theory I am now expounding, the propriety of measure 690 as a musical-perceptual ConteXT for itself-as-EVent.

The question remains, however, to what extent the event of that measure should be considered "practically" locatable in its own context. Most of us would agree that the demands I might make on an advanced music student are not to be made of "the listener," and many of us will also suppose that any phenomenological theory of music, in our present understanding of "phenomenology," will primarily address "the listener," a fictive person whose role vis-à-vis the *Eroica* differs from that of the first flutist, cellist, or conductor playing it, or Beethoven composing it. We do suppose that the perceptions of "the listener" have some real and important relation to the things a composer does, and to things a performer does, but we would not want to equate the roles of composer, performer, and listener, at least not in our culture as it is today for better or for worse. The issue of "the listener" in this connection seems crucial to me. I shall return to it at length in Part V of this chapter.

Meanwhile, I should recall that locatability is only *one* of the matters involved when we stipulate a ConteXT for the EVent(s) of a musical perception. Even when all the events at issue are locatable, what we perceive—the p of our basic formula—depends on the context as well. Thus, to repeat an earlier point, the a-minor chord of Example 4.1c generates one perception in its own context, and a quite different perception in the context of Example 4.1c as a whole. In the analysis of a passage from Schubert that occupies Part III of this chapter, we shall have the occasion to study some actual musical EVents whose perceptual significances shift radically as their ConteXTs expand and/or contract in various musical dimensions.[23]

Now let us return to the Basic Formula, p = (EV,CXT,P-R-LIST,ST-LIST), and devote some attention to P-R-LIST. This argument, it will be recalled, is a list of pairs (p_i,r_i), each pair specifying a perception p_i and a relation r_i which p bears to p_i. For example, p might "deny" p_1, "confirm" p_2, "imply" p_3, "support" p_4, and "succeed" p_5; the P-R-LIST for p would then include the pairs (p_1,denial), (p_2,confirmation), (p_3,implication), (p_4,support), and (p_5,succession). These pairs model the idea that we perceive p_i-being-denied, p_2-being-confirmed, etc. as essential parts of our p-perception.

The P-R-LIST enables us to model recursive aspects of perception-structuring; as we saw in earlier discussion, that is a powerful and characteristic feature of the model. Earlier, for example, we could speak of Perception(a) as perceiving Perception (b)-being-implied, while Perception(b) perceived Perception(a)-being-realized. The P-R-LIST for Perception(a) thus contained the pair (Perception(b),implication), while the P-R-LIST for Perception(b) contained the pair (Perception(a),realization).

Eventually it may be necessary to formulate rules that determine when certain recursive P-R configurations are malformed. A few such rules may already appear obvious, but I would urge extreme caution in the matter. After studying Parts III and IV of this chapter, the reader will see why I want to proceed so carefully. There we shall see that the geometry and logic of musical perception are not easily inferable from the geometry of Euclid or Descartes and the logic of Zermelo/Fraenkel or Gödel/Bernays.

In any event, we must not declare to be "malformed" loops that are simply infinite, like the implication/realization loop for Perceptions (a) and (b), or the trysting loop for Siegmund and Sieglinde. While exploring the Wagnerian loop, we investigated two ways to prevent an EVALuator from getting trapped in the loop; the same expedients are available for the implication/realization loop, and for a large class of similarly structured loops. The first expedient is to apply higher-level parsing to the environment before attempting to EVALuate the perception-strings. The parser would spot the loop and supply the EVALuator with a symbol like " . . . " or "(etc.)" to finish off with, once a certain number of trips around the loop had made the recursive structure clear.

The second expedient is to break off EVALuation upon a trigger signal from an external interrupt, thus: Siegmund's watching Sieglinde's watching Siegmund's watching Sieglinde's watching Siegmund's suddenly hearing Hunding. Just like Hunding's tubas, our string quartet's a-minor triad from Example 4.1c could function as this sort of external interrupt. The a-minor triad as a signal *from outside the listener* could break off the chain of (a)'s implication of (b)'s realization of (a)'s implication of (b)'s realization of (a)'s implication denied by (c). If the quartet were to play Signal(b) instead of Signal(c), the C-major eight-three chord could

23. The reader who wants to explore the abstract theory of ConteXTs farther will be interested in an extended study by Raphael Eric Atlas, "The Diachronic Recognition of Enharmonic Equivalence: A Theory and its Application to Five Instrumental Movements by W. A. Mozart" (Ph.D. diss., Yale University, 1983). This work explicitly and systematically investigates the roles of varying musical contexts in building perceptions involving enharmonic relationships of all sorts within tonal compositions.

have a similar interrupt-function, stopping EVALuation of the (a)/(b) implication/realization loop and introducing the new Perception(b-yes). We might then perceive (a)'s implication of (b)'s realization of (a)'s implication of (b)'s realization being confirmed by (b-yes). The interrupt function for the a-minor five-three chord of Signal(c), or for the C-major eight-three chord of Signal(b), is an attractive theoretical conceit. The harmonic sonorities as interrupts from acoustic signals external to perception-EVALuation have a *different species of function* from any they might carry as arguments or subarguments within formal p-structures.

The species of function is different because the mechanism of the external interrupt necessarily presupposes, as an implicit feature of its model, an aspect of musical time that is not a mental construction of the listener; *some* temporal exigencies impinge upon the listener *from without*. Personally, I like the metaphor of that model very much. The alternate expedient for keeping the EVALuator out of infinite loops, the preliminary parser, does not necessarily presuppose any musical time external to the mind of the listener; the parser, along with the EVALuator et al., is metaphorically part of the apparatus through which a listener can build purely mental categories of space and time for the music perceived.

We return once more to the Basic Formula, p = (EV,CXT,P-R-LIST,ST-LIST), and focus now upon ST-LIST, the list of statements s_1, s_2, . . . s_K made in some stipulated language L. Describing the ensemble of statements as a "list" is only a formatting convention here; the statements might, for example, be abstracted to represent an annotated two-dimensional graph. More generally, the language L might be a composite of several graphic and notational systems with a symbolic textual discourse, and also with a vernacular discourse like everyday English. The language might involve instead or as well poetic sayings or writings; it might involve Freudian free-associations. It might involve gestural "statements" from other communicative systems not usually brought under the rubric of "language," gestures like writing down original compositional material, or performing musical passages. In Part V, I shall devote quite a bit of attention to the notion of composing and performing as means for making perception-statements; I shall more or less withhold that attention until then.

Imagining our utterances or gestures formatted as a "list" is a programming convenience, as I said before; it is not of-the-essence for our model. More of-the-essence, and more contentious, is the idea that a perception—as modeled by the basic formula—necessarily involves utterances or gestures of some kind. With this feature of the model I am asserting *inter alia* that formal musical perceptions are what are sometimes called "apperceptions," since each one embodies "the process of understanding by which newly observed qualities of an object are related to past experience."[24] The model goes even farther in asserting a specifically linguistic component, in a broad sense, for the way in which past experience is actively brought to bear on observation. Our sense of the past, in making perception-statements, is thereby necessarily involved with sociocultural forces that shaped the language L, and our acquisition of that language. In particular, to the extent

24. This is one of the meanings for "apperception" given in *The American Heritage Dictionary of the English Language* (New York: American Heritage Publishing Co., Inc., 1969), 63.

that the language L involves the language of any music theory, that means we must be ready to consider the context CXT for perception p as having a *theoretical* component, along with whatever psychoacoustic component it may possess. To illustrate the point, let us consider the acoustic signal produced by a piano playing the score in Example 4.5a.

Example 4.5

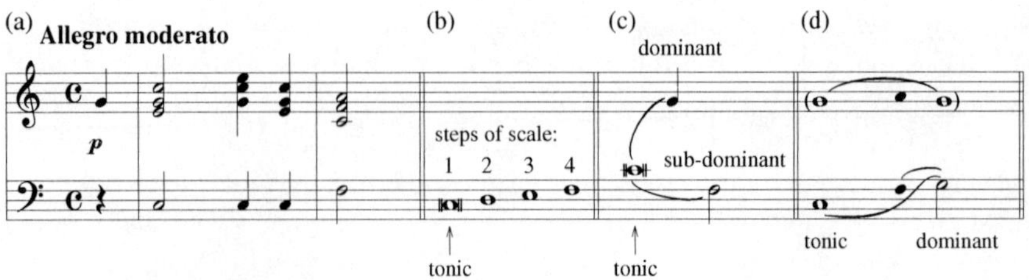

Calling that signal "Signal 5," let us talk about what we might perceive on hearing its last chord. One listener, hearing that event in that context, may say, "I hear a fourth-degree harmony." This statement, an element of a ST-LIST for a pertinent p, implicitly invokes a theoretical context in which the bass F is *four steps up a C major scale* from the C below it. The theoretical context can be symbolized in the manner of Example 4.5b. The "music" of Example 4.5b is not projected by Signal 5, yet it is just as much a part of the CXT for the perception under examination; it allows the listener to hear "degrees" and to hear the F in the bass as the "fourth" one. Example 4.5b carries a long historical/cultural shadow involving the tetrachordal analysis of the major scale, the Rule of the Octave, and other esoterica of which the listener may well be "unaware."

Another listener may want to hear the same chord in the same acoustic context as a "subdominant." To use that term on a statement-list for a suitable formal p, this listener will invoke a *different* theoretical component as part of the CXT; Example 4.5c would serve the purpose. In that example, the bass F of the EVent in question is displayed lying the-interval-of-a-dominant *below* its theoretical tonic C, a middle C which has "already" generated the G that lies the-interval-of-a-dominant above it. This is what the term "subdominant" means, when used properly. It casts a long historical shadow involving Continental harmonic theories of the eighteenth and nineteenth centuries, along with their sociocultural contexts. The theoretical tonic of Example 4.5c is middle C, not viola C as in Example 4.5b. The listener who invokes the "subdominant" context of Example 4.5c will probably also invoke another theoretical context, an "octave equivalence" context that relates the middle C of Example 4.5c in some special way to the C an octave lower, the viola C that figures in the acoustic bass of Signal 5 itself. Indeed, Example 4.5c itself already presupposes a context of octave equivalence, since it assumes that the-interval-of-a-dominant corresponds to the harmonic ratio 2:3; that interval is an octave smaller than the theoretically "correct" harmonic interval given by the ratio 1:3; a ratio of unity-to-aliquot-part or fundamental-frequency-to-partial-frequency. The historical shadow of octave-equivalence in this sort of context includes important speculative work by Descartes, Rameau, and D'Alembert.

A third listener might perceive the final event of Signal 5 as a "dominant preparation," thereby invoking the theoretical ConteXT of Example 4.5d, with its Schenkerian shadows. The G in the bass of Example 4.5d may or may not eventuate in the acoustic continuation from Signal 5; that is irrelevant, since the G in the *theoretical* context is *already* part of "what is perceived" at the end of Signal 5 by the listener who hears a "dominant preparation." As a linguistic resource, the theoretical G of Example 4.5d has no more and no less to do with acoustic signals than does the middle C of Example 4.5c, or the D of Example 4.5b; those are equally linguistic resources, enabling our other listeners to make other kinds of perception-STatements in other theoretical languages.

Part III: A Passage from Schubert

To illustrate what the model of Part II can bring out in analysis, I shall discuss some aspects of Schubert's song *Morgengruß* that are characteristically addressed by that model. Example 4.6 transcribes aspects of the strophe, and gives the concomitant text for the first stanza. I shall assume that the reader knows the piece well enough not to need more reminders of the complete music and text.[25]

Example 4.6

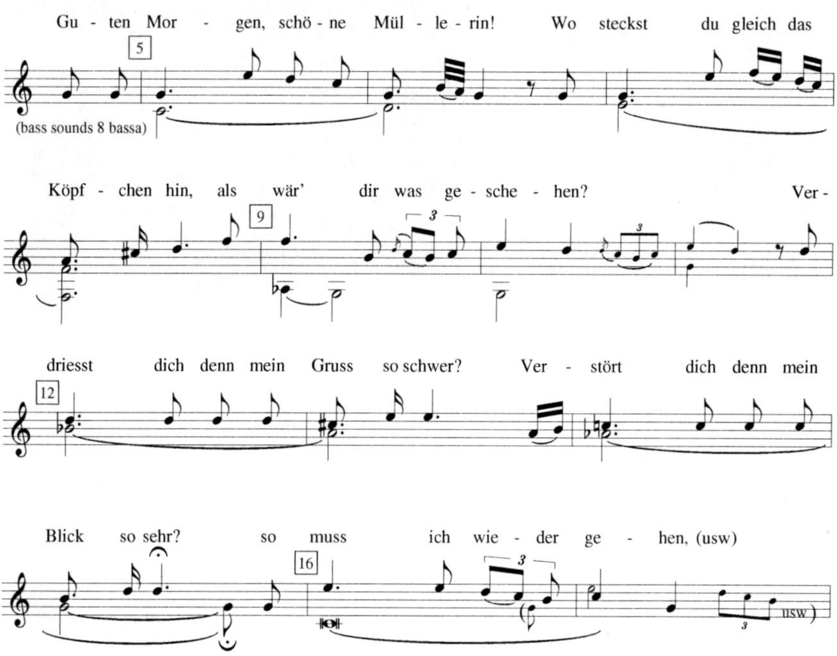

25. The impetus for my discussion comes from a long unpublished essay I wrote on this piece, and on the methodology of analysis, in 1974. Fred Lerdahl and Ray Jackendoff generously credit the essay during their interesting analysis of the strophe in *A Generative Theory of Tonal Music* (Cambridge,

Example 4.7 tabulates aspects of the formal perceptions I propose to discuss. The perceptions are listed as p_1 through p_9 in the left-hand column of the example. Each perception, following the model, involves a family of EVents, a ConteXT for that family, a Perception-Relation-LIST, and a STatement-LIST. EVents are located by entries in the second column of the example; ConteXTs are located by entries in the third column. "Tonal theory" in some heuristic sense is understood as a component of each ConteXT. Selected pairs from the P-R-LISTs are entered in the fourth column of the example, and selected STatements from the ST-LISTs are entered in the fifth column, by reference to graphic examples that will presently be forthcoming.

Example 4.7

p	EV	CXT	Selected P-R Pairs	Selected Statements
p_1	m12	m12		Ex. 4.8.1
p_2	m12	m9–12	(p_1, terminal inclusion) (V-percept, questioning)	Ex. 4.8.2
p_{3a}	m12–13	m12–13	(p_1, incipital inclusion) (p_4, implication)	Ex. 4.8.3
p_{3b}	m12–13	m9–13	(p_2, denial) (p_{3a}, reinforcement)	Ex. 4.8.3
p_4	m12–13	m12–13 plus expected m14	(p_{3a}, realization) (earlier d tonicization, elaboration)	Ex. 4.8.4
p_5	m9–13	m9–13 plus expected continuation	(p_4, medial inclusion), (p_4, reinforcement) (p_{3b}, reinforcement), (p_2, virtual annihilation)	Ex 4.8.5
p_{6a}	m14	m12–14	(p_4, confirmation and elaboration) (p_{6b}, implication)	Ex 4.8.6
p_{6b}	m14	m12–14 plus expected m15 (in d minor)	(p_{6a}, realization), (p_{7a}, modification)	As in the commentary
p_{7a}	m14	m12–14 plus expected m15 (seq.)	(p_{6b}, modification), (p_{3a}, sequential expansion)	Ex. 4.8.7
p_{7b}	m14–15	m12–15	(p_{7a}, confirmation), (p_{6b}, denial) (p_5, confirmation) (via p_{6a})	As in the commentary

Mass.: The MIT Press, 1983), 264–269. Their analysis illustrates excellently the resources and powers of their theory. Since it uses extensively a different language L from mine, it "perceives" things differently; otherwise, I do not sense any major incompatibilities between their readings and mine. Their methodological approach to ambiguous readings definitely does differ from mine, both as expressed in the unpublished essay and as I shall develop it over Parts III and IV of this chapter.

The 1974 essay devoted a good deal of attention to the four-strophe form of the song. Thereby it found a large-scale sense of balance about the temporal extents of tonic and dominant in the song, a balance that resolves on a very high rhythmic level some of the discomfort Lerdahl and Jackendoff feel about those extents in the context of the-strophe-once-around. I too feel that discomfort in that context. The discussion in Part III here will not engage any context as extensive as even one strophe.

Example 4.7 cont.

p	EV	CXT	Selected P-R Pairs	Selected Statements
p_8	m14–15	m9–15	(A♭–G in bass of m9, expanded recapulation), (p_9, support)	Ex. 4.8.8
p_9	m9–15	m9–15 plus expected m16	(p_2, confirmation), (p_{3b}, denial), (p_8, support), (p_5, qualification)	Ex. 4.8.9

The perception p_1 in Example 4.7, for instance, addresses the EVents of measure 12 in the ConteXT of measure 12 (and tonal theory). So, in the row of Example 4.7 headed by "p_1" on the left, "m.12" is entered in the second column, the column of EVents, and "m.12" is also entered in the third column, the column of ConteXTs. Nothing is entered in the fourth column, the column of salient P-R pairs for p_1. This inferentially asserts that it is not crucial to hear p_1 in relation to other perceptions hereabouts, in order to perceive "what we are hearing when we hear measure 12 in its own context."

Example 4.8

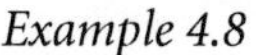

What STatements can we make about "what we are hearing when we hear measure 12 in its own context," understanding also a context of tonal theory? Here is one: the measure elaborates g^6 harmony, with a D in the principal upper voice. That statement is entered in the fifth column of Example 4.7, the column of salient STatements about p_1. To save space, the English sentence is represented on the table by a reference to Example 4.8.1, an example that projects the sense of the statement in a compact graphic format.

Parts 4.8.1, 4.8.2, and so on of Example 4.8 correspond to the perceptions p_1, p_2, and so on of Example 4.7. Our exegesis of the first row from Example 4.7 is now complete: p_1 perceives measure 12 in its own context and in the context of tonal theory; therein the events elaborate g minor harmony with B♭3 in the bass and D5 in a principal melodic voice.

We hear quite different and various other things about measure 12 when we hear the events of that measure in a variety of *other*, more extensive, contexts. The whole point of the present exercise is exactly to examine with some precision the *variety* of formal perceptions that are generated by such a variety of formal CXTs for the EVents of measure 12, and for other related families of EVents. It is meaningless—or at the very least thoroughly arbitrary—to invoke C major and its dominant, or d minor and its subdominant, when we are talking about perceiving measure 12 *in its own context*. Whether or not we *wish* to utter perception-statements about measure-12-in-its-own-context is another matter. I do, because I find the formal perception p_1 a useful entity to have at hand for the P-R-LISTS of other, broader, perceptions. To speak roughly in traditional terminology, I find it useful to be able to refer to "the g^6," when I want to, without having to attribute any degree-function or other function in any key to the harmony and its root. A footnote later on will develop the methodological point.

There are other kinds of perception-statements I might make about the events of measure 12. For example, I might remark on the density of attacks in the accompaniment: only one pitch is attacked at a time, and the attacks come one-per-written-eighth-note. But I will probably not remark on those features of measure 12 *in the context of measure 12 alone*, that is without comparing it to other events, especially immediately-preceding events, in larger contexts. I would certainly not have the sense that the bass of measure 12 lies "in a high register" when I listen to that measure in its own context *only*. (By the italicized word, I intend more precisely a phenomenological context which makes me aware of my own singing voice, a pretty poor bass that comfortably reaches a fourth higher.) The things I am pretending to notice here, about the attack-densities and the register of the bass "in measure 12," are not features of "measure 12" at all; they are, rather, matters that involve how what-I-notice-in-measure-12 engages in Perception-Relations with what-I-notice-elsewhere, all wrapped up in broader ConteXTs. Our model enables me to be precise and formal about these matters.

The perception p_2, in Example 4.7, engages one broader ConteXT for the EVents of measure 12, that is the context of measures 9–12. In *that* context, one's attention *is* drawn to the attack-texture and bass register of the accompaniment in measure 12, and it would be appropriate to utter pertinent statements about those matters on the ST-LIST for p_2. On the P-R-LIST for p_2, one might then refer to perceptions involving the accompaniment textures for measures 9–10, for measure 11, for measures 9–10–11, and so on, as those perceptions relate to p_2. To save space, I have not selected such statements and relations for coverage in the ST and P-R columns of Example 4.7.

On that example, the P-R-LIST for p_2 does contain the pair (p_1,terminal inclusion); this pair perceives the time-span over which p_1 "happens" as a terminal segment within the time-span over which p_2 "happens." The P-R-LIST for p_2 on the example also contains the pair (V-percept, questioning); this pair notices a perception of "dominant" at hand (in retention) and perceives measure 12 as a challenge to the "dominant," *in the context of measures 9–12.* The specific context is crucial; we are not talking about measures 12–13, or measures 12–15, or measures 9–15, and so on. One might ask why the context of measures 9–12, that is the ConteXT for p_2, is well-formed, considering the strong phrase articulation between the second quarter of measure 11 and the pickup to measure 12. That is a good question. To address it in my own hearing, I would point to the persistence of the G root over all four measures, and also to the persistence of the pitch D5 in the principal melodic voice, from the vocal cadence in measure 10 through the entire vocal part of measure 12. In making this response, I refine the pair (V-percept, questioning) to at least three component pairs: (5th-degree-root-percept, prolongation), (D5-melody-percept, prolongation), and (leading-tone-percept, denial). The statements I would make about this state of affairs are covered symbolically by the graphic format of Figure 4.8.2. On that example, the V root and melodic D5 have prolongational slurs leading into their symbolic representations. The denial of the leading-tone function is depicted by the flat-symbol on the figuration for the harmony. A question mark and exclamation point after the flat symbol express confusion about the denial of leading-tone function in a context that otherwise clearly prolongs "dominant" sensations.

Some critical readers may be saying impatiently, "Why all this fuss about a confusing role for the event of measure 12 in a context that bridges a large phrase articulation very awkwardly? Why go to such trouble to perceive the harmony as a confusing minor-V, when it is so clear as iv-of-ii within its *own* phrase boundary?" The remainder of Part III will satisfy such critics, I hope, making it clear why I want to construct p_2 and assert it as a significant perception here. For the time being, we can note that our model will accommodate very well the hostile reactions of these critics upon being confronted by p_2. The model analyzes their denial-of-p_2 as *itself* something-we-perceive in the music. We perceive it specifically when we hear measure 12 as the beginning of a new phrase in a context which both continues "normally" and, also, retains our impression of p_2 (so that p_2 is around to be attacked).

Perception p_{3a} in Example 4.7, hears measure 12 "as the beginning of a new phrase . . . which . . . continues 'normally,'" and Perception p_{3b} extends the ConteXT for p_{3a} backwards so as to be able to retain (and attack) p_2. The pair (p_2,denial) appears on the P-R-LIST for p_{3b}. The critics' denial is p_{3b}'s denial.

p_{3a} hears the EVents of measures 12–13 in their own ConteXT. The musical phrase of measures 12–13 coincides with one complete verse of the text; that is part of the EVent and part of the ConteXT. The outer voices and the harmony implied by the ConteXT are portrayed by the symbolic STatement of Example 4.8.3. In this

ConteXT, the harmony of measure 12 is iv^6 of d minor. d minor, in *this* context (mm. 12–13) is not ii-of-C major; there is no hint of C major tonality in the context of the two measures themselves. Example 4.8.3 suggests the way in which p_{3b} denies p_2 by the annotation "*not* V $^{6}_{\flat}$!"

Beyond Example 4.8.3, we will also want to image on the STatement-LISTs for p_{3a} and p_{3b} various other STatements involving various Perception-Relations on their P-R-LISTs. For instance we might STate, on hearing measures 12–13 in their own context, "Oh, *now* I hear where that g minor six-chord is going." That STatement involves *inter alia* the pair (p_1,incipital inclusion), a pair on the P-R-LIST of p_{3a}. The time-span of p_{3a} continues the time-span of p_1, the span in which one perceives "that g minor six-chord." We might also STate, on hearing measures 12–13 in their own context, "d minor is being tonicized." This STatement involves a mentally constructed d minor tonic, at measure 14 or thereabouts, on which the dominant-of-d in measure 13 will discharge. The mental construction is symbolized in Example 4.8.4, a sketch that pertains to a perception p_4, a perception of the tonicization satisfied in protension. The pair (p_4,implication) appears on the P-R-LIST for p_{3a} and of course the pair (p_{3a},realization) appears on the P-R-LIST for p_4.

On listening to measures 12–13 in the context of measures 9–13, we might also STate, "Aha! So the g minor six chord is *not* a confusing minor dominant of C major; it is rather iv-of-ii in a C-major progression that tonicizes ii." This STatement, the Statement of the Critical Readers, can be imagined on the ST-LIST for p_{3b}. The pairs (p_2,denial) and (p_{3a},reinforcement) accordingly appear on the P-R-LIST for p_{3b}.[26] In connection with the Critical Readers, one would put on the ST-LIST of p_{3b} additional statements, for example: "There is a big phrase boundary between measure 11 and the pickup to measure 12."

Perception p_4 hears the d minor tonic that we expect to continue from the EVents of measures 12–13. We discussed earlier the pairs (p_4,implication) and (p_{3a},realization) on the P-R-LISTS for p_{3a} and $p_{4,}$ respectively. The recursive structure is by now familiar. The d minor tonic event in Example 4.8.4 appears with diamond-shaped noteheads; this symbolizes its contingency in protension only, so far as the STatement being made is concerned; Example 4.8.4 STates *inter alia* that the events of measures 12–13 are about to discharge on a constructed d minor tonic event.

The mentally constructed d minor tonic here interrelates with a d minor harmony we heard earlier. That harmony was tonicized via a fleeting C♯ in the vocal line of measure 8, the first chromatic note of the song. p_4 thus expands and elaborates upon an earlier perception of tonicized-d. The pair (earlier d tonicization, elaboration) appears on the P-R-LIST for p_4. It would be more exact to introduce in this connection a new perception p_{4a} whose ConteXT includes measure-8-in-retention as well as measures 12–13 and 14-in-protension.

Perception p_5 models our effort to make sense of tonicized-d-minor (p_4) following directly upon a prolonged dominant-of-C perceived over measures 9–11.

26. Example 4.8.3 should technically be annotated some more to show how p_{3b}, perceiving C major tonality in its larger context, would analyze the harmony in the key of "C:ii," rather than in the key of d.

We hear that the melodic D5 of measure 13, the D5, which also figures as the diamond-shaped goal of melodic tonicization in Example 4.8.4, prolongs the D5 where the voice signed off in measure 10, a D5 introduced and cadenced on as the fifth of the dominant harmony there. And the other diamond-shaped note of Example 4.8.4, the D4 that is the fundamental bass for the tonicization there, can be heard as part of a bass arpeggiation within the dominant harmony. Hearing these things, we expect that the tonicized d minor of p_4 (of Example 4.8.4), having arisen in a larger context as an elaboration of dominant harmony, will again return to dominant harmony. The statement made by the preceding sentence is elaborated and symbolically sketched in Example 4.8.5, to which reference is made on the ST-LIST for p_5. The diamond-shaped notes on the example portray contextual elements we construct protensively on hearing the EVents of measures 9–13. A slur extends to the right of the melodic D5 within the ii harmony; that symbol suggests that we mentally prolong the melodic D5 through the protensive dominant-of-C that follows; the slurred D5 thereby resumes its earlier role as fifth-of-a-dominant-harmony.

Example 4.8.5 embeds Example 4.8.4 within its middle, and the larger progression "makes good sense" of the smaller. Our model reflects these observations by putting the pairs (p_4,medial inclusion) and (p_4,reinforcement) on the P-R-LIST for p_5. That P-R-LIST also contains the pairs (p_{3b},reinforcement) and (p_2,virtual annihilation). That is to say, p_5 (Example 4.8.5) continues and mightily intensifies the denial of p_2 that began with the construction of p_{3b}. On Example 4.8.5, the bracket, the parentheses, and the filled-in noteheads suggest how the g minor six-chord is *here* perceived as completely forward-looking, inflecting a subsequent (protensive) d minor harmony; in this perception, the g minor chord has no direct prolongational relation to the dominant harmony that precedes it. p_5, perceiving these things about the g minor six-chord, perceives that-p_2-is-virtually-annihilated.[27]

Perception p_{6a} addresses our hearing how the EVents of measure 14, in the ConteXT of measures 12–14, confirm and elaborate the earlier perception p_4. (p_4,confirmation and elaboration) appears on the P-R-LIST for p_{6a}. Example 4.8.6 confirms and elaborates Example 4.8.4 in three stages labeled (a), (b), and (c). Stage (a) shows the protensive d minor tonic of Example 4.8.4 arriving; the inner voices of the mentally constructed triad are filled in. Stage (b) inflects the top voice of stage (a) by a (passing) seventh. Stage (c) inverts the voices of stage (b), leaving the passing seventh in the melody; stage (c) also replaces the A natural in the harmony of stages (a) and (b) by the chromatic variant A flat. The bass, alto, and so-

27. When I refer to "the g minor chord," I demonstrate the utility of having earlier constructed p_1 to reference such a mental object. p_1, which is constructed in the ConteXT of measure-12-by-itself, enables me to refer to a "g minor chord" that is neither a "minor dominant of C major" nor a "subdominant of d minor." Then I can use my language L effectively, to say that p_5 hears the g minor chord as a subdominant of d (= ii/C), not as a minor dominant of C. If I substitute "the subdominant of d" for "the g minor chord" in the preceding sentence, I make p_5 hear tautologously in my language L. If I substitute "the minor dominant of C" for "the g minor chord" in the same sentence, I make p_5 hear in a linguistically erroneous fashion.

Classical theories of consonance and/or triadic root-functionality are very relevant to my claim, that I can perceive "the g minor chord" in its own context. (It does not require "preparation" and/or "resolution" in any larger context, in order to have a traditional "meaning.")

prano voices of stage (c) are projected by the actual acoustic signals of measure 14. The persisting diamond-shaped D4 of stage (c) is a mental construct; it represents the discharge of the d minor tonicization on the harmony of measure 14 as a permissible representative for a d minor root function. The harmony of stage (c) is thus perceived (by perception p_{6a}!) as an inverted and chromatically altered d^7 chord, the d being mentally constructed in the ConteXT of measures 12–14.

Perceiving the C5 of Example 4.8.6 as a "passing seventh" within a constructed d harmony in a context of d tonicity, we will construct another perception protensively, a perception that hears the "passing" accomplished. Perception p_{6b} puts $_{6a}$ together, in this way, with the expectation of B♭4 to come in the melody and G3 to come in the bass, presumably at measure 15. (p_{6b},implication) appears on the P-R-LIST for p_{6a}. G3 and B♭4 are specifically implied by p_{6a} as follows. The A♭ in the acoustic bass of measure 14 is perceived by p_{6a} as *dissonant*, a diminished fifth of a d harmony. It should therefore resolve, we expect, to G3 in the bass of measure 15. The C in the melody of acoustic measure 14 is likewise perceived by p_{6a} as dissonant, a passing seventh. It should therefore resolve, we expect, to B♭4 in the melody of measure 15. We expect B♭ rather than B natural, because the ConteXT for p_{6b} includes a presumption of contextual d minor tonicity, as a theoretical-psychological component. That aspect of p_{6b}'s ConteXT is explicitly noted in Example 4.7. We imagine the symbolic STatements for p_{6b} to include Example 4.8.6 followed by a diamond-shaped B♭4-over-G3 at hypothetical-measure-15.[28]

Perception p_{6b} has on its P-R-LIST the pair (p_{6a},realization). p_{6b} also has on its P-R-LIST a pair (p_{7a},modification). The perception p_{7a} addresses the same EVents in the same temporal ConteXT as p_{6b}, that is the events of measure 14 in the context of measures 12–14 plus an expected measure 15. But p_{7a} expects quite different things from p_{6b}. What p_{7a} expects is symbolized by Example 4.8.7. As the example shows, p_{7a} expects both the outer voices to step down from measure 14 to measure 15; in this p_{7a} agrees with p_{6b}. p_{7a}, however, does not expect to continue "in d minor" past measure 14, and it awaits B natural, not B flat, in the melody of measure 15. In those expectations p_{7a} disagrees with p_{6b}. So the two temporally coextensive perceptions modify each other. The pair (p_{6b},modification) appears on the P-R-LIST for p_{7a}.

p_{7a} expects B natural, not B flat, and p_{7a} is not concerned with maintaining a d minor context, because the perception is listening for *sequential patterns* in *its* ConteXT. This feature of the perception is symbolized by the annotation "(seq.)" in the CXT column of Example 4.7. Perceiving the acoustic signal of measure 14 in the context of measures 12–14, p_{7a} recognizes that the text of measure 14 is analo-

28. Idiomatic harmony in d minor for the B♭-over-G, consistent with the level of complexity introduced into that key by stage (c) of Example 4.8.6, is quite conceivable. For instance, the B♭-over-G could be harmonized by iv^7, giving rise to an elaboration of p_{6b} through the following progression: iv^6(m12), V(m13), i $^{4}_{3\flat}$ (m. 14 as stage(c) of Example 4.8.6), iv^7 (harmonizing the protensive B♭-over-G at hypothetical-measure-15), V^4_2, i^6, and so on.

The harmonic exercise is not sheer pedantry. Our "language L" includes the discourse of traditional tonal theory, and the urge to work out a reasonable harmonization is the urge to show that the STatement of p_{6b} involving B♭-over-G in d minor is in fact a grammatical (i.e., possible) construction in the language L.

gous to the text of measure 12 in a context where a complete sentence underlay measures 12–13; p_{7a} also recognizes that the acoustic harmony of measure 14 has the same intervallic structure as the acoustic harmony of measure 12. Accordingly, p_{7a} expects that measure 15 will continue from measure 14 by analogy with the way measure 13 continued from measure 12: measure 15 will finish the sentence begun in measure 14, and measures 14–15 will project the progression iv^6 V in "c minor" just as measures 12–13 projected the same progression in d minor.

p_{7a} in its context (Example 4.8.7) thus perceives p_{3a} (Example 4.8.3) becoming expanded sequentially. The pair (p_{3a},sequential expansion) appears on the P-R-LIST for p_{7a}. Example 4.8.7 asserts a local tonic of c minor, not C major, for measures 14-and-expected-15. That is because c minor, not C major, is the literal sequential analog for the d minor tonic of p_{3a} (measures 12–13); p_{7a} knows nothing of any larger context involving C major tonality. Example 4.8.7 has a question mark on the progression from its "d minor" of measures 12–13 to its "c minor" of measures 14–15; there is no traditional tonal syntax that makes the progression "logical," especially at the transition from a cadential dominant of d in measure 13 to a subdominant of c in measure 14. It would not help the "logic" much to invoke C major in this connection. The problem is that p_{7a} perceives the harmony of measure 14 as a subdominant of c (or C), and that function has no clear relation in the context (of p_{7a}) to the dominant of d which precedes it.

p_{7a} thereby modifies p_{6b} in yet another way. For p_{6b} senses nothing problematic about the progression from measure 13 to measure 14. p_{6b} perceives V of d progressing very logically to a substitute harmony for a d tonic triad, as indicated in stages (a)-(b)-(c) of Example 4.8.6 earlier. The intermodifications of P_{7a} and p_{6b} in this connection involve something like Rameau's *double emploi* brought into our present model. In one perception, p_{7a}, the acoustic signal of measure 14 signifies an "f chord." In another perception, p_{6b}—actually already in p_{6a}—the same stimulus signifies a "d chord." The perceptions p_{7a} and p_{6b} that carry these significations address events and contexts that are coextensive in cursor-time: both involve the EVents of measure 14 in the ConteXT of measures 12–14 plus an expected measure 15.

To say these things about the two distinct mental objects (or acts), that is about p_{7a} and p_{6b}, is very different from having to assert that there is one acoustic object, "the chord of measure 14," which "is" both an f chord and a d chord "at the same time." I put "is" and "at the same time" in quotation marks to draw special attention to the inadequacy of traditional temporal parlance here, which speaks as if the cursor-time over which measure 14 extends were the *only* temporal frame involved in our constructing, processing, and interrelating the two mental objects p_{6b} and p_{7a}. I shall have much more to say on such methodological points during Part IV.

Perception p_{7b} notices that the acoustic signal continues from measures 12–14 through acoustic measure 15 according to the protensive model of p_{7a} to a dominant of c (or C) with B natural, not B flat, in the melody. Thus, (p_{7a},confirmation) appears on its P-R-LIST. The acoustic event of measure 15 denies the protensive B flat that p_{6b} constructed for *its* (expected) measure 15. Accordingly, the pair (p_{6b}, denial) appears on the P-R-LIST for p_{7b}. p_{7b} does not, however, deny p_{6a}. Indeed, it uses the d root of p_{6a} to confirm the expectations of p_5: p_{7b} perceives that the diamond-shaped notes of Example 4.8.5 are in fact eventuating over the acoustic signal of measures 14–15 just as p_5 had imagined they would, the d-chord of p_5 being represented by the acoustic signal of measure 14 according to the perception of p_{6a} (Example 4.8.6). This activity on the part of p_{7b} is symbolized by the pair (p_5,confirmation (via P_{6a})), which appears on its P-R-LIST.

In confirming both p_{7a} and p_5-cum-p_{6a} the perception p_{7b} confirms both the f chord in measure 14 of p_{7a} and the d chord in measure 14 of p_5-cum-p_{6a}. Our model has no problem in handling this logic, since "the f chord in measure 14 of p_{7a}" and "the d chord in measure 14 of p_{6a}" *are different objects* in our model; "the diamond-shaped d-chord in protensive measure 14 of p_5" is yet another object. p_{7b} notices that measure 15, in its text and its acoustic signal, does complete the parallelism of measures 14–15 with measures 12–13 according to the protensive model of p_{7a}; measure 14 of p_{7a} is a subdominant of the local tonic that governs measures 14–15, just as measure 12 is a subdominant of the local tonic that governs measures 12–13. p_{7b} *also* perceives that the protensive constructions of p_5 (Example 4.8.5) do in fact come to pass over measures 12–15, via the mental processing of p_{6a} (Example 4.8.6) that allows the signal of measure 14 to be perceived as a d harmony. There is no logical contradiction in any of this: we are *not* saying that p_{7b} perceives *one* object as "both an f chord and a d chord at the same time."

Perception p_8 puts the A♭–G in the bass of measures 14–15 into a broad enough context so that the gesture can be heard as an expanded recapitulation of the A♭–G in the bass of measure 9. A P-R pair for p_8 expresses the relationship. Example 4.8.8 makes a symbolic STatement about ways in which the two approaches to G-in-the-bass are similar. In the broad context of measures 9–15 we identify both Gs as dominants of C major; Example 4.8.8 labels the two dominants. p_8 should thereby be understood to enter into suitable Perception-Relations (not shown in Example 4.7) with p_5. p_5 (Example 4.8.5) heard the span of measures 9–15 as an elaboration of dominant harmony in C major, and p_8 (Example 4.8.8) now supports the notion, and is supported by it.

Example 4.7 does not include our earlier perception of A♭–G in the bass at measure 9. Intuitively, we can notice many accented aspects of the gesture; these intuitions could be reflected by suitable Perception-Relations and STatements if we wanted to work them out formally for our model. We notice, for instance, that the bass line and harmony move in dotted half notes from the voice entrance up to the A♭ of measure 9, at which event the bass or the harmony start to move in quarters (as does the accompaniment texture). We notice the unusually great acoustic dissonance and the chordal chromaticism in the harmony over the A♭ of measure 9, given the context of measures 5–9 (or of measures 1–9). We notice the leap of the bass into the A♭ of measure 9, as contrasted with the essentially conjunct motion of the bass during measures 5–8. We notice that the G in the bass of measure 9 is the first large-scale dominant of the strophe (and of the piece); it is the melodic and rhythmic goal of the bass line in the context of measures 5–11. We notice that the vocal F at the bar line of measure 9, a tone prolonged above the A♭–G gesture in the bass there, is the melodic climax of the vocal line in the context of measures 5–9, and of measures 5–11. We notice that this vocal F is dissonant over its essential bass, the G of measure 9. We notice that the vocal F sets a subjunctive verb. If we pursue the matter, we shall notice curious things about the nonresolving pseudo-resolutions of that F in the context of measures 5–11, and curious things about the dramatic irony of the text in that connection, an irony which makes the contrary-to-factness of the subjunctive *itself* contrary to fact: "as if something *were* the matter"—as if *nothing* were the matter!

Such observations, and others like them, enrich the P-R-LIST and ST-LIST of the earlier A♭–G perception that engages the EVents of measure 9; thereby p_8 is itself indirectly enriched. And thereby further salient perceptions, pursuant to these matters, could be added to Example 4.7. For instance, we shall now certainly notice in the ConteXT of measures 5–15 how the "dominant" EVents of measures 9–15 elaborate the subjunctive verb of measure 9 by a series of *questions*: each verse of text that closes during measures 9–15 ends with a question mark. It is possible therewith to hear the high F of the voice in measure 9 essentially still unresolved at measure 15, an understood "questioning" dominant seventh within the large-scale dominant elaboration at hand. This perception is confirmed by the acoustic signal of measures 16–17, where the high vocal F resolves to a high vocal E in a matching rhythmic motive, as the large-scale dominant harmony resolves to a large-scale tonic and the subjunctive doubt resolves into obligation. To bring out the last-mentioned relationship, Schubert displaces the natural text stresses in setting the rhyming verses 3 and 6 of the poem: he sets "als *wär'* dir (was geschehen)" and "so *muß* ich (wieder gehen)," not "als wär' dir was ge*scheh*en" and "so muß ich wieder *geh*en."[29]

Example 4.8.8 indicates succinctly how the "dominant" region of the strophe, measures 9–15, is also the "chromatic" region of the strophe; this large-scale dominant is thematically bound up with the chromaticism, as much as it is with contrary-to-fact questioning and the unresolved high F of measure 9. Consequently, perception p_8 supports another perception p_9 that projects a more chromatic interpretation of the large-scale dominant than we have hitherto examined. The pair (p_9,support) appears on the P-R-LIST for P_8.

Example 4.8.9 sketches a symbolic STatement for p_9, engaging the EVents of measures 9–15 in their own ConteXT along with the ConteXT of the protensive resolution to follow at expected-measure-16. As Example 4.8.9 hears things, the harmonic function of "that g minor chord" in measure 12 is not iv-of-ii after all,

29. N.B.: the youth does not "go." Rather he repeats and extends "I must go" over the remainder of the strophe. Even then he does not go, but remains to sing three more strophes. My unpublished typescript analyzes and interrelates these matters, along with the concomitant E–D–C round between voice and piano, that sets "so muß ich wieder gehen." In my analysis, the round expands into recurrent large-level descents from the vocal E of measure 16 and so on in one strophe, through the vocal D of measure 10–12 in the next strophe, to the vocal C of measure 17 and so on in that next strophe. The E of measure 16-in-that-next-strophe reasserts itself over that C just as the E in the foreground round reasserts itself, in one instrument or the other, over the C in the foreground round. The music for the strophe goes around four times, as does the foreground round-motive within each strophe. The youth can only go when the sense of obligation, the *muß*, has been attached to the act of going, the *gehen*. That happens only when the background E of *muß*, measure 16, is linearly connected in the background to the background C of *gehen*, measure 17. The background connection is not accomplished during measures 16–17 of any one strophe; the background line emerges only as the strophes repeat again and again, going *wieder* through the D of measures 10–12. The more often we pass the E of measure 16, as the strophes go around, the less accent we hear the next time around on the neighboring high F of measure 9; the more structural weight, correspondingly, do we feel on the D of measures 10–12.

but, rather, minor-v-just as p_2 originally thought it was. According to the figure at hand, the B♭ in the bass of measure 12 is not a sixth degree of a local tonic d minor, about to resolve as an appoggiatura to the A natural in the bass of measure 13, the fifth degree of that d minor. Rather, the B♭ in the bass of measure 12 is a chordal tone, a chromatically altered member of a large-scale G harmony that controls measures 9–15; the A natural in the bass at measure 13 does not resolve the B♭ but passes chromatically away from it, in transit to A♭. The flatted notes on Example 4.8.9 behave as scale degrees borrowed from c minor: flat-6 at measure 14 moves idiomatically to 5, and flat-7 at measure 12 steps down idiomatically to flat-6 at measure 14 (via the nonessential passing event of measure 13).

In Example 4.8.9, a slur binds the motive G–B♭–A♭–G. This is the minor version of the "Müllerin" motive from the voice in measure 6. In the foreground, the music moves from tonic harmony at the vocal entrance (measure 5) to dominant harmony (measure 6); the foreground dominant is then prolonged by the Müllerin motive. Just so, the music moves on a larger scale from tonic harmony at the beginning of each strophe to the big dominant harmony at measure 9; p_9 then hears that big dominant prolonged by the (minor) Müllerin motive as depicted under the slur of Example 4.8.9.

The pair (p_2,confirmation) is a characteristic member of the P-R-LIST for p_9: what-p_9-perceives includes the perception that p_2 does (did) in fact make sense, even though it was (is) "denied" by p_{3b} and "virtually annihilated" by p_5. We do not have to have recourse to "posthumous rehabilitation" here. p_2 is not necessarily "really" dead, just because p_{3b} and p_5 honestly perceived it as dying and dead. We are now somewhere else, perceiving something else along with p_9. To put the matter more elegantly: p_2, p_{3b}, p_5, and p_9 are not all cohabiting the same phenomenological place at the same phenomenological time. They are different objects (or acts) in different parts of phenomenological space-time, exercising a variety of interrelationships as reflected in our model by a variety of P-R pairs. I shall discuss the methodological point at greater length during Part IV. Meanwhile, we can note that p_9, in confirming p_2, denies p_{3b}. The pair (p_{3b},denial) appears on the P-R-LIST for p_9. p_{3b}, it will be recalled, denied (denies) p_2 by STating: "Aha! That g minor chord is *not* a confusing dominant of C; it is rather iv-of-ii in a progression tonicizing ii." p_{3b} utters this while listening to the EVents of measures 12–13 in the ConteXT of measures 9–13. p_9 in turn denies p_{3b} by STating: "Doch, doch! The g minor chord *is*, after all, a minor dominant of C, a questioning, doubting, chromatic, blue dominant arpeggiating the G root which set in at measure 9." p_9 utters this while listening to the EVents of measures 9–15 in their own ConteXT, anticipating also a protensive measure 16. In thus denying a denial, p_9 mirrors neatly the contrary-to-fact construction in the text that we examined earlier: "as if something were wrong"—as if nothing were wrong.

The pair (p_8,support) appears on the P-R-LIST for p_9; these two perceptions mutually reinforce each other. The P-R-LIST also contains the pair (p_5,qualification). The qualification-relationship, to be more useful, should be analyzed into a number of components. p_9 and p_5 reinforce each other in that both perceive measures 9–15 as an elaboration of dominant harmony in C. (Compare Example 4.8.9 with Example 4.8.5.) p_9 and p_5 disagree, however, as to the manner of the elaboration; their disagreement is reflected in the differing symbols that appear in Examples 4.8.9 and 4.8.5 around measures 12–14, symbols that have been amply discussed already. The reader may wish to review in this connection our earlier exposition of how p_5 "virtually annihilated" p_2. p_9 takes a longer view than p_5, but that does not mean that p_5 "did not happen" or "was wrong," any more than p_2 "did not happen" or "was wrong" when p_5 took a longer view and virtually annihilated it. The urge to deny or otherwise bad-mouth some of one's own "inconvenient" perceptual experiences in this sort of situation will be discussed during Part IV.

Part IV: Methodology

We have already started to note and discuss the ways in which our model enables us to bypass certain false dichotomies in analytic discourse, dichotomies that arise when we implicitly but erroneously suppose that we are discussing *one* phenomenon at one location in phenomenological space-time, when in fact we are discussing *many* phenomena at many distinct such locations. We can review the point by inspecting the "political/legal" table shown in Example 4.9.

Example 4.9

Democrat/plaintiff (bzw Republican and/or defendant)	Republican/defendant (bzw Democrat and/or plaintiff)
(a) the g-minor harmony of measure 12 in *Morgengruß* is	
v of C major (or c minor).	iv of d minor.
(b) The B flat of measure 12 is	
a chordal third of g; $\hat{3}$-of-g = $\hat{3}$-of-(c:v) = $\hat{7}$-of-c.	an appoggiatura to the A of measure 13; $\hat{6}$-of-d-minor moving $\hat{6}$-$\hat{5}$ in that key.
(c) The A in the bass of measure 13 is	
accessory: it passes chromatically from B flat (m12) to A flat (m14) within a descending c-minor scale segment that aims for the G of measure 15.	chordal: it resolves the appoggiatura of (b) above; it carries the harmony V-of-d.
(d) The harmony of measure 14 is	
an f-minor chord, iv of c/C.	a d-minor tonic harmony, with seventh and altered fifth, inverted.
(e) The biggest musical articulation between measure 5 and measure 16 is	
at measure 9, where the chromatic, questioning dominant of C is attained, with its subjunctive 7th, the event is prolonged in all those respects until m16, where the chromaticism and the questions vanish, and the vocal high F resolves to vocal high E as V resolves to I.	at measure 12, where the second phrase of the musical strophe and the second half of the text stanza begin after a strong phrase-articulation involving a long rest in the vocal part.

When we contemplate such political/legal dichotomies, whether introspectively or in debate with other analysts, the discomforts we feel are symptoms of a deficiency in traditional analytic discourse. These discomforts arise whenever we make, about a listening experience, any statement of syntactic form, "The X is . . ." To take a specific case, when we begin Example 4.9(a) by saying, "The harmony of measure 12 is . . . ," we are already falsely constraining our musical perceptions by implicitly asserting that there is *one* phenomenological object called "*the* harmony of measure 12," and we are also constraining our perceptions by saying of this object that it "is," putting it at *one* location in *one* present-tense system that renders falsely coextensive a number of different times: the historical time in which the piece continues to exist for its listeners and performers, every time in which an acoustic signal projects the score of measure 12, the time during which a listener may be forming and processing perception p_1, ditto perception p_2, ditto perceptions p_{3a} and p_{3b}, ditto perception p_4, or p_5, or p_8, or p_9, and so on, *and* the time in which I am now writing this sentence, *and* the time in which you are now reading it. Our model makes us nicely sensitive to the differences among what-happens-in-measure-12-as-a-constituent-part-of-p_1, ditto p_2, ditto p_{3a} and the rest. These are different formal objects within the model, not one object called "*the* harmony of measure 12." Likewise, our model makes us sensitive to the way in which perception-structures p_i can occupy different mental and/or clock times. Even when p_i and p_j impinge upon us at the same mental or clock time, our model allows them to do so separately; indeed, p_i might have the pair (p_j,denial) on its P-R-LIST while p_j simultaneously had (p_i,denial) on *its* P-R-LIST. We discussed earlier how EVALuation of the infinite loop might proceed to termination during this time: a higher-level parser could mentally process the loop prior to EVALuation, arranging for a suitable exit, or else a signal external to mental processing could interrupt and override EVALuation according to some prestructured configuration of the mental system.[30]

Any phenomenological theory should also make us sensitive to the necessity for conceptually distinguishing among various "occupational" times like those mentioned earlier: the time in which measure 12 "is" as I now think about it while writing this article, the time in which measure 12 "is" as you now think about it while reading the article some months later-by-the-clock, the time in which measure 12 "is" when a pianist and a vocalist create a pertinent acoustic signal by certain psychophysical activities, the time in which measure 12 "is" when a listener in a recital hall receives that acoustic signal via certain psychophysical activities, ditto a listener listening to a recording at home—for the first time, the second time, the Nth time, and so on. Each of these occupational contexts builds a different family of mental constructs for perceiving the passage of time, and a phenomenologist will not assume a priori that the time-systems are all functionally isomorphic. Indeed, the transformations that map each occupational time system into the others

30. The metaphor of an obligatory interrupt works well in analyzing *Morgengruß*, when we sense the psychological immanence of the structural downbeat at measure 16. The signal tells us "it is time to be moving on" from the chromatic/dominant/questioning imbroglio of measures 9–15, an impasse portrayed nicely in this reading by the fermata of measure 15. The downbeat moves us on by its high-level rhythmic position, its tonic harmony, its high vocal E, and its new verb *muß*.

should be presumed quite complex, since they ought to reflect both the autonomy and the interdependence of the various activities.

I have called my false dichotomies political/legal because they force us into the position of voting for a slate of candidates, or of rendering verdicts in adversary judicial proceedings, as we respond to music. I find this not just wrong but fantastically wrong. My own meta-methodology includes these rules for analysis: mistrust anything that tells you not to explore an aural impression you have once formed; mistrust anything that tells you not to listen any more to music that once gripped you, as soon as you have heard one thing going on (or two things, or three, four, . . . five hundred . . . things). The false dichotomies run head-on against my meta-rules, and I find the phenomenology of the model an attractive way to avoid the dichotomies without abandoning rational discourse.

The dichotomies illustrate well the kinds of snares and pitfalls the mind is wont to lay for the ear, not so much in connection with the formal constraints of this or that theory—these are usually easy to notice—but much more in connection with our unexamined common habits, habits like our sloppiness in using the words "the" and "is." Another such common habit is our too facile recourse to the Euclidean plane in connection with representational modeling, a recourse often concealed in our taking for granted the useful metaphors of the page and of received notations.

To illustrate the treacherous aspects of our penchant for the Euclidean plane, one need only glance at a score of *Morgengruß*. There one will see within a portion of a Euclidean plane a certain unique notehead at the bar line of measure 12 in the left hand of the piano; this notehead appears to reference a unique "point" of the plane, a point with a unique vertical coordinate and a unique horizontal coordinate in the Cartesian representation of the plane. The geometric metaphors contribute enormously to the fallacious idea that there is one unique object called "the B flat of measure 12," an object that impinges on us at one unique phenomenological time, the time in which the B flat "is." Our fallacious sense of one object at a unique spatial location is prompted by the unique vertical coordinate for the B flat notehead-point on the Euclidean/Cartesian score-plane. Our fallacious sense that only one musical time is involved, in only one musical time-system, is prompted by the unique horizontal coordinate for the same notehead-point in the same notational geometry, and by the one-dimensional representation of time in that notation. In the same mode of understanding, a certain creature that we fallaciously imagine as "*the* harmony of measure 14" is suggested by a certain visual configuration of adjacent points in the plane; this configuration spans and is (essentially) bounded by the vertical lines that frame the representation of "measure 14" as a connected region in Euclidean space. The one-dimensional span that is the projection of that region on the horizontal axis of the Cartesian plane is also connected; it suggests a unique "time" (span) in which we fallaciously suppose our harmony "is." Fallaciously embracing the geometric metaphors, we conclude "logically" enough about our phenomena [*sic*] that "it" [*sic*] cannot be both an f harmony and a d harmony "at the same time." And so we begin trying to deny and suppress various of our perceptual phenomena [*sic*], not realizing that our conceptual tools are inadequate for the analytic task at hand.

Our model helps us to abandon, along with the dichotomies, certain misleading expressions of the species "merely/only/naught but/simply/ . . . " These utterances help us to dismiss inconvenient perceptions as inconsequential. The linguistic mannerism creeps all too seductively into our prose and—worse—into our mental habits as we think about our responses to music. When we fall into such discourse, the puzzling g minor harmony in measure 12, apparently an inconvenient minor dominant in C, turns out to be "naught but" the beginning of a cadence in d minor (= ii-of-C); but then that event, on a yet larger level, turns out to be "merely" part of a large elaboration of v-of-C after all. In this discourse, we shall now notice first of all a malformation: "*The* . . . g minor harmony . . . *to be* . . . ." But we can now also notice the way in which the expressions "naught but" and "merely" sneak in, so that we are enabled to *push away* some of our perceptions at the expense of others, again as if voting or arriving at a verdict. The expressions tell us not to explore further certain aural impressions that once gripped us; the parlance violates my meta-methodology.

True, we will modify our perceptions as we listen through a piece, extending their P-R-LISTS, creating new perceptions in retrospect that may "deny" old ones, and so forth. Perhaps we perform even more radical acts of mental surgery on them. We can certainly modify our perceptions, too, during the time in which we come to know a piece more richly. All this is perfectly reasonable. Indeed, our model has given us good examples of the process at work, for example, in p_9's modifying p_5's modifying p_{3b}'s modifying p_2, both as we listen to the passage and as we come to analyze it more deeply. What is *not* reasonable is any concomitant urge to deny or bad-mouth perceptions we are coming to modify. The defensive anxiety that underlies such an urge is a good clue that there is unresolved psychological business at hand, that the attention of the ear is being busily directed away from something which the mind wants to leave unacknowledged or unexplored. One thinks of Freud's *Zurückdrängen* and *Unterdrückung*.[31]

When we are using words like "merely" to put down certain of our perceptions, we are likely to call other perceptions "important" or "more important." Our perception-model enables us to avoid those locutions, too. They are suspect because

31. Freud, *Vorlesung zur Einführung in die Psychoanalyse* (Berlin: Gustave Kiepenheuer Verlag, 1955), 64–65. Joan Riviere, in *A General Introduction to Psychoanalysis* (New York: Washington Square Press, 1952), 68–69, translates *zurückgedrängt* as "forced back" and *Unterdrückung* as "suppression." Neither term means quite the same to Freud as *Verdrängung* = "repression." Freud uses the words in connection with his analysis of everyday errors *(Fehlleistungen)*. On the second page of the cited passage, he asserts that "a suppression (*Unterdrückung*) of a previous intention to say something is an indispensable condition for the occurrence of a slip of the tongue." On the preceding page, he has told us that the speaker may or may not be aware of the suppressed intention, but in any case "it has been forced back (*zurückgedrängt*). The speaker had determined not to convert the idea into speech and then . . . the tendency which is debarred from expression asserts itself against his will and gains utterance. . . . This is the mechanism of a slip of the tongue *(Versprechen)*."

Earlier, Freud classifies many *Fehlleistungen* as similar to *Versprechen* in mechanism (Freud, p. 18; Riviere, p. 29). One of the errors is *Verhören* = mishearing an auditory event. The one who *verspricht sich* typically remarks: "How stupid of me! Of course *I meant* to say . . ." The one who *verhört sich* typically remarks: "How silly of me! I realize now that what I *really* heard was . . ."

they inferentially put down the percepts that are "unimportant" or "less important." They are also suspect because "importance" is too imprecise a word to be useful in critical discourse. The word casually suggests unspecified criteria of aesthetic value, as if the values had been stated explicitly and the word was descriptive. And—often at the same time—the word can be used carelessly as a synonym for "priority in a syntactic system" or "rank in a formal hierarchy." The two careless usages, compounding each other, can lead the unwary critic to confuse syntactic priority with aesthetic value, a confusion that is particularly dangerous when one is using Schenkerian or post-Schenkerian music theories. The point is worth two examples.

The first example is literary rather than musical; musicians will more clearly appreciate in a literary context the relations between syntactic function and aesthetic significance. Macbeth, having just murdered Duncan, stares at his bloody hand, which he hardly recognizes, and wonders:

> Will all great Neptune's ocean wash this blood
> Clean from my hand? No. This my hand will rather
> The multitudinous seas incarnadine,
> Making the green one red. (Act II, Scene 2)

About the last sentence of this quotation we can formulate a political/legal dichotomy. On the one hand, the word "This," which is the subject of the sentence, is thereby "more important" than the word "multitudinous," which is ("merely") an adjective modifying the object of the verb. On the other hand, "multitudinous" is ("obviously") "more important" than "This." "Multitudinous" is a five-syllable word after two verses that—with the exception of "Neptune's ocean" and "rather"—comprise only monosyllables; it is also a bombastic Latin word after two verses that—again with the exception of "Neptune's ocean"—comprise only common Saxon words; it is thereby the first crest of a compositional wave that begins to surge up at "rather," climaxes on "multitudinous," breaks at "incarnadine," and subsides through the disyllabic "making" into a dissipating surf of Saxon monosyllables, "the green one red." The wave tosses up the repeated Saxon monosyllabic motif, "My haND," and amplifies it into the polysyllabic Latinate surge, "MultituDiNous seas iNcarNaDiNe," finally echoing off into "Making the greeN oNe reD."

So should we then vote for "multitudinous" as more important than "This"? No. We are not voting; we should not construct a mental object called "*the* most important word of the sentence"; we should not predicate of such a mental object the idea that it "*is*," at one unique temporal location; finally, "importance" is a useless term here because we are attempting to make it reference two very different categories at the same time. In one usage, "importance" refers to height on a syntactic parsing-tree, and in the other usage, the same term refers to compositional accentuation in a complex poetic phrase.

Naturally, we are more interested in Shakespeare's compositional procedures, than we are in the fact that his texts usually fit into the paradigms of English syntax. That is not at issue here. What does concern me involves our possibly confusing the *fact that* Shakespeare wrote English, with the *manner in which* he did so. The fact does not distinguish him from myriads of English-users whose texts interest us far less; the manner does so distinguish him, and cannot be separated from his "compositional procedures." So, while it is not interesting that the word "This" is the subject of some abstract English sentence, it is intensely interesting that *Shakespeare* makes "This," used as a substantive noun, the subject of the *particular* sentence whose compositional structure we have been exploring in connection with the multitudinous seas. The grandiose climax of the sentence is not an EVent whose significant ConteXTs and Perception-Relations can be completely excised from contact with the sentence as a whole, from contact in particular with the opening and the subject of the sentence. We do not respond to dramatic poetry by impatiently twiddling our thumbs while the actor gets through the less impressive but unfortunately necessary words, to arrive at the more magnificent and heaven-storming but less "necessary" ones.

An actor who behaves as if we *did* respond that way will be in trouble. For no audience can possibly miss the "importance" of multitudinous," while an untrained or insensitive actor can easily blunt the effect of the passage by not sufficiently exploring and projecting to the audience how the word "This" works for the poetry. Specifically, Macbeth has just wondered if the ocean might wash "this blood" clean from "my hand." He answers, "No." Then he begins a new thought with the word "This." We suppose that "This" is an adjective, and that the noun "blood" will follow as before. Or, if the actor makes us feel that "This" is being used as a noun, we suppose that it stands for "This blood." But as Macbeth continues to speak we do not get the word "blood"; instead we get "This my hand." Not only will the blood never wash off the hand, even worse: "this blood" and "my hand" have fused into a compact and indissoluble union, this-my-hand, a union for which the appositional form in the syntax is a telling metaphor. Macbeth's question concerned three distinct objects, the ocean, the blood, and the hand; his answer condenses the objects into two, the blood-hand and the multitudinous seas. Hand and blood fuse into one, as action and guilt fuse into one for the character. The contraction of the hand and the blood into the blood-hand creates a tight knot of energy; this energy is later released by the expansion of the texture into the polysyllables of "multitudinous" and "incarnadine." (I first became aware of these energy profiles by noticing that I was instinctively clenching my fist as I said "This," and unclenching it, gradually splaying the fingers of my hand to their widest possible extent, as I intoned the words, "multitudinous seas incarnadine." I shall say more about such performance-perceptions later, in Part V.)

So, "This" is indeed the dramatic focus of Macbeth's attention, the poetic subject of Macbeth's discourse as well as the syntactic subject of his sentence, a subject that becomes—as he stares at it—this blood, this guilt, this hand, and this act all in one, compressed into the taut Saxon monosyllable "This," the very antithesis of the orotund Latin polysyllable, "multitudinous." Which word shall we now say is the "more important"? The reader will by now have taken my point: "importance" is not a useful critical expression here, and it particularly misses the mark when it invites us to vote between English sentence-structure and poetic compositional shape.

My second example involves a somewhat analogous critical situation in a musical analysis. In that analysis, a well-formed Schenkerian reading assigns to a certain event a syntactic role as *Kopfton* in an *Urlinie*, apparently ignoring how much "more important" another event sounds. The situation is somewhat analogous to the Shakespeare example because protests about the Schenkerian reading are to some extent methodologically similar to protests about our calling "This" the subject of Macbeth's sentence, when "multitudinous" is clearly so much "more important." One can also protest the pertinence of Schenkerian syntax itself, in a way one does not usually protest English syntax, and I will get to *that* methodological issue later on.

The music is Handel's familiar setting of the carol *Joy to the World*, and the Schenkerian reading is by Allen Forte and Steven E. Gilbert.[32] In connection with this reading the authors bring up a point of Schenkerian syntax: it is not possible to assert a well-formed *Urlinie* that starts on $\hat{8}$, for example, at the word "Joy"; a well-formed *Urlinie* can, however, start on $\hat{5}$, for example, at "world." This *Urlinie* can descend from $\hat{5}$ to $\hat{1}$ with appropriate support from an *Ursatz* while Heaven and angels sing. In contrast, there is no syntactic support from any well-formed *Ursatz* for a putative descent from $\hat{8}$ (Joy) to $\hat{5}$ (world) within an *Urlinie* that might start on $\hat{8}$. As the authors put it, "the steps between $\hat{8}$ and $\hat{5}$ are . . . over a tonic harmony; this contrasts with the full support given the slow descent from $\hat{5}$ to $\hat{1}$ over the last seven measures." The melodic gesture of $\hat{8}$-to-$\hat{5}$-over-a-tonic-pedal is described by the Schenkerian term, "*Leerlauf.*"

The authors' analysis might at first seem utterly inconsistent with the tremendous accentual impact of the musical attack on "Joy." Is not this brilliant impetus the most striking thing about the piece? And in that case, how can one presume to assert that "world" is "more important"? The reader recognizes, I hope, the analogy with "multitudinous" and "This." In my view, the Schenkerian reading does not claim that "world" is "more important" than "Joy"; rather it asserts that "world" is the *Kopfton* for a well-formed Schenkerian *Ursatz*, much as "This" is the subject of a well-formed English sentence in Macbeth's speech.

The critic will go on to demand of analysis that it demonstrate the pertinence of such grammatical observations for our perceptions of the artworks at hand. I have tried to produce relevant discussion for the Shakespeare passage in this regard, and I shall now make the same attempt for the Handel piece.

There, the Schenkerian syntax suggests an interesting metaphorical image. Handel's joy is cosmic. It fills the universe with its radiance, as a divine harmony. It does not move from one location to another. Specifically, it does not leave its heavenly orb and travel to the world through some conductive medium, for example, through some diatonic series articulated in human time, like an *Urlinie*. Rather, it exists in-all-places at-all-times and suffuses all things, the world in particular, with its tonic harmonic resonance. The *Leerlauf* transmits the radiance of this joy as it were like a space heater, through empty space. No conductive medium is necessary. Only in the world, here on $\hat{5}$, can we set about the kind of structural

32. *Introduction to Schenkerian Analysis* (New York: W. W. Norton, 1982), 182–183.

melodic activity that conducts one event to another through *human* time. That is, only here and now can a Schenkerian *Urlinie* get underway, as the upper structural voice of an *Ursatz*.

These metaphors belong squarely within a conceptual tradition that distinguishes the (harmonic) Music of the Universe from (melodic) Human Music, a tradition extending back to Boethius among music theorists. Zarlino carried the tradition into and through the Renaissance. Handel would have been sensitive to it at least through his relationship with Mattheson. And Schenker's mature theory reworks the old metaphor into yet another form: he presents his *Ursatz* as a projection through human time, by idealized human voices, of a categorically prior harmonic structure given by Nature.[33]

Whatever the relevance or irrelevance of this cultural history, the cosmic metaphor gives us a poetic reading that "makes sense" of the Schenkerian syntax presented by Forte and Gilbert, while also making sense of our natural urge to sing the word "Joy," in the musical setting, as brilliantly and radiantly as possible. This reading would be helpful to a number of singers and conductors, as a way of drawing their interest and hence their attention to the vocal problem posed by "world": it is easy for a chorus to run out of steam at this point in the music, after making a slight diminuendo over the first four notes. No self-respecting chorus needs to be told that "Joy" is something special, just as no self-respecting actor needs to be told that "multitudinous" is something special. Most choruses, however, can use some coaching with the delivery of "world" in its context here, just as most actors can use some coaching with their delivery of "This" in context. And it will surely help a chorus to think of "Joy to the world" as *one* event establishing a harmonic resonance that envelops both the continuing joy and the continuing world, rather than as *four* events constituting a melodic journey that begins at joy and *ends* with the world.

A point should be taken up here that was left hanging earlier. We are much freer to reject Schenkerian grammar, as part of a theoretical ConteXT in which to make perceptual STatements about tonal music, than we are to reject traditional English grammar in connection with English poetry. Such is indeed the case. But, while we are comparatively free to accept or reject this or that music theory as part of a perceptual ConteXT, or as part of a language L in which to make STatements about tonal music, we are not so free to accept or reject the notion of *some* music theory, or theories, through which we can discuss things traditionally called "tonics," "dominants," "strong beats," "beats," etc. To the extent that we attribute systematic priority of any kind to such things in tonal music, the sorts of issues we

33. Relevant material from Boethius is translated by Oliver Strunk, *Source Readings in Music History* (New York: W. W. Norton, 1950), 84–85. Gioseffo Zarlino's ideas are succinctly discussed by translators Guy Marco and Claude Palisca in Zarlino, *The Art of Counterpoint, Part Three of Le Istitutioni Harmoniche* (New Haven, Conn.: Yale University Press, 1968), xviii–xxiv. An eighteenth-century version of the Boethian idea appears in Mattheson, *Der vollkommene Capellmeister* (Hamburg: Christian Herold, 1739), 6; Mattheson's prose paraphrases the text from Boethius cited here. The article on Mattheson in the *New Grove Dictionary* mentions the long-continuing friendship and mutual influence of Handel and Mattheson. Heinrich Schenker's remarks about the *Ursatz* appear in *Free Composition*, trans. and ed. E. Oster (New York: Longman, 1979), 10–11.

have been discussing must come up. We shall still have to watch out not to confuse the assertion of systematic priority, for example, for a tonic or a structural downbeat, with the vague locution that the corresponding musical event is "more important" than others.

I have suggested that our urge to make political/legal choices, thereby suppressing certain "less important" perceptions as "naught but" this or that, can be a psychological pushing-away of material deemed inappropriate or disturbing, a kind of *Zurückdrängung* or *Unterdrückung.* In my own experience, I have always found it useful and productive to proceed on this assumption, whenever I feel the urge upon me. But I do not think that *Zurückdrängung* is its only source. Another significant factor is our tendency to confuse arguments about the truth and well-formedness of propositions in the language L, or arguments that urge us to prefer one such proposition over another in the context of L and the score, with arguments attributing relative value or validity to perceptions themselves. An example lies at hand from our discussion of "Joy to the World." In that connection, we can consider Sentences (a), (b), and (c):

(a) "The *Urlinie* for a pertinent *Ursatz* begins on the $\hat{8}$ of 'Joy.'"

(b) "The *Urlinie* for a pertinent *Ursatz* begins on the $\hat{5}$ of 'world.'"

(c) "The *Urlinie* for a pertinent *Ursatz* begins on the $\hat{3}$ of 'And heav'n.'"

Sentence (a) is false; it can be demonstrated false by an appeal to the conventions of Schenkerian language—conventions that define "*Urlinie*" and "*Ursatz*"—along with an appeal to empirical observation directed at a score of the piece—at the noteheads, and so forth. These appeals involve no listening; they require perception only so far as a person must be able to read English or German text and musical scores, to understand the logical arguments. A hypothetical "perception" corresponding to Sentence (a), say p_a = ($\hat{8}$ of "Joy," whole piece, . . . Sentence (a)), could quite properly be dismissed as "malformed." Criticism of p_a, however, should *not* be directed at some vague and wrong-headed notion that p_a makes the EVent of the opening "Joy" seem "too important." Rather, criticism should address the verifiable fact that Sentence (a) is not a true sentence in the understood language L.

Neither Sentence (b) nor Sentence (c) is false, in the sense that Sentence (a) is. However, the logical conjunction of (b) and (c) is false in that sense: within the language L, specific rules tell us that the sentence "(b) and (c)" is false. The truth of (b) logically entails the falsity of (c), and vice versa.

So much for the logic of sentences (b) and (c) within L. When we construct corresponding perceptions p_b and p_c, however, we are *not* within L. We cannot call either perception "true" or "false," even conditional on the other. Both perceptions are well-formed since, *inter alia,* neither Sentence (b) nor Sentence (c) is in itself false (or malformed in L). The matter can stand some elaboration. Let us define the perceptions as p_b = ($\hat{5}$ of "world," whole piece, . . . (p_c, denial), . . . Sentence(b)) and p_c = ($\hat{3}$ of "and," whole piece, . . . (p_b, denial), . . . Sentence (c)). Since Sentence (b) and Sentence (c) are mutually exclusive within L, it is impossible to perceive a well-formed thing called "p_b-and-p_c" at one-and-the-same-time in one-and-the-same-place. But our model does not propose that we consider p_b and p_c to *be* in the same phenomenological place at the same phenomenological time. Quite the contrary: the model enables us and indeed urges us to articulate *different* locations for p_b and p_c in phenomenological space-time. Thus, a political/legal dispute over "p_b? or p_c?" is out of place.

We *can* rationally argue in a political/legal way over grounds for preferring *Sentence* (b) *to Sentence* (c), or vice versa. We can point to aspects of Schenkerian theory, and/or aspects of the score, that make one or the other sentence preferable. Thus, to support a preference for Sentence (b), we could point to the mini-descent from $\hat{5}$ to $\hat{1}$, with full *Ursatz*-type support from the bass and the harmony, that shapes the first cadence of the music (". . . world, the Lord is come"). Or we could point to the lack of bass support under the acoustic attack of the $\hat{3}$ at "And heav'n"; the entrance of the bass voice is delayed so as to support the agogically accented $\hat{5}$ that follows shortly after, on "sing." And so forth. We can also carry out such an argument by invoking the text of the song. Thus, one might try to whip up a reader's enthusiasm for Sentence (b) through the earlier cosmic blarney involving the *Leerlauf*. An opponent might try to arouse a reader's enthusiasm for Sentence (c) by alternative metaphors. No such considerations, though, could argue for preferring one *perception*, p_b or p_c, over the other. One either *has* the perception, or one *doesn't*. I myself much prefer Sentence (b) and do not experience perception p_c, but I can hardly command a person who already experiences p_c not to do so. Anyone who might experience *both* perceptions, at different phenomenological times and places in the listening process, would find the polemic useful for focusing and refining the P-R-LISTS involved.

Another example will help us distinguish the logic of sentences in L from the logic of perceptions in our model. Suppose any common theory of tonal harmony as a component of a language L. Consider two sentences within that language. Sentence XDY reads, "Event X functions harmonically as a dominant of Event Y," and sentence YDX reads, "Event Y functions harmonically as a dominant of Event X." Clearly each sentence is well formed. And, just as clearly, the sentence that is the logical conjunction of XDY with YDX *must* be false. If XDY is true under a certain allowable substitution for X and Y, then YDX must be false under that substitution, and vice versa. We are assured of this without even considering any musical score, let alone doing any listening. Now let us turn our attention to Example 4.10, which sketches a cadence by Siegmund just before the last passage sung by Sieglinde in Act I of *Die Walküre*.

Example 4.10

It seems at first that we have at hand here a perception-structure that involves exactly the sentence just branded as false, that is, the logical conjunction of XDY with YDX. For the X event is evidently perceived to resolve as a dominant seventh into the Y event at the moment of the cadence. (The textual alliteration on the vocal Gs amplifies the effect.) And, *apparently* at the same time and in the same place, we perceive the Y event as a dominant to the X event that immediately precedes it. (The harmony at Y eventually returns, at the end of Sieglinde's passage, to another cadential gesture in G quite like the one that contains the X event.) It seems that we must deny the one perception or the other, in order to avoid a logical paradox.

But our difficulty is only apparent. The confusion arises from our having improperly reified one percept (as opposed to sentence) called XDY and one percept called YDX; the confusion is compounded by the fashion of speaking that makes us believe we have both perceptions "at the same time," so that we try to imagine one composite perception called "the perception of both-XDY-and-YDX." Our model enables us to avoid just these confusions, by articulating a variety of perceptions, at a variety of places in phenomenological space and time. The earlier analysis of an abstract deceptive cadence (Example 4.1) will serve us in good stead here. In connection with Example 4.10, we can formulate the perceptions q_1 through q_6 following, among others.

q_1 = (Event X,
Example 4.10 up the pause,
. . . (q_2, implication) . . . ,
V-of-an-expected-I)

q_2 = (Event X,
Example 4.10 ending with G instead of $e^{\#6}$,
. . . (q_1, realization) . . . ,
cadential dominant)

q_3 = (Event X,
Example 4.10 without the bass and figure for the event at the end,
. . . (q_2, confirmation) . . . ,
cadential dominant)

q_4 = (Event Y,
Events X and Y,
. . . (q_5, implication) . . . ,
dominant of X)

q_5 = (Event Y,
Events X and Y plus a protensive X′ that projects D^7 harmony,
. . . (q_4, realization) . . . ,
dominant in transit from X to X′)

q_6 = (Event Y,
Example 4.10 and on through Sieglinde's passage,
. . . (q_5, confirmation and elaboration) . . . ,
structural dominant in transit from Siegmund's cadential G:V to Sieglinde's)

All these percepts are well formed. Perception q_7 following is *not* well formed:

q_7 = (Event X-and-Y,
Example 4.10,
. . . ,
. . . , XDY, YDX, . . .).

The STatement-LIST for q_7 is malformed within the language L, so q_7 is malformed as a perception. There cannot be any phenomenological place and time where q_7 "is." In contrast to that, one observes how Siegmund's protensive G^5_3 event, involved implicitly in q_1, q_2, and q_3 as that-of-which-X-is-the-dominant, is a different phenomenological object from Sieglinde's Y event, an E raised-sixth, involved in q_4, q_5, and q_6 as that-which-is-a-dominant-of-retained-X.

One more example will focus our attention even more sharply on the discongruity between the logic of sentences-in-the-language-L and the logic of perceptions in our model. A well-known drawing outlines a Gestalt that can be seen as either a rabbit or a duck. In this connection we can construct a visual percept r, perception-of-rabbit, and a visual percept d, perception-of-duck; evidently both r and d are well formed and relevant. One can make *verifiable statements* on a STatement-LIST for r: these are ears; here is the eye; and so on. One can make verifiable statements in the same language about d: this is the bill; here is the eye; and so on. Present-day computer programs (at least in theory) could recognize such features of the drawing, find them well formed, and tell us both "Here is a rabbit" and "Here is a duck" according to stipulated L-criteria for uttering those remarks. However, although "I see a rabbit" and "I see a duck" are both valid perception-utterances, "I see a-rabbit-and-a-duck" is *not*; at least to my knowledge nobody ever sees both animals *at the same time* (in the same phenomenological place). We would not want our computer to tell us "Here is a both-rabbit-and-duck." We would want the machine to know there is no such animal as a both-rabbit-and-duck.

Thus, even though "I perceive rabbit" and "I perceive duck" are both valid perceptions, we cannot infer the validity of "I perceive rabbit-and-duck." We can infer "(I perceive rabbit) and (I perceive duck)," but only under a very special logical interpretation of the conjunctive "and": the meaning of the conjunction here does not imply "at the same time in the same place." That is, we must understand: "Somewhere I perceive rabbit and somewhere I perceive duck." In this linguistic form, the operator "Somewhere I perceive" does not distribute over conjunction of its arguments: "((Somewhere I perceive)(thing 1)) and ((Somewhere I perceive) (thing 2))" does not mean the same as "(Somewhere I perceive)((thing 1) and (thing 2))." So, in particular, "((Somewhere I perceive) (rabbit)) and ((Somewhere I perceive)(duck))" is valid, while "(Somewhere I perceive) (rabbit and duck)" is not only invalid—since I don't—but also malformed, since rabbit-and-duck is not a well-formed object within animal language.

In just the same way, "((Somewhere I perceive)(XDY) and ((Somewhere I perceive)(YDX))" is loosely speaking valid, if we mean by Y here "something I infer from the acoustic signal during the indicated clock-time." But "(Somewhere I perceive)(XDY-and-YDX)" is not valid: there is no such thing as XDY-and-YDX in the language of harmonic theory.

And in just the same way, "((Somewhere I perceive) (a $\hat{5}$ *Urlinie*)) and ((Somewhere I perceive) (a $\hat{3}$ *Urlinie*))" is not malformed, though I do not myself assert it of the Handel composition; however, "(Somewhere I perceive) (both-a-$\hat{5}$-*Urlinie*-and-a-$\hat{3}$-*Urlinie*)" is malformed, since there is no such thing as both-a-$\hat{5}$-*Urlinie*-and-a-$\hat{3}$-*Urlinie* in the language of Schenkerian theory. If we wanted to, we could develop a post-Schenkerian theory in which a piece could logically have more than one "*Urlinie*." Using that new theory as a component within a new language L, we could then render the conjunctive perception well formed. Presumably we would change the vocabulary of our neo-theory and our STatements, since "Ur" no longer seems appropriate.

We should certainly be willing to alter our theoretical discourse in this way, whenever a certain mass of perceptual experience leads us to believe that the alterations might enable us to articulate valuable analytic insights. But we should think long and hard before subjecting a received theoretical discourse to fundamental modification. In changing the language, we risk losing our ability to express some of the features that characterize what is problematic about a tricky perceptual situation. For instance, we could create a new word "dubbit," defined as the Gestaltist drawing recently discussed; by changing my language in this way I could say "I see a dubbit" and thereby "solve the problems" involved in saying both "I see a rabbit" and "I see a duck." But it is just the "problems" in the perceptual situation that we find *characteristic* and *interesting*, worthy of extended analysis; our linguistic expedient has turned the interesting phenomenon into a humdrum affair. So you see a dubbit. Who *cares* if you see a dubbit?

We should generally take the same methodological tack when some of our perceptions about a piece of music involve STatements that are logically incompatible-in-L with other STatements that we articulate in connection with other perceptions. In such a situation, we should generally want our analysis to convey the characteristic multiplicity of the perceptions involved and the characteristic incompatibility of their assertion in-the-same-place at-the-same-time. The rhythm of the dialectic thus engaged will be a significant aspect of our rhythmic response to the music.

Indeed, one of the most interesting features of our model is the way in which it implicitly engages our sense of musical rhythm beyond what is notated. The model suggests, for example, that the rhythmic effect of the passage from *Morgengruß* involves not just aspects of the music traditionally considered as "rhythmic," but also the way in which the various percepts p_1, p_2, p_{3a}, and so on come into mental focus, engage one another in various P-R situations, recede from focus, and leave behind various mental residues, all the while the acoustic signal is proceeding in clock-time. The model is at present not worked out adequately in this direction. It lacks precision compared to traditional models for musical rhythm in the West since the Renaissance. To provide anything like such precision and for other reasons as well, it needs to have worked into it more explicit roles for the various sorts of time, some of them multidimensional, within which the perceptions

p_i are formed, interrelate, and possibly decay in memory. These sorts of time might well include a clock time for the acoustic signal, another Euclidean time within which the listeners' organs react as systems in the sense of classical physics, a phenomenological time whose passage is marked by events that are pertinent changes of state within those organs (e.g., neuron firings or patterns of such firings) a theoretically determined phenomenological time marked by mental constructs called "beats" or "measures" or "breves" or "perfections" or something of the sort (within certain pieces that posit such mensural notions), a processing time in our model within which something metaphorically like EVALuation of p-structures takes place, possibly a time in which our higher-level parser manipulates configurations of p-structures before EVALuation, and possibly a time within which EVALuation is subject to external interrupts carried into the processing system from one or more of the other time-systems just listed.

The project, when sketched this way, may strike the reader as hopelessly extensive. In fact, it strikes me that way. I think that our model, no matter how much development it may undergo, will always remain incomplete and informal in some of its most compelling rhythmic aspects. That is surely a defect in the model regarded as a component within a potential formal theory of music-perception. But it does not damage the model irreparably as a linguistic tool for making analytic statements about preexisting pieces of music. In the discussion of *Morgengruß*, I hope to have exemplified some ways in which I feel the model can in fact convey new and characteristic ideas about aspects of a piece that are undeniably "rhythmic." I used English prose and a few graphics for the purpose. I can imagine using other media as well: poetry, other languages, other kinds of graphic art, theater arts, musical performance of the piece, or of excerpts therefrom, or of a series of examples (with or without commentary), composed *Lehrstücke* of various sorts, and so on, the various media alone or in combination. The graphic conventions of Schenkerian or post-Schenkerian theories, for example, might enable one to represent aspects of p-structures in local ConteXTs by "windows" framing regions of incomplete or tentative graphs. Example 4.8.1 through 4.8.9 suggests such formats. A considerable amount of rhythmic theory could be formalized from the visually manifest interrelationships of such windows-on-graphs. The Euclidean ground underlying such formalization, which is the plane of the page or of the computer monitor, would have to be taken into careful consideration, lest its influence on the theory be underestimated.[34]

Earlier, I suggested that the p-model is helpful for distinguishing between the undefined "importance" of perceptions, and the syntactic priority of elements within a language L that admits such priorities, elements like subjects of sentences,

34. The tree-structures of Lerdahl and Jackendoff, *A Generative Theory*, seem particularly amenable to elaboration through such "windows." Extending their theory in this way might entail modifying their methodology, particularly on matters of linguistic "preference" and perceptual priority. As the reader will have gathered from my earlier remarks on this issue, I believe that modification in this regard would in fact enrich their theory, which in general I find engaging, powerful, and significant. Recent lectures by Lerdahl, along with private communications, lead me to believe that the theory may develop in the direction of something like my "windows," although of course on its own terms, not on mine.

tonic harmonies, strong beats, or *Kopftöne* of *Urlinien*. The model can also distinguish other sorts of priorities that are helpful in avoiding fruitless political/legal controversy. For example, we can define a category called "finality": p_1 is more final than p_2 if the ConteXT of p_1 includes that of p_2 in all respects and also extends beyond it in the clock time of the piece. We can also define "P-R-emblematicity": p_1 is more P-R-emblematic than p_2 if the P-R list of p_1 is longer, or deeper, or more-inclusive in some other defined way, than the P-R-LIST of p_2. We can define "ST-emblematicity" in the same spirit. And so forth. We are free to assign aesthetic values to these categories if we wish: one critic can legitimately believe and claim that more-final perceptions are thereby "more important" (of greater aesthetic value) than less-final perceptions; another critic can as legitimately believe and claim that the more emblematic perceptions are the "more important" ones; and so on.

I argue that discriminations of this sort are methodologically desirable, not because I believe that value judgments are unimportant in the critical context but—on the contrary—precisely because I believe they are so *very* important. We ought to be correspondingly clear about what those values *are*, to ourselves and—where the occasion demands it—to others. That is why we should not mistakenly confuse our values with formal properties of rationalist systems. The confusion can only impoverish and mar both our systematics and our valuations. To put the matter more colloquially: whatever the individual critics of the preceding paragraph believe, they will all know what they are talking about.

Part V: Perception and the Productive Modes of Behavior

At the very beginning of this chapter, I said that I found the trend toward phenomenological studies of music problematic for music theory, particularly in what one might call the sociology of the matter. I shall now pursue that thought.

The problems I want to consider arise from a tradition in studies of perception, to suppose that there is something X that perceives and something Y that is perceived. Typically X is a hypothetical person; sometimes X is a mind that might be God or a computer or an animal.[35] Typically, Y is asserted, explicitly or implicitly, to have a predicate that can be called "reality" or "existence" or "being," or something of the sort. Even Berkeley agrees that a tree Y does always "exist," since God (= X) is always observing it.[36]

Classical European philosophy and Indo-European sentence structure suggest to us that we call X a "subject" and Y an "object," mentally supplying a verb that describes a relationship in which X is doing something to Y-that-is-not-X; X is "observing" Y or "perceiving" Y, or something of that sort.

35. Or a plant? I once saw a fast-action film of a vine that reversed its direction of growth along the ground 180 degrees, and crawled back for some distance in that direction to reach a stake that had been put in the ground there; the vine then proceeded to climb the stake. Did the vine perceive the stake? If not, why not?

36. See Russell, *A History of Western Philosophy* (New York: Simon & Schuster, 1945), 647 and following, for an entertaining discussion of Berkeley's argument.

Husserl proceeds quite differently in these matters, as do other modern philosophers among his precursors, contemporaries, and followers.[37] But they still recognize a distinction of X and Y in some form. Y is crucially not X-itself but rather some thing(s) demonstrably "other"—this tree here now (that is not me), this acoustic signal here as I listen to it over this time span, that is impinging upon me (but is not me), this artwork as I perceive it or understand it, perhaps as Z made it, or even as Z is making it, but *not* (NB) as-it-is-emerging-now-from-me, let alone as-it-is-being-me-and-I-am-being-it.[38]

The habit of distinguishing X from Y in thinking about perception does not in itself pose a danger for music theory; the habit becomes dangerous, though, when we add an assumption that music theories are, or should be, fundamentally perceptual in nature or purpose. That assumption makes us take as a point of departure for music theory (and not just for studies in musical perception) a paradigm in which a "listener" X is "perceiving" some "music" Y that is demonstrably other-than-X. In such imaginings, "the music" Y is profoundly and fundamentally there, as made by some Z, prior to any activity of X-now, even prior to X-now's presence. For X, Y has *Gegebenheit* and *Dasein,* not just *Sinn* and *Anwesenheit.* Roughly speaking, X finds Y given and there, not just sensible and present. That is so even if, in some situations, Z might be X-yesterday or X-thirty-seconds ago.

The X/Y paradigm can accommodate without undue strain the apparatus of Husserl's phenomenology.[39] But it fits very poorly with the present-tense activities of composers and performers. "The music" that a composer is composing right now is not something demonstrably other than the composer; on the contrary, we say precisely that it is something "of the composer." Nor is the music-as-it-is-

37. Miller, *Husserl,* 7–32.

38. I phrase aspects of the sentence to recall Hegel, for it might appear at first that Hegel's phenomenology does precisely obliterate, or attempt to obliterate, the X/Y distinction. In a sense that is true. But the picture it gives of Hegel's procedure is not complete enough. *The Phenomenology of Mind* does not deny subject-perceiving-object and substitute Understanding-understanding-Understanding. Rather, the book portrays a process of enlightenment, a journey that begins at subject-perceiving-object and ends at Understanding-understanding-Understanding. The journey is a very different thing from the destination: a trip from Des Moines to Chicago to New York to Paris to Damascus is not the same thing as Damascus, nor does it deny Des Moines. Damascus is not a substitute for Des Moines in this connection. For "Des Moines" read "Consciousness" or "Perception"; for "Damascus" read "Self-consciousness" or "Understanding." The air carriers and intermediate airports are the dialectic process and the stages of dialectic transition. According to Gadamer, Hegel's *The Phenomenology of Mind* demonstrates "*the necessary transition* [emphasis mine] from consciousness to self-consciousness. . . . R. Wiehl . . . has shown that in looking back from the chapter on 'Force and Understanding,' one must view 'Sense Certainty' as the point of departure: namely, . . . consciousness as yet entirely unconscious of its essential self-consciousness [X thinking 'I perceive Y' and taking it for granted that Y is something not-me] . . . Hegel's claim that the dialectical transitions are *necessary* [emphasis mine] is made good . . . again and again if one reads carefully." Gadamer, *Hegel's Dialectic,* trans. P. C. Smith (New Haven, Conn.: Yale University Press, 1976), 36.

39. Chapter 1 of Miller, *Husserl,* also addresses this issue. The differentiability of Y from X is clear in Husserl's insisting that "the 'direct' objects of our perceptual acts are ordinary physical objects, and not anything else in their stead" (14). Miller continues by citing Husserl's own text: "I perceive the thing, the object of nature, the tree *there* [emphasis mine] in the garden; that and nothing else is the real object of the perceiving 'intention.' . . . an 'inner image' of *the real tree that stands out there* [emphasis mine] *before me* [emphasis mine] is nowise given."

being-composed fundamentally there prior to the activity of the-composer-now; on the contrary, the gestus of composition involves producing something *not* there prior to that activity. This is as true for the *symphonetes,* the collage composer, and the composer of 4′ 33″, as it is for the *phonascus,* the original genius, and the composer of *The Ring*. To be sure, a traditional composer at work can enter into noetic/noematic exchanges, even into subject/object relationships, with sketches or portions of the piece already drafted. Perceptually oriented music theories will then be pertinent to the working procedure, perhaps even useful or indispensable. But the music-as-it-is-being-composed is far from prior to the composer's activity, nor is it something "out there," other than the composer.

Once the music has been composed, it becomes a wholly different phenomenon for the composer. It becomes a trace or a record of past activities. The record has special values and meanings for performers, listeners, and critics, but for the composer as composer-of-the-piece, the trace means precisely what the sight of ski tracks on the hill behind means to a downhill skier who has navigated a treacherous slope, or what a photograph of yourself on the Eiffel Tower means to you if you have just returned from your first trip to Paris. Not just the level of meaning but the kind of meaning is the same in all three cases: "That was me. I was there."

In contrast, the composer-composing might say, "Here I-*cum*-it am-*cum-is*." And the listener-perceiving would characteristically say yet something else: "I am here-now with that music there-now." The listener-perceiving is involved in the X/Y paradigm; the composer-composing is not, nor is the composer-having-composed. The composer as composer does not "perceive" the art work (or "understand" it either, in Hegel's sense); the composer either *is doing* it or *has done* it. Roger Sessions puts this well:

> Composition is a *deed,* an action. . . . The climber in the high mountains is intent upon the steps he is taking, on the practical realization of those steps. . . . [The composer's] psychology is not dissimilar . . . extremely often the completed work is incomprehensible to him immediately after it is finished.
>
> Why? Because his experience in creating the work is incalculably more intense than any later experience he can have from it; because the finished product is, so to speak, the goal of that experience and not in any sense a repetition of it. He cannot relive the compositional experience. . . . And yet he is too close to it to detach himself to the extent necessary to see his work objectively, and to allow it to exert its inherent power over him.[40]

The X/Y paradigm fits poorly in the same ways with the performer in the act of performing. "The music" that this person is playing now is not "over there" for the player; it is not something other-than-me, prior to any activity on my part. As

40. The passage is taken from "The Composer and His Message," a lecture delivered at Princeton University in the fall of 1939, reprinted in Edward T Cone, ed., *Roger Sessions on Music* (Princeton, N.J.: Princeton University Press, 1979), 25–26.

I have modified the sense of the passage by one of my omissions. Sessions writes: "He cannot relive the compositional experience without effort which seems quite irrelevant." I do not see how the experience can be relived at all.

with composing, the gestus of performing involves producing something that is *not* "there" prior to the activity, something "*of* the artist" at the time of creation. To be sure, a traditional performer at work can enter into noetic/noematic exchanges, even subject/object relationships, with parts of the acoustic signal already produced; to that extent perceptually oriented music theories are relevant and useful. But "the music" as what-is-being-played-right-now is far from prior to the performer's activity. Here, even more than in the case of composition, no one can help but recognize "the music," after it becomes separate from the person of the musician, as a trace or record of that person's activities. We commonly use the word "record" in precisely that connection.

There is not space here to explore the ways in which theories of music may be useful to working composers and performers, or to debate the extent to which useful theories in those connections may or may not be those explicitly bound to ways of perceiving preexisting compositions and performances (rather than those bound to general abstract contexts of science, logic, dialectics, et al.). Personally, I believe that music theories of all kinds can be useful beyond analysis and perception as goads to musical action, ways of suggesting what *might* be done, beyond ways of regarding what *has* been done. But I shall leave these issues unexamined any farther, and proceed instead to sum up my polemic point: since "music" is something you *do,* and not just something you *perceive* (or understand), a theory of music can not be developed fully from a theory of musical perception (with or without an ancillary dialectic). At least, so I maintain.[41]

Actually, I am not very sure what a "theory of music" might be, or even a "theory of modern Western art-music," but so far as I can imagine one (of either) that includes a theory of musical perception, I imagine it including the broader study of what we call people's "musical behavior," a category that includes competent listening to be sure, but also competent production and performance. Here I understand production and performance not only in the sense of high art but also as manifest in everyday acts of musical "noodling," and in a whole spectrum of intermediate activities. Under the rubric of noodling I include rhythmic gestures, conscious or unconscious, like patterns of walking, finger-drumming, or nervous scratching; I also include singing, whistling, or humming bits of familiar or invented tunes, or variations on familiar tunes; I also include timbral productions like twanging metal objects, knocking on wooden ones, making vocal or other bodily sounds without pitched fundamentals or direct phonemic significance, blowing on conch-shells, through hose-pipes, through blades of grass, and so on. The range

41. I differ explicitly here with the stance of Lerdahl and Jackendoff. The first sentence of their book reads: "We take the goal of a theory of music to be a *formal description of the musical intuitions of a listener who is experienced in a musical idiom*" (*A Generative Theory*, 1). I am impressed but not persuaded by their arguments on the issues I have just brought up, arguments that can be found explicitly on pages 7–8 of their text and implicitly throughout it.

It is true that the musical intuition of their listener is not "out there" or "other than me" for that person. But the musical intuition is not "the music"; it is not Husserl's demonstrable-*this,* like the "real tree" of note 39. When I listen to *Morgengruß*, "*the music*" *is* (that instance of) *Morgengruß.* That is what I am listening *to* (perceiving); my intuitions, like my ears and my brain, are things I am listening *with* or *through.* For me the song is *given* and *there.*

of activities between noodling and high art would include bad-and-incompetent performances of art, bad-but-somewhat-competent ones (where the performer realizes that a goal has not been attained and has some sense—cognitive or kinetic—of what to do about it), playing in a band or orchestra, or singing in a chorus, at various levels of competence, dancing in more or less structured ways, performing *Lieder* or Gospel or chamber music or jazz or rock, informally, semi-formally, or formally, writing passages or pieces of music for informal, semi-formal, or formal groups to play, or for high school bands, orchestras, choruses, or "shows," improvising solo or in ensemble, putting an ensemble musical score up on the piano rack and "fooling around" with it (making impromptu transcriptions first this way, then that), trying to recover the sound of an ensemble piece from memory by such "fooling around," on piano or synthesizer keyboards, and so on.

The p-model we have been studying does not begin to engage these forms of musical behavior, and it will not do so until we can conceptualize the various activities as formal "utterances" of some kind, in extended "languages L" of some kind. I hinted at such possibilities when I first discussed the "language L" of the p-model, in Part II of this chapter. I shall suggest the possibilities recurrently throughout the material of Part V that follows. I am not sure that "language" is a useful word to retain in this connection, although there are precedents for the usage (e.g., body language, the Language of Love). And even if the p-model "begins to engage" the activities, it will not very likely to able to *model* them.

The activities as listed here bring into focus what I earlier called the sociology of the matter at hand. Anyone who as spent a certain amount of time around contemporary U.S. music departments or conservatories will be aware of many ways in which our institutions—academic and nonacademic—separate competence in creating fresh music, in performing existing music, and in understanding received musical art. We will recognize this separation whether we like it, dislike it, or respond to it with mixed feelings. The reader has gathered that I dislike it. I do admit that it has some conveniences, mainly in that it discourages dilettantism. Its disadvantages, much more serious to my way of thinking, lie in its encouraging young composers, performers, and scholars to concentrate respectively upon producing "effective" sounds, upon exercising mechanical skills, and upon viewing art as something "given" and "there." We should encourage these young people instead to conceive their various activities as interrelated, and in all cases as ways of making *poetic statements*. I shall say a good deal more on the latter subject further on.

Speaking in particular as a professional music theorist, I worry a lot about the many examinations I have attended and given, in which students are certified as competent musical "perceivers" primarily on the basis of the way in which they run critical analyses of given art works, using received languages L that are not music. Sometimes a student becomes paralyzed if I go to the piano, play something, and ask: "Do you mean, like *this?*" Or the student will freeze on being asked to clarify or defend an analytic reading by "fooling around" of this sort at the keyboard. I have often had the feeling that I *would* encounter such blockage if I *did* try to initiate such discourse with an examinee. Remarkably, there seems to be no correlation either way, between the keyboard ability of examinees and their susceptibility to this paralysis.[42]

I am not concerned here about advanced students of music theory proper, who are being examined in their specific proficiency at this or that technique of analysis, or in their acquaintance with the professional or critical literature. I am concerned, rather, with student musicians in general: they are being encouraged by our educational system to dissociate the understanding of music from its production and performance, to associate musical "understanding" with an ability to give approved responses in English, and/or in certain symbolic languages, to art works that are "given" and "there," art works whose species are well agreed-on in advance of any examination. When we certify "understanding music" on this basis, we are behaving like the authorities who certify "understanding French" on the basis of questions asked in English, to be answered in English, about preexisting French texts. (I suppose that one can technically check off (a), (b), (c), (d), or (e) "in French" as well as "in English.") If, on encountering a student certified as "competent in French" on that basis, one says, "Bien. Causons musique," or, "Il me faut sortir. Écrivez-moi alors deux mots," the result may be substantial or total paralysis. The student may then protest: "I don't speak or write French, but I do have a *reading knowledge*." And the student will be justly indignant since we, the authorities ourselves, have propagated the myth that such a monster as "a reading knowledge of French" exists—that it is possible to read French intelligently without speaking or writing it, and that the ability to answer in English questions in English (or baby "French") about preexisting French texts constitutes knowledge *of* French in some way, rather than knowledge *about* French.

Our conceiving (and encountering) "readers" of French who neither speak nor write French is just like our conceiving (and encountering) "listeners" to music who do not make music in any way. Indeed, we conceive (and encounter) "fans" who watch but do not play ball games, and "audiences" for political debates who do not themselves engage in any political activity but, rather, watch "the politicians," listen to "them," and eventually—perhaps—vote. In other times and places, a region was considered "musical" if its inhabitants habitually made music, one way or another, to the best of their various abilities; nowadays and here, regional music "lovers" boast of their "world-class" orchestras (whose members probably commute), their concert series of prestigious recitalists, their improved attendance at concerts (especially expensive fund-raising concerts), their superb hi-fis, their state-of-the-art compact disc players, and so on.

42. In an upper-division analysis course I once taught, there was a student who could play the first piano sonata of Boulez very well. In the course we had been discussing a piano piece by Debussy for two weeks when she came up with an analytic reading that I could not hear at all. I said, "I can't hear what you mean—play it and give me an idea," whereupon she replied, "I don't play the piece." "Well," said I, "I don't mean as you would on a recital; I mean as you did when you heard (such-and-such)." "Oh," she replied, "I haven't played the piece at all; I thought this was a course in *analysis*." This student was more than competent at the piano but still paralyzed. Some students in this sort of situation play atrociously but give it their best try. On the other hand, some students who can play well also give it their best, while some who play badly freeze up (and of course blame that on a lack of keyboard ability).

And our academies are right at hand, to help the "lovers" decide what to enjoy, in their erotic-acquisitive orgies of consumption. ("Pachelbel's Canon in D can be *yours* for only one dollar!" touts a recent advertisement. Poor Pachelbel—he thought it was his. *La donn' è mobile . . .*) Just like the "ability to read" French, the "enjoyment" of music, along with its "appreciation" and to a significant degree even its "understanding," are all part of a great social swell, a movement which threatens to turn us all into critical consumers, rather than enthusiastic practitioners, of human activity. The movement is wrong. The Lord, after all, did not tell Adam and Eve to observe, understand, and appreciate the world; He told them to *replenish* it.

Naturally, one cannot simple-mindedly divorce constructive creation from perceptive understanding, as if the one could occur without the other, or at least without some experience of the other. I have no wish (obviously) to dispute the value of studies in perception, nor do I much disagree with the claim of Lerdahl and Jackendoff, that "Composers and performers must be active listeners as well."[43] I would, however, qualify it so as to read, "Composers and performers will normally *have done* a great deal of expert and active listening, *before* attaining a state of concentrated readiness in which any specific new creative act can transpire." Schoenberg puts the essence of my revision as compactly as one could imagine it: "Theory must never precede creation: 'And the Lord saw that all was well done.'"[44]

Schoenberg is speaking of "theory" here in the sense of "structural evaluation," so the stress in his context falls on the word "well": theoretical *evaluation* follows creation. In the context of my present polemic, I would stress the word "saw" as much or more: first the Lord created, and only then did the Lord *perceive* what He had (already) done. In the same context, Schoenberg's metaphor suggests a powerful elaboration: when the Lord is pleased by what He sees, *He responds to His perception by creating* something more, or something new. Thus:

> And God said, Let the waters . . . be gathered . . . and let the dry land appear: and it was so.
>
> . . . and God saw that it was good.
>
> And God said, Let the earth bring forth grass . . . and the fruit tree . . . and it was so.
>
> *Genesis, 9–11*

Here one could say that the Lord uses past perception as a stimulus to fresh creation, but it is equally important to put it that He uses fresh creation *as a mode of response* to his latest perception. Creation is thus a species of perception-STatement: "LOOKS LIKE it could use some grass and trees." (And it was so.) Many composers will find this creative/perceptive rhythm familiar: one recognizes that a certain part of the composition is the way it ought to be when—and sometimes only when—*another* part of the composition begins to take shape as a consequence.

43. Lerdahl and Jackendoff, *A Generative Theory*, 7.

44. Arnold Schoenberg, *Structural Functions of Harmony* (New York: W. W. Norton, 1954), 194. The quotation is from the essay "Apollonian Evaluation of a Dionysian Epoch."

Making fresh music as a mode of musical perception—this link in the chain of perception-and-creation is missing in the perceptual theories we have so far considered, including my own p-model so far as it has been worked out as yet. Perhaps the link can eventually be forged within the context of received conceptual systems. After all, Husserl calls perception a mental act, and describes it as something extraordinarily creative. I do not see as yet, though, how he might distinguish and relate what we call acts of listening, acts of performing, and acts of composing, as varieties of *perceptual* response in various musical contexts.[45]

The link might be supplied by something like the literary theory of Harold Bloom, who asserts that "the meaning of a poem can only be a poem, but *another poem, a poem not itself.*"[46] The idea as it stands does not transfer easily to music, but that is largely because of problems attaching themselves to the word "meaning" in Bloom's text. Suppose we modify the notion and, now using the word "poem" to mean any crafted artwork, claim that "a poem can only be perceived in the *making* of another poem, a poem not itself."

In that case, when we play excitedly at the piano on returning home after a stimulating concert we are not executing an *aid* to perception, or to the memory of perception; rather, we are *in the very act* of perceiving, the other poem being our impromptu performance. The same is true when we play fascinatedly again and again over the opening of the finale to the *Appassionata*; we are *not* matching the fingers and positions of our right hands to a preconceived "perception" of the theme; rather, we are *in the act of perceiving* the theme as we move the parts of our bodies to play it; the performances that we essay, if sufficiently competent in gesture, embody a process that is our act of perception. And Beethoven's act of making his c minor Piano Concerto was inter alia his perception, at that time, of Mozart's c minor Concerto. The score, his concomitant utterance, was accordingly a species of perception-STatement. (His act was and is—in retention—many other things, too; the act was/is not one object at one place at one time in phenomenological space-time.) Certain attested remarks made by Beethoven about Mozart's piece do not interest us so much, as records of his various perceptions. Our interest is not less because the remarks are verbal, but because they are inferior to Beethoven's concerto as "other poems."

That feature of Beethoven's verbal remarks highlights an important difference of the post-Bloomian view from the Bloomian one. The post-Bloomian view does not exclude critical utterances as poetry. No more does it exclude acts of analysis. The making of an analysis can be an act of perception, in this view, to the extent—and only to the extent—that the analytic report which traces the deed of perception is itself "another poem."

The broad interpretation of "poem" allows us to admit traditional varieties of interpretative studies into the canon of critical perception, thereby weakening the

45. Avenues of phenomenological investigation in this regard are suggested by Judith Lochhead and George Fisher, "The Performer as Theorist: Preparing a Performance of Daria Semegen's Three Pieces for Clarinet and Piano (1968)," *In Theory Only* 6.7 (1982), 23–39.

46. Harold Bloom, *The Anxiety of Influence* (New York: Oxford University Press, 1973), 70.

force of Bloom's original assertion while expanding its domain.[47] The broad interpretation specifically admits under the post-Bloomian rubric not only the score of Beethoven's c minor Concerto, and not only my playing the theme from the finale of the *Appassionata* this way and that, but also analyses like those of Lerdahl and Jackendoff, or like my discourse involving the syntax of Macbeth's sentence. In doing so, the critical approach brings sharply to our attention the need for studies in *the poetics of analysis.* To the degree that analytic records of musical perceptions are poems, ski tracks tracing the poetic deeds that were the perceptions themselves, then critics—if not analysts—must concern themselves with the poetic resources at hand, that is, the sorts of poetic spaces analysts inhabit and the varieties of poetic media through which they move in executing their deeds.

I take this search for poetics to be the core of the critical position projected by James Randall, Elaine Barkin, and Benjamin Boretz in recent years; their writings "about" music merge seamlessly at various moments with critical theory, analysis, more-or-less-traditional "poetry," and verbal musical composition that has close connections with the more explicitly "compositional" activities of Kenneth Gaburo and Robert Ashley, among others.[48] Also concerned with poetics, and closer to Bloom's original sense of "other poems," are the Functional Analysis of Hans Keller,[49] whose ideas considerably antedate Bloom's, and David Antin's "*talk poem* called 'the death of the hired man,' performed at the Baxter Art Gallery at Cal Tech in 1982 on the occasion of Siah Armajani's construction of a poetry lounge (a version of a New England schoolroom, with handcrafted wooden benches and desks, whose tops have lines from Robert Frost's 'Mending Wall' stenciled across them)."[50]

47. I phrase my text here so as to connect with Jonathan Culler's critique of Bloom, interpretation, and the dissonances between them, in *The Pursuit of Signs* (Ithaca, N.Y.: Cornell University Press, 1981), 14, 107–111.

48. Except for the works of Ashley, the recent writings and the compositions are represented by contributions to *Perspectives of New Music,* starting with the Spring/Summer 1972 issue, which contains James Randall's "Compose Yourself: A Manual for the Young," *Perspectives of New Music* 10.2 (1972), 1–12. Among other things, the article projects an attempt to build a very new sort of perceptual ConteXT in which to hear Alberich's opening passage within *Götterdämmerung,* Act II, Scene 1. Barkin is represented by a number of substantial pieces in the subsequent issues of *PNM.* Of special interest in the present connection is " 'play it AS it lays'," which records a perception of Arnold Schoenberg's piano piece, Opus 19, Number VI (vol. 17, no. 2, Spring/Summer 1979, pp. 17–24). The enormous labors of love through which Benjamin Boretz influenced the journal over many years are only hinted at in his modest editorial apologia, "Afterward (: A Foreword)" (vol. 22, Fall/Winter 1983 and Spring/Summer 1984, pp. 557–559). Kenneth Gaburo is celebrated by a large number of contributions to vol. 18 (Fall/Winter 1979 and Spring/Summer 1980, 7–256). The contribution by Gaburo himself is a lecture/composition/performance/talk poem ("Brain: . . . Half A Whole," pp. 215–256). The reader may want to approach it, or to review it, after perusing the discussion of David Antin and Marjorie Perloff later in this article. Pieces by and about Robert Ashley appear in *Formations,* vol. 2, no. 1 (Spring 1985), 14–63. Musicians may not be familiar with this journal; it is published in Madison by the University of Wisconsin Press.

49. FA No. 1: Mozart, K. 421. *The Score* 22 (1958), 56–64.

50. Marjorie Perloff, "Postmodernism and the Impasse of Lyric," *Formations* 1.2 (1984), 43–63, and, in particular, 57.

To characterize the cited writings as *Versuche* toward the poetics of analysis is not to succumb to a superficial impression about their "poetic" manner in the vulgar sense. A casual reader of Randall, Barkin, and Boretz might easily be misled by such an impression, particularly considering the positions they occupy in a dialectic that is at once intellectual, cultural, and historical, a dialectic that involves them along with the writings of Milton Babbitt and the history of *PNM*. In a superficial view of those relationships, Babbitt is "scientific" and "objective," while the next generation is "poetic" and "subjective." The superficial view is not exactly wrong, but it is very far from adequate to engage the critical issues at hand, issues which it hopelessly trivializes. The writings of Babbitt are as much poems, in the broad interpretation of the post-Bloomian view, as are the writings of Randall. In that view, the issue is not *whether* there shall be poems, but rather what *sorts* of poems there shall be, and by what criteria they are to be valued.

Marjorie Perloff focuses the issues very clearly. At the opening of her essay, "Postmodernism and the Impasse of Lyric," she quotes some traditional lamentation by Christopher Clausen, who has these things to say, among others:

> Few doubt that the rise of science has had something to do with displacing [poetry] as a publically important vehicle for those truths that people accept as being centrally important. The attempt to persuade the reading public that figurative, ironic, or connotative modes of thought and discourse retain their value in an age of computer language has not been notably successful. . . . [educated Americans today] undoubtedly believe that anything of real importance can be better said in prose.

Perloff examines brilliantly "the assumptions behind this statement, . . . not untypical of discussions of poetry in our leading journals." The assumptions are: "First, that 'poetry' and 'science' have mutually exclusive modes of discourse. Second, that 'poetry' is the opposite of 'prose.' Third, that poetry once served and should serve as a vehicle for 'truth.' . . . And, fourth, that poetry is inherently 'figurative, ironic, or connotative' and, as such, stands opposed to 'computer language,' which is presumably non-figurative, straightforward, and denotative. . . . the implication is that the 'truth' of poetry is one of subjectivity, of personal feeling and experience."[51]

These observations launch a virtuoso exercise in critical scholarship, including perceptive analyses of poetry by Louis Zukofsky and Gertrude Stein, which culminates in the extended discussion of Antin's talk poem on Frost. Toward the end of her critique, Perloff picks up her original theme:

> By this time, the audience has been brought round to consider, not only the connection between Frost's "hired man" and Antin's, but also between the status of Armajani, who was *hired* [emphasis mine D. L.] to design the poetry lounge, and Antin who was hired to speak in it. . . . Antin's casual talk has been, all along, . . . a critique of Frost's way of writing poetry with reference to Antin's own poetic, his faith that poetry must be based on actual observation and natural language . . . the text puts forward that poetic not by any kind of general statement, but through a

51. Perloff, "Postmodernism," 43.

> series of narratives, images, and discursive patterns so that we are finally not quite sure what we have witnessed: prose discourse or poetry? Lecture or story? Philosophical argument or sleight-of-hand? . . . Antin does not regard "computer language" or "the rise of Science" as the enemy; . . . and although he regards "truths" as indeed of central importance, he is more interested in questions of appropriateness (what does it mean to *do* x [emphasis mine D. L.] in this context?) and inconsistencies [sc. rabbits and ducks D. L.] than in what Clausen calls "the truths of moments, situations, relationships."[52]

My post-Bloomian proposition, that the perception of a poetic work resides in the (active) making of another poetic work, a work that might be a "performance" in traditional terms, is not such an esoteric idea as the barrage of scholarship over the last few pages may have made it seem. To help convey the point, I will copy out a wonderful poem:

—Accori accori accori, uom, a la strada!
—Che ha', fi' de la putta?—I son rubato.
—Chi t'ha rubato?—Una, che par che rada
come rasoi', sì m'ha netto lasciato.
—Or come non le davi de la spada?
—I dare' anzi a me.—Or se' 'mpazzato?
—Non so; che'l dà?—Così mi par che vada:
or t'avess'ella cieco, sciagurato!
—E vedi che ne pare a que' che'l sanno?
—Di' quel, che tu mi rubi.—Or va' con Dio!
—Ma ando pian, ch'i vo' pianger lo danno.
—Che ti diparti?—Con animo rio.
—Tu abbi'l danno con tutto'l malanno!
—Or chi m'ha morto?—E che diavol sacc'io?
—*Cecco Angiolieri (1250–1319)*[53]

In trying to "perceive" the poem so that it makes sense to you, are you not taken by an urge to *perform* it—to read it aloud and act the roles of the three characters, with appropriate vocal modifications? I am. So far as I kinetically sense the vigorous movements of the characters while they converse—which I do to a considerable degree as I am reading their parts—I am also trying to *direct* the scene for a theatrical production, as part of my mode of perception. This is not to say that I

52. Perloff, "Postmodernism," 60–61.

53. The text is taken from G. R. Kay, ed., *The Penguin Book of Italian Verse*, (Harmondsworth, Middlesex: Penguin Books Ltd., 1958). Kay provides a "plain prose translation": "Run, run, run, man, along that street!" "What's wrong, whoreson?" "I've been robbed." "Who robbed you?" "A woman, who shears like a razor, she's left me so bare." "Well, why didn't you have at her with your sword?" "I'd sooner turn it on myself." "Are you mad?" "I don't know; what makes you think so?" "The way you are going on: it's as good as if she had blinded you, you wretch!"

"See how it appears to people who understand?" "Let them know that you rob me." "O go away!" "I'm going, but slowly, for I must weep my loss." "How do you leave me?" "In bad heart." "Well, you can suffer your 'loss' and every illness with it, for all I care!" "Who is killing me now?" "How the devil should I know?"

would consider irrelevant to my perceptions closely reasoned studies of the syntactic structure, the historical contexts of thirteenth-century Italy (including the rise of the vernacular in literature and the development of the sonnet), the intrinsic sound-structure of the text, the rhythms in the changes of speakers, the ways in which those rhythms counterpoint the regularities of the sonnet "form," contributing thereby to the fantastic modulation and theatrical *coup* when the woman herself appears on the scene (talking about perception), and so forth. All of these studies would help clarify, focus, organize, and intensify my perceptions. But they would not shift the essential *modes* of those perceptions. At least I do not think they would: I do not imagine myself "outgrowing" my urge to recite, act, and direct the three characters, once I acquire "sufficient" reflective knowledge about (or Hegelian understanding of) the play that contains them. I only imagine my performance becoming richer, denser, more compelling, more "true." The reader who was interested in my earlier analysis of Macbeth's soliloquy may have experienced such a response there: to the extent one begins by acting or directing Macbeth in response to the text, to that extent one continues perceiving the passage in the same mode; fresh analytic insight (e.g., about "This" or "multitudinous") will not wean one away from a performance mode; it will only improve the performance, or at any rate stimulate more ambitious performances.

A skeptic could point out that I am discussing a play (by Shakespeare) and an unusually theatrical sonnet (by Cecco); it is only natural to respond to *these* works in a theatrical mode. Fair enough, and I do not want to promote a priori any one mode of perception as universally "better" than any other. Only I believe we are in some danger, these days, of ignoring the more productive modes of perception; I think we underestimate seriously the extent to which those modes are alive and active even in situations in which their pertinence is not so immediately apparent as it is with Shakespeare and Cecco, situations in which we think of ourselves as "readers," not as speakers, writers, actors, and directors; as "listeners," not as players and composers.[54]

To illustrate my point, I shall ask you to imagine the following scenario. You are a young warrior of ancient Rome, taking flight from an armed mass of pursuing enemies. Desperately seeking refuge, you burst unwittingly into the Temple of the Vestal Virgins, a shrine forbidden to males under penalty of death. Amazed and irate priestesses surround you. Collecting yourself as best you can, you turn to them and say—what?

Well you certainly do not say "Pardon ME!" presumably tipping your helmet to the ladies and looking about surreptitiously for a convenient exit. At least, you do not say that unless you are the person who composed the College Board Examination in Latin that I took some thirty-five years ago. Of course, the question on that person's examination was not "What did the young man say to the Virgins?" but, rather, "What is the correct translation of '*Ignoscite*' in the above passage?"

We were offered five translations from which to choose. When I read "Pardon me" as the first of the options, I broke out laughing in the examination hall, draw-

54. The cultural-historical bias behind our underestimation is explored by J. Barish, *The Anti-Theatrical Prejudice* (Berkeley: University of California Press, 1981).

ing some indignant attention from the priests of *that* ritual. How nice, I thought, an examiner with a sense of humor. Then, as I read the other four "answers," the awful truth dawned: "Pardon me" was in fact the "correct" answer. Indeed, according to the question posed, I was to support "Pardon ME!" not only as a *plausible* translation for "*Ignoscite*" in the context, but as a *correct* translation, and not only *a* correct translation but *the* correct translation.

The examiner, of course, had thought "PARdon me," or more likely had not been thinking (perceiving) *anything at all* in the theatrical modes my scenario tries to suggest, the modes in which I had been taking in the story as best I could under the examination conditions, both by temperament and because I was myself a young man in a competitive situation being judged by older authorities. The examiner had certainly not stopped to consider all the connections of the expression "pardon me" in modern English usage, and particularly in *conversational* usage. (I doubt the examiner perceived the context in which "*Ignoscite*" appeared as a conversation.) Someone taking in (perceiving) the Latin passage as an actor or a playwright would have written "Forgive my blasphemy," or "Grant me forgiveness," or something of the sort. These translations project the tone of high-minded civic service and civic virtue that is implicit in the stage-set, the costumes, and the events of the drama. "Pardon me," in conversation, is at best bourgeois British colloquialism. When read as "Pardon ME!" it suggests, even worse, the world of slapstick comedy, a movie starring Steve Martin ("Well exCUse *ME*") or Charlie Chaplin (who would be first rate at the helmet-tipping bit, not to mention the escape scenes). In the theatrical modes, "Pardon me" is just as wrong a translation for "*Ignoscite*" here as "One never know, do one?" and it is wrong in exactly the same respects.

The examiner, however, was not testing for the ability to project oneself imaginatively, using a Latin text, into the world of ancient Rome, nor for the ability to bring into such an imaginative reconstruction the linguistic-conceptual matrices of one's own culture. What, after all, does this have to do with an examination "in Latin"? As Perloff would say, note the assumptions. First, an examination "in Latin" is an examination in "reading" Latin, which is separable from conversation, speaking poetry, acting a drama, or writing original Latin text. Second, "reading" amounts to "grammar" and "translation"; as a result the examination "in Latin" becomes an examination *in* English *about* Latin. Third—and in spite of that—an effective command of English is not prerequisite, since "translation" consists of selecting from among five given choices "the correct answer." Subassumptions: five choices are plenty; a translation is an "answer" to some implicit question; each answer is "correct" or "wrong"; only one is "correct" and it is "*the*" correct one. Fourth, an examination "in Latin" can take place in a hushed, cramped setting where the student can neither read aloud nor move about in kinetic response to the texts at hand; sounds and gestures have nothing to do with "Latin."[55] Saddling

55. How many people does one find in modern Italy who do not use gestures as part of their language? Should we assume that earlier inhabitants of the region were more constrained? Did their fascination with rhetoric, when they discovered it, reflect a desire to keep still while they spoke? Did Cicero deliver his speeches without moving a muscle? In court? In the Senate? Or did he just mail Xerox copies of the written texts to the jurors and the Senators, so that they could "read" the speeches as our high school students do?

ourselves with all these assumptions, we then wonder why so many young people who get our schooling perceive something in popular art that they do not find in "the classics"!

Let me put the matter this way: the gesture and English utterance that you make when you act the young Roman in his predicament are not phenomena that are *separable* from your understanding of what "*ignoscite*" can mean in Latin. Just so, the vocal and bodily gestures that you make when you act Macbeth saying "This" are not phenomena that are separable from what you perceive in the scene as a playgoer or reader.[56] Just so, the way you sing or conduct the first four notes of "Joy to the world" is not something that is separable from the way you perceive structural functions for the notes on which you sing "Joy" and "world." Likewise, your perceptions of *Morgengruß* are not separable from how long you wait on the fermata at measure 15 before it feels right to go on, when you sing or accompany the song, or when you transcribe it for piano solo. Your perceptions of the song are likewise not separable from how long you want to dwell on the lonely B flat in the piano at measure 12, before allowing the next note of the accompaniment to enter. (Our formal perceptions p_1 through p_9 intermesh with just such performance activities.) And your perceptions of the "XDY-and-YDX" cadence in *Die Walküre* are not separable from the way you conduct the *fp* dynamic and the change of tempo, nor is either of these separable from the way in which you act Sieglinde's discovery at this moment that her adulterous-lover-to-be, the savior promised her by her father, is in fact her own long-lost brother.[57]

The musical examples just above involve text and/or drama. That helps me make them vivid for nonmusicians—and for musicians, too, in a different way. Still, the reader who reviews my analytic discussions of the Schubert, Handel, and Wagner passages will find that I have said plenty about their purely musical analysis that is inseparable from the purely musical performance issues raised in the preceding paragraph, plenty beyond the literary and theatrical contexts I have also discussed. Those contexts are naturally also appropriate, and enrich the purely musical discussion.

56. I make contact here again with the sorts of ideas expressed by Lochhead and Fisher, "The Performer as Theorist."

57. Wagner's stage directions say that she tears herself loose from Sigmund's embrace in the most extreme intoxication, and confronts him as a model for comparison ("reißt sich in höchster Trunkenheit von ihm und stellt sich ihm gegenüber"). Each twin has been ordained by Wotan to be the mirror and (dominant) support of the other; Sieglinde comes to realize that at just this moment.

All of Sieglinde's deceptive cadences in G are laden with this dramatic import, as are all the G cadences through Act I. Most of them are deceptive. The deceptive ones typically involve harmonies including an E or a C♯ and/or a B♭, as well as a G. The dramatic "presence" of Wotan throughout Act I is often missed in production, both dramatically and in E-bass events of the music beyond the Valhalla theme itself in that key. Audiences must wonder why the lovers can't get down to business sooner. In Act III, Brünnhilde finally gives Sieglinde a good G cadence, as she predicts the birth of Siegfried. Sieglinde can thereupon come out with the redemption theme in G—her big moment both dramatically and vocally. But the Redemption cadence is spoiled and turned deceptive by the E in the bass and the E–E–B♭–C♯ in the trombones that undermine the cadential G's in the drum and bass trumpet, turning them ominous. Sieglinde must flee from her enraged father, also Brünnhilde's enraged father, who is now clearly identified as the source of the deceptive G cadence, the E in the bass, and the diminished-seventh harmony.

Indeed, it is quite possible to approach a nontexted work of music "theatrically" as well. To illustrate the point, I shall coach you in the dramatic role of "F♯/G♭", within the drama that is the first movement of Beethoven's Fifth Symphony. In one of your dual personalities you are F♯, the leading tone of G, fifth degree or dominant of C; in the other of your personalities you are G♭, upper neighbor to F, fourth degree or subdominant of C. C is the tonic of the piece and you are its antipode on the clock-face of the chromatic scale or the circle of fifths.

You enter magnificently, surrounded by a prolonged hammering diminished-seventh chord that is the goal of the entire musical impetus since the first theme got underway. Your chord is the first fortissimo of the piece and the first *tutti* of the piece. (Drum and trumpets are trying in vain to maintain the tonic C against your might.) Your chord is also the most serious chromatic excursion of the piece so far; the earlier tonicizations of iv were local affairs. You enter here wearing your F♯ cloak, as leading tone to G; but you abruptly hurl the cloak away and reveal yourself in a suit underneath as G♭, upper neighbor to F. Your diminished-seventh chord resolves not as V-of-(V-of-C) but as V-of-(V-of-E♭). By your mighty feat of enharmony, you single-handedly achieve the modulation from C minor to E♭ major, from the first thematic group of the exposition to its second thematic group. A new theme enters directly you have resolved, with the solo horn call.

In the reprise you replay this whole scene, with a big variation. You re-enter on your climactic diminished seventh chord as before. Everyone is waiting for you to throw off your F♯ cloak and reveal yourself as G♭. You throw off your F♯ cloak all right, but *now* you are wearing an F♯ suit beneath it! You resolve as leading-tone to G, and your chord resolves as V-of-(V-of-C) after all. The horn cannot deal with this, and the bassoons must manage the horn-call theme as best they can. You have now single-handedly warded off the modulation of the exposition, and kept the reprise in C.[58]

During the development you display even more extraordinary powers. After the first theme has gotten underway in F minor, there ensues a sequence whose local tonics move through the circle of fifths from F, through C, to G minor. F and G are your potential tones of resolution in your dual capacities as G♭ and F♯, respectively; C is your antipode. Once the music gets to G minor, it starts to develop motivically; as the *Entwicklung* tightens, the bass moves by steps up the G minor scale until it reaches—you as F♯! Thereupon a new motivic sequence begins, using material from the second thematic group. This sequence moves *back* through the same segment of the circle of fifths, via the dominants of G, C, and F minor. Once the music gets to F minor, it starts to develop motivically once again; as the *Entwicklung* tightens, the bass moves stepwise up again. The steps up begin in F minor; then, pivoting through B♭ minor, the tonic shifts and the steps finally arrive at a tonicized—*you* in your capacity as G♭! F has now become your leading tone.

And then, after all, you throw off your G♭ cloak and reveal yourself enharmonically as F♯ all the time!! The enharmonic shift takes place when the "becalmed" accordion-type alternations of the you-minor triad in the winds and strings shift to a you-six-three harmony that is spelled as a D triad in first inver-

58. Atlas, "The Diachronic Recognition" (26–27, 32–33) discusses these two passages.

sion. The dynamics here, *piano, sempre diminuendo,* and finally *pianissimo,* are unique in the movement and *antipodal* to the *forte* and *fortissimo* bluster of C minor. Also antipodal is the dead calm, breathing, riding-gently-up-and-down-on-little-waves effect, compared to the frenzied *Sturm und Drang* of C minor. This is "you-country," if one may say that of a phenomenon so oceanic. From the first-inversion D harmony, the way back to C minor is clear for the reprise. You leave your "you-country" as a member of V-of-(V-of-C) after all, playing just the part you refused to assume on your first-act entrance. (But your big *coup* in the reprise is still to come.)

Now that I have coached you in acting F♯/G♭, do you not sense the cogency of the theatrical mode in connection with how you might play or conduct the pertinent music, and how you might make analytic STatements about it? Is not the way you "play" F♯/G♭ (in both senses of the word) inseparable from things-that-you-perceive in Beethoven's piece? Would not "playing" the role of E♭, or the role of F, or other roles, similarly engage things-that-you-perceive in the piece? (Some things would sound different to different characters.)

My skeptic will point out that this symphony is an exceptionally "dramatic" one, and ask how my contentions would fare in connection with less dramatic music. Here, finally, I must call a halt. As I said before, I am not proclaiming the virtues of any one mode of perception over all others. I am only concerned that our society encourages us to ignore some of those modes. To the skeptic I say, "Find me a piece we both like that you are convinced is neither poetic nor dramatic. Then we shall discuss the matter further."

CHAPTER Five

Auf dem Flusse

Image and Background in a Schubert Song

I propose here to explore the relation of musical structure to textual imagery in Schubert's song *Auf dem Flusse*, from *Die Winterreise.* The exploration will have several parts. Section I develops a general critical stance toward the relation of music and text in Schubert's songs, a stance that will underlie the subsequent critical and analytic discourse. Section II offers a reading of the text for this specific song. According to this reading—which I am of course claiming to be Schubert's, on the basis of his setting—the text is in a sense "about" the creation and evaluation of a poetic image; the essential point is to take the two concluding questions, "Mein Herz, in diesem Bache/Erkennst du wohl dein Bild?" and "Ob's unter seiner Rinde/ Wohl auch so reissend schwillt?", as undecided, not rhetorical. The climactic musical events over the second half of the song, which sets those questions, reflect and project the tensions experienced by the singer as he contemplates the answers.

Section III examines some of the ways in which various aspects of the musical texture combine to suggest and elaborate the reading of section II. From a theoretical view, the aspects touched on are of a traditional sort: the length of musical sections vis-à-vis text sections, tonality, modality, the relations of the vocal line to the soprano and bass lines of its accompaniment, and motivic rhythms. Novel, perhaps, is the consideration of such matters in connection with the critical stance of section I, and the sort of reading asserted in section II.

Section IV goes systematically deeper into the tonal and rhythmic structure of the music. This exploration gives rise to reductive sketches that present in themselves striking images, images that appear to relate forcefully to the imagery of the text and the questions concerning it. The relation of my reduction technique to Schenkerian theory, and of my results to Schenker's published sketch for this song, are taken up in an appendix. Section V attempts a consistent and dramatically cogent interpretation of the images and questions raised by the sketches of section IV, as relating to the images and questions of the text.

I. A Critical Stance: The Composer as Actor

> Whatever filled the poet's breast Schubert faithfully represented and transfigured in each of his songs, as none has done before him. Every one of his song compositions is in reality a poem on the poem he set to music. (*The Schubert Reader*, ed. Otto Erich Deutsch, trans. Eric Blom [New York: W. W. Norton, 1947], 875)

Josef von Spaun's eulogy of 1829 fairly represents the critical style of Schubert's sympathetic contemporaries. Today we feel more comfortable with critical discourse of a kind that points to networks of specific events in specific compositions. Still, it would be a mistake to dismiss Spaun's prose as insubstantial and unhelpful. If we read it closely, we will find him asserting propositions that bear directly on the methodology of analysis and criticism.

One might put these propositions as follows. A Schubert song takes as structural premises not only musical syntax, as it was understood at the time, but also the structure of the individual text at hand. The world of the song, then, is not simply a musical world. On the other hand, it is also not simply the textual world translated into music: it not only "represents" this world, says Spaun, but also "transfigures" it. So, if we have as text a poem on X, we should not consider the song to be another, related poem on X. Rather, the song should be considered a poem on the poem-on-X.

Hence, we can understand the song as a poetic "reading" of the poem-on-X that is its text, a reading that employs a particular mimesis of X as a representational means. From this point of view, I find it suggestive to conceive the relations of composer, text, and song as analogous to the relations of actor, script, and dramatic reading.[1]

To exemplify the utility of this analogy, consider the famous pause in *Die Post.* The opening text reads: "Von der Strasse her ein Posthorn klingt./Was hat es, dass es so hoch aufspringt,/mein Herz?/Die Post bringt keinen Brief für dich." Schubert extends the second sentence by repetitions of the text, going through a substantial harmonic excursion and return, using an ostinato springing rhythm throughout. There then follows an abrupt silence for one measure, before the song continues, "Die Post bringt keinen Brief," in minor and with the springing rhythm gone. These gestures involve a mimetic reading of the text by the composer, a reading that is far from a simple musical translation or mere "representation," as Spaun puts it. Imagine an actor performing the text in question as a script. According to Schubert's reading, the actor would elaborate and extend the action associated with the second sentence. He might pace back and forth, rush to the window and back, and so on. Then, as the postman approaches the door or the mailbox, the actor would stop moving during Schubert's pause, tensely cocking an ear to listen for the sound of the letter dropping. He would relax his features in dejection as the postman leaves, and continue the recitation: "Die Post bringt keinen Brief."

1. In making the composer a mimetic actor rather than a more general poetic reader of the text, I go beyond the stance adopted by Edward T. Cone in his heartwarming study *The Composer's Voice* (Berkeley and Los Angeles: University of California Press, 1974).

Contrast this performance with that of another actor, who is seated at a desk on stage, immersed in reading, writing, or composing. He looks up, momentarily distracted, and notes, "Von der Strasse her ein Posthorn klingt." He resumes his activity for a while, then breaks off in ironic amusement and says to himself, in one phrase, "Was hat es, dass es so hoch aufspringt, mein Herz?—Die Post bringt keinen Brief für *dich*." This second reading of the text is surely as plausible as the first. In fact, it would not be difficult to argue that Schubert's setting involves reading into the text a good deal more than the second actor has to.[2]

So while it would be accurate enough to say that Schubert's reading "represents" the text, one cannot go very far critically until one investigates how this particular representation, from among a number of plausible readings, interacts with musical structure to project an overall poetic conception of the poem that is the text. In this regard, for instance, one thinks of the rhythmic complexity of Schubert's composition, with its contrasts of expansion and contraction, of regularity and irregularity, of ostinato clock time, musical-phrase time, and text-line time. One notes the importance of exact rhythmic and metric proportion in the effect of the first actor's scene: his "internal clock," representing his heart in the text, enters into complex relationships with external clocks of the actor's outer world—that is, the postman's springing horse, his rounds, and so on. The second actor's scene has much less of an exact mensural character; it could be delivered much more "in its own time."

In the view I have just proposed, the relation between Müller's poem and Schubert's setting is formally analogous to that, say, between Shakespeare's *Hamlet* and Henry Irving's *Hamlet*. One could not sensibly analyze or criticize Irving's *Hamlet* without referring to Shakespeare's, but it is important not to identify or confuse the distinct artworks.

II. Schubert's Reading of the Text

The text of *Auf dem Flusse* follows the poet's creation of a central image, and his reaction to it. One can fairly say, as I put it in my preliminary remarks, that Schubert's reading is in a sense actually "about" the poet as image-maker and image-questioner. A condensed synopsis of the poem will help clarify the point. The text of the poem can be found in Example 5.1. The song is printed as Plate 5.1 at the end of the chapter.

In stanzas 1 and 2, the poet observes that the stream, which used to rush in a wild bright torrent, has become still, cold, and rigid, with a hard stiff cover ("Rinde"). In stanzas 3 and 4, the poet, as if idly, scratches on the ice the name of his lost beloved, along with the dates of their first meeting and their final separation. He circumscribes the whole with a broken ring.

2. An acquaintance of mine once placed a telephone call and was greeted by an unfamiliar voice saying without preface, "You have the wrong number!" "Yes, I do," said my friend, "but how did you know?" "Nobody ever calls *me*," said the person at the other end and hung up.

In stanza 5, the poet is struck by the image he has "inadvertently" created and investigates its pertinence by posing two questions, questions which might be taken rhetorically. The first question, insofar as it can be taken rhetorically, points out in the picture of the broken ring, guarding within it the name and the dates, the image of the poet's broken heart. The second question, insofar as it can be taken rhetorically, points out a further and potentially optimistic aspect of the image. Just as the vernal torrent of stanzas 1–2 is still rushing on beneath the icy surface of the stream, so the poet's heart is still swelling tumultuously beneath its frozen crust.

I contend, however, that Schubert's reading takes the two questions at face value, rather than rhetorically. The first question asks, "Mein Herz, in diesem Bache/Erkennst du nun dein Bild?" Read rhetorically, this does indeed assert the pertinence of the image; taken at face value, however, it *questions* the pertinence of the image. Is the inscribed stream truly the image of my heart? Taken at face value, the question also calls into issue the poet's capacity to judge the propriety of the image. Does my heart recognize and credit the image, perceiving or judging it as apt? (These nuances can fairly be read into "erkennst du nun." N.B.: *Erkenne dich!* = "Know thyself.")

The second question asks, "(Ob's unter seiner Rinde/Wohl auch so reissend schwillt?" An attempt to take this question on face value seems at first ridiculous: the poet, presumably a student of natural science in the spirit of Goethe, must know that rivers flow beneath their ice in wintertime. Perhaps the stream is small enough to cast the issue in doubt. But this is beside the point. It is clear that neither the geological structure of the stream nor the biological structure of the heart is essentially at issue.

Having said that, one becomes struck by the use of the word "Rinde." The word is in fact a common biological term, used to denote the cortex of the heart. So it is the use of "Rinde" in connection with the stream, not the heart, that is metaphorical. Through this metaphor, the relation of subject and image is inverted. In the first question, the stream was the putative image of the heart; now the heart with its "Rinde" is the putative image of the stream. This device was prepared by the earlier, more descriptive, reference to the "Rinde" of the stream in stanza 2.

At that time, the stream was "du"; the very opening of the poem, in fact, calls attention to the stream in the—as a—second person. By the time we get to the first question in stanza 5, however, there has been a transformation of persons: the heart has become the second person. When we get to the second question, we have just heard "erkennst du wohl dein Bild?" addressed to the heart. Then, since the *Rinde,* in literal usage, belongs to that second-person heart, it is properly "deiner" *Rinde,* not "seiner." From this point of view we can regard the inversion of subject and image, discussed earlier, as a means of transforming and hence avoiding the implicit question, "Ob's unter *deiner* Rinde/Wohl auch so reissend schwillt?" The transformation of second and third persons over the poem also abets this interpenetration of subject and image.

In Schubert's reading, then, I say that the second question is taken to ask: Is there any capacity for flowing torrential warmth left under the frozen exterior of the heart? Or is it frozen solid, through and through? A question not to be asked!

(And it is not asked . . . yet it is.) The stream will melt next spring, returning to the state described in the opening line of the poem. The subglacial flow of the stream, if existent, is a portent linking its future with its past. But will the poet's heart ever thaw, returning to a state "des ersten Grüsses"? Is there some subglacial flow within it that portends such an eventual thaw? And thus, picking up the first question again, *is* the stream, which will thaw next spring, a true image of the heart?

It is the tensions underlying this reading of the questions that, as I suggested earlier, force the expansion of the setting of stanza 5 over the entire second half of the song. In this connection, it is interesting to note that Müller's text contracts at this point, rather than expanding. Stanzas 1 and 2 are paired by their subject matter, and so are stanzas 3 and 4; stanza 5, however, which ends the poem, has no partner. Instead, it asks two questions. The pair of questions thus substitutes, as it were, for a pair of stanzas; this contracts the time involved by a factor of two. One might say that Müller's text ends with an unresolved systole, for which Schubert's song substitutes an enormous diastole.

III. The Song: Mimetic Techniques

This diastole can be observed in Example 5.1, which plots some of the easily perceivable aspects of the musical setting against the coextensive text. In clock time, the crucial point at measure 41 comes more than halfway through the song. But in strophic time, the four strophes that set stanza 5 after this point are equivalent to the four strophes setting stanzas 1–4 before it. In a sense, this musical diastole is consistent with Müller's textual systole. For one can say that the music expands with respect to the text it sets or, taking a relativistic view, one can say that the text contracts with respect to the amount of music that sets it. The latter formulation is consistent with the reading of section II, which had stanza 5 contracted with respect to its emotional and structural implications.

In any case, Schubert, as he approaches the crucial text questions, makes use of temporal contraction in another way. I am referring to the rhythmic scheme that governs the durations of successive strophes. As appears from the "duration" column in Example 5.1, the process of contraction leads directly and unambiguously to strophe 6, the climactically compressed strophe that first sets the climactic final question of our reading. (The two-measure extension of strophe 4, as the *maggiore* ends, does not disturb the sense of the rhythmic scheme.) Strophe 6, as goal of the contraction process, is consistent with what I have asserted to be Schubert's literal, rather than rhetorical, reading of the text questions.

Strophe 6 takes another kind of strong accent because of the key of its opening. In this sort of loose chaconne/passacaglia/variation structure, strophe 6 is the unique strophe that does not begin with a strong downbeat on E minor or E major. It begins with the usual strong downbeat, but in a foreign key. The relation of G♯ minor to E major is clear enough: G♯ harmony represents iii of E major and, as we shall see later, the G♯ in the bass at measure 48 can fit very convincingly into a structural arpeggiation of the E-major (!) triad over the bass line of the song as a

Example 5.1

Bar	Text	Stanza number	Strophe number	Duration	Key	Relation of Voice to Piano	Right-hand Rhythmic Motive
5	Der du so lustig rauschtest, du heller, wilder Fluss, wie still bist du geworden, giebst keinen Scheidegruss!	1	1	9 bars	E minor	Voice doubles bass (low E).	
14	Mit harter, starrer Rinde hast du dich überdeckt, liegst kalt und unbeweglich im Sande ausgestreckt.	2	2	9 bars			
23	In deine Decke grab'ich mit einem spitzen Stein den Namen meiner Liebsten und Stund' und Tag hinein:	3	3	8 bars	E major	Voice (G♯) takes over from RH (G♮); now RH doubles voice.	
31	Den Tag des ersten Grusses, den Tag, an dem ich ging: um Nam' und Zahlen windet sich ein zerbroch'ner Ring.	4	4	10 bars (8 + 2)			*[sic]*
41	Mein Herz, in deisem Bache erkennst du nun dein Bild?	5	5	7 bars	E minor	Voice (B) rises above both hands.	
48	Ob's unter seiner Rinde wohl auch so reissend schwillt?	(5)	6	6 bars	G♯ minor		*[sic]*
54	Mein Herz, etc.	(5)	7	8 bars	E minor	Voice reaches high E; continues in highest register, above both hands.	
62	Ob's unter seiner Rinde, etc.	(5)	8	8 bars			

whole. These functions put strophe 6 into the realm of E major, the key associated with happy memories of earlier times, perhaps springtime, in stanzas 3–4. This tonal function for G♯ minor thus supports a potentially optimistic answer for the concomitant second text question. If indeed a secret E-major deep structure lies *unter der Rinde* of the E-minor surface structure, then the poet's heart does indeed preserve its capacity for warmth and the return of a vernal state.

Of course, the song is not in the major mode, which is to say that the optimistic answer to the questions is ultimately untenable in Schubert's reading. Although, as we shall see presently, it is not so easy to show convincingly *why* the song is not in fact in the major mode once one begins to examine its deeper tonal structure, which hinges not only on the bass G♯ of measure 48 but also on the powerful vocal G♯ at measure 23. To answer that "why," we shall have to explore what is wrong with the image the poet has constructed, what militates against the E-major image suggested by the deep-level structure.

But we must defer this study until sections IV and V. Here we can note that while the G♯ does indeed put the second question into the realm of the happy, warm E-major memories, the tonal material of strophe 6 also, and ambivalently, refers back to the icy, immobile E-minor world of the opening strophes. The G♯-minor world of the sixth strophe specifically recalls the icy harmonies of measures 9–12 and 18–21. Those measures encompass a most desolate part of the E-minor world; the coextensive text includes the words *still . . . geworden, kalt,* and *unbeweglich.* Here (in mm. 9–12) the tones A♯ and D♯ are locally diatonic, as they also are in measures 48–51. So, as it were, we have been warned that those locally diatonic tones can very easily elaborate and return to E minor in this song. With a bit of stimulation, in fact, one can hear how the melodic structure of the bass line in strophe 1 is transformed into the melodic structure of the vocal line in strophes 5 and 6. Example 5.2 provides the stimulus. The reader should not be distracted by the harmonic notation, which will be discussed soon. The main point of the figure is to suggest the *melodic* transformation of the reduced bass line, bars 5–14, into the reduced vocal line, bars 41–54.

From this point of view, the bass G♯ of strophe 6 does not function as a root representing the major third degree of E. Rather, it functions as a means of providing consonant support for the structural tones B and D♯ in the vocal line. And Example 5.2 makes it clear that B and D♯ strongly project the dominant function in E minor. Riemann's notion of "dominant parallel"—"$(D^+)_p$"—furnishes a good label for the G♯ chord in this connection, as Example 5.2 shows.

Example 5.2

The $(D^+)_p$ analysis of the harmony, in asserting dominant function, implicitly rejects an alternate Riemannian analysis of the harmony as Ŧ$^+$, an analysis that would assign the harmony tonic function. The rejected analysis would be the way to assert in Riemannian terms the idea that the bass G♯ represents the third of a structurally prior E-major tonic. Instead the $(D^+)_p$ analysis asserts for the bass G♯ a function as the under-fifth of the voice's D♯, the tone that is in fact the Riemannian root of the harmony. And that root D♯ of the asserted $(D^+)_p$ functions as the third of a structurally prior B-major harmony, a harmony that is in turn the major dominant of a structurally prior E-minor tonic—understanding "E-minor" in our sense now, not Riemann's.

The use of G♯ minor in strophe 6 is strongly qualified, then, not only by a potential optimistic E-major arpeggiation lying *unter der Rinde* of E-minor surface events, but also by the recollection of the icy D♯ and its ultimate root B that lay, *kalt* and *unbeweglich, unter der Rinde* of the right hand, during the E-minor events of strophe 1. In this way, Schubert projects and reinforces his ambivalent reading of the second text question: what *does* lie *unter deiner Rinde*—the E-major world of strophes 3–4 or the E-minor world of strophes 1–2? The use of tonal and modal ambiguity here, as well as the progressive contraction of strophe-lengths, makes it impossible to read the text questions rhetorically. In this connection, note how the *forte* dynamic at measure 48 bursts out from a song that had been *pianissimo* and *pianississimo* up to measure 41, and had risen only to *piano* at that point. One does not sing such *a forte* rhetorically.

We have so far observed that strophe 6 is a climactic goal for a number of musical processes. We have observed in this connection its ambivalence in referring both to the E-major and E-minor worlds, and we have associated this ambivalence with a structural indecision as regards optimistic or pessimistic answers to the questions of the text.

These views of strophe 6 are further confirmed by the development of the right-hand rhythmic motive, which is summarized in the last column of Example 5.1. Once again, strophe 6 is the climactic goal of a process. And, as with the G♯ tonality, the motive-form of strophe 6 has ambivalent references to the two worlds of the song. On the one hand, the thirty-second notes pick up and continue the process of quickening that began with the sixteenths of strophe 3 and continued with the sixteenth-triplets of strophe 4; hence, we could read the motive form of strophe 6 as even more torrentially flowing, befitting an optimistic answer to the question. On the other hand, the thirty-second notes are interrupted by a syncopating rest on the third eighth of the motive: in this respect the motive form resembles the shuddering forms of the pessimistic strophes 1 and 2, just recalled in strophe 5, rather than the smoother, more flowing forms of strophes 3 and 4. The poet's heart is certainly pumping furiously over strophe 6, even faster than it was during its warm beating over strophes 3 and 4, yet the heartbeat here is perhaps more a raging palpitation than a swelling flow.[3] The return of the thirty-second

3. It would be helpful to have some indication as to whether the thirty-second-note groups are to be played slurred, staccato, detached, or even martellato. The resulting effects would heighten the associations of strophe 6, more or less accordingly, with the optimistic or pessimistic worlds of the music. The autograph does not help: its attack symbols (dots plus slurs) stop abruptly, as do those in the published scores, in measure 28. That is why I have written *sic* here and there on Example 5.1.

notes in the final strophe seems to confirm a pessimistic reading for the motive form, though this outcome is of course as yet unheard during strophe 6.

Finally, it is illuminating in this context to examine the doubling relations of voice, right hand, and bass line. These relations are sketched in the penultimate column of Example 5.1. During strophes 1 and 2, the right hand incessantly reiterates $\hat{3}$–$\hat{2}$ in E minor, *kalt und unbeweglich.* Meanwhile, the voice doubles the bass line, which avoids prominent third degrees. The singer seems to be saying, "I am, at this point, only a bass line, *unter der Rinde*; I have nothing to do with that terrible minor *Kopfton* in the right hand."

Consistent with that attitude, the singer thereupon takes a sharp stone and scratches a G♯ on the icy surface of the right hand, at measure 23. Using that G♯, he substitutes a reiterated major $\hat{3}$–$\hat{2}$ for the earlier minor $\hat{3}$–$\hat{2}$ over the next two variations of the strophe. The right hand, transformed by the image-making activity of the poet, momentarily follows him along, abandoning its own preferred minor *Kopfton* while, so to speak, the G♯ image is warm. (It will freeze over again presently.) The singer has insisted on G♯, not G♮ as the structural *Kopfton* for the melody, a feature which all the doubling relations so far emphasize. (While the melodic activity of the third and fourth strophes is more florid than the unadorned G–F♯ gestures of strophes 1 and 2, it is not hard to hear the underlying G♯–F♯ gestures which form the basis for that activity. The underlying $\hat{3}$–$\hat{2}$ will be made clear in the reductions of section IV.)

At measure 38 the voice, detaching itself from the right-hand part, leaps up to B at the cadence, rather than settling on F♯ once more. The rising pitch, coming at the end of all this material, implies a question; it thus foreshadows the explicit questions coming up in the text. The poet silently contemplates the image he has made, as we listen to the extended fluttering of his heart in the rhythmic motive of the piano. Then everything, even the heart itself, is silent for one measure.

Despite the tremendous musical climaxes later on, measure 40 can be taken as the dramatic climax of the composition. When E minor returns at measure 41, with the right-hand motive of the opening, one senses a tragic catastrophe ahead. It is as if the singer, during the silence in measure 40, had already asked himself the questions and answered them negatively. This sense is made all the stronger by the fact that, while the left hand begins to sing like a cello *unter der Rinde* of the right hand at measure 41, the singer himself temporarily remains silent. He is *still geworden* and *unbeweglich;* he cannot double *this* bass line, as it flows warmly on beneath the icy surface of the right hand. His heart ("mein Herz") is *not* like the river bed flowing on beneath.

A Schenkerian approach to the large-scale tonal activity hereabouts is revealing. If at measure 41 the singer were indeed to double the bass—for example, by singing "mein Herz" on low B and E into the bar line of that measure—then the tonic degree E could be heard as closing a Schenkerian *Ursatz,* and furthermore closing that structure in the major mode. Each strophe so far has elaborated the essential melodic gesture $\hat{3}$–$\hat{2}$, in minor or major, with tonic-dominant support. A vocal E, then, at the bar-line of measure 41 after the vocal G♯–F♯ gestures of strophes 3 and 4, would provide a structural melodic first degree with tonic support;

the *Urlinie* and a concomitant *Ursatz* would essentially close. Given the relations of the voice to the right hand, and to the modal character of the music, such a closure would only make musical sense in the major mode here. This would certainly provide a conclusive and optimistic answer for the questions of the text and the subtext as we have discussed it, questions which in fact are only starting to be presented at measure 41. This situation would indeed render the questions purely rhetorical.

This Schenkerian view, then, gives valuable insight here into the tragic structure of the song, in particular into the inability of the voice to double the bass line at measure 41. Still, the singer, while unable to double the bass, does refuse to submit to the right hand's ominous G♮. Rather than double the G♮, abandoning his major *Kopfton,* he continues his quest for a tenable position in the context. He thus sings neither E nor G♮; rather, he holds onto the questioning B of measure 38 as the one melodic tone that is available for him to take into measures 41–42—the B that sets both the broken ring and his heart. That questioning B, in fact, will sound on after the cataclysm of strophe 8 has passed. It sounds in the piano at measure 74, the very last event of the piece, as the poet moves on and away, taking his heart and his questions with him.

From the vocal B of measures 41–42 to the end of the singing—that is, over the entire questioning half of the song—bass, right-hand melody, and vocal line are essentially distinct, despite some partial doublings. In this respect the situation resembles neither strophes 1–2 nor 3–4. Instead a new mode of relationship develops: beginning at the crucial B of "mein Herz," the voice rises above both the other lines, dissociating itself from both the earlier couplings.

Such behavior is not consistent with a supposition that the poet is confirming rhetorically the validity of an image that has been well established. Rather, it supports again, and in a new way, the notion that he is examining, questioning, and criticizing the image he constructed during strophes 3 and 4. Just as he can be imagined getting up from the ice, rising up physically from his position at surface level to stand above his etching and contemplate it, so the tessitura of his melodic line rises, to stand above the entire accompaniment, surface as well as bass. The rising tessitura of the vocal line, in fact, is a feature that persists continuously throughout the entire song from its beginning, not just from measure 41 on. Expanding our interpretation of the rising B as a question mark, at measure 38 and following, we can then interpret this continuous rise in the vocal line, up to the final climax, as the mimesis of a giant structural question mark. And this suits very well the reading of the text that I proposed earlier, in section II.

IV. Deeper Structure

In section III, we investigated a number of musical gestures by which Schubert, in the words of Spaun, "represented and transfigured" the images and questions of the text. Some of these matters involved phenomena progressing over considerable spans of time and bearing strongly on the central aesthetic content of the song. We were able to discuss them without invoking very deep levels of tonal structure in a technical sense. I should now like to show that such representation and transfiguration also permeate events on those deeper levels.

Some preliminary remarks are in order. It will be wise to state explicitly what I hope the analysis so far has made clear, my personal belief that the aesthetic significance of a musical phenomenon in a hierarchic tonal or metric structure should not be correlated a priori, either directly or inversely, with the depth of the structural level at which the phenomenon is manifest.

I do not want to interrupt critical discussion of the song more than is necessary to introduce the reductive sketches I shall be using. As I have already said, technical commentary on those sketches is relegated to an appendix; there, too, I shall discuss various differences between Schenker's diagram of the song in *Der freie Satz* and my own readings. But the reader who has not yet glanced ahead to that appendix should still be provided with a certain minimum of background information for my sketches. Each note on a sketch testifies that I hear the tone of the indicated line (voice, right hand, left hand) as an essential participant in a harmony that essentially governs the rhythmically symbolized span of the piece. The reader, while doubtless disagreeing with some of my assertions, and with some more than others, will nonetheless quickly get the sense of the method by actually performing the sketches—they are explicitly designed for performance by keyboard and possibly voice, in tempo and in the indicated meters. Within reason, some filling-in of the harmony would be unobjectionable. The point is to check the harmonic, linear, and rhythmic-metric assertions of the sketches by ear, both as plausible tonal syntax in themselves and as accurate reportage of tonal and metric structuring within the piece. Time-spans analyzed as expanded or contracted at a given metric level are adjusted to the asserted norm at the appropriate deeper level.

These preliminary observations out of the way, let us turn to Example 5.3, which brings into clearer focus a number of features discussed earlier. Particularly clear is the technique of rhythmic expansion and compression within the large hypermeasures that demarcate the strophes. In this connection, it is curious how the six-measure group of measures 35–41 expands a four-measure group on one metric level (that of the half-strophe), while the six-measure group of measures 48–54 contracts an eight-measure group at a higher metric level (that of the entire strophe). The bass structures of the two passages on Example 5.3 are remarkably similar.

Overall, the bass line of Example 5.3 clarifies the sense in which the strophes constitute a loose chaconne or set of variations. The right-hand line of the example displays clearly its characteristic repeated $\hat{3}$–$\hat{2}$ gestures at this level.

Example 5.4, which reduces Example 5.3 one metric stage further, also shows repeated $\hat{3}$–$\hat{2}$ gestures in the right hand and variational structure among the strophes on that metric level. In addition, it begins to bring into view some curious phenomena. Its bass line descends an octave, from the upper E at the beginning to the lower E at measure 54. The descent takes place using degrees of the major rather

Example 5.3

than the minor mode of E. After reaching the low E at measure 54, the bass of Example 5.4 does begin to sound in the minor mode, but only to confirm a melodic goal already attained, as it were, in E major. Meanwhile the vocal line of the example, which begins essentially by doubling the bass, rises up the octave to the high E at measure 54, in contrary motion to the bass line. This ascent also takes place "in E major"; that is, the vocal line of Example 5.4 sounds firmly in that key when played or sung.

Example 5.4

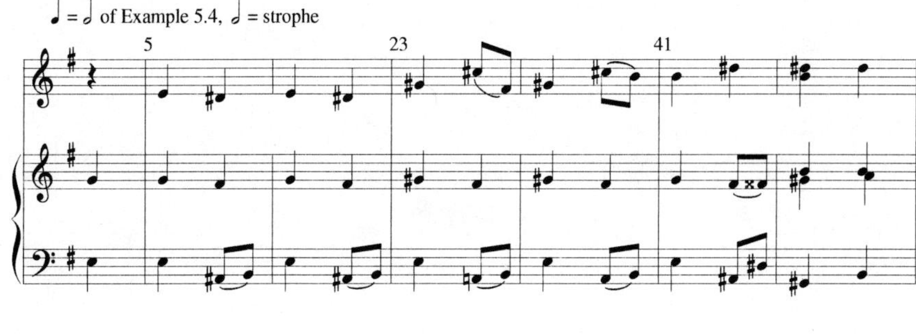

Example 5.5

This phenomenon comes into even sharper focus in Example 5.5, in which the reduction is carried one stage further. The reduced bass line and vocal line, in their mirror relationship, now both sound clearly in the major mode throughout. One notes the structuring force of the G♯ in the voice over strophes 3 and 4, and the G♯ in the bass at the beginning of strophe 6. The vocal G♯ that begins strophe 3, it will be recalled, "corrected" the earlier icy G♮ of the right hand in strophes 1–2. At this metric level the G♮s that occur within the bass line during strophes 7 and 8 disappear, leaving the field completely clear for the major mode as regards the overall structure of the bass line at this level. In the piano part of Example 5.5 one can hear very clearly the essential variation structure underlying the succession of strophes—strophe 6 being exceptional in this respect, as in so many others.

The mirror arpeggiation of voice part and bass, both projecting the major mode, is even more starkly portrayed in Example 5.6. In this final reduction, only the right hand of the accompaniment maintains the minor mode, with its *kalt und unbeweglich* insistence on G♮, G♮, G♮, beating on grimly and incessantly save when momentarily scratched by G♯ in strophes 3–4 and strophe 6.

What a picture! That remark indeed gets back to the point: we are dealing here precisely with the singer as a maker of images, and a critic of images. We have already noted, in section III, how the imagery and its questioning relate to matters of essential melodic structure, modality, and the relation of the vocal line to each of the hands in the piano. Now we have to confront the emergence of these matters on a very deep structural level, and interpret the image which Example 5.6 conveys to us.

Example 5.6

V. Under and Over, Inside and Outside

The vocal part, right-hand part, and bass part of Example 5.6 can be taken to represent respectively the poet, the surface of the ice, and the warm flow beneath the ice. The poet (vocal line) rises over the static, frozen surface of the ice (right hand); the riverbed (bass line), reflecting the poet mirrorwise, descends beneath that surface. Thus *unter der Rinde,* with its E-major arpeggiation downward, is the mirror of *über der Rinde,* with its E-major arpeggiation upwards; *über der Rinde,* or even *ober der Rinde,* is the vantage from which the poet as critic hopes to exert mastery over the image he has created.

In order to interpret Example 5.6 in all its complexity, it will be helpful to distinguish a "false image" and a "true image" that can be read from it. The false image develops from the apparent structural priority enjoyed by the outer voices. "I am like the riverbed, which I reflect," imagines the poet. "As melodically active outer voices, we control the deep structure of the piece in our optimistic E-major mode. The static frozen G♮ of the right hand, prominent though it may be, does not affect our deep structure, where it is only a blue note—and in an inner voice, at that. *Unter der Rinde* lies the E major of the bass, which reflects me and which I reflect, latent though this secret may be in the surface structure of the piece." In this way, the singer reasserts his association with the bass line, and his contrast with the right-hand line, which we discussed earlier in connection with doubling relations. After the B of "mein Herz" the singer can no longer double the bass line, but he hits instead on the ingenious expedient of mirroring it, a relation appropriate to his physical action—standing up—at the beginning of stanza 5.

What makes this optimistic image musically false is the implication that the E-major outer voices of Example 5.6 really control the deep structure of the music. If they did, we would hear the piece in E major, and since we clearly hear the piece in E minor, the image cannot be valid. What makes the image poetically false is its misplaced obsession with the categories of "over" and "under." While these categories are appropriate to characterize the relation of icy surface to riverbed, and of right hand to left hand, they are not appropriate to the cortex of the heart and its interior chambers, nor to the relation of vocal line and bass line combined to the right-hand line of Example 5.6.

The correct categories in both the latter cases are not "over" and "under," but rather "outside" and "inside." It is this misfit of categories that provides a negative answer for the question, "in diesem Bache erkennst du nun dein Bild?" The stream, that is, is not a valid image for the heart. We have just discussed some reasons why. The poet senses such reasons with tension and alarm but is unable to analyze them; presumably the analysis would be too painful.

The true image of Example 5.6, then, proceeds on the basis of "outside" and "inside." The poet, by entering into relation with the stream, has coupled his vocal line with the bass line to form a hull *(Rinde)* of "outer voices," ostensibly active and in E major. But the static "inner voice," which the right hand projects as the kernel at the heart of this *Rinde,* tells us better: its innermost secret is G♮, G♮, G♮, as indeed was foretold by the opening motive of the right hand in the piece. Within the elaborately constructed exterior show of motion and warmth, the poet's heart is frozen solid forever. This must be so, since it is only and preeminently the right-hand line of Example 5.6 that can make us hear the piece with a deep structure in the minor mode.[4] Ironically enough, it is the poet's very creation of the false image for Example 5.6, with its pairing of outer voices against an inner voice, that enables the true image to assert itself.

4. Schenker's analysis asserts otherwise; he hears the structural *Kopfton* for the *Urlinie* only at the vocal G♮ in measure 53. I am convinced that he errs here. The whole discussion so far indicates why I feel it is essential to attach basic structural weight to the opening G♮ in the right hand (which Schenker omits from his sketch). Example 5.6 treats the G♮ as a *Kopfton,* beginning an *Urlinie* that will eventually descend and close. That hearing, the reader will recall, made excellent sense of the failure of the voice to double the bass line at the return of the *minore* in measure 41. What is at issue here is not the presence or absence of an *Urlinie,* but rather the function of the G♮ in the right hand at the opening. If there is to be an *Urlinie,* it ought to begin there.

Afterword

On page 112, I discuss the word *Rinde*, saying it "is in fact a common biological term, used to denote the cortex of the heart. So it is the use of *Rinde* in connection with the stream, not the heart that is metaphorical." These remarks have generated some powerful and interesting criticism by a number of readers, including Anthony Newcomb.[5] Still I am disposed to stick to my guns on the specific point. *Rinde* is in fact a common biological term. It is used for the bark of a tree, the shell of a crustacean, the crust on a pastry or a loaf of bread, and the rind of a cheese. In addition, it is used in specifically anatomical contexts to mean the cortex of an organ: *rindenartig* and *rindig* translate as "cortical" and "corticose" in those contexts.

In all these usages, the *Rinde* has three salient features. First, it is a curved surface surrounding completely the entire volume of a three-dimensional object; it is not a flat planar surface extending over the top of a spatial region, as ice is when it covers a stream. Second, the object that is surrounded by the *Rinde* is alive, or recently alive, or at least characteristically organic. (Perhaps we should consider French cheese rather than German cheese in this connection.) Third, the *Rinde* protects the object from injury, in the manner of armor.

In my personal dictionaries (Heath and Muret-Sanders, 1910), I find no usage for *Rinde* that is not consistent with each of the three features discussed here. In contrast, the use of *Rinde* for the ice does not fit easily with any of the features. As already noted, the ice is a flat planar surface, not a curved surface bounding an enclosed volume. The stream is not literally, but only metaphorically, alive; it was only metaphorically recently alive; it is technically organic in the sense that water is composed of the organic elements hydrogen and oxygen, but it is not characteristically organic beyond that, except metaphorically. Finally, although a stream does develop its ice as the crayfish develops its shell, we do not normally think of the ice as having a protective function, defending the stream from accident or attack. (The *American Heritage Dictionary* [New York, American Heritage, 1969], 1536–1537, gives *rendh–* as the Indo-European root for English "rind," and specifically brings out the issue of attack: "*rendh–*. To tear up. . . . 2. Germanic _*rind–_ in Old English *rind(e)*, rind (< "thing torn off"): RIND." This way of regarding the *Rinde*, from the viewpoint of the aggressor, seems all too depressingly Indo-European.)

In sum, I am still very comfortable with the idea that "it is the use of *Rinde* in connection with the stream that is metaphorical." The word appropriate for the ice in literal discourse would be *Decke*, not *Rinde*. The *Rinde* metaphor does not lie far from common speech of a flowery sort, but that observation makes me feel the force of the metaphor all the more strongly. Here, though, I must draw back from exploring the fascinating contentions which *that* idea suggests, and point out that I really have nothing to "prove" with all my linguistic commentary, except that it would seem reasonable to imagine Schubert finding in Müller's text an interpene-

5. Newcomb's splendid article can be found in Walter Frisch, ed., *Schubert: Critical and Analytical Studies* (Lincoln: University of Nebraska Press, 1986).

tration of object and image over the last stanza, a relationship projecting a subtle misfit of "underneath (the ice)" with "inside (the heart)."

I am sure that Müller was sensitive to that metaphorical dissonance; no mere adventurer, he assumed an official post as teacher and ducal librarian at Dessau in 1819, the year after he completed the *Müller-Lieder*. My belief that Schubert was also sensitive to these matters must rest upon the manner in which I read various aspects of his musical structure. I do not really care, of course, to what extent Schubert was a fine critic of Müller's text. I do care how well he "acted" that script *per musica*, and so I have only to show that the ideas about "under the surface" and "around the kernel," ideas that emerge in my musical analysis, do engage things that can be legitimately (if not necessarily) read from the text. The musical analysis itself is amply problematic.

Appendix

As mentioned in section IV, the basic method of the reductions is to proceed from one metric level to the next, setting down at each stage as few notes as possible to represent an essential harmony governing each rhythmic unit at the pertinent metric level. At each stage, I find it important to make the sketch performable, give or take a few figures and/or some continuo-like harmonic realization. In general, one can usually proceed in a straightforward way from one metric level to the next.

At times, one must adjust expansions or contractions to an asserted metric norm at the next level. The technique can be inferred from the pertinent relations of Example 5.3 to Example 5.4, and so on. Interpretations as to what is expanded and what is contracted, at which metric level, are not always as clear in other pieces as they are here, where the basic strophe-model provides clear large downbeats and a referential rhythmic matrix.

Example 5.7

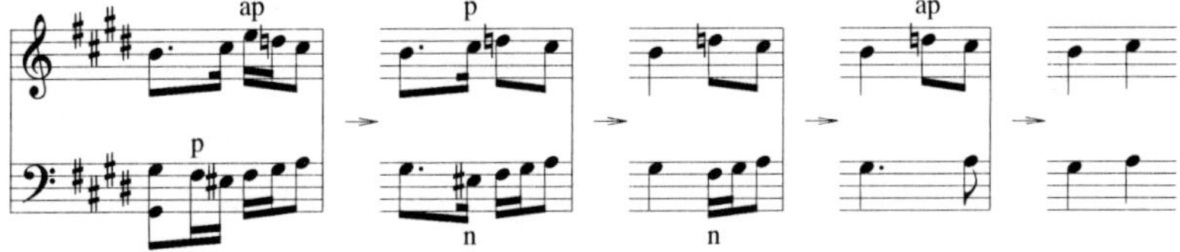

At times, also, one must juggle several rhythmic levels at once. The systematic elimination of accessory tones, proceeding from the more detailed to the broader metric levels, will generally lead to a clear choice of essential tones at the broadest level under consideration. Example 5.7 illustrates the technique, using a tricky passage of the song, measures 27–28. The harmony at the bar line of measure 28 indicates that the high E is an appoggiatura to the D natural at this metric level, and not an essential constituent of the E^6 harmony on a larger level. An alternate reading, to the latter effect, might be worked out; it would lead to the same end result.

As in most reductive methods of tonal analysis, a given event may project a variety of functions with respect to a variety of nested or overlapping contexts in which it is embedded. One is free to read, or not to read, any a priori aesthetic value into the largest or most final of such contexts, beyond its formal status as the largest or most final. In *Auf dem Flusse,* for example, my method yields a variety of functions in a variety of contexts for the six-four chord in measures 9–10. Considering the context spanned by the B triad at the end of measure 8 and the G♯^{7} chord at the beginning of measure 11, for instance, one can hear the six-four chords as passing through. This context is certainly not the most powerful one functioning over strophe 1; still, the notion that the A♯ in the bass of the six-four can pass down from B to G♯ is clearly suggestive in connection with the approach to the climactic G♯ in the bass of strophe 6. Note the disposition of registers in the bass line from measure 44 to measure 48, the latter picking up in register the A♯ from measure 45. We have earlier discussed the G♯ harmony of measure 48 as, *inter alia,* a substitute for the B harmony; this consideration lends support to the idea of passing from one to the other.

An overlapping context, that of measures 9 through 12 in isolation, suggests that the G♯^{7} chord is a returning neighbor to the six-four chord, which then resolves in D♯ minor following the standard cadential formula. Example 5.8 displays the analysis. In this context the A♯ of the bass is essential, not passing, and the F♯ and D♯ above are suspensions, not essential tones.

Example 5.8

Example 5.9

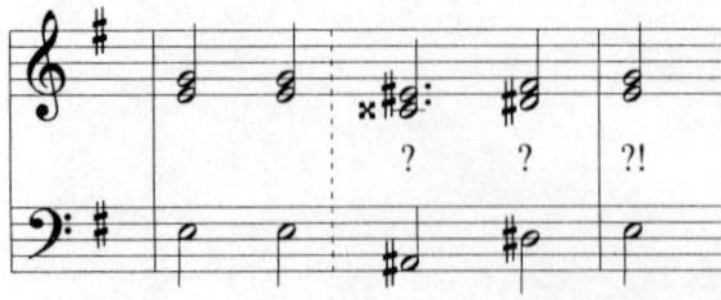

The implications of Example 5.8, however, disappear in a larger context that includes all of strophe 1 and the beginning of strophe 2. Here the overall harmony of the metric unit defined by measures 5–6 is clearly E minor, as is the overall harmony of measures 7–8, and that of measures 14–15. In addition, there are large pulses at the bar lines of measures 5 and 14, along with a subordinate pulse at measure 9 and still lesser pulses at measures 7 and 12. An attempt to fit the reading of

Example 5.8 into this larger context using my method would result in the syntactic impossibility of Example 5.9.

In this context, the weight of the measure-pair 12–13 must clearly be carried by the B chord, functioning as dominant of the following E, and not by the D♯ chord. Then the A♯$^{6}_{4}$ can be heard, in *this* (!) context, to inflect the structural B chord that follows it, as in Example 5.10.

Example 5.10

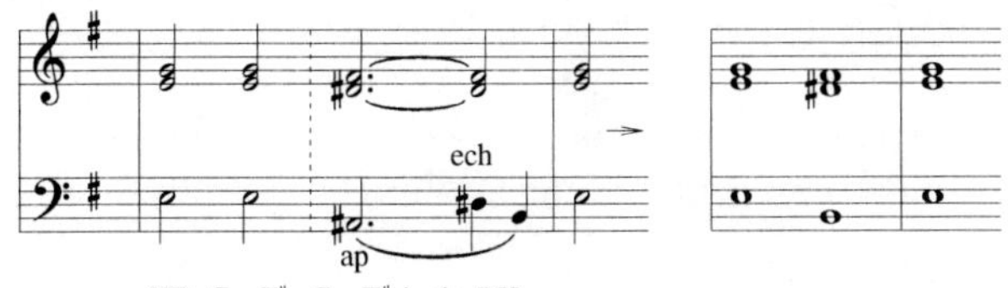

Example 5.11

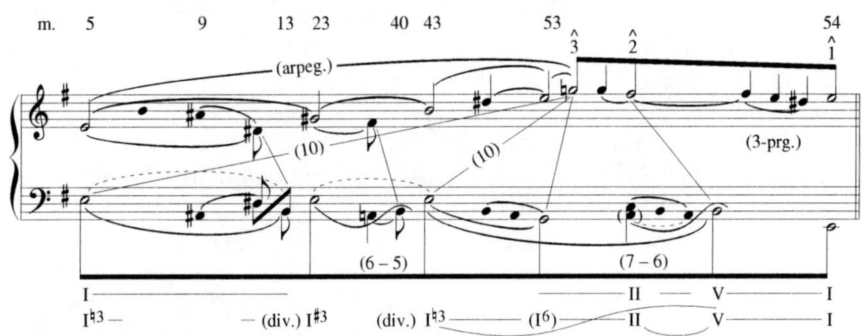

My methods and symbology suffer here, I think, in comparison with Schenker's. Because of the priority I assign metric hierarchies in the reduction process, I am unable (so far as I can see) to assign the D♯ cadence the tonal (as opposed to metric) weight I hear it bearing in the larger context. Schenker's symbology, not so strictly bound to metric hierarchies, does a much better job of demonstrating the simultaneous functioning and interpenetration of the disparate contexts portrayed in my Examples 5.8 and 5.10. His sketch is reproduced as Example 5.11.[6]

I have already discussed in note 5 my dissatisfaction with Schenker's *Urlinie*, which begins at measure 53 and closes in measure 54. As I said there, it seems dramatically essential that an *Urlinie*, if there is to be one, should begin exactly with the opening G natural in the right hand. (This would destroy the theoretical point of Schenker's figure, which is to exemplify arpeggiation in the structural upper voice before the onset of the *Urlinie* proper.) A *Kopfton* in measure 1 could of course later be transferred into the voice at measure 53. The vocal high E of measure 54 could then transfer back to the upper right hand E of measure 70, finish-

6. Heinrich Schenker, *Free Composition*, trans. and ed. Ernst Oster, vol. 2 (New York: Longman, 1979), fig. 40, 2.

ing the proposed *Urlinie* in the proper register (and instrument). The advantages of listening for an *Urlinie,* particularly around measure 41, have already been discussed. On the other hand, the immobile frozen G♮ projected by the right hand of my Example 5.6, a G♮ that does not descend, has a symbolic and dramatic value, too. Example 5.6 is, of course, utterly un-Schenkerian.

The other substantial divergence of my musical results from Schenker's involves the bass G♯ at measure 48, governing the beat at the onset of strophe 6. Almost all my discussion, particularly around Example 5.1 and Example 5.6, has pointed to the necessity of including that G♯ in the large structure of the bass arpeggiation over the song, given my reading. Without the G♯ there is no "secret" E-major bass structure to mirror the E-major vocal structure in Example 5.6, and the dramatic force of the various processes converging climactically onto strophe 6 is largely dissipated.

The priority I attribute to metric hierarchies would force me in any case to write the bass G♯ at measure 48, since it carries the downbeat of its strophe. Schenker's use of the G♮ in the bass of measure 53 for his *Bassbrechung* is inconceivable in the context of my method. I think Schenker was repelled on principle by the idea of mixture in the *Bassbrechung.* He also evidently wanted good local bass support for the third degree of his *Urlinie.* Perhaps, too, he heard the G♯ harmony very strongly as a "dominant parallel" in the sense of Example 5.2. Be that as it may, my methods are well suited to throwing light on the dramatic meaning of measure 48 and its environs, while Schenker's sketch jumps uncomfortably, to my critical taste, from measure 41 to measure 52.

It goes without saying that any reductive method of analysis for tonal music owes an inestimable debt to Schenker's work. I have felt, therefore, some obligation to clarify my departures both from his method and from his reading of this piece. My own method, which I have been using for some time, combines aspects of Schenkerian technique with metric considerations first suggested to me by Andrew Imbrie at Berkeley in the early 1960s. The published sketches that mine most closely resemble, I think, are those presented by Imbrie in his article on "'Extra' Measures and Metrical Ambiguity in Beethoven," *Beethoven Studies [I],* ed. Alan Tyson (New York: W. W. Norton, 1973), 45–66.

I do not consider my method worked out into a theory. It does have strong theoretical implications. I do not feel completely comfortable with all of these, nor do I always find the analytic readings produced by my harmonic-metric consistency at all levels more suggestive than alternate readings assigning more priority to higher-level voice leading. I find it important to make my sketches "performable," as opposed to conceptual, but I am not sure why I feel that way.

Important publications that bear on the theoretical assumptions I seem to be making include Edward T. Cone, *Musical Form and Musical Performance* (New York: W. W. Norton, 1968); Arthur J. Komar, *Theory of Suspensions* (Princeton: Princeton University Press, 1971); Maury Yeston, *The Stratification of Musical Rhythm* (New Haven, Conn.: Yale University Press, 1976); and Fred Lerdahl and Ray Jackendoff, *A Generative Theory of Tonal Music* (Cambridge, Mass.: MIT Press, 1983).

Plate 5.1 Schubert, *Auf dem Flusse.*

(continued)

Plate 5.1 cont.

Plate 5.1 cont.

(continued)

Plate 5.1 cont.

Plate 5.1 cont.

CHAPTER Six

Ihr Bild

Ich stand in dunkeln Träumen und starrt' ihr Bildnis an, und das geliebte Antlitz heimlich zu leben begann.	I stood in gloomy reverie and stared at her picture, and the beloved face secretly began to come to life.
Um ihre Lippen zog sich ein Lächeln wunderbar, und wie von Wehmuthsthränen ergläntzte ihr Augenpaar.	About her lips there began to play a magical smile, and, as if with melancholy tears, her two eyes gleamed.
Auch meine Tränen flossen mir von den Wangen herab,— und ach! ich kann es nicht glauben dass ich dich verloren hab'!	My tears, too, flowed down my cheeks,— and ah! I cannot believe that I have lost you!

When I start to analyze a piece with text, I have found the following exercise to be fruitful. (1) I read the text, then (2) (if I don't know the music well,) I listen to the music until it sounds familiar, then (3) away from text and musical score, I write out a précis for "what is going on," for "what happens" in the piece. (It is important for me actually to write out the précis, not just to say it to myself.) Then (4) I check my written précis carefully against the text, and take note of any discrepancies I observe. Such discrepancies are often a good point of entry for further study of the piece. If any readers wish to carry out the exercise for themselves in connection with *Ihr Bild*, this will be a good point to do so, returning to the present essay after writing out a précis and checking it against the text.

Having frequently brought *Ihr Bild* into classes for musical analysis—including classes comprising quite sophisticated and advanced student musicians, I can report that a very large preponderance of the précis run along the following lines.

"The speaker is terribly depressed over the loss of his beloved. As he stares at her picture, he tries to deny his loss by imagining signs of life in the portrait. When he imagines her eyes gleaming with melancholy tears—'I miss you so'—he notices that the tears are in his eyes, and he is thrust back into his depressed state. No longer able to maintain his illusion, he bursts out in a cry of grief."

Such a summary captures a good deal of the piece's affective content. But, when carefully compared with the text, the précis is still crucially deficient. We can explore the matter by asking, where "is" the speaker? According to the sample précis above, he "is" standing and staring at the picture. But that is not what the poem gives us. The speaker, rather, "is" presently telling (himself and us) how he was standing and staring.

This may at first seem like an overpunctilious cavil. The sense of gloom and despair in the piece is so immanent that we take the past tense of the text, on first encounter, as a literary substitute for a present-tense narration. "I was standing and staring (just as I am doing now), and the picture began to live (just as it is doing now)," and so forth. The implicit inference is that the speaker has often gone through the ritual described, is going through it now as he speaks, and will continue to go through it forever, as if he were inhabiting Dante's Inferno. The inference is perfectly plausible, but it still does not adequately engage the actual tense systems manifest in the text.

For the poem does have a present tense, which it distinguishes sharply from its narrative simple-past. The present tense bursts forth in the last couplet, when the persona exclaims, "I *can* not believe, that I *have* lost you!" I italicize *have* as well as *can*. The auxiliary for the perfect tense is present tense, and the perfect tense, like the present, has never appeared before in the poem. The cry of grief does not only burst through the illusion that the woman is (was) "alive," it also bursts through the speaker's efforts to distance his grief and loss, putting it somewhere else. "I *was* standing and staring," (then and there), "and the picture *began* to come to life," (then and there), "and a smile *appeared*, and her eyes *gleamed*," (then and there). "And my tears, too, *flowed*" (even in this verse, very crucially, then and there—it's not as if I were crying *now*). But of course the speaker is crying now, and his present-tense grief finally bursts through when he cannot hold his distance, his "then and there," away from the raw emotion. Thus, throughout the entire piece, up until the final couplet of text, the "then and there" is conspicuously not "here and now."[1]

True, *we* may feel that the grief is "here and now" despite the speaker's efforts to distance it. That is why a typical précis puts the action of the piece into a present tense. (I discussed the phenomenon two paragraphs above.) But the persona does not acknowledge any "here and now" at all, until the final couplet.

We can synopsize such observations in what I have called "the Speaker's Map" of the poem's tenses.

1. Distancing is also manifest in the speaker's references, during the first two stanzas of text, to "her" portrait, "the" beloved visage, "her" lips, and "her" eyes. There is no "you" in the poem until the final verse.

The Speaker's Map

("1." = first couplet; "2." = second couplet)

Past 2	Past 1	Present
	first stanza	
	1. his gloom	
	2. she came to life	
middle stanza,		
1. her lips		
2. her eyes		
	final stanza	
	1. back in gloom	
		2. outcry

Past 1 is the time in which the speaker "was standing" and so on.; Past 2 is an earlier time in which the couple were together, in which she was "alive" for him. The animated face of the portrait invokes such a time, prior to the time of Past 1, and the persona, while immersed in Past 1, experienced an illusion that he was back in Past 2. The map helps us to see how cleverly Heine set up a "false" ABA form, a form that would be manifest if only his final couplet took place in Past 1. But, having constructed his false ABA, Heine then shatters it ironically with his final couplet.

Now let us examine "the Singer's Map," a map that logs the tonal profiles of the sung phrases, phrases that set the textual couplets.

The Singer's Map

Past 2	Past 1	Present
	first stanza	
	1. b♭: i→V	
	2. B♭: I and cadence	
middle stanza		
1. G♭ tonicized		
2. G♭ bis		
	final stanza	
	1. b♭: i→V	
		2. B♭: I and cadence

At first glance, it seems as if Schubert made a dreadful mistake. He appears to have been fooled by Heine's "false ABA," into composing an actual musical ABA: the music for the final couplet of sung text, for the shattering present-tense outcry of grief, exactly recapitulates the optimistic major-key music for the second couplet of the first stanza, where the picture began to come to life in Past 1.

But Schubert's setting—no matter how he arrived at it—is in fact highly sophisticated. It is also absolutely straightforward. Rather than presenting some stylized manifestation of grief, Schubert shows us the persona, in the present tense, literally not believing that he has lost his beloved. "I *can not believe* that I have lost you," he sings, and the music enacts his disbelief—not just his inability to accept the loss, but even more, his refusal to accept it. "Even now, I can make the picture come to life again—using just the same music with which it came to life in couplet 2 of stanza 1. I can do that whenever I want to—and as long as I can do that, I have not lost you."

Schubert's setting thus elevates Heine's pathetic puppet into a figure of some tragic stature. For Heine's speaker, the sudden incursion of the present tense, at his outcry of grief, completely demolishes the whole impotent ritual of stanzas 1 and 2. Schubert's singer, in marked contrast, refuses to accept or even acknowledge his present "reality"; he immerses himself instead, by an act of will, in a Dante-esque cycle of obsession. He is fated, by this heroic act of will, to enact again and again throughout eternity the ritual described in stanzas 1 and 2—for, without that ritual, there will be no occasion for the picture to "come to life" again and again.[2] And he accepts—nay embraces—his fate. Where we characterized the final couplet of Heine's speaker as an "outcry," the final phrase of Schubert's singer is better characterized as a "denial" (of reality).

Once we grasp what Schubert's setting is up to, we can appreciate the extraordinary effect of the final couplet in Schubert's setting, where the major-key tonic recapitulation enters into a frightful and continually growing cognitive dissonance against the devastating incursion of Heine's present tense. "No!" we want to exclaim, as the major music enters once more, blissfully proceeding exactly through its allotted phrase, "No! No!"

And that dissonance is precisely what is discharged for us by the final piano epilogue, now loud (rather than soft as was the parallel epilogue after the first stanza), now minor (rather than major), now with a full orchestral treatment, trombones and all (rather than a churchy sort of harmonium texture). The final chord, with its seven tones, is the densest chord in the piece, and it is the only complete tonic minor triad in the piece. After "I can not believe that I have lost you," the piano clearly states "But you *have* lost her." The final epilogue is Schubert's formal equivalent for the present tense of Heine's final couplet: it crashes in on the singer's "mistaken" musical ABA and demolishes it.

And nevertheless—does the singer "hear" the piano? To put the matter another way: does the piano epilogue happen "inside" the singer, betokening a final internal collapse despite the singer's effort to maintain his optimistic illusion? In that case, the vocalist might let us sense such an emotional collapse in his physical demeanor after he has finished singing. Or is the piano an ironist in its final epilogue, addressing the singer and/or the audience from "outside" the singer? In that case, the vocalist might take good care to maintain the "optimistic" stance of his physical presence after the singing is over, "not hearing" the piano epilogue at all as he stares blissfully up and out into cloud-cuckoo land.

Considering the role of the final epilogue, we will need to augment the tense systems of the art work yet again, extending the Singer's Map to what we shall call "the Music's Map."

2. To be able to make the picture "come to life" again whenever he wants, the persona must also be able to make it "die" whenever he needs to, killing off his beloved again and again (to put it brutally). Adequately to explore the psychology and sociology of that observation would require a complete and extended essay in its own right. I hope that the present study may provide a good point of departure for anyone interested in writing such an essay.

The Music's Map

Past 2	Past 1	present A	present B
	first stanza		
	1. b♭: i→V		
	2. B♭: I cad.		
middle stanza			
G♭ toniciz.			
	1. b♭: i→V		
		2. B♭: I cad.	
			piano epilogue

The Music's Map distinguishes two present tenses. Present A is the singer's present tense, the tense in which he sings "I can not believe" using the earlier B♭ major music. One could call this "the present of denial" or "the delusional present." Present B is the piano's present tense, the present of "reality," the present in which the piano's crashing minor epilogue comments, "but you *have* really lost her." Present B definitively leads us, the audience, out of the piece. Perhaps it leads the singer out as well (depending upon the interpretations recently discussed). Alternatively (depending upon those interpretations), the singer, "not hearing" the piano epilogue, may be hopelessly trapped inside the piece by the link between the final B♭ major phrase and the second phrase of stanza 1, in Past 1.

The piano, playing solo over a more or less extended amount of time, frames every sung phrase of the piece. Except for the final piano epilogue I have not put any of this solo material onto the Music's Map, because—except for that epilogue—each piano solo seems plausibly consistent with the singer's journey through the tenses of the piece: the piano (up to the final epilogue) can be analyzed as if "with" the singer, in whatever part of the map the singer is traversing. So, for instance, the little echoing "winking" figure in the middle of measure 18 is easily taken to be "with" the singer in Past 2. The same goes for the "winking" figure in the middle of measure 22. Then the heavy transformation of the figure in measures 23–24—combined there with the motif of "the two B flats"—modulates from the G♭ major ambience of Past 2, back to the b♭ minor ambience of Past 1 (couplet 1), and this musical move goes "with" the singer on his return from Past 2 to Past 1.

Even the mysterious opening of the piece, presenting the motif of the two B flats as a temporarily disembodied phenomenon, can be heard as "plausibly consistent" with the Past 1 of the singer's opening phrase that follows. In that connection, the two B flats of the piano introduction can be heard to foreshadow the initial and final B flats of the singer's initial slow turn figure ("*Ich stand* . . . (Träu-)*men*). But the motif of the two B flats, presented so mysteriously as the music begins, while "consistent" with a location in Past 1, does seem to mean something more.[3] Schenker takes the two B flats, with a rest between, as a means for making listeners perform the auditory equivalent of *staring* at the pitch; thus "we feel ourselves

3. The two B flats are the subject of a fine study by Joseph Kerman, "A Romantic Detail in Schubert's *Schwanengesang*," *Musical Quarterly* 48 (1962), 36–49. The article is revised and reprinted in *Schubert: Critical and Analytical Studies*, ed. Walter Frisch, paperback printing (Lincoln: University of Nebraska Press, 1996), 48–64.

wonderfully transported to the side of the unhappy lover, who stands there . . . staring at the portrait . . . ."[4] Following Schenker's lead a bit farther, one might identify the two B flats with all the acts of staring that permeate the piece: we are staring at the persona, who is "here and now" staring at himself as he stood "then and there" in Past 1, staring at the portrait until it began to stare back at him, tears in its eyes. During the piano epilogue, however one interprets it, we will be struck by the way in which the vocalist (if performing well) stares out into the audience.

My own inclination is to hear the two B flats of the opening two measures (and everywhere else) as a symbolic tolling of funeral bells.[5] True, we do not know that the beloved is dead. From Heine's poem alone, we could easily understand the loss as a broken marriage engagement, rather than the physical death of the beloved.[6] And yet the music seems a good deal more funereal than the poem, and the idea of tolling bells seems apt. Even if the beloved has not physically died, the singer seems to be treating her absence as if she had. (Even in the poem by itself, the person does that to a certain extent—dying is, after all, the obverse of "coming to life.")

The bells, in my hearing, toll at every solo comment by the piano except for the two epilogues.[7] The piano's interjection at measures 7–8 (with pickup) tolls on C rather than on B♭. At the beginning of the G♭ music for the middle stanza, though the piano is not playing solo we still hear the two B flats tolling in measures 15 and 16, above the melodic line that doubles the singer. The "winking" motif in the piano halfway through measure 18 combines with the same motif in measure 22, to produce "the two B flats" at a higher rhythmic level. And then at measures 23–24 the two B flats are heavily recapitulated from measures 1–2, as we return to Past 1 for the beginning of the final stanza.

The motif of "the two B flats" appears not only in such foreground passages but also at very high rhythmic levels of the composition. The motif engages, for instance, the two big B♭ major cadences—at measure 12, and again at measure 34. It also engages the way in which measures 23–24 correspond, as a "second B♭" on a

4. Heinrich Schenker, "Franz Schubert, Ihr Bild," trans. William Pastille with the same title in the journal *Sonus,* 6.2 (1986), 31–37. Kerman, in "A Romantic Detail," discusses Schenker's idea skeptically but enthusiastically.

5. Kerman, in "A Romantic Detail," counts as an antecedent for the introduction to "Ihr Bild" (written in 1828) the introduction to a little-known song Schubert wrote in 1824, "Gondelfahrer" (The Gondolier). There, some "chiming" octaves in the introduction are later revealed to be explicit extra-musical symbols when they recur and are developed in the music that sets the text: "Vom Markustürme tönte/Der Spruch der Mitternacht." ("From the tower of Saint Mark's [Cathedral in Venice] resounded the pealing of midnight.") "Spruch" seems impossible to translate here—Kerman translates "tönte der Spruch" as "chimed the knell," which makes the Mayrhofer text too funereal for my taste—perhaps Kerman was transferring a funereal feeling from "Ihr Bild," or from Mayrhofer's other works in general, or perhaps he was under the influence of Gray's *Elegy* (in which case one might translate "tolled the knell").

Later on in Kerman's essay, though, he discourages all efforts to pin the Motif of the two B flats in "Ihr Bild" down to any extramusical symbolism whatsoever.

6. In early-nineteenth-century Germany, engaged couples exchanged portraits. Heine suffered a broken engagement, and the motif of the broken engagement is widespread in his poetry.

7. Although not explicitly "tolling," both epilogues are consistent in character with the beloved's death: the first epilogue is in the nature of "religious uplift," and the second, trombones and all, is amply funereal in its own right.

Example 6.1

high rhythmic level, to measures 1–2. The motivic effect of measure 23, as a "second B♭ beat" for measure 1, is strongly brought out by a rhythmic (but non-Schenkerian) reduction of the music, as in Example 6.1.

Already on rhythmic level (c) of the piece, one hears quite powerfully not only the tolling of the B flats at the beginning of each hypermeasure but also, at a higher level, the tolling of two B♭ "hyperbeats" at measure 1 and at measure 23. At rhythmic level (d)—talk about funerals!—the effect of the two B♭ "hyperbeats" is even stronger.

Yet we must not lean too hard on the structure of Example 6.1. Level (d) indicates why. On that level, the B♭ major cadences have disappeared completely from the scene. Level (d) hears the background musical action of the piece as G♭-displacing-F, then G♭-returning-to-F, while B flats continually toll along as pedal tones. That musical gesture represents the progression from Past 1 into Past 2, followed by the return from Past 2, back into Past 1. So level (d) is "taken in" by Heine's false ABA: it represents faithfully the hearing that is responsible for the inadequate sample précis discussed at the beginning of this chapter, the précis that contained no awareness of any present tense(s) in the work. In that connection, Example 6.1 is in fact very useful to our critique. It specifically demonstrates how a Newtonian chronometry, when brought up to the piece, is inadequate to engage the richness of the work's temporality (or temporalities). It will be interesting, then, to review a variety of Schenkerian background readings that have been proposed for the music. F–G♭–F is not admissible as a Schenkerian *Urlinie*, so each of these readings necessarily confronts the question, what is the overall "action" of the piece through some temporal medium other than Newtonian chronometry?

Schenker himself, in the essay already referenced, proposed an "*Urlinie*" for the work.[8] The line starts out with a gesture spanning a melodic fourth, from the B♭ of "stand" (m. 3), through the A of "Träu-" (m. 4) and the G♭ of "starrt'" (m. 5), to the F of "an" (m. 6). The *Urlinie* then soars up to an imaginary F an octave above, at the top of the treble clef—one might fantasy a soft tremolo of orchestral violins on the pitch during measures 9 and 10—and from there it descends through a melodic fifth during measure 11, through the E♭ of "heim-", the D of "le-", and the C of "-ben", to arrive at measure 12 on the cadential B♭ of "-gann."

There are musical problems with this *Urlinie*. The A natural of "Träu-" surely returns as a lower neighbor to the B♭ that follows it ("-men"), rather than moving down an augmented second to the G♭ of "starrt'." That is not simply a matter of abstract theory, which abstractly "prohibits" melodic motion across an augmented second: Schubert writes a slur under the piano doubling from "stand" to "-men," he writes another slur on the accompaniment from "und" to "an," and the syntactic construction of the text—I was doing X (slurred), "und" I was doing Y (slurred)—is not propitious for any melodic connection here (abstractly "legal" or no) between A natural and G♭ across the "und." Then, too, the "imaginary" high F of the proposed *Urlinie*, while highly poetic, seems a suspicious addition to Schubert's music.

Schenker's *Urlinie* continues onward from measure 12. (His essay was written in 1921, and he had not yet developed the mature theories of *Der Freie Satz* [1935] that are promulgated today—with some justice—as "Schenker.") He brackets the melodic descent of a third, from the B♭ of measure 15 ("ihre"), through A♭ to the G♭ of measure 16 ("sich"). The bracket, in the notation he was using at the time of his essay, indicates a segment of his "*Urlinie*." That is a good idea, for it enables us to get down from B♭ to G♭ via A♭, instead of having to traverse the A♮ of "Träu-." One might accordingly consider emending Schenker's *Urlinie*, so that it begins with this B♭–A♭–G♭ in Past 2, hits its F in Past 1 (at "-ab" in m. 28), and then continues on into Present A, via the imaginary high F and the E♭–D–C–B♭ of measures 33–34 ("dich verloren hab'!"). The suggested emendation also shores up a problem with Schenker's analysis, which unduly downplays the third stanza of the piece.[9] As

8. Schenker's article on "Ihr Bild" gives this as his "Figure 9," which appears on page 37 of Pastille's translation, at the end of the essay, prefaced only by the curt paragraph [*sic*], "Here is the Urlinie:"

9. His sketch describes the structure from the beginning of the third stanza to measure 34 as "like measures 3–12." Of course, the sketch, projecting the poet-as-hero, also omits any reference to the final piano epilogue after the vocal cadence of measure 34. Schenker's verbal discussion of the epilogue is

emended, Schenker's *Urlinie* would only begin acting for real in Past 2, not at the beginning of the piece.

Despite its problems, Schenker's analysis has strong virtues. It integrates into one background action a large-scale melodic gesture that extends from Past 2 through Past 1 into Present A, traversing G♭ major music, b♭ minor music, and B♭ major music in one grand overall sweep, thus engaging the singer's temporal and tonal journey much more extensively than did Level (d) of Example 6.1—or will other *Urlinie* readings we shall consider soon. In Schenker's reading (as emended), the singer is much more a protagonist of the drama than he is at Level (d) of Example 6.1—or in several other background readings. Schenker's *Urlinie* ends in major, with the singer's last sung note; Schenker clearly believes that Present A is the *emotionally* "real" present, despite the piano epilogue, and that makes the singer more heroic, than do several other readings—a feature which will endear itself to vocalists.[10]

Carl Schachter also hears *Urlinie* closure on the sung B flats at the B♭ major cadences of measures 12 and 34.[11] Accordingly, he also believes (like Schenker) that Present A (at m. 34 and following) is the "real" present of the piece, as opposed to Present B. His *Urlinie* does not have the majestic sweep of Schenker's octave. (On the other hand, it is more consistent with Schenker's mature theories.) Rather than descending through an octave, Schachter's *Urlinie* goes $\hat{3}$–$\hat{2}$–$\hat{1}$ in B♭ major: the bass D natural of measure 9 gets transferred into the upper register, where it is sung during measures 10 and 11; then it descends through C (on the last quarter of measure 11) to the B♭ at the beginning of measure 12.

According to this *Urlinie*, the principal action of the piece is "to make the picture come to life" (again and again, as happens in Present A during mm. 31–34). The background structure of the piece is now completely major, taking place during measures 9–12 and (again) during measures 31–34. Past 2 is ignored as a

perfunctory and unsatisfactory. ("But the composer's prophetic vision sees farther. He withdraws the wave of major. At one time it could support an interlude; now it can do so no longer. [D. L.: Why not? Running out of text did not stop Schubert from continuing his music, recycling used text as pertinent, in many of his other songs. Schenker does not explicitly notice the change to present tense in the poem.] Gloomy minor engulfs the whole inner landscape . . .") I wonder if Schenker, on further thought, would have been so ready to imagine the piano postlude as part of a sentimental "*inner* landscape," rather than an ironic "*outer* reality." Perhaps so—Schenker was after all in many ways a nineteenth-century soul, at home with the Romantic dramatic aesthetics of Goethe, Coleridge, and Carlyle, alienated in many ways from early-twentieth-century modes of irony and *Sachlichkeit.*

10. "The unfortunate lover still clings to the last bridges that lead to his beloved with the desperate cry: 'Und ach! ich kann es nicht glauben, dass ich dich verloren hab'!' and the major recounts this. Has he really lost her as long as he still feels this way?" Schenker, "Ihr Bild," trans. Pastille, 36–37. Schenker is beautifully sensitive to the emotional nuances of the final situation, though his analysis takes no explicit notice of tense systems in the text—he describes the poem's events in the present tense throughout his essay.

11. [Carl Schachter presented this reading of "Ihr Bild" during a lecture, "Structure as Foreground: 'das Drama des Ursatzes,'" delivered at Harvard University during the 1991–1992 academic year. A partial representation of Schachter's reading (one that includes the m. 12 cadence but not the cadence at m. 34) can be found in the published version of the talk, "Structure as Foreground: 'das Drama des Ursatzes,'" in *Schenker Studies 2,* edited by Carl Schachter and Hedi Siegel (Cambridge: Cambridge University Press, 1999), 298–314. The work is discussed on pages 299–302. E.G.]

complete "red herring"—in this respect, the reading is quite the opposite of Level (d) in Example 6.1, which wholeheartedly enacts Heine's false ABA progression from Past 1 to Past 2 and back to Past 1, incorrectly asserting that dramatic progression to be the main action of the piece.

As a "heroic" reading of the piece that is also syntactically well formed according to Schenker's mature theories, Schachter's reading can not be faulted. I am somewhat uncomfortable, though, to feel an implicitly asserted "through" (Ur) action for the piece which is confined so strictly to the B♭ major sections. After all, I think that most of us feel the piece to be "in b flat minor," not "in B flat major," and Schachter's structural background does not engage that intuition, which must then be regarded as part of what is "denied" by the heroic protagonist of his reading.

Allen Forte and Steven Gilbert seize just this bull by the horns, in asserting a B flat minor *Urlinie* for the music.[12] They write explicitly, "Analysis of mm. 1–8 should yield the progression ($\hat{3}$/i)–($\hat{2}$/V) which is continued in the ensuing measures thus: (♮$\hat{3}$/V)–($\hat{2}$/V)–($\hat{1}$/I). Notice that at no point in the song does the raised form of scale degree 3 have full harmonic support—and for that reason (in addition to the obvious fact that the song is in B♭ minor) the flatted form takes precedence structurally."[13] Their *Urlinie* goes $\hat{3}$–$\hat{2}$–$\hat{1}$ in b flat minor. It starts on the vocal D♭ of measure 3 [*sic*!], and descends through the vocal C of measure 4, as reverberated by the piano during measures 6–7, reaching its ultimate goal with the vocal B♭ of measure 12. The major harmony at measure 12 is a *tierce de Picardie* in their large-scale b-flat minor structure, not a defining mode for the piece as a whole. Forte's and Gilbert's *Urlinie* thus covers the entire extent of Past 1, both the minor and the major couplets. On repetition, it also covers the move from Past 1 into Present A during stanza 3. And, finally, even though the *Urlinie* ends with the singer's major cadence(s), Forte and Gilbert nevertheless implicitly locate themselves within Present B, when they refer to "the obvious fact that the song is in B♭ minor." From this vantage point the singer's B♭ major is a delusion and denial of b♭ minor "reality."

We may well wonder how to interpret the structural priority that Forte and Gilbert lay on the note D♭ of measure 3. What could be being enacted here, as regards the text? Still, as they point out, that is the one minor third degree of B flat that Schenkerian melodic theory has available to seize on during measures 1–8.[14] And if we assign high priority to an intuition that the piece "really" is in B flat minor, rather than B flat major, locating ourselves at least implicitly in Present B, like Forte and Gilbert, we shall have to analyze some sort of B flat minor structur-

12. Allen Forte and Steven E. Gilbert, *Introduction to Schenkerian Analysis* (New York: W. W. Norton, 1982).

13. Forte and Gilbert, *Introduction,* 218.

14. To my ear, the sense of the minor mode in the song is established much more by the minor *sixth* degree of the key (G♭), than the minor third (D♭). However, that is not easy to reflect in the background of a Schenkerian sketch.

Some German theorists of the nineteenth century proposed a "major/minor" mode consisting of major tonic and major dominant triads, along with a minor subdominant triad. This mode would fit the harmonic world of *Ihr Bild* quite well. But I do not feel that it could be invoked to "solve" any problematic issues of the sort we have been discussing. The issue of major versus minor tonality is at the forefront of the song, and nothing can be "solved" by pretending that there is no such conflict in the piece, hauling in a "major/minor" mode to achieve some sort of abstract "synthesis."

ing about the music. Furthermore, as already noted, the reading of Example 6.1 is not fully satisfactory in that regard.

An extreme B flat minor reading of the music was suggested to me by William Pastille (the translator of Schenker's essay) in the context of a colloquium I gave at Cornell some dozen years ago. I can not locate the sketch he made at the time, and in any case I do not want to hold him to it now, after so many years have passed during which his views may have changed. I shall, rather, use my memory of his general idea as the basis for an exemplary sketch of my own that I shall present here as Example 6.2.

Example 6.2

The *Urlinie* of Example 6.2, which comprises the beamed open note heads in the lower register of the treble staff, almost buys into Heine's red herring, the "false" ABA of Example 6.1, level (d). The *Urlinie*'s F of measure 6 ("an") is inflected by a neighboring G♭ during stanza 2 (say at "sich" in m. 16); the G♭ then returns to F (at m. 24 and following). The B♭ major cadences of the singer happen "above" the melodic Ur-gesture F-G♭–F, as indicated by the various solid noteheads of Example 6.2 in the upper register. So far the musical analysis is not much more than a recasting, with Schenkerian symbols, of the "chronometric" story told in Example 6.1. But then a remarkable idea emerges on Example 6.2: the final piano epilogue picks up the open-notehead F of the *Urlinie* and moves it stepwise down in B flat minor, during measures 35–36. The cadential rhythm of the melody in the two piano epilogues, in measures 13–14 and in measures 35–36, is a clear variation of the singer's cadential rhythm in measures 11–12 and measures 33–34. Accordingly, the *Urlinie* closure at the end of Example 6.2 is saying, "This is the true cadence of the piece; this is where the cadential rhythm bites home, in B flat minor."

Pastille's *Urlinie* is suspended on F, with a neighboring G♭, through the entire sung part of the piece. There is no essential structural motion of the *Urlinie* here, through fourteen-plus-eight-plus-twelve measures of music. The whole essential motion of the *Urlinie* takes place with a giant rush over the last two measures of the piece, after the singer has signed off, where the *Urlinie* plunges wildly down, finally free of the false ABA as "reality" rushes in. We are not talking, of course, about the "delusional reality" of Present A, but rather the "real reality" of Present B. The "reality" in which the *Urlinie* of Example 6.2 plunges down at the end is the "reality" that says, "But you *have* lost her," the "reality" that makes us somehow hear the piece as "really" in B♭ minor, not B♭ major.

The rhythmic rush with which the *Urlinie* plunges down, at the end of Example 6.2, is consistent with the rhythmic profiles of some of Schenker's mature background sketches (for instance his sketch for *Auf dem Flusse*, discussed in an earlier chapter in this book, where his entire *Urlinie* rushes down very close to the end of the song, indeed actually only starting close to the song's end as well).[15] Here, the rushing down of the *Urlinie* over the last two measures of the piece enacts particularly well an appropriate reading of the drama.

Less consistent with Schenker's mature productions is the register of the *Urlinie* in Example 6.2, an "inner voice" of the sketch. For myself, I do not find that an insuperable problem as a matter of abstract principle: it seems to me there are pieces in which it makes sense to think of the *Urlinie* as something more like a "tenor" (in the Renaissance sense) than a "solo melody" in the common-practice style. My ideas about *Auf dem Flusse*, as regards the piano right hand, engaged this notion. My ideas about Robert Schumann's *Auf einer Burg*, in a later chapter, will engage the notion again. In general, I am particularly willing to accept the plausibility of an inner-voice *Urlinie* when I am analyzing a piece with text, if there is something *innig* about the text that can plausibly be enacted by an "inner-voice" *Urlinie*. That is, of course, the case with *Ihr Bild*.

The *Urlinie* of Example 6.2 might at first glance seem somewhat problematic in Schenkerian terms as regards his concept of an "obligatory register" in which all notes of an *Urlinie* must coexist. But I think a plausible case can be made for the bass-clef register an octave below the written *Urlinie* of the example, particularly if the F of that line is effectively heard in that register when the male vocalist sings it.

All this said, I am not quite convinced by the *Urlinie* of Example 6.2, although I find it remarkably ingenious and plausible. As the reader has gathered, I am not completely comfortable with any of the proposed *Urlinien* so far discussed (which

15. The rhythm of a mature Schenkerian *Urlinie* is something like the historical rhythm in which we are accustomed to name the kings and queens of England, or the emperors of Rome. When speaking such a list as if it had some sort of historical *Vernunft*, we do not pause and dwell for a much longer time on say the name of Queen Victoria, simply because she reigned for a longer chronometric span than did most of her fellow sovereigns. The list has a serial logic and rhythm of its own, one not controlled (beyond very loose bounds) by Newtonian chronometry. We are accustomed to such discourse as, "and then nothing much happened for the next fifty years, at which time Marcus Aurelius came to power," even though we have no intention of discussing fifty (more) years in connection with Aurelius's reign.

Many scholars who criticize Schenker for not respecting a Newtonian chronometry of acoustical sound in his analytical sketches are not sufficiently aware, I think—if aware at all—of the Hegelian historicist tradition in which his views of temporality were formed. One can criticize Hegelian theories of temporality in light of more modern and less German views of temporality (and more modern and less German music than that of Schubert, Beethoven, et al.), but one will not so easily be able to assert that Hegelian temporality is irrelevant to the music of Beethoven, Schubert, and their German contemporaries among composers. The issues are somewhat like those of "early music" performance practice. The acoustical differences between Beethoven's pianos and a modern Steinway can be revealing. Robert Cogan, in *New Images of Musical Sound* (Cambridge, Mass.: Harvard University Press, 1984), demonstrates this through his "PHOTO[S] 6" and the surrounding commentary on pages 49–56. A modern pianist in the United States, even if not intending to perform Opus 109 on a Beethoven fortepiano, is nonetheless well advised to heed the acoustical analysis. (That is so even if one believes that Beethoven was in fact as dissatisfied with his instruments as he sometimes asserted.) Similarly, a modern pianist in the United States, even if not intending to project Schenker's analysis of Opus 101 in performance, is nonetheless well advised to be sensitive to the publication of Hegel's *Logic* in 1817, the same year in which the sonata was published. Hegelian temporality was in the German air at the time.

are all those I have heard entertained). My problem with Example 6.2 is that it seems to me to underplay the B♭ major cadences too drastically, to undercut the role of the speaker/singer as protagonist too much. My reaction here is the obverse of my reaction to Schachter's analysis, which seemed to me to highlight too vividly the major cadences of the speaker/singer, at the expense of my intuition that the song "really is" in B flat minor, not major. (Perhaps it "was" in B flat major, in some pertinent past-tense location, perhaps it "delusionally is" in B flat major, in Present A, but as I finish listening to the piece I am inclined to sense a more determinative influence from Present B.)

The reader may perhaps be asking, what is the point of all my obsessive speculation about Schenkerian background readings—along with the non-Schenkerian "chronometric" analysis of Example 6.1? Am I being obscurantist, throwing forth all these suggestions but not promulgating any one of them as my own preference? "After all," one sometimes hears, "the performers must make choices, one way or another."

Elsewhere, I have argued that such a remark seriously underestimates and misapprehends the resources available to good and thoughtful performers, even in apparently highly constrained contexts.[16] In any case, my intention is not to waffle on performance choices, but, rather, to show a menu of reasonable and sensitive options available to performers, enacting and enacted by a variety of poetic readings, within which a singer and a pianist may (and must) find a location that both find satisfying for the occasion of any particular performance. Failing physical ineptitude on my part, a reader would feel no qualms about my personal location(s) while hearing me perform as a pianist, accompanying a singer whose own location(s) were compatible with mine.

16. David Lewin, *Generalized Musical Intervals and Transformations* (New Haven, Conn.: Yale University Press, 1987), 96.

Plate 6.1 Schubert, *Ihr Bild.*

Plate 6.1 cont.

PART III

The Schumanns

The first chapter in this section addresses Clara Schumann's setting of "Ich stand in dunkeln Träumen," the poem set by Schubert as *Ihr Bild*, discussed in the previous chapters. Most readers probably know the Schubert setting and accordingly conceive it as a sort of "definitive" reading for the poem. Schumann's setting is quite something else but—as I hope to show—just as cogent a musical reading (or, as I prefer, "enactment *per musica*"), a powerfully original conception both sophisticated and skillful.

The second and third chapters address two of Robert Schumann's settings that share a particular technical feature. In *Anfangs wollt' ich fast verzagen*, and also in *Auf einer Burg*, I hear a large-scale ambivalence between Phrygian modality and functional modern minor tonality, that is between A Phrygian and D minor, or between E Phrygian and A minor. In each song, I hear the musical ambivalence enacting certain relationships between the persona's past and present. Theoretical matters involving Schenkerian analysis come to the fore; I touch on some, if only in a cursory way, to suggest paths for more thorough investigation.

All three of the chapters in this section are published here for the first time.

CHAPTER Seven

Clara Schumann's Setting of "Ich stand"

Plate 7.1 (set at the end of the chapter) gives a score for Schumann's piece. Heine's text, and my English translation, can be found at the beginning of the previous chapter in this book, on Schubert's setting of the poem as *Ihr Bild.*

Clara Wieck, already for some years a well-known concert pianist, was married to Robert Schumann on September 12, 1840, the day before her twenty-first birthday.[1] Her majority was an important feature in the context, for the lovers' courtship had been protracted and difficult, made particularly tense by the extremely forceful and hostile opposition of her father who, pursuing a sadistically vindictive campaign of hatred and slander on personal, professional, and legal levels, had forced the lovers to remain anxiously separated for several years.[2]

In a diary entry for December 5, 1840, the young woman wrote: "We have been married a quarter of a year today, and it is the happiest quarter of a year of my life."[3] Apparently she began to compose songs only after her marriage, for the first three that we know of were presented to Robert as a gift for Christmas that year.[4] One of the three was her setting of Heine's "Ich stand in dunkeln Träumen."[5]

After having read the earlier chapter in this book on Schubert's setting of the poem, some readers may find her choice of text puzzling—to say the least. In what

1. Nancy B. Reich, *Clara Schumann, the Artist and the Woman* (Ithaca, N.Y.: Cornell University Press, 1985; paperback edition 1987), 102.
2. Salient events of the courtship, and of Wieck's father's labors to shatter the lovers' relationship, are recounted by Reich in *Clara Schumann* over her chapters 3 and 4.
3. Reich, *Clara Schumann*, 104.
4. Reich, *Clara Schumann*, 248. The songs were first published, together with nine of Robert's, under his name as his Opus 37. Clara had begun collecting texts, along with Robert, in 1839 (p. 247), but either she did not compose music for any songs before her marriage, or else she later suppressed such songs as she may have written during that period. The notebook of fair-copied songs that she began in 1843 eventually expanded to include "all the songs she composed between 1840 and 1853 [but none from any earlier time]. Thus an authoritative record of the songs she thought worthy of preserving survives" (247–248).
5. The title "Ihr Bild" seems to have been invented by Schubert (or perhaps by one of his publishers). Apparently it does not appear anywhere else, among references to Heine's poem.

way is such a devastatingly tragic conception appropriate to what should be a joyous occasion? The answer lies, of course, in Schumann's own setting of the text. It was Schubert's song, not Heine's text, that gave us the sense of a devastatingly tragic conception. As we shall see, Schumann's music in fact enacts a joyous reading of the same text—a reading, furthermore, which fits particularly well the personal circumstances of the composer and her spouse in September–December 1840.[6]

As I see the matter, the impetus for Schumann's setting comes from retrospective thoughts about the recent period of separation during which both she and Robert must, on many occasions, have enacted the scene described by Heine at the beginning of his poem—one lover stood in melancholy reverie, gazing at the other's portrait.[7] Clara, in particular, would remember having so stood and gazed, and she would surely remember having had fantasies—as she did so—of Robert's (perhaps simultaneously) standing and gazing at her portrait.

The fusion of genders in this remembered scene seems a fertile topic for several possible species of postmodern critical analysis. As a technical matter the fusion of genders, in the fantasy described, situates Clara's voice very comfortably with respect to the gendering of Heine's text—the presumed "he" who speaks in the poem, who was (N.B. not "is!") gazing at "her" picture, was Robert; and the "she" of the text was Clara. He was gazing at her picture, which seemed to him to come to life, enter his presence, and gaze at him—just as, in fact, she was actually gazing at him (his picture) at the very time (so runs her fantasy) that he was imagining her doing it. But the whole fantasy of Robert's staring so at her portrait was the creation of (the younger) Clara, who was standing and staring at his portrait until it appeared to "come to life" in the fantasy that she generated.[8] And then there is also a present-tense fantasy for Clara in 1840, married and secure, while she is composing her song with all these memories and past fantasies in mind, as a present fantasy-memory.

The idea behind Schumann's setting works well not only with Heine's gendering but also with his tense systems. One imagines Clara and Robert in the past (what I called "Past 1" of the poem), saying to themselves, after staring at the portraits, "Oh, I *can* not believe that I have lost you!" This interesting twist puts Heine's "delusional" present tense (what I called "Present A" of the poem) back into the past—Past 1 of the poem. But there was no delusion there for the Schumanns. In fact, they had not lost each other! On the contrary, their mutual constancy, their refusal to believe that they were lost, far from being a pathetic or tragic delusion, paid off—they were right all the time, in refusing to submit to despair and give up!

6. Did Schumann know Schubert's setting of 1828? So far as I am aware, we do not know. During the 1830s, Robert had written various reviews of Schubert's "last compositions" for the *Neue Zeitschrift* without mentioning the *Schwanengesang*. It might have been another story, however, in 1840. Even in the 1830s, Schubert was well known in Germany as a composer of songs.

7. As mentioned during the discussion of Schubert's song, German couples of the early nineteenth century exchanged portraits (rather than, say, rings) as tokens of engagement. Clara and Robert considered themselves engaged as of August 14, 1837 (Reich, *Clara Schumann*, p. 76), somewhat over three years before their marriage. She was seventeen years old at the time.

8. One should not discount the possibility that the separated lovers had agreed on certain definite times at which they were both to gaze simultaneously at each others' portraits, each knowing that the other would simultaneously be doing so.

This aspect of Schumann's reading fits extremely well with the formal equivalence between Heine's stanza 1, couplet 2, and stanza 3, couplet 2—where the poet "demolishes" his false ABA. For Schumann, as for Schubert's singer, there is nothing false about the ABA at all. Schumann's setting ingests Heine's present tense into Past 1, in the manner just described. In *Schumann's* present tense (as of December 1840), there is no rationale for crying out "I can not believe I have lost you"—the matter has already been decided for three rapturous months of wedlock, with a glowing future in prospect.

Accordingly, Schumann's piano postlude essentially recapitulates her piano introduction, framing her joyous present memory of the lovers' past constancy, as portrayed by her treatment of Heine's text. There is no spectacular confrontation between her piano epilogue and any earlier material.

The composer's conception, in addressing this love song to her husband as a gift, thus has its origin in the same impulse that governs Verdi and Boito's Desdemona, just before the first act love duet in *Otello*: "quanti tormenti, quanti mesti sospiri e quanta speme ci condusse ai soavi abbracciamenti! Oh! come è dolce il mormorare insieme: te ne rammenti!"[9] The joy Schumann feels in her song is strikingly projected by the chronometric reduction of Example 7.1.

Example 7.1

On the treble staff, the piano right hand is represented with stems down, and the vocal part with stems up. Slurs demarcate the couplets of the poem. Rhythmically, every couplet without exception takes four measures of music to deliver. Hyper-hypermetrically, the couplets are generally set as in measures 6–9, 10–14, and 24–27: these begin on the first hyperbeat of a hyper-hypermeasure, and end on the fourth hyperbeat of the same hyper-hypermeasure. If we read the beginning of measure 20 as the beginning of a hyper-hypermeasure, the fourth couplet of text

9. How many torments, how many gloomy sighs, and how much hoping led us [finally] to [our] sweet embraces! Ah! how sweet it is, murmuring to each other, "Do you remember?"

(mm. 20–23) will conform to the norm just described. If, on the other hand, we put the stronger hyper-hyperbeat at the beginning of measure 18, rather than measure 20, then the fourth couplet, while still ending on the last hyperbeat of its hyper-hypermeasure, will begin not at the downbeat of its sextuple hyper-hypermetric span (mm. 18–23), but rather one-third of the way through that span.

In any case—no matter whether we assign measure 20 or measure 18 the greater hyper-hypermetric accent—the setting of the third couplet (mm. 16–19) will not conform to the norm. If we put the greater accent on measure 20, we will analyze measures 16–19 as the last four measures of a six-measure hyper-hypermetric group; if we put the greater accent on measure 18, we will analyze measures 16–19 as the last two measures of one four-measure hyper-hypermeasure, plus the first two measures of the next hyper-hypermeasure.

The hypermetric uniqueness and ambiguity about this couplet is particularly striking because it engages the high vocal E♭ on Example 7.1 at measure 18. That E♭ is supported by a return to tonic harmony (albeit in first inversion), after a considerable excursion to the dominant realm over the eight preceding measures. Although a high E♭ appears in the vocal part of the example at measure 12, the note there is within the dominant realm and—despite the octave relation with its bass—is harmonized not as a tonic, but as a fourth degree of the dominant region. So the high E♭ in the voice at measure 18 sounds as if it should be a large structural tonic return, a dramatic dénouement. But the return is undermined by the hyper-hypermetric techniques just discussed. The actual tonic dénouement is deferred until the high E♭ of measure 28, where the hypermetric stress is unequivocal.

Indeed, the harmony at measure 28 of Example 7.1—first-inversion tonic—is the same as the harmony at measure 18, and the voice part of Example 7.1 assiduously remains below its high E♭ during the whole ten measures between. That suggests a very revealing exercise: Play Example 7.1 at the keyboard up through measure 17; then leap directly therefrom to measure 28 of the example, continuing to play from there on. Alternately, play through measure 19; then leap directly therefrom to measure 30 of the example, continuing to play from there on. Readers who perform this exercise will, I think, be quite struck by how seamless the musical suture is. But what is the point of this unusual construction? Why does Schumann, with a mysterious smile at measure 18 ("ein Lächeln wunderbar"), defer her dramatic dénouement to measure 28?

The answer is forthcoming on taking thought about the intervening span of material in both text and music. The text for measures 20–27, the text that would be excised by the suturing of the experiment, is precisely the text in which all the weeping took place, as first the portrait's eyes gleamed, and then the persona felt his own tears coursing down his cheeks. The music for measures 20–27, the music that would be excised by the suturing of the experiment, is precisely that music during which there is a serious threat of modulation, first to g minor (mm. 20–23), then to A♭ major (m. 24), and then to c minor (mm. 25–27).[10] The suture tells us that the tears were ultimately irrelevant, that the lovers remained steadfast in E♭

10. The tonicization of the dominant, during measures 10–13, is something else. This dominant is not experienced as a "threat" to the tonic.

major throughout their ordeal, refusing to believe that they had lost each other—as indeed they exclaim(ed) just at the "real" downbeat of measure 28.

I have appended a third staff below the main two staffs of Example 7.1, during measures 20–27. There I have sketched a melodic and hypermetric cantus extracted from the vocal part of the example during those measures. One hears very clearly the reference, on this higher rhythmic-metric level, to the melodic-rhythmic foreground of measures 1–3 (and mm. 31–33). The cantus is a slightly varied version of the principal thematic motif in the right hand of the piano during the introduction to the piece—material that reappears as an epilogue. Schumann thus frames her song with piano solos that say all our weeping was swept away as ephemeral by our joyous victory over adversity, when we remained steadfast throughout the bad times.[11]

11. I wonder if there was not some private meaning of this motive that the couple shared. I wonder, too, about the motive of measures 14–15. It seems curiously familiar, though I cannot put my finger on any source. This motive, appearing in a two-measure piano interlude, gives rise to the hypermetric ambiguity concerning measure 18 and measure 20.

Plate 7.1 C. Schumann, "Ich stand."

Plate 7.1 cont.

17
zog sich ein Lä - cheln wun - der - bar, und wie von Weh - muths
21
thrä - nen er - glänz - te ihr Au - gen - paar. Auch mei - ne Thrä - nen
25
flos - sen mir von den Wang - en her - ab. und ach, ich kann's nicht
29
rit.
glau - ben, dass ich Dich ver - lo - ren hab'!
rit.

(continued)

Plate 7.1 cont.

CHAPTER Eight

R. Schumann's *Anfangs wollt' ich*

A Study in Phrygian and Modern Minor

Anfangs wollt' ich fast verzagen, Und ich glaubt', ich trüg' es nie, Und ich hab' es doch getragen— Aber fragt mich nur nicht: wie?	At first I almost wanted to give up And I thought I could never bear it. And yet I *have* borne it— Just do not ask me, "How?"

The above translation is mine. Plate 8.1 (see the end of this chapter) gives a score.

Heine is said to have written the poem about a pair of tight shoes—"tragen" means "to wear" as well as "to bear."[1] I shall not spend time on this, nor more generally on the sardonic aspects of Heine's psychology, because Schumann appears to have set the song very much in earnest, taking the text at face value.

Nor shall I devote much attention to the chorale texture of the music, even to the specific chorale that appears to be referenced.[2] That topic would require a separate article in its own right. I shall only note that the chorale-like texturing immerses Schumann's music in an ambience of devotion and supplication, suggesting that the heavy burden was borne only after intense prayer.[3] This observation makes the last verse of text in the song even more puzzling than it already is in the

1. "Die Persiflage Heines, der seine Verse über ein Paar Lackschuhe . . . dichtete." Dietrich Fischer-Dieskau, *Robert Schumann: Wort und Musik, Das Vokalwerk* (Stuttgart: Deutsche Verlags-Anstalt, 1981), 49. Fischer-Dieskau does not cite any source. ["Heine's humor . . . led him to write these lines about a pair of patent leather shoes." Dietrich Fischer-Diekau, *Robert Schumann: Words and Music: The Vocal Compositions*, trans. Reinhard G. Pauly (Portland, Ore.: Amadeus Press, 1988), 50.]
2. The opening phrase in the voice virtually quotes the melody of the opening phrase from "Wer nur den lieben Gott lässt walten." The immediately subsequent pure seventh degree in the chorale melody possibly also suggested emphasis on that degree, both melodic and harmonic, in later phrases of Schumann's song.
3. The text for "Wer nur den lieben Gott lässt walten" (No. 181 in the C. P. E. Bach collection) supports that notion. Especially pertinent seem the verses "den wird Er wunderbar erhalten / in allem Kreuz und Traurigkeit." The "separate article in its own right" would have to deal at length with the historical development of the chorale genre before, during, and after the time of J. S. Bach, devoting particular attention to the developing relations between public ceremony and private spiritual introspection within the genre.

poem: if the burden was eventually borne through prayer, why not just say so? Perhaps the persona made some very private and difficult sacrifice or penance to ensure the efficacy of the prayer. But that seems a curiously Catholic idea to suggest in the context of a Lutheran chorale.

My main focus will be on the cadence structure of the music, and on the issue of its modality. Specifically, to what extent (in what ways) do we (or can we) hear the final cadence upon the dominant of functional d minor? And to what extent (in what ways) do we (or can we) hear the final cadence on a Phrygian tonic?[4]

I have formulated these questions carefully and self-consciously. In particular, I mean to reject the question, “Do we hear a dominant of d *or* a tonic of Phrygian a?” As I remarked in an earlier chapter, such false dichotomies “force us into the position of voting for a slate of candidates, or of rendering verdicts in adversary judicial proceedings, as we respond to music. I find this not just wrong but fantastically wrong.”[5] I do not want to suggest that all music, as a general principle, can or should be considered a priori ambiguous as to key or mode. I do want to claim that this particular music can be so considered, and that such consideration can reveal interesting aspects of the particular song. Specifically, I believe that the interplay of d minor with Phrygian a allegorizes central dramatic features in Schumann’s reading of the text.

> I can’t go on. I’ll go on.
> —Samuel Beckett, *The Unnameable*

A good way to begin studying those features is to observe the strength of the tonic d minor cadence that supports the end of verse 2 at “nie,” halfway through the poem. The power of the harmonic closure there is intensified by the melody over verse 2 as a whole: after the first D of the voice in measure 5 resolves the vocal C♯ from measure 4, the voice repeats D again and again, and yet again, before closing off with F–E–D in measure 6. The phenomenon is particularly striking when one sings the vocal line without accompaniment, from the beginning through “nie.” To be sure, the accompaniment’s top line, bass line, and harmony are all much more active than is the voice during measures 5–6. But those activities—indeed all such accompaniment activities throughout measures 1–6—clearly outline and support middleground d-minor structuring that cadences in the foreground at “nie.”

The powerful d minor tonic closure and cadence show us how things were “at first” for the persona. The unbearable d minor tonic seems (seemed) here to stay. The cadence on “nie” gives a D in the voice supported by a root-position d minor $^{5}_{3}$ harmony in the accompaniment—a unique such event in the piece. (Later on we shall have more to say about that.)

4. Before the final cadence of the song, A major triads are always unambiguous functional dominants of d minor. The A major triads in measures 1 and 3 are not very weighty in that respect, but the (half-)cadential A major triads in measures 2 and 4 are. There is not much to conclude from this as yet, as regards d-minor and a-Phrygian hearings of the end, but the observation is worth putting down for future reference.

5. “Music Theory, Phenomenology, and Modes of Perception,” chapter 4 of the present volume. The cited text appears on page 81.

But the song, like the person, does go on. And at the final cadence, which rhymes with the "nie" cadence in both text and vocal rhythm, both song and person reach something else, something that is not-d-minor-tonic.[6]

What happens when we hear it as a functional d minor dominant? That hearing goes well with the word "wie?" in the poem, very literally the "last word" there, a word that—as Heine emphasizes—can be a question in itself. Heine could have written perfectly syntactically, "Aber fragt mich nur nicht wie." (Just do not ask me how.) Instead, he emphasized the questioning activity by writing "Aber fragt mich nur nicht, wie?" (Just do not ask me, "How?") The colon before "wie" in the text as sung seems to be Schumann's; it intensifies the point all the more. Hearing the final chord as a functional dominant in this context, we take the final question as awaiting an answer—presumably on the tonic of d minor. But of course the song itself, like the persona, is not going to give us an answer.[7] The unresolved suspense of the situation is not allegorized so well when we hear the final chord as a Phrygian tonic, which does provide a final resolution to the musical situation.

On the other hand, the Phrygian tonic hearing, in providing just such a resolution, better allegorizes the sense of solution and closure that can be read into the end of Heine's text. The first two verses of that text have the character of a *problem*, while the final two verses of text suggest a *resolution*—however tortuous—of the problem. To the extent that the d-minor of "nie" is heard as *problematic* rather than expository, to the extent that the final cadence is heard as *solving* the problem, to that extent we are inclined to hear the cadence as a new tonic, rather than as a dominant of the problem key. After all, it is the people being addressed by the persona who are tempted (one supposes) to ask the question, "wie?" It is not the persona who asks the question. Indeed the final sentence of text is *not* interrogative; it is imperative. The person commands the people being addressed *not* to ask the question. The inference is clear: if the question is asked, the person intends not to answer it.

6. The reader may feel that I am making too much out of a conventional Bach-chorale-style cadence on "nie." To be sure, many Bach chorales begin with one or more phrases making emphatic cadences in the main key, sometimes ending on the tonic harmony in each phrase, sometimes alternating dominant half-cadences (as at m. 4 of Schumann's song) with tonic authentic cadences (as at m. 6). There are also Bach models whose final cadences, like Schumann's here, are not on the opening tonic harmony—whether one interprets such a cadence as on a functional nontonic Stufe of the main key or on the tonic of a different ecclesiastical mode with the same diatonic set of notes. An informative and imaginative study by Lori Burns, *Bach's Modal Chorales* (Stuyvesant, N.Y.: Pendragon Press, 1995), will be of interest to those wishing to pursue issues of modality in Bach's chorales.

But I do not find such stylistic aspects of Bach's practice very cogent as criteria that can govern in any decisive way an analysis of how Schumann's music reads Heine's text. At most, Bach's procedures in those respects would have suggested possible resources to Schumann; they would not have directed him on how to use which of those resources in setting this particular poem, beyond the very first vocal cadence in measure 4 (which sets the chorale melody being quoted).

7. *Mit Myrthen und Rosen*, the song that directly follows *Anfangs* in the cycle, sets out a strong D major tonality from its beginning on. This might suggest a musical answer for a suspenseful dominant-of-d-minor on "wie?" But I do not find the idea convincing: I do not sense how the text of *Mit Myrthen* might suggest any concomitant dramatic resolution to the question, "wie?"

The D major of *Mit Myrthen* and the A major of *Berg und Burgen schau'n herunter*, the song that precedes *Anfangs* in the cycle, both seem equally consistent musically with a functional dominant-of-d-minor hearing for the final cadence of *Anfangs*, and with a tonic-Phrygian-a hearing.

Let us call the people to whom the persona is speaking "the audience," to have a convenient name for them. The name is more than convenient—I want it to remind us that we, reading the poem and listening to the song, are to some extent among those people. The discussion so far leads to the following reading.

The audience is curious and in suspense at the end of the song. It hears the final chord as a dominant. To the extent that we feel ourselves as audience, being addressed by the persona, we are primed to hear the final chord as a dominant of d minor—wanting to ask, "wie?" The persona, in contrast, feels no suspense, having resolved a problem from the past, a problem allegorized by the earlier unbearable tonic cadence in d minor. The person hears the final chord as a solution, a closure, and hence a new tonic. To the extent that we are empathizing with this protagonist, we are primed to hear the final chord as Phrygian tonic.

The effect of the song's close is much inflected by the strong emphasis on the note C during its second half. Verse 3 of the poem rhymes with verse 1, and the vocal line for verse 3 (mm. 7–8) replicates the vocal line for verse 1 (mm. 2–3), with only a slight rhythmic variation in the opening two notes, right up to the final two notes of the phrases. There, the melodically cadential C♯–A of measure 4 is replaced by the two C naturals of measure 8, just where the textual endrhyme occurs—the first endrhyme of the poem. Those C naturals tell us that the vocal line is now going to head downward, away from the insistent melodic D of measures 3, 4, 5, 6, and 7. The setting of "doch (ge)tragen" emphasizes the critical melodic motion from the last D of the vocal line ("doch") , to the first C ("tra(gen)")—the idea is, *no longer* D *but* C. The cadential emphasis on the repeated C naturals in the voice at measure 8 is reinforced by a complete authentic cadence in C major on the crucial third beat of measure 8, where we hear C natural in the voice rather than C sharp. The modulation to C major, rather than F major, is unusual in common-practice d-minor tonality.[8] As verse 4 begins immediately afterward, the vocal part through measure 9 insists again and again on the C natural attained in measure 8, in pointed contrast to the insistent vocal D that began setting verse 2 in measure 5.

The C naturals just discussed are syntactically consistent with either a d-minor hearing for the end of the song, or with a hearing in Phrygian a. Either way, the C naturals participate in a large linear structure that is manifest in the vocal part, from the D of measures 3–7, through the C natural of measures 8–9, to B♭ and A over the last two measures. In Phrygian a, there is no conceptual problem asserting this gesture as some sort of modal "*Urlinie*," beyond the problem of bringing the Schenkerian term into a modal-but-not-tonal ambience at all.[9] In a fully Schenkerian view of functional d minor, a stepwise descent from $\hat{8}$ to $\hat{5}$ at the end

8. The question of structural parallel octaves, from the D-over-D cadence in measure 6 ("nie"), to the C-over-C cadence in measure 8 ("tragen"), raises interesting technical problems for voice-leading analysis, whether in a functional-d-minor reading, or in an a-Phrygian reading of the piece's close. We shall investigate some of these later.

9. Lori Burns explores just this problem in *Bach's Modal Chorales.* Although she does not assert a $\hat{4}$–$\hat{3}$–$\hat{2}$–$\hat{1}$ *Urlinie* for any Phrygian chorale by Bach, that is not because of any theoretical feature of her system; rather, she does not find any Phrygian chorale by Bach that exhibits such a structure. She does assert a $\hat{4}$–$\hat{3}$–$\hat{2}$–$\hat{1}$ *Urlinie* for the Mixolydian chorale, "Dies sind die heiligen Zehn Gebot," BWV 298, and her system has no problem in accommodating the structure.

of a piece cannot be asserted as the end of an "*Urlinie*," and this does raise a problem for interpretation. Presumably one is not content, without substantial further comment, simply to assert that the piece "closes" structurally with the d-minor $\hat{3}$–$\hat{2}$–$\hat{1}$ of measure 6, to assert that the whole second half of the piece—the "I'll go on" half—the "doch" half—is some sort of coda to measure 6. And yet there hardly seems any musical alternative to that reading, in the fully Schenkerian view.[10] So a traditional Schenkerian reading of the music does need substantial further comment, to make its sense suitably allegorical in the ambience of the poem.

Example 8.1

Examples 8.1a and 8.1b are voice-leading analyses for Phrygian-a and d-minor hearings of the song, respectively. I have tried to make Example 8.1a support as strong a purely Phrygian reading as possible. And I have tried to make Example 8.1b as strongly Schenkerian as possible. A number of other readings seem possible between those two poles, adjusting various features of the two analyses in one direction or another.

The *Urlinie* considerations just discussed are manifest in the visual symbols of the examples. Example 8.1a asserts the $\hat{4}$–$\hat{3}$–$\hat{2}$–$\hat{1}$ Phrygian *Urlinie* discussed above. The descent through $\hat{3}$ to $\hat{2}$ to $\hat{1}$ is supported by the background bass motion $\hat{6}$–$\hat{7}$–$\hat{8}$. I have tried to emphasize this structural role for the bass F by asserting F, not D, as the principal note in the background bass even at the opening of the song. There is no background $\hat{3}$–$\hat{2}$–$\hat{1}$ in d minor here at all; the F–E–D of "trüg' es nie" happens at a subordinate level, embellishing a background D-over-F. The problem of structural parallel octaves, from the "nie" cadence to the "tragen" cadence, is finessed

10. Burns (*Bach's Modal Chorales*, 17–21) has a salient discussion of Schenker's insistence that the melody for "Gelobet seist du, Jesu Christ" should be analyzed and harmonized in functional C major, rather than in a Mixolydian G. Schenker criticizes not only Bellermann but also J. S. Bach himself in this regard, offering his own harmonization in C major as more "natural."

here because the structural counterpoint instead asserts the C of "tragen" as a fifth over the background F, not an octave over pure $\hat{7}$ of d minor.

I have used a similar expedient, to analyze around the parallel-octave problem in Example 8.1b, even though neither the bass F nor the vocal C is an "Ur" note of that reading. Example 8.1b highlights the way in which this functional-tonal hearing removes the second half of the song from the background of voice-leading structure. One might say that in this reading, "all the action" of the music happens before verse 3, where in Example 8.1a "all the action" happened after verse 2.

I said above that "a number of other readings seem possible between [the] two poles [of Examples 8.1a and 8.1b], adjusting various features of the two analyses in one direction or another." An interesting idea would be to hear an *Ursatz* that combines the F–E–D over D–A–D of Example 8.1b, with the D–C–B♭–A over F–G–A of Example 8.1a, thereby spreading "background" action (in some extended sense of the term) over the song as a whole. This *Ursatz* would assert the sixth-descent F–E–D–C–B♭–A over the bass D–A–D–F–G–A. The structure would be neither strictly functional tonally, nor strictly Phrygian as an expanded cadence. It would be some sort of tertium quid, so far as canonical models for modal and tonal cadence-structures are concerned. The idea seems consistent with a point of view espoused by Dahlhaus:

> There is a relationship between a and e [in traditional Aeolian and Phrygian modes], but it does not include the dependence of one degree upon the other. The fifth-relation is nothing but a bilateral relation, and it was perceived as such [in pertinent historical times] without e being related to a as a dominant or a to e as a subdominant. A listener who has grown up in the tradition of major-minor tonality may find it difficult to discontinue hearing a sense of alignment in degree relationships, but to do so is not impossible.[11]

Nevertheless, I am not completely happy with the sort of urbane permissiveness inherent in Dahlhaus's remarks, as an approach to the present song. For one thing, Schumann and his times are different matters from Palestrina and his times. Even more salient for me personally is my sense that there are strong tonal alignments in the song at hand: there is no question but that A *is* dominant of D through the whole first half of the piece; nor (to my ear) is there any question that by the end of the song, the persona is hearing a Phrygian solution to the d minor problem, the D now being a (Phrygian) subdominant of A. To the extent that we identify with the persona (and do not simply remain "audience" asking the person "wie?"), we will (or at least can) hear the Phrygian hearing. Characteristic for the song, I believe, is a certain rhythm or progression, from the one unambiguous hearing to the other—or at least the possibility of the other.

The graphic symbols of Example 8.1a by themselves do not capture such a rhythm or progression. Neither do the symbols of Example 8.1b. Nor would the symbols of the "compromise" analysis discussed earlier—with the melodic

11. Carl Dahlhaus, *Studies on the Origin of Harmonic Tonality*, trans. Robert O. Gjerdingen (Princeton, N.J.: Princeton University Press, 1990), 223. Quoted and discussed by Burns in *Bach's Modal Chorales*, 13–15.

sixth-line F–E–D–C–B♭–A in the background. In each case, the notion of *an Ursatz,* however echt-Schenkerian or post-pseudo-quasi-Schenkerian, works against representing or even adequately acknowledging the rhythm or progression being discussed.

It would be nice to have a theoretical-analytic system for representing structural voice-leading that responded better to this issue. I can imagine a sort of morphing hypertext that moved from one window like Example 8.1b, to another window like Example 8.1a, in some pertinent way. But at present I cannot work out this notion as anything more solid than a fantasy.[12] In this connection it would be penny-wise and pound-foolish to abandon the notion of "an" *Ursatz* altogether, as somehow "irrelevant" to some soi-disant "more sophisticated" hearing. Any background analysis does crucial work in specifying just what some metastable hearing of the piece is. Without a background analysis, we should be reduced to more or less impressionistic discussion of large-scale voice-leading possibilities, and such a return to pre-Schenkerian hermeneutics (as if Schenker had never happened) would surely lower, rather than raise, the level of sophistication in our discourse.

12. I engage related issues in my "Music Theory, Phenomenology, and Modes of Perception," cited earlier (Chapter 4 in this book). Most of the pertinent discussion there is in Part IV of the chapter (pp. 79–93).

Plate 8.1 R. Schumann, *Anfangs wollt' ich.*

CHAPTER Nine

Auf einer Burg

Eingeschlafen auf der Lauer Oben ist der alte Ritter; Drüben gehen Regenscheuer, Und der Wald rauscht durch das Gitter.	Fallen asleep on his watch up there is the old knight. Yonder, rainstorms pass by, and the woods rustle through the lattice-work.
Eingewachsen Bart und Haare, Und versteinert Brust und Krause, Sitzt er viele hundert Jahre Oben in der stillen Klause.	Overgrown his beard and hair, petrified his breast and ruffles, he has been sitting many centuries up there in his silent cell.
Draußen ist es still und friedlich, Alle sind in's Tal gezogen, Waldesvögel einsam singen In den leeren Fensterbogen.	Without, it is still and peaceful; everyone has gone down into the valley. Solitary wood-birds sing in the empty window-arches.
Eine Hochzeit fährt da unten Auf dem Rhein in Sonnenscheine, Musikanten spielen munter, Und die schöne Braut, die weinet.	A wedding party is traveling down there along the Rhine, in sunshine. Musicians are playing gaily, and the beautiful bride—she is weeping.

Warrior knights are, among other things, supposed to rescue damsels in distress. But the old knight in Eichendorff's poem is oblivious to the damsel in distress who passes by literally under his nose. The time is out of joint—as the music is perhaps remarking via the syncopations in its C major episodes.[1]

1. Karen A. Hindenlang argues a fully allegorical and political meaning for the poem, in her article, "Eichendorff's *Auf einer Burg* and Schumann's *Liederkreis*, Opus 39," *The Journal of Musicology* 8 (1990), 570–587. She argues that the old knight is Friedrich Barbarossa himself, on guard in his secret cavern within the Kyffhäuser (a mountain in the Thuringian Harz), "awaiting his opportunity to return and lead the German people in their time of need" (575). The bride represents *Germania*: "a

Is the bride distressed? I think it is safe—even necessary—to suppose that she is, in one way or another. The ending of the poem makes no sense if her tears are tears of joy. We are clearly meant to be shocked and brought up short by a sense of puzzlement about the ending—literally, about the last word.[2] The sense of uncertainty that we feel in this connection is, I shall soon argue, projected strongly by the music of Schumann's setting

The poem is laden with sharp antitheses. The statue is "oben" in a high fortress, surrounded by woods; the wedding party is "da unten" in the river valley. The statue is old and male, the bride young and female. The statue "lives" only in the past, the bride is very much in the present—and as a bride, she also invokes our sense of the future. The statue is a warrior, the bride a civilian. The statue, white with petrifaction, remains rigid and frozen; the bride, in her white gown, is pliant and warm. The statue is confined and motionless; the bride moves swiftly along the river. The statue is in a dark chamber; the bride is in bright sunshine. The statue is alone; the bride is surrounded by a noisy throng of people. A few birds pipe mournfully to the statue, and they are "solitary"; the musicians of the wedding party play lustily for the bride, and they are immersed in a highly social noisy throng. Rainstorms pass by the statue "over yonder" (drüben); the weeping of the bride, which also passes him by, is by way of contrast very much in the foreground of the poetic scene.[3]

In this connection, one may reasonably look for aspects of the song that project musical contrasts of a similar sort. The present chapter proposes such a contrast, specifically an antithesis between "ancient" e-Phrygian modality and "modern" functional a-minor tonality.[4] The musical interplay of these organizations

woman, a conventional symbol for a nation, who is also a bride, an ancient symbol for the Christian church, sails by on the one river which represents the course of German history. Above her [Hindenlang rationalizes at some length the geographical impossibilities involved in such an allegorical juxtaposition of the Rhine with the Harz mountains] is the saviour of the German people, the single figure who could restore political stability, religious harmony, and the peace of a vanished golden age. A new era is at hand. Yet, while the river flows through time, the ancient king remains frozen in time. The bride and the knight . . . are kept apart. And the bride, quite understandably, weeps" (580–581).

2. Karlheinz Schlager, in "Erstarrte Idylle, Schumanns Eichendorff-Verständnis im Lied op. 39/VII (auf einer Burg)," *Archiv für Musikwissenschaft*, 23.2 (1976), 119–132, devotes some attention to this topic. "The final verse remains open for interpretation: is it joy, stirred-up feelings, or the perception that the [emotional] ground is giving way beneath her feet, that has overtaken the bride and causes her to weep? In any case it gives rise to a discombobulating impetus, like the unexpectedly ironic echo [at the end of] many a Heine poem" (122). (Die Schlußzeile steht der Interpretation offen: Ist es Freude, Rührung oder die Erkenntnis des schwankenden Grundes, die Braut befallen hat und zum Weinen bringt? Es ist in jedem Fall ein Moment der Irritation, ähnlich dem unerwartet ironischen Ausklang vieler Heine-Gedichte . . . .) While Schlager does not rule out tears of joy—as I do—he appends a suggestive footnote to the first sentence above: "The [eponymous] Weeping Bride, in [one of] Eichendorff's *Romances*, bewails her destiny, to have obtained as husband a man she does not love." (ibid.) (*Die weinende Braut* aus den *Romanzen* EICHENDORFFS beklagt das Schicksal, einen ungeliebten Mann zum Gatten zu bekommen.)
3. I am indebted to Deborah Stein, who pointed out many of these antitheses in a lecture on Schumann's Eichendorff *Liederkreis* given in November 1983, at the meeting of the Society for Music Theory in New Haven. I have added some further antitheses of my own.
4. Deborah Stein (see note 3) proposed a contrast between two functional keys, e minor and a minor, the music modulating from one to the other during each of the two strophes. Her idea provided a consid-

enacts the idea that "the statue 'lives' in the past," while "the bride is very much in the present." To the point in this connection is the shadowy presence of the narrating persona in the poem. This person is situated at an ambivalent level. For him—like those in the wedding party—the statue is "oben," and he thus views the ancient world of chivalry from the standpoint of present-day reality. But also for him—like the statue—the wedding-party is going past "da unten," and he remains—like the statue—a detached observer of the present-day crisis, viewing that crisis sub specie aeternitatis rather than as an active participant in its peripateia.[5] In my reading, the ambiguity between a minor and e-Phrygian modalities enacts and is enacted by this dual nature of the ambivalent narrating persona. The uncertainty that we feel at the end of the poem as to why the bride is weeping, an uncertainty to which I alluded earlier, is also well projected by the musical ambivalence just proposed.

The reader will recall in this connection my analysis of *Anfangs wollt' ich fast verzagen*. In fact, I undertook that analysis partly as a preliminary exercise for the present one: I wanted to show that Schumann was sensitive to intrinsic ambiguities between modern minor half-cadences and full cadences in a sixteenth-century sort of Phrygian mode, and willing to exploit them when the musical device suited his dramatic purposes.

That said, some differences between *Auf einer Burg* and *Anfangs wollt' ich* should be examined at once. First of all, the music of *Anfangs* is through-composed, while *Auf einer Burg* comprises two parallel strophes that project essentially the same music. Then too, *Anfangs* progresses harmonically from its beginning to its end, as i → V in minor, or as iv → i♯ in Phrygian. In contrast, *Auf einer Burg* prolongs one *Stufe* through each of its two strophes (and hence through its entirety), projecting a harmonically static v—♯ in minor, or i —♯ in Phrygian.[6] Finally, the song that follows *Anfangs* in its cycle, *Mit Myrthen und Rosen*, while in the (major) key for

erable impetus for my own. I modify her idea because I cannot hear a modulation from functional-e-minor at the beginning of the song, to an unambiguous functional-a-minor at its end. The final cadence of the song, in my hearing, must be *ambiguous* as to E or A centricity, and any E centricity there must perforce be Phrygian, not functionally tonal.

Hindenlang (*Auf einer Burg*, 582) writes that "the tonality is under the modal influence of E aeolian," but I cannot hear what she means, beyond the prominence of D natural as a scale degree in the music—equally consistent with e-Phrygian, and more so when interacting harmonically with various F-naturals approaching the final cadence. She believes that the end of the song has been "misidentified" by analysts who have considered it Phrygian, while "the ear easily recognizes the unmistakable . . . sound of . . . the true [a minor] dominant" (ibid.) My ear is not so easily convinced as hers is. Nor do I think that Palestrina's ear would easily have recognized the unmistakable sound of a true a-minor dominant. The reference to Palestrina's ear will be picked up later on.

5. Schlager ("Erstarrte Idylle," 121) observes: "It is this . . . view from an elevated vantage point that is also relied upon in many paintings by Caspar David Friedrich, where a figure in the foreground is set off in shadowy relief against an infinitely extending landscape." (Es ist dies . . . Blick von einem erhöhten Standpunkt aus, der auch von vielen Gemälden Caspar David Friedrichs [1774–1840] vertraut ist, in denen eine Gestalt im Vordergrund sich silhouettenhaft vor einer endlos weiten Landschaft . . . abhebt.) Schlager, however, does not discuss the view upward from the vantage-point of Eichendorff's narrator, upward toward the statue. I take this duality of view, both up and down, to be a significant aspect of the poem (and the music).

6. I rule out hearing the strophe as a "modulation" that begins in functional e-minor and ends on a nontonal e-Phrygian. If I am to hear the song as tonally functional, I want to hear it in a minor, not "e minor."

which the final chord of *Anfangs* is a dominant, is not related in any obvious motivic or thematic way to *Anfangs*. In contrast, the song that follows *Auf einer Burg* in its cycle, *In der Fremde* (2), is very strongly related motivically and thematically to *Auf einer Burg*. Even more: just that motivic-thematic work, at the beginning of *In der Fremde* (2), keeps alive and active the ambiguity between a-tonicity and e-tonicity that I have asserted of *Auf einer Burg*. Specifically, the E–A–B–C figure of *In der Fremde*, measures 2–3, clearly presents the basic melodic motif of *Auf einer Burg*, here "in a minor" rather than "e minor" or "e Phrygian." And then measures 4–5 of *In der Fremde* transpose the same motif "back" to the original e-level of *Auf einer Burg*, measures 1–2. The immediate juxtaposition and progression of a-level and e-level motif-forms, over measures 2–5 of *In der Fremde*, recalls very strongly the middle of *Auf einer Burg*, where the piano interlude (mm. 18–21) begins by presenting the motif and its sequel "in a," and this is immediately followed by the beginning of the second strophe (mm. 22–25), which transposes measures 18–21 so as to present the motif and its sequel "back in e."

Thus, although the final cadence of *In der Fremde* (2) is very conclusively in functional a-minor (with *tierce de Picardie*), one should be wary, I think, of trying to make the opening measures of that song carry too much weight, in determining the resolution of any ambiguity between a-minor and e-Phrygian just heard in *Auf einer Burg*. Whatever modal ambiguities of this sort one hears in *Auf einer Burg* strongly continue into the beginning of *In der Fremde* (2), to be resolved musically in favor of functional a-minor only at the end of *In der Fremde*. The two songs are thus in some sense a pair of musical pieces. And the pair, as such, is to be heard in a functional a-minor, when analyzed in retrospect from the ending of *In der Fremde*.

Why then analyze *Auf einer Burg* as if it were an independent piece? Here I must plead that *Auf einer Burg* projects such a strong phenomenological presence in its own right, as to render uncomfortable any notion that it is merely—or even primarily—in the nature of a musical prelude (dominant preparation) for the tonic downbeat at the end of the next song. To support my plea, I would point out that *Auf einer Burg* is surely the more weighty of the two songs from virtually any aesthetic point of view other than that of an abstract functional dominant-and-tonic.[7] In this connection, though there are certain points of contact between the two poems (*rauschen, Wald,* singing birds, *Einsamkeit,* and the like), these are fairly common materials of the poetic genre at hand, whereas the text of *In der Fremde*, as a putative "resolution" for the preceding poem, is not well able to surmount the overwhelming fact that the statue and the wedding party are gone, leaving us with our questions, once *Auf einer Burg* has concluded.

Then, too, the musical *Stimmung* of *Auf einer Burg* is solemn, majestic, labored, learned, and heavily thoughtful, while the music of *In der Fremde* is more scherzoso—despite the delicate tempo indication and the serious subject matter of the text. This relation between the two songs makes it difficult to put too much aesthetic weight on the second song of the pair, as if they were say a prelude and fugue. A better model, to my way of thinking, would be two *Stollen* (for the two strophes

7. Even here, one might argue abstractly that the (hyper)metric weight of a functional V → I progression can be taken by the dominant harmony, rather than the tonic, in suitable contexts.

of *Auf einer Burg*), followed by an *Abgesang* (*In der Fremde*). Using that model, I can argue that the two *Stollen* might project Phrygian tonics or functional tonal dominants ambivalently, and that the *Abgesang* (at its end) releases the tension of the ambivalence, providing a function tonal cadence by way of conclusion.

A Phrygian Voice-leading *Ursatz* for the Strophe of *Auf einer Burg*

So far I have treated the idea of "Phrygian structure" somewhat impressionistically. I have pointed out (in note 4) the emphasis on harmonies containing D natural and F natural, approaching the final cadence of the strophe. This sort of observation could be worked out in more detail to show that the final cadence, as a musical gesture, conforms to various of the cadence formulas categorized as "Phrygian" by German theorists of the seventeenth and eighteenth centuries (e.g., Herbst, Printz, Walther, Kirnberger, Türk, Knecht, and Vogler).[8] Other gestural aspects of the strophe, besides its final cadence, are also stylistically typical of large-scale Phrygian organization. In particular, strong opening and final cadences on e, together with secondary medial cadences on C and a, are very frequently found in compositions of the sixteenth century commonly classified as Phrygian. Idiomatic, too, is the use of a-minor harmony as a means to prolong cadential e harmony, as it does to some extent approaching the final cadence of the strophe, and also—particularly—as it does in the piano interlude between the two strophes. Then, too, the pairing of principal motif entries "on e" with imitative entries "on a"—as in measure 3, or in the piano interlude—is a characteristic aspect of sixteenth-century "Phrygian" rhetoric.[9]

Although the gestural features discussed in the preceding paragraph are more than impressionistic, they seem only incidental side-references, poetic obeisances if you will, in the context of a Schenkerian analysis that would hear both strophes of *Auf einer Burg* as prolongations of functional a-minor V harmony in a Schenkerian sense, preliminary features within a functional a-minor *Ursatz* whose *Kopfton* occurs (only) within *In der Fremde* and whose final closure occurs (only) at the end of *In der Fremde*.[10] I intend to show now that if we restrict our musical attention to the strophe of *Auf einer Burg* itself, as a smaller context for musical perception, then we can find a quasi-Schenkerian voice-leading *Ursatz* for that strophe-in-itself, which can legitimately be asserted as a "Phrygian *Ursatz*" for that context.

Such a voice-leading *Ursatz* can be only "quasi" Schenkerian, because its structural upper voice, corresponding to events in the vocal part of the song, can not

8. A useful summary discussion of these theorists' cadence formulas can be found in Lori Burns, *Bach's Modal Chorales* (Stuyvesant, N.Y.: Pendragon Press, 1995), 187–218.

9. Typical "Phrygian" character, in all respects discussed during the preceding paragraph, can be observed in the *Sanctus* from Palestrina's mass *Sine nomine*, or the *Hosanna* from his mass *Repleatur os meum laude*. There are, of course, many other compositions of this sort. Many were highly regarded by Schumann, as attested by his letter to D. G. Otten, April 2, 1849: "some pieces must be left for the minority, for the few . . . truly artistic minds, and they have Palestrina, Bach, Beethoven's last quartets, etc." The excerpt from the letter appears in *Robert Schumann, On Music and Musicians*, ed. Konrad Wolff, trans. Paul Rosenfeld (New York: Pantheon Books, 1946), 92.

10. I shall discuss later on why it is problematic to assert a *Kopfton* for any Schenkerian a-minor *Ursatz* within *Auf einer Burg* itself.

close on the tone E. The vocal part, that is, does not carry a large-scale structural $\hat{3}$–$\hat{2}$–$\hat{1}$ descent (or other conjunct descent to $\hat{1}$ from $\hat{8}$ or $\hat{5}$) that would be well-formed as a Schenkerian *Urlinie* for a Phrygian structure. Nevertheless, I intend to assert such a $\hat{3}$–$\hat{2}$–$\hat{1}$ in a structural inner voice. While not in conformity with Schenker's restrictions on the behavior of a functionally tonal *Urlinie*, my inner-voice *Urlinie* is idiomatic, where it lies, as a structural tenor or cantus firmus for a composition in Renaissance modal style. It also comports nicely with Schumann's interest in musically "innig" phenomena.

Example 9.1

Example 9.1 is a collection of voice-leading sketches that address my point. Example 9.1(a) is a high-level middleground sketch. Measure numbers for the first strophe appear above the music. (Those for the second strophe are respectively 21 measures later: 22, 26, 35, 36, 37.) After the cadential E harmony arrives at measure 16 on the example, alternate possible continuations are sketched in brackets: one "resolves" the E harmony as a dominant in functional a minor; the other prolongs the E harmony as a Phrygian tonic, in the manner of the music following measure 37.

Example 9.1(b) works out, at a more detailed middleground level, the structural voice-leading from measure 9 to measure 14. The a minor harmony shown at measure 14 on the example does not assert itself strongly as a local tonic; rather, it sounds as vi of the C major *Stufe* from measure 9. The *Zug* in the upper voice of Example 9.1(b) goes $\hat{5}$–$\hat{6}$–$\hat{7}$–$\hat{8}$ within the C *Stufe*; the parallel tenths below go $\hat{3}$–$\hat{4}$–$\hat{5}$–$\hat{6}$ within the C *Stufe*. In neither the *Zug* nor the lower parallel line is the G raised to G♯ as it approaches A. (Nor is F raised to F♯ in the lower line.) The structural a-minor harmony as vi-of-C is portrayed very summarily on Example 9.1(a).[11]

The rhythmic aspect of Example 9.1(a) is worth noting. Rhythmic dilations like the one that begins at measure 14 on the sketch are a strong resource (as well as a problematical aspect) of Schenkerian analysis, a resource (and a problem) shared by my quasi-Schenkerian sketch. The sketch asserts two structural harmonies compressed into the climactic chord of measure 14, which occupies a rhythmic psychological time commensurate with that taken up by the first eight measures of the piece. Here the temporal foreshortening enacts the text well, as the exigencies of the temporal present surge in on the narrator, who has hitherto identified himself with the statue, undergoing the endless stately and balanced processions of time past.

Example 9.1(c) reduces Example 9.1(a) to a level closely approaching an *Ursatz.* Measure numbers are again given for the first strophe; the second strophe can be analyzed in the same way, with measures 22, 35, and 37. A Phrygian *Urlinie* is beamed in the alto voice of the treble clef. The *Urlinie* is supported contrapuntally by the beamed notes of the bass beneath it. Of course, one cannot speak of a "*Brechung*" (arpeggiation) here; that is a familiar aspect of "Phrygian" cadence formulas, since the fifth degree of the Phrygian mode does not carry a perfect fifth within the scale.

Examples 9.1(d) and (e) reduce the formula even farther. As regards the treble clef of Example 9.1(d), Carl Schachter has pointed out that the notes G–C–B–G♯ compose out the secondary melodic motif of the piece—as heard in the voice over measures 3 and 4 ("Oben ist der alte Ritter").[12] Example 9.1(e) reduces the structure to my Phrygian *Urlinie* and its bass support, plus a descant involving the vocal part of the song. The descant descends from $\hat{5}$ of e harmony to #$\hat{3}$ of E harmony, filled in by a passing $\hat{4}$.

Schachter's brilliant observation is completely convincing to my ear, where it seems quite compatible with my Phrygian reading even though he hears *Auf einer Burg* completely tonally, prolonging a functional dominant of a minor that resolves within *In der Fremde.* Unconvinced by my Phrygian analysis of the strophe-in-itself, Schachter pointed out that the F natural on my Examples 9.1(c)(d)(e) is not sung by the voice, and he was uncomfortable with a reading that allows such a thing to happen. Some fourteen years later, I still do not have a response to Schachter's criticism that satisfies me, reading the relation of singer to accompaniment in some way that gives the piano something to "enact" in producing the F naturals on Examples 9.1(d) and (e).

And yet, as I have already indicated, I am uncomfortable with a reading that does not allow any possibility of musical closure at the end of *Auf einer Burg.* While I feel that *In der Fremde* adequately resolves the psychological uncertainties we feel

11. Because of these features, the singer's high C in measure 14 cannot signal the beginning of a functional a-minor *Urlinie* for *Auf einer Burg* (or for the pair AeB-plus-IdF). There is not adequate a-minor root support for such an analysis. On Example 9.1(a), the harmonic progression of the fourth, fifth, and sixth quarter-notes projects a contrapuntal 5–6 over a C continuo bass, followed by a D root bass.

12. Private correspondence, following the New Haven meeting of 1983, cited in note 3.

at the end of *Auf einer Burg*, I do not want to hear the earlier song's voice-leading and harmonic structure only as a preliminary for *In der Fremde*. Such uncertainties are well captured, to my ear, when we enquire of Example 9.1(e), in what ways is this a complete Phrygian piece? And in what ways is it a dominant for some a-minor tonic to come? Here, it seems essential to me that we do not ask: "Is this a complete Phrygian piece? Or is it a dominant for some a-minor tonic to come?" I touched on the methodological point earlier, in connection with *Anfangs wollt' ich*. If we demand that Example 9.1(e) project either a complete Phrygian piece, or an incomplete tonal piece, but not some tertium quid, then I feel we are not doing justice to the sensations with which we are left at the end of *Auf einer Burg*.

While on the subject of motivic expansion, we should note the motivic aspect of the final cadence in the bass line, which is particularly strong at the end of the second strophe: starting at the A in measure 35, the bass then proceeds to D, then to F, then to E. The melodic figure A–D–F–E, beginning with the fifth-leap down from A to D, sounds to my ear as a pertinently transposed rhythmically augmented—and otherwise rhythmically transformed—permutation of the *Kopfmotiv* B–E–F♯–G. The "d-minor" transpositional level, A–D–E–F, is gesturally pertinent to the preparation for a Phrygian cadence.

Earlier (in note 10) I promised to discuss why it is problematic to assert a *Kopfton* for any Schenkerian a-minor *Ursatz* within *Auf einer Burg* itself. Note 11, along with pertinent discussion of Example 9.1(a) and (b), pointed out why it would be difficult to assert the singer's high C of measure 14 as such a *Kopfton*. Within the strophe itself, no other candidate comes into consideration. There remains the a-minor material within the piano interlude. One might, for example, try to assert the piano's C of measure 21 as such a *Kopfton*, or even the piano's high E of measures 18–19, which could then conceivably be picked up by the singer's high E at the opening of *In der Fremde*. All these candidates have solid a-minor local root support.

Before all else, I should say that any attempt to locate a functional a-minor *Kopfton* within the piano interlude of *Auf einer Burg* slips by my Phrygian *Ursatz* as unnoticed as the bride slips past the statue. I asserted my *Ursatz* as an *Ursatz* for the strophe, not for the song as a whole (including the piano interlude).

That said, I should voice some discomfort at the dramatic idea of an *Ursatz* that begins during the unique 4 measures, halfway through the song, where the singer is not singing—all the more so because those 4 measures form an interlude between two musically parallel strophes. My discomfort is like Schachter's at the F natural in my Phrygian *Urlinie*, only much more so.[13]

And that said, I should add that there does seem a definite poetic value in the thought that the piano, when left to its own devices within *Auf einer Burg*, is eager

13. The 5-line *Ursatz* proposed by Pastille for Schubert's *Ihr Bild* is open to something like the same questioning. Pastille's $\hat{4}$–$\hat{3}$–$\hat{2}$–$\hat{1}$ occurs during the piano epilogue there. But that epilogue is "the last word" in a number of dramatically central ways, as we saw. It is not at all the same as the earlier interlude within that song, to which the epilogue makes sharp contrasts in mode, texture, and dynamics. Furthermore, Pastille's *Kopfton* is very much the property of the voice, and there is excellent dramatic support for the idea that the voice's unwillingness to close $\hat{4}$–$\hat{3}$–$\hat{2}$–$\hat{1}$ in the *minor* mode enacts a dramatic refusal to accept the "reality" of the persona's situation, a reality which the piano emphasizes in its epilogue.

to interpret the music in functional a minor. So eager, in fact, that it cannot wait for the voice to cadence melodically on G♯, in measure 17, before making its own would-be authentic cadence in a minor.[14] The enactment here, I believe, is something like this: so far, the narrating persona (say "Eichendorff") has identified himself with the statue—austere, remote, disinvolved, regarding the scene sub specie aeternitatis. But as the persona stops narrating, the piano enacts his sudden awareness of himself as existing in the present, a present in which music is functionally tonal, in which—as Hindenlang puts it—"the ear easily recognizes the unmistakable . . . sound of . . . the true [a minor] dominant."[15] Tonal hearing wants to summon the statue's E triad to action, making it relevant to the present, where it should "resolve." But so far as the statue himself is concerned, the cadential E triad is a perfectly static tonic, requiring no further action whatsoever. As the statue hears the piano interlude—if indeed he hears it at all—the a-minor harmony is merely an idiomatic means of prolonging a Phrygian E tonic. And the narrating persona, to the extent he continues identifying with the "observing" statue, can hear the a-minor interlude in the same way. We only know that the persona has trouble in doing so, because the a-minor harmony comes in too soon, too anxiously, in measure 17. And our impression is later reinforced by the way in which the opening of *In der Fremde* resumes and develops the anxious toggling between a-tonic and e-tonic that we heard over measures 18–25 of *Auf einer Burg*.

The role of the piano interlude sheds considerable light on the effect of Schumann's strophic setting. The musical effect is especially striking because the poem itself is so urgently progressive in its second half, particularly when it swings into its final quatrain. If you were a composer setting the poem, and knew no earlier settings, you would be unlikely to conceive your music in two similar strophes for the two halves of the text. Schumann, that is, must have had a strong "idea" in making his setting strophic.

I think his idea was this: after the piano, during its interlude, has enacted the narrator's sudden awareness of himself as existing in the present, a present in which music is functionally tonal, the reprise of the possibly-Phrygian music for the second strophe makes us more and more uncomfortable. It specifically evades the issue that the piano interlude has just brought so forcefully to our attention. While the narrator is delivering the second half of the text, the music seems content to root itself "back in the past" again, retreating into the narrator's pose sub specie aeternitatis, refusing to deal explicitly with the "presentness" of a-minor hearing. The Phrygian reading for the second strophe thereby builds up enormous tension, seemingly at odds with the concomitant "presentness" of its text, above all the text that concerns the wedding party. Just this tension will be released by *In der Fremde*.

14. The bass A of measures 17–18 is the lowest note of the piece so far. (The poem is soon to "go down" into the valley.) No note sounds lower than that A until the very last bass note of the piece—conspicuously not A but a possibly-Phrygian contra-E.

15. The Hindenlang quote appears in note 4.

Plate 9.1 R. Schumann, *Auf einer Burg.*

Plate 9.1 cont.

20
p
Drau - ßen ist es still und fried - lich, al - le sind ins
p
25
Tal ge - zo - gen, Wal - des - vö - gel ein - sam sin - gen in den lee - ren Fen - ster - bo - gen.
30
Ei - ne Hoch - zeit fährt da un - ten auf dem Rhein im Son - nen - schei - ne,
34
ritard.
Mu - si - kan - ten spie - len mun - ter, und die schö - ne Braut, die wei - net.
ritard.

PART IV

Wagner

"Amfortas's Prayer" was written as a birthday tribute for Joseph Kerman—from whom I learned a great deal about analyzing music drama of all kinds. It was published in *19th Century Music,* vol. 7, no. 3 (1984). Focusing on the third act prayer, the chapter engages other passages as well. It also addresses more general features of the music-drama, in particular the interrelation between two worlds in the story and two worlds in the music. One of the musical worlds pertains to scale degrees, the other pertains to the function-theories of Hugo Riemann. I suggest that a particular enharmonic seam in the musical fabric (between B natural and C flat) allows a listener to pass from one dramatic world to the other, as Parsifal is able to pass from Monsalvat (in Gothic Spain) to Klingsor's magic castle (in Moorish Spain) and back.

"Some Notes on Analyzing Wagner" was also published by *19th Century Music*, vol. 16, no. 1 (1992). It extrapolates Riemann's function theories into the more general sorts of transformational theories that I expounded in *Generalized Musical Intervals and Transformations* (New Haven, Conn.: Yale University Press, 1987). I try to show how such transformations can metaphorically or allegorically enact aspects of *The Ring* and *Parsifal.*

The chapter on *Tristan* was written for the present book. Francis Fergusson stresses the drama of passion that, to be sure, is the progressive aspect of the work. (Fergusson interestingly contrasts Wagner's drama with Racine's *Bérénice.*) But *Tristan* contains as well a drama of action, very much in the manner of Scribe (although Wagner no doubt imagined his model to be Schiller). The dramas of passion and action are enacted by two modes of musical organization, crudely identifiable as "atonal" and "tonal." Rather than trying to locate a critical *point d'appui* somewhere along the spectrum of action: passion::tonality:atonality, I attempt a more dialectic stance that allows full play to both modes of organization.

CHAPTER Ten

Amfortas's Prayer to Titurel and the Role of D in *Parsifal*

The Tonal Spaces of the Drama and the Enharmonic C♭/B

The section of the drama to which the title of this chapter refers is Act III, measures 933–993. This section begins with the change to a D-minor key signature and the first entrance of the new *Weihegruß* motive, as Titurel's coffin is opened and all break into a woeful cry. There follow, with some tonal substitutions we shall presently explore, two *Stollen* in D minor and an *Abgesang* in D major. The *Abgesang* turns back to D minor as it approaches the final cadence of the section, at measure 993. The cadential formula in the vocal part is especially conventional; the spectacularly deceptive cadence at "*Ruh*!" is all the more wrenching.

The musical Bar Form sets an equally formulaic prayer in the text:

Stollen: My father, . . . most blessed among heroes . . . thou purest one, . . . I gave thee death!
Stollen: O, as thou now . . . beholdest the Redeemer, entreat Him . . . to bestow death finally upon me.
Abgesang: Only this mercy! . . . I cry to thee; cry thou to Him: "Redeemer, grant rest to my son!"

The formulas of the prayer are in thrilling dramatic dissonance against the bizarre, well-nigh blasphemous, network of substitutional transformations it employs. The father has died for the sins of the son; following this, the sainted father, *Hochgesegneter der Helden*, is to assume the role of the Holy Mother, blessed among women; he is asked to intercede with the Redeemer for the sinner Amfortas, now and in the hour of his death.[1]

The symbolic substitutions in the spiritual drama interact with transformational substitutions in the tonal realm. Just as the father in the formulaic prayer is inflected substitutionally, first by the Holy Son who died for our sins and then by the Holy Mother who intercedes in our behalf, so is the D minor/major of the for-

1. Amfortas could still address the Redeemer directly in Act I, without such intercession. Wagner emphasizes the point by building Amfortas's first act aria to its climax precisely at the words: "*Du Allerbarmer! Ach, erbarmen!*" (I, 1393–1396).

mulaic Bar structure inflected substitutionally, first by the thorny D♯ minor of the first *Stollen* and then by the consoling D♭ major of the second *Stollen* and *Abgesang*. I do not want to push any harder the analogy of the chromatic keys with the members of the Holy Family. Mainly, I wish to draw attention just to the idea of transformational substitution in both text and music, substitution in each case within a highly formalized structure.

Example 10.1 clarifies both the substitutions and the classic formality of the music. One might even say "neoclassic": we could almost take this *Außensatz* as the plan for an aria by Gluck, if we ignore the chromatic substitutions and the harmonic activity of the inner voices.[2]

The numbered brackets on Example 10.1 indicate tonal substitutions other than interchanges of D minor with D major. Bracket 1 asserts that the D♯ minor of the music substitutes for the D minor of the example over measure 939. Bracket 2 again asserts the functioning of D♯ minor as a substitute for D minor, now in a more indirect way. Over measures 947–952, various Stufen of D♯ in the music substitute for the corresponding Stufen of D in the example. So, for example, the F♯-minor harmony in the music of measure 947 is a substitute for the F-major harmony of the example: altered III of D♯ minor for III of D minor. (The alteration, A♮ for A♯, reflects the persistent residual force of D-minor scale degrees.) Similarly, the G♯ harmony in the music of measure 949 is analyzed as IV of D♯ minor, substituting for the IV of D minor that appears in Example 10.1. The B-major chord of the music at measure 950 substitutes for the B♭-major chord of Example 10.1: VI of D♯ for VI of D. The substitutions of measures 951–952 are trickier, as the scale degrees of D minor intrude more and more into the music. Example 10.1 asserts the somewhat "modal" progression which I hear underlying the passages.

2. My reading of the Bar Form here differs from that proposed by Alfred Lorenz in his monumental study, *Das Geheimnis der Form bei Richard Wagner, Band IV: Der Musikalische Aufbau von Richard Wagner's "Parsifal"* (Berlin, 1933), 176. Lorenz extends the *Abgesang* of his Bar through the grisly cadence at measure 993, where the Prayer itself, as a set piece, ends. His Bar includes not only the D-minor Prayer proper, but also the highly chromatic (E-minor?) choral fragment that follows, *etwas beschleunigend,* during which the knights press ever closer in upon Amfortas with their nightmarish commands. Lorenz's Bar then continues yet farther, through the even more chromatic—virtually atonal—music of Amfortas's raging despair, during which he violently exposes his wound to the knights and frantically urges them to slay him, all *lebhaft*. Lorenz uses the word *Verzweiflung* to label the entire passage from the opening up of the coffin up to the entrance of Parsifal, though Wagner uses the word only in connection with the raging atonal music toward the end. (The word appears in the stage directions where the *lebhaft* music begins.) Obviously, I hear nothing of Lorenz's extended Bar Form. I am sympathetic to his difficulties in accommodating the *beschleunigend* and *lebhaft* passages within his theoretical model. Still, it is essential in my reading that the Prayer should close very strongly, as an internally coherent set piece, right at measure 993, where the prayer text ends. And it seems ruinous to suggest to the actor playing Amfortas that *Verzweiflung* should somehow dominate the tender, fantastic, and intimate pathos of the prayer itself. (Consider how one would light these sections of the drama!)

I have been critical of Lorenz here, and I shall again be critical later, whenever I find it important to contest his assertions. My critical attitude does not arise from a low opinion of his achievement. Lorenz was the first to provide solid critical ground for our intuitions that Wagner's mature music dramas are organic unities. Even more important, he was the first to sense and claim that these dramas could be analyzed in that connection. Any critic whose work still generates lively contention fifty years after its publication must have been doing something right!

Example 10.1

Stollen 1.
(Weihegruß)
Stollen 2.
(Engel)
(Liebesmahl)
(Durch Mitleid)
Abgesang.
(Mit-Leid)

The first *Stollen*, in sum, develops the musical idea of D♯ minor-for-D minor, along with the textual idea that Titurel has died in the place of Amfortas. *("Der einzig ich sterben wollt', dir gab ich den Tod!")* The second *Stollen* and the *Abgesang* develop the ideas of D♭ major-for-D minor and D♭ major-for-D major, along with the fantastic conceit that Titurel, a *Stellvertreter* for *a Stellvertreterin,* might substitute for the Holy Mother, interceding with the Redeemer on Amfortas's behalf. The musical idea of D♭ major-for-D major is "dual" to the idea of D♯ minor-for-D minor. There does not seem to be any analogous duality in the symbolic substitutions of the text.

Bracket 3 on Example 10.1 asserts D♭ major as a substitute for D minor around measure 959. The D♭ major *Engel* motive of measures 959–960 is "corrected" into D major at measures 962–964; thereby, one might consider analyzing D♭ major as a substitute for D major, not D minor. The substitution for D major will emerge later, in the *Abgesang*. It is indeed being prepared here; nevertheless, the analysis of Example 10.1, that is, the D-minor model for measures 958–961, predominates in my ear. That is not only because some D-minor scale degrees, especially F and C, persist over the music of those measures but also because the music projects a strong transformational relation between the D-minor *Weihegruß* motive and the D♭-major *Engel* motive. The *Weihegruß* of measures 933–935 recurs to open the second *Stollen* at measures 956–958, except that the fifth degree of D minor is changed at measure 958, in both the melody and the harmony, to the fifth degree of D♭ major. Then the rhythm and the bass arpeggiation of the *Weihegruß* recur again immediately at measures 959–960, but now the music is completely in D♭ and the melodic intervals of the *Weihegruß* are compressed into those of the *Engel* motive.[3]

Let me draw particular attention to the way in which Wagner prepares this first substitution of D♭ for D within the Prayer. He does not simply state D♭ major with the entrance of the *Engel* motive itself, at measure 959. Rather, he prepares D♭-for-D-as-tonic, by using A♭-for-A-as-dominant in measure 958. We have already noted the transitional variant of the *Weihegruß* to which this gives rise. The idea of A♭-for-A-as-dominant will become progressively more significant as we approach the end of the opera.

The potency of the idea is already manifest in the events connected with bracket 4 on Example 10.1. Starting at the D major of measure 962, the music moves back toward D minor, searching for a cadence in that key. Measures 965½–967½

3. Lorenz draws special attention to this motivic transformation *(Parsifal*, 176). He does not discuss the implications of the tonal substitution, D♭-for-D. With reluctance, I forego discussing the connections between the rising half-step sequence of the *Engel* motive here, and its earlier such sequences in the drama. In general, I shall have to forego such discussions except where they impinge directly upon my announced topics. The *Weihegruß* is related not only to the *Engel* motive but also to the *Liebesmahl.* For instance, the melody of measures 942–943½ retrogrades exactly the first six notes of the (transposed) *Liebesmahl.* Despite the transposition and reharmonization, one recognizes the expanding series of falling diatonic intervals here, retrograding the contracting series of rising intervals that characterizes the beginning of the *Liebesmahl* as a sort of scenario-like source-motive: M3, m3, (M?!)tone, (m?!)tone, semitone. The metaphoric logic of the retrograde relation is clear enough. Amfortas is "pushing back" his obligation to conduct the service.

elaborate the cadence-seeking F–E gesture in the melody.[4] A half-cadence on the "dominant of D" is finally attained at measure 969, according to Example 10.1. Still according to the figure, this "dominant" is then prolonged, together with the "E" of the F–E gesture; then at measure 972½ the entire F–E gesture recurs in the melody, now with a "dominant" bass at measure 973½. Following that, there is yet another half-cadence in D minor at measures 974–976, with the cadence-seeking E in the top voice. All very clear, except that the actual music under bracket 4 appears in A♭, substituting for the "dominant of D." Once again, the substitution A♭-for-A-as-dominant appears. And now its structural weightiness is quite apparent. For the A♭ music at measures 969–970 presents the *Liebesmahl* motive itself in its original key, that is, the *Hauptmotif* of the entire music drama. And this is not all; the last half-cadence just discussed, back in D minor again at measures 975–976, clearly refers to the beginning of the *Thorenspruch* motive, specifically to the pedal A-as-dominant that summons the *Thorenspruch*, together with the harmony that launches the *Thorenspruch* on the text word "*Mitleid*" of that motive. It is appropriate that the music of measure 975, essentially repeated at measure 976, sets the repeated word "*Tod!*" in the text: Amfortas, longing throughout the D-minor Prayer for death to put him out of his misery, had already come to believe in Act I that the promised savior of the *Thorenspruch* was none other than Death himself.

At this point, it will be useful to consider some broad and abstract structural implications of the tonal relations we have just been discussing. Wagner has informed us, via bracket 4, that the A♭that substitutes for A-as-dominant is in fact the very A♭ that is the tonic key of the drama. When this A♭ appears in a dominant role, it suggests tonicizing a subdominant D♭ from which one might build a final plagal cadence for the opera. But, since A♭-as-dominant is a substitute for A-as-dominant, since it inflects D♭ only as a substitute for D-as-local-tonic, the abstract possibility arises that D itself might serve as a functional (substitute) subdominant, so that the alternative plagal cadence might proceed from D-for-D♭ to A♭-as-tonic. And, in fact, the idea that we are awaiting D as the structural key for an ultimate cadence is supported by the structure of the *Thorenspruch*. That motive begins over a sustained dominant of D and tells us to await something. We can presume the "something" in question to involve a tonicized D. Indeed, the extended *Thorenspruch*, extended to include the text "*harre sein, den ich erkor,*" does cadence in D, although it does not tell us just who the *reine Thor* is to be.[5] Later on in this

4. The F–E gesture arises locally from measures 936–937. The harmony of measures 965½–967½ reminds us that the melodic gesture was embedded in the motives of *Öde* (III, 1–2) and *Waffenschmuck* (the transformation of Parsifal's horn call, at III, 169–171, that directly precedes his third act entrance).

5. Over Act I, the *Thorenspruch* music occurs only in D, introduced by a sustained A dominant, right up until the end of the Grail scene. The motive occurs in this way four times. It first appears at measures 177–182, where Gurnemanz opines, "Thoren wir, auf Lind'rung zu hoffen, wo einzig Heilung lindert!" The words are prophetic of the events at the end of the third act. The musical play on "Heilung lindert" and "Herzeleide" is nice. The next *Thorenspruch* occurs at I, 318–327, where we learn the text, up through "der reine Thor." Amfortas diffracts and tropes both the music and the text; he says he

chapter we shall see how these abstract ideas are worked out concretely at the close of the music-drama itself.

Bracket 5 on Example 10.1 analyzes the D♭-major music at the opening of the *Abgesang* as a substitute for the D-major music we expect here, the music that finally does come at measures 986 and following, prepared at measures 983–985 by the return of the cadence-seeking melodic F–E over A-as-dominant. A fine touch at measure 978 is the reversal of the F–E gesture to E–F, caused by the slippage from D major to D♭. As before, the D♭ tonic substitution is prepared here by a preliminary substitution of A♭ for A-as-dominant.

Wagner's use of the major mode to portray the most sublime extremity of pathos is especially in the spirit of Gluck. One can hardly take *sehr langsam* slowly enough. Along with Wolzogen and against Lorenz, I take the new theme of the *Abgesang* to be derived from the *2. Herzeleide* or *Liebesweh* motive. The correspondences of rhythm and contour are decisive. (The earlier motive has also become associated with an extreme slowdown to *sehr langsam,* around II, 947–950.) Amfortas has killed his father as Parsifal has killed his mother (II, 923–926). The motivic association reminds us that Amfortas, along with everybody else, never mentions his mother. We have already noted how, during the Prayer, he deputizes his father to assume a maternal role.

The tonal double-take of the *Abgesang*, presenting new thematic material first in D♭-for-D and then in D itself, is prepared by the analogous presentation of the *Engel* motive toward the beginning of the second *Stollen*. In the second *Stollen*, D♭ major and its dominant were analyzed as substitutes for D minor and its dominant; in the *Abgesang*, D♭ major substitutes for the expected (Gluckian) D major.

Beyond the five brackets on Example 10.1, I have also labeled the cadential Mystic Chord of measure 993 with a numeral: 6. Although I do not pretend to assert an exact event in D for which this chord substitutes, I do hear it clearly as part of a "five-flat" world that enjoys a kinship with the substitutional D♭ major. The kinship functions because we are familiar with D♭ as a substitute region, and the chord of measure 993 is obviously a substitute chord. If we want to, we can find the same pitch-class configuration within the D♭ region of the Prayer, underlying for instance all of measure 979 ("*einz'ge Gnade*"), or at the attack of the second quarter in measure 981. But I would not make too much of this: at measure 993,

has come to believe that the promised savior is Death. As we have noted, this belief underlies the D-minor tonicity of Amfortas's Prayer in Act III, where he pleads for death (especially in mm. 975–976, on the word "*Tod!*" over the opening *Thorenspruch* chord). The third *Thorenspruch* in Act I occurs at measures 727–735; Gurnemanz is reporting the story of its origin. Text and music are here extended for the first time, through "den ich erkor." The squires echo the first half of the *Thorenspruch;* this is the first choral music in the opera. The fourth *Thorenspruch* occurs at measures 1404–1411; here, the invisible boys' choir sings the extended music and text, as Amfortas sinks back in a faint after finishing his rant. I am not sure what is supposed to be going on here. Presumably the invisible chorus is inside Amfortas's head; but the music is also audible to the knights on stage, who comment upon it. If they are hearing it miraculously, they seem awfully calm about the miracle. Only during the last thirty-one measures of Act I does the *Thorenspruch* appear in keys other than D. During this brief span, it appears in A, in C♯, and several times in B. These peripatetic tonal wanderings fit the dramatic situation: both Parsifal and Gurnemanz significantly misapprehend the situation at hand. The upshot is that we are all the more convinced of D as the "correct" key for the *Thorenspruch.*

the focus of stage activity flashes back to the knights, away from Amfortas, so we are bound to take in the sonority to a large extent as pertaining to the B♭-minor funeral world of the knights, only indirectly related to Amfortas's private D♭ fantasy.[6]

This concludes our survey of the annotations on Example 10.1. Let us review it briefly. Brackets 1 and 2 show how D♯ minor is used as a substitute for D minor during parts of the first *Stollen*. The substitution prepares the later dual substitution of D♭ major for D major in the *Abgesang* (at bracket 5). Because of the dual relationship, the D♭-for-D major substitution, when it occurs at the beginning of the *Abgesang*, is felt to be balancing and compensating, hence, more weighty and cadential than it would be without the dual foreshadowing. During the second *Stollen*, an intermediate substitution is given rein: D♭ major for D minor (brackets 3 and 4). An important aspect of this substitution is the concomitant substitution of A♭ for A-as-dominant (at m. 958 and during bracket 4; later also approaching the opening of the *Abgesang*): Wagner identifies A♭ in this connection as the *Liebesmahl* A♭, the tonic of the opera. Furthermore, he identifies A in this connection as the dominant that summons the *Thorenspruch*. The abstract implication of these identifications is that A♭-or A-as-dominant will summon a tonicized D♭-or-D, fulfilling the prophecy of the *Thorenspruch;* at that point, the subdominant D♭-or-D can cadence plagally into A♭-as-tonic (*Liebesmahl*), and the opera can end with the communion service itself. Amfortas believes that the obligatory D♭-or-D is his own death, for which he pleads eloquently during the Prayer and the subsequent *Verzweiflung*. But the knights know better, as the deceptive cadence of measure 993 tells us, denying Amfortas his D cadence with a gruesome shock. For if Amfortas dies, cadentially tonicizing D♭-or-D, who will be left to uncover the Grail, that is, to execute the obligatory plagal cadence from D♭-or-D to A♭-as-tonic?

Of course, we know the solution to this problem. It is Parsifal, the *reine Thor* of the prophecy, who is to take on himself the indicated subdominant weight of D-or-D♭, just as he takes Amfortas's office on himself; in that capacity he will perform the plagal cadence and uncover the Grail. This is the point of the tonal plan for III, 1030–1088. A major, to become dominant of D, underlies the events of measures 1030–1056, from Parsifal's appearance to the change of key signature at measure 1057, where the Parsifal motive is stated broadly in D major as Parsifal takes command of the stage. The curing of Amfortas's wound is "thrown away" on the stage, during the A-major passage. Our analysis shows us the logic here: it is not the pain of the physical wound that Amfortas finds unbearable, and it is not the healing of the wound that the drama makes obligatory. Rather, it is Amfortas's inability to perform his office that he finds unbearable, and it is the relieving of Amfortas from that duty that is the obligatory event. So the healing of the physical wound is underplayed on stage during the A-major music; then Parsifal explains: "Be healed and absolved, *for I shall now administer thy office.*" The future-tense nuance is important, according to my reading; the Schirmer translation ("I do hold

6. The similar sonorities earlier in the act, at III, 777 and III, 795ff., would no doubt reward study in this connection. III, 795ff., like sonority 6 of Example 10.1, leads to an entrance of the *Glockenlaute* figure. Both the earlier sonorities, like sonority 6 of the example, intrude upon a locally very stable D tonic. The earlier D tonic is the tonality at the end of the Good Friday music; the sonorities certainly have to do with the approach of the funeral procession.

thy Office now") is inadequate. The "office" is not a static *position* of royalty; it is, rather, *a performance*, that is, unveiling the Grail and conducting the service. Parsifal, while speaking these words, is not yet performing the office; he begins to perform it precisely at measure 1057, where A major yields as dominant to D major, where Parsifal takes over the stage from Amfortas, displaying the Spear, the emblem of office that legitimizes his authority. This is the obligatory "subdominant" beat, the long-awaited D of the *Thorenspruch;* once it has arrived the music can move "plagally" to a final tonic A♭, in which the *Liebesmahl* service can be performed correctly once more. The A major of measures. 1030–1056 is the familiar dominant preparation for the D-as-D♭ of measure 1057.

The idea that the D-major beat of measure 1057 fulfills the *Thorenspruch is* made clear by the six preceding measures of stretto on the *Thorenspruch Kopf*. We have heard this stretto before. A more extended version led to Parsifal's coronation earlier in the act; there, the stretto led to a similar triumphant display of the Parsifal theme, then in B major as Parsifal reached an important preliminary goal in fulfilling the prophecy. The way to D often leads through B in this drama.[7] The D major of measures 1057 and following reminds us, too, that Parsifal first seized control of the spear, toward the end of the second act, in D major. (And that D came out of the B *ambiance* in Klingsor's realm.)

Following the big D-major wash at III, 1057–1060, the harmony roves chromatically, not approaching a cadence until measures 1080–1081 ("*Grales Welle*"). The preceding two measures indicate that this cadence "should" be in A minor, landing on an A-minor $^{6}_{4}$ chord at the bar line of measure 1080. Instead, A♭ major substitutes for A minor. The substitution is the "dominant" version of the D♭ major-for-D minor substitution encountered during the second *Stollen* of Amfortas's Prayer. The A and A♭ tonalities here are then to be taken as dominants. And, indeed, the cadential A♭ harmony of measure 1081 is stated as a dominant ninth chord. (It has the Mystic Chord from m. 993 over an A♭ bass.) Not only is the A♭ chord a dominant, it is a highly thematic dominant, specifically the dominant that introduces the *Thorenspruch*. So A♭-as-*Thorenspruch-dominant* substitutes for A-as-*Thorenspruch-dominant,* all according to the abstract network of ideas discussed earlier.

Thus, when the music reaches the "D-major" chord of the transposed *Thorenspruch* motive, three measures later, we do not hear that harmony only, or even primarily, as an E𝄫 Neapolitan of a tonic D♭. Rather, the harmony is also, and primarily, a restoration on a larger scale of a *real* D major, restored from the substitute D♭. We know that the *Thorenspruch* is fulfilled by D, not D♭. From this chord in measure 1084, a chain of *Liebesmahl* incipits leads directly to the tonic A♭ downbeat four measures later. The stage action concomitant with this obligatory structural D-to-A♭ progression is the obligatory structural gesture of the opera: Parsifal, firmly in command of the office, discharges his foreordained duty by directing the unveiling of the Grail.

7. Or is it to E𝄫 through C♭? And if so, how can E𝄫, as altered fifth degree of A♭, major, have a "plagal" function? I shall discuss the C♭/B enharmony and the methodological problems of substitute degrees and substitute functions later at length.

I am puzzled by the harmonies of measures 1084–1087, the measures that span this D-to-A♭ progression. Why should the huge A♭ arrival, so strongly plagal on a large scale, be approached locally from its dominant, E♭ in measure 1087? And why should that E♭ be preceded by its own dominant in measure 1086? I am not sure exactly what Wagner had in mind here, but two considerations seem to the point.

First, in performing his office, Parsifal is performing the function last carried out correctly by Titurel, and Titurel directs the unveiling of the Grail from a dominant vantage point. He sings over a tonicized E♭ pedal at I, 1246–1258 ("*Mein Sohn* . . ."); he sings a cadence in E♭ at I, 1417–1418 (*den Gral!*"); and this generates an E♭ pedal that leads directly to the unveiling itself. So Parsifal in Act III, singing "*Enthüllet den Gral, offnet den Schrein!*" approaches A♭ locally from E♭ harmony with a certain consistency. Perhaps E♭ is the key that unlocks the shrine?

The second, and related, consideration is this: the chain of *Liebesmahl* incipits that act as *Leitmotiven* over measures 1084–1087, leading the music and, hence, the harmony from D to A♭, does not constitute a new motivic idea. Rather, it arises transformationally from a similar motivic chain that closed the first act Prelude over an E♭ dominant pedal. Example 10.2 shows the transformational relation.

Example 10.2

As Example 10.2b shows, the harmony of III, 1084–1087 is to a large extent determined by the triadic structure of the *Leitmotif* succession. And as the relation of Example 10.2b to Example 10.2a shows, the *Leitmotif* succession in III, 1085–1087 is rigorously derived from that of I, 106–109 by the following rules: substitute D for D♭; substitute A for A♭; omit the D♭ of I, 108–109. The first two of these rules should be familiar to us by now! In particular, they result in the substitution of a D-minor triad outline, at III, 1085, for the D♭-major triad outline at I, 106. It is perhaps relevant that the D♭ and B♭ triads of Example 10.2a are arpeggiated over an E♭ pedal, and so cannot realize their plagal harmonic potential; in contrast, the D-major, D-minor, and B♭ triads of Example 10.2b are free of any dominant pedal, and so have the potential to project any plagal function they may be carrying. (This must be phrased very carefully.) We have already noted that III, 1084 is approached, both locally and on a large scale, as a strongly plagal event.

Still, it is hard to override the more natural reading one constructs from the four measures of Example 10.2b in their own context, along with the tonic A♭: in the context of these measures alone, D major is major of D minor, D minor is *Leittonwechselklang* of B♭ major, and B♭ major is dominant of E♭, which in turn is dominant of the tonic A♭. Lorenz certainly hears this natural reading. Indeed, he appears to infer from it that the mass of D-minor events from Amfortas's Prayer on function in the large just as III, 1085 does in the small, as *Leittonwechsel* for the dominant of the dominant. Thence he infers a large-scale progression governing the second half of Act III, comprising the B♭-minor funeral music, the D-minor "*Verzweiflung*," and the A♭-major tonic. He analyzes this progression as S_p, (Đ) [D], T. So his D minor plays a large structural role as a (dominant of the) dominant, not as a (substitute) subdominant.[8] This reading does extreme violence to all the plagal features of the large-scale D; it surely goes too far. Besides, his progression is abstractly bizarre: his (Đ) [D] tonicizes a large-scale E♭ that never appears, unless Lorenz means the solitary E♭ harmony of Example 10.2b to carry the structural dominant weight for the entire second half of Act III.

But, just as Lorenz's dominant reading for D minor goes too far as a large-scale phenomenon, so my plagal reading of III, 1084–1086 goes too far as a local reading, insofar as it denies *any* force to the obvious local reading (Đ$^{+}$Đ D) [D]; T. Still, I think the plagal local reading needs to be suggested and investigated, if only because the more "natural" local reading makes the music sound so unbearably banal. It seems more legitimate to attempt inferring a local reading from a large-scale one, as I am doing here, than to attempt an inference in the reverse direction, as Lorenz appears to have done.

One further word of caution is in order. While Example 10.2 may legitimately be used to help us entertain the plagal local reading, the example cannot be used to "prove" the "correctness" of that reading. One cannot legitimately infer from an isomorphism in motivic scale-step function (as between Examples 10.2a and 10.2b) an isomorphism in harmonic Riemann function. Later in this chapter I shall devote considerable attention to the point.

Whatever the meanings of the local dominant functions at III, 1086–1087 (and I do not claim to have fathomed them fully), it is clear that once past the tonic A♭ downbeat, we are in a paradise of plagal luxury. A few of the events deserve special commentary in the context of this essay. The A♭ cadence of measures 1092–1094 is answered by the texturally parallel D♭-to-A♭ cadence of measures 1100–1102; the resulting I V / IV I progression is itself, on a larger scale, a "plagal" version of the more familiar "authentic" I IV / V I formula. This brings us harmonically to measure 1106, where the *Thorenspruch* music commences yet once more with A♭-as-dominant. And once more the music breaks off on the D-major harmony, locally a Neapolitan but globally a restored substitute for D♭.

At last the awesome plagal potential of D major is fully unleashed, as the music moves halfway around the circle of fifths in an unbroken chain of plagal cadences all the way from D to A♭. B is notated, along the way, as enharmonically equivalent to C♭. The timbres of the voices, and their spatial placement in the theater, ascend steadily along with the ascending fifths that connect adjacent keys in the plagal chain. The penultimate key in that chain, D♭, is prolonged and elaborated; as a result, the approach to A♭ at the curtain close is locally as well as structurally heavily plagal.

8. *Parsifal*, 182.

We can reflect the plagal power of D major here by labeling its function as (S(S(S(S(S(S)))))). After all, that is precisely what we hear. Expressed in this way, the function of D major as a superamplification of "S" becomes manifest and vivid.

Lorenz insists emphatically that the enharmonic shift from B to C♭ is purely notational in this chain, that we ought to hear D major for what it "really" is, E♭♭, the better to appreciate the ride around the circle of fifths.[9] In a certain sense, he has an obvious point. But he misses an analytic component of the situation, and he courts a theoretical danger. The analytic component is the highly thematic character of the enharmony B/C♭ in the music drama as a whole.[10] The theoretical danger involves the uses and misuses of Riemann theory, particularly as it interacts with Stufen theories. The theoretical problems here are central to Wagner study and of intrinsic interest, so I shall examine them at some length.

We can start by observing that the function (S(S(S(S(S(S)))))) does indeed make the harmony of measure 1109 come out as E♭♭, if we count five scale degrees per "S," back from the eventual tonic A♭. To bolster Lorenz's point even more, we can observe that the harmony of measure 1109, even if functioning globally as a substitute for D♭, surely functions locally as a Neapolitan of D♭, and this makes it again E♭♭. Now, since we locally approach the harmony at issue, from the tonic A♭, as an E♭♭ harmony, and since we locally return from it, to the tonic A♭, still as an E♭♭ harmony, then why not just *call* it an E♭♭ harmony? Why keep insisting that it is a D harmony?

A provisional answer is, because D clearly has a strong global plagal function here, in which it substitutes for D♭, the paradigmatic subdominant of A♭. Hence, the harmony at issue should receive the same letter name as D♭, rather than the same letter name as E♭. But, one might respond, why should it receive a letter name *at all*? And this gets to the heart of the issue.

9. *Parsifal*, 180.

10. It underlies the function of the second act, as we shall see later. An interesting manifestation of the enharmony on a local scale is the music of I, 147–160, where Gurnemanz prods the dramatic action out of its A♭ lethargy for the first time after the curtain rises, getting it "Jetzt auf!" Obviously the "B-major" key of measures 147–150 is purely notational, that is, "really" C♭ major. But "Heil euch!" at measure 158 is equally obviously sung on C and A♭, not on D♭♭ and B♭♭; we can certainly remember where C and A♭ are, after hearing the music of the drama so far. The harmony of "Heil!" *is* prepared by its dominant, which is therefore a dominant of C (not of D♭♭). And the high and low C♭s of the vocal line that begin the passage are clearly the same pitches as the high and low B♮s of the vocal line later on, within the dominant-of-C harmony. So there is a real enharmonic shift within the passage. It is significant that this is our *first* move away from A♭, and that it takes us to and through the enharmonic C♭/B. I would put the moment of shift at "*Zeit ist's*." The specific augmented triad here suggests Klingsor's realm, and so does the locution. (Cf. "Die Zeit ist da.") Without this enharmonic shift (N.B.), the first *Thorenspruch* music of the drama (mm. 177–182) would come out in E♭♭, not D! This state of affairs is also thematic, and bound to the C♭/B enharmony. Abstractly, if we get to C♭ and then rise a minor third, we will land at E♭♭ unless C♭ has undergone the thematic enharmonic shift to B; in that case, we will end up on D. The ramifications of that abstract idea will be examined in depth later on. They have a great deal to do with the "plagal D" of Act III, particularly as it involves the Spear.

For the great virtue and power of Riemann function theory, which is also the source of its problems and difficulties, is precisely its ability to avoid assigning letter names (i.e., implicit scale-degree functions) to its objects. Let us consider the chord of III, 1109 from this point of view. As a global substitute for the pure subdominant its function can be expressed by "♯S." Approached locally as the Neapolitan of the same subdominant, its function is °$\mathcal{S}$(S). Left locally via six plagal cadences into the tonic, its function is (S(S(S(S(S(S)))))). Now all of these various contextual functions demonstrate various aspects of the chord's S-ishness. In none of these contexts does the chord have anything the least bit T-ish or D-ish about it. However, when we assign the chord the letter name E♭♭ (and not D), it is hard to avoid the implication that the chord executes certain tonal functions we conventionally associate with the fifth, and not the fourth, degree of A♭. But that implication is not accurate. Or more precisely, I believe the implication to be inaccurate as regards the particular harmonic event under examination. Hence, I want to avoid the danger of even suggesting such an implication. I do not feel that it is so dangerous to label with a fourth-degree letter name an event I hear with powerful subdominant Riemann function(s). But strictly speaking, that is a matter of convention. One might ask why we should necessarily identify subdominant Riemann function *a priori* with fourth-degree scale function, and I for one do not believe there is a good answer to that question in the abstract. I would only argue that analytic discourse becomes awkward if we do not attach letter-name labels to harmonies in a piece we are discussing, that it is hard to avoid implicity asserting degree functions when we use the letter names, and that in referring to an event which lies one, two, or six "S-stages" from a Riemann "T" in various of its contextual relationships, we court less implicit danger if we conventionally use a fourth-degree letter name than we would if we used a fifth-degree letter name.

The danger, if we strictly identify Riemannian Ds and Ss with motions through four or five measured scale degrees, is that we can end up with glaringly false "logical syllogisms." For example: as (S(S(S(S(S(S)))))), the harmony "is" E♭♭; but E♭♭ represents the fifth scale degree of the tonic A♭; "therefore" E♭♭ has some sort of Riemannian D-function; and "therefore" six plagal cadences piled consecutively one on another execute a "dominant" function. Or: as °$\mathcal{S}$(S), the Neapolitan of the subdominant, the harmony "is" E♭♭; but E♭♭ (etc.); "therefore" the Neapolitan of the subdominant has a dominant effect.

The false syllogisms demonstrate an important theoretical point. The nature and logic of Riemannian tonal space are not isomorphic with the nature and logic of scale-degree space. The musical objects and relations that Riemann isolates and discusses are not simply the old objects and relations dressed up in new packages with new labels; they are essentially different objects and relations, embedded in an essentially different geometry. That is so even if in some contexts the two spaces may coexist locally without apparent conflict; in this way the surface of a Mobius strip would locally resemble the surface of a cylinder to an ant who had not fully explored the global logic of the space.

Though we may be prepared to take this point in intellectually, we must still work to appreciate fully the extent to which it impinges upon our immediate perceptual experience in listening to Wagner. It is indeed the basis for many of his best conjuring tricks.

Example 10.3

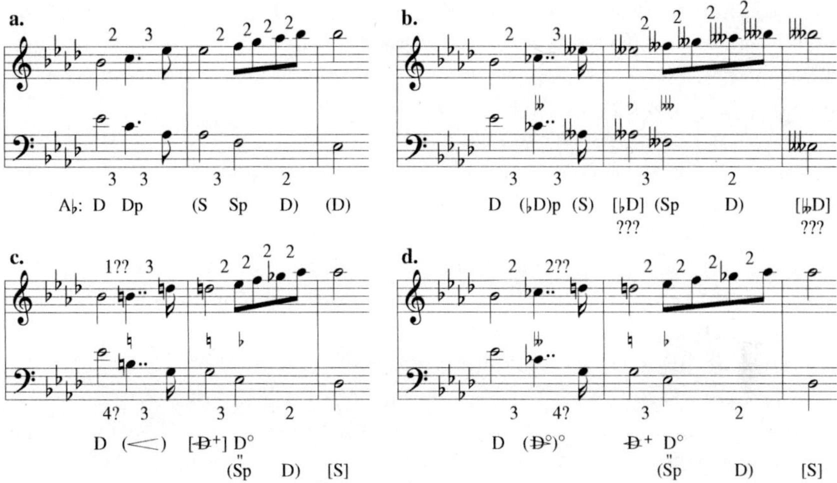

Consider Example 10.3a, a schematic representation of the Grail motive prolonging a dominant function in A♭ major. Scalar distances are written as numerals between notes of the outer voices: "2" means some species of second; "3" means some species of third; etc. Beneath Example 10.3a, a legitimate Riemann analysis appears.

Example 10.3b displays a chromatic transformation of Example 10.3a, spelled so as to preserve all the scalar distances of Example 10.3a. The Riemann analysis beneath Example 10.3b attempts to follow the resulting degree relationships along, so as to accommodate itself isomorphically to the Riemann analysis of Example 10.3a. Thus, the third harmony of Example 10.3b, for instance, is analyzed as some species of A harmony, accordingly in an S-relation to the opening E♭ harmony, just as the third harmony of Example 10.3a was in an S-relation to the first harmony of Example 10.3a. But this analysis is clearly untenable. We hear too strongly that the "A♭♭" of the third harmony, in Example 10.3b, is the same pitch-class as the G that appeared as the third of the opening triad. Hence, the third harmony *prolongs* the (function of the) first harmony; it is not a subdominant for it. Likewise, given the overriding A♭ tonality, there is no way we can hear the final chord of Example 10.3b as projecting a *dominant* function in A♭, prolonging the function of the opening harmony. Rather, we must hear the final chord as the subdominant of A♭, and the music of Example 10.3b overall as in motion from D to S functions.

Example 10.3c re-spells Example 10.3b with Wagner's spelling. The passage is III, 1098–1099, which is where the Grail begins to shine; it is the "modulation" from V to IV within the large plagal formula I V / IV I, which we discussed earlier. The Riemann analysis beneath Example 10.3c clearly does justice to the essence of the passage *as we perceive it in Riemann space*: the passage as a whole begins by prolonging the opening D-function; the passage then pivots on the fourth harmony and moves on to tonicize the closing S-function. The analysis recognizes the D-function of the pivotal fourth harmony, a triad involving the same root and fifth as the opening D-function harmony. The Riemann analysis of Example 10.3b was oblivious to that aspect of the progression. On the other hand, in order to do minimal justice to the passage as an object of Riemann space, the analysis of Example 10.3c must do violence to the passage as an object in motivic Stufen space: the degree distances between the outer voices of the opening two chords are changed.

Example 10.3d is an alternate reading of the passage, re-spelling the second chord enharmonically. Its Riemann analysis portrays more effectively than Example 10.3c the aural connection between the second and the fourth harmonies, and the functional proportion: harmony 4 is to harmony 3 as harmony 2 is to harmony 1. Like Example 10.3c, 10.3d does justice to the passage as an object in Riemann space, and like Example 10.3c it thereby does violence to the passage as an object in motivic Stufen space.

Now, all this is not to say that the intervallic structure of Example 10.3b is "wrong." On the contrary, it is absolutely right as concerns the musical object in Stufen space; its correctness in that space is what makes the magic trick come off. In that space, the final harmony is indeed on E♭♭♭. What *is* "wrong" is to infer, from the letter name in Stufen space, an isomorphically determined function in Riemann space, as in the erroneous Riemann analysis for Example 10.3b. The E♭♭♭ chord does *not* have a dominant function. Indeed, strictly speaking, the E♭♭♭ chord does not have a subdominant function either. It simply *does not exist as an object in Riemann space*, although it does in Stufen space. If we imagine pressing together between our fingers a section of a Mobius strip and a section of a cylindrical loop, then the E♭♭♭ chord can be imagined metaphorically on some part of the loop that diverges from the strip, and the subdominant function can be imagined on some part of the strip that diverges from the loop, as an imagined opaque projector shines the actual music to project upon both the loop and the strip.

The illusion that the E♭♭♭ chord has a subdominant function, while also reflecting the persistence of the fifth degree we can associate with the opening dominant function of the passage, is exactly the illusion on which Wagner's magic relies; it depends on our willingness to suppose an isomorphism of Riemann space with degree space. From this illusion, we infer that we have heard a dominant triad become a subdominant triad before our very ears. And there are plenty of critics to supply us with mystic effusions and vulgar profundities, to argue a Brummagem sublimity for the sleight-of-hand.

Other critics, on hearing the middleground inconsistency within Stufen space, become hostile; they infer, from Wagner's fondness for magic tricks, that his entire craft is naught but shoddy Kitsch. But that sort of critique equally fails to do justice to the passage at hand. There is in fact no enharmonic relation between the E♭♭♭ triad of Example 10.3b and the D♭ triad of Example 10.3c–d. The former triad exists only in Stufen space; the latter exists only in Riemann space (so far as the context of the example itself is concerned).

There is to be sure a functional enharmonic relation on which the trick relies, but it is not the relation of E♭♭♭ with D♭. It is, rather, the enharmonic equivalence of C♭ with B. Example 10.3c and 10.3d make this clear. The functional enharmonic shift occurs either just before or just after the second chord of the passage. Our ears have started to follow the Grail motive in Stufen space, as in Example 10.3b. But by the third or fourth harmony, and certainly by the final harmony, we realize that we are perceiving *another object*, an object in Riemann space. We move from one space to another, in our perception, without being fully aware that we have done so until some time after. Reconstructing the passage as an object of Riemann space, after it is over, we find the necessary enharmonic shift to have occurred around (or before or after) the C♭/B harmony. Since the two musical spaces do not conform isomorphically over this passage, there must be a flaw, a splice, a hidden seam, to create the impression that they do. This flaw, this splice or hidden seam, is the enharmonic shift from C♭ to B. It enables us to slide smoothly from one space to the other under the illusion of isomorphic continuity.

As I pointed out earlier, the enharmonic identification of C♭ with B is *thematic* in the drama, and it is thematic in precisely this way. That is, we recognize it as a topographical or geological feature of the spaces in which the music moves, a fault in the terrain through which we can move from Stufen space to Riemann space and back. Very frequently, we encounter the enharmony embedded in a melodic or harmonic augmented-triad complex: E♭–C♭/B–G. Such is the case in the passage just examined (Examples 10.3c–d). Such, too, was the case with the enharmonic C♭/B at "*Zeit ist's*" in Act I (m. 151), discussed in note 10. Klingsor's music is saturated with that augmented-triad complex. The music of Examples 10.3c–d recalls Klingsor and the events of Act II in moving from E♭ to C♭/B to G (and back to E♭) harmonies.

Indeed, Klingsor's magic C♭/B castle is itself an embodiment of the geographical metaphor. It is a "flaw," a "splice," a "hidden seam." It is a "topographical . . . feature of the spaces in which the music moves," "a fault in the terrain through which we can move" from one space of the drama to another and back. The castle is on the border between the Gothic, diatonic Stufen world of Monsalvat, Act I, and the Arabian, chromatic, Riemann-transformational world of magic and miracle. In the diatonic Stufen space of the Grail brotherhood in Act I, we do not go wrong if we measure topography by scale degrees. But the magic and miracle of things has been lost; we know it only in story (Gurnemanz) and as a residual trauma (Kundry, Amfortas). In this Stufen-world, things are exactly as they seem, for all the miracles have been expropriated by the forces of evil. Only by voyaging to and through the magic C♭/B castle, the seam that permits an interface with the other world, can Parsifal ultimately repatriate the miraculous for the forces of good, returning with the Spear.

And the Spear brings us back again to the role of D, the miraculous plagal D that enables Parsifal, wielding the Spear at the end of Act III, to relieve Amfortas of his office and open the shrine, cadencing into A♭; the miraculous D with which Parsifal repossesses the Spear from Klingsor at the end of Act II, the "plagal D" that launched us into this lengthy theoretical excursion.[11] The excursion, in fact, now allows us to analyze very carefully the large-scale magic trick that makes the "pla-

11. The "plagal Spear" figures a good deal in Act I, but there it is only Stufen-plagal, not miracle-plagal. I mean it is associated mainly with D♭ and D♭ major, not with D and D major. Indeed, when the *Speer* motive first appears within the opening *Liebesmahl* of the opera, it points firmly in measure 4 at the fresh tone D♭, a D♭ that replaces the D♮ we heard within the C-minor *Schmerzensfigur* a measure

gal D" work. We progress in Stufen space from the A♭ major of Act I to the C♭ tonality that opens Act II; this C♭ represents the normal minor third of A♭ in Stufen space. But then, during Act II, C♭ undergoes the thematic-enharmonic transformation to B, Klingsor's castle acting as the topographic interface just discussed. I think one can even locate the exact moment at which the enharmonic shift occurs: the moment of the kiss. Once the enharmonic shift has occurred, Parsifal can seize the Spear in D major, the third of B minor. In passing through the enharmonic splice C♭/B, we have lost one degree of A♭, just as we lost a degree in Examples 10.3c–d, traversing the same splice. So when we return to Stufen space in Act III, we find that the Spear's D major in fact represents a fourth degree, not a fifth degree, of A♭, despite the fact that we traversed two rising minor third progressions to get to that D major. In Examples 10.3c–d, we traversed two falling thirds in the root-progression E♭–C♭/B–G, and we found we had fallen a sixth instead of a fifth; just so the large-scale progressions now under discussion, A♭–C♭/B–D, rises two thirds and finds itself having risen a fourth, not a fifth. In each case, the breakdown in the logic of Stufen geometry occurs because of a transition through the thematic enharmonic splice C♭/B, the flaw that allows Stufen space to communicate effectively with Riemann function space.

We have noted that the relation E♭–C♭/B–G is often manifest in the drama. So, of course, is the relation of A♭–C♭/B–D. We have just discussed one of its very large-scale manifestations. In that manifestation, we are quite sure that the enharmonic shift actually occurs in Act II, so that we hear B–D and not C♭–E𝄫 thereafter. That is confirmed in Act III by the coronation in B, the motion from B to D during the Good Friday music, and the mass of "plagal D" events, including the return of the *Thorenspruch* stretto from the B-major coronation scene, to prepare Parsifal's big D-major takeover just before the final unveiling of the Grail. The D minor/major of Amfortas's Prayer is heard in this larger context.

Example 10.4

In some of the early manifestations of the formula A♭–C♭/B–D, it is not so clear that an enharmonic shift actually occurs; we can indeed hear C♭–E𝄫. This is a possibility before we have made the trip through Klingsor's castle. For example, consider the treatment of the Faith motive as it is introduced in the first act Prelude. Example 10.4 schematizes aspects of I, 45–55; a quarter note of the example represents a measure of the music.

As the example shows, traditional Stufen analysis is perfectly adequate here. The sequence moves from A♭ through C♭ to E𝄫, and the remainder of the passage

earlier. The D♭ of the *Speer* motive has a strong plagal effect, leading the *Liebesmahl* to its cadence. Later on, at the beginning of Gurnemanz's narrative, the D♭ Stufen-function of the spear and its motive takes on massive harmonic weight (I, 506–507, "Oh, wundenwundervoller heiliger Speer!").

works itself out with perfect logic in Stufen space. There are no functional enharmonic relations. Wagner spells E♭♭ major as D major, over measures 51–52, but that is only a notational convenience. (Perhaps he also intended it as a sort of "conceptual" gesture, to foreshadow later events in D. Then, too, the increased timbral resonance of the trombone pickup into measure 51 makes it hard to believe that the sounds notated as A and D are "really" so remote as B♭♭ and E♭♭.)

Conceptual and timbral subtleties aside, it is clear that the E♭♭-major harmony of Example 10.4 is in a substitutional relation to the E♭-minor cadential harmony under the fermata. The two harmonies represent variant third degrees of C♭ and hence, indirectly, variant degrees of A♭. If we graph the consecutive local tonics of Example 10.4, then the "correct" graph is Example 10.5a, not Example 10.5b.

Example 10.5

We are tempted to consider Example 10.5b here only in hindsight, because of various subsequent objects and events in Riemann space. (Those include a later enharmonic shift on C♭/B within the first act Prelude itself.) But as of I, 45 we know only Stufen space. Listening to Example 10.5, one hears immediately that a paradigmatic "subsequent object" is the *Zauber* motive. Example 10.6 displays that motive in the form that most closely links it with Example 10.5.

Example 10.6

As the example indicates, this form of *Zauber* appears spanning the kiss attack (a felicitous term) at II, 986. Wagner writes no key signature from measure 972 to measure 1041; most of this music is highly chromatic and vagrant. Wagner notates Example 10.6 an enharmonic comma away, writing B♮ where Example 10.6 has C♭, and so on. Kundry has just cadenced in the local key of C♭, and her vocal cadence on the word "*Kuß*" at measure 983 is notated as a C♭; thereupon Wagner begins notating the orchestra in B, making the notational shift at that key word. Here we are at the very crux of the enharmonic shift involving C♭ and B in Act II, and hence in the opera as a whole. In contrast to our sense of Example 10.5, we are highly unsure as to whether the indicated note on Example 10.6 "should" be spelled D♮ or E♭♭, or even C♯♯. More exactly, we hardly care about the issue, so immersed are we in the thick of Riemann space at the very brink of the C♭/B interface.[12]

12. The orchestration makes measure 983, where Kundry sings "*Kuß*," a convenient place to change the notation enharmonically. It seems clear, though, that the actual moment at which the magic shift occurs is at first lip contact, which I take to be the bar line of measure 986, as indicated in Example 10.6. That is one reason I am quite willing to shift the spelling of Example 10.6 by an enharmonic comma from Wagner's practical notation.

And yet at other moments in Act I and Act II, we do puzzle over the spelling of the indicated tone in the *Zauber* motive. The motive engages Stufen space because we associate it with the opening of the *Liebesmahl,* particularly when it appears at the pitch-class level of Example 10.5 and Example 10.6. We can recall the role the Grail motive played in connection with Example 10.3 earlier: it engaged our discussion of that passage with Stufen space. *Zauber,* in its relation to the *Liebesmahl,* plays an analogous role, engaging our perception (for instance) of Example 10.6 with Stufen space.

Indeed, the dramatic action of the opera involves precisely "bringing the magic back" to the communion service. Significantly, it is not clear just what the Stufen transformation is that "brings *Zauber* back to the *Liebesmahl.*" One can certainly consider each of the possibilities shown in Example 10.7a–c.

Example 10.7

Examples 10.7a and 10.7b are equally compatible with the kiss harmonization. Example 10.7a conforms with Example 10.5a; Example 10.7b is one of the "subsequent objects" that suggests Example 10.5b. Example 10.7c clings desperately to the "logic" of motivic Stufen space; like Example 10.3b earlier, it thereby leads us to a functional absurdity in Riemann space.

Thus, with suitable reservations and qualifications, we can find an interesting transformation in the character of the pitch class D/E𝄫 over the drama. In Example 10.4 it is unambiguously E𝄫, a third degree of C♭ and, hence, indirectly a fifth degree of A♭. In Example 10.6, the function of the pitch class as a degree of A♭, is virtually indecipherable: it may be D or E𝄫 or even C♯♯. By the end of the opera, the pitch class is D, a global substitute for D♭, that executes formidable S-function in Riemann space.

Amfortas's Prayer, while ineffectual as a prayer, plays a vital role in establishing the substitutional role of D vis-à-vis D♭. We already know by this time that D is not E𝄫; what we learn from the Prayer is that D is henceforth a plagal substitute for D♭; it will not become a leading tone to E♭ (as in Example 10.5b and Example 10.7b). The puzzling local events of Example 10.2 qualify that assertion a bit, but they do not substantially disturb its large-scale validity. Amfortas does not know how to use his plagal D, but Parsifal does, and that relationship legitimizes Parsifal's takeover from Amfortas as much as does his possession of the D-ish spear. Amfortas gives to Parsifal something essential about the plagal D, something that does not directly involve the Spear. Parsifal tells us just this in the text that precedes his big D-major takeover at III, 1057: "Gesegnet sei dein [plagal D] Leiden, das Mitleid's höchste [plagal D] Kraft, und reinsten Wissens [plagal D] Macht dem zagen Thoren gab!"

CHAPTER Eleven

Some Notes on Analyzing Wagner

The Ring *and* Parsifal

Example 11.la sketches the Tarnhelm motive from *Das Rheingold* as first heard; Example 11.lb sketches the modulating middle section of the Valhalla theme, again as first heard. For many years I had sensed some underlying relation between the two passages, without being able to put my finger on it. In my recent book, *Generalized Musical Intervals and Transformations,* I tried to work out a suitable relationship using networks of *Klang* transformations. Example 11.2 reproduces figure 8.2 from the book.[1] There is a misprint: what is incorrectly written as "(G ,-)" on the left of Example 11.2a should be written as "(G♯,-)."

Example 11.1

a. Tarnhelm motive, *Das Rheingold,* sc. 3, mm. 37ff.

b. Modulating section of Valhalla theme, *Das Rheingold,* sc. 2, mm. 5ff.

1. David Lewin, *Generalized Musical Intervals and Transformations* (New Haven, Conn.: Yale University Press, 1987), 179.

Example 11.2

a.

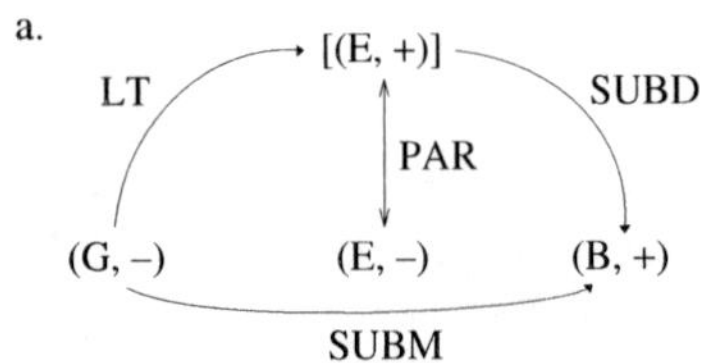

b.

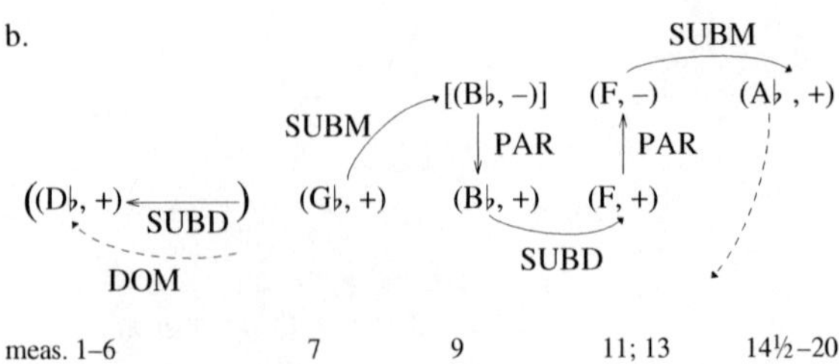

The bracketed harmonies on the example are understood as interpolated transformational stages in the networks. LT signifies Riemann's *Leittonwechsel* transformation: the two notes spanning the minor third of a triad are preserved, while the third note moves a semitone to form a new triad of the opposite mode. The transformation SUBM makes a given triad the submediant in the key of the transformed triad. I was eager to assert SUBM between the opening and final harmonies of Example 11.2a; this made me assert B major, but not B minor, to be functional at the end of Example 11.1a. (Wagner uses both major and minor harmonizations in the course of the *Ring* and *Tristan.*)

In the book (on page 178), I say that Examples 2a and 2b "make visually clear a strong functional relationship" between the two passages, "a relationship which it is difficult to express in words." The relationship is difficult to express because the analysis is bad. It is bad for at least three methodological reasons that I can spot. Criticism (a): There is no point asserting "a strong relationship" without being able to specify just what the relationship *is.* All things are "related" in the Great Chain of Being. Criticism (b): Example 11.2 does not lead us deeper into the music of Example 11.1, or into other pertinent music, or into dramatic ideas about the *Ring.* Criticism (c): Example 11.2a, as it stands, is technically malformed by the criteria of *GMIT.* (The criteria are developed only later in the book, but that is beside the point in this connection.) While I felt the dissatisfactions of criticisms (a) and (b) most keenly, I was unable to make progress until I became aware of (c) as well; this gave me a point of departure for improvement. Example 11.3 will help us to explore the specific way in which Example 11.2a is malformed.

It is true, as Example 11.2a asserts, that G♯ minor is the submediant of B major, and that the *Leittonwechsel* of G♯ minor is the subdominant of B major. Symbolically, the equation of Example 11.3a is true: applying the transformation SUBM to the *particular Klang* G♯ minor has the same effect as applying, to that *particular Klang,* first the transformation LT and then the transformation SUBD. But the

Example 11.3

a. true: (g♯) SUBM = ([g♯]LT) SUBD
B = (E) SUBD; correct
b. false: (any *Klang*) SUBM = ([that *Klang*]LT) SUBD
c. false e.g.: (C) SUBM = ([C]LT) SUBD
e = (e) SUBD ??; wrong.
d. false: SUBM = LT SUBD

equation of Example 11.3b is *not* true. In *general*, if one applies SUBM to a *Klang*, the result will *not* be the same as if one applies first LT and then SUBD. Example 11.3c shows how this works when the *Klang* in question is, for example, C major; applying SUBM to C major yields a different result than does applying first LT and then SUBD. The chord of which C major is the submediant is not the same as the chord of which the *Leittonwechsel* of C major is the subdominant.

Because the equations of Examples 11.3b and 11.3c are false, the functional equation of Example 11.3d is false. And so the configuration of arrows and arrow-labels on Example 11.2a is malformed by the criteria of GMIT (9.2.1 [D], p. 195). As soon as I noticed the malformation, it occurred to me that the SUBM arrows of Example 11.2 were problematic in other ways as well. The SUBM arrow of Example 11.2a, for instance, was forcing me to assert B major and ignore B minor, where Wagner's music suggests both B major and B minor equally. Bringing B minor into Example 11.2a along with B major forms a suggestive analogy to the F major and F minor of Example 11.2b. Then, too, why should I assert a SUBM relation in Example 11.2b between G♭ major and the bracketed B♭ minor? Why not assert a *Leittonwechsel* here, making another suggestive analogy between Examples 11.2a and 11.2b? Rethinking my analysis along these lines, I quickly arrived at the new network analyses of Example 11.4.

Example 11.4

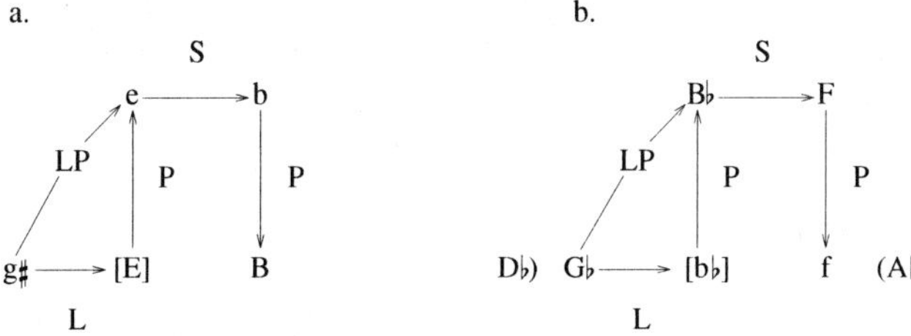

In these graphs the *Leittonwechsel*, subdominant, and parallel transformations have been abbreviated as L, S, and P respectively. The new analyses are much better than the old. They specifically respond to each of the three earlier criticisms. In response to criticism (c), the graphs of Example 11.4 are well formed. I particularly emphasize this point because when a graph is well formed, one is apt simply to take that for granted. I want to stress once more that it was just this criterion that enabled me to work out the better analyses, with consequences we shall shortly examine.

The new analyses also respond to criticism (a). A very specific relationship can now be asserted between the two passages: they admit of *isographic* analyses under the interpretations of Example 11.4. That is, the configurations of nodes and arrows are the same, on Example 11.4a as on Example 11.4b; furthermore, there is a certain privileged way of relating transformations that makes the transformations of Example 11.4b analogous to those of Example 11.4a as they label their respective arrows. Here the privileged relationship is very strong—it is absolute identity. To the extent that transformations here play the role of extended formal "intervals," there is a quite precise sense in which Examples 11.4a and 11.4b demonstrate the same tune in different modes. That is, they run through the same configuration of "moves," differing only in the place where they begin their journeys. One asserts a specific and very strong relationship when one makes precise a sense in which the Tarnhelm and the modulating section of Valhalla can be described as "the same tune in different modes."

Finally, this way of regarding the two passages leads suggestively deeper into the music, responding to criticism (b). One reason I had felt a relationship between Tarnhelm and Valhalla in the first place was that the two thematic ideas grow to interact more and more as the *Ring* progresses. Example 11.5 shows the passage in which one first becomes strongly aware of the interaction, the climax to act II, scene 2, in *Die Walküre*.

Example 11.5 Die Walküre, Act II, scene 2, climax.

WOTAN (mit bittrem Grimm sich aufrichtend)
So nimm meinen Se - gen, Nib - lun - gen Sohn!
ff
dim.
p
più p

There is not space here to discuss the Tristan harmony that engulfs the opening A♭ minor, or the Gold motive at the end, or the fantastic rhythmic detail, or all aspects of the vocal line. That being said, one can hear clearly enough that the opening Tristan harmony enlarges A♭ minor, and one hears E minor at the end. The large progression of A♭ minor to E minor evidently elaborates the first two harmonies of the Tarnhelm motive. Furthermore, the notes with stems up on the top staff of Example 11.5 clearly constitute a transformation of Valhalla—the opening, rather than the middle section of that theme. Example 11.6 works the transformation out in some detail.

Example 11.6a puts the opening of the Valhalla theme in A♭ major and indicates the most accented harmonic gesture of the two measures, namely the inflec-

Example 11.6 Transformations of Valhalla theme.

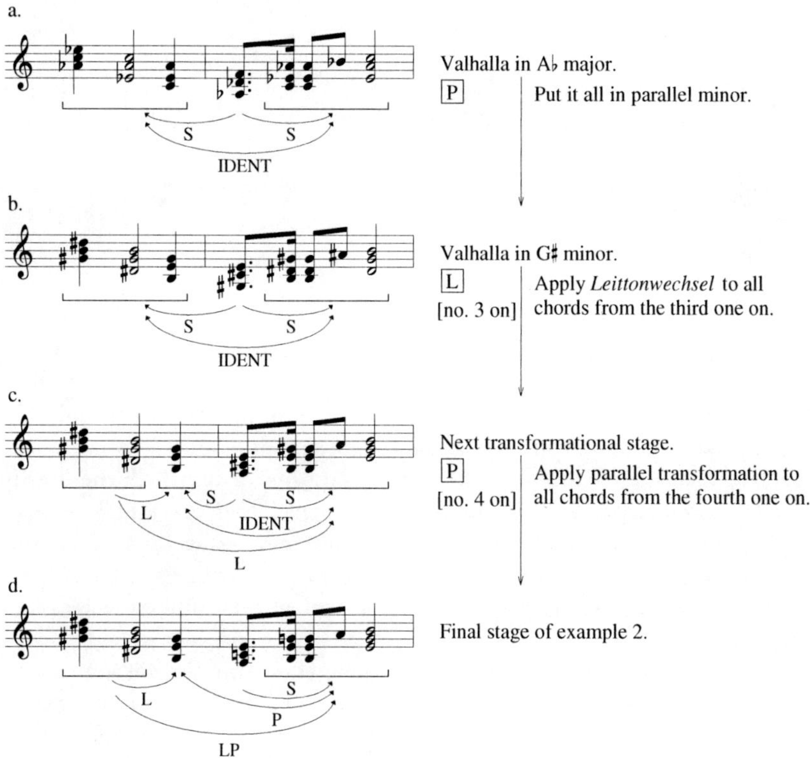

tion of the tonic by its subdominant.[2] One gets from Example 11.6a to Example 11.6b by following the first descending P-arrow at the right of the example: Example 11.6b puts all of Example 11.6a into the parallel minor. To get from Example 11.6b to Example 11.6c, one then follows the descending L-arrow: Example 11.6c transforms the chords of Example 11.6b into their respective *Leittonwechsels*, starting from the third chord on. Then Example 11.6d transforms the chords of Example 11.6d into their parallels, starting from the fourth chord on. The effect of the various vertical arrows is logged by the transformational analyses that build up beneath Examples 11.6b, 11.6c, and 11.6d. The various transformations involved here, namely S, P, and L, are exactly the transformations involved in the earlier networks of Example 11.4, networks that established a strongly isographic relationship between the Tarnhelm and the middle section of the Valhalla theme.

Example 11.7 emphasizes that aspect of the analysis by juxtaposing two networks. Example 11.7a reproduces Example 11.4a, the Tarnhelm analysis, which is

2. The dominant harmony that supports the penultimate note of Example 11.6a is omitted on the sketch. To include it, and to carry along its transformations through the later stages of Example 11.6, would be to complicate the analysis needlessly for present purposes. The omission is not to be construed as an implicit assertion that less-accented, smaller-scale harmonic features, such as those supporting melodic passing tones, are "less important" in some unspecified aesthetic sense.

Example 11.7

a.

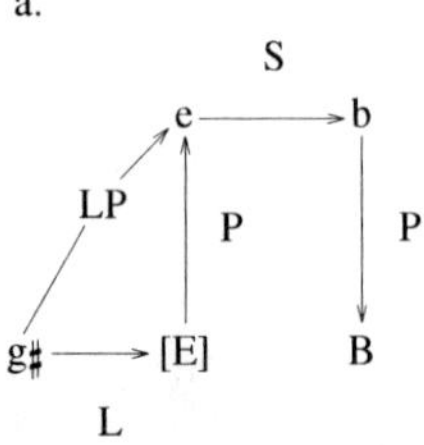

b.

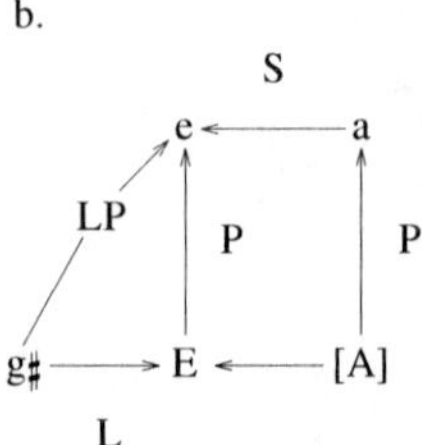

isographic to the middle section of the Valhalla theme. Example 11.7b puts into analogous form the transformational analysis from beneath Example 11.6d; this is the analysis of the Tarnhelm-infected Valhalla *Kopf* at "So nimm meinen Segen."

Example 11.7 shows how the gradual corruption of the pure Valhalla theme, logged by the progressive transformational encrustations of Examples 11.6a, b, c, and d, is actually the systematic working out of a transformational scheme already implicit within the middle section of the Valhalla theme itself; that middle section, in its isography with the Tarnhelm motive, already contains the potential for Valhalla's corruption. Just so does the progressive deformation of Dorian Gray's portrait merely log the potential for corruption already implicit in the narcissism of the beautiful youth himself.

Indeed, the "bitter rage" of Wotan in Example 11.5 is aroused not so much by the frustration of his plan as by his dawning awareness of the corruption necessarily inherent in the plan itself. The very idea of Valhalla contains at its center the source of its own corruption, and Wotan's becoming aware of the fact here moves him beyond political action, suffering, and anger to tragic self-awareness.

There is a significant technical feature of the work so far that contributes to problems in this sort of post-Riemann transformational analysis. In Example 11.2b, we saw G♭ major analyzed as the submediant of B♭ minor, whereas in Example 11.4b, an alternate analysis of the same passage, G♭ major was analyzed as the *Leittonwechsel* of B♭ minor. One can easily imagine other contexts in which one could assert yet other Riemann-type relationships between the two *Klänge*. For example, G♭ major is the parallel of G♭ minor, which might progress along a chain of subdominants through D♭ minor, A♭ minor, and E♭ minor to B♭ minor; in this context one could assert B♭ minor as "PSSSS" of G♭ major. To sum the matter up, there is no unique Riemann-type relationship abstractly specified by the notion of starting at G♭ major and arriving at B♭ minor; the system makes a number of transformations conceptually available, each of which abstractly carries G♭ major to B♭ minor. In mathematical language, one says that the pertinent group of transformations "is not simply transitive."

Wagner interweaves such multiple relationships with particular craft. To explore some of his art, we shall now examine a number of interrelated passages from *Parsifal*. Example 11.8a shows aspects of the opening, which presents the Communion theme. The theme is written under one slur; essentially following Lorenz,

Example 11.8 Parsifal.

I have articulated it into three sections, namely an incipit motive, the *Schmerzensfigur,* and the Spear motive.

Example 11.8b aligns beneath the Communion theme the first statement of the Grail motive in the opera. The alignment shows how the Grail harmonies reference and summarize salient features from the overlying incipit and Spear motives. The Grail, as heard in Example 11.8b, does not reference the central *Schmerzensfigur* of Example 11.8a at all.

Below Example 11.8b appears a harmonic analysis. The final cadence, which involves characteristic scale activity not taken directly from the overlaid portion of Example 11.8a, is analyzed using traditional scale degrees, Roman ii, V, and I. Up until that final cadence, the M-arrows assert each harmony of Example 11.8b as the mediant of the next. The chain of M-arrows coexists comfortably with the chain of falling diatonic thirds in the trombones, and with the regular rhythm of the harmonic changes during this portion of Example 11.8b.[3] Abstractly, one could assert the progression from A♭ major to F minor as a "relative" relation, and likewise the relation from D♭ major to B♭ minor. Since the progression from F minor to D♭ major, however, cannot be analyzed as a "relative" relation, such an analysis would break the chain just discussed. The break in the chain would feel particularly uncomfortable, because a smooth and homogeneous transition from F minor to D♭ major, in the middle of Example 11.8b, serves the very particular purpose of gliding unnoticeably over the missing *Schmerzensfigur* references. It seems awkward to draw attention to the lacuna, which would happen to the extent one hears the f–D♭ progression in the middle of Example 11.8b as somehow specially marked. The critical point is all the more cogent when one observes that the most likely abstract candidate for an f–D♭ relation here, other than the M-relation of Example 11.8b, would be specifically a *Leittonwechsel* relation. The *Leittonwechsel is* the most characteristic harmonic feature of the *Schmerzensfigur* in Example 11.8a; there the *Leittonwechsel* supports a climactic downbeat when the high A♭ moves to high G. To hear f–D♭ in Example 11.8b as a *Leittonwechsel* would then be to draw particular attention to a *Schmerzensfigur* that is missing at this point, rather than to glide surreptitiously over its absence.[4]

Example 11.8c, also aligned beneath Example 11.8a, shows the special role reserved for the *Leittonwechsel* relation in the context of the Communion. Contour, dynamics, and floating-versus-beating metrics spotlight the climactic *Leittonwechsel* from A♭ major to C minor, and the return to A♭ by *Leittonwechsel.* As Example 11.8c suggests, the progression inflects the theme as a whole, not simply the *Schmerzensfigur* and its immediate continuation. The *Schmerzensfigur* is, to be sure, the special focus of the relation; one wonders if Wagner was consciously exploiting a pun on *Leidton.*

3. The chain of falling thirds in the trombones is the source of the "Helpful Kundry" motive.

4. If one plays over the incipit and Spear motives of Example 11.8a without the *Schmerzensfigur,* connecting the end of the incipit bracket directly to the beginning of the Spear bracket, one can hear the f–D♭ progression as a *Leittonwechsel.* One can specifically hear the agogically accented D♭ of the Spear melody stepping up from the C within the incipit material, rather than stepping down from the E♭ of the missing *Schmerzensfigur.* The analysis is latently possible to that extent and worth exploring to that degree.

Example 11.9 Parsifal.

Example 11.9a shows the consequent, C-minor variant of the Communion theme. Below this, Example 11.9b aligns a succession of harmonies that can be inferred from the melodic activity—one must remember that the tempo for the written quarter note is "Sehr langsam." The harmonic analysis below Example 11.9b shows how profoundly the structure of the theme has changed, in the pertinent transformational system.[5] At the very beginning of Example 11.9b, the progression from C minor to A♭ major is not analyzed as a mediant relation, following the precedent of A♭–f at the beginning of Example 11.8b; rather, the c–A♭ that opens Example 11.9b is analyzed as *a Leittonwechsel*. That is because we associate the specific tonality-and-harmony of C minor, in relation to the tonality-and-harmony of A♭ major, with the paradigm of the *Schmerzensfigur* in Example 11.8c, and the large-scale *Leittonwechsel* relation that spreads out over Example 11.8c therefrom. Unlike Example 11.8a, the theme of Example 11.9a is articulated by several different slurs; the first of these slurs sets off the opening c–A♭ progression just discussed.

The leading tone of C minor appears climactically at the proper moment in Example 11.9a. Because of the augmented second in the melody, supported by the slurring of the theme here, however, one does not hear C-minor return before the *sforzando* on the high B. Instead the A♭ remains frozen in the melodic line, continuing to project A♭-major harmony, so that when the *sforzando* B♮ occurs, the effect is to change A♭ major to the parallel A♭ minor, as indicated by the P-arrow below Example 11.9b. As the exact intervals of the *Schmerzensfigur* are subsequently recapitulated, the earlier A♭ of the melody in Example 11.9a continues frozen under the B♮, so that the implied harmony moves on from A♭ minor to E major, via a new *Leittonwechsel*. The end of the *Schmerzensfigur* finally restores the melodic G, but by now the harmony has changed so that the melodic move from A♭ to G sounds in a local context of E harmony: the effect is from E major to E minor, as indicated by the second P-arrow beneath Example 11.9b. The Spear motive returns us to the local tonic, now C minor, as did the Spear motive before, in A♭. In Example 11.9a the C-minor version of the motive is changed so as to put extra emphasis on the early return of E♭ in the melody; the change is supported by the end of the second slur in the theme. The overall harmonic effect, from E minor at the end of the *Schmerzensfigur*, is through C major and back to C minor via yet another L transformation and yet another P transformation.

Overall, then, the transformations below the left side of Example 11.9b go through a complete cycle of alternating Ls and Ps, starting and ending at C minor. Once C minor has returned, it is confirmed by a scale-degree, dominant–tonic

5. One might go so far as to say that the analysis calls into question the extent to which Example 11.9a should be called a "variant" of Example 11.8a, rather than a new idea. Exploring the question, one notes that the two melodies, if analyzed as series of diatonic places, coincide exactly in their intervals up to the fourth note of the Spear motive. Both melodies rise a third from their point of departure, then rise another third, then rise a step and repeat the note, rise a step, rise a step, fall a step, and so forth. In the system of transformations containing such gestures, the melodies have isographic profiles. There is, thus, a profound divergence between the diatonic world of the music and its Riemann-functional world. The reader will find that idea developed at greater length in "Amfortas's Prayer to Titurel and the Role of D in *Parsifal*: The Tonal Spaces of the Drama and the Enharmonic C♭/B," the preceding chapter of this volume.

progression as indicated, supported by the third slur of Example 11.9a. The melody within that slur crescendos to another *sforzando* on the low B of that dominant, restoring the leading-tone function of the B in C minor. By association of dynamics, and by octave equivalence of extreme registers in the melodic ambitus, the gesture recalls the earlier frustration of C-minor leading-tone function in the upper register at the climax, where we heard local A♭-major and local A♭-minor harmony.

The foregoing discussion has clarified, I think, what an error it would be to assume that the first arrow beneath Example 11.9b should bear the same transformational label as does the first arrow beneath Example 11.8b, simply because Example 11.9a begins as a diatonic transposition of 11.8a. Example 11.8b shows a chain of diatonic mediant relations supporting the first and last sections of the theme; the chain of mediants is immersed in the larger-scale diatonic *Leittonwechsel* of Example 11.8c, which bursts into the foreground to interrupt the chain of mediants during the *Schmerzensfigur*. Example 11.9b shows a thoroughly chromatic chain of alternating L and P transforms, owing its closure to a mathematical symmetry rather than a diatonic context. Example 11.9b may be regarded as a trope on the *Schmerzensfigur*, which provides both the L idea, and the idea of moving to C minor as a setting for Example 11.9, whence the whole system of alternating Ls and Ps arises via the A♭–B♮ relation as discussed.[6]

Just as Example 11.8b is the version of the Grail motive that goes with Example 11.8a, so Example 11.9c is the version of the Grail that goes with Example 11.9a. One sees how Example 11.9c fits Example 11.9a precisely because of the analysis that underlies Example 11.9b. Example 11.9c occurs almost at the end of the entire opera, eight measures before the final chorus, at the stage direction "Allmähliche sanfte Erleuchtung des 'Grales'" (gradual soft illumination of the Grail).

In the *Ring*, the L and P relations of the Tarnhelm are involved in the corruption of Valhalla. In *Parsifal* the same transformations become equally associated with suffering, minor, and chromaticism; however, they lead *through* suffering to salvation, *durch Mitleid wissend*. The musical difference, I think, is that the L and P relations of *Parsifal* chain together and eventually build complete cycles that return to their points of departure, as in Examples 11.9b and 11.9c. In the *Ring*, the open-ended application of LP rather disrupts and destroys, as in the relation of Examples 11.6d to 11.6a.

6. The reader is again referred to the chapter in this book entitled "Amfortas's Prayer," apropos the diatonic-and-Riemannian worlds of the drama. Important work on the form-building potential of L-and-P chains, and of such transformational algebra in general, has been carried through by Brian Hyer in a recent study, *Tonal Intuitions in Tristan and Isolde* (Ph.D. diss., Yale University, 1989); also idem, "Reimag(in)ing Riemann," *Journal of Music Theory* 39.1 (1995), 101–138.

CHAPTER Twelve

Tristan

Well-Made Play and Theater of Passion; The Teleology of Functional Tonality and the Self-Propagation of Transformational Atonality

> If one thinks of *Tristan und Isolde* as simply another love-story, one can see that it is plotted on the serviceable principles of the well-made play. The first act is an exposition of the basic conflict, that between the love of Tristan and Isolde and their moral obligation, especially to King Mark. It ends with an incident which raises the suspense: they kiss just as the ship docks, and the curtain falls with a burst of musical excitement. The second act is built on top of the first, and shows the overt deed which the first act promised. This act also ends with an exciting event, the betrayal and the stabbing; and the second act curtain marks the "climax" of the conflict. The third act is the denouement: all is resolved, or dissolved, in death.
>
> The single purpose of this scheme, thus abstractly understood, is to hold and excite the audience by means of the *facts* of the story. It would have been equally useful as the framework for a drama of ethical motivation, like Racinian tragedy; the same facts, in the same order, might have been used to present the life of the reasoning soul in its struggle with inclination, instead of the invisible life of passion transcending recognizable reality altogether. Thus the plot of the opera as "intrigue" shows something about Wagner's relation to the audience, and something about the well-made play, but very little about his real principles of composition.
>
> —Francis Fergusson in *The Idea of a Theater*
> (Garden City, N.Y.: Doubleday & Company, 1953), 91

Fergusson asserts that the "single purpose" of the well-made play is "to hold and excite the audience," the better to render them receptive for the rhythms and flows of the "real" dramaturgy, which follows "the action of passion."[1] For him, the well-made play is thus a device to abet the drama of passion, rather than a partner of that drama in a dialectic process.

I disagree with his assertion. I believe that there is instead an essential dialectic tension between the two species of dramaturgy in the work, and I find that this dialectic tension specifically enacts and is enacted by a musical dialectic that persists

1. Fergusson formulates his very impressive extended critique of *Tristan* so as to exemplify "the action and theater of passion" (Chapter 3, 80–109), in contrast to Racine's *Bérénice*, which exemplifies "the action and theater of reason" (Chapter 2, 54–80).

throughout the drama, a dialectic between the traditional teleology of tonality, on the one hand, and, on the other, the propensity of abstract intervallic structuring ("atonality") to saturate its environs through self-propagation. The present chapter elaborates my claim.

To be sure, from a historical (or perhaps historicist) point of view the Scribean well-made play, as a vehicle for serious dramatic composition in 1858, was a tired old nag, while the new drama of passion was a fresh fire-breathing steed.[2] A critic's attention, in studying a work of art, is naturally drawn to the historically new, the radical, the revolutionary, at the expense of the old, the worn, the conservative or reactionary. That is quite proper, and indeed from a political point of view (going beyond historicism), such criticism helps alert us to aspects of the artwork that continue to exercise a powerful influence—for good or for ill—on the future behavior of related cultures. In the case of Wagner, the political observation is particularly relevant for our own present-day culture.

One therefore naturally wants to devote ample attention to the theater-of-the-future in Wagner's dramatic conceptions, just as one wants to devote ample attention to the "music of the future" therein. And that brings me back to my central claim: just as the "music of the future" interacts dialectically with aspects of traditional tonality in *Tristan*, so does his "theater of the future" interact dialectically with his well-made play. Furthermore, the simile is not a mere static analogy: each of the two dialectics, musical and theatrical, *enacts* the other allegorically as the drama progresses.

The literature of musical analysis for *Tristan* is vast, and I do not believe I shall have any particular music-analytic observation to make that has not already been made as well or better by someone else.[3] At most, I may have one fresh observation. But fresh observations per se are not what I intend by the analytic commentary that fol-

2. Scribe did not die until 1861, but most of his 350-plus plays were composed and acclaimed long before that. Several of the most popular were already written in the early 1820s—for example, *L'Ours et le Pacha* (1820), *Mon Oncle César* (1821), and *Valérie* (1822). An ambitious young man of the theater living and working in Paris during the years 1839–1842—Wagner, for example—would certainly have been impressed by Scribe's influence, and he would have received strong impressions from Scribe's plays produced during that period, for example, *La Calonie* (1840), *Le Verre d'Eau* (1840), and *Une Chaîne* (1841).

3. A useful apparatus for bibliographic reference up to 1985 appears at the end of *Wagner: Prelude and Transfiguration from Tristan and Isolde*, ed. Robert Bailey (New York: W. W. Norton, 1985), 305–307. The volume itself is a first-rate compendium of assorted matters relevant to *Tristan* studies: historical background; the composer's own program notes; pertinent scores; the composer's preliminary draft sketches, with analytic commentary; four critical essays; twelve analytical essays; bibliography.

Bailey's title refers to the first act introduction (*Einleitung*) as the "Prelude" (*Vorspiel*), despite Wagner's use of the then-unusual former term in the orchestral score for the staged drama. Almost all modern concert performances in English-speaking countries use the more conventional title; Wagner also apparently used it whenever he referred to the concert version. But most modern performances—departing from Wagner's usage—also refer to the "Transfiguration" (*Verklärung*) as the "*Liebestod*," and Bailey is amply sensitive to that distinction, discussing it explicitly at some length (41–43). Bailey does discuss—quite aptly—Wagner's use of the term *Einleitung*, but only in two tangential sentences (121). Later on we shall explore a sense in which the music before the first act curtain-rise is indeed a structural "introduction" to the dialectic of the drama, rather than a "prelude" to it.

lows. Rather, I wish to draw explicit attention to the double dialectic I am asserting, as the dialectic works itself out in a variety of contexts through the music-drama.

Most of the music-analytic literature on the drama falls into one of two categories. The main branch, which has flourished since the time of the drama's composition and continues to flourish today, has tried to explicate the musical discourse by referring it to one or several canonical theories of tonal music, suitably extending such theories as necessary.[4] The other branch has flourished more recently in North America, where a variety of studies have appeared which analyze the musical discourse as thoroughly "atonal"—that is, as governed by intervallic patternings without necessary functional tonal implications.[5] Exceptional in this respect is the dissertation by Brian Hyer, which falls clearly neither into the one camp nor the other: Hyer moves freely back and forth between "tonal" and "atonal" modes of analysis, both of which contribute to his overall hearing.[6] He does not, however, lay particular emphasis on a specifically dialectic process in this connection. Nor does he explicitly attempt to link any such musical dialectic with a theatrical dialectic between the well-made play and the drama-of-passion.

Examples 12.1 through 12.5, and the commentary that follows them, will explore the "tonal" side of my musical dialectic. I should apologize to musically sophisticated readers for reviewing material that will be so familiar to them, but I am eager to make my ideas accessible to readers who are musically literate but not professional. Even for the cognoscenti, it may perhaps be of some interest to hear the *alte Weise* sound yet once again, in a somewhat different key.

Example 12.1

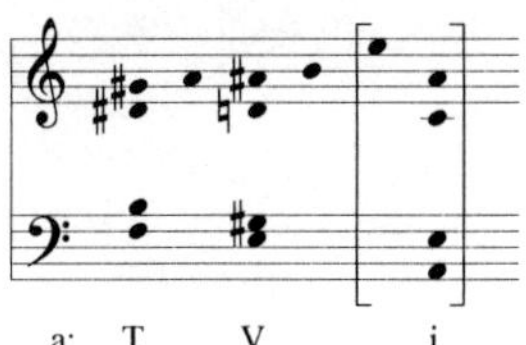

Example 12.1 sketches a harmonic progression heard frequently during the drama. It first appears during the second and third measures of the first-act Introduction, where it is the first harmonic progression heard in the drama—heard before the curtain rises. Below the notes, the progression is analyzed in a minor. "T" stands

4. Such canonical theories include figured-bass theory, fundamental-bass theory, Riemannian function theory, and Schenkerian theory.

5. One of the earliest and most influential of such studies appears within Benjamin Boretz's *Meta-Variations: Studies in the Foundations of Musical Thought*, a Ph.D. dissertation written at Princeton University in 1970. I mention it here because it is not listed in Bailey's bibliography (as described in note 3). Bailey's collection of essays includes a much slighter piece by Milton Babbitt, to represent this critical category. (Babbitt is of course a central cultural figure in this context.) A revised version of Boretz's dissertation appears in *Perspectives of New Music*, vols. 8–11 (Fall/Winter 1969 through Spring/Summer 1973). Boretz's *Tristan* analysis appears in vol. 11, no. 1 (Fall 1972), 159–217.

6. Brian Hyer, *Tonal Intuitions in "Tristan und Isolde"* (Ph.D. dissertation, Yale University, 1989). There is a great deal more to the dissertation; we shall come back to it in another connection later on.

for "Tristan Chord"; it is not clear what harmonic function—if any—the chord assumes in the key. (A great deal of controversy in the literature has been generated by this ambiguity.) The a minor tonic harmony of the analysis appears on the example in brackets: the harmony does not actually sound in the music but is present only by analytic implication, so to speak, as the goal of the harmonic progression.[7]

Example 12.2

Example 12.2 sketches a harmonic progression that appears at the climax of the first act Introduction—still and again before the curtain rises. (a) of the example gives a stripped-down version of the music itself (with augmented rhythmic notation); (b) of the example puts the harmonic progression of (a), without the repeat, into a more normative form. Below the notes of (b), the progression is analyzed in e♭ minor. "T" again stands for "Tristan Chord"; the T is parenthesized because the harmonic function of the Chord is unambiguous in this context—it functions as a seventh-chord on the second degree of e♭ minor. The first harmony over the bass B♭ functions as a dominant-ninth chord in e♭ minor; the soprano C♭, picking up the C♭ of the Tristan Chord, moves as a chromatic appoggiatura to C natural, and the raised ninth of the dominant harmony then resolves to the raised tenth in the first bracketed harmony, as raised-sixth-degree to raised-seventh-degree in the key of e♭ minor. The e♭ minor tonic harmony of the analysis appears on the example in brackets: like the bracketed a minor chord of Example 12.1, the e♭ minor chord here does not actually sound in the music but is present only by analytic implication, so to speak, as the goal of the harmonic progression.

Example 12.3

Example 12.3 is a rhythmically simplified sketch for the music at the very end of the Introduction and (after the double bar) at the very beginning of the first

7. Hyer makes a good deal of this phenomenon, taking it as a point of departure for a fascinating semiotic analysis of the music, and an equally fascinating semiotic critique of Rameau's fundamental bass theory. We shall return to the phenomenon (although without Hyer's semiotic component) later in this chapter.

scene on stage. The curtain begins to rise exactly at the beginning of the example, and has risen fully by the end of the example, where we see Isolde and Brangäne on board the ship. The notes with stems up, after the double bar, are the beginning of the young sailor's song ("Westwärts [schweift der Blick]"). We do not see him; his voice comes down from above the stage, atop the ship's mast.

Below the notes of Example 12.3, the progression is analyzed in c minor. "T" stands once again for "Tristan Chord"; the chord is there by implication as the arpeggiated sum of the notes bracketed over the "T" symbol. The c minor tonic root, after the double bar, appears on the example in brackets: like the bracketed a minor chord of Example 12.1 and the bracketed e♭ minor chord of Example 12.2b, the tonic bass root c does not actually sound in the music here but is present only by analytic implication, so to speak, as the goal of the harmonic progression.

Example 12.4

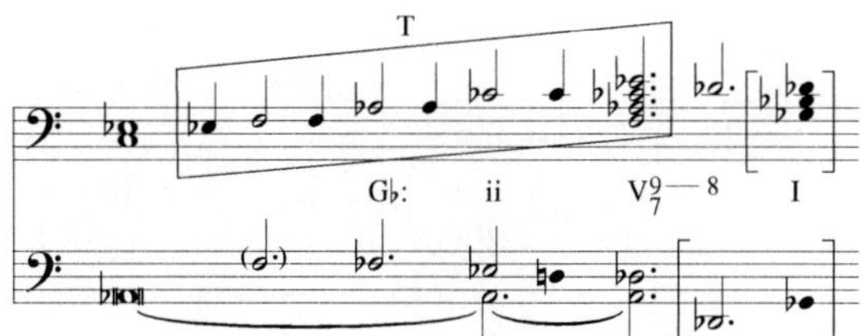

Example 12.4 sketches a passage from the middle of the second act (and of the entire music-drama). The notes in the upper staff with stems up come from Tristan's vocal line as he sings "O sink hernieder, Nacht der Liebe." "T" stands once again for "Tristan Chord." The chord exists by implication as the arpeggiated sum of Tristan's sung notes, within the box under the "T" symbol on the example. The Chord also appears—enclosed in the same box—as a simultaneity within the G♭ major dominant ninth harmony under Tristan's high E♭. This event is marked by the first downbeat for Isolde's voice in the passage, and it is also marked by the winds' entering just here. The G♭ major tonic harmony of the analysis appears on the example in brackets: like the tonic chords or roots of earlier examples, the G♭ major chord does not actually sound in the music but is present only by analytic implication, so to speak, as the local goal of the harmonic progression. The notes in the bottom staff with stems up will be discussed later.

Example 12.5

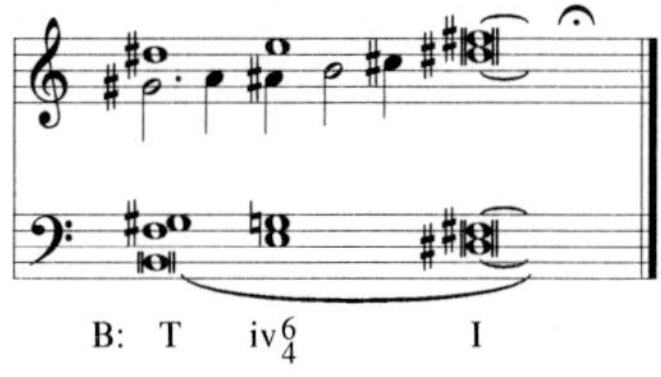

Example 12.5 sketches the harmonic progression at the close of the drama. The curtain does not fall until the fermata at the very end. During the notes before the fermata "Mark blesses the bodies."

Below the notes, the progression is analyzed in B major. "T," as before, stands for "Tristan Chord." The B major tonic harmony of the analysis, unlike the implied tonic chords or roots in the earlier examples, appears explicitly at the end of the progression (and of the music-drama). Unlike the harmonic cadences of Examples 12.1 through 12.4 above, this one is plagal: the local tonic harmony is approached from its subdominant, not its dominant.

Examples 12.1 through 12.5 show the Tristan chord as a "bone in the throat" for traditional functional tonality, the musical analog of the well-made play. In this world, the world of teleological action and purpose, there are clear dramatic obligations to be discharged and goals to be attained. In the music of this world, dissonant harmonies must push on toward well-defined tonal goals, ultimately resolving cadentially to consonances within well-defined keys. The Tristan Chord in particular, intrinsically dissonant and often unclear in tonal function, resolves—more correctly, the well-made music keeps trying to resolve it—within one local key or another. The tonal resolutions of the Chord in Examples 12.1 through 12.5, within local keys of a minor, e♭ minor, c minor, G♭ major, and B major, are typical. Many more such examples can be found, probably involving well-nigh each of the twenty-four possible keys. The Chord, in this context, enacts an aspect of the Tristan-Isolde (*Liebestod*) relationship, a relationship that disrupts the well-defined social-political roles and goals of the well-made play. Isolde is a princess, betrothed to a king in a politically arranged marriage. Tristan is a loyal kinsman, vassal, and knight to that king, a former wartime enemy of Isolde's, a courtier who has conceived and been sent forth on an important political errand. The love relationship, enacting and enacted by the Tristan Chord (*inter alia*), is a "bone in the throat" for all obligations and goals of this sort as they attempt to confront it in one way or another.

In the music, we can hear how provisional and unsatisfactory such attempts are, through the sheer variety of contextual local keys that try to make the chord "resolve." Neither the (bracketed) a minor of Example 12.1, nor the (bracketed) e♭ minor of Example 12.2, nor the (bracketed) c minor of Example 12.3, nor the (bracketed) G♭ major of Example 12.4, nor any other such provisional local tonic key during the course of the drama, nor even (as I shall argue) the explicit "final" B major of Example 12.5, succeed in laying the Tristan Chord to rest. The chord asserts itself, as itself, through and despite all such attempts to rationalize it in the goal-driven world of functional tonality. A telling point, in this connection, is made by the incessant appearance of the term "(bracketed)" in the preceding sentence. While the would-be keys of Examples 12.1–4, and many other such moments, are perfectly clearly defined "by analytic implication"—and arguably "heard" in that sense, through some suitable cognitive mechanism—the actual tonic harmonies themselves are typically deferred, held in abeyance as the music continues around or past them.

Hyer formulates excellent and extended original commentary around just this point.[8] He puts particular emphasis on the observation that by and large the would-be "tonic keys," in contexts like those of Examples 12.1–4, are defined not by the acoustic assertion of their tonic harmonies but, rather, by the acoustic direction of the musical flow into the *dominants* of the would-be tonic harmonies—

8. *Tonal Intuitions*, cited in note 6.

generally dominant-seventh chords. (More rarely, the music flows towards the subdominants of the keys.) Such dominant chords (dominant-seventh chords) are typical semiotic markers, Hyer observes, defining their would-be keys by pointing at their absent tonic chords. In this connection, the Tristan Chords that precede the cadential dominants of examples 1–4 (and other such contexts in the music of the drama) possess in themselves a semiotic role as signs pointing at the dominant-sevenths to come. A frontispiece to Hyer's dissertation reproduces a cartoon portraying a road sign that reads "Sign Ahead."

The music of Example 12.5 is somewhat of an exception to these observations. Here the key and tonic harmony of B major have already been amply established before the example begins; and the note B that underlies the entire bass of Example 12.5 prolongs the bass of that preceding tonic. The Tristan Chord at the beginning of the example thus does not have a forward-pointing function; instead, it extends an already established local tonic. To the point, in that connection, is the subdominant (rather than dominant) inflection of the tonic in the example. Then, too, Wagner is making a reference here to the Tarnhelm Motiv from *Das Rheingold*, an inter-opus reference that invokes the idea of "(magical) transformation" in general.

The B major tonic of Example 12.5, as an acoustic presence rather than a semiotic absence, executes to some extent the canonical "ending" function for a traditional tonal opera in mid-nineteenth-century Europe. There is perhaps something perfunctory about it in that connection, despite the beauty of the music hereabouts. By this point in the drama, in any case, we are not going to hear B major as an *overall* tonic for the music-drama, so the would-be key does not really lay the Tristan Chord and the love-relation to tonal rest. Indeed, there are good grounds for hearing the B major as an elaboration of the note B within the Tristan Chord itself: the third act begins in f minor, and f is a note of the Tristan Chord; Isolde's Transfiguration (*Mild und Leise*) begins in A♭ major, and A♭ is a note of the Tristan Chord; the Transfiguration and the entire music-drama end in B major, and B is a note of the Chord. We shall soon have a great deal more to say about the Tristan Chord as an "atonal" *Ding an sich* of this sort.

The "perfunctory" aspect of the ending tonic, with the somewhat bathetically inadequate idea of "finally laying the Tristan Chord to rest," enacts and is enacted by Mark's blessing the corpses. The Biedermeier spirituality recalls the ending of the *Flying Dutchman*, where the music is quite similar (though in another key) as the Dutchman and Senta rise up into the heavens. (The original ending for *Siegfried's Tod*, heavily influenced by Fichte's optimism before Wagner had encountered the ideas of Schopenhauer, featured Brünnhilde leading Siegfried by the hand in a refulgent apotheosis, as the lovers ascended to Valhalla.) Indeed, at the end of *Tristan*, the B major music works a good deal better in the theater than does the ostentatious blessing on stage.[9] I think we can accept B major, by this point in the musical symphony, as another would-be tonic key that inflects the Tristan Chord and the world of the *Liebestod* more generally, "resolving" the Chord and the love-relation only in the Biedermeier world of the survivors. Mark survives and

9. I am told that there is a sketch for the ending of *Parsifal* where the corpse of Titurel rises from its coffin and makes the Sign of the Cross over all and sundry—or is that Kundry? If so, we can be grateful that Wagner, for the final version, revised this conception.

"means well," but he does not necessarily speak for us—at least he does not speak for more than one aspect of our attitudes towards the drama. In that capacity he executes the theatrical function proper to survivors at the end of Shakespearean tragedies—Edgar and Albany, for example, at the end of *Lear*, or Horatio and Fortinbras at the end of *Hamlet.*

∾

The Tristan Chord, when heard as a feature of the "well-made" tonal music, is a dissonance requiring resolution. As such a dissonance it can be compared to, say, a diminished seventh chord in Bach or an augmented sixth chord in Mozart. But it can also be heard "atonally," as a symbolic musical *Ding an sich.* When the Chord persists in sounding itself again and again during the drama, in Examples 12.1–5, and in other passages of this sort, the various would-be "keys" come to sound more and more not (so much only) as well-made "resolutions" of the Chord, but (also) as an agglomeration of phenomena *accessory* to the Chord-as-*Ding-an-sich.* In this hearing, the "keys" gather around the Chord, ornamenting and inflecting it all to its greater glory and musical autonomy.[10]

The Chord also becomes involved, from the very beginning of the first act introduction, in transformational sorts of generative musical processes that unfold its own intervallic structure, without reference to any sorts of traditional "well-made" tonal functions.

In these ways the Chord enacts—and is enacted by—the love relation of Tristan and Isolde, for which I shall use the term *Liebestod.*[11] From within the dramatic world of the *Liebestod*, all the obligations and goals of the well-made play—obligations involving the shipboard voyage, Isolde's marriage, the hunting party, the attempted suicide of the first act, and so forth—are viewed as mere occasions to assert and propagate the *Liebestod* over all its contexts and surroundings. Just so does the Chord assert and propagate itself through all the would-be "resolving" keys of the "well-made music." So do various other motifs, configurations, and intervallic transformations that come to be associated with intervallic generative processes that affect the Chord.

Examples 12.6 through 12.10 and the commentary that follows them, will explore this "atonal" side of my musical dialectic. I extend my apologies again to musically sophisticated readers for whom much of the material will be familiar. I do believe that my dialectics will generate some new musical observations relating *O sink hernieder* to the opening of the first act introduction.

Example 12.6a shows what I shall call the "central dyad" of the Tristan Chord, the dyad {G♯,B}. Example 12.6b arpeggiates the Chord in close position, where the central dyad appears in the temporal and registral center of the Chord. The dyad appears on the example with open note heads. Example 12.6c arpeggiates the dominant-

10. We have already noted, for instance, how the keys of f minor, A♭ major, and B major, as they provide a musical frame for the overall actions of the third act, also elaborate various constituent tones of the Chord—F, A♭ (G♯), and B.

11. As Bailey demonstrates (41–43), Wagner himself used the term *Liebestod* only in this broad dramatic sense, and when he applied it to a specific musical passage from the drama, he applied it only to the first act introduction, which was thus for him both a "Prelude" and a "Liebestod" at once.

Example 12.6

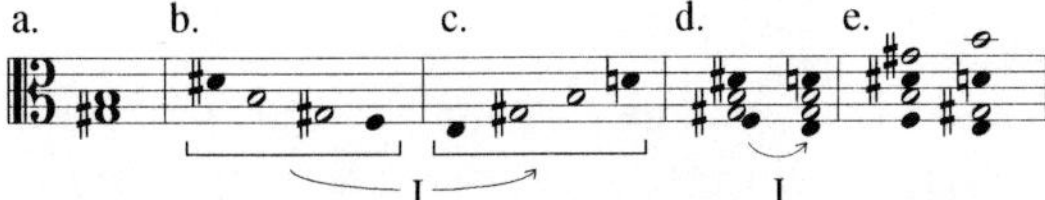

seventh harmony on root E (dominant of a minor) in close position. As we hear from examples 12.6b and 12.6c, the E-root dominant-seventh is the intervallic inversion of the Tristan Chord; the particular level of inversion preserves the central dyad as such. The inversional transformation is symbolized by the arrow labeled "I" that links Example 12.6b to Example 12.6c. Example 12.6d telescopes the arpeggiated chords of 12.6b and 12.6c into adjacent (I-related) simultaneities. Example 12.6e redistributes the notes of 12.6d, putting some notes into different registers but preserving the harmonic sense of the progression. 12.6e gives the actual pitches of the basic progression in measures 2–3 of the drama, as they appeared in Example 12.1. Despite the redistribution of pitches into new registers, the voice-leading that involves the central dyad in 12.6e projects the role of that dyad as a symmetrical center-of-inversion for the context: the open notehead G♯ of the Tristan Chord moves up three semitones to the open notehead B of the E-root dominant seventh chord, and the open notehead B of the Tristan Chord moves down 3 semitones to the open notehead G♯ of the E-root dominant seventh chord.

Example 12.7

Example 12.7a uses open and filled-in noteheads for a new purpose. In the left "measure" of the example we hear two harmonies: first the Tristan Chord appears—in the compact spacing used earlier. Then three tones of that Chord are sustained, while the central G♯ moves minimally toward central B, up by semitone to A. As suggested by the I-arrow on Example 12.7a, the second symbolic "measure" of the example I-inverts the first measure. Here we hear the E-root dominant seventh chord; then three tones of that chord are sustained, while B moves down by semitone to A♯.

The first measure of Example 12.7b is the same as the first measure of 12.7a. The R-arrow from 12.7a to 12.7b indicates that the second measure of 12.7b retrogrades the second measure of 12.7a. On Example 12.7b itself, an RI-arrow signifies that the second measure of 12.7b is the retrograde-inversion of the first—"inversion" still and again being understood as about the central dyad.

When the notes of Example 12.7b are redistributed in register, they give exactly the nonbracketed notes of Example 12.1. This analysis shows, then, that the most paradigmatic progression involving the Tristan Chord can be generated more or less completely by "atonal" intervallic means, given the structure of the Chord itself plus the idea of moving notes by semitone (as in the first measure of Example

12.7a).[12] Specifically, in the analysis that leads from Example 12.6 through Example 12.7 into the nonbracketed portion of Example 12.1, the "key of a minor" plays no *constructive* role whatsoever.

I put "constructive" in italics because, immersed in our culture—and to the extent that our culture still prolongs certain aspects of mid-nineteenth-century listening—we will certainly register an impression that the harmony of Example 12.6c is a familiar sound in traditional a-minor tonal compositions, and that its central dyad {G♯,B} comprises the two tones of the a minor scale, which are diatonically adjacent to the tonic tone A in a context that is meaningful at the approach to a traditional contrapuntal cadence (clausula). But these are not, strictly speaking, constructive features of "the analysis that leads from Example 12.6 through Example 12.7 into the nonbracketed portion of Example 12.1." That analysis does perfectly well on its own terms, given the Tristan Chord as a *Ding an sich*, the idea of the {G♯,B} dyad as "central" (in a close registral spacing of the Tristan Chord), and the idea of voice-leading by semitone (as discussed earlier and in note 12).

It would be possible to adopt a sort of hybrid approach to the analysis of Example 12.1, starting with the presumption of a-minor functional tonality, then valorizing the semiotic role of the E-root dominant seventh in that context, and valorizing the dyad {G♯,B} because its two notes paradigmatically converge by diatonic melodic steps upon the tonic note at cadences in the key of a minor. We could then "deduce" (or generate) the Tristan Chord as the intervallic inversion, about the diatonically significant G♯-and-B, of the tonally functional E-root dominant seventh chord. This is essentially Hyer's point of view and analytic procedure. He has many compelling observations from that point of view, as regards Example 12.1 and many other musical passages of that sort in the drama.

But the point of view is not adequate by itself for my dialectic purposes here. In Hyer's reading, the Tristan Chord is anything but a musical *Ding an sich*—on the contrary, it is an elaborate derivation from the tonally significant E-root dominant seventh, plus the idea of inversion about the tonally significant dyad {G♯,B}. And for the purposes of my dialectic reading, one should be able (though not obliged) to hear the Chord as a generative atonal *Ding an sich*. On this dialectic branch, the generating Chord can indeed act as an *Einheit*, giving rise to tonal impressions in a minor (as the manipulations of Examples 12.6 and 12.7 give rise to structures that we associate with such impressions). On this dialectic branch, then, where the Chord-an-sich is an *Einheit*, the impression of a-minor tonality arises as a *Gegensatz*. This branch of the dialectic valorizes in particular the significance of the Chord-an-sich as the first harmony that we hear in the piece. In Hyer's reading—which I am happy to hear on another branch of the overall dialectic—the presumptions of a minor, deferred by a listener past the Tristan Chord itself until the end of the first complete phrase, work as an *Einheit*; the Chord-itself-as-Ding-an-sich then becomes a *Gegensatz*. My reading of the artwork wants to maintain both modes of hearing the music, music to enact and be enacted by both modes of

12. The latter "given" can be regarded as a logical consequence of dividing the octave into twelve equal parts; in that respect, it is itself an "atonal" feature of the musical discourse, whatever the historical developments through which such a division of the octave came into practice.

drama—the well-made play (for tonality as *Einheit*) and the theater of passion (for atonal propagation of the Chord-an-sich as *Einheit*).[13]

Example 12.8

Example 12.8, continuing a thoroughgoing "atonal" mode of analysis for the first act introduction, is articulated into three components, labeled with the numbers 1, 2, and 3. Component 1, which appears beamed together on the example, is the Motive of Longing, heard at the very beginning of the music-drama. The Motive's characteristic rhythm is not transcribed by the example, but the rhythmic phenomenology is suggested: the fermata, which the example places on the Motive's high F, during which the dynamic swells, symbolizes the long duration of that note.

Component 2 of the example summarizes the role of the central dyad {G♯,B} during the harmonic progression that follows (in the winds), the progression of Example 12.1. The bracket that links the end of component 1 to the beginning of component 2 indicates that the D♯ that ends component 1 sounds together with the first notes of component 2 (within the Tristan Chord). After a substantial and tension-laden rest in the music, component 3 is heard.

Component 3 can be heard as a diatonic transposition of component 1 in the key of a minor. But we are eschewing all such observations, for the moment, in our "atonal" analysis. Atonally, component 3 is not quite "right" as a transposition of component 1: its opening leap is by nine semitones up, where the leap of component 1 was by eight semitones. The atonal analysis has then to ask, what causes this slight deformation in the Motive? The notation of component 3 on the example suggests that a response must involve the role of the central dyad {B,G♯}: those tones appear with open noteheads to span the opening leap of component 3 in the example, thereby recalling the same tones B and G♯ that sounded together at the beginning of component 2 (inside the Tristan Chord). So the atonal "deformation" of component 3 involves the persistent structuring power of the central dyad. (Actually, as we shall see presently, the nine-semitone leap of component 3 is atonally normative—the atonal "deformation" resides rather in the eight-semitone leap of component 1.)

Example 12.9

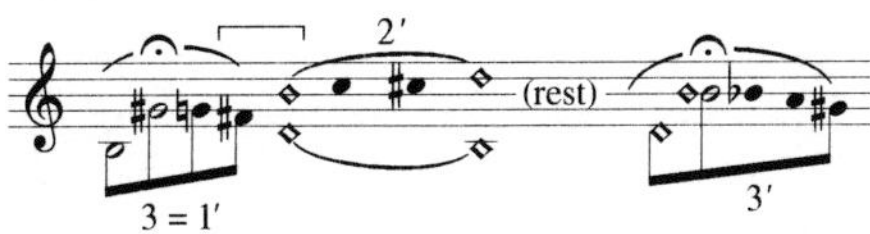

13. It is of course eminently proper for Hyer to assign the priority that he does to tonal hearing, in a dissertation that proclaims its topic to be "*Intuitions of Tonality* in 'Tristan und Isolde,'" rather than "Tristan und Isolde" in general.

Example 12.9 continues analyzing the music past component 3 of Example 12.8. On Example 12.9, that motive is marked "3 = 1′", indicating that the third component of Example 12.8 is the first component of Example 12.9. Components 2′ and 3′ of Example 12.9 correspond, respectively, to components 2 and 3 of Example 12.8. Roughly speaking, Example 12.9 transposes example 8 up by three semitones. The structuring aspect of "three semitones" here resides in the role of the three-semitone interval that spans the central dyad.[14]

The new central dyad of Example 12.9 is accordingly {B,D}—the transposition of the three-semitone dyad {G♯,B} up by three semitones. B and D are marked on Example 12.9 by diamond-shaped open noteheads, to signify that function. The diamond-shaped notes accordingly structure component 2′ and the nine-semitone leap at the beginning of component 3′.

Component 3′ as a whole is not quite a literal transposition of component 3. The new motive-form continues its chromatic slide by one more note than did component 3 (or component 1). According to those earlier models, the descending tail of component 3′ "should be" B–B♭–A. But component 3′ continues one note farther, so that its descending chromatic tail is B–B♭–A–G♯. Manifest here is the structuring role of the original central dyad {G♯,B}, which accordingly appears with round open noteheads on component 3′ of Example 12.9. The four-note chromatic tail B–B♭–A–G♯ specifically retrogrades (in register) the rising four-note chromatic melody G♯–A–A♯–B of Example 12.8, component 2. That was the melody that rode over the paradigmatic harmonic progression of Example 12.1, the first harmonic progression of the piece, as that progression set into motion the Tristan Chord, the first harmony of the piece.

These inflections are significant and powerful in the atonal structuring. For, left to itself (so to speak), the normative model for components 1 and 2 would continue to proliferate mechanically, transposing itself up by three semitones again and again. Example 12.10 suggests such hypothetical mechanical proliferation of the atonal structuring.

Example 12.10

We do not need to invoke tonality (yet), to find a rationale for breaking the mechanical behavior of Example 12.10. We have just noted how various features of the atonal structuring in themselves (the central dyad {G♯,B} in particular) extend the chromatic tail of component 3′ by an extra note, thereby bringing to a halt the machinery of Example 12.10 at the place marked "NB" three-quarters of the way

14. The three-semitone interval is, beyond that, a conspicuous feature of the Tristan Chord in close position (shown as such in Example 12.6a)—the Chord in that position has three semitones not only between G♯ and B but also between F and G♯. The tonal signification of the latter interval, as a diatonic augmented "second" rather than as a minor "third," is irrelevant to the purely atonal analysis at hand.

through the example. Since the Motive of Longing here (component 3′) comes to rest on G♯, not A, the form of the Tristan Chord that continues the music therefrom must include G♯, not A, and that involves further transformations of the subsequent harmonic profile. As we shall see presently, "G♯ not A" is a powerfully thematic idea for the musical structuring.[15]

In that connection, we can observe at once the other "NB" on Example 12.10, at the very first note of the example. The note is G♯, not A. But A sounds in the actual music (as on Example 12.8). The substitution at the first "NB" of Example 12.10 shows how eager the atonal world of the music is, to dispense with A the better to highlight G♯, and that phenomenon—finally—does impinge on the tonal world of the musical structuring. For, as we noted in Example 12.1, the note A is the putative tonic for the opening phrase of the piece. Thus, the opening note A is a "bone in the throat" for the atonal structuring, for the "music of the future" in the drama—much as the Tristan Chord was a bone in the throat for traditional functional tonality, for the "well-made tonal" structuring.

It is not necessary, in this connection, to attribute an immediate tonic function to the opening note A of the piece—a relatively short pickup to the accented long high F that follows. The tonal impression of a minor adheres to the opening phrase as a whole, after we have reached the E-root dominant seventh, in a manner already discussed. Having traversed the opening phrase, we can then tonally rationalize the transformation of component 1, Example 12.8, into component 1′, Example 12.9, by hearing the opening leap of the latter as diatonically transposing the opening leap of the former. So the transformation that generates component 3′ is doubly determined: atonally, it is determined by the role of the central dyad {G♯,B}; tonally, it is determined by the diatonic transposition in a-minor. Only as the machinery of Example 12.10 becomes more and more of an implicit presence do we become sensitive to the idea of A-not-G♯ as a "bone in the throat" for the atonal structuring.

This hostile intrusion of A-not-G♯ into the atonal structuring of Example 12.10 warns us not to derogate the world of well-made functional tonality in the drama, as if it were no more than a serviceable frame for the music-of-the-future. The musical intrusion enacts and is enacted by the theatrical point I made in my original critique of Fergusson: it will not do to write off the well-made play simply as a device to focus the attention and excitement of the audience on a pure ("real") drama of passion. The well-made artistic media do not serve the media-of-the-future in either dimension; they contest them and are contested by them.

In the atonal world of the music, then, the opening Motive of Longing (component 1 of Example 12.8) "should" sound as at the beginning of Example 12.10—with G♯-not-A. And indeed the theater-of-passion, through the rest of the drama, labors mightily to transform the motive "back" (from the atonal point of view) to G♯–F–E–D♯, or (enharmonically) A♭–F–F♭–E♭. Example 12.2 showed this emendation occurring at the climax to the first act introduction: the revised motive ap-

15. Bailey's analytical study of Wagner's sketches and drafts is superb on this issue (*Prelude and Transfiguration*, 126ff.).

pears on the bottom staff of Example 12.2a with stems up. Significantly, the revised motive is played by the cellos (who had played the original version of the motive at the opening of the drama, without other instruments present). In Example 12.2a, which begins "*più forte*," the cellos are reinforced by three horns and (*fortissimo*) bass clarinet; then, when the whole progression repeats *fortissimo*, the cellos are supported by all four horns (*fortissimo*) and both bassoons.

Significantly, as well, Example 12.2 depicts one of the very few places in the drama where the Tristan Chord appears with its most plausibly rationalized intrinsic tonal function—as a seventh-chord on the second degree of e♭ minor. As it were, in the music of Example 12.2 the well-made tonal component of the drama is saying: "If you insist, O atonal world, that the Motive of Longing should begin with A♭-not-A, then I will modulate to e♭ minor—where that will work just fine tonally, and where the Tristan Chord, too, will feel right at home tonally."

But the bracketed e♭ minor tonic harmony, at the end of Example 12.2b, never eventuates in the music. Instead, there follows a yet-again-repeated Tristan Chord, now sustained *fortissimo* by the full orchestra. And then that climactic Tristan Chord dissipates in volume, tempo, and orchestral texture, leading to a varied return of the a-minor progression from Example 12.1. As it were, in this music the atonal world of the drama is saying: "No, I refuse to accept your modulation, O tonal world. The Tristan Chord is *not* a functional ii^7 harmony in e♭ minor, it belongs rather in your would-be a-minor, where it can more properly exercise its atonal function as a bone-in-the-throat *Ding an sich*."

These imaginary conversations illustrate what I have in mind, when I assert in the drama an essential "dialectic tension" between well-made tonal music and atonal music-of-the-future.

The music of Example 12.4 (*O sink hernieder, Nacht der Liebe*, from the second act love duet) strongly exercises the same dialectic process. Reviewing Example 12.4, the reader will observe that I have included a melodic line with stems up in the lower staff. This line, together with the opening bass A♭, enables us to trace out the "atonally preferred" form of the Motive—A♭–F–F♭–E♭. I say "trace out," intending an analytic construction, because no single instrument produces all of those notes. The opening bass A♭ of Example 12.4 is in the cellos; the parenthesized F (in the register of Example 12.4) is sung by Tristan (on the word *sink*); the following F♭ and E♭ are in the violas. The violas then continue chromatically on downward in register, through the unstemmed D natural of the example to the stem-down D♭, as the A♭ major tonality at the opening of the example swings into G♭ major.

Here the tonal/atonal dialectic works as follows. The A♭ major tonic chord at the beginning of Example 12.4 is very firmly established as a local tonic of its key, at considerable length, before the example begins. Globally, in comparison to the a-minor ambience at the beginning of the music-drama, this is an emphatic way of asserting "A♭-not-A": both tones are represented in the global context as tonics of keys. Locally, there is a very strong discharge of dramatic tension (*Entspannung*) as the music settles into an extended peaceful pulsing of the strings on the A♭ major harmony before Tristan's vocal entrance. The musical *Entspannung* enacts and is enacted by the lovers' settling into a flowery bank—finally alone by themselves and at rest after the hectic physical and acoustic frenzy that marked the beginning of their clandestine meeting.

Example 12.11

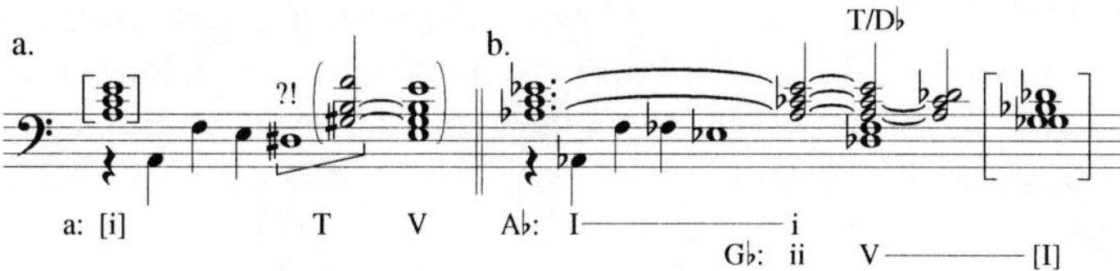

Examples 12.11 and 12.12 will help us analyze the musical *Entspannung* beyond matters already mentioned. Example 12.11a symbolizes aspects of the music that opens the drama, the beginning of the first act introduction. The bracketed a-minor triad at the left does not sound in the music; rather, it symbolizes a retroactive determination to hear the entire opening phrase in the key of a minor.[16] The next four notes symbolize the Motive of Longing that opens the actual music, placed in a lower register so as to contrast with later events in that register. The first three notes of the Motive work fine within the bracketed a-minor harmony. The final note of the Motive, the D♯, is marked with a question mark and an exclamation point. It dissonates radically with the bracketed a-minor chord. The parenthesized material to the right of the example represents what happens "after" the intruding D♯.[17] D♯ is immersed in the Tristan Chord, which emphasizes the intruding character of D♯ by heightening the dissonance level even more. Then the dissonance resolves by semitone voice-leading into the dominant harmony of a-minor, also in parentheses. The seventh of the dominant harmony, which sounds in the music, is omitted on the example, and the tonal rationale that the example presents for the Tristan Chord is only one of several viable such rationales that have been proposed and argued in the literature. Despite those limitations, the example still clearly manifests a sense of the Tristan Chord as tonal bone-in-the-throat.

Example 12.11b, reworking Example 12.4, contrasts with Example 12.11a in many ways. First, the A♭ major harmony at the left of Example 12.11b actually sounds in the music; indeed it sounds at great length and with the textural *Entspannung* already mentioned. Within this A♭ harmony, the Motive of Longing is varied so as to begin on A♭, not A; this is the canonical "atonal" form of the Motive discussed earlier (e.g., in connection with Example 12.10). The Motive as a whole now works fine with the harmony that embeds and supports it. In particular, the final D♯ = E♭ of the Motive now consonates reposefully with the harmony—strikingly unlike the D♯ of Example 12.11a. Consequently, there is no harmonic force to drive the music onward from the E♭ of Example 12.11b, as there was from

16. Such a determination on a much larger level—a determination to hear the entire Introduction in the key of a minor—is symbolized by a beamed open notehead for the opening note A of the drama in the structural bass of a Schenkerian analysis by William Mitchell (reprinted by Bailey, *Prelude and Transfiguration*, 243). Hyer (*Tonal Intuitions*) criticizes Mitchell's analysis.

17. The D♯ that happens "before" finishes the Motive of Longing in the cellos; the D♯ that happens "after" sounds in the English horn, as the winds enter on the Tristan Chord.

the D♯ of Example 12.11a. There is instead a complete and reposeful self-contained closure at the bass E♭ of Example 12.11b, symbolized by the large slur under the entire left-hand side of the example.

We shall come back to the right-hand side of the example in a while, but let us first pause for some commentary. The closure and consonance at the end of the transformed Motive of Longing enacts and is enacted by the dramatic *Entspannung* at hand. The reposeful closure marks the nearest that the musical drama ever gets to a synthesis of dialectic tension between the well-made tonal world and the atonal world. The musical synthesis can be described as follows. On Example 12.11b, during the E♭ at the end of the long slur, the well-made tonal component of the music is saying, as it were, "If you insist, O atonal world, that the Motive of Longing should begin with A♭-not-A, then I will modulate the drama to the key of A♭ major, where that transformation of the Motive will work just fine tonally—as regards both the A♭ at the beginning of the Motive and the E♭ = D♯ at its end." And the atonal component of the music is saying, as it were, "If there is to be functional tonality in the music for this drama, the harmony must accommodate and support the G♯ = A♭ (but not A) that I want to have at the beginning of the Motive of Longing. So I am happy with the harmony of Example 12.11b, and can accept it peacefully, without making dissonance on the D♯ = E♭ of the Motive." In this way, both tonal and atonal worlds in the music achieve their goals vis-à-vis the Motive; they are both—for the moment—at rest. They have not abandoned a condition of dialectic tension between them; rather they have found—for the moment—a mutually satisfying synthesis of that tension, as regards the Motive of Longing.

The musical synthesis enacts and is enacted by the nearest the theatrical drama ever gets to a dialectic synthesis that might mitigate its tension between the "real" world and the passion-world. As the lovers sink onto the flowery bank in their embrace, they have momentarily achieved their passion-goal within the "real" world. Specifically, they have managed to meet in privacy by means of an intrigue within the "real" world, and the intrigue has—for the moment—succeeded.[18] It seems, momentarily, as if the lovers' passion is not necessarily a bone-in-the-throat for the well-made play, since a familiar sort of well-made intrigue within that play can—apparently—accommodate their passion.

To be sure, this condition is temporary; it will not last. Theatrically, as note 18 has just pointed out, the well-made audience "knows" that the intrigue is doomed to fail through Morold's treachery. And the audience for the theater-of-passion comes as well to realize, during the dialog that follows here, that the *Liebestod* relation cannot possibly fulfil itself within the "real world." Indeed, the lovers themselves come to articulate just that insight, during the dialog:

> (Isolde:) Herz an Herz dir, Mund an Mund; (Tristan:) eines Atems ein'ger Bund; (Both:) bricht mein Blick sich wonnerblindet, erbleicht die Welt mit ihrem Blenden,

18. True, within the well-made play the audience "knows" of Morold's treachery, in setting up the lovers' meeting. But Tristan does not, and Isolde, although warned by Brangäne within the well-made play, has refused to accept the warning. The lovers do get to meet in private within the real world, which was in a sense Isolde's point when she earlier rejected Brangäne's warning, hailing the goddess of Love as "des Weltenwerden Walterin" (the ruler of worldly destiny).

(I:) die uns der Tag trügend erhellt, (T:) zu täuschendem Wahn entgegengestellt, (Both:) selbst dann bin ich die Welt.

([As I lie with my] heart upon your heart, mouth upon mouth, bound together in one breath, my vision [both lovers are singing] is transformed, dazzled by rapture. The World, with its glitter, fades away—the world that lying Day illuminated for us, a false model set up to deceive us. Then I myself [both are singing] am "the World.")

Musically, too, the audience knows that the *Entspannung* projected on the left half of Example 12.11b will not last. While the A♭ tonality has made its peace with the revised version for the Motive of Longing, that tonality has not yet accommodated the Tristan Chord. The chord, while not so dissonant within A♭ tonality as it was within a minor, is still dissonant. The musical point is made on the right half of Example 12.11b. To get from the tonic A♭ harmony to the Tristan Chord, the music has first to accommodate the C♭ of the Chord, which moves the tonal ambience from A♭ major to a♭ minor (marked "i" on the example)—and even then the note F within the Tristan Chord, heard tonally, implies a modulation. On Example 12.11b the Chord is treated as the upper four voices of a dominant-ninth harmony within the new local tonality of G♭ major. The harmonic analysis of the example notes that the "V^9" of that key is heard as "T/D♭," the Tristan Chord over a D♭ fundamental bass.

The musical disruption is not so violent, in the well-made tonal world, as the disruption in Example 12.11a. Still, the Tristan Chord of Example 12.11b betokens a certain instability within the would-be A♭ tonality. That is significant, since the A♭ tonality spreads out over a large section of the music that follows Example 12.11b, during the remainder of the lovers' meeting.[19] Even after "Selbst bin ich die Welt," which is set to a quite atonal succession of roving diminished-seventh chords, culminating at "Welt" in a full-orchestral climax upon a supremely "atonal" Tristan Chord, the music very soon returns to an A♭-major cadence and coda, at "Niewiedererwachens wahnlos hold bewußster Wunsch." Example 12.12a gives the music, in a hypothetical version that would complete the implied plagal cadence in A♭ major, as indicated by the bracketed material at the end.

And now Example 12.12b shows how "the Tristan Chord . . . betokens a certain instability within the would-be A♭ tonality," here just as in Example 12.11b. The music of Example 12.12b continues from Example 12.12a according to the progression of Example 12.11b, to a Tristan-Chord-over-bass-D♭, which—as a dominant-ninth sonority—betokens a modulation to G♭ major. The modulation then ensues, as the lovers stop singing for some time, while Brangäne sings the first section of her Watch, music based on the "Träume" motive (Example 12.12c, which overlaps the end of Example 12.12b). The harmonic point of the Träume Motive is to show the Tristan Chord resolving diatonically in G♭ major, into dominant harmony. Brangäne's Watch, which wanders about a good deal harmonically, neverthe-

19. In particular, A♭ major tonality there becomes identified with the "Mild und Leise" music that will recur—beginning in A♭ major—during the scene of Isolde's Transformation toward the end of the entire drama. (Neither during the second act love duet, nor during Isolde's third act Transformation, does the A♭ tonality maintain itself through what follows the "Mild und Leise" music.)

Example 12.12

less settles definitively into G♭ major or G♭ (f♯) minor tonality at all its main tonal moorings.

A particular point just made deserves special emphasis: the Tristan Chord, spelled {F,A♭,C♭,E♭}, while still dissonant within G♭ major, is *diatonic* there—it does not disrupt the scale of the key.[20] So the well-made tonal music and the atonal music enact a dialectic synthesis about G♭ major and the Tristan Chord as *Ding-an-sich*, very like the earlier such dialectic about A♭ major and the Motive-of-Longing-with-A♭.

At the end of Example 12.12b and the beginning of Example 12.12c, the well-made tonal component of the music is saying, as it were, "If you insist, O atonal world, that the Tristan Chord should be a primary constructive element for harmony, then I will modulate the drama to the key of G♭ major, where the Chord will work just fine in a traditionally functional tonal role." And the atonal component of the music is saying, as it were, "If there is to be functional tonality in the music for this drama, the harmony must accommodate and support my Tristan Chord. So I am happy with G♭ major, and can accept it peacefully." In this way, both tonal and atonal worlds in the music achieve their goals vis-à-vis the Chord; they are both—for the moment—at rest. They have not abandoned a condition of dialectic tension between them; rather they have found—for the moment—a mutually satisfying synthesis of that tension, as regards the Tristan Chord.

The synthesis, however, is only temporary, as the Chord is not destined to fulfill a traditional well-made tonal-functional role. It is, rather, destined to be a tonal bone-in-the-throat, just as the *Liebestod* relation in the theater-of-passion is destined to reject the would-be well-made "solution" to the problem of the *Liebestod* through the second act plot intrigue. The *Liebestod,* rejecting the deceptions of "Day," will go on to reject even the well-made "solution" to its problems offered by

20. The same is true for the key of e♭ minor. This was demonstrated in Example 12.2b, which showed the Tristan Chord resolving diatonically to the dominant of e♭ minor at the climax of the first act introduction. But the major tonality of G♭ better suits the temporary *Entspannung* of the second act love scene.

King Mark toward the very end of the third act: although Mark means well with his efforts to find a place for the lovers within the "real" world, the *Liebestod* would not have been satisfied by the real-world solution he has prepared—to divorce Isolde and let her marry Tristan. The irony of the moment—that the death of the lovers "need not have happened"—exists *only* within the well-made play. Within the theater-of-passion, Mark's "solution" is a pathetic irrelevancy; the *Liebestod,* in that theater, must press on to its predestined end, the dissolution of all worldly existence in Death. Just so, the Tristan Chord in the music can at best only provisionally accept any functional commerce with the well-made world of tonal functionality—a commerce being provisionally negotiated during Example 12.12bc.

In this connection, we should observe that A♭ major and G♭ major can not both govern the overall tonality of the love duet at the same time. Despite all the passes being made at dialectic "reconciliation" of the tonal and atonal musical worlds, there is still a certain uncertainty—well portrayed on stage by the anxiety in Brangäne's warnings—about the security of the reconciliation. The diagram below will help us explore that uncertainty a bit more deeply.

A♭ major ↔ "atonal" Motive of Longing ↔ Tristan Chord ↔ G♭ major

Each double-arrow on the diagram indicates a particular species of compatibility. A♭ major is compatible with the Motive of Longing that begins on A♭-not-A. That form of the Motive, leaping from A♭ up to F and then sinking down through a chromatically passing F♭ to end on E♭, is highly compatible with the Tristan Chord: the motive-form as described begins with notes A♭ and F, and passes chromatically down to its ending on the note E♭; the salient notes A♭, F, and E♭ are all constituent notes of the Tristan Chord. The Tristan Chord, as discussed at some length earlier, can assume a clear traditional diatonic function in the key of G♭ major.

But the double-arrow relation, in the diagram, is not transitive. A♭ major is not quite compatible with the Tristan Chord; the atonal form of the Longing Motive is not compatible with G♭ major; and of course A♭ major and G♭ major can not reign over the tonal world at the same time. One senses, then, a slight wavering to and fro during the pertinent span of the second act music—most audibly, perhaps, as the music under examination oscillates gently back and forth around A♭ major and G♭ major.

By way of conclusion, we do well to observe that the musical dialectics examined above are presented to the audience strictly before the theatrical/textual dialectics. That is the main dramaturgical business of the first-act Introduction. The reader may wish to review the commentary around Examples 12.1 through 12.3, and Examples 12.6 through 12.10, with this thought in mind. One sees why Wagner writes "Introduction" rather than "Prelude" in the orchestral score, and why Wagner, whenever he used the term *Liebestod* "as the title for an orchestral excerpt, . . . consistently and exclusively used it for the Prelude [*sic*] to Act I."[21]

21. Bailey, *Prelude and Transfiguration*, 41.

PART V

Brahms

CHAPTER Thirteen

Die Schwestern

(Author's note: This chapter is published here for the first time.)

The text of "Die Schwestern," from Mörike's *Gedichte,* 1838, with my translation is given here. The annotations are mostly taken from George Bozarth.[1] Plate 13.1 (at the end of the chapter) gives a score for the song.

Wir Schwestern zwei, wir schönen, So gleich von Angesicht, So gleicht kein Ei dem andern, Kein Stern dem andern nicht.	We two sisters, we pretty ones, So alike in appearance, No egg so resembles another, Nor any star another.
Wir Schwestern zwei, wir schönen, Wir haben lichtbraune Haar,[2] Und flichst du sie in Einen Zopf,[3] Man kennt sie nicht für wahr.	We two sisters, we pretty ones, We have light brown hair, And if you weave it into one braid Nobody can tell it apart.
Wir Schwestern zwei, wir schönen, Wir tragen gleich Gewand, Spazieren auf dem Wiesenplan Und singen Hand in Hand.	We two sisters, we pretty ones, We wear the same clothes, We walk in the meadow And sing hand in hand.

(continued)

1. George Bozarth, "Brahms's Duets for Soprano and Alto, op. 61," *Studia Musicologica* 25 (1983), 191–210. The article gives useful, engrossing information on the poem's and the song's dates, sources, sketches, and general development through the compositional process. It includes as well some trenchant analytical and critical commentary. Bozarth provides the text, with his translation and annotations, on page 208. The article has a number of unfortunate misprints. After consultation with Bozarth, I have simply corrected those in my text.
2. Brahms changed "lichtbraun" to "nußbraun" (nut-brown). Bozarth ("Brahms's Duets," 195) speculates that the changed adjective better describes some particular singers Brahms had in mind.
3. "Und flichtst" (and if you wove) in later editions of the *Gedichte* (1856, 1867), and in the song. Brahms's piece was published in 1874; Bozarth makes a convincing case that the composer had completed a first version by the late 1850s. Author's annotation: The text emphasizes the *Einheit* of the sisters by capitalizing "Einen." The same happens in later verses with "Einer" and "Einem." The song has "einen / einer / einem."

Wir Schwestern zwei, wir schönen, Wir spinnen in die Wett', Wir sitzen an Einer Kunkel, Wir schlafen in Einem Bett.[4]	We two sisters, we pretty ones, We spin in emulation, We share one distaff, We sleep in one bed.
O Schwestern zwei, ihr schönen! Wie hat sich das Blättchen gewend't![5] Ihr liebet einerlei Liebchen— Jetzt hat das Liedel ein End'.[6]	Oh sisters twain, you pretty ones, How the tables have turned! You love the same sweetheart— Now the little song has an end.

Numbers of voices address us, some in succession and some in overlay.[7] Of these, we shall devote particular attention to Mörike's sisters, Mörike's raisonneur, Brahms's sisters, Brahms's raisonneur, and the singers who perform the duet.

Mörike's Sisters

These sisters speak, during stanzas 1–4 of the poem, with one voice. True, a live reading could be imagined in which one speaker reads (say) stanzas 1 and 3, while another reads stanzas 2 and 4. Still, the text does not individuate two distinct voices in that way—equally imaginable is a live reading in which one speaker reads stanzas 1 and 2 while another reads stanzas 3 and 4, or a live reading in which one speaker reads stanzas 1 and 4 while another reads stanzas 2 and 3.

Mörike's Raisonneur

During stanza 5 of the poem, we hear a different voice. The text does not itself preclude the possibility of two or more personae as raisonneurs. But the text does not particularly suggest that possibility either.[8] Given the cultural conventions of the time and the place, I think that most of us will take the voice of Mörike's raisonneur in the poem to be that of one person, a person decidedly older than the sisters, and male—representing the mature wisdom of its society.[9] While the voice does not explicitly point a moral, it does suggest such pointing. The raisonneur knows what the sisters do not, or at least he can say what they cannot; he knows

4. "Und schlafen" in a later edition (1867).
5. Brahms changed "gewend't" to "gewandt." Bozarth and others observe the wry twist this gives to the final rhyme (or assonance) of the poem.
6. The 1856 and 1867 editions each have (different) slight variations on this text.
7. Using the word "voices," I mean to invoke the formidable work of Edward T. Cone exploring this notion, above all in The *Composer's Voice* (Berkeley: University of California Press, 1974).
8. Bozarth ("Brahms's Duets," 198) refers to my "raisonneur" as "the narrator." Brahms's setting, where the text is delivered by two singers, is another matter—a matter to be discussed later.
9. Brahms's setting, which assigns the raisonneur's text to female singers—the singers who have just impersonated the sisters—is particularly striking in this connection. The matter will be discussed in due course.

better than they how life arranges itself, and he speaks with absolute authority. This is the voice that, in the poem by Hillaire Belloc, tells those of us who are disobedient children always to hold fast to Nurse, "for fear of finding something worse," the voice that presents us with the naughty children of *Struwwelpeter*. It is the voice of the omniscient and omnipotent poet who, having created his dolls, can play with them in any way he chooses, often—as here—with a decidedly sadistic amusement.[10]

What, then, *is* the moral being pointed? I find at least three interrelated components suggested by the poem.

1. Sexual maturity demands competitive individuation.
2. In the Hegelian logic of things, *Einheit* leads perforce to *Entzweiung*.
3. In "modern" (i.e., nineteenth-century European capitalist) society, *Gemeinschaft* is childish and/or peasant-like; it must and will be superseded by a competitive struggle among individual adult agents.

The Biedermeier assumptions underlying each of these three components deserve some discussion. The vulgar Darwinism of component (1) is manifest enough. It presupposes the social impossibility of a polygamous *ménage à trois*, although one might suppose plenty of room in the sisters' well-upholstered bed for their gentleman friend.[11] The Darwinism is "vulgar" because there is no strictly *genetic* value in sexual competition between the sisters if they are identical twins—a possibility that is more than consistent with the text.[12]

The Hegelian logic of things, in component (2), is even more obviously a social construct in which the raisonneur's moral is embedded. True enough, the story does demonstrate how the sisters' unity in all things must perforce lead to an identical choice of mate. But that does not necessarily entail an *Entzweiung*, absent the vulgar Darwinism of component (1), or the capitalist ethic of component (3). Necessary for an *Entzweiung* is the presumption that the sisters cannot share their mate, as they share everything else.

The capitalist ethic of component (3) cannot yet be separated clearly from the vulgar Darwinism of component (1). Nevertheless, I want to articulate it now as an independent idea, because I intend later on to bring some matters of Brechtian stagecraft into my discussion of Brahms's setting, and to talk about the Biedermeier ambience in which we might presume the singers to be performing their song. For the time being, it suffices to note that Mörike's remarks to friends, on writing the poem, can easily be read as suffused with an anxiously—and I would say nastily—patronizing class-consciousness toward young peasant girls, and indeed toward the whole question of "folk" poetry.[13]

10. Bozarth's chronicle ("Brahms's Duets," 197–198) seems strongly consistent with the ideas just advanced, as regards the expressed views of Mörike and his friends. A reading of Mörike's poem by Kristina Muxfeld, to be discussed in an Appendix, is not inconsistent with those ideas, although it raises other possibilities as well.
11. I am grateful to Peter Wollny for having pointed this out, in classroom discussion.
12. More than consistent in light of verse 3, "So gleicht kein Ei dem andern."
13. Bozarth, "Brahms's Duets," 197–198.

Let us now turn to Brahms's setting, having commented on Mörike's sisters and Mörike's raisonneur.

Brahms's Sisters

These sisters, unlike Mörike's, are *entzweit* from the beginning on. They sing as two distinct voices, soprano and alto, and they sing different notes except at the very beginning and at the very end of each musical strophe. The idea of *Einheit* is not realized in any identity of their *musical* voices.[14] Rather, it is represented by their singing almost exclusively note-against-note, as they deliver the same text at the same time. *Einheit* is also represented by the almost exclusively consonant character of the vertical musical intervals they produce, in so singing.

There is only one exception to this, while the sisters are singing (that is, over the first four strophes of the song). They depart from note-against-note singing *only* when singing "wir schönen," and they *always* so depart whenever singing "wir schönen," the alto always making a little melismatic flourish. Furthermore, the sisters sing in vertical dissonance *only* at the first "schön-" of each strophe, where they *always* dissonate.[15] The alto makes the dissonance (e.g., at the beginning of measure 2), and the soprano resolves it (e.g., at the beginning of measure 3). We sense that the alto is the "naughty" child, and the soprano the "good" one. As early as measures 2–3, Brahms thus individuates the sisters by more than tessitura alone; he also introduces the dramatic motif of conflict and its resolution. Repeating the text "wir schönen," Brahms enables each sister to take the fore in turn—first the mischievously dissonating alto (possibly jealous of the soprano's high G), then the well-behaved resolving soprano. "How pretty I am!" and then "How pretty *I* am!" The unctuous legato here, surrounded by staccato notes, makes a very "pretty" effect, particularly if taken at a leisurely Viennese tempo rather than a brisk northern pace.[16]

Example 13.1

The intervallic formula governing the dissonance treatment is 2–3, as sketched on Example 13.1a. This is the source of the dissonance treatment for "Ihr liebet einerlei Liebchen" in the last strophe, as sketched on Example 13.1b. Here the musical conflict breaks out in earnest, as the voices clamber upward each alternately over the other, each dissonating and then resolving as the other bumps it down. One easily visualizes Brahms's sisters—die schönen, die schönen—alternately pushing

14. Brahms's text underlay, interestingly, does not preserve Mörike's capitalizations for "Einen," or "Einer," or "Einem," capitalizations pointed out in note (c) to the poem's text.

15. I count vertical fourths between the sisters as consonant. They always appear in either $^{8}_{5}$ or $^{6}_{3}$ structures over the bass. Bozarth draws attention to the dissonance ("Brahms's Duets," 202–203).

16. Cynthia Gonzales pointed this out in class discussion.

and shoving their way, each in front of the other.[17] We must observe, though, that the text here does not belong to the sisters themselves. Rather it belongs to the raisonneur. The musical link between Example 13.1a and Example 13.1b thereby crucially involves the *singers* who are performing the song, first as they present or represent the sisters during strophes 1–4 (as in Example 13.1a), then as they present or represent the raisonneur in strophe 5 (as in Example 13.1b). We shall have much more to say later on about the role of the singers-as-such. First, let us devote attention to Brahms's raisonneur, especially in the context of Mörike's.

Brahms's Raisonneur

I will continue to use singular nouns and verbs when referring to this persona, whom I will continue to gender as male. I do so partly for convenience, to avoid having to use both singular and plural forms, or both female and male, at each reference to the persona. I also do so partly because Brahms's raisonneur builds upon Mörike's, whom I definitely feel to be a male individual. Mainly, though, I want to use singular male word-forms so as to highlight for the reader the discongruities of my doing so, whenever attention focuses on the two female singers who project the voice of the one male persona.[18]

To be sure, one could interpret Brahms's raisonneur as plural or female. Thus, one might imagine that the raisonneur's voice is that of the two sisters in their inmost thoughts, each covertly voicing to herself thoughts and information she could not voice publicly, in the hearing of the other. Raphael Atlas suggests such a reading: "These new personas are the individuals behind the double image, three-dimensional creatures ironically addressing the twin doll-figures which have concealed them until now. . . . The sisters bring their competition into the open only to close the case immediately."[19] Or one might imagine Brahms's raisonneur to be an older, more experienced woman, or a pair of such women—perhaps the sisters themselves, looking back at a later time.[20] I think that such ideas could work in performance. But I still prefer to think of Brahms's raisonneur as singular and male, projecting the text of Mörike's omniscient male voice. That leads to a formal Brecht-

17. The voices also each make little melismas, singing two eighths on a syllable against a quarter in the other voice. The soprano is now the actively melismatic voice; it has three such melismas during the fight, while the alto has only one. The soprano caps off this behavior with a final climactic melisma on "End," in the final verse, reaching its high G for the last time.

    Bozarth (ibid.) points out that the 2–3 on "schönen" was not present on Brahms's early sketches, but only appeared after Brahms had sketched the "ihr liebet" passage.

18. Discongruous, too, is the age of the raisonneur, whom I have imagined as older than the sisters, an authority figure. The singers, who have just impersonated the young sisters, must now represent the mature raisonneur—whom, of course, they cannot "impersonate" in the same way. Much more will be said later on this subject.

19. Raphael Atlas, "Text and Musical Gesture in Brahms's Vocal Duets and Quartets with Piano," *Journal of Musicology* 10.2 (Spring 1992), 231–260. Atlas's commentary on *Die Schwestern* appears on pages 240–242.

20. Lara Pellegrinelli suggested these ideas in a class.

ian *Alienation* (*Verfremdung*) between the singers-as-actors, and the material they have to deliver in the fifth strophe. I find the Alienation Effect particularly convincing here, and I shall have a good deal more to say on the subject later.

The voice of Brahms's raisonneur is clearly marked off musically by the change of mode during strophe 5. In that strophe, verses 2 and 4 of the text are set, with some variations, as major parallels to the second and fourth verses of earlier, minor, strophes. In particular, the extended G major cadence of verse 4 in strophe 5, at which the raisonneur's text comes to an emphatic "End," extends a major parallel version of the g minor cadences that closed the singing at the end of each earlier strophe.[21]

The third verse of text in the raisonneur's strophe is set by the musical fight discussed earlier. The vocal parts conspicuously do not parallel the third verses of earlier strophes. Instead, as pointed out before, they draw a contrapuntal impetus from the 2–3 figure of "wir schönen, wir schönen," a figure taken from the first verses of earlier strophes. A rationale for the a minor tonicization and cadence, at the end of the raisonneur's third verse, will be presented later. As we shall see, the a minor cadence can be referred back to the F major harmony heard at the end of the third verse in each earlier strophe. But that reference will not be what one would call "parallel" musically.

The first verse of strophe 5 does not parallel the first verses of earlier strophes either. To be sure, the parallelism is there in the first complete measure of strophe 5. But measures 2 and 3 of strophe 5 depart sharply from paralleling the earlier model. These measures of strophe 5 specifically do not tonicize iii in G major, as measures 2–3 of earlier strophes tonicized III in g minor. If they did, the soprano would have an F♯ at the beginning of measure 2 in strophe 5, rather than an F natural. The possibility is sketched in Example 13.2.

Example 13.2

The reader who sings over Example 13.2 will notice how difficult it is to produce the soprano's F♯ at the beginning of measure 2. The difficulty is not simply in vocal technique. (For many sopranos, the F♯ lies at the break between throat and head registers of the voice.) The difficulty is much more a matter of psychology: F natural is the thematic continuation for the soprano singer, after reaching the high G of the arpeggio in measure 1. The soprano's F natural at measure 2 of strophe 5 does not "parallel" the earlier F naturals of the *minore*, it preserves them.

More will be said later about the thematic character of F natural throughout the song.[22] Here—at measure 2 of the final strophe—we shall focus upon the dif-

21. The turn back to g minor at the end of the final ritornello in the piano, after the fifth strophe, is another matter. This is no longer the raisonneur's music proper. Later discussion will engage the "voice" of the piano, yet another persona in the song.

22. Comments by Natalie Boisvert originally suggested this exploration to me.

ference in tonal function, from the F natural at measure 2 of earlier strophes. In g minor, F natural—within the diatonic descending scale—has a strong harmonic function as $\hat{5}$ of III. In G major, F natural is chromatic, and its main harmonic function is as $\hat{4}$ of IV. These functions are manifest in Brahms's music. In the final strophe, the "schön" F natural of the soprano in measure 2 is no longer a dominant, intensified as such by its dissonant minor seventh in the alto. The alto sister is no longer on the scene; the alto singer is still with us, but she is now a part of the raisonneur's voice. In that capacity, she does not dissonate with the soprano singer but, rather, participates in a consonant $^6_3$ harmony, taking the third above the bass, in consonant fourth-relation to the soprano above. The F harmony is no longer a dominant of B$\flat$ (= III of g); it is now a subdominant of C (= IV of G). And the harmony of measure 3, in the raisonneur's strophe, does not resolve the harmony of measure 2—as did the harmony of measure 3 in earlier strophes. Rather, the harmony of the raisonneur's measure 3 leads IV of C to V^6_5 of C, prolonging the F natural as a (chromatic) dissonant seventh; the moment of resolution is thereby deferred to the beginning of measure 4, where the second verse of the raisonneur's text begins. Although the F of the raisonneur's measure 3 is a dissonant seventh of its harmony, there is no dissonance between the voices of the singers, who are now jointly presenting the voice of Brahms's raisonneur, rather than individually articulating the voices of Brahms's sisters. The absence of dissonance between the two voices highlights the subsequent 2–3 figures in the musical fight during verse 3 of the raisonneur's strophe, making those dissonances all the fresher when they eventually do appear.

Brahms gives us one final 2–3 formula at the very end of the sung text, extending the G major cadence at the repetition of "Liedel ein." The 2–3 figure here plays its traditional role as a formula in a (decorated) suspension clausula approaching a unison cadence on G. "This," says the raisonneur, "is where such dissonant 2–3 figures will eventually get you, O sisters—to the end of your saccharine relationship." The raisonneur, representing the mature wisdom of his culture, has presumably studied "Palestrina style," a particular construct of that culture.[23] Very neat is the assonance of "Liedel ein" with "Liebchen," where the 2–3 figure was most recently heard before.

The Singers: Acting Technique

Brahms indicates that they are to be female, with differing ("ungleich") vocal qualities. He could, of course, have set the piece for matching voices had he wished to do so—for two sopranos or two altos. I think most of us imagine the singers as young, at least young enough so that they can impersonate Brahms's sisters, based

23. The interested reader will find pertinent discussion of Brahms's exposure to Bellermann's counterpoint treatise, and to other theoretical publications involving earlier music, in the appendix for an article of mine, "Brahms, his Past, and Modes of Music Theory." The article appears on pages 13–27 of *Brahms Studies, Analytical and Historical Perspectives*, ed. George S. Bozarth (Oxford: Clarendon Press, 1990). The appendix occupies pages 25–27.

as those are on Mörike's. But then in what terms do the singers, whom we have just heard impersonating young girls, present the voice of an authoritative single male raisonneur during strophe 5? They surely do not impersonate him, in the same way they "impersonate" the sisters.[24]

A related question, already raised briefly, involves the musical fight during verse 3 of the final strophe. On what dramatic terms can the singers behave musically like fighting sisters, when they are actually delivering text that belongs to a different persona, text that refers to the sisters as "ihr," not as "wir"?

I find the notion of Epic acting style, in the sense of Brecht, a cogent way to explore these questions. The singers, in this view, are not being the raisonneur in the final strophe. Nor are they being the sisters in verse 3 of that strophe. Rather, they are being singers throughout the strophe. In so being, they are showing us how a raisonneur who represents the authority of mature male wisdom in their society (Mörike, for example) responds to the picture painted in strophes 1 through 4. And then, during the musical fight, they are showing us how the sisters will behave when they learn the true state of affairs. Better yet, in Brechtian terms, they are showing us how the raisonneur did so respond, and how he imagined the sisters would behave when they learned the truth.

A useful reference work for those unfamiliar with Brecht's theories (in other than their vulgarized popular forms) is Martin Esslin's *Brecht: The Man and His Work*.[25] An extended quotation from Esslin will be to the point here:

> The basis of the Brechtian technique of acting is the conception that the actor should not regard himself [herself/themselves, passim] as impersonating the character so much as *narrating* the actions of another person at a definite time in the past. To illustrate these actions and to make them fully understood by the audience he goes through the motions the character made, imitates the tone of his voice, repeats his facial expression, but only to the extent of *quoting* them. The Brechtian style of acting is acting in quotation marks.
>
> Brecht liked to illustrate his basic concept of acting by the example of an everyday occurrence one might observe in any large town. A street accident has happened. A crowd has collected on the scene, and an eyewitness is telling the bystanders what has taken place: he wants to indicate that the old man who has been run over walked very slowly, so he will imitate his gait to show exactly what he means. He is in fact *quoting* the old man's walk. And he is quoting only *those elements* of the old man's movements which are *relevant* to the situation he wants to describe. The eyewitness concerned is far from wanting to *impersonate* the victim: "He never forgets, nor does he allow anyone to forget, that he is not the one whose action is being demonstrated [i.e. who 'is being' run over], but the one who demonstrates it." [The quotation from Brecht is cited here by Esslin.] The character who

24. The question can be avoided, to be sure, by supposing Brahms's raisonneurs to be plural and female, along lines discussed earlier. My point here will be that we do not have to avoid the question. Indeed, meeting it head-on, I hope to show that we can read some interesting extra dimensions into the dramaturgy of the song's presentation.

25. Martin Esslin, *Brecht: The Man and His Work* (Garden City, N.Y.: Anchor Books, Doubleday & Company, Inc., 1961). Esslin gives a very complete bibliography of all pertinent writings in German and in English as of that time.

> is being shown and the actor who demonstrates him remain clearly differentiated. And the actor retains his freedom to *comment* on the actions of the person whose behavior he is displaying.[26]

The same bystander might then go on to show how the driver of the car reacted in horror when—too late—she saw the old man; how the driver twisted frantically at the steering wheel as the car skidded out of control; and so forth. The bystander, that is, can move freely from presenting one character to presenting another character, so long as a suitable story is there to make the connection plausible.

We are in fact used to accepting this style of acting within the domain of classical Greek tragedy, where it is codified by the convention of the Messenger. Think, for example of the messenger who narrates the death of Jocasta and the reactions of Oedipus, in the Sophocles drama. If you review the speech, you will find that there is an enormous amount of "acting" to be done there. But we never believe that the messenger "is" Jocasta, or that he "is" Oedipus. He shows us, rather, how they behaved (past tense). That, one notes, does not destroy the overwhelming emotional and dramatic force of the speech, when well presented. To be sure, the actor who plays Oedipus may act as if he "is" Oedipus, soliciting our identification. (I do not believe that he must or even necessarily should do so, but the role certainly can admit an Illusionist acting style.) The Greek theater, in that important respect, is not necessarily an Epic Theater as a whole. Less so is Shakespearean theater as a whole. Even there, however, we find Shakespeare paying tribute to Epic (probably Senecan) acting style in such set pieces as the player's speech in Hamlet about Pyrrhus, Priam, and Hecuba, and one presumes that Shakespeare expected us to find the player's presentation moving, as Hamlet does. (The complexity of this scene involves an actual actor impersonating—in Illusionist non-Epic style—the character of a German actor visiting Hamlet's court, who in turn gives an Epic performance of his Senecan text.)

The notorious Alienation Effect, in this connection, arises from any of many possible devices that might be used to project strongly to an audience the distinction between presenting actor and character presented. The Alienation helps make it clear that the actor is not being, but showing, the character. Brahms's singers are thus Alienated from my raisonneur by manifestly being two, and being female—and, I think, by ideally being young enough so that we have already accepted them as impersonating the sisters, in distinction to the raisonneur. (This Alienation disappears, or is substantially weakened, in readings that do not number and gender the raisonneur as one male persona.) Then, during the musical fight in verse 3 of the final strophe, the singers are Alienated from the fighting sisters whom they show to us, because by now we have shifted gears, and suppose the singers to be showing us the raisonneur, not the sisters. (They are showing us the sisters, so to speak, in the raisonneur's imagination.) The text, with "ihr liebet" instead of "wir lieben," reinforces that Alienation.

An interesting feature of my reading is that, over the first four strophes, we accept the singers as indeed impersonating the sisters, in Romantic-Illusionist acting

26. Esslin, *Brecht*, 130.

style. The ironic jar when the raisonneur's voice suddenly enters the scene (with concomitant changes in the music) is all the more intense because the acting style now abruptly also shifts, from Romantic-Illusionist to Epic. Brahms's subtle individuations of the sisters during strophes 1 through 4, as discussed earlier, prepare us for the surprise discovery that the singers are not, in fact, the sisters.

So far I have commented on Epic acting as a matter of sheer technique. Now it is time to bring the sociopolitical aspects of Brechtian theory into the picture, along with other pertinent sociopolitical considerations. We shall see, in fact, that the singers are *not* ideal Epic actors in the sense of Brechtian theater. They lack a crucial aspect of that style; specifically, they lack an ironic and self-consciously critical attitude toward the society in which they are immersed.

The Singers: Sociopolitical Contexts

> Hartlaub [in 1837] was correct to suggest [to Mörike, after reading the poem,] that, rather than being sung by a dayworker's daughter in a spinning room, these verses should be set for a pair of "edle Dirnen," or sung with piano accompaniment in a bourgeois living room.
>
> This is, of course, exactly what Brahms did in the late 1850s.[27]

Most of us, when left to our own fantasies, will go along with Hartlaub's second alternative, I think, when we imagine who is performing the song. We imagine the singers to be girls or quite young women, very likely actual sisters in a bourgeois household. The girls are singing Brahms's music in their Biedermeier German (Austrian, Swiss) parlor, probably accompanied by their mother or an older sister at the piano. They are performing for "the grown-ups," including their father and very likely some after-dinner guests as well. The performance is an occasion to display skills appropriate to their social position as unmarried young bourgeois females, and it is thereby also an occasion to solicit and win appreciative praise from their elders, not only for those skills but also for the charm with which they display themselves, prettily dressed (in identical dresses) and prettily singing—die schönen, die schönen. I can even see them joining hands and doing a modest but cute little dance turn during each ritornello in the piano.

No wonder they hate each other. They can hardly wait for the musical fight in the last strophe, which gives each a sanctioned opportunity to upstage her sibling

27. Bozarth, "Brahms's Duets," 198–199. For background on Wilhelm Hartlaub and his friendship with Mörike, Bozarth refers to Renate von Heydebrand, *Eduard Mörikes Gedichtwerk* (Stuttgart: J.B. Metzlersche Verlagsbuchhandlung, 1972). The cited remarks by Hartlaub appear on page 248 of von Heydebrand's book. "edle Dirnen" would be "aristocratic young damsels." That seems quite incompatible with the alternative "bourgeois living-room" to which Hartlaub refers. The nobility and the peasantry share a feudal ambience quite foreign to that parlor, so important a feature of the Biedermeier capitalist ethic discussed earlier. The edle Dirnen will reappear in the Appendix to this chapter, where they comport well with an interesting reading of Mörike's poem by Kristina Muxfeld.

while "showing," in good Epic fashion, how the sisters-in-the-song will behave (or rather, in the past tense, how the raisonneur thought they would behave). I remarked earlier that during the fight one "easily visualizes Brahms's sisters—die schönen, die schönen—alternately pushing and shoving their way, each in front of the other." That idea was not quite exact. It is, I think, the singers, not the sisters, whom one visualizes in this connection. True enough, the singers, in so behaving, are showing us (as Epic actors) the behavior of the sisters. But it is the singers, not the sisters, who are actually spoiling for a fight—a fight for which Brahms's piece gives them a welcome opportunity. (No doubt the grown-ups will find the "mock" combat of the singers highly amusing and charming.)

In expressing their antagonism as competitive individuals who can no longer be constrained by an artificial *Gemeinschaft*, the singers are executing precisely the agenda demanded by the "moral" of Mörike's raisonneur: they are exemplifying the Biedermeier lessons of vulgar Darwinian competition, of Hegelian *Entzweiung*, and of mature capitalistic individuation. No wonder that this performance will be received with enthusiastic approbation by the grown-ups who concur with those cultural morals, identifying with the "mature wisdom" of the raisonneur. One may even imagine the grown-ups, after the singers' performance, remarking not only on how pretty the girls are, but on "how much they have grown,"—that is, how well they are learning the cultural lessons proper for young female adults, how well they "understand" the message of the raisonneur whose behavior they are portraying in their Epic presentation.

It is now past time that I acknowledge my indebtedness to Ruth Solie, writing on Schumann's *Frauenliebe* :

> Because nineteenth-century listeners expected music to carry messages, the [*Frauenliebe*] songs would have been understood in their own time to be doing "cultural work," and indeed would have been used by their culture in ways that made that work explicit and gave social sanction to their message.[28]
>
> Songs such as the *Frauenliebe* cycle have in their presentational character a stronger and more immediate power to convey such cultural messages than any literature could. They have, that is, considerable performative meaning. Though actually conveying the sentiments of men, they are of course to be performed by a woman, in a small and intimate room in someone's home, before people who are known to her and some of whom might be potential suitors; she is unlikely to be a professional singer but, rather, someone's daughter or niece or cousin—an ordinary woman, significantly enough—and she sings, in the native tongue and contemporary idiom of herself and her hearers, texts which seem already to have been popular favorites, no doubt to an audience of approvingly nodding heads.[29]

Just so our young singers, while executing the agenda implicit in the raisonneur's "moral," thereby soliciting and winning the approbation of the grown-ups,

28. Ruth A. Solie, "Whose Life? The Gendered Self in Schumann's *Frauenliebe* Songs," in *Music and Text: Critical Inquiries*, ed. Steven Paul Scher (Cambridge, England: Cambridge University Press, 1992), 219–240. The cited text is from page 219.

29. Solie, "*Frauenliebe*," 226.

are seducing and charming their audience, rather than stimulating their audience to critique its own society. And that aspect of our singers' behavior is quintessentially un-Brechtian. The Brechtian acting style is not only a matter of technique; it also demands that actors challenge their audiences so as to elicit such social critiques.

> [Brecht thought of the epic theatre as one] which aimed at awakening the spectator's critical faculty, which concentrated on showing mankind from the point of view of social relationships. . . .
>
> A narrative theatre, he argues, can show far more than just the way people act and suffer. . . . It can comment on the action. By keeping the spectator in a critical frame of mind it prevents him from seeing the conflict entirely from the point of view of the characters involved in it and from accepting their passions and motives as being conditioned by "eternal human nature." Such a theatre will make the audience see the contradictions in the existing state of society; it might even make them ask themselves how such a society might be changed.[30]

Now our young Biedermeier singers, as we have seen, actually encourage their audience—the "grown-ups"—to see the conflict entirely from the point of view of one of the characters in their text, namely the raisonneur. And they encourage their audience to accept the sisters' passions and motives, when conflict breaks out during the musical fight, as being conditioned by "eternal human nature." Far from making the grown-ups see contradictions in the existing state of their society, the Biedermeier young singers encourage them in their belief that all is quite as it should be: How charmingly the girls show how "mature" they are getting, how well they understand and appreciate the raisonneur's moral!

But is everything quite as it should be? What do we think, what should we think of a society that looks with encouragement and amused approbation upon the rupturing of friendship and family ties—of sisterly love and *Gemeinschaft*—all in the name of some eternally established and necessarily competitive "individualism"? The Biedermeier singers do not press those questions upon their audience, the grown-ups in the parlor, yet Brahms's composition is pressing the questions upon me as a member of his audience—a point to which I shall soon return.

Far from challenging the grown-ups, the singers rather retreat from the dangerously overt combat of their third verse in the final strophe. If the nasty sibling antagonism underlying the musical fight were allowed to persist through the end of the song, the grown-ups would likely feel a certain unease, perhaps even discomfort. And that would endanger the impression the singers must leave, as sweet young things obedient to the proper social norms of their culture. Hence the retreat portrayed halfway through the final piano epilogue: the G major of the Epic acting style, now becoming uncomfortable for the singers, disappears as suddenly as it had emerged; the music reverts to the Illusionist g minor folk style where the singers "are" the sisters. "We are just sweet young things after all," the singers seem

30. Esslin, *Brecht*, 142. Esslin goes on to argue that Brecht was mistaken to suppose that such critical questioning need necessarily lead to Marxist answers. I find no such overt supposition in Brecht's writings—the relation between the dramaturgical and political aspects of his life seems to me a good deal more subtle.

to be saying, "perish the thought that we should be upsetting you or making you think. We are just here to be cute and to amuse you—we are, in fact, the sisters."

But the device, while presumably working for the grown-ups who are the singers' audience, does not work so well for us, Brahms's audience. We sense a certain awkwardness, a certain clumsiness, as if the singers, having remained in G major a bit too long, were trying too late to get back into their little dance routine and thereby botching it, slightly marring the final effect of their Biedermeier show. This clumsiness could be performed "cutely," to be sure, and so "in character." That said, we should observe that such a manner of speaking treats the singers not as actors in their own show, but rather as characters in Brahms's show. Now we are thinking of Brahms as Epic dramatist. Rather than "being" the singers, he shows us how they behave(d); and, to boot, he fulfills the Brechtian role of social critic in so doing.[31] By keeping us in a critical frame of mind (to paraphrase the earlier quotation from Esslin), Brahms prevents us from seeing the conflicts (conflicts between the singers, conflicts between the singers and their grown-up audience) entirely from the point of view of the characters involved (the singers and the grown-ups). He prevents us from accepting their passions and motives (the jealous envy of the singers, their desire to show themselves off, the smug self-assurance of the grown-ups, and so forth) as being conditioned by "eternal human nature." Brahms thereby makes us see contradictions in the state of (his—to some extent still our) society; he might even make us ask ourselves how such a society might be changed. And so the singers do not have the last word, the "End," after all; the last word belongs to Brahms (who naturally identifies himself with the accompanist at the piano, finally free to put in his two cents worth now that the singers have stopped).

The Singers: Final Thoughts

By "the singers," I shall always (continue to) refer to the people whom I have imagined as bourgeois young females of the nineteenth century. We have seen how these people function dramatically in several ways, and it will be wise to summarize our observations in that connection.

1. They can impersonate the sisters, in Illusionist acting style.
2. In Epic acting style, they can present the raisonneur's voice, showing us the raisonneur issuing his moral, showing us how he imagined the sisters fighting.

31. One might wonder: How could Brahms possibly "be" the young female singers, anyway? To explore the sense of my remark, let a skeptical reader compare Brahms to Wagner in this respect. Most of us, I believe, will agree that Wagner is at his most Wagnerian precisely when he is "being" Isolde, or Brünnhilde, or Wotan, or Sachs, or even Alberich, and so on. And we know what we mean by that manner of speaking. The Wagnerian theater was one of Brecht's most formidable targets.

I wonder what would have happened if Brahms had lived on into an age when he could have read and seen Brecht's dramas. Personally, I think he could have made fantastic music-drama with a script like *Mother Courage*. (The duet *Edward* gives some hint of specific possibilities there.) Of course, he and Brecht would have had terrible fights over the role of the music.

3. They can also "present" the sisters, in Epic acting style, rather than impersonating them. They clearly do this in the musical fight within the strophe. Later on, I shall argue that they also do this, to some degree, in the earlier strophes.
4. They can figure as "characters" themselves in an Epic dramatic presentation by Brahms, a presentation that makes us aware of a social critique taking note of the singers' behavior.

Since the word "singers" is now so overloaded with reference, we shall need a different term for people who might be performing the vocal parts of the piece today. I shall call them "current-day vocalists," thus distinguishing them from "the singers," who will always be the girls in the Biedermeier parlor.

Musical Matters: Introductory

The rest of this chapter involves more technical musical explorations. I shall first propose a basically four-square rhythmic/metric setting, embodying a folkish *Vierhebigkeit*, as a template that underlies Brahms's actual music. This will enable us to explore in more detail the composer's techniques of phrase extension, and how they abet his presentation of the drama.

The "*Vierer*" of my four-square setting will embody certain decisions about melodic and harmonic priorities—indeed, the rhythmic exercise will force such decisions. And those, in turn, will clarify and support a Schenkerian reading for the music.[32]

My particular reading brings out a certain Dorian quality about the g minor strophes, and that will lead to a more thorough exploration of the piece's F naturals as thematic entities, an issue already broached earlier.

The Dorian F major *Stufe*, VII of the g Dorian mode, can be inverted into a functional a minor *Stufe*, ii of the G major mode. The pitch-class inversion has one center at E-and-F; it also leaves invariant the pitch-class dyad {A,C}. Thereby it performs a *Leittonwechsel* on the F major and a minor *Stufen*. The other center of the same inversion is at B♭-and-B♮; the inversion leaves invariant the pitch-class dyad {G,D} and thereby transforms the g minor *Klang* into the G major one. These abstract Riemannian matters will be applied analytically, to see how the music for the third verse of the final strophe, the music for the musical fight, can be heard as a transformation of the music for the third verses of the earlier g minor (g Dorian) strophes. The textual and dramatic consequences will be explored.[33]

32. I shall not refer specifically, in connection with the activities so far described, to William Rothstein's monumental achievement, *Phrase Rhythm in Tonal Music* (New York: Schirmer Books, 1989). Nor do I suppose that he would agree with all of my specific assertions and readings. But my attitude toward the activities described is strongly conditioned by his ideas.

33. Edward Gollin suggested the idea to me, that one could hear G major in the piece as an inversional transformation of the earlier g minor. He also proposed that the transformation allegorized the image of "gewandt." His initiative stimulated me to explore the inversional transformation just described, of F-*Stufe* into a-*Stufe*.

Other inversional relations are also of interest. Inversion-about-A transforms the E♭ of the alto's "schönen" into the D♯ of the piano left hand under "liebet."[34] Inversion-about-G transforms, some into others, various G-modes latent in the piece's high-level structure. These matters will also be examined.

Musical Matters: The Four-Square Version

Example 13.3

Example 13.3 shows a four-square version of the music for the g-minor strophes, complete with piano ritornello. The "four-square version" will also be called "the sisters' song." There is no reason to suppose that Brahms ever sketched any such thing, or that this music precedes the final version in any other sort of chronological sense.[35] But it is a useful hypothetical version, because it emphasizes the "folkish" character of the sisters, an important aspect of the drama. Its rhythmic/metric character projects a manner in which the sisters might have sung, if sisters and singers were in fact the same. The four-square version is also interesting musically in the sheer fact that it can be inferred from Brahms's piece without doing much violence to melody or harmony. That enables us to analyze Brahms's music as if it were a "transformation" of the four-square version—a stimulating exercise, as we shall soon see.

Brackets above the top staff of Example 13.3 set apart what is sung, from the piano ritornello. Concomitant text for the sung music will shortly appear on a separate figure. Symbols (a) through (e) mark, for future commentary, places where Brahms's actual setting extends the four-square version. (I shall take the liberty of

34. This idea, too, was suggested by Edward Gollin.

35. Bozarth ("Brahms's Duets," 207) gives what he calls a "reconstruction" of a "Simple Strophic Setting" for the g minor strophes, based on autograph and sketch material. The reconstruction already essentially includes all the extensions of my "four-square version" that appear in the published score.

speaking in this manner here and later. We must recall that I am really discussing how the four-square version contracts Brahms's setting, but the analytic myth of the reverse transformation will be stimulating, as noted earlier.)

We can comment on symbol (e) at once, since it does not involve text-setting. So well-oiled is Brahms's technical machinery—Joseph Kerman once compared it to a Rolls-Royce engine—that without going through the present exercise we might not even have noticed the "extra" two eighth notes in the phrase, extending the four-square setting by one beat. But if we were trying to dance to Brahms's ritornello, we would notice the extra beat at once! Any musician who has ever accompanied a beginning or intermediate classical ballet class will recall the physical havoc wreaked on traditional choreography by such a "ninth beat" in the middle of an apparently eight-beat phrase. I suggested earlier that one could visualize the singers doing a little dance-turn during the ritornello, and I think the image comes in useful here, even if one does not attempt to stage an actual dance turn. The extra beat at (e) on Example 13.3 then indicates a glitch in the singers' impersonation of the sisters. (The sisters' dance on Example 13.3 is a perfectly conventional eight-beat affair, easily executed.) Perhaps the singers, caught up in their own rivalry, momentarily stumble in their impersonation of the sisters' *Einheit*. Perhaps one singer makes a deliberate error in her routine that will make the other look clumsy. One might even imagine one of the singers—I should say the alto in the first ritornello—giving the other a surreptitious kick beneath their swirling Dirndls, to make the other stumble and appear clumsy to the grown-ups. In subsequent occurrences of the ritornello, the singers could then alternately trade surreptitious kicks. In any case, the glitch is some sort of Alienation device, to make us sense—if at first only subliminally—that the singers are not, in fact, the sisters they are pretending to impersonate.

Example 13.4 examines the specifics of Brahms's other "expansions" from the singers' song. The symbols (a) through (d) key in to the places similarly marked on Example 13.3. On Example 13.4(a) the text and rhythm for the sisters' song appear above; below that are aligned rhythm and text for the corresponding span of Brahms's song. The harmonic plan (for both versions of the song) is aligned still farther beneath. Commentary then appears, summarizing the ways in which harmony and text are prolonged in Brahms's setting. Finally, the total durational "expansion," from the sisters' song to Brahms's, is noted.

Examples 13.4(b) through (d) follow the same format as Example 13.4(a). The analysis for Example 13.4(b) needs further discussion, but first we should note the progressive character of Brahms's rhythmic expansions.

Example 13.4(a) expands by two quarters.

Example 13.4(b) expands by two quarters.

Example 13.4(c) expands by four quarters.

Example 13.4(d) expands by four quarters.

Example 13.3(e), in the ritornello, expands by one quarter.

Example 13.4(a) for the next stanza expands by two quarters.

Example 13.4

a.

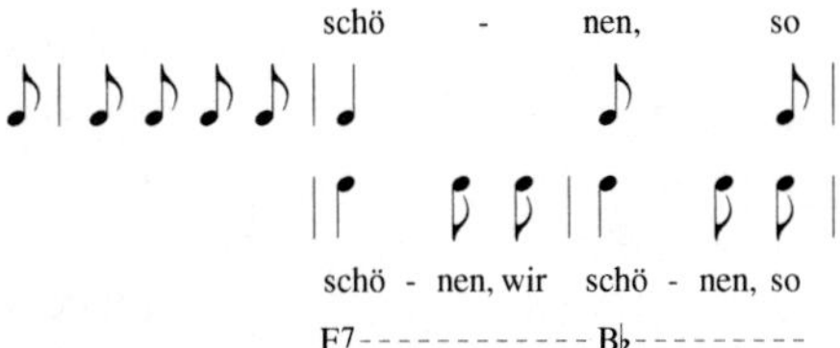
schö - nen, so
schö - nen, wir schö - nen, so
F7------------ B♭---------

harmony: F^7 prolonged 1 quarter; B♭ prolonged 1 quarter.
text: "wir schönen" repeated.
total expansion: 2 quarters

b.

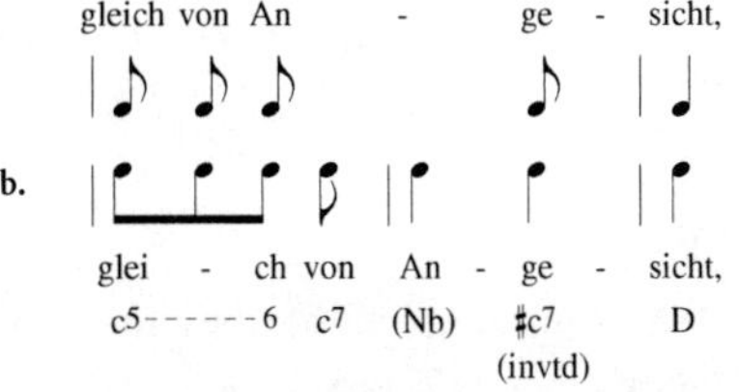
gleich von An - ge - sicht,
glei - ch von An - ge - sicht,
c5------6 c7 (Nb) ♯c7 D
(invtd)

(NOT D—(Nb)—D. The cadential V arrives only at "-sicht.")
harmony: c^7 prolonged up to c♯^{7} (g♯$^4_3$) for 3 eighths; c♯^{7} prolonged 1 eighth.
text: "gleich" prolonged 2 eighths via melisma;
"An-" and "-ge-" each augmented from eighth to quarter.
total expansion: 2 quarters

c.

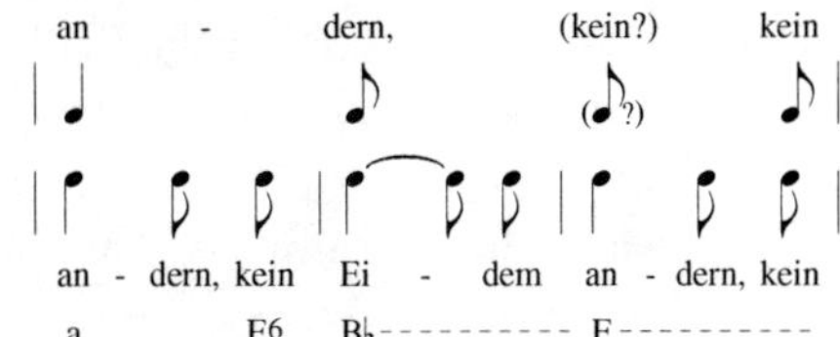
an - dern, (kein?) kein
an - dern, kein Ei - dem an - dern, kein
a F6 B♭---------- F----------

harmony: a minor prolonged 2 eighths (counting the F^6 as part of the prolongation);
B♭ and F each prolonged 3 eighths.
text: "kein Ei dem andern" repeated.
total expansion: 4 quarters

d.

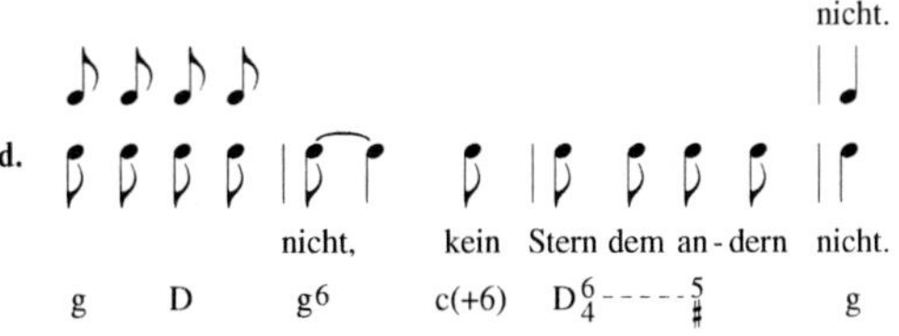
nicht.
nicht, kein Stern dem an-dern nicht.
g D g6 c(+6) D$^6_4$-----$^5_♯$ g

harmony: deceptive cadence at g^6 generates an extending cadential phrase.
text: "kein Stern dem andern" repeated.
total expansion: 4 quarters

And so forth. Beginning with each ritornello, and continuing through each subsequent stanza up to the last, successive expansions are by one, two, two, four, and four quarters. We shall see later that the musical fight in the last strophe expands its four-square model by eight quarters.

Now I shall comment on my analytic note ("NOT D—(Nb)—D") for Example

13.4(b). The harmonic underlay I give, "c7 (Nb) ♯c7 (inverted)," reflects the structural sense I hear in my four-square version for this music. In that version, the bass line rises stepwise from first to fifth degree of the g minor scale, reaching the cadential fifth degree only at "-sicht." The $g\sharp^{4}_{3}$ harmony just before "-sicht" works as an inverted diminished-seventh harmony on c♯. The C♯, as it were, belongs in the continuo bass—chromatically filling in the rising step from C to D in the bass line. The G of the $g\sharp^{4}_{3}$ reanimates, as it were, the fundamental bass at a higher middleground level; it touches the background tonic G once more just before the *Quintzug* G–D in the bass reaches a dominant *Teiler* at the D of "-sicht."

In this reading, Brahms's D harmony at "An-" is not a *Teiler*, but a foreground voice-leading event. It provides neighbor notes for the ♯c7 harmony that follows—hence, Example 13.4(b) analyzes it as "(Nb)." More specifically—looking at the score now—a c7 harmony is reached at "von." It may at first seem as if it is passing on to a structural D *Teiler* harmony at "An-", but I am rejecting that analysis. Rather, I hear the c7 being prolonged as follows:

The soprano's B♭ at "von," within the c7 harmony, is neighbored by the A of "An-," and then returns to B♭ at "-ge-," within the c♯7 harmony.

The alto's G at "von", within the c7 harmony, is neighbored by the F♯ of "An-," and then returns to G at "-ge-," within the c♯7 harmony. This gesture is doubled by the piano RH, except that the returning G at "-ge-" is *untergeworfen* into the bass by the harmonic inversion.

The RH's E♭ at "von," within the c7 harmony, is neighbored by the RH D of "An-" and then returns, at "-ge-," to E natural within the c♯7 harmony.

The LH's C at "von," within the c7 harmony, is neighbored by the bass D of "An-," and then returns to C♯ at "-ge-," within the c♯7 harmony. (The C♯, as noted earlier, is the note that "belongs" in the continuo bass.)[36]

If, as I argue, the D major harmony at "An-" is not the *Teiler* that one might well mistake it for at first (before hearing the music for "-ge-sicht,"), then why did Brahms use just that harmony at that place? I think he wished to suggest the possibility of a structural arrival in the music a measure earlier than it actually comes. The dramaturgical point, I believe, is to suggest to the listener the possibility of a rhythmically and metrically "four-square" song, a song the sisters—rather than the singers—might have sung, a song that the singers are not in fact presenting to us. Indeed, precisely the song of Example 13.3 hereabouts. The music for measures 4–5.1 in Brahms's piece is exactly the same as the music for measures 3–4.1 in Example 13.3, "the sisters' song," except that Brahms's accompaniment repeats its c minor figure on the last eighth of his measure 4, while the accompaniment for the sisters' song puts the diminished-seventh harmony on the last eighth of its measure

36. This reading succeeds well in keeping structural tension going through to the end of the phrase. It delivers the text, in that regard, a lot more idiomatically than the reading which arrives at V prematurely, on "An-". Thus: not "so glei—ch von AN ( ) ge ( ) sicht," a reading almost impossible to deliver idiomatically with the long quantity of Brahms's quarter note on "-ge-," but rather "so glei—ch von An-ge—sicht." The weight on "-sicht," in the latter delivery, is quantitative rather than stressed. The delivery *draws out* "Angesicht" without particularly stressing any of its syllables.

3, to contract and square off the sense of the entire phrase that Brahms actually wrote. In particular, the music for the voice parts in measures 4–5.1 of Brahms is exactly the same as the music for the voice parts in measures 3–4.1 of Example 13.3.

Brahms's text-setting helps us to continue listening through the false arrival on "An-." If the arrival were real, and the music really four-square, then why not set the text as on the top part of Example 13.4(b)? The false arrival is thus not meant to fool us completely, but only to suggest, as I have put it, the possibility of a four-square version. And the melisma on "gleich," preventing the four-square text-setting of Example 13.4(b), is a device that works against the four-square version, a device that we may therefore presume to belong to the singers, the more cosmopolitan young bourgeoises, rather than the naive sisters.

I think that expansions (a), (c), and (d) of Example 13.4, as well as expansion (b), all have a similar dramatic purpose. In successfully playing with the rhythmically square rhetoric of the sisters' song, the expansions introduce Alienating material into the singers' performance. The folkish sisters would certainly not have the sophistication to execute such rhythmic maneuvers at all, let alone to bring them off so smoothly, with such grace and charm.

Example 13.5

Example 13.5 gives a four-square version for the final strophe, without ritornello. I shall call this "the raisonneur's song." The title is convenient in the context of the present critique, although my raisonneur would certainly be sophisticated enough to make his own rhythmic/metric expansions on a four-square version. "His" four-square version is in large part, I think, an inference from the four-square sisters' song, plus the strophic character of text and music throughout the poem and piece.

The expansions of Brahms's piece at (f) and (g) of Example 13.5 can be analyzed straightforwardly enough now, after the work on Example 13.3 and Examples 13.4(a)(b). Brahms's music at (f) of Example 13.5 expands the four-square version by two quarters, like (a) of Example 13.4. And Brahms's music at (g) of Example 13.5 also expands the four-square version by two quarters, like (b) of Example 13.4. The expansion process now continues formalistically enough: where

Brahms's music for (c) and (d), in earlier strophes, expanded its four-square models by four quarters each, his music for (h) and (i) of the final strophe expands its four-square models by eight quarters each. But formalism is not the whole story. We shall pick the matter up later.

Example 13.5(i) does not need special commentary; the reader can easily enough hear and work out how Brahms extends his final cadence. Special commentary for passage (h) is provided by Example 13.6.

Example 13.6

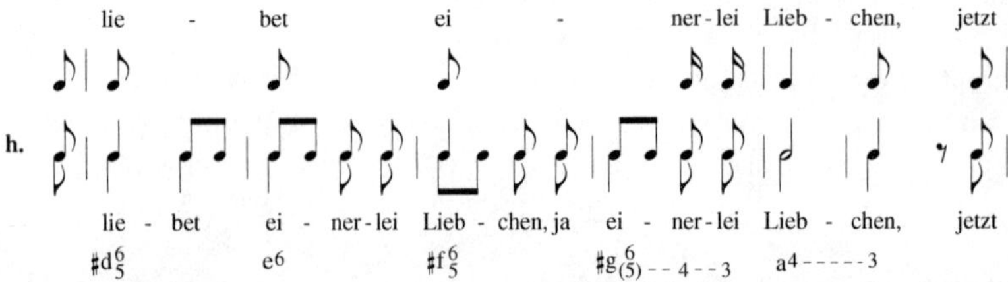

harmony: Each harmony of the raisonneur's song, up to a minor, is rhythmically augmented doubly in Brahms's song, from eighth-note to half-note duration. The rhythmically extended harmonies are elaborated contrapuntally, using the 2–3 formulas between the voices as a framework for a chain of Übergreifungen. This adds 4-times-3 eighths, that is, 12 eighths, to the Brahms version. NB: Brahms needs extra time to sound C-over-B and later E-over-D, in the chain of 2–3 formulas. There is no time for those dissonances on Example 13.5.

Then the a-minor measure of the raisonneur's song is rhythmically augmented singly in Brahms's song. This adds 4 eighths to the Brahms version. So in all, the 2-measure phrase of the raisonneur's song expands by (12 + 4) eighths, or 8 quarters (4 measures).

text: "einerlei Liebchen" becomes "einerlei Liebchen, ja einerlei Liebchen."

The expansions at (h) and (i), by eight quarters (four measures) each instead of four quarters (two measures) each, are not simply a formalistic game. The extra hierarchical level of temporal expansion goes well with the extra hierarchical levels of complexity in the dramatic representation. No longer impersonating the sisters (adding some covertly Alienating expansions of their own), the singers are now showing us how the raisonneur imagined that the sisters would behave upon discovering the true state of affairs, and the singers are at the same time showing the behavior of the sisters-as-imagined-by-the-raisonneur. On top of all that, as suggested earlier, the singers are having a "real" fight between themselves-as-the-Biedermeier-young-ladies, revealing themselves as characters being presented Epically by Brahms the dramatist. This amount of complexity in the dramatic representation is not easily confined within the same time-span used before, in a much simpler dramatic situation.

Musical Matters: Schenkerian Structure

Example 13.7(a) gives a Schenkerian analysis for the music of the g minor strophes (without ritornello); Example 13.7(b) gives an analysis for the G major strophe.

Example 13.7

In Example 13.7(a), while the opening bass G moves stepwise up (through a "virtual" C♯ as already discussed) to D, the upper voice on the sketch descends through the normal g minor scale in tonally functional counterpoint—F and E♭ over the bass A, D over B♭, C over C, B♭ over C and C♯, and finally a high middleground A over the bass *Teiler* D. Schenker declares that such a 7-*Zug* always stands for the step of a second that the seventh inverts.[37] So I presume he would have read the essential motion here from the opening low G4 on the top staff, with open notehead and stem down, to the next open-notehead-stem-down on the staff, A4 over the *Teiler*. My stem-down A4 eventually connects to the later stem-down B♭4, which I have marked as $\hat{3}$ of an *Urlinie*. I can abstractly imagine ("in theory") analyzing the strophe as having an *Urlinie* that starts on this $\hat{3}$, where the preceding stems-down open-noteheads at G4 and A4 would prepare that $\hat{3}$ in an *Anstieg*. But I do not like the musical effect. The reading does not seem to involve much of the musical activity in the strophe at a high enough structural level of the analysis, and the eventual $\hat{3}$–$\hat{2}$–$\hat{1}$ of the *Urlinie* it asserts seems a pusillanimous affair as projected in the music. I am much more persuaded by the octave *Urlinie* I sketch on Example 13.7(a).

In this reading, the F5 I have marked as $\hat{7}$ picks up the high G5 marked as $\hat{8}$, as the D harmony changes from major to minor. This already has a Dorian sound: the idiomatic harmonic function for F natural in functional g minor is (as noted earlier) $\hat{5}$ of III, not $\hat{3}$ of v. F5, stepping down from G5 earlier on at "wir schönen," was indeed treated as $\hat{5}$ of III. But the F natural I have marked as the background $\hat{7}$ on Example 13.7, while again stepping down from G5 in the background (beamed upward stems), has a perceptibly more Dorian character. The Dorian sense is intensified by the background E natural and D natural that follow, marked $\hat{6}$ and $\hat{5}$. In functional g minor one does not descend from F natural to D by way of E natural.

37. Heinrich Schenker, *Free Composition*, trans. and ed. Ernst Oster (New York: Longman, 1979), 74.

It would be possible to read this F–E–D segment as a $\hat{3}$–$\hat{2}$–$\hat{1}$ *Zug* within a d minor *Stufe*. My analysis assents to the persistence of the d minor *Stufe* at the background level in the bass: the first bass D with beamed stem down connects to the next bass G with beamed stem down; a downwards slur connects that bass D through the intervening bass A and bass F with open noteheads, until the beamed G takes over from the beamed D. If one reads the F–E–D of my *Urlinie* as a $\hat{3}$–$\hat{2}$–$\hat{1}$ *Zug* in d minor, the following C5 in my *Urlinie* (marked $\hat{4}$) would be a passing seventh within the d minor middleground harmony.

But I prefer a different reading, as indicated on Example 13.7(a). Within the far-background d *Stufe*, I like to hear a slightly more foreground-level F *Stufe*. This emphasizes the Dorian character of the music all the more, because my reading allows the crucial F natural marked $\hat{7}$ to expand into its own *Stufe*, as VII of g minor. Aspects of the *Stufe* are bracketed in the example. The span from $\hat{7}$ to $\hat{4}$ of my *Urlinie* is connected by a slur; this analyzes the linear segment on a middleground level as a scalewise descent from-F-to-C within the Dorian F major *Stufe* (rather than a descent from-F-to-D, followed by a passing C, within the d minor *Stufe*). In the bass beneath, I have connected the open notehead A and the open notehead F by a slur above, as participants in my Dorian F *Stufe*. That *Stufe* is then subsumed into the larger-level d minor *Stufe*, before the tonic G *Stufe* reappears. So the F natural in the bass of my sketch is not beamed into the "*Baßbrechung*" of my *Ursatz*. (One could hardly speak of a "*Brechung*" in that case!) For later purposes, it will be useful to note that the Dorian span of my musical analysis (F major within d minor) is exactly coextensive with the third verse of text in the stanza.

The Dorian aspects of the music project a "folkish" character, consistent with the picture of the sisters being presented. Logically enough, the Dorian music disappears in the final strophe, where the folkish sisters have disappeared and the raisonneur has taken over in G major. In that strophe, the Dorian music is replaced by the music for the fight, coextensive with the third verse of text in the final stanza. We shall later explore that substitution in greater detail.

First, though, we should look over Example 13.7(b). I have parenthesized the D5 marked $\hat{5}$ in my *Urlinie* for the strophe. That is because the singers do not sing it. I believe that it belongs nevertheless: the rest of the *Urlinie*, through its octave descent, is very plausibly projected by the singers. To help us hear the parenthesized D5 at the D cadence, we can listen to the upper notes in the piano RH over measures 2–6.1 of the strophe: they project very clearly the stepwise linear motion F–E–D an octave below that segment of my *Urlinie*. In particular the accompaniment line lands emphatically on D4 at "-wandt!", where the earlier g minor strophes had F♯4 at "-sicht" etc. The sudden drop in dynamic level in the accompaniment right at "-wandt!" provides a subtle sort of negative accent for the occasion: the accompanist should take good care to drop to the piano dynamic exactly as indicated on the score, at the beginning of the measure, not—like the singers—on its last eighth. The accompanist's sudden dynamic drop is in some sense a musical projection of the parenthesis I have put onto Example 13.7(b), around the D in my *Urlinie*.

The third verse of the stanza is now set, not by Dorian music, but by an elaborate extension of C5, the $\hat{4}$ of my *Urlinie*. Example 13.7(b) shows how the C5 is prolonged as $\hat{3}$ within a local a minor *Stufe*, ii of G major. During this span the structural bass rises stepwise from E to A, as indicated by the upward slur. The stepwise rise occurs "in a minor": E–F♯–G♯–A. The bass D♯ inflects the E at the beginning of this gesture. On the upper staff of the example, parallel sixths rise stepwise ("in a minor") above the opening notes of the bass gesture: (B above D♯, then) C above E, D above F♯, E above G♯. As the bass reaches the local tonic A of the a-minor *Stufe*, the voices fall back to A and C. Starting at C-over-bass-E, the example graphs the story as an elaborated arpeggiation of a-minor harmony: C5 rises stepwise to E5, which then drops down to A4-and-C5. The little beam on the example asserts that arpeggiation.

My *Ursatz*, having prolonged its C5 by a -minor harmony, projecting $\hat{4}$-over-ii in G major, moves on to B4 over D in the bass, executing the conventional progression of ii to a cadential-$^6_4$ as the *Ursatz* approaches its final dominant and tonic.

Musical Matters: Das Blättchen Gewandt

Edward Gollin, as mentioned earlier, suggested hearing the raisonneur's G major as a Riemannian inversion of the sisters' g minor, allegorizing the image of "das Blättchen gewandt." The idea works very well as a way of relating the a-minor fight music, in the G major strophe, to the F major Dorian music of the earlier g minor strophes. As we have noted, the passages occur at analogous positions within their respective stanzas, each setting the third verse of its 4-verse stanza. Inversional thinking will help us to hear much more going on.

Example 13.8

Example 13.8 aligns analytic sketches for the two passages at issue. On the top staff of the example we see the *Urlinie* segment F–E–D–C from Example 13.7(a); A and F lie below just as in the bass of Example 13.7(a). The top staff thus represents everything bracketed on Example 13.7(a) as the Dorian span of the music.

On the bottom staff of Example 13.8, we see a sketch for the fight music in the final strophe. Pertinent symbols are taken over from Example 13.7(b). The lower line of Example 13.8, E–F♯–G♯–A, represents the pertinent bass span from Example 13.7(b). C and E, with stems up, represent aspects of the arpeggiation-within-ii depicted on the top staff of Example 13.7(b).

The visual layout of Example 13.8 makes manifest a strong inversional relation between the Dorian music and the fight music. The inversion transforms F to E and vice versa. It is the same (pitch-class) inversion that transforms B♭ to B and exchanges D and G. Thus it is the inversion that exchanges the G major *Klang* with the Riemannian "d minor" *Unterklang*—that is, with our g minor. In the process, which exchanges pitch-classes F with E and A with C, the F major *Klang* is transformed into the Riemannian "e minor" *Unterklang*—that is, our a minor. Thus, the VII *Stufe* of g minor is transformed into the ii *Stufe* of G major. The folkish F-major of the sisters' Dorian music is thereby transformed into the functional a-minor music of the fight, allegorizing yet further the notion of "das Blättchen gewandt."

The counterpoint of the top staff on Example 13.8 takes place "within F major," and the counterpoint of the bottom staff "within a minor." Hence, though the *Stufen* are inverted (including the half-notes of the example, all harmonic tones), the quarter-notes on the bottom staff of Example 13.8 do not invert those on the top staff "exactly"—that is, semitone-for-semitone. The counterpoint inverts (in the intervallic sense) only diatonically, as is clear from the symmetry on the visual fields of the two staffs.[38]

Gollin also drew attention to the enharmonic transformation of E♭, at "schönen" in the opening strophe, to D♯, at "liebet" of the final strophe. This transformation, he pointed out, is also a species of *Wendung*. Indeed, E♭ is the "flattest" pitch class of the piece, while D♯ is the "sharpest." E♭ is not paired with D♯ by the inversion studied so far, of G into D and vice versa. But E♭ and D♯ are paired by another pitch-class inversion, namely inversion-about-A. That idea is interesting to work with.

In Example 13.7(a), we can follow the E♭ of "schönen" stepwise down, through D, C, and B♭, to arrive at A, the central pitch-class of the inversion. And on Example 13.7(b), we can follow the D♯ under "liebet" stepwise up, through E, F♯, and G♯, to arrive at A, the central pitch-class of the inversion. The analogy is very striking. The semitone/whole-tone relations within the respective linear gestures are exact: E♭–D–C–B♭–A moves down by minor second, two major seconds, and another minor second; D♯–E–F♯–G♯–A moves up by exactly the same chain of diatonic intervals.

The cited linear segments reinforce the idea of "*Wendung*" even farther. But they do not interact as clearly with the Schenker analysis (or any Riemann analysis), as did the F-major and a-minor *Stufen* discussed earlier. E♭–D–C–B♭–A, in Example 13.7(a), does not pair very well in tonal function with D♯–E–F♯–G♯–A on Example 13.7(b). Nor do the two sections of the text seem to correspond in any clear and strong way, as did the third verses of the respective strophes in connection with the inversion of F-major *Stufe* to a-minor. I feel that I have not yet fully worked out this topic.

Yet another inversional relation can be heard in the piece's structure, one that I have worked out more to my own satisfaction. That is inversion-about-G. The inversion has a sort of a priori plausibility, G being the tonic note of the piece. But

38. Curiously, the individual voices of Example 13.8 do relate exactly, semitone-for-semitone, under other transformations. The quarter-note voice of the lower staff on the example, E–F♯–G♯–A, moving through two whole steps and a half-step, is an exact transposed retrograde of the quarter-note voice on the top staff, F–E–D–C, which moves through a half-step and two whole steps. If we "unretrograde" the a-minor tetrachord we get A–G♯–F♯–E, a transposition of F–E–D–C by pitch-class interval 4 (minus 8 mod 12). And the half-note voice on the lower staff, C–E, can also be analyzed as a transposed retrograde of A–F, the half-note voice on the upper staff. Only the interval of transposition is different: E–C transposes A–F by pitch-class interval 7, not 4. So under transposed-retrogression, the top staff of Example 13.8 does not invert as a whole into the bottom staff.

there is a lot more than that, to the structuring force of the transformation. To hear what I mean, we can listen to the three different octave-species that structure Examples 13.7(a) and 13.7(b):

G–F–E♭–D–C–B♭–A–(G) is manifest at the beginning of Example 13.7(a), governing the first half of the text stanza (through "-sicht"). I shall call this octave-species (somewhat carelessly), the (G) "Aeolian mode."

G–F–E–D–C–B♭–A–G is manifest over Example 13.7(a) as a whole; it governs the *Urlinie* for the strophe. I shall call this octave-species (somewhat carelessly), the (G) "Dorian mode."

G–F–E–D–C–B–A–G is manifest over Example 13.7(b) as a whole; it governs the *Urlinie* for the strophe. I shall call this octave-species (somewhat carelessly), the (G) "Mixolydian mode."

Now under inversion-about-G, the G-Dorian mode inverts into itself, while Aeolian and Mixolydian modes invert each into the other. More specifically, the Mixolydian descent in Example 13.7(b) can be asserted as a retrograde-inversion-about-G of the Aeolian descent in Example 13.7(a). This closes up a symmetry in the modal structure of the piece as a whole. It also projects, in its retrograde-inversional transformation, two different sorts of "*Wendung*."

Closing Thoughts: The Rocket Motive and the Piano

By "the rocket motive" I shall mean a rising arpeggiation in continuous eighth notes through at least four consecutive notes of a triadic harmony. It appears:

1. in the vocal parts at the beginning of (the first verse in) every strophe.
2. sim. at the beginning of the third verse in every g minor strophe.
3. in the piano part, inverted, during the first verse of text for strophes 3 and 4.
4. sim. during the third verse of text for strophes 3 and 4.

Thus, some form of the motive appears—in voices or piano or both—at the beginning of each strophe, and also at the beginning of verse 3 in each of the (four-verse) strophes. That is a strong aspect of "*Vierhebigkeit*" in the setting, a four-square feature that supports the rhetorical investigations I earlier took in that regard.

The voices never present the motive in inversion; the piano always does so, except in the bass of the fight scene. As early as the beginning of the third strophe, the inverted piano motives foreshadow the "*Wendungen*" of the final strophe. We can take the prime form of the motive to signify the sisters. At first we might suppose that to mean "Wir Schwestern"; later on, after we hear "Ihr Schwestern," "we sisters" will broaden to "the sisters," or even "the singers-as-the-sisters." The inverted form of the motive is the sole property of the piano, a voice we earlier identified with Brahms's presence in the music as super-ironist (beyond the raisonneur). During strophes 3 and 4, the comments of the piano in the inverted motivic contour are pointing us towards the "downer" in the last strophe.

During the musical fight, the piano presents prime forms of the motive in the bass register, where we have never heard them before. This depicts, in my reading, how a male raisonneur was imagining how the sisters would fight when they discovered the truth: the prime forms of the motive are still given to the narrating voice(s), which is now that of the raisonneur. The mirror texture of prime-versus-inverted motive forms in the accompaniment tone-paints a sort of "cross-eyed" image, suitable for the fighting sisters—or, even better, the fighting singers pretending to be fighting sisters in the raisonneur's imagination. It also pits Brahms (inverted forms in the RH) against the raisonneur in the LH, manifesting Brahms as "superironist."

Appendix

I gave a lecture on the preceding material for the Music Department of Yale University in October 1996. After the lecture, Kristina Muxfeld of that department proposed that Mörike might well have intended his poem as a satire on the decadent aristocracy of his time, and particularly on the prevalence of lesbianism among its young women. This would certainly make good sense of Hartlaub's reference to the possibility of "edle Dirnen" performing a musical setting of the poem, as well as the (alternate) possibility of young bourgeoises.

Muxfeld points out that in contemporary German usage, "Liebchen" refers only to a female. Such usages change rapidly, though, and Grimm's Dictionary explicitly allows a "Liebchen" to be either female or male, providing several examples of explicitly male Liebchen in early nineteenth-century poetic usage (including examples from Friedrich Müller and Grillparzer).

Muxfeld believes that "einerlei Liebchen," in particular, suggests the possibility of an incestuous narcissistic relationship between the "edle Dirnen." My Heath dictionary, under "einerlei," as an adjective gives "of one sort; one and the same; immaterial" (and as an adverb, "all the same"). Muret-Saunders gives "of the same sort or kind or description; identical." This does not seem to me determinative, one way or the other. Muxfeld's reading calls into question my ideas about *Entzweiung* and individuation, essential for my Brechtian interpretations of Brahms's piece—however one reads Mörike's poem. Her proposed reading for "einerlei" would need to explain what sense is made in that context by the preceding verse, "Wie hat sich das Blättchen gewend't!" If the sisters have indeed become narcissistic lesbian lovers, that would seem only the logical endpoint of their behavior earlier in the poem (sc. in their younger days), rather than a sudden reversal in the status quo ante.

In this chapter, I have supposed that Brahms—whatever Mörike's and Hartlaub's ideas—imagined his singers to be young bourgeoises in a Biedermeier living room, and not "edle Dirnen." My supposition had very significant consequences for my Brechtian readings involving those singers. Given the conventions of usage reported by Grimm, I can easily imagine Brahms reading past the word "Liebchen" without being particularly struck by modern usage, any more than we imagine the hero Frederick, in *The Pirates of Penzance*, to be homosexual because a chorus refers to his "beauty." My so imagining Brahms is supported by the reactions of several of my acquaintances, native German-speaking musicians who have been familiar with the song for some time. They attest unanimously that they would not themselves refer to a man today as a "Liebchen," but they also attest unanimously that they had always assumed the Liebchen in Mörike's text to be male. A native German-speaking professor of German literature not familiar with Brahms's setting, familiar with Mörike in general but not remembering the specific poem, read "the same boy-friend" and, while allowing on questioning that the Liebchen of 1838 could be female, denied any priority for female over male in the context; the professor also denied that "einerlei" suggested "of the same type as yourself" in the context. (The same professor pointed out words in the text that Hartlaub would have read as "edle": "Gewand" for "Kleid" and "Wiesenplan" for "Wiese." Perhaps Hartlaub supposed his edle Dirnen, while reciting Mörike's verses, to be playing at peasants, in the manner of Marie Antoinette as shepherdess at the Petit Trianon.)

To be sure, the force of "straight" social conventions works to conceal any such sexual imaginings as those Muxfeld attributes to Mörike. My supposition is that any such ideas, whatever their pertinence to Mörike, were just as concealed from Brahms, as they were from my contemporary German-speaking interlocutors.

I also supposed Brahms to have conceived a raisonneur and to have conceived him as a singular male authority figure. Muxfeld's reading of Mörike, while consistent with a male and singular raisonneur in Mörike's poem, is consistent with other possibilities—as are the suggestions of Atlas and Pellegrinelli cited in notes 19–20. An extreme version of Muxfeld's ideas would assert what I have called the "musical fight" at "Ihr liebet" to be no fight at all, but rather a musical representation of an erotic encounter between the incestuous sisters—there being no third "Liebchen," male or female. (I am not sure to what degree Muxfeld means to endorse such a reading, beyond suggesting its possibility.) In this case Brahms's sisters, as well as Mörike's, would be involved in the musical imagery. Much of my own reading would disappear—not only the existence of a fight but also the idea of *Entzweiung*, the distinction (and alienation) of Brahms's singers from his sisters in an Epic presentation (as contrasted with the Romantic-Illusionist identification of actor/singer with sister), the Biedermeier parlor as theater and its grown-ups as audience, the necessary distinction of "Ihr" from "Wir," and with all that the necessity for any raisonneur at all, of whatever gender and number. The possibility of a raisonneur would remain, but the "moral" being drawn would be decidedly a different affair, what with such an exultant triumph of *Einheit* over competitive individualism.

I find it hard to hear, at "Ihr liebet," a musical enactment of incestuous lesbianism in an aristocratic milieu. That seems to me not to comport well with the somewhat vulgar oom-pahing in G major, suddenly louder and heavier, that Brahms gives us in the piano at the beginning of his final strophe. The musical gesture seems to me a good deal more appropriate for the entrance, as a new persona, of a self-satisfied, hale-and-hearty (and no doubt somewhat portly), bourgeois older male authority figure—a "grown-up."

Plate 13.1 Brahms, *Die Schwestern.*

Sop.
Allegretto
Wir Schwest-ern zwei, wir Schö - nen, wir schö - nen, so gleich___ von An - ge -
Alto
Wir Schwest-ern zwei, wir schö - nen, wir schö - nen, so gleich___ von An - ge -
Allegretto
p
sicht, so gleicht kein Ei dem an - dern, kein Ei___ dem an - dern, kein Stern dem an-dern
sicht, so gleicht kein Ei dem an - dern, kein Ei___ dem an - dern, kein Stern dem an-dern
nicht,__ kein Stern dem an-dern nicht.
nicht,__ kein Stern dem an-dern nicht.
p legg.
f

Plate 13.1 cont.

Stanza 3
Wir Schwest-ern zwei, wir schö - nen, wir schö - nen, wir tra - gen gleich Ge -
Wir Schwest-ern zwei, wir schö - nen, wir schö - nen, wir tra - gen gleich Ge -
wand, spa - zie - ren auf dem Wie - sen - plan, dem Wie - sen - plan, und sin - gen Hand in
wand, spa - zie - ren auf dem Wie - sen - plan, dem Wie - sen - plan, und sin - gen Hand in
Hand, und sin - gen Hand in Hand.
Hand, und sin - gen Hand in Hand.
p
f

(continued)

Plate 13.1 cont.

Stanza 5

f
O Schwest-ern zwei, irh schö - nen, ihr schö - nen! wie hat sich das Blätt - chen ge -
f
O Schwes-tern zwei, ihr schö - nen, ihr schö - nen! wie hat sich das Blätt - chen ge -
poco f
p
wandt! ihr lie - bet et - ner-lei Lieb - chen, ja e - - ner-lei Leib -
p
wandt! ihr lie - bet ei - ner-lei Lieb - chen, ja ei - ner-lei Lieb -
p
p
chen - jetzt hat das Lie - del ein End, jetzt hat das Lie - del, das Lie - del
p
chen - jetzt hat das Lie - del ein End, jetzt hat das Lie - del, das Lie - del
p
dim.

Plate 13.1 cont.

PART VI

Schoenberg

Works by Schoenberg were the subjects of my first publications involving music with text. Only later did I discover that some of the attitudes I brought to these analyses would be interesting to bring up as well to the more traditional repertory of Lieder and opera. Throughout my academic career, I have continued to publish studies of Schoenberg's vocal works, which I have always found an inexhaustible source of ideas about music with text.

The first chapter of this section, "Womens' Voices and the Fundamental Bass," is a relatively recent piece—it was published in 1992, in the *Journal of Musicology*, vol. 10, no. 4. As the title indicates, it is not primarily about Schoenberg at all. But it does involve considerable discussion of the vocal movements from the Second Quartet. I put it first in this section partly because its point of view is more general than that of my other essays involving Schoenberg's music, and partly because the Second Quartet is the earliest composed of Schoenberg's pieces that are addressed in the present book.

The chapter on Opus 15, Number XI, "Towards the Analysis of a Schoenberg Song," appeared in *Perspectives of New Music*, vol. 12 (1973–1974). The chapter on Opus 15, Number VII was published by *in theory only,* in vol. 6, no. 1 (1981). The same journal, in vol. 6, no. 4 (1982), published the chapter on "Vocal Meter," which includes a rhythmic analysis for the vocal part of Opus 15, Number V. The three chapters give an adequate sampling of my work on the *Hanging Gardens* cycle. The chapter on vocal meter also includes rhythmic analysis of passages from *Pierrot* and *Herzgewächse.*

The chapter on the first scene of *Moses und Aron* was published by *Perspectives of New Music* in vol. 6, no. 1 (1967). It has already been reprinted on several occasions, but I think it will stand yet another reprinting for the occasion of this book. It discusses the large-scale musical organization of an operatic scene by the composer, and it specifically addresses the role of serialism in that connection—an issue that will be picked up again in connection with the study of Milton Babbitt's *Philomel*, in the next section of this book.

Interested readers can find further analytic observations on *Pierrot* in "Some Notes on *Pierrot Lunaire*," in *Music Theory in Concept and Practice* (Rochester: University of Rochester Press, 1997), 433–457, an article that applies to the analysis some theoretical techniques I developed only over the past decade or so. Interested readers can also find observations on *Moses und Aron*, Act I, Scene 3, in "Inversional Balance in Schoenberg's Music," *Perspectives of New Music*, vol. 6, no. 1 (1967), 1–21. I decided not to reprint either of these articles in the present book and not to publish any of several new ones on which I have been working. The book as it stands already contains an adequate and reasonably representative sampling of my work on Schoenberg.

CHAPTER Fourteen

Women's Voices and the Fundamental Bass

Lawrence Kramer has recently offered a striking Freudian trope for discussing musical form and sexuality in Wagnerian and post-Wagnerian music.[1] Analyzing Isolde's Transfiguration in particular, Kramer observes that the passage

> conforms in every detail to the Freudian language of love. The ego-libido that was invested in the beloved as object-libido now flows back onto the subject and becomes ego-libido once more, yielding a flood of narcissistic pleasure so overwhelming that the ego drowns in it. . . . The movement of psychosexual regression is also embodied in the "regressive," that is the recapitulatory character of the Transfiguration as a whole. The music returns Isolde to the scene of her fullest earlier rapture.[2]

To the extent that the notion of Freudian regression is pertinent, it suggests a return on Isolde's part to a pregenital phase of sexuality.[3] Perhaps that suggestion prompted the idea that Kramer proposes next:

> Isolde's dispersal of Tristan's image—and her own awareness—into the unqualified movement of "hochste Lust" also testifies to a weakening of gender boundaries. In its original form, the A♭ portion of the Transfiguration is first sung by Tristan. Isolde follows with a parallel passage, omitted in the Transfiguration, in which she repeats virtually the whole of Tristan's line. This strophic articulation of the lovers' desire acts as a denial of sexual difference—and its inequalities. As desiring subjects, Tristan and Isolde are indistinguishable. . . . By returning [in the Transfiguration] to Tristan's strophe but omitting her own, Isolde reaffirms that the subject of desire is indifferent to gender, that the true human being, to recall Wagner's dictum, is both male and female. . . . Throughout the opera, as has often been noted, Wagner

1. Lawrence Kramer, *Music as Cultural Practice 1800–1900* (Berkeley: University of California Press, 1990).
2. Kramer, *Music as Cultural Practice*, 164. The liquid imagery is an essential feature of his model.
3. One could say, to a phase of oral sexuality. Viewing Isolde's *Liebestod* as an exercise in oral gratification certainly seems more than plausible.

> portrays Tristan and Isolde in terms that reverse certain deeply entrenched gender roles. . . . "O sink' hernieder, Nacht der Liebe" perfectly epitomizes the mobility of gender between Tristan and Isolde. The crisscrossing arpeggiations [of the Tristan Chord] in the vocal lines intimate a sexual difference that is also a sexual sameness. Masculine and feminine overlap as mirror images of each other, and this just as the lovers ask for a forgetfulness in which their separate identities will fade away ("gib Vergessen, daß ich lebe"). . . . [The lovers] are constituted as subjects by a desire that overflows all boundaries, and for which gender is finally no more than a pretext.[4]

Kramer's blurring of gender boundaries was surely felt by those who put Peter Behrens's *Der Kuß* on the cover of the Dover orchestral score.[5] The idea seems suggestive in a number of ways. Yet I have an insurmountable problem in accepting it. For I cannot imagine the Transfiguration being sung by a male voice. I cannot imagine Tristan singing it, any more than I can imagine King Mark—or Manrico or di Luna. This is music that I cannot hear without the female voice, any more than I can hear the Mendelssohn violin concerto without a solo violin. The instrument that sings Isolde's Transfiguration is the instrument—or the forerunner of the instrument—that sings Salome and the persona of *Erwartung*. For the time being, I mean only to point out that we cannot imagine those instruments as male voices.[6]

Susan McClary, in her recent book, pushes the matter considerably farther.[7] She views Salome and the person of *Erwartung* as exemplars within a line of pieces by male composers that feature madwomen as solo singers. This line includes Lucia and extends back to Monteverdi's lamenting Nymph.[8] Isolde is brought into the group with a bit of effort.[9] McClary discerns in this genre a strategy for male avant-garde composers:

> If we review the portraits of famous madwomen in music, we find that the signs of their madness are usually among the favorite techniques of the avant-garde: strategies that for each style hover at the extremes, strategies that most successfully exceed the verbal component of dramatic music and that transgress conventions of "normal" procedures. . . . the very qualities regarded as evidence of superior [musical] imagination—even of genius—in each period of music are, when enacted on stage, often projected onto madwomen.[10]

McClary devotes particular attention to Schoenberg and to *Erwartung* in this connection.

4. Kramer, *Music as Cultural Practice*, 164–165.
5. I am grateful to Daniel Beller-McKenna for this observation.
6. Salome seems to me a particularly telling example. I can easily imagine a variation of the story in which the nymphet is a boy. (And I can easily imagine Wilde imagining that.) But I cannot imagine as a boy's voice the voice that sings in Scene 3, the duet with Jochanaan. The boy's voice does not have within it the foundation for the ever-transforming motive "Lass mich deinen Mund küssen, Jochanaan," not to mention much of Salome's preceding music.
7. Susan McClary, *Feminine Endings: Music, Gender, and Sexuality* (Minneapolis: University of Minnesota Press, 1991).
8. McClary, *Feminine Endings*, 80–111 (Chapter 4: "Excess and Frame: The Musical Representation of Madwomen").
9. McClary, *Feminine Endings*, 100.
10. McClary, *Feminine Endings*, 101.

> What Schenker continued to hold as sacrosanct—rational tonal procedure, dissonance regulation, and laws of necessary closure—Schoenberg perceived as oppressive conventions, rather than immutable or natural. Yet throughout [the *Harmonielehre*], Schoenberg also reveals how terrifying it was to identify himself with those forces that had traditionally served to destabilize tonal certainty—dissonance, chromaticism, excess—but which were inevitably quashed in accordance with narrative propriety. In effect, he allies himself with what had always been defined as the "feminine" side of all the binary oppositions governing tonal procedures and narratives.
>
> . . . But he is careful . . . to avoid the obvious and conventional mapping of these musical [binarisms] onto gender. He chooses rather to define the oppositions in accordance with images of resistance against oppressive political authority . . . , aligning himself with the properly masculine business of revolution.[11]

There follows a lengthy quotation from the *Harmonielehre,* about the fundamental tone as "sovereign," "supreme lord," and "progenitor," imposing its "will" on its "dependents" and "subjects." The fundamental tone need not endure, any more than a conqueror need endure as dictator; the struggle between rival fundamentals has something very characteristic about it as well. "This precondition, that everything emanates from the [fundamental] tone, can just as well be suspended, since one is constantly reminded of it anyway by every tone."[12]

McClary then returns to her point, that despite the masculine heroics of such mythologizing, the musical radicalism of *Erwartung* is quite another story:

> His metaphorical surrogate in *Erwartung—the* piece in which he committed his supreme violation, his break with tonality—was . . . the figure of the madwoman. The political revolutionary of *Theory of Harmony* . . . is nowhere to be seen. Schoenberg's celebrated "emancipation of the dissonance" is self-consciously presented as the liberation of the female lunatic, of the feminine moment of desire and dread that had driven most nineteenth-century narratives. . . . Stripped of the possibility of resolution or the intervention of hegemonic control, desire in its rawest, most murderous form runs rampant through the piece.[13]

McClary could well have added that *Erwartung* was composed at lightning speed toward the end of 1909, while *Die Glückliche Hand,* the music-drama that *does* embody Schoenberg's myth of heroic masculine struggle and revolution, took until November 1913 to complete, although it was begun immediately after the composer finished *Erwartung.*

McClary's essay squarely addresses my insistence that the voices of Salome and the person of *Erwartung* are female rather than gender-free. The essay suggests that what appears to me prima facie as an acoustic apperception is actually a culturally conditioned phenomenon. I think there is a good deal to the point, and I shall return to related matters later on.

11. McClary, *Feminine Endings*, 105.
12. McClary, *Feminine Endings*, 105–106. I think McClary misses the extent to which the fundamental tone as patriarchal "progenitor" enacts a gender role here, as well as and in connection with its political role. I shall return to the point later, in connection with my central discussion of Rameau.
13. McClary, *Feminine Endings*, 107–108.

Nevertheless, McClary's thesis does not do so well with Isolde, who is "mad" only by a considerable stretch of the imagination. Isolde plays "maddeningly in the cracks of tonal social convention," says McClary. While Isolde "is not presented as a dominatrix . . . she does befuddle and seduce poor Tristan by means of her chromatic excess, and she too (like Lucia and Salome) achieves transcendence in the absence of the phallus."[14] But none of this argues Isolde's insanity, even—nay especially—if one accepts the dubious "befuddle and seduce." It argues only Isolde's resemblance to the other heroines in attitudes toward certain musical conventions, and in respect of a certain transcendent character. If those traits are defining signals for madness, then Isolde is simply mad by definition, and her tautological inclusion on a list of madwomen provides no useful support for McClary's thesis.

I think there is a broader category than "madwoman" in this context, a category that one can formulate and study without denying the force of McClary's ideas about madwomen. Rather than "mad," I suggest that Isolde during her final music is more aptly described as ecstatic, transported, enraptured, perhaps even Delphic. Of course, those states are akin to madness. But then madness is also akin to those states. They are all states of "transcendence," and I shall expropriate that term from McClary as a useful rubric here.

The transcendent woman's voice, as McClary points out in the case of madwomen, transcends both musical and social conventions. Furthermore, it transcends its accompaniment in my acoustical sense, climbing over it.[15] This is one reason that I must hear the voice as female, given our cultural metaphors for "above" and "below" in music.

McClary's study essentially restricts itself to opera, but I hear the transcendent woman's voice elsewhere as well. It sounds, for instance, in the two final movements of Schoenberg's second string quartet, Opus 10. These pieces in some respects fit Schoenberg's stylistic crisis better than does *Erwartung.* McClary asserts *Erwartung* as "the piece in which [Schoenberg] committed his supreme violation, his break with tonality." But that is too tendentious. By the time Schoenberg composed the opera, he had already finished the last movement of the quartet Opus 10, the song "Am Strande," the two songs Opus 14, the Hanging Gardens songs Opus 15, the three piano pieces Opus 11, and the five orchestra pieces Opus 16. One can argue about where "his break with tonality" occurred (if anywhere!), depending on one's definition of "tonality." In any case, the last two movements of Opus 10 seem to me closer to the crucial spiritual event than does the opera, coming after Opus 16. The third movement of the quartet, *Litanei,* is one of the last pieces with key signature; the fourth movement, *Entrueckung,* is one of the first pieces without key signature.

The voice in *Litanei* is surely the transcendent woman's voice. At its entrance it appears magically from within its accompaniment, doubling the second violin an octave below the first violin. The acoustic effect is one of the most astonishing in music: the voice seems to rise Delphically from out of the quartet as the ensemble "begins to speak" for the first time in its history, as well as in the piece. A male voice

14. McClary, *Feminine Endings,* 100.

15. Lat. transcendere = Eng. to climb, step, or pass over.

could not emerge from the violins "over" the ensemble in this way.[16] The vocal discourse is in the chromatic style of Wagner/Strauss. In the climactic leap of "nimm mir die liebe" one recognizes Kundry's "lachte," a gesture that will return in the "Hilfe" of *Erwartung*.[17] More generally, the vocal line strings together significant leitmotifs and transformations thereof, carrying the burden of the piece forward. Some of the motifs are diatonic, and the voice can make tonal cadences with them when it so desires, for example, at "nur die qual." On the other hand, the voice can also transform just those motives so as to move away from tonal security into "*schwebende*" sorts of harmony, for example, at the final "gib mir dein glück!"

The technique is no different in kind—only in quality—from the way in which Salome takes her original motive for "Lass mich deinen Mund küssen, Jochanaan," a clear elaboration of local dominant harmony, and progressively transforms it into a Protean modulatory device that leads the music of Scene 3 into ever higher and more chromatic tonal regions, with spectacularly reckless abandon. But the woman of *Litanei is* not "mad" like Salome. (Nor is she "bad.") She is grief-stricken, devotional, exhausted, at the end of her tether, athirst for spiritual renewal. In all those respects her transcendent musical prayer articulates the feelings of George, or of Schoenberg at this time, much more than those of any imagined female "character."

And yet the transcendent musical voice must be a woman's voice. It must specifically rise above the ensemble, well over the usual bass register. It must project an upper-register *Hauptstimme* that controls the flow of musical events with a motivic through-line, specifically wresting control of that flow away from any fundamental bass. The harmony is turned *schwebend* by the final vocal cadence at "gib mir dein glück," composing out the motivic neighbor G♭–G♮ on *gib* and *glück;* only after that does the violin return the G♮ to G♭, and it is only at this point that the cadential E♭-minor six-four chord can appear, returning the music to its tonic home. The final crescendo to *fff* on the E♭-minor triad is well-nigh unbearable. Will the prayer be answered? Will the person be relieved of the lowering E♭-minor grief "die sie umdüstert?" We do not know: the transcendent voice has disappeared and we are left with the sense of her ever-heavier burden.

The persona of *Entrueckung* is also not "mad." George is presumably recording an experience of poetic raptus, or possibly a sexual transport, or possibly elements of both. Schoenberg, writing no key signature and beginning completely "atonally" for the first time in an extended piece, was doubtless portraying his own sense of being carried away by the musical "breeze from another planet." As before, the voices of George and Schoenberg seem to merge with the female voice of the singer, in a Kramer-like "gender-free" complex. Kramer's Freudian regression, difficult to

16. Beethoven's male voice, in pointed contrast, does not "give voice to" the orchestra, emerging "from inside it." His male singer interrupts the orchestra, disputing the orchestral material so far.

17. At "*liebe*" in *Litanei*, the leap—from high C to middle B—outdoes Kundry in both registers. Kundry leaps only from high B to middle C. Curiously, the leap in *Erwartung* retreats back to Kundry's exact pitches—high B and middle C♯—rather than extending the leap yet farther. Perhaps Schoenberg was making some point, consciously or unconsciously, in his reference to Kundry's "*lachte*" here. The singer will certainly notice the reference. Is there something Christlike (for the singer) about the body of her lover? The text refers to God—if only through colloquial expressions—in the lines immediately preceding and immediately following the scream.

spot in the text of *Litanei,* can certainly be found in the text of *Entrueckung,* which can legitimately be asserted to involve sexuality in at least some senses of the term.[18]

But still and again, notwithstanding these Kramerian motifs, the voice that sings is necessarily a woman's voice, not a man's voice. When the voice enters with its rising D4–G4–A4–C5 motive at "Ich fühle luft" (mm. 21–23), we hear the gesture recalling a familiar constructive melodic motive from movements 2 and 3, well before we construe it as a "bass" for the accompanying stringed instruments.[19] When this music returns climactically (mm. 110ff.), D2–G2–A2–C3 does become a strong bass in the low register of the cello, carrying a full orchestral treatment of the theme, fortissimo, in the strings. But now the voice in its upper register soars ecstatically free of the ensemble, stringing together various pitch classes from the inner voices of the theme's verticalities to form a melodic setting for the final words of text, "heiligen stimme."

Just before the climax, at the instruments' reprise of the *Ich löse mich* theme (mm. 100ff.), the voice sings not the *Ich löse mich* melody but a new idea that strings together *Ich fühle luft* tetrachords: C♯4–F♯4–G♯4–B4–D♯4–G♯4–A#4–C♯5 (Ich bin ein funke nur vom hei-). The line goes on, after B4 again, to distort the tetrachord in a characteristic Salome-like way: E♯4–A4–B4–D♯5 ([hei]-ligen feu-).

The *Ich löse mich* theme is introduced by a characteristic progression of verticalities, at measures 51–52 and again at measures 99–100. The fourth-chord (G2, F3,B♭3,C4) "resolves" into the fourth-chord (F♯2,F♯3,B3,C♯4). One hears the vertical fourth-chords derived from the melodic-motivic tetrachord D4–G4–A4–C5 of *Ich fühle luft,* a tetrachord already familiar as a melodic motive from earlier movements. "Harmony," that is, is perceived here primarily as verticalized soprano melody. And what about the semitone voice-leading that connects the vertical chords? One hears the semitones being controlled at measures 51–52 not by the G2–F♯2 in the bass, settling into the eventual tonic note of the piece, but rather by the voice's melodic semitone C4–B3 setting the text "Ich lö-" for the beginning of the theme.[20]

At the reprise of the theme the situation is similar, except that the *Ich löse* theme is given to the violins in octaves; we still associate the theme with the voice, even though the singer is momentarily silent across the bar line of measure 100. The C–B gesture in the upper strings must be brought out in performance: C is prolonged over measures 97–99; C moves to B at measure 100. All the strings crescendo continuously over measures 96–99, but only the first violin is given any specific dynamic marking during this process. The dynamic marking, forte, applies to the C5 in the first violin at the bar line of measure 97, where the voice is momentarily also singing that pitch. The subsequent figuration in the first violin keeps C alive in various registers through measure 99; in that measure the viola sits

18. One would not be surprised to encounter in *Salome* or *Elektra* any local segment of the music from the theme "Ich löse mich in tönen," especially from the continuation at "kreisend" to the cadence at "ergebend."

19. The upper strings, descending in contrary motion to the rising vocal motive, support in their stratospheric registers the descending formants of the vowels in "Ich fühle luft." Thereby the upper strings amplify the vocal pronouncement as principal melody, rather than providing material against which the voice sounds as a "bass."

20. The voice line continues with pitch-class semitones: C4–B3–A♯4–A4–. The bass line, after sounding G2-F♯2 in measures 51–52, rises by these motivic semitones all the way up to E3 in measure 59.

heavily on C4 as well. Those Cs must be led carefully to the Bs in the violins at the beginning of measure 100, especially C4 to B3. The *piano subito* can help. In this way, the performers will enable the listener to catch the beginning of the melodic reprise for "Ich löse mich," avoiding undue emphasis on the bass motion from G to F♯ that could too easily project an omnivorous "tonic downbeat" on the bass F♯. The instrumental *Hauptstimme* going into measure 100 is C–B, *subito p*, not G–F♯ with tonic *Entspannung*. Rather than "release," one senses an increase in pressure, pushing "*alla breve; etwas bewegter als das erste mal*" toward the climax ten measures later.

Tonic *Entspannung* occurs only at measure 120, after that climax, and *after the transcendent woman's voice has left the piece.* At measure 120, the fourth-chord (G2,F3,C4,F4,B♭4) resolves, *Sehr ruhig*, to the enharmonic F♯ triad (F♯2,C♯4,F♯4, B♭4)—or to the minor triad halfway through m. 120 when B♭4 "resolves" to A4. One hears how the C, in the familiar fourth-chord over G, no longer moves to B, when G moves to F♯ in the bass. C now moves only to C♯. And B♭, rather than moving to B, sustains over the F♯ bass—either as an enharmonic A♯ or as a chromatic suspension to A natural over F♯. The singer having vanished into outer space, a fundamental bass for the piece can finally assert itself. (And the fundamental bass for the quartet as a whole can finally reassert itself.)

The *Ich löse mich* theme provides another spectacular example of the voice's freedom from the fundamental bass. About halfway through the theme, at "lobes" (m. 62), the harmony latches on to a dominant four-three of F♯, a sonority already used to articulate "tönen" (mm. 54–55). The lower three strings, hearing that they are once again on a functional dominant for their would-be "tonic" F♯ fundamental, seize on the chord and sit there for four measures, the cello dropping down at once to C♯2 so as to put the harmony in root position. Nowhere else in the quartet is there such an extensive static prolongation of any dominant harmony. After the cello drops down to C♯, the voice—doubled by the first violin—sings the text "dem großen atem wunschlos mich ergebend" on the tones E4–G4–E4–{D♯4–D4}–F4–E4–D4–D♯4–E4–E4–C4. The vocal line, as one hears even without the rhythm—and even more so with the rhythm—makes a strong melodic cadence in C major. Over the prolonged C♯7 harmony, of course, many of its notes sound "blue," especially G and E. But when the cadence comes, at "-gebend" (m. 66), it is the voice's C-major melody, not the fundamental bass F♯, that carries the day. At the bar line of measure 66 the cello, instead of leaping from its "dominant" C♯2 to some note of a "tonic" F♯ harmony, sinks down from C♯2 (enharmonically respelled D♭2) to the open C string, and a C-major triad supports the penultimate vocal note E4. Furthermore, the cello gesture here (D♭2–C2) is precisely the beginning of the melody *Ich löse mich*, transposed a pitch-class semitone so as to begin D♭–C rather than C–B. The transpositional interval is the complement of the semitone that opens the melody: C becomes the second note of the tune (the note that takes the metric accent), rather than the first note. The cello continues past measure 66 to play the first seven notes of *Ich löse mich*, with the correct contour and rhythm; the viola enters in stretto with yet another transposition; stretto entries of the melodic motive continue for some time thereafter with rhythmic diminutions, involving the first violin as well as the viola and the cello. The text associated with the stretto motive is "Ich löse mich in tönen," and it can hardly be coincidental that the cello entry which begins at the pickup to the C-major cadence of measure 66 is marked not just "*express.*" but also "(*Ton!*)." This is one of the "tones" in which the voice is *gelöst* (dissolved, unbound, set free); the problem of the C♯7 harmony under the C-major vocal line is also *gelöst* (solved or resolved), and the music here is specifically *gelöst* (absolved, set free) from any F♯ obligations of the "dominant seventh" harmony.[21]

After the singer has left the piece, after the cadence on the F♯ triad at measure 120, the C♯7 passage returns as coda material (mm. 128–133). The C-major resolution is quoted there (m. 134), but without the melodic stretto entries on "Ich löse mich." Equally telling, the C-major triad is played only by the violins, so that the bass of the harmony is on C4, not C2. The bass of the C♯7 harmony is on C♯3, not C♯2; from C♯3 the cello line descends (can descend) chromatically downward, to and past the low F♯2. The beginning of the chromatic descent, C3–C3–B2–B♭2–, does produce the series of pitch classes that is associated with the transposed form of "*Ich löse mich,*" but the contour is wrong, the rhythm is wrong, and there is a rest in the cello at the crucial bar line of measure 134, where the C-major triad appears above the violins. In short, the bass C♯ from measure 128 on is now much more strongly a fifth degree of the fundamental F♯, and the C♯7 is allowed to assert itself much more as a "real" dominant, now that the transcendent voice has left the piece.

The sorts of observations I have been making on the quartet amplify the sense in which I feel that the transcendent voice is a female voice. A male voice, singing an octave lower, could not have the same kind of relations with the bass line, the presence or absence of fundamental bass activity, the derivation of "harmonic" verticalities from melodic motives, and so forth. The female voice is typically acoustically free of what we conceive as a functional bass line—whether continuo or fundamental bass—and that is less typically true of the male voice.

∾

"Typically" is a tricky word here, mixing physiological statistics with cultural norms. The real catch lies in "what we conceive . . . as a bass," and I shall return to that later on. Meanwhile, an analysis of "typically" will serve as a useful bridge into the following part of this chapter.

One observes that men and women "typically" (physiologically/statistically) center their *everyday speaking* voices within respectively lower and higher registers. We are no doubt somewhat conditioned thereby to hearing their *musical* "voices" in those respective registers.

21. A comparison with a passage from Wagner's *Todesverkündigung (Walküre* II/4) is interesting. In measures 42–44 Brünnhilde sings "Nur Todgeweihten taugt mein Anblick," arpeggiating an E♭-major triad. The harmonies of the Fate motif beneath her are E minor and E♭7. Then over measures 45–47, as the Fate harmonies sequence to G♭ minor and F7, Brünnhilde sings "Wer mich erschaut, der scheidet vom Lebens Licht," arpeggiating an F-major triad. According to the earlier model for this music, we should now hear the Death Motive in A♭ minor. However, we go into B♭ major instead (at *"Licht")*, with material from the Valhalla theme. Of course, B♭ major comes in perfectly "well" locally after F7 in the accompaniment. The point is, B♭ major is not the normative continuation here. And we are prepared for a B♭ cadence here specifically by the configuration of the transcendent woman's vocal line—arpeggiating E♭ and then F triads. As evidenced in her melody, she "knows" we are going to cadence in B♭ , rather than moving on to A♭ minor. Just so does the woman in *Entrueckung,* as evidenced in her melody, "know" we are going to cadence in C at "mich ergebend," rather than F♯.

But here one must take particular care. Our musics are not "natural phenomena," like everyday speaking. All singing styles, in particular, are highly stylized in comparison to everyday speech. Why should not this stylization include "low" singing for women and "high" singing for men? Indeed, male falsetto singing is prevalent and stylistically normative in much recent popular music. Then, too, a number of contemporary women singers have learned to extend their usable ranges down an octave or more by singing into the vocal fry. One need not be an anthropologist to imagine a culture in which women sing low notes and men sing high notes, at least in certain culturally designated styles (sacred, artistic, magical, or whatever). In fact, our culture could supply pertinent gender myths—which are always at hand—to sanction such proceedings. Zarlino, for instance, compares the vocal ranges to the Four Elements. In his view, the lowest voice represents Earth and the highest voice Fire.[22] As we all know, women are more "earthy" than men, and men are more "fiery" than women—and that is why the women sing bass and the men soprano, in our imaginary culture.

The anthropological exercise highlights a particular cultural norm in the idea that "the female voice is *typically* acoustically free of what we conceive as a functional bass line," and the idea that this "is less *typically* true of the male voice." The idea presupposes that females and males, when singing in stylized fashion, will do so in registers that center about the centers of their physiologically/statistically "natural" speaking voices.

One recognizes a residue of Enlightenment thought in such a valuation of "nature." And that is only fitting, for we are about to turn our attention to Rameau in connection with the idea of "what we conceive as a functional bass line." Let us turn specifically to the *Traité,* and to its very beginning.[23] After some preliminary material, Rameau begins the body of the entire work—Book I, Chapter 1—as follows:

> Music is the science of sounds; consequently sound is the principal material of music.[24]

We are, that is, in the realm of the "natural." The next sentence (paragraph) subordinates melody to harmony, and goes on to equate harmony with music:

> People ordinarily divide music into Harmony and Melody, even though the latter is but a part of the former, and it suffices to understand Harmony to be perfectly instructed in all aspects of music, as will be demonstrated in the following.[25]

22. Gioseffo Zarlino, *Istitutioni harmoniche* (Venice: Senese, 1573), 281–282. The notion is expounded in Part III, Chapter 58. (Trans. Guy A. Marco and Claude V. Palisca, *The Art of Counterpoint* [New Haven, Conn.: Yale University Press, 1968], 178–180.)

23. Jean Phillippe Rameau, *Traité de l'harmonie* (Paris: Ballard, 1722). (Trans. Philip Gossett, *Treatise on Harmony* [New York: Dover Publications, 1971].) In the quotations that follow, I provide my own translations.

24. Rameau, *Traité,* 1: "La musique est la Science des Sons; par consequent le Son est le principal objet de la Musique."

25. Rameau, *Traité,* 1: "On divise ordinairement la Musique en Harmonie & Melodie, quoique celle-cy ne soit qu'une partie de l'autre, & qu'il suffise de connoître l'Harmonie, pour être parfaitement instruit de toutes les proprietez de la Musique, comme it sera prouvé dans la suite."

The next paragraph tells us how to begin studying harmony (and therefore music, and therefore sound). We must study how to relate higher notes to lower notes:

> We shall leave to Physics the concern of defining sound; in Harmony we classify it only as low [grave] or high [acute], without regard for either its amplitude or its duration; and *it is upon the relation of high sounds to low ones, that all understanding of Harmony should be based* [emphasis D. L.].[26]

We do not, NB, study how to refer "bass" sounds to higher ones (as, for example, I was doing, passim, in my discussion of Schoenberg's Op. 10). The neophyte who asks what "grave" and "acute" sounds may be is answered by the following sentence and paragraph:

> Grave sounds are the lower ones, *like those produced by male voices;* and acute sounds are the higher ones, *like those produced by female voices* [emphasis D. L.].[27]

In sum, sound = music = harmony, and harmony is characterized by the relating of what women might sing, in upper registers, to what men can sing in lower registers.[28]

Very soon, of course, there ensues a significant qualification: the "bass" under discussion here is rather a fundamental bass than a continuo bass. We might therefore understand "C harmony" when a woman is singing C in an upper register while a man is singing E in a lower register. But we shall not refer the man's E to the woman's C; rather, we shall refer both to some hypothetical C in a yet-lower register, a fundamental-bass C that is "*sous-entendue*" beneath the (E,C) dyad. The woman's upper-register C here is a "root-representative" [my term], but it is not the root itself. "The root itself," once we get beyond basic dyadic consonances, seems to mean something like "any root-representative in a sufficiently low register," where "sufficiently low" means at or below the continuo bass. The point remains that the man *could* sing such a "root itself," even if he is not at present doing so; the woman *could not*. More precisely, she "could not" if she is forced to remain centered around her "natural speaking" register, not extending that register down by singing into her vocal fry (or using electronic modification, etc.).

Not only, according to Rameau, are women's voices to be referred to the idealized male voice of the fundamental bass for their musical meaning; the idealized

26. Rameau, *Traité*, 2: "Nous laisserons à la Physique le soin de définir le Son; dans l'Harmonie on le distingue seulement en grave & en aigu, sans arrêter à sa force ny à sa durée; & c'est sur le rapport des Sons aigus aux graves, que toutes les connoissances de l'Harmonie doivent être fondées."
27. Rameau, *Traité*, 2: "Les Sons graves sont les plus bas, comme ceux qui sont rendus par les voix mâles, & les aigus sont les plus élevez, comme ceux qui sont rendus par les voix féminines."
28. The opposition of *grave/aigu* has an interesting relation to French speech in this context. When speaking French, if one pauses in the middle of a sentence, one makes a rising tone at the pause. And if one wishes to indicate the end of a sentence, one makes a falling tone. Thus: En parlant français [rising tone] on fait de temps en temps une pause [rising tone], en y élevant le ton de la voix [rising tone] si l'on n'a pas encore atteint [rising tone] à la fin de la phrase [falling tone]. Thus "un tone grave" is something that a French speaker will associate—if only subliminally—with ideas of completion and cadence, while "un ton aigu" is associated with a lack of syntactic completion.

male voice actually *engenders* the women's voices. Considering an entire unit string divided into 2, 3, 4, 5, 6, or 8 aliquot parts, Rameau imagines strings whose lengths ½, ⅓, . . . ⅛ represent the aliquot divisors of the unit string. He then says,

> each partial string comes from the first one, because these parts are contained in that single first string; hence the sounds produced by the divisor strings are engendered by the first sound, which is consequently their source and foundation.[29]

The male sound, that is, gives birth to the harmonious female sound, which is one of its parts, going so far as to expropriate from the female the characteristic act of parturition. The notion recalls the birth of Eve from Adam's rib. It is difficult to imagine a more essential species of control.

To see how radically Rameau's tonal theory transformed the received metaphors of its recent past, one can compare Zarlino's discussion of four-part vocal texture in *Istitutioni,* Part III, Chapter 58. Zarlino, as already noted, identifies the four voices with the four elements:

> As every physical body is composed of the elements, so every perfect [musical] composition is composed of the elemental parts. The lowest voice is called the bass; it is analogous to the element of earth, which is the lowest of the elements. The next part in ascending order is the tenor, which is analogous to water. It is just above the earth and united to it; similarly the tenor immediately follows the bass, and its low tones are indistinguishable from the high tones of the bass. The next voice part above the tenor is called by some the contratenor, by others the contralto or alto. Its position, third and central among the voices, is analogous to that of air; as air blends in a certain way with water and fire, so the low alto tones blend with the high tenor tones, while the high alto tones blend with the low tones of the fourth and highest voice, the canto. This voice, called by some the soprano because of its supreme position, is analogous to fire, which follows air and holds the highest place.[30]

29. Rameau, *Traité,* 5: "chaque partie de ces cordes provient de la premiere, puisque ces parties sont contenuës dans cette corde premiere & unique; donc les Sons que doivent rendre ces cordes divisées, sont engendrez du premier Son, qui en est par consequent le principe & le fondement." The quotation is from Book I, Chapter 3, Article 1, "On the source of harmony or the fundamental sound (Du principe de l'Harmonie ou du Son fondamental)."

30. Marco and Palisca, *Counterpoint,* 178. Zarlino, *Istitutioni,* 281: "si come ogni Corpo misto di eßi [Elementi] si compone; cosi si compone si queste ogni perfetta cantilena. La onde le parti pia grave nominarono Basso, ilquale attribuiremo allo Elemento della Terra: conciosia che: si come la Terra tra gli altri Elementi tiene illuogo infimo; cosi it Basso occupa it luogo pia grave della cantilena. A questa, procedendo alquanto pia in suso verso l'acuto, accommodarono un'altra parte & la chiamarono Tenore, it quale aßimigliaremo all'Acqua; la quale; si come immediatamente segue, nell'ordine de gli Elementi, dopo la Terra & e con essa abbraciata: cosi nell'ordine delle dette parti il Tenore senza alcun mezo segue it Basso, & le sue chorde gravi non sono in cosa veruna differenti da quelle del Basso, poste in acuto. Simigliamente accommodarono la Terza parte sopra it Tenore, la quale alcuni chiamano Contratenore, alcuni Contralto, & altri la nominano Alto: & la posero nel terzo luogo, che e mezano nella cantilena; & si puo aßimigliare veramente all'Aria; it quale; si come si conviene con l'Acqua & col Fuoco in alcune qualita: cosi anco le chorde gravi dell'Alto convengano con le acute del Tenore, & le acute convengano con le gravi della Quarta parte posta pia in acuto, chiamata Canto. Questo accommodarono nel luogo supremo della cantilena: la onde dal luogo che tiene, alcuni etiandio la chiamano Soprano, it quale potremo aßimigliare al Fuoco, che segue immediatamente dopo l'Aria, nelgrado supremo di tale ordine."

Here each voice has its independent and coordinate place in the scheme of things; no voice "engenders" or "is engendered by" any other. The metaphorical view continues as Zarlino elaborates the natures and proper functions of the various voices:

> The soprano—being the highest of the parts—is most penetrating to the ear and is heard above all the others. As fire nourishes and is the cause of all natural things produced for the ornamentation and conservation of the world, the composer strives to have his upper voice be decorative, beautiful and elegant, so that it will nourish and satisfy the souls of listeners. As the earth is the foundation of other elements, the bass has the function of sustaining and stabilizing, fortifying and giving growth to the other parts. It is the foundation of the harmony and for this reason is called bass, as if to say the base and sustenance of the other parts. . . .
>
> The Tenor, which is the next part above the bass, is the part that governs and regulates the composition and maintains the mode upon which it is based. It must have elegant movements so arranged that they observe the natural order of the mode, whether this is first, second, third, or another. Its cadences must be placed on the proper tones and introduced with good reason.
>
> When the air is illuminated by the sun's rays, it brightens and makes everything smile here below. Similarly, when the alto is well ordered and composed, ornamented with beautiful and elegant passages, it adorns and beautifies the composition.[31]

While the bass "is the foundation of the harmony," that is a technical aspect of its function, rather than a reason to assign it metaphorically generative priority. The bass's function is vital, indeed, but no more vital than that of the tenor, which "governs and regulates the composition and maintains the mode upon which it is based," or the soprano, which is to "nourish and satisfy the souls of listeners." One would hardly judge a piece of music successful from which listeners came away feeling aesthetically starved and dissatisfied, even if the treatment of harmony and mode were "correct."

To be sure, Zarlino is presumably imagining a *Klangideal* of men's and boys' voices, so the question of women's voices need not obtrude itself into his remarks about the "soprano" and "alto" vis-à-vis the lower parts. Rameau, in contrast, ex-

31. Marco and Palisca, *Counterpoint*, 179–180. Zarlino, *Istitutioni*, 282: "[il Soprano,] che e piu acuto d'ogn'altra parte, & piu penetrativo all'Udito, farsi udire anco prima d'ogn'altra: la onde si come'! Fuoco nutrisce, & e cagione di far spdurre ogni cosa naturale, che si trova ad ornamento, et a conservatione del Mondo; cosi il Compositore si sforzara di fare, che la Parte acita del la sua cantilena habbia bello, ornato et elegante procedere di maniera a che nutrisca, & pasci l'animo di quelli, che ascoltano. Et si come la Terra e posta per il fundamento de gli altri Elementi; cosi il Basso ha tal proprieta, che sostiene, stabilisce, fortifica & da accrescimento alle altri parti; conciosiache e posto per Basa & fondamento dell'Harmonia; onde e detto Basso, quai Basa, & sostenimento dell'altre parti. . . . Il Tenore segue immediatamente il Basso verso l'acuto, ilquale e quella parte, che regge, & governa la cantilena, & e quella, che mantiene il Modo sopra il quale e fondata; & si debbe comporre con eleganti movimenti, & con tale ordine, che osservi la natura del Modo, nelquale e composto: sia primo, secondo, terzo, over altro quai si voglia osservando di far le Cadenze a i luoghi propij, & con propo sito. Ma si come, essendo l'Aria illuminata da i raggi del Sole, ogni cosa rasserena & ogni cosa si vede ridere di qua giu, & esser pina di allegrezza; cosi quando l'Alto e bene ordinato, & ben composto, ornato di belli, & eleganti passaggi, adorna sempre, & fa vaga la cantilena; . . ."

plicitly refers on several occasions to women's voices in the upper register; beyond that, his *Klangideal* often involves an idealized *Außensatz* comprising "melody" and "harmony"—and for him, melody is naught but a "partie" of harmony (see note 25), just as the higher partial strings, characteristically sung by women's voices, are "parties" of the fundamental (see note 29).

∾

I would much prefer to let the chapter end here, allowing readers to respond in various ways to the ideas and the material it presents. But, while wishing to leave readers free to do so, I feel it would be disingenuous of me not to indicate some of my own responses.

Do I believe that the material somehow devalues traditional tonal music? No, the music stands on its own without the aid of Rameau's theory, or of any other metaphors advanced to discuss it. The same goes for music involving the "transcendent woman's voice" as conceived by male composers coming out of a fundamental bass tradition.

Do I believe that the material devalues traditional fundamental-bass theory? Yes, so far as such theory asserts musical structure to be based on the subordination of higher sounds to lower ones.

Do I believe that we should stop using the constructs and concepts of traditional harmonic theory, in teaching chorale harmonization or other sorts of strict tonal writing? Do I believe we should stop teaching such things? No, to both questions. Such pedagogy can make musicians sensitive to how harmony can urge on or hold back a melodic or other textural flow of events. There are good arguments for studying the musical techniques in historically distanced styles, so as to minimize the amount of compositional ego a student invests in the enterprise. Beyond that, many people still want to perform traditional tonal music, and many people still want to discuss it in a critical or scholarly way; it is a good idea for such people to have had experience in writing tonal exercises, hearing in what ways the various exercises work or do not work. A certain amount of traditional theoretical vocabulary is well-nigh unavoidable if the material is to be taught; to avoid terms like root, root-position, authentic/half cadence, and so forth would be unbearably constraining. The vocabulary is pedagogically effective. It is also conceptually pertinent so far as the relevant composers—from Haydn and Mozart on, at any rate—used similar terminology in conceptualizing their own harmonic practices.

What, in connection with tonal pedagogy, do I feel this chapter suggests? Above all, that women musicians should not be imprinted with a sense that events in a bass register are "not in their musical voices." Male musicians, by and large, have less of a problem hearing soprano events "in their voices," because we spoke and sang in that register as children.[32] Then too, a number of male musicians will be

32. Certainly one of the most formative experiences in my own musical development was singing in chorus over twelve years of grade school and high school, passing through the four parts from soprano to bass. A teacher does well to be self-conscious about the fact that the experience of the changing voice, normal for men, is foreign to a woman's routine musical development.

So far as a man hears his own internalized soprano voice to be the voice of a child, that makes it all the easier to conceive the soprano as "dependent" on the lower voice of the grown man. I re-

sensitive to overtones of the notes they sing, and many of the lower overtones "in our voices" will lie in alto or soprano registers.[33]

What resources are available, to avoid imprinting women musicians in this way? Ideally, first of all, no student should be instructed in tonal theory or strict tonal composition, who is not already fluent at the keyboard. People who have incorporated a keyboard instrument into their musical body image will hear themselves producing sound in any register, and interrelated sounds in all. Very ideally, the essay suggests to me that each female/male student would also do well to have some fluency on a solo bass/treble instrument; such experience would extend the student's internalized sense of a personal musical "singing" voice beyond the "typical" everyday speaking register.

Beyond that, tonal harmony can be presented less as a projection of roots from lower to upper registers, and more as a way of interrelating triadic structuring with melodic/rhythmic parsing. In such a conceptual picture, triadic roots in lower registers do indeed play a certain marked role—particularly at cadences. But a root playing that role need not be conceived as an a prioristic generator for structure in a melody; rather, the root can as well be conceptualized as a response to a perceived

member vividly how, as a young boy singing soprano, I would look at the "big boys" singing bass and wonder impatiently how I could ever endure to pass the years waiting until I would be so grown-up myself as to sing bass.

33. This experience, too, is likely to encourage males in imagining soprano or alto events somehow subordinated to their own. Rameau, whose attention was directed to overtones only after he had written the *Traité,* reports in the *Nouveau système* that he listened to the sound of harmonic overtones in his own voice, had other musicians do the same, and thereafter had "not doubted for a moment that this was the true principle of a Fundamental Bass, which I would have discovered again from this experience alone." The pertinent passage appears at the very beginning of the Preface. Jean Phillippe Rameau, *Nouveau système de musique théorique* (Paris: Ballard, 1726), iii: "Si la Basse-Fondamentale proposée dans le *Traité de l'Harmonie,* paroit aux Musiciens, un objet digne de leur attention; que n'en présumeront-ils pas, lorsque par leur propre experience ils seront convaincus qu'elle leur est naturelle, qu'elle leur suggere tout ce qu'ils imaginent en Musique, & qu'en un mot, son Principe subsiste dans leur voix même? Il y a effectivement en nous un germe d'Harmonie, dont apparament on ne s'est point encore apperçu: Il est cependant facile de s'en appercevoir dans une Corde, dans un Tuyeau, &c. dont la resonance fait entendre trois Sons differents à la fois (Cette experience est citée par differents Auteurs); puisqu'en supposant ce même effet dans tous les corps Sonores, on doit par consequent le supposer dans un Son de nôtre voix, quand même il n'y seroit pas sensible; mais pour en être plus assuré, j'en ay fait moymême l'experience, & je l'ay proposé à plusieurs Musiciens, qui, comme moy, ont distingué ces trois Sons differents dans un Son de leur voix; de sorte qu'après cela, je n'ay pas douté un moment que ce ne fut-là le veritable Principe d'une Basse-Fondamentale, dont je ne devois encore la découverte qu'à la seule experience." (If the Fundamental Bass proposed in the *Traité de l'Harmonie* should seem to musicians a subject worthy of their attention, what would they not suppose, if they were to be convinced through their own experience that it is innate to them, that it suggests to them everything that they conceive in music, and that—in a word—its principle subsists in their very own voices? In fact, there is indeed within us a germ of Harmony, which apparently no one has noticed so far. It is, nevertheless, easy to notice in a string, in a pipe, etc., whose resonance sounds three different tones at a time (this experience has been cited by various authors). Supposing then the same effect in any resonant body, we should consequently suppose it in a tone of our own voices, even if it should not be perceptible. But to be more sure in this matter, I myself essayed the experiment, and suggested it to several musicians who—like myself—distinguished these three different tones within one tone of their voices. As a result, from then on, I have not doubted for a moment that this was the true principle of a Fundamental Bass, which I would have discovered again from this experience alone.)

melodic structuring—even at times a symptom that such perception is going on. Some aspects of Schenkerian theory (not all) are well adapted for such an approach. But the view is not particularly Schenkerian in itself, as the C-major cadence in the Schoenberg quartet, responding to aspects of the vocal line, will testify.[34] Indeed, the view is not even particularly "modern." Mattheson's critiques of Rameau, for example, are quite to the point in this connection.[35] And, so far as eighteenth-century composition itself is concerned, one thinks of various chorale harmonizations by J. S. Bach, who parses a given melody (e.g., *Herzlich thut mich verlangen)* so as to end on a Phrygian first degree in one setting, and on the third degree of a major key in another.[36]

34. In connection with the C-major parsing of "dem großen atem wunschlos mich ergebend," beginning on E4–G4–E4, interested readers are invited to note the climactic E5–(D♯5–F♯5)–G5 several measures earlier, at "kreisend, webend." The G5 (m. 58) is the highest note so far in the vocal part, which begins at measure 21.

35. A number of them are collected and commented on by Erwin R. Jacobi in *Jean Philippe Rameau, Complete Theoretical Writings,* vol. 6 (American Institute of Musicology, 1972). Mattheson is sensitive in particular to the sexual metaphors of Rameau's discourse. "Rameau sagt in seinem Tractat von der Harmonie, S. 139: Sie werde zum ersten gezeuget. Das gebe ich gerne zu. Das erste Kind aber, so gezeuget wird, muss doch Vater and Mutter haben. Nun vertritt ja hier der Klang allein des Vaters, and die Melodie allein der Mutter Stelle. Nichts ist deutlicher! Er sagt ferner, man müsse schlechterdings die Regeln der Melodie aus der Harmonie nehmen, und gestehet hergegen S. 142: Es sey fast unmöglich, gewisse Regeln davon zu geben: obgleich die höchste Vollkommenheit in der Melodie stecke, ohne welche die schönste Harmonie bisweilen abgeschmackt herauskomme. Arme Leute, wo nehmen?" The text is cited by Jacobi in the *Writings,* xxii–xxiii. (Rameau says in his *Treatise on Harmony,* page 139, that it [Harmony, rather than Melody] is the first to be engendered. [The reference is to Chapter 19 in Book II of the *Traité.*] I concede that willingly. But the first child, in order to be born, must still have [both] a father and a mother. Now here in fact the Fundamental Bass alone plays the role of father, and Melody alone that of mother. Nothing could be clearer. Later on, he says that we must unequivocally derive the rules of Melody from Harmony. But then, contrariwise, he confesses on page 142 [in Chapter 20] that it is almost impossible to give definite rules for it [Melody], even though the highest perfection is invested in Melody, without which the most beautiful harmony would turn out to be insipid. Alas, what are we to do?) The translation is mine.

36. The phenomenon is among many discussed by Lori Burns in "J. S. Bach's Chorale Harmonizations of Modal Cantus Firmi" (Ph.D. dissertation, Harvard, 1991), a thorough theoretical investigation of its subject involving an original analytic/theoretical method.

CHAPTER Fifteen

Toward the Analysis of a Schoenberg Song (Op. 15, No. XI)

Example 15.1

a	Als wir hinter dem bebluemten tore	exposition
b	endlich nur das eigne hauchen spuerten.	
c	warden uns erdachte seligkeiten?	problem
a	Ich erinnere, dass wie schwache rohre	action
d	beide stumm zu beben wir begannen	
b	wenn wir leis nur an uns ruehrten	
d	und dass unsre augen rannen—	
c	So verbleibest du mir lang zu seiten.	"dénouement"

The poem has a clear two-part form, as narrative, which is supported by the endrhyme scheme. Example 15.1 shows what I mean. I have put "dénouement" in quotes, for the end of the poem does not resolve the problem or indicate the outcome of the action to our satisfaction. More questions remain unanswered than answered; we do not know, for instance, whether the tears were of joy or grief or both; we do not know what happened after the lovers remained side by side for a long time; mainly we do not know the answer to the question posed in the text, "warden uns erdachte seligkeiten?" The narrative form and endrhyme scheme (as illustrated by Example 15.1) associate that question with the last line of text, heightening that paradox.

One might, within Example 15.1, also put "action" in quotes, as referring to lines 4–7. The natural sense of urgency or drive one would attach to this part of the narrative is greatly undercut by the qualifying "Ich erinnere, dass." Introducing the present tense into the apparent narrative past of the poem so far draws our attention toward what is happening now (the poet is remembering) at the expense of what happened then (the described "action" which, however, is now something over with).[1]

Without delving farther into the poem itself yet, let us note some broad aspects of Schoenberg's setting, viewed in light of the poetic analysis so far. First, one notes that Schoenberg composed four vocal phrases, one to go with each of the narrative sections of the poem. Vocal phrase 1, measures 8–10, sets the textual exposition. Vocal phrase 2, measures 11–12, sets the problem of the narrative. Vocal phrase 3, to my hearing, comprises measures 13–19, all of the material of the "action" lines 4–7 of the poem.[2] And vocal phrase 4, measures 21–23, sets the "dénouement," the final line of text.

Having noted this, we must make some immediate qualifications, for it is clear that the musical functions of the four vocal phrases do not correspond in a 1-to-1 fashion with the narrative functions of the coincident sections of text. Vocal phrase 1, setting the narrative exposition, has comparatively little in the way of musical exposition (we shall examine later how the musical material of the phrase is developed out of the piano introduction). Vocal phrase 3 provides a definite musical answer to the question of vocal phrase 2, ending on a substantial cadence. Measures 18½–19 of the vocal line are a definite musical answer to measure 12. Beyond that, the entire vocal line of measures 16–19 contains (among other things) a reworking and transformation of the entire vocal line of measures 11–12. Schoenberg, then, has set the text so that the music for line 7 (rather than line 8) answers the music for the question of line 3. Line 7, rather than 8, then supports what sense of dénouement there is musically. Correspondingly, vocal phrase 4 has no musical work to do as a dénouement; musically it is a coda, rather than an outcome, referring back to the music for line 1 of the text rather than line 3.

Any attempt to identify the four vocal phrases simply and completely with the four sections of the poetic narrative is thus not tenable from a rhetorical point of view.[3] Let us now view the large shape of the piece from a different perspective: its

1. Compare the same technique at the end of Heine's *Ihr Bild:* "Und, ach, ich *kann* es nicht glauben . . ."

The effect is of course very different, as is Schubert's response from Schoenberg's. If one studies Schubert carelessly, one might believe he was insensitive to the point, proceeding to finish off a simple-minded musical ABA that sets the tragic present-tense final line to the same major-key music that had previously accompanied the singer's optimistic delusion, as described in his past-tense narrative. The apparent simple-mindedness conceals a devastating dramatic sophistication. The point is that Schubert takes the singer absolutely literally at the final line of text: "I *cannot* believe I have lost you"; hence I will continue to sing just as I did before. The musical equivalent of Heine's change of tense is delayed and given to the piano in the following little epilogue, now minor rather than major, loud rather than soft, as reality crashes in on the pipe dream: "You lose, buddy, because you really *have* lost her!"

Let the reader take care, then, when we shortly find Schoenberg likewise apparently "missetting" George's rhetoric.

2. One might consider separating off measures 18–19 as a separate phrase, setting line 7 alone, after an earlier phrase setting lines 4 through 6. The special focus on line 7 of the text is evident, but it is impossible for me to hear the phrase that begins at measure 13 as adequately cadenced by measures 16–17 alone. Needless to say, this ground will be covered in great detail later on.

3. Whether this is a defect, a clever subtlety, or an aesthetically neutral aspect of the work is a critical question which it would seem premature to answer at this point.

large metric structure. Here we find clear large beats at measures 1-, 8+, 13-, and 20, producing the form diagrammed in Example 15.2.

Example 15.2

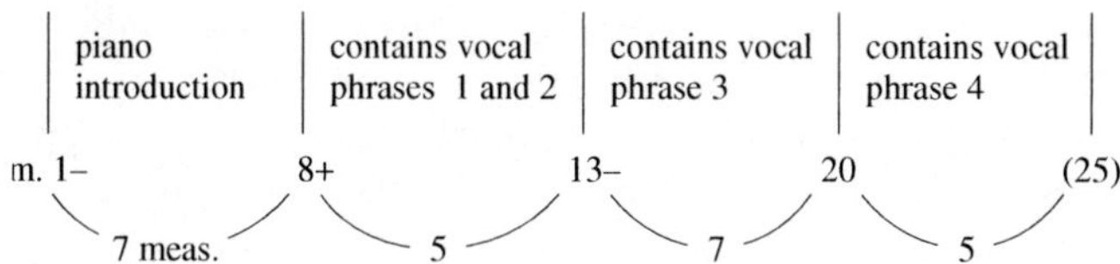

The diagram projects a strong duple structure: 7-plus-5 measures, followed by 7-plus-5 measures. That structure is supported by the strongest reprises in the music: the major/minor triad at measure 13- reprising the right hand of the opening; the augmented repetition of vocal phrase 1, from measure 8+, following the beat at measure 20. The reprise of the major/minor triad at measure 13- also coincides with the text "Ich erinnere." That is a happy means of pointing the musical reprise, but it is also very suggestive in light of our earlier analysis about the function of "Ich erinnere" in the text. It is the unique present-tense verb of the poem, and it is withheld for three lines so as to undercut the functionality of the ensuing narrative past action. By the musical correspondence of the major/minor triads, the "present-tense" context of the poem is thus identified strongly with the music of the piano introduction (which, however, preceded the voice's delivery of its first three lines of text in the narrative past tense).

In that connection, "Ich erinnere" is also identified with the theatrical aspect of the singer's silence over the opening seven measures of music. Whatever we are to imagine going on in the singer's mind during that span of time evidently has something to do with "remembering," and something to do with setting a present-tense mode for the work in distinction to the narrative past of the singer's opening text. (The singer's remaining silent over this amount of sheer chronological time is quite striking theatrically, not to mention that the gesture takes up over a quarter of the piece.)

Associating "Ich erinnere" in this way with the piano introduction, it seems consistent to regard the overall musicodramatic form of the piece as involved with working around the musical gestures of the piano introduction, rather than simply having to provide a "resolution" for line 3 of the poem. The musical action of vocal phrase 3, measures 13–20, specifically corresponds to the piano introduction in the duple structure of Example 15.2. So the big vocal cadence preceding measure 20, the large downbeat on the bar line of measure 20, and the coda character of the music following that measure all begin to seem logical in this context, where they were earlier only puzzling. We should note that a functional regular meter (in fact the written meter) sets in strongly, for the first time, with the turning of vocal phrase 3 toward its cadence and the subsequent beat at measure 20. This phenomenon sets in exactly at measure 16, with the turning down of the melodic line in the voice from its climax at measure 15. The written bar lines for measures 16, 17, 19, and of course 20 itself are all clearly audible, as is the written meter hereabouts.

(This span also involves the portion of the vocal line that picks up and eventually answers the question-music from mm. 11–12.) The clarity of local metric definition from measures 16–20 is in notable contrast to the preceding metrically floating music of the song.

Evidently the large metric sketch of Example 15.2 is getting us significantly farther in relating text and music organically. Beyond the points already made, the duple metric structure manifested by Example 15.2 appears to reflect various "duple" senses in the overall organization of the text—most notably the narrative structure "exposition/problem; action/dénouement" and the supportive endrhyme structure "ab/c? adbd/c." Naturally the correspondence of musical metric structure with text here is not simple or 1-to-1 (the text lacks provision for anything corresponding to the music of the piano introduction). But the duple feeling of Example 15.2, as such, is arguably in the spirit of the poem.

Now that we have opened an avenue of approach to the song as a whole, we can start looking at the music in detail, having some sense of the large composition into which these elements are to fit. In light of the preceding discussion, it would not be amiss to plunge right into the all-important piano introduction in this case. The very strong thematic profile of the opening would also make such an approach appropriate here. (As a general rule, I believe one should not necessarily begin analyzing a piece by plunging into the opening measures.) Nevertheless, I should like to choose a different mode of entry into the music even in this case: the large melodic construction of the vocal line. In general, I would mistrust any analysis of a song that did not at some point investigate that aspect of the work (as well as the overall relations of text to music). In particular, the voice is so exposed in this song, and the peculiar character of the vocal line in relation to its extreme registers is so striking, that one is almost invited to begin here by the composer. As we shall see later, the large gestures of the melody in the vocal line are intimately related to basic intervallic structures exposed in the piano introduction and developed throughout the piece in the small as well as in the large.

Example 15.3

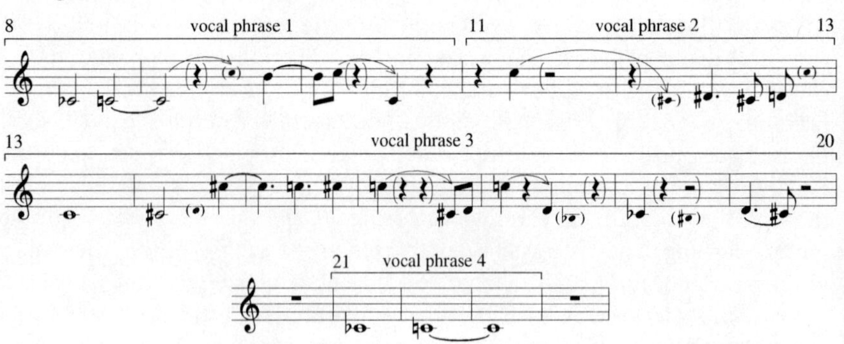

Example 15.3, then, is a rough sketch indicating how the vocal line is melodically organized around certain crucial half-step relations about middle C in the

lower register, and the same pitch-class relations an octave higher. The vocal phrases are constructed around these half-step relations in the extreme registers, with vocal "elevators" rising or falling between the extreme registers. The "elevators" are indicated by arrows in Example 15.3.

Vocal phrase 1 begins by exposing a C♭–C relation in the low register at length, then takes a swift elevator up an octave to dwell on the B–C relation in the upper register, then takes a gently subsiding triplet elevator back down to touch the low C again at the cadence. Vocal phrase 2 reattacks the high C forcefully, then drifts down the octave to cadence on low D. The latter pitch is connected to the earlier low C♭–C via C♯; the low D is also inflected by its upper auxiliary D♯. The high C is touched once again immediately following the cadential low D; evidently this gesture has to do with the question (problem) of the text, structurally as well as locally (the leap upwards matches the rising pitch of the question mark). Vocal phrase 3 sets off with a strong C–C♯ relation in the lower octave; after touching the low D once more, the voice shoots up to expose the C–C♯ relation in the upper octave at great length—this being the melodic climax of the entire vocal line, appearing however shortly before the height of the text "action" (we will discuss that later). The voice is unable to maintain the high C♯ and subsides back to its oft-stated high C (the "action" leading nowhere new); that high C takes a characteristic downward-drifting elevator to the lower register for yet a third and fourth time (mm. 16–17), and vocal phrase 3 cadences strongly, at measure 19, on the low C♯, with considerable conjunct melodic convergence on that tone. The low D (associating overall with the cadence of phrase 2, m. 12) is now heard as appoggiatura to the cadential C♯ in measure 19. The power of the cadence in measures 18–19, as gathering together earlier material, is enhanced by the return of the voice, at the pickup to measure 18, to the low C♭ on which it originally began (m. 8) and which it has not touched since, having remained essentially above it all the time. Vocal phrase 4, as musical coda, returns to the original C♭–C gesture of measures 8–9, with the upper octave no longer in the picture.

We can summarize, in one sense, as follows: the most critical half-step relations on which the vocal melodic structure hangs are B–C (or C♭–C) and C–C♯. The resultant basic cluster B–C–C♯ is extended upward (in the lower register only) to include D as a structural auxiliary to C♯ (cadence on D at m. 12 "resolving" to cadence on C♯ with D as appoggiatura at m. 19, etc.). In the upper register, the tones B, C and C♯ of the basic cluster are very strongly set off. C♯ is the melodic climax of the entire line, and one can note that the upper B♭ is the only tone missing from the total gamut of the voice's range over the song.

A harmonic realization of the above structural observations can be noted, embedded within the little "motto" which occurs first in the piano introduction and recurs twice at later points in the piece (see Example 15.4).

The basic cluster B–C–C♯, together with F, forms a pitch-class collection, which I will denote by "X." In Example 15.4, X is represented by a certain chord. The "neighboring" cluster C–C♯–D, together with F, forms a pitch-class collection, which I label "N." N is also represented by a chord in Example 15.4. That N is to be heard as a neighbor to X (rather than vice versa) will become abundantly clear in

Example 15.4

the sequel; this is also consistent with the primacy of B, C and C♯ in the large structure of the vocal line, with D as neighbor to C♯ in the lower register. The progression of the N-chord to the X-chord in Example 15.4 summarizes important semitone relations that are familiar from our earlier discussion of the large vocal melody: D-to-D♭ (C♯) in the bass, C♯-to-C in the soprano, and C-to-B in the tenor voices of the chords. The pedal F of Example 15.4, an element of both N and X, is absent from the large vocal schema of Example 15.3. We shall comment later on the significance of the absence of any powerful F (or any F at all after m. 9) from the vocal line.

Considering the actual aural effect of the opening of the piece, Example 15.4 appears a somewhat artificial way of introducing the reader to one of the important intervallic ideas (N-to-X) of the piece. However, it does make an immediate hook-up to the preceding discussion of the large vocal line. Beyond that, the recurring motto of Example 15.4 becomes progressively more and more important as a Leitmotif in the song. The medial chord of the motto (an altered Tristan chord?!) has a strong autonomy in the piece. In the sequel, I will call it the "magic chord." This chord, in fact, has a definite function within the cycle as a whole. (It would be out of place to explore this at length here, but the interested reader may be referred to measure 8 of song No. I, and to four measures before the end of song No. XV, as a point of departure in this connection, the latter with particular reference to measure 20 of No. XI. As we shall note later, the magic chord has a certain "framing" function within No. XI somewhat analogous to the frame for the entire cycle created by the moments cited in songs Nos. I and XV. For reference to other motifs of this song that recur throughout the cycle, the reader is referred to Jan Maegaard's valuable dissertation, *Studien zur Entwicklung des dodekaphonen Satzes bei Arnold Schoenberg,* Wilhelm Hansen, 1972.)

Example 15.5

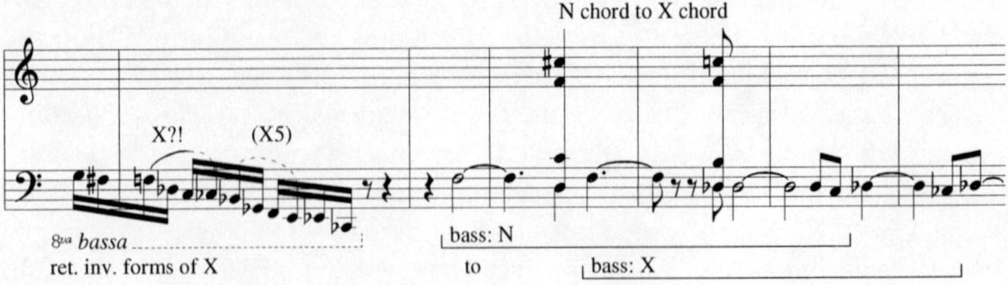

Example 15.5 demonstrates the wider, and basic, constructive role of X and N-to-X within the piano introduction. The N-to-X relation, heard chordally within the motto, is subsequently "prolonged" melodically in the bass line. The left hand at the opening of the piece consists of a chain of linear X-forms (retrograde-inverted, if we take F–D♭–C–C♭ as a basic linear form for X). Overlapping that chain, one finds prime melodic forms of X; in particular, X at its basic pitch-class level can be found at the written bar line of measure 1. (I would not make much of this, but perhaps it is a subtle reason for the placement of that written—but hardly audible—bar line.)

Example 15.6

Another prominent feature of the piano introduction is the motif which I will call "T" (for major/minor triad). Example 15.6 shows how this motif is developed over the opening five measures. T has a preferred linear form (B♭–D♭–F–D), as did X. For present purposes, we will not concern ourselves with the problem that we sometimes hear T-forms identified with their "roots," and sometimes not, over the piece. (I will defer a general discussion of tonality in the context of this song until later, in note 10.) Example 15.6 sidesteps the problem by indicating how T is transposed first by three semitones, then by four, referring those intervals back to the first two intervals of the linear T motif itself. In this way, we can avoid attributing a D♭ "root" to the second T-form of Example 15.6, and an F "root" to the third form at a moment where one hears a different "root" overall if one listens tonally.

Example 15.7

Example 15.7 shows how the basic form of T can be heard as moving into the bass of the motto, and thence can be analyzed as underlying the remainder of the entire first half of the song up to measure 13, where the original thematic T-form is reprised. This involves hearing the C and C♭ of measures 5–6 as passing—between tones of T—rather than as essential (elements of N-to-X). There is, of course, no reason why the tones should not have such an ambiguous function. Later we will analyze them as lower auxiliaries to D♭ too, in connection with still another motif.

Example 15.7 is an attractive conceit in light of our earlier discussion (following Example 15.2) of the relation of measures 13ff. to the piano introduction. To get at this again, let us imagine a hypothetical song whose first six measures are identical with those of the actual song, and which then proceeds as follows: the piano right hand remains silent in measure 7; the piano left hand goes down to (bass clef) B♭ somewhere in measure 7 or at measure 8; the voice enters at that moment on the text "Ich erinnere." I contend that something like this hypothetical music underlies the actual effect of measures 1 to 13, and that Example 15.7 illustrates how the arrival of the B♭ beat in the left hand is delayed for five measures, while the voice covers the narrative-past portion of the text that precedes the delayed present-tense "Ich erinnere." That seems very consistent with the virtual cessation of activity in the piano part after the initial voice entrance until measure 13, and the striking effusion of pianistic activity immediately thereafter.

In my "hypothetical song," I omitted the piano right hand of measure 7. Obviously, the shock of that music distracts our attention from the leisurely sinking of the left hand down to the "hypothetical B♭" of "hypothetical measure 7 or 8." In that sense, the right hand of measure 7 is to be related to the entrance of the voice with actual text other than "hypothetical 'Ich erinnere'" at measure 8. The substantial accent of measure 7 is then a theatrical cue to singer (and audience): "stop standing there and musing; start telling your story (in the past tense)." Anyone who has ever sung in public will recognize that, to the singer, measure 7 will have an analogous effect to that which the stage manager's call of "places!" has on an actor. Thus, the rhythmic pickup at measure 8: the singer, being aroused, sails into his narrative (rather than singing "Ich erinnere" to himself).

Example 15.8

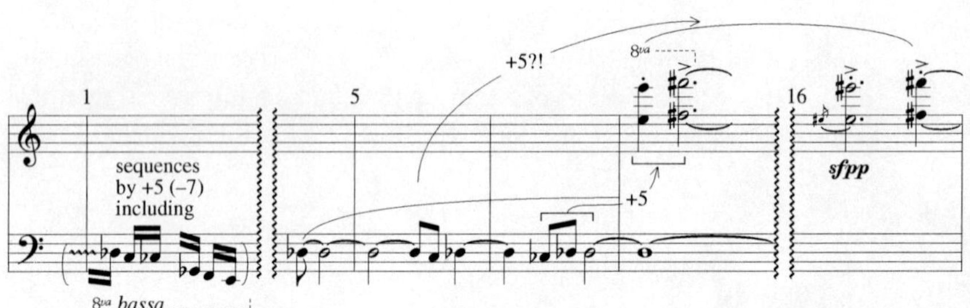

In this connection, one notes the picking up of measure 7 by measure 16 in the piano right hand. This relation is very audible in the overall textural context of the song. Example 15.8 attempts to place the resultant E–E♯–F♯ complex in a wider frame of reference, in a five-semitone relation to the basic B–C–C♯. The actual reference of Example 15.8 to the piano bass of measures 4–6 is strained; it might be more pertinent to hear the large-scale relation of measure 7 to measure 16 in connection with the large B–C and C–C♯ gestures of the vocal line, to which measures 4–6 can in turn be related. On the other hand, one immediately hears measure 7 in a five-semitone relation to the C♭–D♭ of measure 6 (as indicated on Example 15.8). Considering that measure 7 is so sharply unrelated to measures 1–6 in any number of other respects, at least that much is to the point. The idea of picking up the disturbing measure 7 at measure 16 ties in nicely with the idea of measure 16 being the point at which the piece abandons the climactic measure 15 and begins its approach to the big cadence and downbeat at measures 19–20, with strong metric regularity.

In discussing the effect of measure 7, we should draw even more attention to its "fourthy" sound (i.e., five semitones) in relation to the bass. The actual fourth D♭ (C♯)-against-F♯ will persist for a long time in the accompaniment. Beyond that, the auxiliaries C♭ and E, from which D♭ and F♯ are respectively approached, build up the total sound in an even more fourthy way. Namely, one hears the total complex of C♯–F♯–B–E, harmonically equivalent to a fourth-chord. That sound seems related, in my ear, to the orgy of fourths in the cascades following measure 13. More specifically, measures 13ff. "unleash" the fourths that were a prominent structural feature of the beginning and end of the piano introduction, but otherwise not developed there (our attention focusing on magic chord, N-to-X, and T at the expense of the fourths during the bulk of the introduction).

Example 15.9

The idea of "structural transposition by five semitones," related to the fourthy sounds just discussed, is used as a means of connection across the rest in measure 2, to get to the magic chord. Example 15.9 shows how the chain of major thirds, transposing by five, continues into the right-hand part of the chord. (The preparation, over the opening measure, for the tritone in the left-hand part of the chord will be discussed later.)

Example 15.10

While on the subject of fourths, it is appropriate to label a new motif Y in which a fourth is conspicuous. Example 15.10 shows this motif, which figures, along with a transposed form, in the piano introduction. I have chosen to label the left-hand form as "prime" and the right-hand form as "transposed," even though the latter is more immediately audible and will remain more prominent over the piece. The form that I label "Y" contains what I consider to be the "tonic" minor third of the piece, F–D, and the "tonic" fourth C♯–F♯. The pitch-class complex

D–F–D♭ appears both in the prime form of the N-to-X idea (cf. Example 15.5) and the prime form of the T idea (cf. Example 15.7). In some sense, D–F–D♭ is the "tonic minor/major third" of the piece, so that it is consistent to label as the prime form of Y that form that contains those pitch-classes. "Y7" is then the "dominant" form of Y, as G♯–C♯ is the "dominant" of C♯–F♯, C–A the "dominant" of F–D, and so on. (I do not wish to discuss here how seriously or frivolously I am invoking the notion of "dominant" in this context, beyond availing myself of a certain conceptual ease it affords. Note 10 will pick up that train of thought.)

Example 15.10 illustrates how, in order to subsume the shock of measure 7 into a Y-form answering the earlier Y7, we must hear the C and C♭ of the bass in measures 5–6 as auxiliaries to the D♭, entailing dramatic tension against our earlier ways of hearing those tones: as essential tones prolonging N-to-X, or as passing tones in the sense of Example 15.7, within T.

Example 15.11

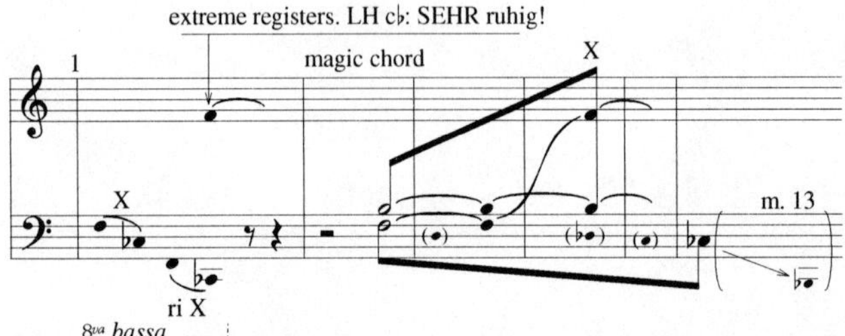

Example 15.11 illustrates the importance of the tritone F–B over the piano introduction. The tritone is latent in measure 1, and provides strong continuity into the left-hand part of the magic chord in measure 2. The tritone is of course embedded harmonically not only within the magic chord but also within the X chord. The tritone also spans the preferred linear form of X, F–D♭–C–C♭, a feature that appears locally in the left-hand figuration of the opening, and more significantly in connection with the overall structure of the bass line from measure 2 to measure 6 (the C♭ there being "about to resolve" to the B♭ in m. 13).

Let us examine now the way in which the piano introduction prepares vocal phrase 1. It is pertinent to review Example 15.4 in this connection, recalling the voice-leading features of the N-to-X chordal progression. The alto voice of the two chords remains on F. The soprano voice moves from C♯ to C, a gesture that is also embedded melodically within Y7 (Example 15.10). The bass moves from D to D♭, a gesture that is also embedded within Y (Example 15.10) and T (Example 15.7). The remaining semitone gesture involved in the voice-leading of N-to-X chords is C-to-B in the tenor voice. And it is that gesture, embedded in an inner voice of the motto and not embedded in any other significant motif as yet, which the voice seizes on at its entrance as the basis for the large melodic structure of its first phrase (cf. Example 15.3, vocal phrase 1). This symbolizes the dramatic detachment of the singer's original explicit thoughts from the central ideas of the introduction (while nevertheless providing some basis for continuity acoustically).

Example 15.12

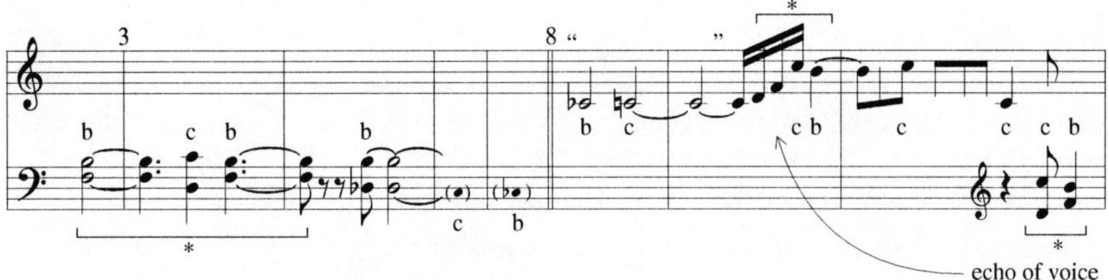

Example 15.12 shows in more detail how carefully the B–C relations in vocal phrase 1 are integrated with material from the piano. Aside from the melodic oscillations of B with C, one notes the use of the left-hand material from measure 3 (marked with asterisks in Example 15.12) to provide the rising "elevator" for the voice in measure 9. This is confirmed by the recurrence of the motto an octave higher shortly thereafter, solidifying B–C in the upper vocal octave. (It will be noted that the asterisked material is not a central motive of the piece, but an acoustical association.)

In connection with our dramatic analysis so far, dwelling on B–C has the concomitant effect of inhibiting the B (C♭) from moving down to B♭ with a big beat, as in the "hypothetical song." It should not be necessary at this point to rehash the argument as to why this is an appropriate thing for the voice to be doing while singing its opening lines of text, before "Ich erinnere" and the low B♭ at measure 13. A fine touch here is the use of B♭ in the vocal line of measure 8 as a passing tone. This emphasizes even more the fact that C♭ is not resolving to B♭. (There are no more B♭s in the music until m. 13.)

Aside from the melodic and rhythmic accents on the C♭s of measure 8, another factor that makes it clear that B♭ is a passing tone here is the power of the "A♭major/minor triad," that is, T10 . . . in the vocal line of measure 8. Example 15.13 shows how T10 recurs at the climax of the phrase, and how it moves on to T2 at the cadence.

Example 15.13

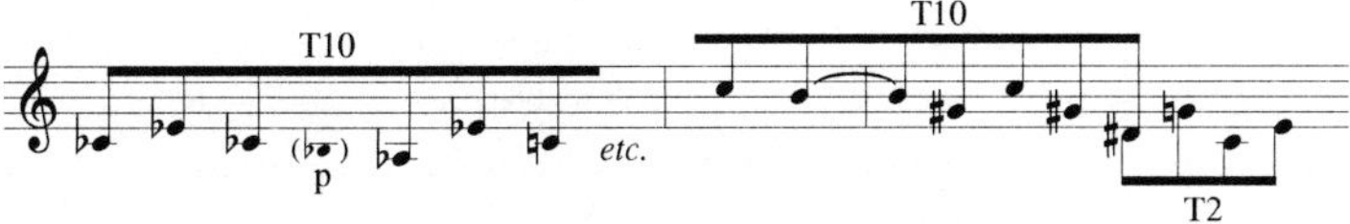

Perhaps the gesture T10-to-T2 can be heard as a "dominant" version of the earlier T3-to-T7 (right hand, mm. 2–5, as in Example 15.6). The phrase need not rely on that relation to any great extent, however. A much more potent aspect of the motive structure here is the reference to Y-forms diagrammed in Example 15.14.

Example 15.14

Since Y is a mirror of itself, there is some general ambiguity as to the proper labeling of Y forms (as transpositions or inversions one of another). Here, later analysis will show that the form labeled "Y6" in Example 15.14 is indeed to be considered as a transposition (rather than an inversion) of Y. Specifically, it is to be heard as a semitone "too low," that is, a semitone lower than the Y7 that the piano played in the top line of measures 2–5 (Example 15.10). This already seems plausible, since the notes involved are the highest of piano and voice so far in the piece, respectively, discounting the piano right hand of measures 7ff. Later events will clinch the relationship. The other Y-form of Example 15.14 I have analyzed as an inversion, rather than a transposition. First, the overall sense of the vocal phrase is that the lower register moves up, while the upper register moves down. Second, that sense is reinforced by the move from D♯ up to E at the end of the phrase, answering the slightly earlier move from G♯ down to G, in measure 10. Third, the sense of the B–C relation in the lower register is that B moves up to C; the sense in the upper register is that C moves down to the heavily accented B of measure 9, despite the "teaser" high C that recurs in measure 10. All of this indicates a basic inversional sense underlying the phrase. And when one notes that a center of inversion is specifically B-and-C, this clinches the choice of notation, "B-and-C" being melodically the essence of the phrase.[4]

Example 15.15

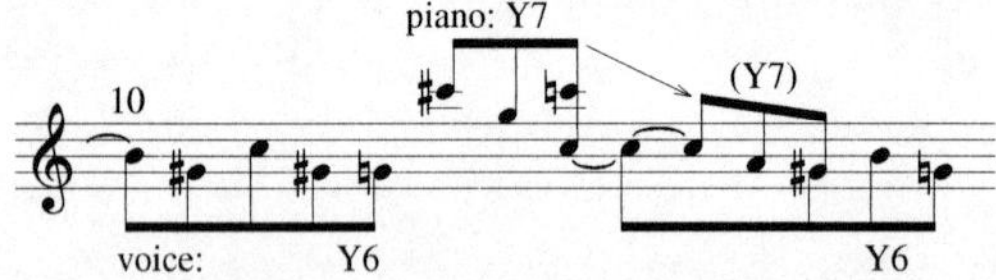

Example 15.15 continues to work with the idea that the Y6 of measure 10 is heard as "a semitone too low," below the earlier Y7 of the piano. At the end of measure 10, on top of the vocal cadence, the piano comes in with a reprise of the motto. The top line of the piano here thus reinitiates Y7. Since the voice has just sung Y6 in its upper register, the effect is of the piano's "correcting" the voice. The voice reenters, picking up the C of Y7 from the piano and finishing off Y7 correctly with the C–A–G♯ of measure 11 (compare the melodic line of mm. 3½–4½). However, the voice cannot maintain Y at the 7-level, and immediately slips back down again to Y6 as measure 11 goes along. We shall return later to the dramatic "meaning" of these gestures, summarized in Example 15.15.

Meanwhile, we return to discuss the oscillating C–A of measures 8–9, the gesture on which the voice part of the entire song will later end, at measures 22–23.

4. This discussion may seem pointlessly pedantic to some. I can only urge my own conviction that careless notation, chosen without examination of the aural function of the phenomena involved, can lead to substantial musical confusion. Thus, for example, "I♯" for "V/iv," and so on. In this passage (m. 10) one can find many Y-forms about on the page, and in each case one can call the form either a transposition or an inversion of Y. I would consider all forms beyond the two I have discussed aurally tenuous if not downright nonexistent. Careless notation (of these, or of the two I have noted) would create "relationships" on paper that could well confuse the ear of the analyst.

Example 15.16

The gesture does not fit snugly into a larger familiar motif immediately surrounding it. I would approach it through the notion that C–A is to be heard as the "dominant form" of the "tonic" minor third F–D. We have had similar oscillation on F–D earlier in the piece; Example 15.16 shows what I mean. When the C–A stops oscillating in measure 9, the next notes we hear are D and F, although this is a very local event. Finally, the context in which we are presently most familiar with C–A is that of Y7, within which the minor third is embedded. Example 15.15, and earlier discussion, indicated the importance of relating Y7 to Y6, "down a semitone," within the vocal line. The corresponding minor third embedded within Y6 is B–G♯, or C♭–A♭, and the oscillating C–A of measures 8–9 is readily heard as being a semitone above the earlier C♭s and A♭s of the vocal line. The relation recurs in the upper register near the opening of vocal phrase 2, where the high C–A will subside to the high G♯–B as Y7 overall subsides to Y6. Thus the oscillating C–A of measures 8–9 can be indirectly but convincingly related to the C–A of Y7 abstractly; and the original choice of the "7" in the label for Y7 already reflected the notion that the minor third C–A of Y7 was the "dominant" of the basic minor third F–D.

Example 15.17

Example 15.18

Example 15.19

Examples 15.17 through 15.19 continue the motivic analysis of vocal phrase 2 beyond where we left it in Example 15.15. Example 15.17 demonstrates N7-to-X7, the "dominant" form of N-to-X, within the line (just as Y7 earlier was the "dominant" of Y). Example 15.18 shows how N7, besides moving to X7, also can be heard to slip down a semitone to N6 within the line. This is in analogy with Y7 earlier

slipping down to Y6 (the slipping minor thirds involved being the C–A and G♯–B embedded in each pair of 7-to-6 motifs).

Example 15.19 shows how N1 governs the approach to the cadence of the phrase thereafter; also how N1-to-X1 is involved with the "question mark" of the high C after the cadential low D, and with the connection to the low C that begins vocal phrase 3. N1-to-X1 is of course "a semitone too high" in the low register here. We recall that the latter half of phrase 1 and the opening of phrase 2 involved Y6, "a semitone too low" in the upper register. Each of these reciprocal gestures involves specific basic tones of the vocal line. Y6-instead-of-Y7, in the upper register, involves high tones C–B instead of C♯–C, while (N1-to-X1)-instead-of-(N-to-X), in the low register, involves low tones C♯–C instead of C–B. Both these substitutions are quite audible in context. In the upper register, "C–B rather than C♯–C" is very clear (cf. Example 15.15). In the lower register, it is not very hard to locate the low C♯s of measure 12 and the low C of measure 13 with reference to the low C♭s and Cs of measure 8, particularly as one is singing. Of course, the motivic context in which the tones are embedded relies heavily on the piano introduction.

We can review all of this as follows: after the piano introduction, which forms a large metric unit of the piece, the next large metric unit comprises the first two vocal phrases, measures 8–13, as indicated in Example 15.2 earlier. That unit has an overall symmetrical melodic "action." The upper register is brought "down a semitone": high C instead of high C♯, C–B relation instead of C♯–C relation, Y6 instead of Y7, including reference back to the music of the piano introduction. The lower register is brought "up a semitone": low C instead of low C♭, C♯–C relation instead of C–B relation, N1-to-X1 instead of N-to-X, including some reference back and also possibly allowing the first low C of measure 13 in the voice.

That overall action, for the second metric unit of the song, is completed on the last eighth of measure 12, if one accepts the high C there as a substitute for the low C. The piano evidently does, since it comes in with its long-delayed low B♭ beat at that moment. It is only after that, however, that the voice completes its total melodic action in register (which is of the essence of that action), hitting the low C of measure 13. The high C at the end of measure 12 is thus, aptly, a musical question mark: does the low C♯ resolve to the high C? This ties up with a consistent reluctance on the part of the voice, through the metric unit of measures 8-to-13, to sing C♯-to-C in either register (cf. Example 15.15 again). The putative motion of low C♯ to high C in measure 12 is weakened by the evident resolution of the C♯ to the D immediately preceding the high C. On the other hand, if that C were only low, one would have no trouble hearing the earlier C♯s resolving to it through the intervening D, particularly with the aid of the strong beat provided by the piano. However the low C would be grotesque vocally as setting the end of a question. Thus, it might be conceivable to consider the final C of measure 12 as "really" low, but displaced an octave by the pitching of the question at that moment. The piano presumably "hears" it that way. One might conjecture that the piano is very keen on the motivic support (N1-to-X1) by which the C♯ can be carried to C. For the piano's introduction featured N-to-X strongly (Example 15.5); the last thing the piano played before the end of measure 12 was a strong N-to-X within the motto at measures 10–11; and the piano has just heard the voice sing a clear N7-to-X7

(Example 15.17). The piano, then, might strongly expect or desire that the N1 of Example 15.19 will move on to X1, producing a pitch-class C. To the extent that N, X and N-to-X are pitch-class ideas, independent of register, the piano might not care so much which C the voice actually provides.

The voice of course does care, and the beat within the vocal line is delayed until the low C that opens vocal phrase 3. This definitely completes the "overall action" for the metric unit of measures 8–13, discussed earlier, by providing C♯–C and N1-to-X1 in the low register. The force of the beat also involves simply providing some C♯-to-C within the vocal line in register. (This, however, "ought to happen" in the upper register and will later on.) Although the singer will hear a beat on the second eighth of measure 13, the beat provided by the piano's low B♭ two eighths earlier is clearly overriding to my ear, in the total context. It is as if the push of the piano's beat gives the singer encouragement, once he has heard the low B♭, to sing low C and "Ich erinnere," instead of high C and a question mark. "*Now* I'm beginning to remember!"

We have reached a crucial articulation in both text and music. Starting with the text, we can find at least three related but distinct dramatic components of "Ich erinnere," to which we can attach Roman numerals for convenience in future discussion.

I. The audience—and possibly the singer—becomes aware of the singer as an actor in the present, rather than the past.

II. The audience—and possibly the singer—becomes aware of the singer's specific present action of "remembering" (something).

III. The singer becomes conscious, at this moment but not earlier, of specific past events—or more likely feelings—hitherto inaccessible to his recall. In this context, lines 4–7 of the poem really are "action." Only the true action takes place in the present, as the singer strives to recall the pertinent memories. The apparent past "action," the narrated past behavior of the lovers, is a formal screen for that true present action. Such, at any rate, is the dramatic reading that Schoenberg's setting projects to me; further expansion, with musical references, will follow.

Musical support, around measure 13, for the above three dramatic components is to be noted as follows :

- I. becoming aware of the singer as an actor in the present
  - A. the immediacy of the low B♭ beat
  - B. similarly, to a lesser extent, for the low C vocal beat on "Ich"
  - C. the (heightened) resumption of activity in the piano at measure 13, following its essentially complete suspension during the whole time the singer has been singing (in the past tense) so far;
- II. becoming aware of the action of "remembering" (something)
  - A. recollection in the piano of earlier piano music
    - 1. recall of the opening pitch-class B♭ strongly

2. recall of the concomitant T-motif at its original pitch-class level (to recur yet again in the right hand a measure later)
3. recall of the original thematic contour and (to a sufficient extent) rhythm of the T-motif at the opening of the piece, to recur through measures 14–15 *passim* as the T-motif is transposed about

B. recollection in the voice of earlier piano music: recall of the thematic T-contour-and-rhythm associated with transpositions of that motif. The contour and rhythm continue to dominate the whole voice part of measures 13–14, up to the second quarter of measure 15, even after the intervals of T disappear.

C. recollection in the voice of earlier vocal music
1. recall of the low C from vocal phrase 1 passim, and especially from the cadence of that phrase at the end of measure 10.
2. recall, in measure 13, of T2 as a collection (c major/minor triad), from the T2 surrounding the low C of measure 10;

III. the singer's remembering specific past events—or feelings—hitherto inaccessible to his memory: completion of the low C♯–C gesture from measure 12 to measure 13 in the vocal line. This is something the singer has so far been notably unable to accomplish (cf. Example 15.15 and various earlier discussions). It touches off a formidable workout of C-and-C♯ throughout the whole vocal line up through measure 17. The workout thus presumably corresponds musically to at least some of the "true action" discussed earlier—of trying to bring specific hitherto inaccessible memories into present consciousness.

We shall note other, more subtle, "remembering" gestures around measure 13 later. Almost all the musical features cited here involve music recalled from the piano introduction. We discussed the relation of measure 13 and following to that introduction earlier. It is appropriate to continue that discussion now. In the context of the above Roman-numeral components, particularly I and II, the dramatic symbolism of "remembering" music from the piano introduction is ambiguous. Does the singer remember this music? Or just the audience? What does it mean if the singer does, or does not, remember that music? These matters need some critical decisions (by the performers—consciously or intuitively—as much as, or more than by the analyst).

One can approach the problem as follows: are we to take the piano introduction as symbolizing a reality external to the singer (e.g., "what actually happened before the song begins"?). Or are we to take it as a projection of the singer's internal present musings, thoughts and feelings quite likely unconscious or pre-conscious? In the first case, "becoming aware of the singer as an actor in the present" and "becoming aware of the singer as a 'rememberer'" (I and II earlier) are things that the audience does at measure 13 but not the singer himself. In the second case, awareness in those respects dawns on the singer right along with the audience.

The interpretation that satisfies me best is some amalgam of the above two extremes. I feel that the singer has definitely lost, by the end of the song, whatever awareness he had at measures 13ff. of being "in the present." Hence, his return to the "past tense" music of measure 8 at measure 21. This gives a very definite dramatic function to that reprise. As noted earlier, the reprise is otherwise puzzling, if one considers only the abstract form and rhyme scheme of the text, associating line 8 with line 3 rather than line 1. This observation tends to support the piano as "external" to the voice. On the other hand, the climactic attainment of the high C♯, with its concomitant Y7, in measure 15 after the singer's earlier inabilities in these respects, does indicate to me some sort of psychological breakthrough. To the extent that it suggests subconscious matter rising into consciousness (or almost) at that moment, it favors the interpretation of the piano as "internal" to the singer musically. A both/and approach to the problem is consistent with the idea that "what actually happened in the past" seems hard to separate, in this song, from the present memories and recall abilities of the singer—as if the singer were trying to get at the emotionally essential features of a past incident in the course of "objective" narrative description, as he might, say, in talking to a psychotherapist. By my reading, the singer almost succeeds in this internal quest (m. 15), but can't quite follow through (m. 15 comes too soon in the text; something more is required, etc.). Then the essential emotional recall slips away (mm. 16–17) and, by the end of the song, the singer is right back where he started at measure 8, only more so. The last line of text is very appropriate to go with the image of emotional paralysis here. Curiously, the poet there addresses his beloved directly, and for the first time: "so verbliebest du." In this reading, the frustration of the singer, following measure 15, would be strongly signaled by the frustration of the pornographic interest of reader or audience, aroused over lines 4 through 6 of the poem and then progressively frustrated by lines 7 and 8.

In sum, I take the symbolic function of the piano, through the song, as being both external and internal to the singer, in an inseparable bind. I can entertain other consistent possible solutions, though. However, having raised the issue, I do not feel the obligation to go into them.[5]

C♯ having been connected to C in the low register, from measure 12 to measure 13, the singer's work of remembering hitherto inaccessible material (III earlier) proceeds by reversing the direction of that gesture. C is raised to C♯ in the

5. The external/internal function of the accompaniment is a general problem to confront in the analysis of any song. Sometimes the solution is obvious. It is not so (to take an interesting comparison) at the end of Schubert's *Ihr Bild,* discussed in note 1. If the piano there is taken to be "inside" the singer, the *minore* of the epilogue symbolizes the internal overwhelming of the man by the grief he has just consciously refused to acknowledge. In this case, the singer must approach the preceding *maggiore* vocal cadence with that in mind, and then possibly even perform some sort of theatrical "take" after he stops singing (if he can do so in good taste). If, on the other hand, the piano is "outside" the singer, the *minore* epilogue is purely ironic, directed to the audience. In this case, the singer must take care to point the irony by maintaining the theatrical projection of his "happy" cadence with complete conviction after he has stopped singing, "not hearing" the epilogue at all.

The dramatic situation and problem here are very similar to those at the death of Lear: does he realize that Cordelia is really dead and die of grief, or does he die from the strain of actually maintaining his optimistic fantasy that she may return to life? As with Lear, it seems to me that the problem in *Ihr Bild* cannot be definitely resolved by analysis; on the other hand, the performer must confront the problem (consciously or intuitively) and somehow resolve it for himself if the piece is to work in performance.

lower register, with strong support from T-motif forms. The singer does not have the "right key" for T (i.e., "B♭"), but does have the appropriate thematic contour and rhythm that has so far identified T when appearing as an incipit motif. His statement of T2 in measure 13 thus contrasts sharply with his earlier T2 in measure 10: there the T motif was being used as a cadence motif, rather than an incipit, and the singer did not produce the thematic contour. The forcefulness with which the singer retrieves the low C from measure 10 as a basis for subsequent action is striking.

The low C♯ in the voice at measure 14 is carried in by the T-motif play, but is not melodically or rhythmically powerful on its own, as part of the critical C–C♯ action. It receives overwhelming support from the piano, though. One can hear the low C♯ of the piano at the bar line of measure 14 goading the voice along impatiently in that regard. The growing excitement of the singer is now evident in the progressive expansions of the thematic T-contour, with different intervals, leading into measure 15 and the high C♯. I refer to the contours that begin in measure 13 and proceed: C–E♭–G–E, C♯–E–G♯–D, D–G–C♯–G♯. The low D of measure 14 overlaps the last two contours above, further tightening the excitement. The low D, as a point of departure for a T-contour, is of course either "wrong" or "premature." It distracts from the C–C♯ gesture by suggesting that C♯, as yet not firmly established, may be only a passing tone going up to D. The reader may recall our earlier discussion of the roles of C♯, D and C at the cadence of measure 12; evidently the singer still has that low D in his ear here.

But the effect of low D is quickly obliterated by the vocal attainment—at last!—of the high D♯ at the end of measure 14, with enormous melodic and rhythmic accent. This amounts to a C–C♯ gesture on a grand scale, as it carries all the earlier high Cs of the vocal line up to this melodically climactic C♯.[6] Along with the C♯, the voice "remembers" Y7, from the piano introduction, with a vengeance. This entails a glorification of C-to-C♯ in the upper octave through measure 15. All these features are of course in notable contrast to earlier events concerning the vocal line.

Measure 15 is clearly not only a melodic climax, but also the span of maximal dramatic achievement for the voice, in "remembering specific matter hitherto inaccessible." Whether the achievement is in some sense sufficient is debatable. On the one hand, one could argue that the whole song so far has been pointing toward the voice's reaching C♯, C-to-C♯ and Y7 in the upper octave, and the voice has now attained all of them. According to this view, the remainder of the song could be

6. The fresh sonority of the fourth-and-tritone elevator D–G–C♯ used to get to the upper octave here is extremely effective. The same interval structure will be used as a descending elevator C♯–G♯–D at the end of measure 15, thus framing the climactic measure 15 with those sonorities.

There are other fourth-and-tritone sonorities around, both locally and earlier. For me, the strongest local association to the voice's D–G–C♯ of measure 14 is the equally fresh A–B♭–E♭ of the piano right hand in measure 13. This, in turn, could lead back to earlier gestures in the vocal line (we will pursue that matter later). The X complex contains such a sonority (F, C, B), as does the magic chord (F, B, E).

Those are not weighty matters to my ear. In connection with the D–G–C♯ of measure 14, I am mainly aware of the freshness of the sound preparing and framing the melodic climax, and beyond that primarily of the melodic functions of the individual notes involved: the low D and high C♯ as discussed in the body of the paper; the G between as having to do with the earlier G♯ of measure 14 and the later G♯ of measure 15—these recalling the G♯s and Gs of the voice in measures 10–11.

taken dramatically as a relaxation after this achievement, subsiding back to the original state of repose for the voice. One could effectively stage-light a performance according to this notion: piano introduction in semidarkness; dim light up for measure 8, growing in intensity to a period of maximal illumination (a good metaphor) during measure 15; thence dimming again to the level of measure 8 at measure 21; thence a slow fade with a blackout either at measure 24 or at "measure 25" (the piano goes off the keyboard there).

On the other hand, I prefer to argue that the achievement of measure 15, while substantial, represents only a plateau of dramatic accomplishment; that the expected advance beyond that plateau is frustrated at measure 16 and through the following music. After the ending of measure 12 and the tentative rise of C♯ to D in the lower register of the voice at measure 14, one might expect the vocal line, after reaching the high C♯ "plateau" in measure 15, to push one up to D, and perhaps even beyond. After all, the narrated "action" here is still going strong in the text. In this connection, the play with various levels of the major/minor triad in the piano over measures 13–15 is suggestive: the "C♯ triad" of measure 14 in the bass moving up in some sense to the "D triad" in the right hand a measure later.[7] In general, the notion that the vocal line fails to attain high D (and/or beyond) after measure 15 is suggestive in light of the cadence in the voice at m. 19. There the low D, picked up from the end of measure 12, moves down as appoggiatura to the low C♯, and D fails to establish itself, ultimately, even in the low register.

But we do not need to entertain speculations about missing high notes to appreciate various manifestly frustrating (rather than relaxing) things about the attack of measure 16 and the music that follows. The recurrence of C–A in the voice at measure 16, after the C–A of measure 15, recalls the "oscillating C–A" of measures 8–9, a gesture that will return in measures 22–23 with an even greater sense of stasis. At measure 16, the oscillating C–A is embedded in a greater oscillation of all of Y7 over measure 15–16¼. The resulting aura of diffidence and hesitancy about Y7 itself is in marked contrast to the direct and energetic drive of the voice from measure 13 into measure 15. If one were to take Y7 at measure 15 as a definitive achievement, there should not be so much vacillation hereabouts, oscillating on the motif itself, with the oscillating C–A recalling the static "past-tense" of measure 8. In fact, Y7 continues to drift away back into the darkness through the opening of measure 17. Example 15.20 shows what I mean.

Example 15.20

Beyond that, measure 16 is a distinct reference back to measures 11–12 in the voice, transformed so as to lose a good deal of motivic and local contour profile. Measure 17 is yet another such gesture, carrying the liquidation a step farther in

7. I am not attributing "roots" to all the major/minor triads. The preceding references are just convenient shorthand. I would simply claim that the weight of each T-form hereabouts is carried psychoacoustically, in the context, by the lowest note of the form, which is also the initial note.

both respects.[8] One cannot easily claim that these musical references back to measures 11–12 connote only "relaxation" rather than "frustration." For, at the attack of the voice in measure 11, the high C–A–G♯ was crucially involved with the singer's failure to attain C♯, C–C♯ and Y7, and the slippage from the piano's high C♯ to the singer's high C (see Example 15.15 and pertinent earlier discussion). At the opening of measure 16 in the voice, we have exactly the same "frustrating" features present: the voice singing high C–A–G♯, failing to maintain C♯, C-to-C♯, and Y7, and allowing the earlier high C♯s to slip down to C. The slippage down to C here is particularly poignant if one feels any implication that the voice might instead have risen even higher than C♯, instead of falling back from it.

The music of measure 11 set the first part of "the question" in the text. The urgency of the question is much dissipated, in my hearing, by the liquidations of the music in the vocal part at measures 16–17. Instead of "remembering the answer," the singer appears to be "forgetting the question!"[9] This forgetful drifting off in the music of measures 16–17 is strikingly inapposite to the text there—pornographic interest should be reaching peak intensity over exactly this text. But by the time we get to the critical "und" at the end of measure 17, we are back on the fuzzy low C♭ where the voice began measure 8 (the piano bass assisting that reference with a hint of "A♭ major/minor triad" under the "und" C♭).

A number of other features about the attack of measure 16 can be discussed in this connection. The mechanical pattern in the piano right hand of measure 15 is abruptly interrupted, frustrating an expected C♯ (NB!) and "F♯ major/minor triad" at the bar line of measure 16. The latter will subsequently be picked up by the voice in measure 18. The C in the voice, at the bar line of measure 16, can be heard (among many other things) as a substitute for the thwarted C♯ in the piano right hand there; this is very much in keeping with earlier discussion of the voice's C.

We have noted that the vocal part, at measure 16, refers back to measure 11. The interrupting E♯–F♯ of the piano right hand at measure 16 throws us back even farther, to measure 7. That was a point before the voice even began to sing. In fact, it was specifically the singer's cue for his opening entrance. This seems interesting in light of the later references to measure 8 at the end of measure 17 and at measures 21ff., but I can't quite formulate my specific reaction.

Another frustrating aspect of measure 16 is the abrupt cessation of thirty-second-note activity in the piano figuration, except for a few following rebounds to that shock. The initiation of the flowing thirty-seconds during measure 13, after five essentially inactive measures for the piano, was a strong textural element associated with "Ich erinnere." The abrupt choking-off of the rhythmic flow at mea-

8. What in the world does this "whole-tone music" have to do with the present song?! Actually, I think I hear a reference to No. VIII of the cycle. That song began with energetic whole-tone music. Its initial text was: "Wenn ich heut nicht deinen Leib beruehre," and there seems to be an arguable sonorous association to the text here, now that the moment is at hand: "wenn wir leis nur an uns ruehrten."

9. A particularly fine point in the technique of destroying that urgency is the resetting of the low D-to-high C leap across the bar line of measure 17. The new context, rhetorical and metric, completely destroys the questioning force that adhered to that leap at the end of measure 12. Note the dynamics going into the bar line of measure 17. In fact, the D–C leap has already had its back broken across the bar line of measure 16.

sure 16, then, would logically symbolize an abrupt frustration of the crucial memory flow.

Finally, it is notable that, for the first time in the piece, a regular meter becomes aurally functional right at the bar line of measure 16, and remains so at least through the attack of measure 20. It is interesting that this unambiguous and persistent meter, conforming to the time signature of the piece, is established by the voice alone (through its unimpeded recurring half-measure rhythmic motive in mm. 16 and 17). This is a strong clue that "something definitive happens" at the bar line of measure 16. That notion is not consistent with the idea that measures 16ff. constitute a "gradual relaxation from the achievement of 15"; but it is highly consistent with the idea that the voice's high C at measure 16, and the accompanying click-back in the piano, represent a definitive frustration of whatever might have been a consequence of the voice's having attained measure 15, in terms of pushing on beyond that plateau.

It is likely the low B♭ in measure 17 that triggers the singer's awareness of getting so hopelessly adrift from the motivic ambience of the song, corresponding with his psychological drifting away from the question of measure 11. Perhaps he recalls here the low B♭ beat of the piano preceding measure 13, which had triggered "Ich erinnere" there, as well as or even more than the opening B♭ of the song. At any rate, motivic activity in the voice definitely picks up over measures 18–19, leading into the strongest vocal cadence the singer is to achieve. To the extent that the low B♭ of measure 17 is a signal to the singer recalling the piano's B♭ preceding measure 13, it would play an analogous role, musically, to the syntactic role of the word "dass" in the text of line 7, feebly but distinctly trying to get back to "Ich erinnere, dass." The voice's low B♭ is of course about to recur on that "dass," in measure 18, initiating an "*ersatz* T-reprise" which hooks up to the T-reprise in measure 13 more definitely.

If we take the low B♭ of measure 17 as the point where the singer begins "remembering" (something) again, instead of forgetting, the following C♭ "und," with its reference to measure 8, would be a musical analog of "where am I? Let's see . . . I was telling this story." The following vocal B♭–D♭, T8 structure, and thematic T contour, constituting a false reprise of the basic T-gesture, would be a musical analog to: "Oh yes, I remember . . . I was trying to remember something (at m. 13)." But he only remembers *that* he was trying to remember (something), not *what* it was that he was trying to recall. In any case, singing the original "B♭ major/minor triad" has nothing to do with anything in the vocal line so far—it is much too late in the song for the singer to appropriate that gesture here. Beyond that, his memory of the thematic gesture itself is imperfect (he doesn't remember m. 13 very well). He gets the contour and the opening B♭–D♭, but actually winds up singing a form of T8, an "F♯ triad." Does he perchance remember this as the level of T that "should have been" completed by the piano right hand going into the frustrating measure 16 earlier? Does he perhaps have some vague tonal sense that the piece "was in F♯ minor" earlier, and should end up in that "key" now?

One can sum up here by saying that, having gone completely adrift from the song in measure 17, the singer then begins to pull himself back, particularly in terms of "remembering something" (cf. II of the earlier dramatic analysis). First, he remembers that he is singing this song (low C♭ at the end of m. 17, referring to m. 8); then he remembers that he is supposed to be remembering something (low B♭, "dass," T8 of m. 18 referring back to m. 13, etc.). He does not yet remember, though, just what it is that he is supposed to be remembering. But he is certainly cranking his memory engine, after the disastrous stall of measures 16–17.

The gathering up of these musical reminiscences is very helpful in building toward the cadence coming up. Coincidentally, the low C♭ and B♭ of the voice in measure 18 provide a very useful melodic point of departure for a conjunct rise up to the cadential C♯ of measure 19 (converged on from above via D♯ and the D-appoggiatura).

Motivically, we have left off at the F♯ in the voice at measure 18. Once the singer gets there, he succeeds in remembering the question-cadence of measure 12, from the corresponding F♯ of that measure. This memory is much more central to his important task, and the subsequent tones, in repermuting the N1-to-X1 configuration, do provide a musical answer of sorts to the question-cadence of measure 12. Most notably, the cadential D of measure 12 now becomes an appoggiatura to the cadential C♯ of measure 19, so that the singer does at least "get back to C♯" in some sense after the frustrating Cs of measures 16–17. Of course the C♯ of measure 19, being low, is not a complete equivalent by any means for re-attaining the high C♯ (much less doing anything beyond that). Nevertheless, even the low C♯ has not before been stabilized. It has always had, from its introduction in measure 12 on in the vocal part, a certain tendency to move on up to D in the lower register; hence, finally stabilizing the vocal low C♯ does represent a definite achievement—definitively moving the low Cs of measures 8, 9, 10 and 13 up to that C♯ over the vocal line as a whole so far. The D–C♯ cadential gesture of the voice in measure 19 is given weighty support by the bass of the motto in the accompaniment hereabouts. D-to-D♭ (C♯) is an important component of the N-to-X chords, as we are reminded here; and the bass D♭ of the X-chord in measure 19 doubles the singer's cadential C♯.

In sum, the vocal cadence in measure 19 does represent some sort of pertinent present memory achievement on the part of the singer. Unfortunately, that musical achievement is subsequently thwarted by the ultimate return of the vocal line to the irrevocable low Cs of measures 22–23. Once more, the singer's effort to establish and maintain C♯ at the expense of C has been frustrated, this time finally, and once more the singer drifts off (now in rhythmic augmentation) on repeated Cs, C–A oscillation, and so on, after failing to maintain C♯. The overall effect of the reprise of measure 8 in measures 21ff. has been discussed earlier.

Another matter of interest here is the inverted T-contour F♯–D♯–B♯–D through which the voice approaches the cadential appoggiatura. Since prime forms of the T-contour have had a strong melodic incipit character in the song, the inverted contour is effective for cadencing. But, as with the preceding B♭–D♭–A–F♯, the intervals are "wrong." Specifically "wrong" is the B♯: if it were B, the inversion of T would be intervallically exact. The B♯ is, of course, necessarily tied up with the approach to the C♯ of measure 19, and thence to the whole C-and-C♯ story over the piece, as we have just discussed at length. The intervallically "wrong" F♯–D♯–

B♯–D, like the preceding B♭–D♭–A–F♯, seems to have to do with the singer's problems in remembering. Note how forcefully the piano "corrects" the inverted motive immediately after, with its C–A–F–G♯ leading right into the big beat of measure 20 (much more on this subject later). Also, the rhythmic/metric aspect of the T-contours in the voice here does not fit well with the original (thematic) T rhythmic/metric sense. In fact, one notes that the only place in the song where the voice succeeds in singing a T-contour with either the "right" intervals or something like the "right" rhythmic/metric sense is precisely at "Ich erinnere": there, both the intervals and the rhythmic/metric sense are "right." So we may presume that the "wrong" intervals and rhythmic/metric sense accompanying the T-contours in measures 18–19 have to do with the idea mentioned earlier: the singer remembers that, but not what, he is supposed to be remembering. Thus, while the approach to the cadence in measure 19 does succeed in doing something musically about the question of measure 12, it fails to cope adequately with the "T-problem," even while sharply raising that issue. In this respect, then, the cadence is inconclusive enough to be overridden by the piano's cadence into measure 20, as we shall discuss later.

It may be helpful to go over the dramatic interpretation of the vocal line from measure 16 on once more, this time in specific connection with the three aspects of "Ich erinnere" to which I earlier attached Roman numeral labels. It will be convenient to take up II first: the audience's—and possibly the singer's—awareness of the singer as a "rememberer" in the present. From measure 16 on, as earlier, the audience, at least, will be very aware of the singer in that capacity, if we do not specify exactly what it is that he is to be remembering during that time. In measures 16–17, the singer is hard at work forgetting not only measure 11 and its question, but even what the music of the song as a whole should sound like. This forgetting (in the present) is the necessary obverse of remembering (in the present), if such remembering is to constitute any achievement. From this point of view, the end of measure 17—just before "und"—is a psychological climax of the song: it is the moment of maximal forgetfulness, from which the singer subsequently pulls himself out to at least some extent. That corresponds well with the text, since line 6 is the climax of the narrative action, and the peak of pornographic interest. The notion also corresponds well with the idea expounded earlier that measure 15 is not completely satisfying as a climax for the song, but seems, rather, a plateau from which one might push on to a pinnacle or fall into the abyss of measure 17. The audience's, and singer's, awareness of the singer as rememberer, from the end of measure 17 through the cadence in measure 19, has been discussed already. Whether or not the singer (as opposed to the audience) consciously remembers measure 8 at measure 21 seems debatable. I believe that the singer himself is not conscious of the reference. The "meaning" of the piano part around the crucial beat of measure 20 is of course involved here, and we shall return to this point later, after examining that music. In any case, the singer is certainly aware of himself as a rememberer at least from measure 18 through the cadence of measure 19, and he actually and consciously achieves a certain amount of dramatic work in that capacity. The audience will be completely aware of the singer as rememberer (or forgetter, which is to them the same) all the way through to the end of the piece.

To that extent, singer and audience, respectively, will be aware of the singer a fortiori as an actor in the present rather than the past (I of our earlier analysis). Let us now consider III: the singer's effort to remember specific events or feelings hitherto inaccessible to his consciousness. Musically this appears to be connected at least with establishing C♯, establishing Y7, moving C to C♯, doing all this in the upper octave, and so on, as undertaken in the vocal line of measures 13–15. The bar line of measure 16 is an abrupt and definite frustration, according to my reading. The cadence of measure 19 does succeed in establishing the low C♯, superseding earlier low Cs in the vocal line, but even that achievement is ultimately frustrated by the return to low C in measures 22–23. And, to the extent one feels that the necessary musical breakthrough would involve pushing beyond measure 15, or bringing more material into the vocal line, the frustration of the singer's desired action is all the greater.[10]

10. A notable component of the stability/instability of C♯ throughout the piece, to my ear, is the clear tonal sense of the music at moments involving important C♯s and D♭s. Although one can hear a B♭ root for some time into measure 1, the first really convincing root feeling I have in the piece is that attached to the X-chord in measure 4, and the subsequently prolonged D♭ in the bass. Here D♭ is heard as a solid root (stability), but also with a very clear dominant function (instability). Whenever the motto recurs in the piano one hears the bass of the X-chord in the same way. Y7, with its central melodic C♯-C relation, is going on in the tune during the motto, and the soprano C of the X-chord (the crucial melodic C of Y7 that sinks from C♯) can be heard harmonically as a frozen leading-tone to the root D♭ of the harmony. This seems cogently connected with the character of the C–C♯ relations in the song as a whole.

If we follow the bass line from measure 4½ on, we can note that the established "dominant" D♭ remains as a pedal (explicit or implicit) up to the B♭ beat preceding measure 13. This reinforces the notion of Example 15.7—that that beat can be heard as having been delayed from where it might hypothetically have entered in measure 7 or measure 8. The piano part of measures 13–19 can be (very fancifully) glossed tonally as a highly elaborate variation on the root progression "B♭ to V/f♯" that underlay the piano introduction. (It helps to have other points of contact relating those spans of the music, as discussed earlier in connection with Example 15.2, etc.) In that connection, we note that the X-chord of the motto in measure 19, which sustains the D♭ (V/F♯) root, is back for the first time in its original register—in contrast to the two earlier chords of the motto in measure 18—and that the crucial D♭ in the bass of that chord doubles the crucial cadential C♯ of the voice.

To repeat: the strong root sense affords "stability" to C♯; the clear dominant function, however, makes it "unstable." That is, one expects C♯ to resolve harmonically to f♯. This hardly happens at measure 20 (where it "should"), but from measure 21½ on, one can indeed hear an implied f♯ harmony. Or is this a second-inversion effect still implying a functional C♯ root? In any case, if one had to pick a key in which to hear the entire song, it would surely be f♯. (Does that have something to do with the interrupted T8 in the piano right hand going into m. 16, and the subsequent T8 in the voice of m. 18?)

In general, now, I feel that tonality functions in this work mainly as one means of clarifying, enriching and qualifying a basically contextual ("atonal") structure. This in the sense of the preceding remarks. Another example: the basic minor/major third (D,F,D♭), common to prime levels of both N-to-X- and T-motifs, is presented in strong tonal contexts at the opening of the song, embedded in those motifs: D♭–F–D in the right hand of measure 1, embedded within T, as "♭3–5–♮3 in B♭"; D–F–D♭ in the bass of the motto, measures 3–4, as "6–♯7–5 of f♯." I am sure this is pertinent to my hearing F–D as the "tonic minor third" of the piece.

If one tried to push tonal analysis, however, beyond such considerations, I believe the results would be either too general ("the song is in f♯, largely over a V pedal, with some reference to ♯iii"), or too speculative, or too mechanical and irrelevant. What, for instance, is one to make, tonally, of the big beat at the bar line of measure 20, where the dominant X-chord evidently "resolves"? How

So far, in discussing the music of measures 13 to the end, I have concentrated mainly on the vocal line, referring to the accompaniment only where that reinforces or qualifies certain aspects of the voice. This seems a reasonable approach, since the vocal line up to measure 13 was virtually unaccompanied, and also since the piano and the voice, over the first half of the song, were presented as musically autonomous instruments. We must now return to measure 13 and examine the piano part of the latter half of the song. Along with that, we shall investigate further ways in which the two instruments interact, musically and dramatically.

The T-forms in the piano, measures 13–15, have already been discussed to some extent. One observes that the succession T-to-T3 in the left hand, measures 13–14, reprises the identical succession of the right hand, measures 1–3 (see Example 15.6). So more than simply T itself is recalled from the opening of the piece here. T3 is naturally all the stronger at measure 14 for having the thematic contour and rhythm attached. The doubling of the left hand with the voice here draws attention to the singer's first tentative C-to-C♯ gesture (mm. 13 to 14), and also to how feeble a role the voice nonetheless still plays in setting up its own C♯ here. The voice's C♯ needs a "nudge" from the piano, just as the voice needed the low B♭ "nudge," a measure earlier, to sing the low C. The voice is making progress, though: its time lag behind the piano's nudges is down to a triplet eighth instead of a quarter note's duration.

My first reaction to the left-hand octaves in measures 13–14 was that they were only to help the long notes sustain. But this was not very convincing. The lower register (at least on a grand piano) has enough power not to require the doubling, particularly when it is so easy for a listener to follow the familiar T-motifs. Perhaps the octaves look ahead to the right hand of measure 16, which in turn looks back to measure 7, and thence to all the F♯ and C♯ octaves in measures 8–10 and 21–24. I cannot focus those speculations more cogently at present. More clear is the observation that the left hand of measure 13, the octaves included, can be regarded as a reprise not just of the opening T-motif of the piece, but also of the subsequent F–D "echo" in the bass of measures 2–3, an octave lower. The reprise, that is, includes the notion of transferring the descending-third half of T by an octave. More generally involved is the idea that the descending third somehow "recurs." We have noticed that phenomenon before in the context of what I have called "oscillation." Example 15.16 indicated a plausible relation between the F–D under consideration here and the ubiquitous oscillating C–A thirds. In that light, perhaps the rhythmic relation between the left-hand octaves in measures 13–14 and the voice part in measures 22–23 is significant. All of this seems to the point regarding at least the octaves

far does one get into the song by calling the chord of measure 20 "a substitute for i^6 in f♯" or "an altered III in f♯, as substitute for i"? These descriptions have something to do with the harmonic effect of the bass tone, but ignore the all-important magic chord in the upper voices, marked considerably higher dynamically and split off from the low tone in the notation. It can be argued (as we shall later on) that it makes more sense to consider the bass "nonharmonic" here, the basic harmony being the magic chord. In any case, even from the tonal point of view above, how can the X-chord, as dominant, "resolve" into a chord that still maintains the harmonic effect of the tritone F (E♯)–B? Of course it can (and does), but the effect can not be explained completely—or even substantially—by tonality.

in measure 13. The dramatic meaning of presenting the double F–D there in the form of octaves, rather than echo or oscillation, would bear some investigating.

The A–B♭–E♭ in the right hand, measure 13, has been discussed in note 6, in connection with the D–G–C♯ of the voice in measure 14, and so on. As with the latter configuration, the A–B♭–E♭ provides a very fresh sound, particularly so in its register. The fourth-plus-tritone effect can be intellectually related to a motivic idea we shall discuss later in connection with the subsequent cascade figurations. This is not very interesting to my ear, however. As with the D–G–C♯ in note 6, I am mainly aware of the functions of the individual tones involved, considering the harmony as having more a coloristic accenting function that a motivic one. The B♭ and E♭ anticipate tones of the subsequent broken fourth-chord. The high A moves to the A♭ of the fourth-chord, and I can hear a reference to the melodic A–G♯ of Y7 (piano, mm. 4½–5; voice, m. 11).

The rhythm of the A–B♭–E♭ gesture is important. Both vocal phrases 1 and 2 contain significant melodic halts midway: on the voice's B, last quarter of measure 9, and on the G, last quarter of measure 11. In each case, the rhythmic motif "(𝄾) ♩ ♩ (♩)" was an important aspect of the voice's getting underway again within each phrase: that rhythm on G♯–C–G♯ of measure 10, on F♯–C♯–D♯ of measure 12. Here the same rhythmic motif appears yet once more as the piano gets underway after its long quietus, and as the singer's crucial recollections gets underway.

We turn now to the thirty-second-note figuration. The "fourthy" sounds generally recall the "fourthy" aspects of the piano introduction discussed earlier. Specifically, the overall harmonic effect of measures 6–7 is recalled (picking up what was earlier an interruptive event). Also the transpositions-by-5 are recalled from the left hand of measure 1. The latter association is supported by the (once again, and for the first time since) flowing rhythm, by the downwards-flowing overall contour of the cascades, and by the sequential character of the figuration. The latter becomes, in fact, a chain of exact sequences (by five semitones) when the left hand takes over the figuration in measure 15, heading into the low register of measure 1. The left hand of the opening, as well as the right hand, is thus also reprised significantly by the music of measures 13ff.

In order to analyze the overall effect of the cascades more closely, it is helpful to divide the basic motif (e.g., A♭–E♭–B♭–F–B on the last quarter of m. 14) into two components. "α" will denote the downward component of the motif, always comprising two fourths down (e.g., A♭–E♭–B♭ of the above cited motif-form); "β" will denote the upward component (e.g., F–B of the cited form). β hops a tritone (up) on its first two appearances, thereafter a fourth (up). α drops out at the crucial bar line of measure 16; β continues sporadically for some time thereafter. Because of the pauses on each β-component at regular rhythmic intervals, it is easy to hear successive β-components relating each to the next, across the intervening α-components. Example 15.21 charts the pitch-class aspects of that "β-story," through measure 15.

The example clarifies that there are two parts to the "β-story" here, corresponding to before and after the last quarter of measure 14 (where the hands switch motifs, the T-motif recurs once more in the right hand, and—!—the voice hits its crucial high C♯). In part 2 of the story (after the bar line of m. 15, in the left hand),

Example 15.21

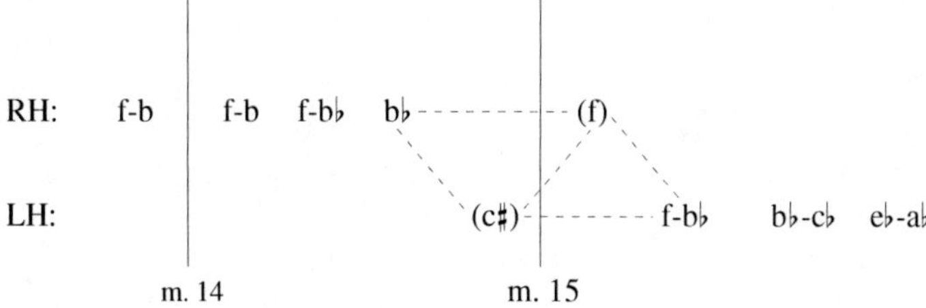

the β-components build up a fourth-chord: F–B♭, B♭–E♭, E♭–A♭. This is evidently related to the fourths of the α-component. In fact, F–B♭–E♭–A♭ is a literal pitch-class retrograde of the first α-gesture A♭–E♭–B♭(–F) in the right hand, on the last quarter of measure 13. So we defer consideration of part 2 of the β-story until later, when we have also examined the α-story.

For part 1 of the β-story (Example 15.21, right hand, up to m. 15), the essential gesture is evidently the progression of the tritone F–B (or B–F) to the fourth F–B♭ (or fifth B♭–F). The "fifth B♭–F," as indicated by a dotted line on Example 15.21, does not appear with the characteristic β-rhythm, but it does appear with the correct β-contour across the bar line of measure 15, where it can be identified as the fifth spanned by the original T-motif. Other events around the bar line of measure 15—indicated by other dotted lines on Example 15.21—indicate that this identification is proper.

Having made that identification, we can further relate the total gesture "F–B to F–B♭" with the overall bass line from measure 2 to measure 13, as discussed in connection with Example 15.7 earlier, and also in connection with Example 15.11. The magic chord of measure 2 was the strongest early manifestation of the harmonic power of the tritone F–B, and it is interesting to note, in this connection, a certain harmonic influence of the magic chord in the music surrounding the β-tritones of measures 13–14. I have indicated this in Example 15.22. The magic chord harmonies there, in each case, are prefaced by identical pick-up harmonies, which I have labeled with an asterisk.

Example 15.22

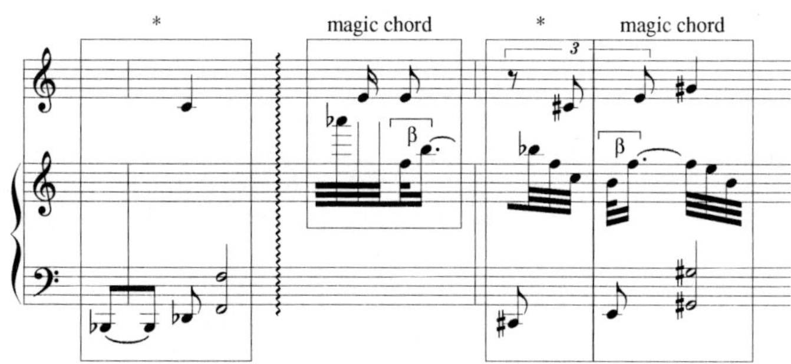

From the point of view just discussed, part 1 of the β-story is a highly condensed reprise of an essential feature of the total gesture underlying "piano introduction-to-m. 13 B♭." This condensed reprise also leads to a B♭ beat and recurrence of T—namely, those in the right hand at the end of measure 14.[11] Once again, it is very much to the point that the voice hits its crucial high C♯ right after that right-hand B♭ beat (following its earlier "lagging" behavior, with respect to the piano, at the beginning of measure 13 and again at the beginning of m. 14). The B♭s and Fs of the piano also provide quite audible "root support" for the voice's high C♯, which the piano also momentarily doubles.

Part 2 of the β-story is related to the α-story as discussed earlier; the surplus fourths of measures 16–17 are also part of that complex. At this point, then, we return to study the story of the α-component as a point of departure. Since the α-components go by so fast, I hear each of them primarily simply as spanning a certain segment of the circle of fourths, building up in relation one to another in that context. In analyzing the overall α-story (and what will subsequently happen to the β-fourths), it is helpful to plot each α-component along an abstract circle of fourths. Example 15.23 is the result, up through measure 15.

In Example 15.23, C♯ has been taken as twelve o'clock on the circle of fourths with some forethought. The reason will become very clear later. Meanwhile, it may be to the point to recall the importance of C♯ for the voice throughout the song. In the example, the numbers labeling all arrows, except for "β2," refer to successive appearances of the α-component. So the arrow labeled "1" denotes the first appearance of the α-component: A♭–E♭–B♭ (–F?) in the last quarter of measure 13. The arrow labeled "2" denotes the second α-component: B♭–F–C in the first quarter of measure 14. And so on. The arrow labeled "β2" denotes the F–B♭–E♭–A♭ built up by part 2 of the β-story during measure 15.

The diagram manifests some interesting structural features. First is the inversional balance of the whole system, C♯ being one of the centers of inversion. The repetition of arrows 3 and 4 by arrows 5 and 6 on the right side of the circle is balanced by arrow β2, which repeats the corresponding left-side segment of the circle (although in retrograde). Second, all α-arrows go counterclockwise, while the β2-arrow goes clockwise. Third, the pitch-classes G and (especially) C♯, the centers of the inversional balance, remain as yet uninvolved in the scene, while all other pitch-classes have now been involved.

The relevance of that analysis is immediately confirmed by the next two appearances of β-fourths in measures 16–17: D–G and G–C. This constructs the

11. Another, more abstract, way of regarding the phenomenon just discussed would take as a point of departure the chordal form of N-to-X embedded within the motto. That progression contains the semitone gestures D-to-D♭, C♯-to-C and C-to-B, each heard against the pedal tone F (see Example 15.4). It is those gestures, of course, which are melodically prolonged by the bass line of measures 2–6. If we follow the indicated expansion process one stage farther, we arrive at the gesture B-to-B♭, to be heard against the pedal tone F. That gesture is, of course, "part 1 of the β-story." From this point of view, we have abstractly related the gestures of the N-to-X idea to the B♭-f within T, as a sort of boundary for those gestures.

This abstract formulation is an intellectually elegant way of tying up the apparently independent ideas of T and N-to-X. More to the point, it evidently (in light of the preceding discussion) has a good deal to do with actual important events of the music. "Part 1 of the β-story," in this sense, helps to confirm retroactively the pertinence of that abstract idea in analyzing the relation of the piano introduction (bass line measures 2–6) with the low B♭ before measure 13, as discussed in connection with Example 15.7.

Example 15.23

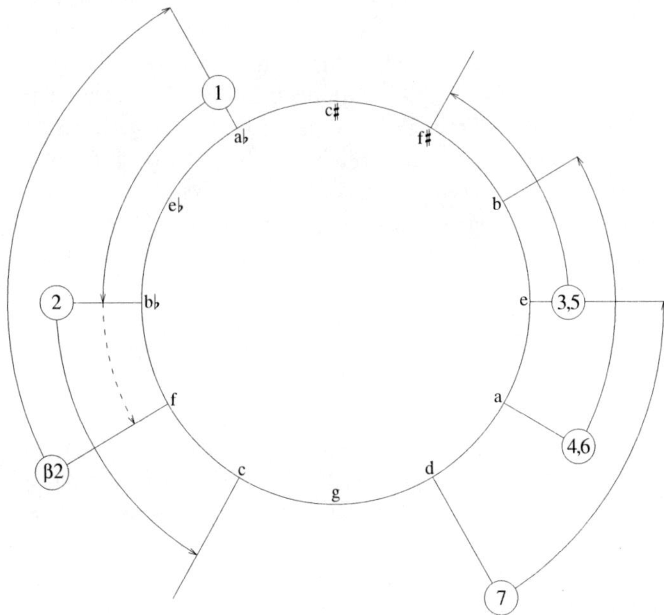

(clockwise) arrow D–G–C that "closes the link" at the bottom of the circle of Example 15.23 around G as one of the centers of inversion. Evidently, what remains to be done, in this game, is to "close the link" correspondingly at the top of the circle—by either G♯–C♯–F♯ or its retrograde—around the all-important center C♯.

But the β-component is apparently unable to make that link. Instead it hits E♭–A♭ once more at the end of measure 17. That was as close as a β-fourth ever got to the top of the circle of Example 15.23. It is where the β2 arrow left off, on the circle, just before the abrupt break at measure 16; thus E♭–A♭ at the end of measure 17 can recall the final low fourth of measure 15, just before the crucial break-off. And the fourth E♭–A♭ is also where the whole story of Example 15.23 began, in retrograde (arrow 1.) Beyond all this, the fourth at the end of measure 17, by providing "root support" for the voice there, helps to throw the whole ambience of the song back to measure 8, away from whatever work remains to be accomplished here.

Nevertheless, the crucial link is closed. Locally, this is accomplished (counterclockwise) by the upper register of the piano part: F♯ of measure 16, C♯–G♯ of measure 18. Note the contribution of the registration, and the rest, in the variant of the motto, as making this connection aurally possible. The link is accomplished more powerfully later on, this time going clockwise, from the right-hand G♯ of measure 20 into the continuation C♯, F♯, etc. in the right hand thereafter. It is easy to identify the G♯ of measure 18 with that of measure 20 in the piano right hand, because of the magic chord that supports each one. Since the melodic fragment of measure 19 in the piano may be heard as transitional, and since the E♯ of measure 16 can be heard as an appoggiatura to the following F♯, we can in fact claim with some justice that the overall gesture F♯–C♯–G♯–C♯–F♯ is the essence of the piano melody from the crucial break at measure 16 right to the end of the piece. This sheds some light on why the fourth C♯–F♯ is melodically active from measures 21¾ on, while it was only present in the harmony at measures 8–10. It is not that hard, indeed, to hear the rising C♯–F♯ fourths in the right hand at measures 21¾ff. as variants of the rising fourths of the β-components earlier. This particularly when the rhythm is slowed down so much in other respects around measures 22ff. And it is also not difficult to hear, at measure 18, the familiar C♯–G♯ fourth of the motto, and Y7, in relation to the preceding orgy of fourths generally.

It is, in fact, of importance that the fourths just mentioned are the crucial melodic fourth of the motto and Y7 (C♯–G♯, the "dominant" fourth of the piece), and the crucial harmonic fourth C♯–F♯ of measures 7–10 and 22ff. (the "tonic" fourth). The point is that the play of fourths discussed in connection with Example 15.23 sets up those two fourths very clearly. That preparation, focussing on C♯ as center-of-inversion and the "missing link" fourths C♯–G♯ and C♯–F♯, sets up the thematic gestures of measures 18 and 22ff. in such a way as to interact cogently with the voice's struggle to maintain C♯ after the bar line of measure 16. It may be recalled that the motto in the piano at measures 10–11 was tied up with the voice's failure to attain C♯ (etc.) there. Correspondingly, some of that flavor will carry over to measure 18.[12]

It remains to investigate various events surrounding the big beat at the bar line of measure 20. I take the harmony of the beat to be simply the magic chord, with the extra A in the bass only a *Klirrton* in its harmonic aspect. (See earlier remarks, in 10, on the—to me wrongheaded—"tonal analysis" of this chord. And observe again the notation of the chord and the dynamic indications.) The low tone does

12. Does one hear the voice F♯ at measure 18 as connecting to the piano's subsequent C♯–G♯ in this context? Perhaps, to the extent particularly that one can hook up the voice F♯ to the piano F♯ of measure 16. But connecting voice to piano notes melodically does not feel right in this context. More to the point might be the relation between the voice F♯ at measure 18 and the vocal cadence on C♯ in measure 19, producing an F♯–C♯ fourth within the structure of the vocal line itself. This is audible enough, especially if one picks up the hint from the D♭ two notes before the F♯ (and the root sense V–i of the T8 form??). One could emphasize the latter features by vocal accents ("dass UNS-re AU—-gen"). But that would be gross, and would contradict the dynamic indication. The effect, if there, should be subliminal.

The F♯ of the voice in measure 18 is certainly important in recalling to singer and listener the question and music of measure 12, as discussed earlier. The entrance of the motto in the piano here seems particularly effective. I have not analyzed that to my own satisfaction, but I am sure that it involves the assonance of *augen* with the earlier *hauchen*. The motto comes in much sooner here, after the triggering text sonority. There is a component of the poem involved which we have not discussed: the *hauchen* was *das eigne* while the *augen* are *unsre*. The shifting persons (wir, das eigne, spuerten, uns, ich, wir, . . . , du, mir) as well as tenses bear some consideration. Curiously, *Ihr Bild* also brings in *dich* suddenly at the end.

Until the discussion around Example 15.23, our examination of Schoenberg's constructive techniques in this song focused on what might be called "proto-serial" motivic and intervallic procedures. Example 15.23 and so on dealt with a constructive use of total chromaticism itself, and in an inversionally balanced context. The interested reader can find a more general theoretical exposition of such matters, and a wider range of musical examples, in my article "Inversional Balance as an Organizing Force in Schoenberg's Music and Thought," *Perspectives of New Music* 6.2 (1968), 1–21. The present song illustrates very well "the two principles of serialism and 'tonic inversional balance' of the total chromatic . . . side by side."

lower the center of gravity of the sound and provide a thicker density appropriate to the psychological sense of resolution here. The low A also has certain motivic functions, which we shall examine later. But the basic harmony remains simply the magic chord to my ear. The cessation of the bass sixteenths on the eighth-note low F of measure 21, at the end of the slur, supports this hearing. That low F, of course, reproduces the magic chord once more under the sustained notes of the right hand, the *Klirrton* now having vanished.

The peculiarly satisfying effect of the magic chord here has to do with a number of motivic features. Here I use the term "motivic" in an almost purely Wagnerian sense. The chord itself, the motto in which it is embedded, and the concomitant melodic fragment on top of the motto have all been established as a Leitmotif in the full sense of that term. If we examine the three appearances of that Leitmotif in the song, we notice something very pertinent to the effect of its last appearance here.

The features common to all three appearances of the Leitmotif are the chordal progression N–magic chord–X, the melodic line C♯–G♯–C over those chords, and the subsequent melodic "tail" (C–)A–G♯. Let us call this complex the "nucleus" of the Leitmotif.

In measures 2½–5½, the nucleus was preceded by a metrically weighty magic chord, while the melodic tail drifted off into nothingness. Emphasis here was thus focused on the magic chord at the expense of the nucleus, even to the extent that one heard the N and X chords as accessory to the preceding magic chord to a considerable extent.

As the music developed, though, N-to-X became a very important germ for the organic growth of the intervallic structure. By the time the Leitmotif next appeared, in measures 10–11, the weighty magic chord preceding the nucleus had accordingly disappeared, and one heard the medial magic chord of the nucleus, between N and X, as essentially "passing," its duration being an apparently expressive rather than structural feature of the music there (like a written-out fermata). The tail of the nucleus drifted off again, this time in the vocal line of measure 11. Here again, as earlier, the X-chord went (locally) "nowhere."

In measures 18–20, now, these aspects of the Leitmotif are radically transformed. An "extra" magic chord, beyond the one within the nucleus, reappears with great metric weight, as in measure 2, only now at the end of the nucleus, not at the beginning. The X-chord, which had both times broken off before, "going nowhere," now leads purposefully right into the weighty magic chord. And the melodic tail C–A–G♯, which had earlier simply drifted off both times, now points very purposefully toward the G♯, which carries a strong beat. In getting to that G♯, the tail is transformed. The T7-form, which underlay the right hand in measures 4–5, is now given a strong melodic profile by the insertion of the F into the melodic contour. This produces a linear form of T7, and with the thematic T-contour, but in inversion.

The effect of the inverted T-contour is of course strongly cadential. See my earlier remarks on the voice's F♯–D♯–B♯–D. In discussing the latter, we noted how the piano here "corrects" the intervals of inverted-T. We also identified the failure of the voice to sing "right" T-intervals in measures 18–19 with the singer's inability to remember what he is supposed to be remembering; and we noted that the T-contours which he sings in fact highlight that issue here. The intervallically exact inverted-T in the piano, then, which is also much "better" as regards its rhythmic/metric sense, should give us a clue to just what it is that was eluding the singer in measures 18–19, and in his memories more generally. From that standpoint, the fact that the piano's inverted-T leads directly and forcefully into the magic chord is suggestive. Specifically, it suggests that the magic chord symbolizes at least a significant part of those memories inaccessible to the singer's present consciousness. (Hence the strong cadence and downbeat at measure 20, overriding the dramatically inadequate vocal cadence in measure 19.) To fortify this thesis, let us review some other aspects of the behavior of that chord in the piece.

In general, the magic chord, which is so weighty at its first appearance in measure 2 as to render N and X its accessories, never develops into an organic generative feature of the intervallic structure, the way that N-to-X does. It is an autonomous sonority, and it recedes very much into the background of one's aural attention as N-to-X begins to take over. In particular, the magic chord is very little in prominence during the entire time the voice is singing. The "passing" magic chord over the bar line at measure 11 has been noted; but one also notes that this is the only place between the singer's entrance and his cadence at measure 19 where he is silent for longer than the eighth-rest he needs to breathe occasionally. And the voice's rest across the bar line of measure 11 coincides exactly with the time the magic chord is sounding. The magic chord in measure 18 is more problematic in this regard (cf. note 12, especially the remarks at the end) but does not draw attention unduly away from the voice; one is too accustomed, by this time, to the nuclear magic chord of the motto, as passing between N and X. The magic chord does not appear explicitly elsewhere between measure 8 and measure 19½, although it does exercise a definite harmonic effect around the bar line of measure 14, where the singer is getting into the thick of his remembering (see Example 15.22). It may be significant that the magic chord recurs "almost explicitly" on the second quarter of measure 21, at a moment when the voice is singing one of its tones. This is a unique such event of the piece. But the bass F is two octaves too low, and the upper three tones of the chord are not reattacked along with the F (and are acoustically much attenuated by this time), so that it is dubious to claim that the voice is actually "supported by the magic chord" here in the full sense of that idea.

In fact, the piece notably lacks any moment at which the magic chord supports any emphatic (not to say climactic) vocal achievement. Compare *Tristan*, and its chord, in that respect! N-to-X, ignoring the passing magic chord between, is an intervallic gesture with whose ramifications the voice is highly involved. See particularly Examples 15.3 and 15.4, and the surrounding discussion; then of course also Examples 15.17, 15.18 and 15.19. In that context, the big magic chord of measure 2½, before the voice is in, precedes N-to-X and draws weight away from it. And the big magic chord of measure 20, after the voice is "out" (in some sense), follows N-to-X and in fact "resolves" it, again drawing weight away from it. The magic chord is to that extent "outside the piece" as far as the singer's consciousness is concerned. The fact that the magic chord is autonomous, rather than generative, also helps keep it "outside the piece" for the singer.

These observations lend considerable support to our earlier idea, that the magic chord is indeed very much involved symbolically with those memories inaccessible to the singer's present consciousness, hence, in a sense "outside the song" as far as his awareness is concerned. The weighty chords at measure 2½ and especially at measure 20 make excellent dramatic sense from that point of view, as does the vocal rest across the bar line of measure 11. Conceivably, some music involving the singer's remembering the magic chord was what lay ahead, above the plateau of measure 15, had the singer succeeded in making the breakthrough. Example 15.22 showed how the singer was already getting a whiff of that idea as he built up toward measure 15. In this connection, the vocal line in measure 19 does stabilize the low C♯, achieving something—and something to do with the text question—but notably fails to do anything about remembering the magic chord. Perhaps the whole point of measure 18 is that the voice doesn't hear the chord in the piano. The cadence at measure 19 is very feminine, and is immediately overwhelmed metrically by the accent of the subsequent (unsung) chord at measure 20. Also, the cadential C♯ of the voice in measure 19 doubles the bass ("root") of the X-chord, which promptly drives on to resolve into the magic chord after the voice has stopped singing.

As discussed earlier, one could analyze the dramatic situation at measure 20 in two extreme ways, depending on whether one takes measure 20 (and other piano solo sections) as being "external" or "internal" to the singer. Or, as I prefer, one can mix these extreme modes: the beat at measure 20 is external, in that it says ironically to the audience: "he will never remember this." But the beat is also psychologically internal: the singer is overwhelmed by the realization (possibly not conscious) that his internal search has failed, and he gives up at this point. The reader, if so inclined, can review here earlier speculation on the singer's psychology following measure 21.

The notion of the singer's psychic energy draining away after the beat of measure 20 is effectively tone-painted by the bass line there. (More simply, the bass line also tone-paints the tears of the text.) The reference of the bass line in measure 20 to the bass line at the opening of the piece also suggests the idea that the singer is "right back where he started" (only more so).

As for the actual tones of this "contrabass clarinet" passage: one can take as a point of departure the strong melodic sense of A-to-G♯ going into measure 20 in the right hand of the piano. That A–G♯ is locally embedded in the inverted T7 motif, but more emphatically functions as the end of the "tail" of the Leitmotif nucleus, that is, as the end of the familiar melodic Y7. At the moment that this A resolves to G♯, at the bar line of measure 20, the "contrabass clarinet" A enters under the G♯, keeping the relationship in the air harmonically. When the clarinet a finally moves, it repeats the A–G♯ gesture and continues on chromatically to G♮. By the end of the measure, the clarinet is back on A an octave lower; the line now once more moves down chromatically through G♯ to G, and now keeps going on to F♯. Considering that the point of departure for all this was the A–G♯ at the end of Y7, the "tail" of the Leitmotif, I can hear a clear reference here to the vocal line of measures 11–12, where the voice began with the "tail" of the Leitmotif and extended the A–G♯ down chromatically, through G, to F♯. It was notably at that F♯ that the voice earlier picked up the music of measure 12, in measure 18½. So the bass line is tying up some unfinished business here, supplying a reference to the first half of the question-music of measures 11–12, with the "right notes" (the voice having recalled the "wrong notes" for that reference in mm. 16 and 17). If we look a bit more closely, we can find in the contrabass clarinet line, across the bar line of measure 21, an explicit Y7 form (D♭–C–A-G♯) whose tail is extended to create the gesture C–A–G♯–G–F♯ (and, eventually, F). This comes very close to the voice in measures 11–12, up to the pivotal F♯. Only the voice did not hook that F♯ up to any subsequent F.

In that Y7 is the "dominant" of Y, the third C–A the "dominant" of the third F–D, and so on, we can try by extension to consider the gesture C–A–G♯–G–F♯ (and, eventually, F) to be the "dominant form" of the gesture F–D–D♭–C–C♭ (and, eventually, B♭). The latter gesture is immediately recognized as the one familiar from many earlier discussions of the bass line in measures 2–6 (etc.—and eventually m. 13). So the music of the first half of the question (mm. 11–12 up to F♯) is the "dominant" of that bass line gesture, and it is exactly that music that the voice has so much trouble with in measures 16–17. Once the voice gets to the F♯, in measure 18, it can remember the rest of measure 12 quite effectively. The piano (in its contrabass clarinet line) of course has no trouble in remembering C–A–G♯–G–F♯. And the piano gets that F♯ down to F, which the voice was unable to do. This is the "dominant" gesture to "getting C♭ down to B♭," at which the piano has also been successful earlier.

In connection with the absence of any F from the vocal line after the F♯ of measure 12, we can note that there are several places where F would be a highly appropriate note to sing, motivically. An F immediately or soon after that F♯ would be motivically consistent, in fact. Referring back to Examples 15.17, 15.18, and 15.19, we note that the voice line of these measures includes motivic gestures N7-to-X7 and N1-to-X1, and also N6, but that N6 does not progress on to X6 (which would put an F after the F♯ of m. 12). At the end of measure 14, an F rather than a G would be motivically expected after the D, in light of the progressive play with T-forms going on in the voice line from measure 13 up to this point. Finally, in measure 18, after the voice's B♭–D♭, one certainly "expects" the prime form of T; and hence F after the D♭.

Can one conclude from this that "getting the F♯ of measure 12 down to F" is something which also has to do with frustration for the singer? If he ever did sing the F, would the magic chord appear over it? It is suggestive to speculate around these ideas, but I don't feel one could conclude too much definitely. Curiously enough, the "missing F" from the voice part after measure 12 (in fact after m. 9) might also relate to the high B♭ missing from the voice's gamut over the piece. Should the voice move down from the high C♭ to that missing high B♭, as he "ought," in order to execute the "dominant" gesture F♯-to-F, as the piano does execute those gestures?[13] In spite of note 13, I would answer "no" to the preceding question. Nevertheless, the observation that B♭ and F are two conspicuous missing tones in the

13. Can one read this idea into a connection of the high Cs of the voice, measures 16–17, to the low C♭ of "und" and thence the subsequent low B♭, with abortive T-motif there to represent "Ich erinnere" (by "dass")? Perhaps. But if so, the gesture could be executed more clearly. The low B♭ of course cannot substitute completely for the high B♭ in any case.

See my dramatic analysis earlier of the singer's psychology at and following "und." Insofar as a C–C♭–B♭ gesture, with a T-form beginning on the B♭, recalls the approach to the beat of measure 13 from the bass of measures 5–6, the singer's gesture here would be part of his remembering the measure 13 beat here—that is, remembering that he is supposed to be remembering something. But, though I can entertain it, I am far from convinced by the melodic analysis that initiated this note.

vocal line is somehow suggestive in light of the overall structural role of just those tones, and in relation to each other, in the piano part. This seems, at any rate, a further manifestation of the dissociation of voice from accompaniment action.

A few more points remain to be noted in connection with the bass line of measures 20–21 (and beyond). The A–G♯ gesture, governing the right-hand approach to measure 20, appearing harmonically at that bar line and initiating the continuation of the bass line as just discussed, also appears in the relation of the retrograde-inverted X-forms A–G♯–G–E♭ and A♭–G–F♯–D in the "contrabass clarinet" line. The A of the first form naturally receives great accent; the A♭ of the second form of course receives less, but is still audible, since one groups the 16ths motivically in blocks of four. The intervening block of four sixteenths is a (retrograde-inverted) N-form, not an X-form. Since one expects X-forms exclusively, because of the reference to measure 1, this draws some attention to the minor (rather than major) third involved in that form. Hence, a subtle motivic accent is given to the recurrence of the tone A, the minor third C–A, the Y7 in which that C–A is embedded, and the gesture C–A–G♯–G–F♯ (eventually F). The Y7 is eventually "answered" by Y at its prime level: F♯–D–F in the bass of measure 21, then all subsequent C♯s and F♯s ad lib. Y becomes somewhat stronger here if one can hear back, past the "contrabass clarinet" solo, to the D–F–D♭ of the preceding motto bass line. But I wouldn't worry about that. The prime form of Y is in any case somewhat of an abstraction, based on the prominence of Y7 in the music, together with the notion that the C–A and G♯–C♯ components of Y7 are to be heard as "dominants" of the "tonic" minor third F–D and fourth C♯–F♯.

I am left with a lot of loose ends. One I feel I should pick up. The reader may have got the impression, from Example 15.22, that there is some harmonic technique consistently governing the total texture of measures 13–15, or of the song as a whole. I haven't found any such technique. I believe there is none, but I would be happy to be proved wrong.

One should return here, if not earlier, to reexamine the thematically pregnant opening measure of the piece and the way it qualifies for a listener the material that follows. The opening of No. XI, though, sounds much less autonomous when heard right after the ending of No. X. N.B. not only the G and A♯ there, but also the preceding chain of fifths in the bass, continuing right on into the sequences at the opening of No. XI. This, of course, all to the greater glory of the magic chord in measure 2.

Other loose ends, musical or dramatic, the reader can pick up on his own, if so inclined. It would be dreary to review yet again and further qualify how appropriate Schoenberg's handling of the text is, in spite of his apparent "missettings" of it. One could continue going over and tying up aspects of the piece indefinitely. I think it is quite of the essence of this piece, as with most of Schoenberg's work, that one can never tie everything up in a neat package, particularly in a "linear" prose discussion. The title of this chapter reflects my conviction. I will be satisfied if I have succeeded in setting in resonance, within the reader, certain musicodramatic ideas that I feel pertain to the work.

Plate 15.1 Schoenberg, Op. 15, No. XI. Used by permission of Belmont Music Publishers.

Plate 15.1 cont.

(continued)

Plate 15.1 cont.

20
ppp
So ver-blie-best du mir lang zu Sei - ten.
8
pp
pppp

CHAPTER Sixteen

A Way into Schoenberg's Opus 15, Number VII

Angst und hoffen wechselnd mich beklemmen,	Anguish and hope in turn seize me.
Meine worte sich in seufzer dehnen,	My words trail off in sighing.
Mich bedrängt so ungestümes sehnen,	Such tempestuous longing assails me
Daß ich mich an rast und schlaf nicht kehre,	that I do not turn to rest or sleep,
Daß mein lager tränen schwemmen,	that tears flood my couch,
Daß ich jede freude von mir wehre,	that I ward off every pleasure,
Daß ich keines freundes trost begehre.	that I seek no friend's consolation.

The poem, an exploration of an affective disorder, is in two parts. The first three lines expose the affects involved: *Angst and Hoffen wechselnd, ungestümes Sehnen.* The last four lines catalogue the resulting symptoms: *das ich . . ., das mein . . .,* and so on. The end-rhyme supports this articulation of the poem into 3 + 4 lines: *a b b / c a c c.*

The design is somewhat unbalanced, befitting the subject matter. From the rhyme scheme, it would appear that line 4 was an "extra" line: were it removed, the rhyme would balance as *a b b /a c c.* Furthermore, the removal of line 4 would not greatly change the descriptive sense of the text; line 5, in fact, recapitulates the descriptive content of line 4, rather more "poetically."

A second, and subtler, source of imbalance in the poem is the content of line 2: the poet is already presenting a symptom before having finished exposing the affects responsible. If line 2 began with "daß," and/or did not rhyme with line 3, we might even consider articulating the poem into 2 lines (affect, symptom) plus 5 lines (affect, *so . . . daß* symptom, symptom, symptom, symptom). As it is, the 3 + 4 articulation maintains itself, but line 2 does create a strong medial contrast between lines 1 and 3, against the rhyme scheme. And that contrast foreshadows the already overextended symptomology of the last four lines.

In these connections, the broad outlines of Schoenberg's setting are very striking. The music articulates three, rather than two, large sections:

Section 1: *Nicht zu rasch*, 6 measures, setting lines 1–3

Section 2: *Langsamer,* 7 measures, lines 4–6

Section 3: *Sehr langsam,* 6 or 7 2/4 measures, line 7 alone.

The overloaded lines 4–7 have meiosized into two sections of music, each commensurate with the musical unit setting lines 1–3. In this reading, the "extra" line of text is not the fourth, but the seventh. The inflated articulation of this line, off and away from lines 4–6, draws attention to this particular symptom as contrasted with the others, and one can admire the psychological surety of the composer's musical processes here, bringing to light important aspects of the text which are not so apparent at first reading.

First, the narcissistically defensive loneliness of line 7 becomes an enormously accented and apparently (see later remarks) final stage of a psychological progression through the song. The stage attained is that in which the poet can get along "perfectly well" (i.e., perfectly miserably) without anybody's helpful concern. The importance of this psychological state in the overall effect of the song is reflected by Schoenberg's setting of the piano part. The right hand can get along perfectly well without the helpful support of the left.

But it would not be accurate to analyze the psychological state just discussed as completely final in the song. The poet "does not seek the consolation of any friend." But, as the music moves into the final chords, we are reminded that there is certainly *one* friend from whom the poet seeks something, and that something is not just sympathy. The themes of emotional need and interpersonal relationship, implicitly underlying the generation of *Angst, Hoffen,* and *ungestümes Sehnen*, are absent from the fourth through sixth lines of the poem; they are introduced explicitly only in line 7. Schoenberg, picking up this feature of the text, blows up line 7 into an *Abgesang* as well as a coda: his music demonstrates that *Angst und Hoffen* are a psychological *result* (mm. 18–19), as well as a cause (m. 1). This closes a psychological circle: "Alternating anguish and expectation, and tempestuous longing, have driven me to such a state that I sigh while speaking, cannot sleep, sob at night, am totally depressed. (And—m. 14—so that) I do not seek the consolation of any friend. (For there is only one friend who can satisfy my wants, and that not with consolation; it is just this need which has led me to my state of—m. 18—alternating anguish and expectation.)"

But the song is no more completely recursive than completely linear. This is primarily due to the enormous loss of energy that occurs over the course of the music, and particularly throughout the third section. The piece indeed traces a psychological circle, but while it is tightly wound over the first third of its trip *(Nicht zu rasch),* it has begun to loosen a bit over the second third (*Langsamer*), and is imminently about to give up the ghost by the time it reaches its home stretch (*Sehr langsam*); the piece barely manages to pull into the station at measure 19 with its last bit of energy. The circular journey has worked itself out dynamically into total exhaustion.

Schoenberg must have taken his cue for this conception from the unbalancing line 2, "meine Worte sich in Seufzer dehnen." The sighing motive of the piano in the last section, in particular, clearly recalls the sighing motive of the piano in measures $2\frac{1}{2}$–$3\frac{1}{2}$ and $3\frac{1}{2}$–$4\frac{1}{2}$, associated with that text.[1] But not only does section 3 in itself portray "sighing," the song *as a whole*, with its continual exhaustion of energy, and its quantum leap past measure 14 in that respect, also manifests the phenomenon described in line 2 exactly and literally: the singer's words extend (past m. 14) and expand into sighing. I do not know what one could call this device of text-setting; "tone-painting" seems grossly inadequate.[2]

Many of the features that brake or extend the music from line 4 on are obvious enough. One that is perhaps not so immediately evident is the rhythmic articulation of the text, line by line. In the voice part, each line of text is set as a subphrase, and these subphrases are articulated by rests (with one exception, to be discussed later). Section 1 establishes an eighth rest, *Nicht zu rasch,* as a norm in this regard; that is, such rests separate line 2 from line 1 and line 3 from line 2. Striking, then, is the lack of any vocal rest to mark the largest structural division so far, between lines 3 and 4 at the bar line of measure 7. Naturally, a whole host of important musical and textual features are involved in this phenomenon; in our present context we can (for the moment) simply observe that Schoenberg is, among other things, contracting the duration between lines, the better later to extend (*dehnen*). For, from the bar line of measure 7 on, the expanding pattern is clear and direct:

before line 4, there is no rest;

before line 5, there is a sixteenth rest, *Langsamer*;

before line 6, there is an eighth rest, *Langsamer*;

before line 7, there is a quarter rest, *Sehr langsam.*

Since we do not fully respond to the change of tempo at measure 14 until past that quarter rest, we can actually hear an even longer rest there, still in the *Langsamer* tempo. With this in mind, one notes that the progression of rests tabulated above spans exactly the second (*Langsamer*) section of the song and, indeed, is one of its characteristic features, contrasting with the regular eighth rests, *Nicht zu rasch*, of section 1. (I am grateful to Mr. David Lyttle for having brought this aspect of the piece to my attention.)

For those to whom this pattern may seem artificial, it will suffice to read lines 4 through 7 of the poem aloud, using Schoenberg's rhythms while conducting the musical downbeat at the beginning of each line of text. The coincidence of these downbeats with the rests under discussion projects the gasping *Seufzer* of the singer, in the most literally physical sense, as they undergo progressively greater *Dehnung.*

The progression aims at the vocal quarter rest of measure 14, one of the most important features in Schoenberg's separation of line 7 from the others, and hence

1. The situation is complicated by the skewed phrase-structure of voice and piano in the first section of the song, and by other musical associations involved with the piano part of measures $13\frac{1}{2}$–$14\frac{1}{2}$. The footnoted sentence should not be taken as asserting anything more than it actually states.
2. The device seems to me to have an interesting methodological kinship with the "Theory of Types" that Russell and Whitehead were developing in mathematical logic at just this time. The logical theory investigates statements that make assertions about their own structure and behavior. The song explores a condition of which it is itself a symptom.

in his conception of the song as a whole.[3] The quarter rest is in turn involved with a whole complex of striking rhythmic features surrounding the bar line of measure 14. As a point of departure for their investigation, we can observe that the rest participates in apparently extending the normal duple measure of the music to a unique triple measure. The triple measure is in fact quite audible (not just visible) within the voice part itself, despite the further metric complications introduced by the piano hereabouts. Still considering the voice part itself, one can relate this (apparent) metric extension to the immediately preceding three-measure group of measures 11–13; the three-measure group extends the normal two-measure group which, up through measure 10, has been the metric module setting each line of text. If we now investigate how this three-measure group itself came into being, we will become aware that the technique of rhythmic augmentation, clear enough by measures 18–19, actually sets in as early as measure 12 itself. That is, measures 12–13 in the voice part "ought to be" only one measure (in pitch content, they specifically refer to the voice and then soprano piano part of m. 2); it is the augmentation technique that extends the one-measure model to two here, and thereby the two-measure group to a three-measure group.

What makes it difficult to notice this phenomenon on first hearing is the dotted rhythms of measure 12, continuing from the last half of measure 11. If the four pitches of measure 12 were equal eighths, augmenting the first half of measure 2 literally, the aural effect of the augmentation would be overwhelming. The rhythmic variant smooths over the critical joint between measures 11 and 12, reinforcing the already linking text doggerel of "je-de freu-de," and the linking pitch pattern of broken thirds, along with the locally recurrent A4. All this (but particularly the rhythmic variant of the augmented measure) makes measure 12 sound very much like an extension of measure 11, so that one hears the group (locally and initially) as "11-and-12, then 13." This largely covers the onset of the augmentation technique exactly at the bar line of measure 12, a phenomenon which led to our preceding analysis of the metric group as "11, then 12-and-13." As I shall explore shortly, it is important for Schoenberg's purposes that the listener only gradually become responsive to the augmentation underlying measures 12–19 of the piece.

Example 16.1

3. To my ear, there is a hint that the progression of rests actually continues beyond this point, to the vocal half rest of measure 17. This can be heard as a pause between the cadence of measure 16 (in the voice) and the unsung but imagined text *"Angst"* over the chord of measure 18. Later discussion will clarify the impression more formally. But the effect, if heard, is only a subtle afterthought; there is no question that the quarter rest of measure 14 is the "definitive" vocal rest of the piece.

Example 16.1 investigates these matters in greater detail. Example 16.1a presents a hypothetical "normal" vocal setting for lines 6 and 7 of the text, using Schoenberg's pitches and following the rhythmic and metric norms established by the first section of the song.[4] Example 16.1b simply augments the material from the pitches of measure 12 on. The first two-measure model of Example 16.1a is thereby transformed into a three-measure group, along the lines already discussed. The second two-measure model of 16.1a, however, transforms into a four-measure group, since the augmentation affects the entire model here. At this point, one recognizes the genesis of the quarter rest at measure 14: part of this complex, it augments the eighth rest of the basic model for setting a line of text.

Example 16.1c transcribes the rhythm and meter of the song itself. The three-measure group of Example 16.1b carries through as such to 16.1c, with the rhythmic variation already discussed. The four-measure group of 16.1b, however, becomes condensed into a second three-measure group of 1c. The first two measures of that four-measure group specifically condense into the single 3/4 measure of 16.1c: measure 14 of the song. This is why I earlier referred to that measure as an "apparent" expansion of a normal 2/4 measure: one can certainly hear it as such, but one can also hear it, in other contexts, as a contraction of a pair of such measures.

The two modes of hearing measure 14 function at different times in one's listening, a feature much to Schoenberg's technical purpose in sustaining the musical impulse through such a long and slow final section, having already lost so much energy at measure 14. That is, the augmentation in the vocal line of measures 12–13 is to a large extent locally covered, as discussed earlier, so that measure 14 as one comes into it is heard more in contrast with Example 16.1a than with Example 16.1b. In that connection, the measure sounds extended and dragging, with a beat too many. This sense, coming on top of the tempo change, strongly contributes to a feeling of substantial energy loss as one swings into the final section. Continuing to listen past measure 14, however, one becomes gradually aware of the augmentation in the voice part, confirmed by measures 18–19. In the process, one compares one's residual impressions of measure 14 more and more not with the model of Example 16.1a directly, but, rather, with Example 16.1b. In this context, the measure sounds contracted on a broader metric level, missing one beat, suggesting subsequent relaxation. In a similar way, but on a broader rhythmic level, as one becomes more and more responsive to the augmentation, one hears the three-measure group of measures 14–16, the second three-measure group of Example 16.1c, not only as an expanded relaxation of the corresponding normal two-measure group of Example 16.1a, but also, and progressively more, as a contracted tautening of the corresponding four-measure group of Example 16.1b. This, too, generates an urge for substantial rhythmic relaxation following measure 16. It is just these reservoirs of energy, in my hearing, that enable the singer to keep going for so long, so slowly and with so little mate-

4. In the present connection, I am not making any functional normative distinction between 6/8 and 2/4 measures (of section 1). The discussion at hand will involve beats only at the half-measure level or higher, not within the half-measures themselves.

rial after measure 14, projecting at such length the sighing *Dehnung* discussed earlier.[5]

Returning to Example 16.1: the condensation of 16.1b into 16.1c is specifically effected by the setting of "keines freundes": the eighth notes of 16.1b here become "dis-augmented," reverting to the sixteenths of the original model 16.1a, in forming the last beat of measure 14. If it were not for this specific transformation, Example 16.1c would be hardly distinguishable from 16.1b in overall metric effect. It is a telling psychological detail that the singer's abrupt shift of metric level should be triggered by "keines freundes"—the significance of that text in Schoenberg's conception was discussed earlier. It is, I maintain, equally no coincidence that the original shift of metric levels in the vocal line, at measure 12, was triggered by the assonating "freude." George points to the association himself by the parallel placement of "jede freude" in line 6 with "keines freundes" in line 7, although the words in the poem do not set off anything like the rhythmic/metric complexities of the music hereabouts, complexities forcefully pointing the singer's emotional discombobulation in relation to *the* friend, along the lines discussed earlier.

Returning to Example 16.1 once more: the vocal line, having projected measures 11–13 and 14–16 as three-measure groups, will naturally group the following tacet as yet another. This notion is parenthetically sketched at the end of Example 16.1c. There is nothing in the piano part to contradict such a metric reading of measures 17–19, and I hear that reading very strongly in the music as a whole. The "sighing" chord of measure 17 (identifiable as such from the bar lines of m. 3 and especially m. 4, where it underlies and doubles "*seuf-*") takes the stress of the entire group. Both the *Angst* and *Hoffen* chords, thereafter, are metrically weak afterbeats to the sigh on this rhythmic level. The effect fits neatly with the earlier discussion of the role the latter two chords play here, in contrast to their impetuous dramatic role at measure 1.

Example 16.1c thus presents three groups of three measures each, which begin with an eighth rest, a quarter rest, and (as symbolically sketched) a half rest, respectively. This is the notion I was getting at, less formally, in note 3. It relies, of course, on the supposition that the singer "participates," somehow, in measures 18–19 but not in measure 17.

Having reached this stage in the rhythmic analysis of measures 12–19, we can begin to attack some of the analytic problems raised by the piano part hereabouts, starting with the four-chord motive across the bar line of measure 14. This figure, whose beginning articulates the opening of section 3 a quarter note "early," is rich in associative functions. Some are local, involving reference to the voice in measures 12–13 and to the augmentation process more widely; I shall return to these later. For the moment, I shall focus on the larger-scale associations, recalling material directly from section 1: it is these associations that make us respond to the motive as initiating a "new section" of the piece, rather than simply extending and echoing the voice part of measures 12–13.

5. Of course the unwinding of the rhythmic/metric complexities in the piano part after in the piano part after measure 14 also contributes to the kinesis of the music as a whole, but it does not particularly help the singer in sustaining the vocal through-line.

I have already observed that the figure recalls the piano motive of measures 2½–3½. The closeness of the transposed pitch-fit is involved in the association. So is the dynamic swell and fall, portraying sighing. But perhaps strongest is the sense of the motive as characteristically going across the (audible) bar line defined by the voice in each case, what I have earlier called the "skew" fit of the instruments.

The figure also, however, strongly recalls the total content of measure 2 in the piano. Relevant are the untransposed pitch identity of the upper lines, the articulation between the second and third chords of the group, and the tenuto mark on the B♭ of the third chord, in each case. (Yes, the B♭ in m. 2, as in the original Universal Edition, not the G as "corrected" in the *Gesamt Ausgabe.*) The association is further fortified by the transformational link of the voice part in measures 12–13.

In sum, the motive under consideration strongly recalls both the four eighth-notes spanning measure 2, metrically a strong pair of eighths followed by a weak pair, and also—simultaneously—the four eighths linking the last and first halves (respectively) of measures 2 and 3, metrically a weak eighth-pair followed by a strong. The motive thereby becomes "skew," in the sense I have used the term here, against itself! The unique rests in the piano part of measures 13–14 fittingly frame and highlight this gesture which, to my ear, underlies the inordinate amount of tension projected here, tension sufficient to sustain the unwinding of the piano part so slowly, with so little material, over the rest of the song.

That is, there would already be considerable obvious rhythmic and metric tension about the placement of the motive in relation to the piano part immediately preceding, and to the voice part hereabouts (which, as I have noted, is itself considerably convoluted). And, taking the motive as framed by the rests out of the surrounding context, there would still be considerable tension generated by its internal rhythmic irregularity, compounded by the sudden tempo change. What raises the level of tension to the nth degree beyond all this is the further internal metric "self-skewness" of the motive as referred back to the prototypes of section 1, giving it a metric character which is not just ambivalent but strictly self-contradictory: we are not at all "unsure" of the metric relation between the first and second chord-pairs of the figure; rather, we are "sure" that the relation is strong to weak, following the model of measure 2, and we are also "sure" that the relation is weak to strong, following the model of measures 2½–3½. The motive syncopates against itself, even while syncopating with everything else in hearing around measure 14.[6]

6. To be sure, there are other associations with section 1 involving parts of the motive, but no others I can hear so obviously involving the motive as a whole, that is as a *Leitmotif.* In any case, no further associations I hear substantially change the "self-skew" character of the figure as heard in the light of section 1 and, in fact, some further associations quite reinforce that character (an example appears later in this note). That section 3 should take "consequent" matter, from mm. 2 and 3, as a principal motivic point of departure befits its thematic function as an *Abgesang.* This contrasts to the second *Stollen,* which began at measure 7 with a strongly recognizable and extended variation on the "antecedent" matter from measure 1.

These broad outlines, firm as they are, are qualified by further associative nuances, not even yet considering nonassociative factors in the music. For example, the freshness of the piano attack on the first three-note chord of the motive, after the preceding trailing-off in the piano part, certainly recalls the effect of the attack on the first chord of the piece. This strengthens the overall strong-to-weak metric sense of the motive. On the other hand, the return to an augmented triad containing B♭ as-

If we look for a textual clue to this musical state of affairs, we can find it logically enough over the crucial pair of eighth-notes, in the last half of measure 2, that pivotally connect the two models for the motive. The key word is *beklemmen.* A person presenting *Beklemmung* as a medical symptom would not simply be generally feeling anxiously oppressed, but would be complaining of such sensations specifically in the chest, affecting the heart and/or the breathing, that is, of arrhythmia. Such a condition would naturally result in spasmodic and rhythmically erratic syncopation, and this is precisely what we have been examining in connection with the piano part in section 3.[7] The idea of "skew" syncopation in the piece begins precisely under the text "beklemmen," with the pair of eighth-notes that led us to the word. Those eighth-notes, in turn, initiate the "sighing" motive of measures 2½–3½, whose role in the *Dehnung* of section 3 has already been mentioned. The sighing of section 3 (in the piano at least) is then "beklemmt." The extra dimension makes these *Seufzer* better translated as "groans." The notion of *Beklemmung* also gives the pianist a certain hint as to how to perform the inverted carets midway through measures 2 and 3. This is useful background for an eventual performance confrontation with the bar line of measure 7, where the caret reappears, now at the end of a measure, indeed a whole section—a feature that is surprising in the present context, and will bear further study later on.

At present, though, we should return to discuss the motive further, as it associates in a local, as well as a large-scale context. The point of departure for such exploration is evidently the relation of the motive to the vocal line of measures 12–13. I noted earlier how that line initiated the process of rhythmic augmentation persisting through the rest of the piece. I also noted how the effect was largely covered at that point by the techniques making measure 12 sound as an extension of measure 11. It is only with the entrance of the piano's motive that the impact of what happened in measures 12–13 begins—and only begins—to dawn on the listener. The rhythmic augmentation, while *beklemmt,* is now clear. For the moment, though, the listener largely responds to it as an apparently new feature of section 3, belonging to the piano with its motive as incipit for the section. Yet to the extent that the motive also reverberates and amplifies the vocal line of measures 12–13, one begins (and just begins) to become aware that the augmentation in the piano is instead a comment on a rhythmic/metric process initiated and controlled by the voice, as discussed earlier in connection with Example 16.1. In that discussion, it became clear how important it was that the rhythmic structure of the vocal line over measures 12–19 dawn on the listener only gradually; the piano motive begins the process of enlightenment. The powerful large-level associations of the motive discussed earlier prevent the secret from coming out too soon: we are too busy

sociates the third chord of the motive equally strongly with the first chord of the piece, strengthening the overall weak-to-strong sense of the motive. All of this works to the greater glory of the metric paradox by now sufficiently discussed. It is perfectly logical that there should be fragmentary "antecedent" associations here back to m. 1, as well as larger-level and over-riding "consequent" ones: the motive provides a forceful beginning for its own new section which, on a larger and overriding level, is an *Abgesang* for the song as a whole.

7. Cf. Beethoven's treatment of the subject: the "*beklemmt*" violin during the middle section of the Cavatina from the B♭ Quartet, Op. 130.

sorting out the complexities of the motive-as-incipit to be very immediately receptive to its function as commentator on measures 12–13. But when the motive recurs over the following measures to accompany the entire last line of the text, we have more leisure to aurally ponder why just this material should be so persistent. And, aided by the text link of *keines freundes* back to *jede freude,* which has had plenty of time to sink in by the end of measure 15, we can hear the piano, by measure 16, much more explicitly as a *beklemmt* commentator on measures 12–13. The galling ruminations of the piano over section 3 thus underlie and unify the chain of associations, from *jede freude,* through *keines freundes,* to the friend, and back to *Angst und Hoffen,* discussed earlier as closing a psychological circle in the piece. And, beyond simply linking these ideas, the associative technique of the music projects the *gradual* way in which the existence and the binding power of the chain dawn and grow.

Hearing the piano motive as an amplified reverberation of the voice in measures 12–13 adds even further complexity to its already complex internal metric sense. We have noted that the relation of the first chord-pair to the second within the motive is heard both as strong-to-weak (specifically "1–2"), following the model of measure 2, and also as weak-to-strong (specifically "–2 | 1"), following measures 2½–3½. The association with measures 12–13, the latter two measures of a three-measure group in the voice, suggests yet another metric context in which the motive might be heard: as "–2–3" of a large triple gesture.

It is not easy, though, to hear where the preceding "1" of such a gesture, at the appropriate rhythmic level, could be heard in the music, even isolating the piano part. One could, to be sure, force such a reading by leaning especially hard on the piano's G halfway through measure 12, hearing not just a functional strong quarter, but a "strong measure" beginning there. But the profile of the surrounding melodic contour and dynamics makes this seem far too artificial to my ear. Note that the same problem arises if one tries to lead into the motive as "–2 | 1."

The problem can be avoided by imagining that one accompanying "instrument" trails off ametrically into the rest in measure 13, and a new "instrument" enters after the rest to play the motive: the new instrument can pan in "out of the blue" in its own metric context, specifically as if beginning the second measure of either a two- or a three-measure group. The latter "–2–3" idea, unfortunately, still will not work out: even milking the syncopation for all it is worth, one could not avoid hearing the first chord of the subsequently repeated motive as the (duly syncopated) "1" to which such an extended anacrusis would lead; this would result in a much sharper immediate metric transformation of the motive than the musico-dramatic context can support. That is, the "gradual" sense of the unwinding would be violated as the motive, including no downbeat at this metric level on its first appearance (as "–2–3"), would immediately thereafter begin with a downbeat "1" on its second appearance. (The eighth-rests, while suggestive, are just not long enough to function as "beats," down or no, on this metric level, where the "beat" corresponds to an entire measure at the *Langsamer* tempo.)

So the possibility of hearing the motive as "–2–3," reverberating measures 12–13, is ultimately untenable to my ear. It is still useful I think, for two reasons. First, it can help the pianist play the motive without unduly over-projecting it as either strong-to-weak or weak-to-strong, maintaining the important tension of the *Beklemmung*. Second, it helps the pianist, frustrated finally in any attempt to project "–2–3" here, to feel a corresponding release at the end of the piece, where an analogous potential strong/weak or weak/strong ambivalence about measures 18–19 is very successfully resolved by hearing the *Angst* and *Hoffen* chords as "–2–3" of a three-measure group. Example 16.1c, in fact, indicated how that three-measure group is naturally commensurate with the vocal three-measure group of measures 11–13. It makes a certain sense, then, to attempt to refer the motive, as both a reverberation of measures 12–13 and a pianistic point of departure leading to the piano's solo cadence of measures 18–19, to the "–2–3" metric prototype underlying the vocal span of music so linked. There is a sense, that is, in which the motive "ought to" scan as "–2–3" on this level; the fact that it cannot should be savored in that connection. This is, of course, another and further complicating aspect of the *Beklemmung* hereabouts.

Example 16.2 shows how the pianist, without having to come in "out of the blue," can still rebar his part so as to attack measure 13½ as if beginning a measure. The trick is to consider the first half of measure 11 as if it were a third beat of measure 10, following the suggestion of measure 9. The larger meter can then be worked out so as to project the two "measures" of the motive on its first entrance as either strong-to-weak (Ex. 16.2a) or weak-to-strong (Ex. 16.2b).

I would caution a pianist against over-projecting the rebarring, though, in either version. First, Schoenberg's phrasing, as well as the inertia of the hitherto heavily duple measures, works considerably against hearing measures 10–11½ unequivocally as a "triple measure." (Nor is any other rebarring of the passage any more plausible.) Beyond that, neither Example 16.2a nor Example 16.2b allows one to hear the two "measures" of the motive on first appearance as "–2 | 1" or "–2–3." This was discussed earlier. Example 16.2b does allow the motive to enter weak-to-strong, but only as "–3 | 1," which does not adequately represent the metric sense of the augmented reference to measures 2½–3½. In any case, one should presumably not try to project any one chosen "solution" to these ambiguities at measure 13½; one should on the contrary try to keep them all in the air, at least up to measure 17. Note that this involves maintaining (to the extent possible) the ability to hear the first half of the motive as if it were the second measure of a two- or three-measure group. And that, in turn, involves being able to dispense entirely with the rebarring of Example 16.2, simply letting the music trail off from measure 11 to measure 13½ in the piano, in metrically unorganized quarters; then coming in on a cold "second measure" of a measure-group at measure 13½. It would be helpful to have a dynamic after the *diminuendo* of measure 12, to compare to the *piano* attack of measure 13½. But perhaps Schoenberg was wiser to give the pianist some leeway here for personal maneuvering, to achieve a suitable balance among all the ambiguous metric sensations at hand.

The outcome of all the rhythmic, metric, and associative finesses we have been discussing is to strengthen all the more the downbeat effect of the pulse at the bar line of measure 17. There we recognize a completely unambiguous association to the bar line events of measure 3 and especially measure 4, with the *Seufzer* chord extending the singer's words. This association makes it clear that measure 17 is un-

Example 16.2

questionably stressed metrically at its appropriate motivic rhythmic level. And that rhythmic level is now clear, there being no further syncopations from here on to confuse our perception of the straightforward augmentation.

Interacting strongly with these factors is the pitch organization of the music over the final section of the piece. The *Seufzer* chord at the bar line of measure 17 is a goal of the wedging process that has been converging audibly from measure 13½ on.

Example 16.3

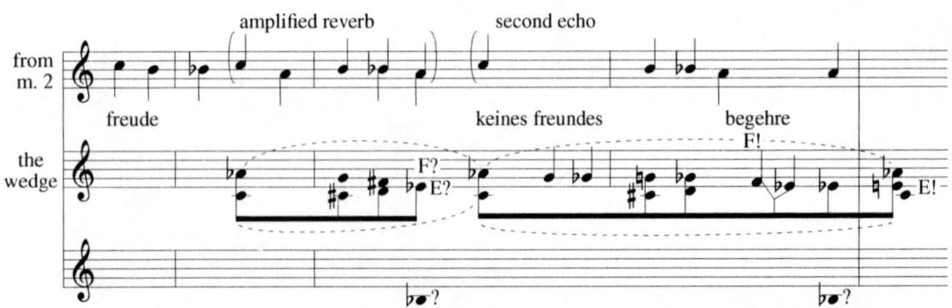

Example 16.3 attempts to expose and clarify this process, starting from pertinent elements of the voice part in measure 12. The motive involves two wedges, one between the outer and one between the lower two voices in the piano part. Example 16.3 clarifies what I hear to be the case: the former wedge is greatly subordinate to the latter, which is identified on the diagram as "the" wedge. The primary function of the top voice in the motive is rather displayed as continuing to reverberate the voice part of measures 12–13, the material arising from measure 2 and setting off the augmentation process at *freude*. The material, in this view, forms a descant for the upper voice of the "real" wedge, which starts from the C4 and A♭4 in the first chord of the motive.

Following Example 16.3 along, we note that the first attempt of the wedge to converge is frustrated by the last chord of the motive in measure 14. (As with other disruptive sonorities in the song, the chord has *Hoffen* rather than *Angst* structure.) Several things are "wrong" about this chord. For convenient later reference, we can tabulate the following "errors":

1. The chord does not follow the mechanical pattern of semitone-convergence established by the first three chords of the motive. If it did, it should read A4–F4–E♭4.
2. Specifically missing from the above norm is F4. Although E♭ is present (as is the descant A) the wedge cannot continue as long as the F, wedge-partner for the E♭, is missing.
3. Instead of the F, the chord contains B♭3. This tone apparently participates in none of the essential tonal activity for the phrase that the example sketches.

The poetic effect of the disruption, with its reference to "*Hoffen*," is strong enough, but the tonal function of the particular disruption in evidence is not yet clear in any positive sense.

As a result of these "errors," the wedge fails to continue converging to the indicated goal of (unison) E4. So we go back to the first chord of the motive and try again. Now, as Example 16.3 indicates, the voice leaves the descant line and moves into the upper line of the wedge itself, exactly at "keines freundes." The voice continues to take control over the upper line of the wedge, so that by the time we pass the penultimate chord of the motive at measure 15½ the situation is much changed. Specifically, in contrast to the earlier "errors" we have here the following "corrections":

1. The voice now arpeggiates, all on its own, the chord A–F–E♭, which "should have been there" all along as the final chord of the motive. It does so with a cadential sign-off at "begehre." The word-play, about the *begehrte* sonority, is a nice touch.
2. The weight of this vocal cadence goes especially on F4, and very much in relation to the following E♭4, the two providing the missing member-pair of the wedge. The relation is particularly highlighted because the voice has been generally drifting down in semitones, in its overall structure, since the C5 of measure 12. One expects the F to continue this drift, at least touching on E before E♭ enters the vocal scene. One expects this all the more since the fifth and sixth lines of the text have previously cadenced with descending semitones. Indeed, every preceding line of text has cadenced with some form of the pitch-class interval 1 or 11. The F–E♭ cadential gesture is thus much highlighted. And, in particular, it is tied in a very complex fashion to the E for which the E♭ "substitutes" at the cadence. That is, of course, the E to which the wedge as a whole is to converge, to which the F-and-E♭ pair of the wedge, in particular, are about to "resolve"—the E4 at the bar line of measure 17.
3. The "misfit" final chord of the motive, with its B♭3, does recur in the piano, but its disruptive effect on the wedge is much attenuated. The chord is now heard as a pick-up from the immediately preceding vocal cadence on "*begehre*," leading into the chord at the bar line of measure 17. The misfit chord, besides being heard after the "correct" harmony of "*begehre*," no longer has an accent mark, nor is it followed by a rest; it is preceded by an inverted caret (the *Beklemmung* symbol) and pushes strongly forward, away from the preceding three chords of the motive and toward the following *Seufzer* chord.

As a result of these developments, the wedge now can and does converge. This confirms and contributes to the downbeat at the beginning of measure 17, which has been discussed in other connections. The tonal effect is much enhanced by the recurrence of the C and the A♭ in the *Seufzer* chord there, symmetrically disposed about the wedge-goal E and referring back to the Cs and A♭s from which the wedge has twice begun to converge. This, as indicated by the dotted slurs in Example 16.3, ties together all of the wedging action from measure 13½ to measure 17. The *Seufzer* chord at measure 17 thus retroactively organizes the most directive overall tonal feature of the "sighing" final section of the song.[8]

It remains, in connection with Example 16.3, to ponder the tonal function of B♭3 in the "misfit" chord of the motive. The note does not "fit into" the wedge. Or does it? If one ignores register, the B♭ as a pitch-class is its own partner in the pitch-class inversion-about-E: in fact, that operation cannot be distinguished functionally from pitch-class inversion about B♭—both rules reflect C into A♭, C♯ into G, etc. In this sense, the B♭ is as much of a "tonic representative" for the pitch-class inversion as is the E; it can stand by itself to that extent.

It would not be comfortable to let it so stand here, though. We are very aware of the pitches in register as we hear the wedge, not only the pitch-classes involved. From that point of view, the problematic B♭3 of Example 16.3 "ought to be" answered by B♭4. And this in fact actually occurs: the answering B♭ is just that one which appears in the middle of the *Angst* chord of measure 18, and recurs in the following *Hoffen* chord. Those chords are indeed almost completely symmetrical about that B♭, continuing to project the same pitch-*class* inversion as did the wedge, now represented with pitch center B♭4 rather than E4. Only the *Hoffen* chord is slightly asymmetrical, continuing to display the disruptive behavior which chords of this form have exhibited over the piece.

Example 16.4

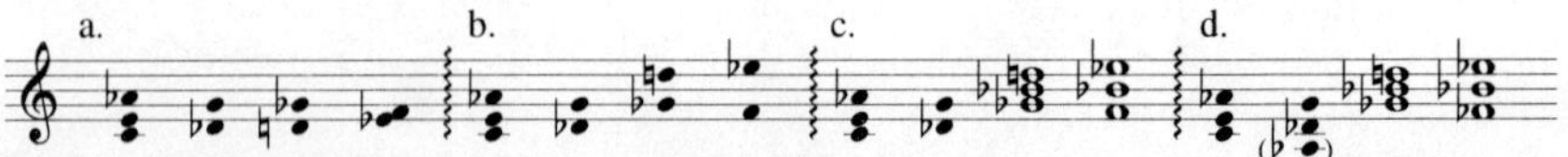

Example 16.4 works out these matters more systematically, analyzing the tonal content of measures 17–19 as a somewhat transformed and diffracted reverberation of the wedge. Example 16.4a shows the wedge making another pass at converging, up to the F–E♭ that was earlier so touchy. In 16.4b, this model is transformed by inverting the last intervals of the wedge, so that they center about B♭4 rather than E4. The pitch-class structure of the wedge is not affected thereby: the same pitch-class inversion is still being projected. This notion is further reinforced in Example 16.4c by the addition of the local pitch center B♭s themselves. Considering the power of the preceding pitch-center E4 at measure 17, this gesture (so to speak) composes-out the equation: pitch-class inversion about E equals pitch-class inversion about B♭.

Example 16.4d has the tonal content of the three measures themselves. The two *Hoffen* chords disrupt the stability of the inversion. The A♭3 of the first is the transposed analog of the misfit B♭3 in Example 16.3; we may take it as analogously "rep-

8. I am deliberately avoiding casting the present remarks into more Schenkerian terminology. Those who may wish to invoke such terminology are of course free to do so. I can see the point. But, personally, I think that Schenkerian assertions would be theoretically contentious here and would not yield much analytic mileage in describing the music beyond what has already been said without them.

resenting" the A♭ an octave higher, particularly as the latter appears in an augmented triad. More striking is the "wrongness" of the final *Hoffen* chord (which is, of course, the original structure from the latter half of m. 1): the "wrong note" here is F♭, as a substitute for F♮. Example 16.4 makes this reading of the chord quite plain.

The F♮ that "ought to be" in the final chord as wedge-partner for the E♭ that is there, projects once more the pair F–E♭ with which the converging wedge earlier had such difficulty, which the voice finally succeeded in supplying at its final cadence. When we recall, from (2) of the earlier "corrections" list (p. 333), that we "expected" E♮ rather than E♭ as the last note for the voice, the whole matter is tightly tied up: the pitch-class pair F-and-E♭ is thematically bound with the play of discombobulating substitutions. The E, or F♭, between them can, in varying contexts, be heard as one of the centers for the "tonic inversion" of the piece, a center to which the F and the E♭, as wedge-partners, can "resolve" (this as, e.g., at m. 17). But in other contexts, the F♭ can be heard as a wrong note, substituting for F in the inversionally balanced pair F–E♭ (this, e.g., as in the preceding discussion of the F♭ of Ex. 16.4d, in the context of the rest of Ex. 16.4). That actual F♭ in measure 19 is, to be sure, heard this way. But it is *also* heard the other way simultaneously: recalling and reverberating the "tonic" E from measure 17. That is, the bass of the final chord of the piece is at one and the same time a wrong blue-note and a tonic!

The potentiality for this ambivalence was naturally already latent in measure 1: that measure as a whole stakes out inversion-about-B♭ clearly enough, with the F♭ as disruptive substitute for F. The spelling supports that reading (F♭ rather than E♮, although Schoenberg does have some general preference for spelling major sevenths rather than diminished octaves). Note, too, the visual symmetry of the notation about the B♭ on the center line of the treble (right hand) staff. The visual symmetry is reflected by enough pitch symmetry so that one takes in the aural equivalent. What is not yet suggested strongly, in measure 1, is the other branch of the ultimate ambiguity at measure 19: that the F♭, perhaps respelled as E♮, can also have a tonic, rather than blue-note function, as another center of balance for the tonic pitch-class inversion. It is the establishment of just that other branch of the ambiguity with which the final section of the piece is so concerned in its pitch-structure, so that the final F♭ in measure 19 can be heard in relation to the E of the *Seufzer* chord in measure 17. The close of the song thus leads the singer to a sort of meta-stable equilibrium in her juggling of the relations of *Hoffen* (m. 19) to *Angst* (m. 18), via the *Seufzer* (m. 17) the situation generates; all this is worked out from the suggestions of the initial impetus itself.[9]

9. I find it irresistible, at this point, to quote Schoenberg himself on his text settings ("The Relationship to the Text," 1912): "inspired by the sound of the first words of the text, I had composed many of my songs straight through to the end without troubling myself in the slightest about the continuation of the poetic events. . . . It then turned out . . . that I had never done greater justice to the poet than when, guided by my first direct contact with the sound of the beginning, I divined everything that obviously had to follow this first sound with inevitability." The article is reprinted *in Style and Idea,* ed. Leonard Stein (New York: St. Martin's Press, 1975), 141–145.

The reader has possibly been wondering at what point I will direct notice to my own article on "Inversional Balance as an Organizing Force in Schoenberg's Music and Thought," *Perspectives of New Music* 6/2 (Spring/Summer 1968): 1–21. Now. The interested reader should also be referred to:

The pitch structure exposed in measure 1 continues to develop logically through the remainder of the opening subphrase. The two minor thirds in the first half of measure 2 balance each other by inversion about B♭, a feature that is projected aurally by the way in which the voice contours the broken thirds and visually by the spelling of the second third. The piano ends its subphrase here, stopping short of the voice with the inverted caret that signals the *Beklemmung* to come, as that word of text appears. Piano and voice remain askew for the rest of the first section. The voice continues its subphrase through to the end of the measure. Worried, as it were, by its earlier "mistake" of E♭–F♭ for E♭–F, it gives that touchy pitch-class pair another try in inversion, so producing F♭–E♭ for F–E♭. The tenuto indication over the piano's B♭ here (*not* under the G!) belongs to the associative complex: This picks up the B♭ center of inversion from measure 1, specifically from the middle of *Hoffen,* recurring now in the middle of *beklemmen.* The musical treatment makes it clear poetically that it is *Hoffen,* which is responsible for the *Beklemmung,* not *Angst.*

The failure of the blue-note F♭ to correct itself here indicates that its inversional imbalance will be a strong generative feature in the music (leading ultimately to the solution of m. 19 in connection with m. 17, but also leading elsewhere first, as we shall see presently). Indeed, this failure makes the F♭-for-F-natural issue of the highest moment: not only does the "mistake" repeat itself, it intensifies itself by the big rhythmic/metric accent that establishes the F♭ powerfully in the upper register of the voice. This gives rise to an "erroneous" structural line carrying the voice over its first subphrase: from the D of Angst, through the E♭ of *Hoffen,* to the F♭-rather-than-F of *beklemmen.* A good deal of the large tonal action of the piece can be fruitfully regarded as working around the problem posed by this "erroneous" gesture. The problem can be stated as follows: given a strong D-to-E♭ as a point of departure, to follow this by F-not-F♭.

One notes such work going on first in the piano under the third line of text. Having abandoned its high register after the D5–E♭5 of measure 1, the piano returns to that register next only at measure 5, where its E5 picks up the "wrong note" in this connection. An effort to hear across, from the E♭5 of measure 1 to the E5 of measure 5 in the piano, is aided by the possibility of hearing measures 4½–5 as a varied retrograde of measures 1½–2½ (across the caret). Having thus picked up the "wrong" note at measure 5, the piano now very clearly projects the idea of "F-not-F♭ via the transformation of measures 5½–6½, in relation to measures 4½–5½. The E5 (or F♭) of measure 5 is thereby "corrected" to F5 on the second eighth of measure 6. The correction is celebrated in the last half of measure 6: after the by now familiar lead-off of the first three thirds, one hears the crucial D–E♭–F

my remarks on song Number XI of this cycle in "Toward the Analysis of a Schoenberg Song," Chapter 15 of the present volume; Jan Maegaard, *Studien zur Entwicklung des dodekaphonen Satzes bei Arnold Schoenberg* (Copenhagen: Hansen, 1972); and Edward T. Cone, "Sound and Syntax," *Perspectives of New Music* 13/1 (Fall/Winter): 21–40.

This essay was written in 1975. During the intervening time an interesting article on Opus 15, by Richard Domek, appeared in *College Music Symposium* 19/2 (Fall 1979): 111–128. In the final section of his article, Domek engages some of the same material from No. VII that I discuss in the present chapter, and he relates this material to a larger overview of the cycle as a whole.

itself in the upper register. The piano breaks off here with a *beklemmt* caret, but the D–E♭–F is passed on to the voice, to begin the new large section of the song at measure 7.[10]

With this event, the linear incipit figure of minor second-major second finds its downbeat, as well as its "correct" pitch-class level. That figure has been ubiquitous as an intervallic incipit since measure 2. Every subphrase, in fact, has led off with it: vocal C♯–D–E in measure 3, vocal A–B♭–C in measure 5, and piano B♭–C♭–C♯ in measures 4½, 5½, and 6½.[11] The "clicking into place" of the figure metrically, as well as transpositionally, at the bar line of measure 7 is a strong indication that the voice, in the new section of the song, is ready to take over initiative from the piano in working on the problem at hand. The downbeat vocal D4 of measure 7 specifically refers us to the downbeat vocal D5 of measure 1, the only other vocal downbeat in the song that begins a line of text: we are dealing with that D, and the problem arising from the "erroneous" structural line that began there, as the voice gets underway here.

Let us restate yet once more the problem that the piano solved in the first section of the song, which the voice is to deal with presently: given a strong D-and-E♭; to follow this by F-not-F♭. The strength of D-and-E♭ as a point of departure for the voice hereabouts is plain enough: the new lines of text at measure 7 and at measure 9 both depart therefrom. Beyond that, the voice cadenced on a strong D–E♭ at the end of measure 6, going on without pause into the opening D–E♭ of measure 7. (The piano also keeps the two pitch-classes in the air through mm. 7–8½ in the inner voice of its chords.)

Going on in the voice part, one is strongly aware of "F-not-F♭" at the cadence in measure 8. The cadential E-up-to-F is striking, for one thing, because it is the only line-ending in the text at which the voice cadences upwards. This cadence is, in fact, more than a local event; it very strongly summarizes an overall tonal motion for its entire two-measure vocal subphrase. The vocal line of measures 7–8 articulates naturally into two segments: "Daß ich mich an rast" and "und schlaf nicht kehre."

The first segment is symmetrical about F♭ and pauses momentarily on that pitch at its end, thus moving the D–E♭ of "daß ich" temporarily up to the "wrong" note F♭. The situation is then "corrected" by the second segment, which is symmetrical about F, ends on the F, and indeed wedges in on the F, with the final local cadential gesture of E-to-that-F that I have just discussed. The cadence figure thus

10. Note again in this connection that there is no vocal rest at the beginning of measure 7, a feature that helps the singer pick up where the piano left off. The absence of a rest also tone-paints the local text, particularly if the singer can actually get from measure 5 through measure 8 without taking a breath. In that case, the exhaustion to which the text refers will be quite audible in the vocal quality.

What is the dynamic in the piano at the end of measure 6? Does the *ritard* go into the new tempo or under it? How is the *ritard* to be paced? It would be nice to have definite answers to these questions, but there do not appear to be any.

11. Over the piano's G–B♭ in measure 2 we heard the "wrong" F♭ of *beklemmen.* Under the G–B♭, when it returns in m. 3, we hear E4 in the voice. This makes it plausible to regard that E, like the F♭4 at the end of measure 1, as a "wrong" E: one that "should be" an F. One can then further regard the C♯–D–E in the voice at measure 3, the first occurrence of the *incipit* figure, as being already charged with an urge to "correct" itself by moving up a semitone, following the "correction" of its E (F♭) to F. That urge would then specifically discharge at the D–E♭–F with which the voice begins measure 7.

summarizes the relation of the two segments whose progression, one to the next, composes-out the idea of "F-not-F♭, following D–E♭ as point of departure."[12]

Having accomplished its work in the lower octave over measures 7–8, the voice is now ready for the *scène à faire* in the upper octave, over measures 9–10. This is a touchier matter, recalling much more directly the *Hoffen* and *Beklemmung* issues of measures 1–2. But, with the aid of the melisma (unique in the song) to get up the octave from the already established F4 to the high-F-instead-of-high-E, the voice manages the task, albeit in highly *beklemmt* rhythmic fashion. The notion of *Beklemmung* is particularly apt because the line of text is, uniquely, missing one foot. This, to me, is clearly the climax of the piece. Although the voice has been on higher pitches (about which more later), it did not have to work so hard to get to them, nor was its work so dramatically thematic. And, this climax past, the voice immediately begins to head for the final cadence, aiming for the augmentation material of measures 12–13 that will work itself out to that cadence. Having accomplished the job of "correcting" F♭ to F, in both octaves, the voice is willing and eager to supply the "correct" F–E♭ for the wedge at measure 16, as discussed earlier. It will be left to the piano at that point to "say" for the singer what the singer cannot consciously "say" to herself: this "corrected" F-and-E♭ pair itself can be heard resolving, through *begehre* and beyond, all to the greater ultimate glory of E as tonic center of inversion at measure 17. The F having thus resolved to E, the "wrong" F♭ of the *Hoffen* in measure 19 will turn out to be in some part "right" after all, as prolonging the tonic E.

The piano is in fact already beginning to warm to that new job over measure 9 and following. Having already finished its "F-not-F♭" work some time ago, it is by no means so taken with that idea now as the voice is. Rather, it is already toying with the notion of letting its F "resolve" back down to E, foreshadowing measure 17.

Example 16.5

By means of the arpeggiated *Hoffen* forms displayed in Example 16.5, the piano plays first with moving F5 down to E5. Then, supporting the vocal thrust up, the E5 with its *Hoffen* form moves back up to F5 with its form, and apparently stays there for good as the piano moves on to its own climax elsewhere. But, after vocal and piano climaxes are past, the arpeggio moves F5 back down (yet again) to E5 with its *Hoffen* form, and leaves off there.[13]

12. A subtle touch here: the gesture has denied E (or F♭) as a local center-of-inversion, for the first segment, replacing it by F as a local center-of-inversion. But E, while "wrong" as a blue substitute for F, is absolutely "right" when functioning as a center-of-inversion, as ultimately at measure 17. So the ambivalence is displayed here. The piano is certainly unhappy about something on the last half of measure 8. Is it about the voice's having denied E as center-of-inversion? The strange behavior of the accompaniment at any rate calls added attention to the cadence of the subphrase.

13. The reader who is familiar with my essay on Number XI of the cycle (the previous chapter of this volume) will recognize familiar material in the top line of the piano from measure 10½ to 11½. Compare the discussion of the approach to measure 20 in the chapter on Number XI. The appear-

The piano then does not really support the voice's large-scale push up from E to F here, beyond the local support it supplies during the melisma itself. The piano is already playing with resolving F to E as well, trying both ideas out alternately. Nevertheless, the accompaniment does in fact project a large structural push up a semitone hereabouts, although E and F are not involved. Example 16.6 sketches what is involved.

Example 16.6

The earlier vocal climax at measure 4, while not so hard-earned as the F5 of measure 10, presented the highest pitch of the voice in the song. It was powerfully accented not only by the rocketing anacrusis, but even more by the octave coupling between voice and piano. The poetic function of the accent was to attach the symbolic *Seufzer* label firmly to the chord in the piano at that moment, but the accent is far greater than necessary for that purpose alone. So strong is it to my ear that I have little trouble hearing the pitch material picked up by the piano in measure 7½–8, as indicated in Example 16.6. This recall of G5 and A♭5 from measure 4 is certainly one of the salient aspects of the particular chords used here as variants of measure 1.

Through that intermediation, one hears the pitch complex in question moving up a semitone to the piano's climax at measure 10½ (anticipated a measure before). Like the earlier vocal climax, that of the piano presents the highest pitch for the instrument in the piece. The climax is also analogously accented by a sharply rising anacrusis. Finally, the striking octave coupling between voice and piano recurs, even more striking now that the voice is an octave below. These large-scale associations, then, project the sense of a powerful push up a semitone at measure 10½ in the piano. Even though the voice's E-to-F is not specifically involved in the pitch structure of the event, the voice's effort is in some sense given support by the parallel gesture in the accompaniment.[14]

ance of such "magic chord" material here indicates a definitive articulation of the action. There is to be no more work on the "F-not-F♭" idea; now we are heading elsewhere (toward m. 17). Compare also the right hand in measure 13 of Number XI.

14. Interesting here is the unique resolution in this song of a *Hoffen* form to a fourth-chord. Indeed, the fourth-chord B♭–E♭–A♭ is the "correct" one to go with the augmented triad from the beginning of measure 7, by analogy to the "correctness" of the final two chords in Example 16.4c. One can hear, latent in the texture of the piano part in measures 9–11½, a good deal of flirting with various possible resolutions of *Hoffen* forms to fourth-chords. The significance of all this cannot, in my view, be satisfactorily discussed in the context of the present song alone. Reference to events in other songs from the cycle would be necessary.

Continuing with Example 16.6 from measure 10½: the model of measure 4 is still followed in transposition. The minor ninth leap down is now composed-out elaborately, via the attacks on the successive quarter-note beats of measures 11–12. The enormous rhythmic expansion of the ninth leap, from the model of measure 4½, lends support to the notion entertained earlier that the pianist can project at least measures 11½–13½ as if an "ametric" cadenza, in the interests of trying to project the beat on measure 13½ as if for a "second measure" of a measure-group.

We can now easily hear the A♭ and the G on the quarter-beats of measure 12 hooking up with the subsequent entrance of "the wedge" from Example 16.3. In this connection, one recognizes the "misfit" chord of the motive as the climax chord from measure 10½, down an octave. The "extraneous" B♭3s of measures 9 and 10, alternating with the B♭4s on the bottom of the climax chords halfway through those measures, are the same B♭3s as the "misfit" B♭s from Example 16.3. They keep alive the potential "tonic" function of the pitch-class B♭, as a center of inversion. The tonic function is represented, in both cases, by allowing the B♭ to hang about as a bass note floating below the rest of the tonal action.

Identifying the misfit chords of Example 16.3 with the climax chord of measure 10½, where Example 16.6 "moved up" a semitone, we can hear Example 16.6 "moving back down" again at measure 17, where the last misfit chord resolves to the *Seufzer* chord. We are moved back down by association to the *Seufzer* of measure 4, the point of departure for Example 16.6.

Thinking over the large-scale relation of measure 4 to measure 10½ to measure 17 as involving the notion of "up a semitone, then back down again," the specific pitches one hears in connection with the large-scale structural "sigh" are surely G♯ (or A♭, of *Seufzer* at m. 4), to the high A of the piano climax in measure 10½, and then back down to the A♭ of measure 17, via the misfit-to-*Seufzer* upper voice. This A♭-and-A relation, in the pitch organization of the piece, seems to go along with the idea of "given D-and-E♭." Example 16.7 indicates what I mean, at least through measure 10. One notes particularly that measures 4½ff., in addition to their "retrograde" character discussed earlier, can also be heard as a varied inversion of measures 22ff. The inversion is about A-and-A♭. And that is the same pitch-class inversion as inversion-about-D-and-E♭. The inversion is apparently being used as a technical means to "compose-out" the function of its central dyad-pair(s), just as the little vocal segments in measures 7–8 "composed-out" their respective centers F♭ and F.

Example 16.7

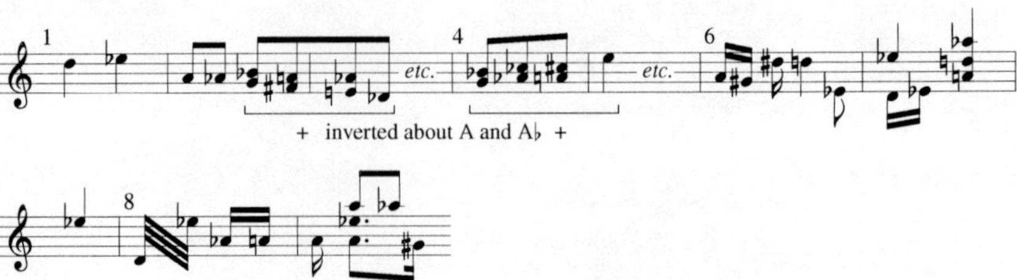

I will stop here, having outlined a "way into" the song, as the title of this chapter promised. A myriad of analytic and performance problems are left untouched. I hope only to have conveyed enough sense of what I perceive as the through-lines of the piece, to indicate a large framework within which such matters may be examined with an ear toward their function in the work as a coherent unity.

Plate 16.1 Schoenberg, Op. 15, No. VII.

Plate 16.1 cont.

11
daß ich je - de Freu - de von mir weh - re,
Sehr langsam
14
daß ich kei-nes Freun-des Trost be - geh - re.

CHAPTER Seventeen

Vocal Meter in Schoenberg's Atonal Music, with a Note on a Serial *Hauptstimme*

During the years 1908 to 1916, Arnold Schoenberg composed a number of important works involving solo voice. Some of these works have a curious feature in common: at the entrance of the vocal part, when its pitches and rhythms begin to interact with those of the text, a regular meter is projected which is in conflict with the written meter of the notation. The vocal meter and the written meter are each at times more or less in conflict with and, at times, more or less supported by the rhythms of the accompanying instruments.

In this practice, Schoenberg was no doubt influenced by Brahms. But one cannot bring to a study of Schoenberg's works from 1908 to 1916 the same presumptions one brings to Brahms's tonal compositions.[1] I propose to focus on three of Schoenberg's pieces that exhibit the characteristic feature described earlier, and to examine critically some rhythmic aspects of their openings. In order of study, the three pieces are Opus 21, Number II ("Columbine" from *Pierrot Lunaire*), Opus 20 ("Herzgewächse"), and Opus 15, Number V ("Saget mir" from *Das Buch der hängenden Gärten*).

I shall not attempt to integrate my observations with pitch structure in any systematic way. Indeed, I shall offer only a few formal generalizations of any sort. Nevertheless, I hope to demonstrate a consistency in Schoenberg's hearing and thinking as he employed this technical feature in diverse compositions, a consistency that can be useful for further investigations into Schoenberg's rhythmic

1. For example, the conflict between the heard 3/2 vocal meter and the written 4/4 meter, at the opening of the song "Immer leiser wird mein Schlummer," Opus 105, Number II, is resolved by the powerful authentic cadence in measures 8–9. The heard meter of the *Hauptstimme* at the beginning of the Horn Trio, Opus 40, is supported by the accompaniment. The opening music is heard in 2/4, which is also the written time signature, but the strong beats that are heard occur consistently a quarter note off the notated strong beats. This state of affairs persists throughout the entire first theme, which elaborates dominant harmony; it is "corrected" by the powerful entrance of the tonic harmony in measure 29, supporting the cadential downbeat of the first theme and providing the initial impulse for the bridge section. The presumptions which we bring to discussions such as the above include our taking as clearly understood such notions as "authentic cadence," "dominant harmony," and "tonic harmony."

practices. To illustrate the point, I will conclude with a comment upon the opening and the reprise in the first movement of the Fourth Quartet, Opus 37.

Let us begin by studying Example 17.1a, a hypothetical setting for the opening two lines of text in "Columbine." The meter of the example, which I shall call the "vocal meter," is clearly supported by traditional aspects of text-setting. Specifically, that meter is supported by accents arising from the text-stresses, the agogically accented notes, and the local high pitches of the *Sprechstimme*. The rhythm-and-contour profile for the second line of text is a variant of the rhythm-and-contour profile for the first line. Indeed, the rhythm of measures 3–4 (except for the grace note) is exactly the same as that of measures 1–2, and the contour of measures 3–4 is an intensified expansion of the contour in measures 1–2.

Example 17.1b intensifies and expands the climactic "Wunder–" even more. The expansion now affects not only contour, but also rhythm and even the regularity of the vocal meter: vocal measure 3 must add a beat to accommodate the rhythmic expansion of the setting. The resulting new rhythmic motive, comprising a dotted quarter and three eighths, will be called the *Wunderrhythmus*; it is bracketed in Example 17.1b. In similar spirit, I shall attach the label of *Mondlichtsrhythmus* to the rhythmic motive comprising an eighth rest, an eighth, a dotted quarter, and another eighth, bracketed in Example 17.1a. Example 17.1b is the opening of the vocal part in the piece, except that Schoenberg writes this material using the metric notation shown in Example 17.1c.

I shall call the meter of Example 17.1c the "written meter," in contrast to the "vocal meter" of Examples 17.1a and 17.1b. The written meter is amply audible in the violin part, which is a dynamically prominent *Hauptstimme*. Up to the final quarter note of the violin in written measure 5, every note of that instrument is either an eighth note, or less, or a dotted quarter, or greater. In this context the notes a dotted quarter or greater take agogic accents, and such notes are attacked at the bar lines of written measures 1, 2, 4, and 5. The A♯ and G♯ of the violin, attacked on the first and third beats of written measure 5, echo its B♭ and G♯ from the first and third beats of written measure 4; this relation supports and projects the written meter. As a further articulation of that meter, the rhythmic figure in the violin that fills written measure 4 can be heard as a variant of the rhythmic figure filling measure 2. One recognizes the latter figure as the *Wunderrhythmus*.

The piano also associates the rhythmic content of written measure 4 with that of written measure 2. The total pattern of attacks in the piano during each of those measures projects the *Mondlichtsrhythmus*. So does the total pattern of attacks in the piano during written measure 5. The *Mondlichtsrhythmus* comprises, of course, the total rhythmic content of written measure 1 in the voice; the rhythmic motive thus functions as a quasi-ostinato that supports and projects the written meter through almost the entire phrase under examination.[2]

2. Readers who go on in the piece will note returns to the *Mondlichtsrhythmus* in the piano, "correctly" placed metrically, within written measures 12, 15, and (particularly) 21. Measure 12, which picks up the *Mondlichtsrhythmus* from the voice and violin in measure 11, is a big cadence preceding a return of the opening violin figure. A *Luftpause* (of about an eighth) between measure 12 and measure 13 is of excellent effect. It enables the pianist to articulate the legato figure of measure 13 away from the staccato *Mondlichtsrhythmus* of measure 12. At measure 21, the *Mondlichtsrhythmus* of the piano

Example 17.1

Having heard the written meter, as well as the vocal meter, functioning constructively in the passage, let us now study how the two metric systems interact. Two, and only two, attack points in the music correspond to the onset of strong quarters in both the vocal and the written meters. These points are at the attacks of the

underlies the same rhythm in the voice; both coincide with the reprise of line 1 in the text, featuring the name of our motive: "des Mondlichts bleiche Blüten . . ."

words "bleiche" and "weißen." Examples 17.1a, b, and c show how these attacks fit both meters. The internal rhyme of the two words at issue is no coincidence. Schoenberg has seized on a structure of sonic correspondences in Hartleben's German text which cuts across the formal metric arrangement of text lines. Example 17.2 portrays salient aspects of that structure. Note how Schoenberg's setting of "Wun–" as a melodic climax raises the pitch of the vowel, so that it more closely resembles the vowel of "Blü–," with which it corresponds in the scheme of the example.

Example 17.2

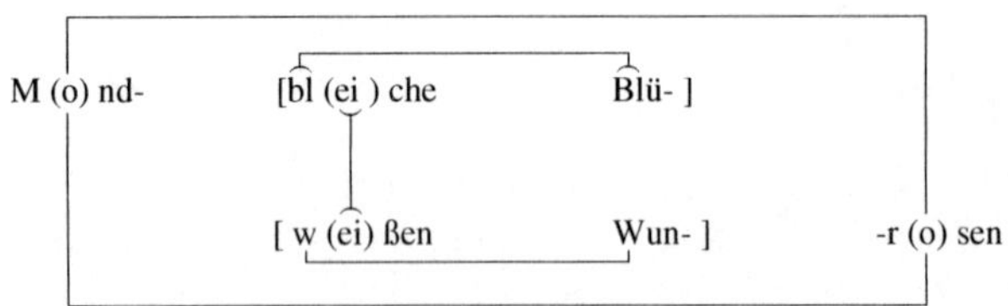

Our attention was drawn to the scheme of Example 17.2 by the unique correspondence of "bleiche" to "weißen" in the relation of vocal and written metric schemes: the attacks of the words uniquely correspond with strong quarters in both the meters. The written meter on its own interacts yet more forcefully with the scheme of Example 17.2. The rhythmic setting of "weißen Wun–" in the vocal part of written measure 4 is exactly the same as the rhythmic setting of "bleiche Blü–" in the vocal part of written measure 2 (save for the grace note). This is a unique correspondence in the phrase: every other written measure has its own indigenous rhythmic profile in the vocal part. I have already noted the rhythmic coincidence of written measures 2 and 4 in the violin part (*Wunderrhythmus*), and also in the piano part (*Mondlichtsrhythmus*); hence the "rhythmic rhyme" of written measure 2 and 4 is virtually complete, interacting with the correspondences of the two bracketed textual elements within Example 17.2.

The vocal meter, unlike the written meter, works against the scheme of Example 17.2, interacting instead with the poetic meter of the text:

Here "weißen" associates primarily with "Mondlichts," the two words taking the initial stresses of their respective isometric lines of text.

The metric structure shown above is manifest in Example 17.1a, the point of departure for studying the vocal meter. The stress on "blei–," subordinate to the textual stresses on "Mond–" and (especially) "wei–," is also subordinate to the musical stresses on those syllables in the vocal meter. (See Ex. 17.1a and b.)

This discussion highlights the unique metric status of "weißen." Its attack occurs at that one point in the phrase which projects both a bar line of the vocal meter and a bar line of the written meter. As a vocal bar line (see Ex. 17.1a and b), "weißen" supports and is supported by the textual correspondences displayed above; as a written bar line (Ex. 17.1c), it supports and is supported by the textual correspondences displayed in Example 17.2. Two observations are in order. First, the interplay between vocal and written meters in the music, the object of inquiry here, reflects and is reflected by the interplay between distinct modes of poetic organization in the text. Second, since the stress at the attack of "weißen" is a unique point of connection in both text and music about which this interplay pivots, one can speak of that attack with assurance as the structural downbeat for the entire phrase. The musical interplay of conflicting vocal and written meters, so cogent in representing diverse structural aspects of the text, is also crucial in defining the structural downbeat.

The melismatic treatment of "Wunder–" deserves some more attention. As noted earlier, it continues the process of intensification and expansion that relates the second pair of vocal measures, in Example 17.1a, to the first pair. The rhythmic expansion of Example 17.1a into Example 17.1b introduces vocal metric irregularity into the setting at the point where the cadential rhythmic figure of "–rosen" answers the textually and rhythmically analogous "Blüten." At the same time, the rhythmic expansion of "Wunder–" also makes the cadential rhythmic figures fit the written meter in exactly the same way. The metric placement of "–rosen," across written bar line 6, agrees with the metric placement of "Blüten," across written bar line 3. So the written meter, which notably does not associate the initial feet of text lines 1 and 2 in their metric placement, notably does so associate the final feet of the two text lines, by virtue precisely of the melisma on "Wunder–."

Example 17.3

The entire complex of interrelationships just studied becomes a thematic aspect of *Pierrot Lunaire* after its introduction in the second song. Example 17.3, for instance, shows how a striking reworking of the idea appears in Number V, "Valse de Chopin," where the chaste longings of "Columbine" are transformed into chords of uncontrollable desire (*wilder Lust Akkorde*).

The *Lustakkorde* are presented by the piano in exactly the rhythm of Example 17.1b. Accordingly, Example 17.3 assigns to this material the vocal meter of the earlier example, which becomes the "piano meter" here. The tempo of Example 17.3 is close to that of Examples 17.1a and b (the composer's metronome marks appear in the examples). The piano meter in the "Valse," like the vocal meter in "Columbine," is heard against a written 3/4 meter. The contending meters, however, fit differently in the waltz. Example 17.3 shows the coincidence of piano-meter bar lines with written-meter bar lines at written measures 16 and 19. Filling each of those written measures in the voice part, at "Wilder Lust" and "eisgen Traum," is a rhythmic figure comprising a dotted quarter, an eighth, and a tied quarter. This is the same rhythmic figure that set "bleiche Blü–" and "weißen Wun–" in the earlier song, where the figure also filled just those measures which followed attacks stressed by both of the contending metric systems. As it were, the *bleiche Blüten* and *weißen Wunderrosen* of "Columbine" have been recalled from memory, transformed into *bleiches Blüten* and *weißen Wunderrosen* by the necrophiliac "Valse."

∾

The approach to the opening of "Columbine" has thus enabled us, among other things, to get a good overall analytic "fix" on a complex passage from the waltz. It would be difficult to get such a clear fix on the overall shape of the *Lustakkorde* passage by plunging at once into its pitch analysis, whether by ear or by a theoretical system. (Ex. 17.3 does not include any pitches from the very active and canonically related winds in the quoted passage.) The concept of "vocal meter" is equally useful in connection with other passages whose pitch structures are notoriously recalcitrant to analysis. Much ink has been spilled, for example, in attempts to find some logical principle underlying the opening of "Herzgewächse," but the strong internal regularity of the rhythm in the vocal part there has not as yet been cited, to the best of my knowledge. Example 17.4 transcribes the opening of the song, with a reduced accompaniment, into a "vocal meter."

The vocal line moves mainly in sixteenth notes, pausing from time to time on notes of greater duration. Every note longer than a dotted sixteenth is either a dotted eighth or, on one occasion, a quarter tied to a sixteenth. The agogically accented dotted eighths recur at regular intervals of time, helping to define the bar lines of vocal measures 5, 6, 7, and 8. After the bar line of vocal measure 8, the next long note occurs two such temporal intervals later, at vocal bar line 9. (The unusual length of this note balances the unusually long time we have had to wait for it.) The bar line at vocal measure 10 will be discussed later.

These features give rise to a strong rhythmic motive in 3/8, within the voice part up to vocal bar line 8. If the 3/8 meter is read backwards from the initial entrance of the voice, the piece is found to open on a downbeat in that meter; the long notes of vocal measures 1 and 2 occur on downbeats of that meter, and the accompaniment rhythms of those two measures are analogously placed with respect to the meter. The vocal meter puts a downbeat on the high F of vocal measure 4; that beat, which interacts nicely with the tonic accent on the pitch, is very useful to the singer as a cue for her entrance on the low F an eighth later. It also provides, as it were, a dotted eighth's worth of the pitch-class F, beginning at vocal bar line 4; thus it fits in nicely with the regularly recurring dotted eighths in the voice at vocal bar lines 5, 6, 7, and 8. The meter shown in Example 17.4 interacts well with the metric scheme of the text:

Meiner müden Sehnsucht blaues Glas
deckt den alten unbestimmten Kummer,
dessen ich genas,
und der nun erstarrt in seinem Schlummer.

Example 17.4

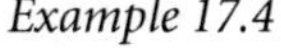

Each of lines 1, 2, and 4 hangs on two principal stresses in the text, a medial stress and a final stress within the line. The stresses of line 1 are on "Sehn–" and "Glas"; these syllables underlie the dotted eighths at vocal bar lines 5 and 6. In line 2 the final stress is on "Kum–"; this underlies the dotted eighth at vocal bar line 8. From the text underlay at vocal bar line 7 we can infer that Schoenberg heard "un–" as the medial stress of line 2. I myself tend to read "al–," not "un–," with that function. Probably Schoenberg was influenced by the assonance of "un–" with "Sehn–" The stress on "un–" also suits his rhythmic motive.[3] The medial stress of line 4 is on "–starrt," which underlies the long note at vocal bar line 9. The final stress on "Schlum–" is one of the factors influencing me to hear vocal bar line 10 where I have written it in Example 17.4. I shall explore other factors presently. Given the text-setting so far, this textual stress, in rhyme with "Kum–," will assert itself to some extent in the music.

The isolated stress "–nas" of text line 3 also asserts itself in the vocal meter, but not so strongly. Clearly, the situation is much more complex as regards this rhythmically deficient line of text. "–nas," where it comes in the text, serves as a medial stress for a hypothetical line 3 that is never completed. "–nas," rhyming with "Glas," also serves as a final stress for this line of text.[4] To put the matter another way: line 3 is clearly incomplete, but it is not clear whether the first or the last half of the line is missing.

Without going deeper into textual analysis, we can say that the stress on "–nas" and the missing material of line 3 generate disruptive metric complexity in the text. The disruptive complications are reflected in the vocal meter of Example 17.4: the stress on "–nas" comes an eighth later than we expect it, given the established rhythmic motive, and it also underlies a dotted sixteenth, rather than a dotted eighth. The earlier setting of the subsidiary stress on "al–" by a dotted sixteenth tells us that such an event does not define a vocal bar line. The effect may be described as follows. The attack on "–nas," rhyming with "Glas," disrupts the 3/8 vocal meter by coming an eighth too late. Because of the text stress and rhyme, and all the more while the sixteenth note is being prolonged through its dot, we imagine a vocal bar line at "–nas" and hence tentatively hear vocal measure 8 as a 2/4 measure. The high F from the bar line of vocal measure 4 returns in the accompaniment under "–nas," which lends support to this hearing. But "und" comes on too soon; we realize that "–nas," like "al–," underlies only a dotted sixteenth, not a dotted eighth. Text and vocal rhythm hurtle on all the way to "–starrt," where we can finally hear our vocal bar line. Then we reinterpret our earlier tentative hearing: vocal measure 8 is not a 2/4 measure but a hemiola of two 3/8 measures into one 3/4 measure. The function of the mini-stress at "–nas" is thus to define the hemiola while suggesting, but not realizing, the possibility of a 2/4 measure in the vocal meter. Vocal measure 9 then realizes the latter possibility.

The articulation of vocal bar line 9, clear enough from the text stress and the rhythmic accent in the voice part, is made even clearer by the inverted caret in the accompaniment. As for the articulation of vocal bar line 10, beyond the effect of the end rhyme and the text stress, we can note the following matters. First, despite the discombobulations of vocal measure 8, a certain motivic inertia has been established that leads us to expect a vocal bar line after hearing a long duration followed by three sixteenth notes in the voice. The vocal bar line on "Schlum–" satis-

3. It is curious that "alten" does not correspond to anything in the French, which reads "mes lasses mélancolies."

4. It is again curious that the rhythmic deficiency of line 3 (and the third lines of later quatrains) does not reflect any feature of the French text. The endrhyme scheme of the German, *a b a b*, also differs from the *a b b a* scheme of the French.

fies that expectation. Second, the texturing of the accompaniment supports a strong articulation at the vocal bar line. The rest in the accompaniment that follows the bar line is twice as long as the only earlier rest in the accompaniment, the rest under "al–"; this stands out in the rather murky sonic fabric of the accompaniment. The triplet eighth rhythm, continued in a mini-ostinato following the bar line, has been heard only once before. That was in conjunction with the F–G♭–E♭ figure preceding the singer's entrance at vocal measure 4. The triplet eighths following vocal bar line 10 feature the same pitch-classes, F–G♭–E♭. The associating rhythmic and pitch-class gestures thus frame the entire vocal part of the text quatrain, both introducing the voice's entrance and commenting upon its exit. In this connection it is not hard to imagine the F on the second triplet eighth of vocal measure 10 as in some way displaced from the vocal bar line, where it "belongs" following the model of vocal measure 4. The E in the voice has presumably displaced it.

And, finally, that vocal E has a number of very powerful pitch functions in the phrase as a whole, functions that support not only a strong stress but even a structural downbeat there. The E is the last of the twelve pitch-classes to be exposed in the voice part; it thus takes an accent of chromatic completion. The way in which the vocal line has introduced new pitch classes earlier contributes strongly to the force of the completion. Specifically, by the attack of the C♯ in vocal measure 7, nine of the twelve pitch classes have been exposed in the voice part. Missing as yet are G♯, C, and E. G♯4 appears in the voice with the stressed syllable "Kum–" at vocal bar line 8; C4 appears on the infamous "–nas," and finally E4 appears at (the pickup to) "Schlum–." Note the inversional symmetry of G♯4 and C4 above and below E4. Thus, by vocal bar line 10, the listener is already strongly primed to hear the introduction of new pitch classes into the voice part as coincident with stresses (or mini-stresses) in the vocal meter. That has been the case, in fact, since the C♯5 of vocal measure 7.

The sense of chromatic completion of the pitch class E is all the stronger because the specific pitch E4 has long been sensed as a "hole" in the tessitura of the vocal melody. The very opening of that melody, up through the E♭4 of vocal measure 6, emphasizes the absence of E4 within the active range D4–G4. The voice then continues to sing either above E4 or below E4; by the end of vocal measure 9 it has sung every pitch in the range B3-B♭4 except that E. (It has also touched C♯5 once and, fleetingly, D5 once.) Thus, the E4 at vocal bar line 10 closes and completes the principal active register of the entire phrase, as well as the abstract total chromatic of pitch classes.

Example 17.5

E4 is near the center of the active register B3-B♭4, which adds to its stability. The exact center of the register is the dyad E4–F4, and it is interesting to entertain the idea that the final E4 of vocal measure 10 somehow balances the initial F4 of vocal measure 4. Indeed, the pitches in the voice part up to "alt–" are strongly balanced by inversion about E4–F4, except that E4 itself is missing from this segment of the voice part (Ex. 17.5). The actual leap from B3 to B♭4 in vocal measure 6, spanning the boundaries of the principal active register at the end of Example 17.4, is also interesting. In this context, the final G♯3 of vocal measure 10, three semitones below B3, presumably answers the C♯5 of vocal measure 7, three semitones above B♭4.

Example 17.6

Example 17.6 cont.

Let us now look at the written meter for this passage, as shown in Example 17.6. In "Columbine," it was not hard to hear musical features of the accompaniment projecting the written meter. Here, it is not so easy. So we shall temporarily defer considering what the musical meaning of the written meter might be, returning to this important critical issue after further rhythmic analysis. Assuming that the written meter means something, if only an abstract idea on Schoenberg's part, I shall proceed formally as I did with "Columbine," looking for places where significant stresses of both metric systems coincide. The following coincidences occur:

1. Vocal bar lines 2, 4, 6, and 8 coincide with quarter-note attacks in the written meter, though they are "second quarters" rather than downbeats of the written 3/4 measures. Vocal bar lines 1, 3, 5, and 7 are all of the quarters of the written meter.
2. The stress on "–nas," which unsuccessfully tries to define a vocal bar line and successfully creates a vocal hemiola, does appear on a written bar line. It is the first attack in the vocal melody to do so.
3. The stress on "–starrt" resumes the pattern of (1): it is a vocal bar line and the attack of a second quarter in a written measure.
4. The attack on "Schlum–," already analyzed in many ways as the main structural downbeat of the phrase, is a unique attack that begins a measure in both the vocal and the written metric systems. In this respect, its metric role is formally analogous to that of the attack on "weiß-" in "Columbine."

From these observations, a consistent reading for the metric action of the phrase can be constructed. That action, achieved at the structural downbeat on "Schlum-," is to bring the evolving written meter (Ex. 17.4) into conformity with the regular written meter (Ex. 17.6). The way in which the action is accomplished is preeminently logical. For, given the abstract problem of a primary meter in 3/4 and a secondary meter in 3/8 whose bar lines coincide with the third and sixth eighths of the primary 3/4 measures, how does one logically transform the secondary system into the primary? First, one transforms a suitable pair of secondary 3/8 measures by a hemiola into a secondary 3/4 measure; this brings the quarters of the hemiola meter into alignment with the quarters of the primary meter, as symbolized by the transformation of Example 17.7a into Example 17.7b.

Example 17.7

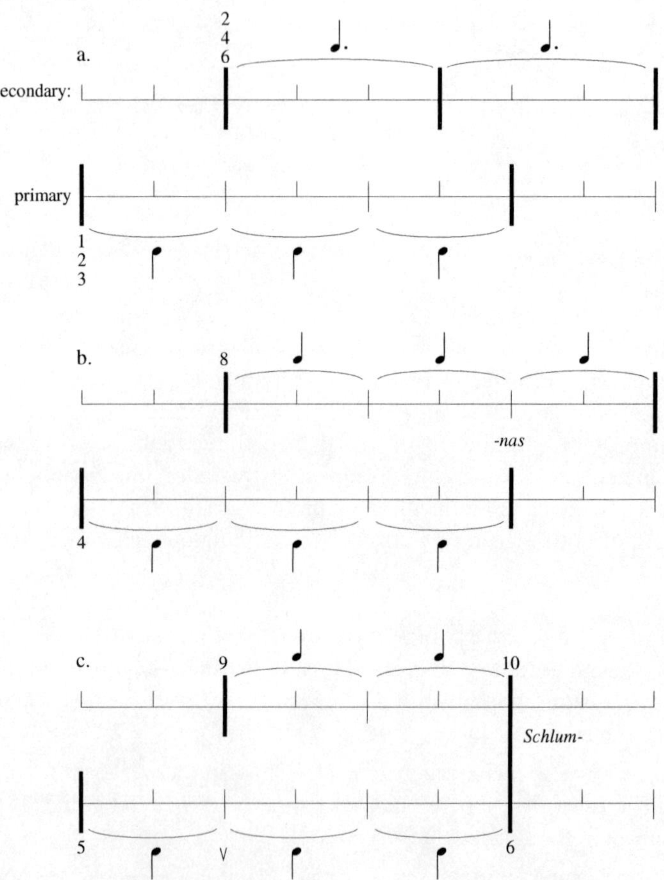

Next, following the transformation of Example 17.7b into Example 17.7c, one takes the new secondary 3/4 and drops a quarter-note beat from it; this brings the bar lines of the two meters together at the end of Example 17.7c. The change from 3/4 to 2/4 in the secondary meter is not a permanent reorientation to a duple metric system; rather, it is a one-time affair, a way of losing one beat, of resetting a watch by one hour, as it were, when crossing a time zone, here the time zone whose boundary separates the two 3/4 meters of Example 17.7b.

Now the abstract "logic" of the transformations just discussed is, in fact, the actual process by which the initial 3/8 vocal meter in "Herzgewächse" is transformed, to reach its structural downbeat at vocal bar line 10. The pattern of vocal bar lines 2, 4, 6, and 8, coinciding with the second quarters of the written measures, sets up the "condition" of the logical problem "given" in Example 17.7a. Pertinent vocal and written bar lines are indicated in the example. The stress on "–nas" is indicated in Example 17.7b. The transformation of 2a into 2b, creating the hemiola and suggesting the possibility of a vocal 2/4 measure, is thus effected by the weaker of the two stresses in the vocal meter which is also a written bar line. And the stronger such stress, on "Schlum-," effects the transformation of 2b into 2c by means of the promised 2/4 vocal measure, which drops a quarter-note beat.

The idea of dropping a beat was, I have no doubt, suggested to the composer by the "missing" half of line 3 in the text, even though the musical manifestation of this idea is deferred from "–nas," where it appears in the text, to "Schlum–," where it appears in the song. Perhaps Schoenberg felt that one definitely senses the loss of a half-line of text only at the end of the quatrain, where the overall rhyme scheme and poetic meter finally become clear.

The fact that the two stresses common to both meters, on "–nas" and on "Schlum–," effect the two transformational gestures of Example 17.7, gestures that govern the metric action of the phrase, creates to my ear the strongest sense in which I "hear" the written meter. That is, I hear an important change of state occurring at written bar line 5, and another important change of state occurring at written bar line 6, where there is also a strong downbeat. The rhythmic relation of those two "transformational beats" itself projects the written meter of the phrase, in conjunction with the rhythmic accent on "–starrt," a subordinate accent in the written meter which articulates the quarter note as a sub-beat.

Beyond that, I think the written meter must be inferred from the way in which the vocal meter transforms itself. That is, the vocal meter, in undergoing its transformations subsequent to vocal bar line 8, behaves as if it were trying to accommodate itself to some other meter, as yet unheard. At "Schlum–" we become aware that this other meter is in fact the written meter, partly because the process of accommodation is now complete, and partly because the rhythm of the two beats through which the transformational process occurs itself projects the written meter. It is as if the vocal meter were a character alone on stage: up to vocal measure 8 it behaves consistently in its own way; then its behavior begins to change, and because of the nature and rhythm of those changes the influence and proximity of another, perhaps more central, character who has not yet appeared on stage can be inferred.

∾

The next piece demonstrates the utility of analyzing vocal meter in connection with the structure of an entire song, not just its opening. Example 17.8a transcribes the vocal rhythms and pitches of Number V from *Das Buch der hängenden Gärten*, setting them in a "vocal meter" with the text beneath.

Example 17.8

The meter of the example generally fits the rhythmic accents of the melody and the text stresses of at least the opening three lines; even more, it displays a basic rhythmic motive that sets each of the first three lines of text, with minor variations from one line to the next. This motive, which fills each of the first three vocal measures, comprises three submodules of two quarters each, thus projecting the vocal meter of $3/2 = 3 \times 2/4$. In the motive, the medial submodule is characteristically the active one, both rhythmically and in registral span. Line 4 of the text is set to a rhythmic transformation of this basic motive. It will be useful to work the transformation out more explicitly as shown in Example 17.8b.

The first stage of Example 17.8b is a hypothetical setting of line 4 following the musical model of vocal measures 1, 2, and 3. This setting, like that of the earlier lines, puts a strong rhythmic accent on the final text stress of the line, here on the word "hole." Stage 2 replaces each 2/4 submodule of stage 1 by a 3/4 submodule, adjusting the internal rhythmic content of each submodule accordingly. This results in a total meter of $9/4 = 3 \times 3/4$, in place of $3/2 = 3 \times 2/4$. The "active" medial submodule is bracketed. The final text stress on "hole" is still respected by this setting. The third stage of Example 17.8b is vocal measure 4 of Example 17.8a. The transformation here exchanges the total rhythmic content of the second and the third submodules. As a result, the third submodule becomes the "active" one. This destabilizes the cadential effect of the line ending by speeding up, rather than slowing down, the rhythm. The cadence is also destabilized by the setting of "ho–" in the middle of a group of eighth notes: the rhythmic accent we expect on that syllable is conspicuously denied.

I will tuck away for future discussion the critical question: what does the far-reaching transformation of the basic motive, into the form of vocal measure 4, have to do with a compositional conception of the song? At present, let me continue with an overview of Example 17.8a, noting only that the rhythmic regularity of vocal measures 1–3 has been forcefully discombobulated by vocal measure 4. In my view, this discombobulation temporarily breaks down the vocal meter completely, so that I analyze the setting of lines 5 and 6, in Example 17.8a, out of any vocal meter. (I am ignoring the written meter for the time being.) What I hear is rather a play of various diffracted 2/4 and 3/4 submodules over lines 5 and 6. The diffracted submodules are displayed in the example by brackets. The alternations and permutations of the submodules develop consistently the ideas underlying the two transformations of Example 17.8b: 2/4 and 3/4 submodules have analogous functions; and submodules may be permuted among themselves. Text lines 5 and 6 are also framed by comparatively long rests, emphasizing their "out of meter" character with respect to the vocal metric scheme of Example 17.8a. It is still interesting that the nonbracketed material of the line 5 setting in the example comprises three quarter-notes in sum, and the nonbracketed material of the line 6 setting comprises two quarters. These are potential submodule durations; perhaps one can imagine submodules of rests to have been split up and wrapped around the two line-settings, to envelop them.

At the end of the text, the singer returns to the motivic 9/4 meter of measure 4, in singing vocal measure 7. Indeed, the motive form that sets line 7 is naught else but the second rhythmic stage of Example 17.8b. Thus, it represents an intermediate link, hitherto missing, between the motive form of vocal measures 1–3 and the form of vocal measure 4. Specifically, it represents the basic motive of vocal measures 1–3 transformed so as to use 3/4 rather than 2/4 submodules; it also represents the rhythmic content of measure 4, but with the "active" submodule restored to its rightful place in the middle of the motive, rather than at its end. (Compare the second stage of Ex. 17.8b to vocal measure 7.)

Because of the latter relation, the cadence on "sohle" can have its proper rhythmic effect, and the song ends. The rhyme of "sohle" with "hole" is no accident, nor is the fact that the rhyming vowels are set by the same pitch, E♭4. I shall soon say a great deal more about this. For the present, it suffices to observe that "sohle" works as a cadence where "hole" did not, and that the transformational structure of the vocal metric scheme is heavily involved in the cadential effect, not just locally (because "soh–" is a half note where "ho–" was an eighth note), but also in the large (because the motive form of vocal measure 7 provides a resolving balance and link between the form of measure 4 and the forms of measures 1–3).

While the medial submodule of vocal measure 7 regains its rhythmically active function, it conspicuously does not regain its registrally active function. It is rather conspicuously inactive registrally, simply treading water in that respect. The final submodule, setting "sohle," is therefore all the more conspicuous for its registral initiative. Indeed, the low A3 is truly spectacular in the context of the entire vocal part. All of the text lines so far have cadenced with a semitone or a whole tone, so the tritone leap is unexpected, particularly at the very end of the song. Furthermore, the listener has, as yet, had no inkling of the low register in the voice which this leap exposes, a register which is "way too low." To some extent, the low A tone-paints the effect of the lady's imagined tread on the poet's cheek; this grinds his face into the mud so that the last note emerges, as it were, *bocca in fango*. But the idea of "way too low" is very thematic in the poem as well. The phrase is metaphorically appropriate, depicting the utter self-abasement of the kingly speaker at the denouement. "Way too low" is also appropriate to describe the vowel pitch of the word "hole" when it appears in the spoken text; that vowel pitch is of course recurring on "sohle." To appreciate the unexpected lowness of "hole," the written text should be consulted:

> Saget mir auf welchem pfade
> heute sie vorüberschreite,
> daß ich aus der reichsten lade
> zarte seidenweben hole,
> rose pflücke and viole,
> daß ich meine wange breite,
> schemel unter ihrer sohle.

Given the meter and rhyme of the text through line 3, we expect the rhyming word "breite" at the end of line 4, where it would make excellent sense. "Hole" not only disrupts the expected rhyme, but it also does so by introducing a vowel pitch that is "way too low," given the pitch of "breite" and indeed the general tessitura of all the vowel pitches over lines 1–4 in the text. So there is a pronounced and, so far, puzzling disruption of the text pattern at the end of line 4. Here we see the source of the disruptive and so far puzzling transformation of the basic rhythmic motive in Schoenberg's setting, from the form of vocal measures 1–3 to that of vocal measure 4.

But what is the dramatic point of these transformations, textual and musical? To see this, consider the situation of the poetic speaker. He is a king, one of the few facts that George's cycle makes clear, and his beloved is within his domain, hence within his absolute power. He wishes to prove his love by a suitable gift. But what gift, in this situation, can be recognized as genuine and truly heartfelt? The king considers three gifts in turn as the poem progresses. First, he considers gossamer silk fabrics: presumably he will spread these out for her to walk on (*zarte seidenweben breite*); the rhyme scheme so far suggests this, as I have noted, and there does not seem to be any other reason for his anxious desire to intercept her with such a presentation while she is taking her daily walk. But can this gift be accepted as a truly heartfelt manifestation of his love? Surely not, for even the most costly and exotic fabrics come cheap to the King of the Hanging Gardens. Such a gift would display only his own power and ego. So "hole" substitutes for "breite" while the king takes thought, already mistrusting his first gift. He will *fetch* the silks, and . . . what? One still expects "in order to spread them before her," given the text and rhyme scheme so far. But, after "hole," the king realizes the inadequacy of this idea, and he abandons it.

The sound of "hole" has triggered the consideration of a truly suitable gift. Logically enough, the two later text lines that end-rhyme with "hole" concern themselves respectively with the second and third possible gifts, of which the third proves satisfactory (to the king). Line 5 considers the gift of flowers that the king has plucked himself. (Only flowers whose names contain the long "o" vowel come into consideration.) This gift is certainly better: after all, even the humblest swain picks flowers for his love. But there is still too much of ostentation in this gift. The king is, after all, the King of the Gardens; these are *his* flowers, not any old flowers he has chanced to find, and their beauty is still and again a manifestation of his power, dominance, and ego.

The final gift is thus deemed worthy in the imagination of the king because the thing being given is precisely his own power, dominance, and ego: he becomes a helpless, submissive object in the very act of giving. This presentation is the sole gift which the absolute monarch can give as a person, not as a potentate. He will indeed spread out something rare for her to walk upon, as seems to have been his original idea with the silks (*zarte seidenweben breite*), but he has come to realize that what must be cast down into the dirt (as low as A3) is his own rare person, rather than any precious object in his regal possession. Thus, "breite" finally appears after all, but only after the complex investigation launched by "hole" has led away from "seidenweben breite" to the solution, "meine wange breite." Perhaps only a series of paintings by Klimt could do full justice to this fantastic conception: the king standing at enormous height in his baroque oriental panoply of majesty and power, then prostrating himself upon the ground (at the vocal portamento in line 6, which traverses the entire throat register of the singer from the heights to the depths), and finally placing carefully on the path before his beloved, with deliberate and humble devotion, the delicate silken luxury of his own cheek, exquisitely shaved, pumiced, perfumed, and rouged for the occasion.

We can now appreciate the overall compositional structure of the vocal meter presented earlier in Example 17.8a, as that structure develops and becomes transformed through the song. The discombobulating metric transformations at vocal measure 4 correspond to the problems raised by the inadequate gift of silks. The temporary loss of the vocal meter and the tentative reshuffling of metric submodules, over lines 5 and 6 in Example 17.8a, correspond to the search for the answer to those problems, that is, the search for the worthy gift. The metric "solution" of vocal measure 7 corresponds to the resolution of the dramatic problems by the discovery of the worthy gift.

The pitch structure of the voice part interacts effectively with the text reading and metric analysis earlier. The melodic phrase that sets line 1 comprises rising whole-steps B4–C♯5–D#5 in the upper register and descending semitones F♯4–F4–E4 in the lower register, until the cadential D4. That tone continues the descent in the lower register, but by whole-step rather than semitone. One naturally becomes curious about the absence of E♭4 in this context. Its absence is made all the more striking by the cadence of vocal measure 2, enharmonically on E♭5–D5. This "corrects" the cadence of measure 1, but in the wrong register. (The king has no problem "being high," but he does have a problem "being low.") At the opening of vocal measure 3, the cadence of measure 2 is retrograded and E♭5 is left hanging high in the air while the voice explores its middle register. The latter exploration continues up to the cadence of vocal measure 4, on the notorious "hole," where the registrally active submodule abruptly carries us down to the crucial E♭4, and to the crucial cadential dyad E♭4–D4. These events would solve the problem posed by the absent E♭4 of measure 1, were it not for the speed of the submodule, depriving "hole" and the E♭4 together of a suitable rhythmic accent for the cadence. The music for line 5 picks up the high register; specifically, it picks up the chromatic ascent D5–E♭5 from vocal measure 3, and continues the chromatic line with E5–F5. The underlying link in the text is effective: "daß ich . . . rose pflücke." The composite line D5–E♭5–E5–F5 sets forth, in retrograde and in too high a register, a gesture that was *not* stated in vocal measure 1, that is F4–E4–E♭4–D4. At line 6, the king prostrates himself. The vocal portamento, already mentioned, appropriately transfers the high register to the low register; the pitch-class F now appears as F4, not F5. And now the gesture F4–E4–E♭4–D4 can appear, once the king has abased himself. It occurs specifically on the text "wange breite," and the crucial E♭4 at last appears with rhythmic support, on the stress of "breite." The E♭4–D4 of "breite" transfers the E♭5–D5 of the rhyming "schreite" down to the proper (i.e., low) register. It also corrects the too-fast E♭4–D4 of "hole," to a metric submodule capable of projecting the text stress with suitable rhythmic accent. Recall that "breite" really belonged, in some sense, at the end of line 4, where "hole" substituted for it with dynamic consequences. The elaborate transformation of the melody for vocal measure 1 into the melody for line 6 deserves exhaustive study in itself. Here it suffices to note that the entire chromatic gesture F♯4–F4–E4–E♭4–D4 is projected, recapitulating the entire low register of vocal measure 1, along with the E♭4 that was missing there. (The F5 that ends line 5 in the voice is connected to the F♯4 that begins line 6 via the accompaniment, which plays F–F♯ in octaves, in the pertinent registers, while the voice pauses between lines 5 and 6.)

The "problem of E♭4" being solved at "breite," the music turns its attention to solving the problem of the vocal meter during line 7, in the manner already analyzed. As far as E♭4 is concerned, vocal measure 7 is a coda, confirming the arrival and stability of that pitch. The reiterated F4–E♭4 is fruitfully heard as a transposition of the "pfade" cadence on E4–D4, following the analogous transposition of "mir, auf welchem" into "daß ich meine." I cannot pursue that topic here to the point of doing it justice.

In sum, the "problem of E♭4" interacts cogently with the earlier textual and metric analysis, as does the careful use of high and low registers in the melody. I would be very pleased at this point if the reader has forgotten that Example 17.8a does not reflect the written meter of the song: this would demonstrate forcefully my point about the utility of "vocal meter" as an analytic tool. I shall content myself with only a brief discussion of the written meter; its detailed analysis would draw us deeply into the musical totality of the song, and I do not have the space here for such extensive work. Example 17.9 shows the first two measures of the piece.

The written meter continues throughout the song in groups of 2 × 3/4 written measures. The downbeats of the 3/4 measures, and of the 6/4 hypermeasures, are somewhat ambiguous in the opening of the song but less ambiguous in the piano part from written measure 3 on. The abstract relation of the written meter to the opening vocal meter of Example 17.8a is similar to that relation studied in the opening of "Herzgewächse": to derive the written meter of "Saget mir" from its opening

Example 17.9

vocal meter, one could hemiola the vocal 3/2 = 3 × 2/4 into 6/4 = 2 × 3/4, and then displace the resulting 6/4 by one beat to come into phase with the written 6/4 = 2 × 3/4. Schoenberg does not carry out that transformation in this song, but it is still interesting to note the similarity of the metric relations that occur within the two pieces. (The relation of vocal to written meter is the reverse, here, from that in "Herzgewächse.")

The accompaniment meter, with its quasi-sequential music, supports the internal rhyme of "Saget" with "pfade" in line 1; later events will similarly support the rhymes of "heute" with "–schreite" in line 2, and of "daß" with "lade" in line 3. Naturally, this situation changes drastically over line 4. (Perhaps the word "zarte" is already wrong: to preserve the internal rhyme we should have something like "leichte seidenweben breite." Perhaps "reichsten" and "seiden–" deserve further textual analysis in connection with this touchy rhyme.)

On "pfade," and similarly later on "–schreite" and on "lade," the text stress is supported by the beginning of a submodule in the vocal meter which corresponds to a bar line (but not to a hyperbar line) of the written meter. This pattern, relating the regular written meter and the regular vocal meter over lines 1–3 in the text, is broken in line 4: "hole" receives neither the stress of a vocal submodule nor the stress of a written bar line.

The written meter exercises more influence over rhythmic events within the vocally ametric lines 5 and 6. "Pflü–," the "–o–" of "viole," and "wan–" each begin both a vocal submodule and a written measure; "pflü–" is unique as the beginning of a written hypermeasure to boot. "Pflü–" is further unique because the accompaniment drops out beneath it.

There is no coincidence of stress between any written measure and any submodule of vocal measure 7. So the "solution" of the metric problem within the internal vocal metric structure of Example 17.8a does not entail bringing the vocal meter and the written meter into alignment. The relation of vocal to written meter in the piece cannot be approached in such a straightforward way. This relationship is complicated by the association of strong recurrent thematic ideas in the piano with the written metric structure. For instance, the piano music of written measures 3–4 recurs climactically at written measure 15, where it is subsequently extended to govern the last four written measures of the accompaniment. Written measures 15–18 basically underlie vocal measure 7, but the climax chord at written bar line 15 is actually attacked earlier, in the middle of "breite." Its prototype, the chord at written bar line 3, was attacked in the middle, not of "–schreite" but of "heute." This association, in the piano music, of "breite" with "heute" seems purposeful, expecially since the "heute . . . –schreite" rhyme has already been pointed by the written meter, at its bar lines 3 and 4.

The piano music that underlies the vocal reprise in line 6 of the text is also a reprise. But the piano, unlike the voice, does not reprise its opening music here. Rather, the piano repeats a theme we have already heard twice before, once roughly underlaying line 3 and once roughly underlaying the first two-thirds of line 4. This theme, as it occurs three times with varying continuations, surely engages the notion of the three gifts; its definitive last appearance under line 6 makes sense in that connection, as does its earlier appearance under line 4. But its apparently premature appearance under line 3 is puzzling in the same connection. (It does tie together the "daß" that begins line 3 with the "daß" that begins line 6.)

Here, in the attempt to find a cogent relation between vocal and written meter, we are in the presence of another rhythmic technique much favored by Schoenberg, which I like to call "time-warp." The general technique may be described as follows: an association is set up between a sequence of gestural events in time-system 1, and a corresponding sequence of events in time-system 2. The rhythms in which the corresponding sequences go by, however, are not the same. The discrepancy may be the result of an algebraic transformation, or it may be nonarithmetic.[5] I have just noted two examples of time-warp in the large formal rhythm of this song; both were of a nonarithmetic character.

For another example of the technique, on a smaller scale and of an algebraic nature, Example 17.9 may again be consulted. The structural line F♯4–F4–E4–D4 of the vocal part is doubled by the upper voice of the piano chords. But the doubling does not underlie the singer exactly; rather the following algebraic scheme obtains:

On the F♯, the piano is a quarter later than the voice.

On the F, the piano is an eighth later.

On the E, piano and voice are synchronous.

On the D, the piano is an eighth earlier than the voice.

In sum, the piano gains an eighth-note on the voice with the entry of each new pitch in the line. Given the vocal part and the synchrony of attacks on the E, the piano rhythm here could actually be "deduced" logically from this scheme. (I would not care to assert, though, that it *should* be conceived as so generated.) The attack of both parts on the E supports the local stress on that note, a mini-stress in

5. Phenomenological matters pertinent to such discrepancies have been discussed by Judy Lochhead in her article, "The Temporal in Beethoven's Opus 135: When Are Ends Beginnings?" *In Theory Only* 4/7 (1979): 3–30. Her dissertation will go farther in this direction. [Lochhead's dissertation at the State University of New York at Stony Brook was completed in 1982 as "The Temporal Structure of Recent Music: A Phenomenological Investigation."]

both the vocal and the written metric systems. More significant over the long run is the fact that, once the E is past, the piano anticipates the next note before the voice sings it. And that note is, very precisely, "not E♭4." So the absence of E♭4 from the cadence of the text line, an absence with powerful implications over the entire song, is not just the singer's idea. Rather, the idea is first suggested by the piano and then accepted by the voice. Is that acceptance willing? Or has the piano, by forging ahead, put something over on the singer? What does the piano represent anyway, so far as the singer and the audience are concerned? I do not propose to answer these questions here but only to indicate, by posing them, that the relation of vocal to written meter (piano meter) in the large structure of this song cannot be analyzed by means as straightforward as those used in discussing earlier examples.

∾

Nevertheless, I hope to have made it abundantly clear by now that "vocal meter" is an important tool toward the analysis of "Saget mir," just as it was an important tool in approaching the passages studied before. In fact, the idea that underlies the notion of vocal meter can be extended fruitfully to the analysis of music by Schoenberg which is neither vocal nor from the "atonal" period 1908–1923. For instance, Example 17.10a transcribes the opening theme of the Fourth Quartet, Opus 37, into an intrinsic "violin I meter."

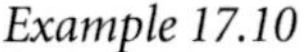
Example 17.10

This meter respects the rhythmic accents within the theme, the accent mark on the F and, most particularly, the stress mark on the A♭. It articulates the tetrachordal structure of the row, one of its several important internal structurings. It interprets the theme as a thrice-stated rhythmic motive, distorted by time-warp upon its second appearance but restored, upon its third, almost to its original form. The motivic equivalence of the first and third measures in the example, with the special stress symbol over the A♭, can hardly be overlooked when one considers the reprise of this theme later in the movement (written measures 165ff.), which occurs in an exact isorhythm but transposed by a (pitch-class) tritone (Ex. 17.10b).

The tritone relation between the opening of measure 1 and the opening of measure 3, in Example 17.10a, is thus expanded to become a giant tritone relation between the entire opening theme (Ex. 17.10a) and its entire reprise (Ex. 17.10b), a very notable constructive feature of the movement as a whole.

The written meter is 4/4 throughout, starting from the beginning of Example 17.10a. It is supported by the attack pattern of the accompaniment over written measures 1–3.[6] At hand, too, is yet a third powerful mode for organizing the rhythms of the theme, though this mode is not metric: that is the palindrome of durations which the theme projects up through its G, shown as Example 17.11.

Example 17.11

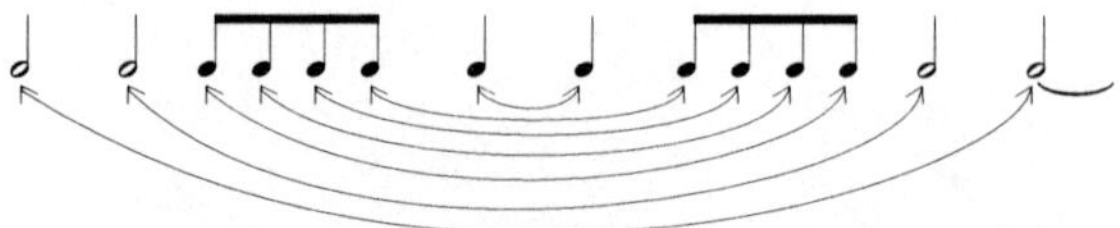

Confronting such a bewildering pile-up of rhythmic systems, we can at least say this: just as Schoenberg considered his extraordinary pitch networks to be "pantonal" rather than "atonal," so can we consider his extraordinary rhythmic networks to arise from the abundant profusion of various metric and other rhythmic structures, rather than from the absence of such structures.[7]

6. Martha MacLean Hyde, "A Theory of Twelve-Tone Meter," *Music Theory Spectrum* 6 (1984):14–51, has also demonstrated cogent interrelations of the 4/4 meter with the segmental structure of the row and its harmonic implications.

7. A profusion of contending potential metric systems, whose influences ebb and flow over the course of a passage, emerges clearly from the analysis of Opus 19, Number VI, which I presented in "Some Investigations into Foreground Rhythmic and Metric Patterning," *Music Theory, Special Topics,* ed. Richmond Browne (New York: Academic Press, 1981), 101–137.

The reader who is familiar with "A Way into Schoenberg's Opus 15, Number VII" (Chapter 16 of the present volume) will recall my attention there to the thematic textual idea of *Beklemmung*, in connection with musical techniques pertinent to some of the matters discussed in the present chapter.

George Fisher's article, "Text and Music in Song VIII of *Das Buch der hängenden Gärten,*" *In Theory Only* 6.2 (1982): 3–15, discusses some implications of the vocal meter, especially over the first three lines of the text, in an illuminating analysis.

Harold Lewin's article, "Schoenberg's *Pierrot Lunaire*: The Rhythmic Relation between Sprechstimme and Instrumental Writing in 'Eine blasse Waescherin,'" *Theory and Practice* 5.1 (1980): 25–39, contains very sensitive discussion of both the piece and the issue the title raises, an issue which has also been of central importance in the present paper. Lewin's approach and mine are interesting to compare, both as they contrast with each other and as they supplement each other. (So far as I know, we are not related.)

Finally, Schoenberg's own article on "Brahms the Progressive" in *Style and Idea,* ed. Leonard Stein (New York: St. Martin's Press, 1975), 398–441, encourages me in many ways to continue the line of thought presented in this chapter.

CHAPTER Eighteen

Moses und Aron
Some General Remarks and Analytic Notes for Act I, Scene 1

The dramatic idea of this work hinges on the paradoxical nature of God: the *Unvorstellbares* that commands itself to be *vorgestellt.* The musical metaphor that reflects (or better defines) the dramatic idea is the nature of the twelve-tone row and system as "musical idea" in Schoenberg's terminology. "The row" or "the musical idea" is not a concrete and specific musical subject or object to be presented for once and for all as referential in sounds and time; it is, rather, an abstraction that manifests itself everywhere ("allgegenwaertiger") in the work. And yet it can only be perceived, or realized, by means of an aggregation of specific *Vorstellungen*, even *Darstellungen*. Or, more exactly, the composer may perceive it as a sort of resonant abstraction, but it remains unrealized and unfulfilled until it is manifested through performance and communicated to an audience by means of material sounds, representing the idea in all its manifold potentialities.

In this connection, the multiple proportion—God : Moses : Aron : Volk equals "the idea" (row) : composer (Schoenberg) : performer : audience—is suggestive. Moses, like Schoenberg, perceives directly and intuitively a sense of divine ("precompositional") order. He cannot communicate this sense directly, however. As he suggests in Act I, Scene 1, he would much prefer to spend his life in simple contemplation of this order. But God commands him to communicate it ("Verkuende!") and he is powerless to resist.

God demands that His order be communicated to the Volk. Yet how can they be taught to love and understand the immaterial and *Unvorstellbares* (the true musical experience)? They will likely mistake this or that specific material manifestation of it (especially when brilliantly performed by Aron) for the idea itself. In fact, this is exactly what happens. To make matters worse, Moses is no performer; he cannot communicate directly to the Volk. As it turns out, he cannot even make himself understood by Aron, his sympathetic performer. This state of affairs is symbolized, of course, by Moses' Sprechstimme as opposed to Aron's coloratura tenor.

In sum, the following dramatic relationships are set up:

God loves the Volk (more than He loves Moses, as we gather from Act I, Scene 1) but cannot communicate with them directly, and they do not know or love Him.

Moses knows and loves God; he does not love the Volk, nor they him, though they fear him; he cannot communicate with the Volk.

Aron does not know God, but wants to love Him; he loves the Volk and is loved by them. Note that, in his love for the Volk, Aron is more like God than is Moses. He communicates easily with them.

Moses and Aron (the crucial link) love each other and think they know each other; as it turns out, they do not. The link breaks down, with tragic consequence.

Aron has dual allegiance: to Moses, whom he respects and tries, at first, to obey; and to the Volk, by which he gets carried away (just as the performer gets carried away by the audience even while intending to concentrate on the composer's wishes). Ultimately, his infatuation with the Volk wins out. (And we must recall that, in his love for the Volk, Aron is closer to God than is Moses in feeling, if not in understanding. Note his "Israels Bestehn bezeuge den Gedanken des Ewigen!" in II.5, mm. 1007ff.)

To what extent the tragic breakdown is due to Moses's inability to communicate clearly enough to Aron, or to Aron's inability to suspect and resist his natural affection for the Volk—this remains an open question at the end of Act II. Schoenberg evidently meant to decide this question, in the third act, in Moses's favor. But the libretto is unconvincing to me. The problem posed by the drama is not whether Moses or Aron is "right," but rather how God can be brought to the Volk. If the triple-play combination of God to Moses to Aron to Volk has broken down between Moses and Aron, and if the Moses-Aron link cannot be repaired, then the catastrophe of the philosophical tragedy has occurred in Act II and the drama is over. If there is a personal tragedy involved, it is surely that of Moses, and he, as well as or instead of Aron, should be the one to die (which in a sense he does at the end of Act II).

Remarks on the Singing-and/or-Speaking Chorus, in General, and in I.1

By opening the opera with the bush scene, Schoenberg first presents the singing-and/or-speaking vocal ensemble as the voice of God. It is important for us to have made this association *before* we encounter the Volk, who will constitute the same sort of vocal mass singing or speaking or both together. The effect is to bind God and the Volk together in a special way which, so to speak, includes both Aron (singing) and Moses (speaking). *Both* Moses and Aron are necessary to realize

God's plan. God's voice is a mixed speaking-and-singing mass, hence He seeks the Volk, who can realize the *Klangideal*. Neither Moses nor Aron, both being individuals rather than masses and vocally restricted to only speaking or only singing, is of real interest or importance to God except as "a tool," a means of focusing the two paradoxically coexistent facets of His nature. The speaking facet is identified with the "unvorstellbar" nature of God, the singing facet with His demand to be "verkuendet." (Note the absence of the Sprechchor under the text "verkuende" at m. 15 of the opening scene, and again at the end of the scene.)

Aron, the singer, is necessary for the "Verkuendigung," then. He can, for instance, pick up the tune of "Dieses Volk ist auserwaehlt . . . " (m. 71 of I.1), without even having heard it, at the end of Act I (m. 898) and feed it to the Volk for a triumphal reprise of the *sung* part of "Dieses Volk" (mm. 919ff.). But he is unaware of the overwhelmingly powerful spoken element going with the sung chorus at measure 71. From the point where Aron takes over from Moses (m. 838), there is no speaking to the end of the act. This reflects Aron's unawareness of the "unvorstellbar" part of God, and the Volk's consequent lack of understanding of it. Aron's text from measure 838 on is a compendium of material ideas and promises; his misreading of the text of measures 71ff. is also symptomatic and disastrous:

Voice of God, mm. 71ff.	*Aron, mm. 898ff.*
Dieses Volk ist auserwaehlt, vor allen Voelkern,	Er hat euch auserwaehlt, vor allen Voelkern
das Volk des einzigen Gottes zu sein,	das Volk des einzigen Gottes zu sein,
	ihm allein zu dienen,
dass es ihn erkenne	keines andern Knecht!
und sich ihm allein ganz widme;	Ihr werdet frei sein
dass es alle Pruefungen bestehe	von Fron and Plage! (!)
denen in Jahrtausenden der Gedanke ausgesetzt ist.	Das gelobt er euch:
Und das verheisse ich dir:	Er wird euch fuehren
Ich will euch dorthin fuehren	in das Land wo Milch and Honig fliesst, and ihr sollt geniessen
wo ihr mit dem Ewigen einig	leiblich was euren Vaetern verheissen geistig. (!)
und allen Voelkern ein Vorbild werdet.	(But cf. Exodus 3:17 . . . ! !)
	(following sung Volk chorus to the same text)

Aron here is surely the virtuoso performer, carried away in front of his audience, adding, as he thinks, expressive embellishments and "interpretation" to a piece he "knows"! Moses is, of course, the writhing composer in the audience at the concert.

In contrast, we immediately identify Moses, in I.1, with the speaking, "unvorstellbar" aspect of God. From a purely theatrical point of view, this involves our understanding those parts of I.1 in which the Sprechchor predominates over the solo singers as particularly intense for Moses. Thus: "Du muss dein Volk befrein" (m. 26) and the entire prophecy (mm. 67–85). It will be noted that these sections are those most crucially involving Moses' duty with respect to God's love for the Volk.

In I.1, Schoenberg uses a variety of means to shift the focus between the solo singers and the Sprechchor, most notably (i) relative dynamics, (ii) entry time with respect to text (who leads off, who follows), (iii) completeness vs. hocketness of text presentation.

Dramatic Structure of I.1

The scene glosses into four dramatic sections:

α: EXPOSITION (1–28). Moses encounters the bush. God commands him: "Verkuende!" (not yet specifically mentioning the Volk). Moses wants to demur, but God tells him he is not free to do so, and more specifically and forcefully commands "Du muss dein Volk befrein!"

β: AGON (29–66). Moses offers a series of objections, God counters them.

γ: THE PROPHECY (67–85) for the Volk.

δ: CODA (86–end). Transition back to the immediate situation, and "Verkuende!"

Serial Background for I.1

Example 18.1 shows the row and its hexachordally related inversion, S_0 and I_0. Hexachords, hexachordal "areas" will be denoted as follows: H_0 is the first (unordered) hexachord of S_0, the second of I_0; h_0 is the first of I_0, the second of S_0. A passage is "in A_0" when the hexachords involved appear as H_0 and h_0, or when rows used are S_0, I_0, R_0, RI_0, or when X and Y ideas (see below) appear at levels derived from S_0 and/or I_0, etc. A_1, A_2, etc. denote the corresponding transpositions of the entire complex A_0

Example 18.1

S_0 and I_0 have the same dyadic segments; also, the chromatic tetrachord 3–4–5–6 of S_0 is the same as 7–8–9–10, reordered, of I_0. Textures reflecting these segmental structures emerge in the scene.

Schoenberg does *not* state any complete row-form in I.1 in a melodic linear way. The first such statement in the opera is reserved for Aron's entrance in I.2. At the prophecy, in I.1, we do get linear melodic statements of hexachords, at 0 level, and with periodic musical construction.

Example 18.2

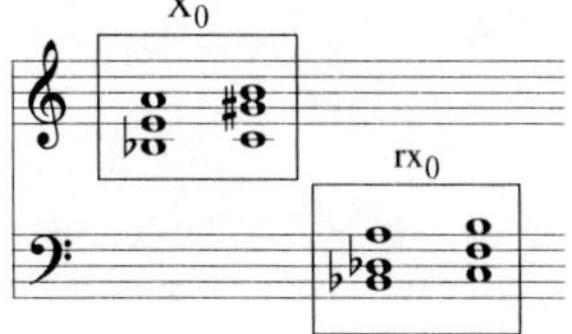

Up to that point, the principal thematic intervallic ideas are those indicated by Examples 18.2 and 18.3. Example 18.2 is the chordal progression X_0 from the first to the last three notes of the row, with answering rx_0. As first presented, the relation sounds more variational than (retrograde) inversional. Later in the scene, as we shall note, when X appears against x rather than rx, Schoenberg makes the inversional relation aurally clear. In the sequel, I will speak of X chords or Xx textures, etc. pretty loosely. It will be noted that any X chord is sufficient to define the row and area in which it appears. This is aurally very helpful in the scene.

Example 18.3

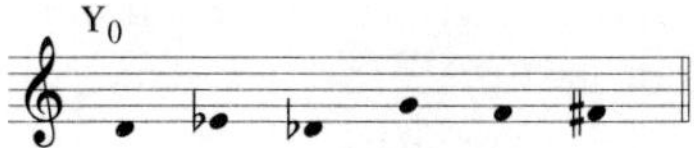

Example 18. 3 shows the melodic idea Y_0, notes 4 through 9 of S_0. The thematic idea has a preferred contour (as in Ex. 18.3) and rhythm, but is subject to some variation in these respects. It can also be split, symmetrically, in half. Note that y_0 (4 through 9 of I_0) is the same, linearly, as rY_1; analogously, $Y_0 = ry_{11}$. These relations can be used to pivot between areas related by 1-or-11 interval, and Schoenberg makes use of the property to do so in the scene (mm. 50½–53½, mm. 67–70, m. 85). In the passages just cited, A_0 is "inflected," in this way, by both A_1 and A_{11}; A_8 is inflected by A_7 . . . (presumably).

The reason for "presumably" is that, although there is only one occurrence of $Y_8 = ry_7$ (so that it is not intrinsically clear which is accessory to the other), the area A_8 is very clearly one of the important secondary areas in the scene, and it is frequently preceded or followed by A_7 or A_9 (without the use of the Y-pivot).

It will be noted that both the X and Y ideas contradict the hexachordal, dyadic and 3–4–5–6 vs. 7–8–9–10 articulations of the row. This abstract "tension of textures" is realized in the scene by the use of musical textures in the chorus that reflect the abstract one. Of course, the X and Y ideas are not only compatible, but serially complementary with each other, and are so employed in the music to a great extent. In the course of the scene, the chorus moves from X texture (with Y obbligato, representing Moses, in the orchestra) at the opening of the scene, to more dyadic textures approaching the prophecy, to linear hexachord statements with fairly dyadic accompaniment at the prophecy, and then returns to its original X texture in the coda.

Analysis of α Section (Exposition)

The chorus sings in A_0 up to the end of the section, where it breaks loose violently into A_5 at "Du muss dein Volk befrein!" (m. 26), generating energy for the following section. The Xx chords belong to the singers. They sing nothing else until "so kannst du nicht anders mehr" (m. 25), where we get a sort of "serial *Zug*" in the women's voices (passing through the row from the first X_0 chord to the second one), and x_0 linearized against y_0 in the men's voices. At measure 26, the singers return to X chords, but in A_5. Here x, rather than rx, is presented against X, bringing out the inversional rather than "variational" relation, as the A_0 area is left. (But all this is greatly covered by the Sprechchor dynamically and in the text-setting.)

The chorus is thus essentially a *static* musical element until the end of the section. This reflects its dramatic position. It is *Moses* who introduces tension into the scene. Correspondingly, Moses's music is very active in the section. He is never accompanied by A_0 row forms here, and he is very modulatory.

(We do not hear the Sprechchor until after we hear Moses speak. This may symbolize the notion that God is not "unvorstellbar" when He is singing to Himself, but only to *human beings*.)

The Y idea belongs to Moses. The characteristic slow, uneven, trudging rhythm laboriously wending its way through small intervals that is generally imposed on presentations of Y seems apt to depict musically the character that appears through Moses's self-descriptions. At Moses's first speech (mm. 8–10), Y_0 is presented melodically in the upper notes of the chords, arrhythmic but with its characteristic contour. It is harmonized by four-note chords from RI_1 and S_{10}. The function of neither the texture nor the row-forms is clear to me, but they certainly do introduce contrast, while presenting a melody that will "go with" the serial area of the chorus.

The melody is, in fact, picked up immediately by the orchestra, in A_0, as obbligato to the following choral statement; presumably this represents Moses listening to the bush.

The local connections into and out of Moses's first speech are smooth, hinging on the tritone E–B♭: that tritone plus D pivots from measure 7 to measure 8; the tritone plus A pivots from measure 10 to measure 11. Contrast, but little tension yet, as the text indicates.

However, Moses is much disturbed by "Verkuende." He launches into his longest and most structured speech of the scene, with very sharp harmonic contrast and quick "harmonic rhythm" (total-chromatic turnover). As we shall see at the end of this chapter, the serial structure of this speech can quite suggestively be regarded as generating the large structure of the whole remainder of the scene; at any rate, it certainly introduces important areas and area relations that will figure later on.

This speech falls into two parts, dividing at measure 21 ("Ich bin alt"). The first part is, rhetorically, in form aba′b′, with the apostrophising of God articulating the a and a′:

a: "Gott meiner Vaeter . . . "

b: "der du ihrem Gedanken . . . "

a′: "mein Gott,"

b′: "noetige mich nicht . . ."

That form is supported by the music. a and a′ correspond in texture. For a, we get a quick run-through of I_9 and R_8, coming to rest in A_5 at b, with a clear thematic texture, X and Y. At a′, we get an analogous quick run-through of I_2, followed at b′ by a return to A_5 in which the serial texture clears up again, this time into dyads in measure 20. In sum, Moses's gesture here is a twofold modulatory excursion, coming to rest in A_5 both times, first with X and Y texture, then with dyad texture.

(A nice psychological touch is provided by the "groaning" modulatory X chords alternating with awful, squashy-noise chords at the 9, 8, and 2 areas, depicting Moses's reaction to the implacable static A_0 X-chords of the chorus.)

Note that it will become clear later on that A_8 and A_5 are the two principal secondary areas of the scene, and that A_9 is "supposed" to inflect A_8 via the 1-relation of areas. Hence, the area progression: 9 8 → 5, 2 → 5 may be "reduced," intellectually, to: 8 → 5, 2 → 5. Thence it will be noted that there is an inversional balance which "motivates" the choice of A_2 to balance A_8 about A_5, "tonicizing" A_5. This idea seems to go nicely with all the previous analysis of the passage, and the actual rows involved, RI_8 and S_2, do have a harmonically inversional relation. Whether one is actually aware of this, or to what extent one is, at measure 16¾ and measure 19, is somewhat hazy, to say the least, but possible to my ear.

There is still a bit of "smooth" connection from measure 15 to measure 16: the texture hints at picking up the oscillating A and B from the chorus melody into the agitated opening of measure 16; these notes recurring as a harmonic pair at the bar line of measure 17, and finally vanishing in effect as the 5-area sets in.

The second part of Moses's speech ("Ich bin alt . . .") begins with a distorted X and Y texture applied to S_8, and proceeds, in measure 22, to a straight run-through of I_9 and RI_9. Measure 21 picks up the F♯–C–F chord of S_8 from the second beat of measure 17, creating an aural link between the two 8-forms. Here, A_8 is the clearly and thematically textured area, just as A_5 was in the first part of the speech; important, since these will become the two principal secondary areas of the scene.

Example 18.4

The pickup of the chorus at measure 23 is definitely "smooth," in view of the preparation of the C–F–B in measure 22 (see Ex. 18.4). The C–F appears to refer back to measure 21 also: while several elements carry over harmonically from measure 20 to measure 21, the striking sense of harmonic change (and local arrival) at measure 21 seems most strongly created by the conjunct move from the melodic E–B–F♯

of measure 20 to the chordal F♯–F–C of measure 21; thus, the fourth C–F is what is moved to at that point. To this extent, Moses is setting up the chorus entrance (unconsciously?) at measure 23, or perhaps they are showing him that he can't escape.

The turn of the chorus to A_5 at measure 26, then, picks up that area from the first part of Moses's preceding speech. Perhaps Moses had a premonition of this most unwelcome command, or perhaps they are hitting him in his vulnerable area. At measures 26–27, Y and y forms appear in the orchestra as before, but now greatly distorted in contour (mirrorwise, as are the X chords in the chorus) probably reflecting Moses's agonized reaction to the chorus's command.

Analysis of β Section (Agon)

Dramatically, the section divides in two at 48½ ("Ich kann denken . . ."). Throughout, the chorus becomes very active in all respects (modulation, new textures, initiative for same). Up to 48½, Moses becomes more and more passive, musically as well as dramatically: here he is not so much raising real problems as offering excuses and evasions. His speeches become shorter and shorter. At 35½, 40½, and 47½, he accepts whatever serial area the chorus has left off on, and the chorus changes area with their replies (this serial situation is quite audible).

At 48½, though, Moses finally articulates a real insight and problem: "Ich kann denken, aber nicht reden." Here, Moses becomes active again musically also. He returns to the original area A_0 "all by himself" (that is, from his own preceding A_9, which he had picked up from the chorus, rather than in response to any immediately preceding nudge from the chorus). The serial return is supported by a sort of reprise of measures 11ff. This finally gives the chorus some pause; it has to stop and think during the modulatory orchestral interlude that follows. The remainder of section β consists of the chorus's answer to this real objection of Moses: first, they bolster his faith and reassure him ("Wie auf diesem Dornbusch . . ."), then they come up with a practical solution ("Aron soll dein Mund sein . . . "). The latter, of course, sets up the central problem of the drama.

(As later metric analysis will attempt to show, "Aron soll dein Mund sein . . . " carries a very big stress; it will be analyzed as *the* big A_8 arrival of the scene. In this respect, it is perhaps of note that when Aron enters, in I.2, he is singing in A_4, an area that is *antipodal* to A_8 with respect to A_0!)

While Moses soon becomes passive after the opening of section β, he is still musically active at measure 29. (Nevertheless, his speech covers only two measures, as opposed to his previous three-with-fermate and five-measure speeches.) Texturally, the gesture of measure 29 is similar to that of measure 19. The trail-off into quintuplets is a familiar aspect of Moses's complaints by now, and the I_9 form at measure 29½ can be heard, to some extent, as recalling the I_9 of measure 22.

"On paper," the preceding S_7 (m. 29) balances the I_9 about the A_8 coming up in the chorus at measure 31. As will become clear in the sequel, this relation is "supposed to be" functional, as are the 1-and-11 area relations between 7-and-8 and 9-and-8.

An aspect of measure 29 that is very audible to me is the emergence of the three-note chromatic "half-of-Y" motive as a musical carrier *across* an articulation,

Example 18.5

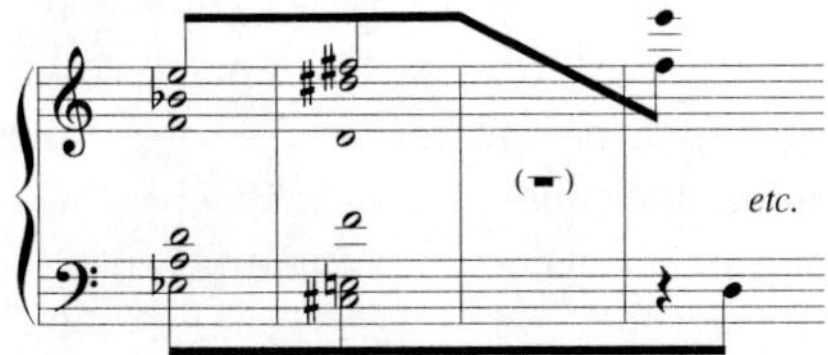

from measures 26–28 *into* measure 29. (Example 18.5 shows what I mean.) Likewise, the same motive carries the B–C♯ trill of measure 30 into the middle C of measure 31, across an articulation. While there are also some binding common-tone relations involved at these moments, we are used to that situation; the *kinetic* use of the three-note motive is new, very effective, and goes well with the activation of the Moses-chorus agon.

The speech of the chorus at measures 31–35 sits in A_8. As noted earlier, this is the "balance point" for Moses's previous S_7 and I_9. A_8, of course, picks up the other main area Moses had already exposed, in the second part of his long speech in section a. In fact, the chord on the last beat of measure 30 can be heard to pick up the relevant chords from that earlier section (second beat of m. 17, first half of m. 21).

The chorus now begins to sing the "inversional" X-against-x (as opposed to the "variational" X-against-rx), just as they did in A_5 ("Du muss dein Volk . . ."), and as they did *not* do in A_0. They do not complete the Xx idea, though; instead, they become very active serially, running through hexachords, Y motives, and so on in more or less mirror fashion.

Moses's next question (m. 35½) is supported by only one chord, a vertical h_8. While he appears to be taking the initiative rhetorically, by asking a question, the musical and serial treatment make it clear that he is really simply treading water, taking his cue from the chorus.

As before in section β, there is a strong kinetic sense about the interchanges between Moses and the chorus here. Moses's chord in measure 35½ sounds "passing," via the B♭–A♭–F♯ in the upper register, measures 35–37. (The serial rationale of the three whole-tones is not clear to me.) Also there is a three-note chromatic carrier from the E–E♭ within Moses's chord to the F–E in the men's voices at measure 36.

The chorus calms down at measures 36–40. (Why? There seems to be some sense of return to the texture preceding m. 8 here. I can't figure out what the idea might be.) They return to simple Xx chords in A_7. The Xx relation is inversional, as it always has been in secondary areas, rather than variational as in A_0.

The A♭ of Moses's "passing" chord in measure 35½ returns as neighbor to the F♯ of measure 37, and this relation is prolonged in register through Moses's subsequent extension of the chorus's A_7 area (again, in spite of his rhetorical "initiative"), up to another local stress (like m. 36½) at measure 41½. There, the chorus lands again on an X-chord, changing area back to A_5. Intensifying the situation of measure 30½, we get here only a mere hint of "X-ness" before other serial textures set in.

The longish choral speech that follows is modulatory, from the familiar A_5 through A_8 (orchestra, m. 43), through A_3 and A_9 (mm. 44, 46). Two features seem to stand out strongly.

First, the chorus begins to pick up dyadic and chromatic-tetrachord (3–4–5–6 and 7–8–9–10 of the row) textures more and more. (N.B. already the line of the chorus bass from m. 36 to 42.) As pointed out in the "serial background" portion of this chapter, these textures are incompatible with the X texture, and we may note again that (except for the mysterious sitting on that texture in mm. 36–40) there has been a progressive liquidation of X sounds in the chorus going on (noted in connection with the amount of X-reference at m. 30¼ and m. 41½). There is some hint of X-sound in the female voices at measures 44–45, but by measure 46 they have very definitely yielded to the dyads and chromatic tetrachords. This seems to have to do with God's turning to thinking about the Volk.

The second feature that stands out strongly in the chorus passage under discussion is that the B♭–A♭–F♯ idea that was introduced in measures 35–37 gets picked up and developed here into E(38)–D(41½)–C(42)–[C–B♭–B]–C(44)–D(45)–E(46½). The medial C–B♭–B is, of course, our friend the three-note "half-of-Y" motive. As I said before, I can't find any serial rationale for this three-whole-steps idea, but it does seem more than fortuitous in the music.

At measure 47½, Moses begins another stock excuse, continuing the chorus area, as he did earlier at measure 35½ and measure 40½. (We might note that the three areas, in order, are A_8, A_7, and A_9. This might be viewed as a composing out of the already cited use of 7 and 9 areas as balanced "accessories" to the 8-area, noted in connection with mm. 29–31. Perhaps both of these are supposed to compose out the "half-of-Y" motive?) His opening chord and quintuplet texture recall the old story of his earlier I_9 statements as measure 22 and measure 29½. But here we are in an *antecedent*, not a *consequent* part of his phrase, and there is a sudden and dramatic break texturally, dynamically, and serially, as he puts his finger on what is *really* troubling him: "Ich kann denken, aber nicht reden." The reprise here has already been mentioned. One notes also that Moses picks up the X and Y ideas that have just been abandoned by the chorus in favor of the dyads and chromatic tetrachords. If we recall that the latter gesture of the chorus was tied up with God's thinking on the Volk, the dramatic appropriateness of Moses's gesture here is clear, though hard to put into words. His X-chords make a particularly strong color contrast after the chords in measure 47 and the first half of measure 48.

There follows a modulatory orchestral interlude (mm. 50½–53½), involving extended chromatic wiggling à la "half-of-Y" or chromatic-tetrachord. The motion is from I_0 (RI_0?) to S_1 (R_1?), demonstrating $Y_1 = ry_0$ for the first time, and thence sequentially through I_7 and S_8, demonstrating the analogous relation $Y_8 = ry_7$. This suggests yet another rationale for the 7-and-9-surrounding-8 area relations already discussed: that it will be an analogous tonicization of the principal secondary area A_8 to the tonicization of A_0 surrounded by A_1 and A_{11} (and Schoenberg will make the latter very clear in the sequel, via the appropriate Y/y symmetries). In this connection, since measures 52–53 is the only passage in the scene that explicitly links A_8 with A_7 or A_9 via a Y-symmetry, we might note that the X-chords that appeared in the chorus S_8 at measure 31 and I_7 at 36¼ are picked up in measures 52–53. (Measures 31 and 36½ were clearly paired by the text, recalling in both cases Moses's original "Einziger, ewiger . . . " although Moses did not use those areas at that time.)

As mentioned earlier, the last choral speech of section β divides in two: bolstering Moses's faith (mm. 53⅔–59½) in A_5; then solving the practical problem via Aron (mm. 59½–67) in A_8, inflected by RI_9 and R_7. A_5 and A_8 are, of course, the two principal secondary areas of the scene, originally exposed in Moses's speech in measures 16–22. And the RI_9 and R_7 inflection of A_8 is by now an old acquaintance. The A_5 and A_8 of this chorus should be taken as the definitive "answer" to Moses's early speech, for Moses does not speak again, and, after this point, everything is very clearly in a basic A_0 (although the chorus does return to A_5 for a bit to begin its coda).

After an initial run-through of S_5, the remainder of the A_5 part of this choral passage is completely based on the dyads of A_5. (In fact the run-through itself is pretty dyadic, especially as accompanied.) All the more striking, then, is the return to inversional Xx chords for the A_8 section at measure 59½. The G♭–C–F of the female voices is a familiar tag for recognizing A_8 (cf. 17¼, 21, 31, 43? 52¾?); the chord is restated at measure 62, where we get overlapping presentations in run-through form of S_8, RI_9, R_7, and I_8. The powerful inversional Xx at measure 59½ is the last time we shall hear such a clear X texture until the coda. Because of the great power of the inversional feeling at measure 59½, and the symmetrical formal arrangement of rows in measures 62–65, the chances of our hearing the RI_9 and R_7 as balanced inversionally about A_8 seem pretty good here, in spite of (or maybe to some extent even because of) the dense texture.

Analysis of Section γ (the Prophecy)

The prophecy is articulated musically, as in the text, into two parts, each beginning with a preliminary announcement of upbeat character: measures 67, 71, 79, 81. Each part builds to a climax at its end. The second part is much more intense than the first in all musical respects.

I have a very clear sense of measure 81 being the "big downbeat" of the scene, rather than measure 71. I can't find any "tonal" reason for this. Other factors seem to indicate that 81 is a more crucial metric articulation than 71. For instance, the setting of "Und das verheisse ich dir" that precedes 81 is such as to make the text, with its built-in strong upbeat character, very clear. The rest that begins measure 81 and the purity and clarity of the sung sound in measure 81, after all the speaking static and noise preceding, create for me an enormous (negative) accent. Probably, too, factors of large-scale metric consistency are operative in my hearing here: as we shall see later, "Aron soll dein Mund sein," "Dieses Volk ist auserwaehlt . . . ," and "Ich will euch dorthin fuehren . . ." (mm. 59½, 71, and 81) are metric articulations on the same level to my hearing, and I certainly hear "Aron soll . . ." as a bigger stress than "Dieses Volk . . . ," which is of course consistent with hearing "Ich will . . ." as also more stressed than "Dieses Volk. . . ." The drama supports the latter readings, I think. "Aron soll . . ." is the release (downbeat) for all the accumulated tension of the problem of Moses involving his inability to communicate. "Dieses Volk . . ." involves vision, but not action or decision, and the section has the character of God taking a very deep breath to come out with a decisive statement of resolve at "Ich will. . . ."

Measures 67–68 present A_0 with a complex texture: in the orchestra, we have X_0 progression in whole notes, Y_0 theme obbligato, and dyads from A_0. The chorus sings the dyads, but only one note from each of the X_0 chords. (As mentioned earlier, the chorus will not return to clear X_0 sound until the coda.) Measures 69–70 are in "sequence" with measures 67–68, in A_{11}, displaying $ry_{11} = Y_0$ (and thus balancing the earlier A_0–A_1 relation at mm. 50½–51, just as A_7 and A_9 have been balanced about A_8. An analogous A_0–A_1 will, in fact, return later.)

The connection from the orchestral I_8 at measure 66 to the choral opening at measure 67 involves not only the carry-over of the G in the bass, but also, to some extent, the common-tone function of the chromatic tetrachord D♯–C♯–D–E between measure 66 and measure 67. The latter relation is noteworthy, since it demonstrates, for the first time, a *segmental* (hence intrinsic serial) relation between I_8 and I_0 (also S_0); this provides a "natural" serial basis for a link between A_0 and the important secondary area A_8. (Cf. the dyads of A_0 that open I.2 and the segment G♯–F♯–G–F of S_4 at Aron's entrance more specifically, m. 98½ff. and Aron's part at mm. 125¾–126. The analogous relation functions here between A_0 and S_4.)

The chromatic tetrachord is also used to slide kinetically into measure 71: F♯–E going to G–F at the bar line in the orchestra.

The emergence of linear hexachords in the *Hauptstimmen* from measures 71–76 was noted earlier; it seems to be the big serial event of the scene, after all the play with X textures, dyads, and chromatic tetrachords in the chorus textures. We are evidently getting close to "the idea," and, logically enough in terms of the sonorous metaphor of the opera, the Sprechchor begins to get very noisy and to take over the lead in presenting the text. The orchestra makes it clear that the accompanying voices are basically derived from a dyadic texture, though various other hints occur, notably of X-chords at "wrong" levels in the choral bass part at measures 71 and 74, and in the alto at measure 75.

At measures 77–78, the serial texture is liquidated, hexachords alone more or less taking over, reflecting the change of character in the text.

Measures 79–80 make another big textual upbeat, with analogous texture to measures 67–68 and measures 69–70.

Measures 81–84 in the sung chorus and orchestra are basically an intensification of the texture of measures 71–76. The relative dynamics of singers and orchestra versus (reinforced!) Sprechchor are disturbing here, but Schoenberg's conception is consistent, in terms of the musical metaphors: As the tonal texture becomes more and more complex, revealing and suggesting infinitely complicated relationships which one would have to strain to sort out under the most favorable conditions, the "unvorstellbar" static rises in a great swell to block Moses's (and our) perception of it.

As the Sprechchor drops out at measure 85, the area shifts to A_1, with measures 67–68-type texture. The orchestral *Hauptstimme* demonstrates $rY_1 = y_0$, balancing the events of 69–70, which demonstrated $ry_{11} = Y_0$. The soprano link B–C, A–B♭ over the bar line into measure 85 is very neat: these are the sevenths associated with the rX_0 progression, and here they are demonstrated as combining to form a chromatic tetrachord!

Analysis of δ Section (Coda)

After having whipped itself into a frenzy of sublimity, the chorus suddenly remembers Moses, who is standing there, doubtless open-mouthed and utterly clobbered. It returns abruptly, without smooth tonal connection, to its misterioso pianissimo texture, to X-chords and then dyads, in A_5. Measure 86 evidently refers back specifically to 36½, 87¾ to 41½, and 88½–89 to 55 (and thence 20), all of these being earlier A_5 moments. The idea is, I think, that the chorus is reminding Moses that all his objections were answered in section β.

I don't know exactly what the A_{10} is doing in measure 90—it certainly provides a fresh kind of contrast for the last return of A_0 at measure 91. A_{10} was used once (and only once) before: this preceding the first return to A_0 (m. 11). The analogy is intellectually attractive, but musically pretty thorny; the texture preceding measure 11 was so different (in fact, unique in the scene, and the four-note chord texture does not reappear until the equally "unique" m. 208 of the second scene: "Reinige dein Denken . . ."). Nevertheless, there may be something in the fact that the common-tone transition from measure 10 to measure 11 was E–B♭-plus-A, and that the same sonority appears at the return to A_0 in measure 91. (However, it is not conspicuous in m. 90.)

The concluding A_0 passage (mm. 91–97) presents X-chords and liquidates the Y-motive. I.e. the bush remains, *sicut erat in principio*; Moses leaves. Interesting are the harmonic tritones formed of the sixth and seventh notes of the rows that appear as a result of the Y liquidation in measures 95 and 96. These tritones *bridge* the hexachords, and perhaps, in terms of the textures we have had so far in the scene, this has something to do with their pertinence as cadential sonorities.

Further Remarks on Some of the Textures

The X-texture seems to be generally associated with God as a mystery, as drawn into Himself. (This is not to be confused with His "unvorstellbar" aspect, which involves human reaction to Him and is pretty clearly identified with speech, rather than with any tonal idea.)

One can make a good case for the dyadic texture as going with God's desire to be "verkuendet," and His thinking of the Volk (which is essentially the same phenomenon). Thus, the first dyadic texture we encounter is at measure 20, under Moses's text: "ihn zu verkuenden." The accompaniment textures for the prophecy (to the extent they are audible) are basically more dyadic than anything else, and here God is certainly thinking of the Volk. Similarly, the dyadic bias of the textures at measures 43ff. appears to go with God's imagining Moses before the Volk. The opening of Scene 2, with its veritable orgy of dyads, seems suggestive here, as heralding and accompanying Aron, who is to accomplish the "Verkuendigung."

But here we run into trouble and inconsistency in our symbolism. For the *most* dyadic chorus texture certainly appears at measures 53–58, where God is thinking about Himself communicating to Moses, not about Moses or Aron communicating to the Volk. And, along with this, we have the spectacular contrast of the X-texture, and *not* dyads, immediately following, at "Aron soll dein Mund sein . . ." According to the reading of the previous paragraph, this seems completely, even perversely, inconsistent.

In sum, I can't make consistent symbolic sense out of the use of the textures. But it is a problem of interpretation that is certainly worth grappling with, since Schoenberg handles these textures so carefully and dynamically in the scene.

Summary and Speculative Metric Analysis of the Scene

Example 18.6 attempts, first, to make sense of the area-structure of the scene, assuming that A_8 and A_5 are the main secondary areas (which is very clear), that A_1 and A_{11} are inversionally balanced accessories to A_0 (which also seems clear) and that A_9 and A_7 are analogous accessories to A_8 (which is at least intellectually convincing, in light of our preceding labors).

The A_2 at measure 19 makes good intellectual sense, as mentioned earlier, if it is regarded as balancing A_8 about A_5, "tonicizing" A_5. The 1 and 10 areas at measures 8–10 remain a puzzle (as does the passage itself—A_1 is certainly "accessory" to A_0 here only by a real stretch of the imagination). This is not too disturbing, since the melodic Y_0 at that point serves to prolong A_0. The 3 area at measure 44 and the 10 area at measure 90 also don't "fit in"; otherwise the area chart seems quite logical.

Additionally, I have attempted, largely "by ear," to articulate the scene into commensurate metric units at a fairly large level; I have indicated these articulations, which overlap the Greek-letter formal divisions of the scene, by dotted lines on the example.

This metric reading seems by and large convincing and suggestive to me. It supports Moses's entries at measure 8 and measure 16, and then indicates how God takes over the important stresses up to Moses's articulation of his "real" problems at 48½. Also, the reading seems to work well, in other respects, with the dramatic kinesis of the scene, and with the importance of A_5 and A_8 as secondary areas. (The mysterious areas at m. 8 and m. 90 are made more mysterious by the metric reading, but this, too, seems appropriate.)

Even a larger metric reading still seems suggestive: taking measure 81 as *the* big downbeat (as discussed earlier), the reading:

1 | 8 16 | 23 31 | 41⅜ 48½ | 59½ 71 | 81 90

appears logical, and stimulates thought. Thus, after the anacrustic A_0 of measure 1, the big measure | 8 16 | is dominated by Moses and his tension against A_0. Measure 23 then provides the first A_0 big downbeat, releasing this tension, as God takes over.

The foreground push from A_0 to A_5 that God then introduces with "Du muss dein Volk befrein . . . " is covered with speech static locally, but works itself out in the large progression from A_0 at measure 23 to A_5 at measure 41⅜ (the next "big

big bar line") through a subsidiary A_8 at measure 31. And this motion, from A_0 to A_5 through A_8, seems also to augment the progression of the opening of Moses's long speech (mm. 16–19, after the preceding choral A_0).

Moses' "Ich kann denken . . . " at 48½ is an A_0 upbeat, on this metric level, to God's downbeat A_8 answer at measure 59½, "Aron soll dein Mund sein." The latter, and the relative stresses at measure 71 and measure 81, were discussed earlier.

Thus, from the first A_0 big-big downbeat at measure 23, we have the following:

0́	8̆	5́	0̆	8́	0̆	0́ ⁀	
23	31	41⅜	48½	59½	71	81	90

and, reducing this, we get:

0	5	8	0
23	41⅜	59½	81

And this big progression makes excellent sense as an expansion of Moses's long early speech (mm. 16–22, together with the preceding A_0 and the following A_0 downbeat at m. 23).

It probably would be helpful to read over the analysis again at this point, following Example 18.6.

Example 18.6

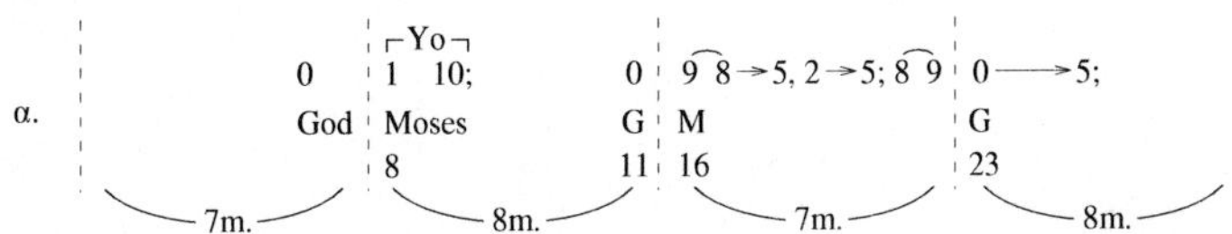

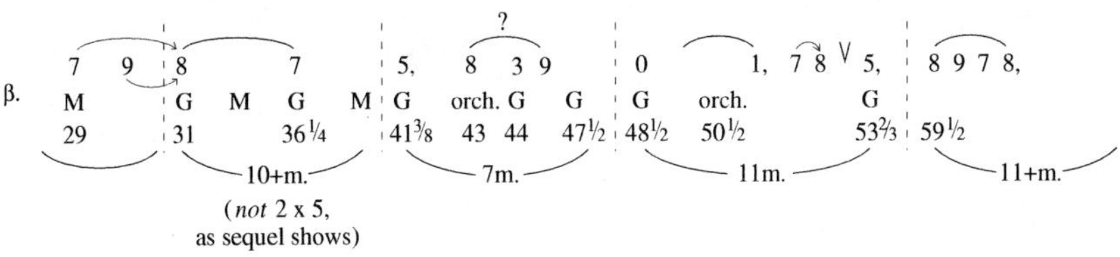

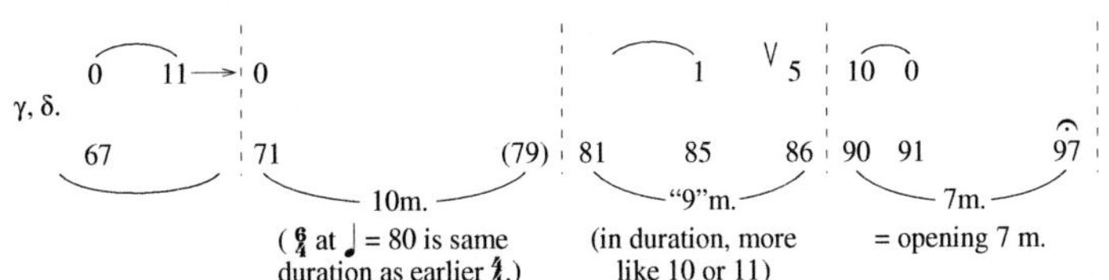

PART VII

Babbitt

This section reprints an article that was published in the *Journal of Music Theory Pedagogy*, vol. 5, no. 2 (1991), 111–132. It transcribed the keynote speech I gave at the meeting of the Society for Music Theory in Cincinnati, November 1991.

Only part of this chapter concerns a specific piece of music-with-text, namely Milton Babbitt's setting of the poem "Philomel" by John Hollander. (Hollander wrote the poem as a libretto for Babbitt.) I decided to reprint the entire article, and not just the Babbitt analysis, because of the way in which the article integrates its analytic observations with a number of more general concerns about music theory that have long preoccupied me, concerns which exercise—and no doubt have long exercised—a decided influence on the ways in which I approach music analysis in general. I find it useful to make those concerns explicit here, somewhat in the way I found it useful to go into the phenomenological issues of the earlier chapter that addressed Schubert's *Morgengruß*.

An appendix notes a reaction by the composer, in personal correspondence, to the central image I find in his work.

CHAPTER Nineteen

Some Problems and Resources of Music Theory

Many years ago I had a student at the keyboard realizing figured bass, while the rest of the class was writing down Roman numerals. At the end of one phrase, the pianist saw Example 19.1a and played something like Example 19.1b. The rest of the class uniformly reported hearing Example 19.1c.

Example 19.1

I had the pianist repeat the realization a couple of times, but nobody else heard anything to change about Example 19.1c. Finally, I put Example 19.1a and the soprano line of Example 19.1b up on the board, much to the class's surprise. "But you shouldn't be surprised," I said. "just a few days ago I was talking about 6-chords, including why our text says not to double the bass. If you remember, I said the idea behind the rule was to keep the bass of the 6-chord from asserting itself as a root. Then I talked about exceptions to the rule. One exception was when the root function would be idiomatic, for instance in the cadence formula ii^6–V. And here is just that formula. That's why you all heard a IV root for the ii^6, especially with the bass of the ii^6 doubled in the soprano here, preceded by its own leading tone."

There was a considerable silence. Then one student raised his hand and said, "Yeah, but that was just theory."

Thirty years later, I am still unable to disentangle the genius of that remark from its imbecility. Both involved the way in which the theory lecture attempted to describe a conceptually structured sound-world that was categorically prior to any particular musical event, score, or experience.

The occasion must have influenced my prose some seven years later in 1968, when I wrote that music theory "attempts to describe the ways in which, given a certain body of literature, composers and listeners appear to have accepted sound as conceptually structured, categorically prior to any one specific piece."[1] Today I am still reasonably satisfied with that view of music theory, and I shall explore various of its aspects in some detail.

Overworked terms create problems for us in describing conceptual sound-structures, and the pursuit of those problems can be enlightening. My book on generalized musical intervals arose in part as an attempt to pursue some of the ways in which the term "interval" has been overworked.[2] The overworked term "minor" was the source of another interesting exploration for me, an exploration I shall begin with another pedagogical story.

Example 19.2

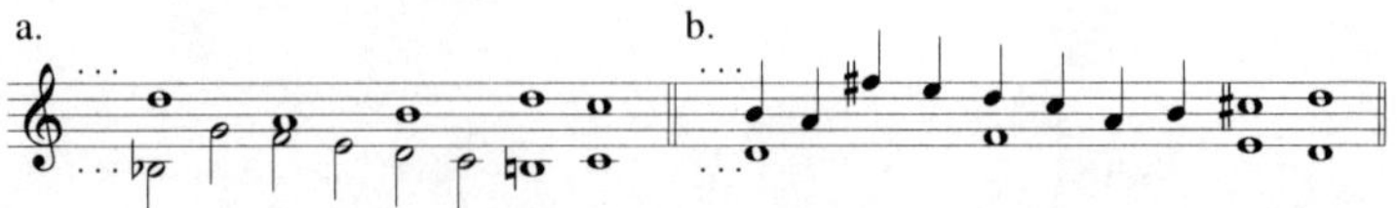

Example 19.2 illustrates typical errors in the exercises that one student, about twenty years ago, was submitting for a first-year class in Jeppesen-style species counterpoint. I kept correcting his papers, indicating why the ficta was inappropriate, and reminding him that Jeppesen forbade the MAJOR sixth leap up, while the MINOR sixth leap up was permitted. We would talk, and he would say he understood. But exercises like Example 19.2 kept coming in. Finally, at one of our agonized critiques, he said to me, "But I AM leaping up the minor sixth; that's why I need the accidentals." When I asked him what he meant, he pointed to something like the beginning of Example 19.2a and said, "You see, B♭ to G, that's G minor." Then, remarkably, he pointed to something like the beginning of Example 19.2b and said, "You see, A to F♯, that's F♯ minor."

For purposes of the first-year course, it was sufficient to remind the student that the word "minor," in this context, describes the acoustic size of the sixth, not its modal or harmonic character. But the incident triggered interesting thoughts for me beyond that. First of all, I noticed how apt for this context was Zarlino's way of describing sixths.[3] When a sixth is regarded as a fourth plus a third, or a third plus a fourth, the smaller sixth is associated with the smaller third, and the larger sixth with the larger third. My student would not have had his problems, had he originally acquired his concepts about sixths from the historically pertinent sound-world of Zarlino, instead of from some subsequent theory that had described sixths as inversions of modally charged thirds. The point about Zarlino is espe-

1. David Lewin, "Behind the Beyond, A Response to Edward T. Cone," *Perspectives of New Music* 7.2 (1969): 59–72. The quoted material is on page 61.
2. Idem, *Generalized Musical Intervals and Transformations* (New Haven, Conn.: Yale University Press, 1987).
3. Gioseffo Zarlino, *Istitutioni harmoniche*, 2nd ed. (Venice: Senese, 1573). Facsimile reproduction (Ridgewood, N.J.: Gregg Press, 1966).

cially interesting because Zarlino himself is already showing sensitivity to modal charges on thirds, both as major or minor consonances above a bass, and as major or minor third degrees in various scales.

Indeed that sensitivity seems to underlie some of the problems Zarlino has describing consonant sixths in "a conceptually structured sound-world . . . categorically prior to any particular musical . . . experience." For him, the larger sixth is conceptually always as in Example 19.3a.

Example 19.3

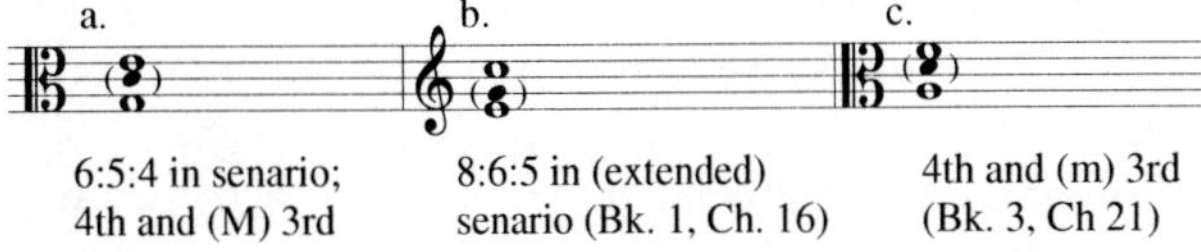

This displays the large consonant sixth as composed from elements of the senario, here 6 and 4 as divided harmonically by the mean term 5. It also displays the sixth as composed from a fourth below plus a third above. Zarlino's problem with the small consonant sixth involves an attempt to preserve both these features of his large sixth. He wants the small sixth to be composed from elements of the senario, as in Example 19.3b; there the small sixth is composed from elements of 8 and 5 of an extended senario, divided by a "mezzano termino harmonico which is 6."[4] From a modern point of view, we can say that he wants the small sixth of Example 19.3b to stay in C major like Example 19.3a, our C major here reflecting Zarlino's conceptual *Urklangwelt* of the senario. At the same time, Zarlino wants his small sixth to be constructed by minor/major analogy with his large sixth, in a manner suggested by the analogy of Example 19.3c with Example 19.3a. He says that the sixths "are composed . . . from the fourth plus the major third, or the minor third."[5] But clearly Zarlino cannot both have the minor/major analogy of Example 19.3c, and remain within the extended senario as in Example 19.3b. That is, he cannot so long as he wants to speak of "THE" minor sixth. Here the term "THE" is problematic, given his conceptual sound-world. Examples 19.3b and 19.3c clearly describe two distinct consonant minor sixths.

Example 19.4

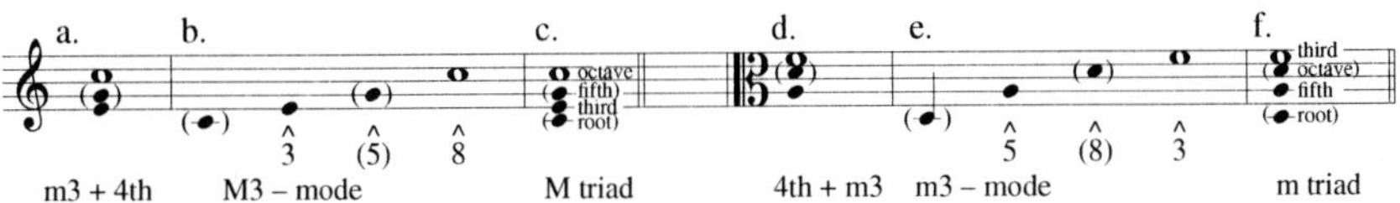

4. Zarlino, *Istitutioni harmoniche*, Book 1, Chapter 16 (33). "Mezzano termino harmonico" COULD simply mean a whole number lying between 8 and 5. Coming where it does, though, the expression seems arch if not tendentious. It recalls the same expression, used to describe the "mezzano termino harmonico" 5 that lies between 6 and 4. In that context, we are surely to understand the "mezzano termino harmonico" as a "harmonic mean."

5. Zarlino, *Istitutioni harmoniche*, Book 3, Chapter 21. "sono composte . . . della Diatesseron et del Ditono, over del Semiditono; . . . " (131).

Examples 19.4a and 19.4d distinguish the sixths as a minor third plus a fourth, or a fourth plus a minor third. Zarlino could have used this terminology, had he wished to. He could also have used the terminology that distinguishes Example 19.4b from Example 19.4e. 19.4b describes one sixth as the span from third to octave in some major-third authentic mode, mediated by the fifth of the mode. 4e describes the other minor sixth as the span from fifth to third in some minor-third authentic mode, mediated by the octave of the mode. Zarlino did not, of course, have at hand the terminology that enables us to describe 19.4c and 19.4f, where the two minor sixths are distinguished as third-to-octave of a major triad, or fifth-to-third of a minor triad. There are a variety of technical reasons why it would have been awkward for Zarlino to have distinguished two minor sixths as in 19.4ad, or as in 19.4be. More important is an overriding conceptual reason: for Zarlino, each consonance must exist as one abstract universal Platonic entity, before it is allowed to enter into a variety of contexts like those of Example 19.4. So in particular "THE" minor sixth must exist, if we are to treat minor sixths as consonances.

Example 19.5

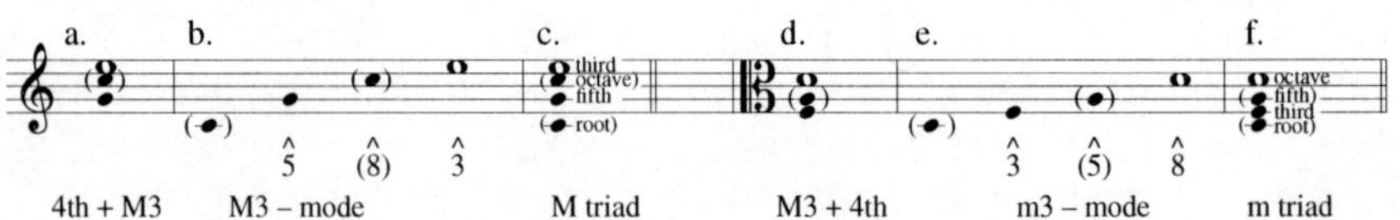

Example 19.5 shows that the same critique can be applied to "THE" consonant major sixth, even though Zarlino has no technical problems with that interval. The distinction between two different major sixths is illustrated by the student's analysis of Example 19.2. The student analyzed Example 19.2a as "B♭ to G, that's G minor." This follows the model of Example 19.5def. The student then tried to analyze Example 19.2b according to the same model: "A to F♯, that's F♯ minor." But this analysis is malformed in a way the other was not. Evidently the A–F♯ leap of Example 19.2b conforms to the model of Example 19.5abc, not 5def. However, the student was unable to say "A to F♯, that's 5–3 in D major." He couldn't say that precisely because he was trying to relate all the things he called minor sixths—that is, all the things we call major sixths—to minor modes and triads. Even sweeping up after the student, we still find the terms "minor" and "major" to be overworked. And, perhaps yet more serious, the term "THE," when applied to "minor sixth" or "major sixth," is improperly restricting the pertinent conceptual sound world. To more fully explore that world you can ask yourself these questions: in what ways is Example 19.5abc the analog of Example 19.4abc? And in what ways is Example 19.5abc the analog of Example 19.4def? Exploring those questions, you will soon hear the four consonant sixths interrelating conceptually among themselves in a very complex way.

I call Examples 19.4 and 19.5 "consonant" sixths because I can imagine the analysis of (b), (c), (e), and (f) being applied, in a more modern context, to various "dissonant" sixths. A large dissonant sixth, for example, is spanned between the fourth degree and the second degree of a major or minor scale. This sixth extends within a dominant seventh harmony, from the seventh of the harmony up to the fifth; it articulates naturally into an augmented fourth below plus a small third above. One hears the sixth when Tamino sings "wie noch kein Auge je gesehn," following the motive of "Dies Bildnis ist bezaubernd schoen." Other dissonant sixths, small and large, extend within dominant ninth harmonies, from the major or minor ninth of the harmony up to the seventh. Such a sixth is spanned from the sixth degree of its scale to the fourth degree, as divided by the second degree.

I pointed out earlier that "for Zarlino, each consonance must exist as one abstract . . . Platonic entity, before it is allowed to enter into a variety of contexts like those of Example 19.4." That involves what I shall call "the Platonic THE" of Zarlino's locution, "THE minor sixth." The world of music theory is full of such Platonic THEs, improperly constraining the discourse.

Example 19.6

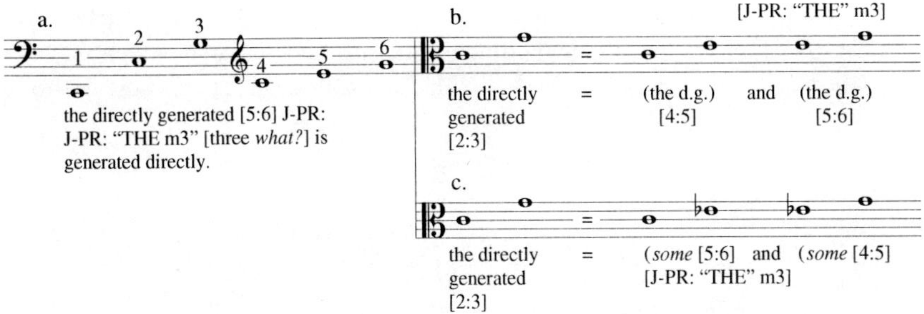

Example 19.6 shows how a Platonic THE confuses Rameau's discussion of "THE minor third" in the *Traité* (Book I, Chapter 3, Article 5). According to Rameau's earlier discussions, the E–G dyad of Example 19.6a should either be assigned a C root, or else no root at all. The same is true for the E–G dyad as it appears in Example 19.6b. There is no reason to assign this E–G dyad the root E. On the other hand, we can intuit good common-sense reasons for assigning the C–E♭ dyad of Example 19.6c the root C. By confounding the two different theoretical dyads under one Platonic rubric, Rameau believes he is able to assert of something called "THE minor 3rd," both that it is directly generated, like the E–G of Examples 19.6ab, and that it has its lower note as a root, like the C–E♭ of Example 19.6c.

Aristoxenus, who was born about the time of Plato's death, is already sensitive to the Platonic THE in music theory. He writes: "the same notation is employed for the tetrachords hyperbolaion, neton, meson, and hypaton. Thus, the signs fail to distinguish the functional differences, and consequently indicate the magnitudes of the intervals, and nothing more. But . . . mere knowledge of magnitudes does not enlighten one as to the functions of the tetrachords, or of the notes, or the differences of the genera, . . . or indeed anything else of the kind."[6] Aristoxenus's specific critique is relevant to present-day discussions of "THE fourth," when we attempt to use that Platonic rubric to cover both the dyad G–C and the dyad C–F in the context of C tonicity.

6. Oliver Strunk, *Source Readings in Music History* (New York: W. W. Norton, 1950), 30–31.

Fétis may well have been sensitive to Aristoxenus's general critique, when, in the *Traité*, he presented his theory of nineteenth-century European tonality.[7] Intervallic magnitudes, he asserts, do have specific fixed Platonic attributes. But so do the degrees of a given scale or mode. Composing in a key involves matching the Platonic characters of the vertical intervals above the bass, with the Platonic characters of the scale-degrees in the bass. A mismatch gives rise to modulation. Thus, to illustrate "THE perfect fourth" as a "natural interval," free from any tonal context, Fétis displays the dyad C–F.[8] However, when "THE perfect fourth" is to be displayed as consonant in the C major system, Fétis represents it by the dyad G–C.[9] In tonal music, the character of Fétis's Platonic fourth matches the character of his Platonic fifth degree in the bass, not his tonic degree. The Platonic characters that Fétis assigns his intervals and scale degrees seem to be his readings of cultural conventions.

I forego discussing a host of technical and ideological problems with Fétis's system. The theory does respond to the problem that worried Aristoxenus; it provides a context in which vertical intervals of the same acoustic size can have a variety of functional meanings, depending on the scale-degrees over which they appear. But Fétis, when he assigns Platonic THEs to scale-degrees, still falls victim to the more general problem of Platonic rubrics.

Example 19.7

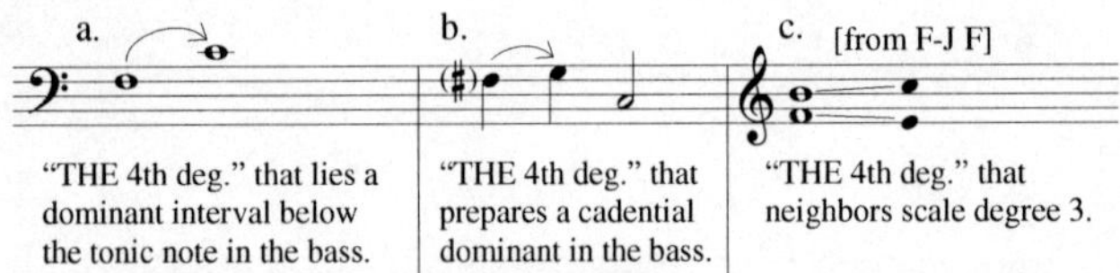

a.
b.
c. [from F-J F]
"THE 4th deg." that lies a dominant interval below the tonic note in the bass.
"THE 4th deg." that prepares a cadential dominant in the bass.
"THE 4th deg." that neighbors scale degree 3.

Examples 19.7a, b, and c show that there are at least three different paradigmatic 4th degrees in C major, even restricting our attention to the bass. The descriptions that underlie the examples are mine. I see no reason why the fourth degree of Example 19.7b can not be raised as well as pure. Fétis runs into conceptual difficulty when he tries to identify all three figures with one paradigmatic Platonic object, "THE fourth degree." The commentary under Example 19.7 gives some sense of his troubles.

FJF talks about one object called "THE fourth degree," that has one "character." This *caractère* "does not exclude the idea of momentary repose." [p. 15; FJF is hearing 19.7a, I think.] "But it may happen that the repose may not occur . . . so that the third, the fifth, the sixth, and the octave can equally well accompany [i.e., sound above] this note." [pp. 15–16; FJF is hearing 19.7b, I think.] The augmented fourth, which is a consonance for FJF, may also accompany "THE fourth degree." FJF gives 19.7c as an example (p. 16). THE character of THE fourth degree is now getting pretty hard to grasp. The augmented fourth of 7c must obey its "appelative" character by continuing as shown, to the event it summons. Is the E of 19.7c then mo-

7. François-Joseph Fétis, *Traité de l'harmonie*, 12th ed. (Paris: Braudus et Cie, 1879).

8. Fétis, *Traité de l'harmonie*, table "des intervalles naturels," page 6.

9. Fétis, *Traité de l'harmonie*, table "des intervalles consonants," page 9.

mentarily reposeful? No, for "THE tonal character of THE third degree [in the bass] is absolutely opposed to any sentiment of repose." [p. 20; as in 19.7c??] And so forth.

The citations are from François-Joseph Fétis, *Traité de l'harmonie*, 12th ed. (Paris: Braudus et Cie, 1879).

In my article on phenomenology and music theory, I went so far as to challenge the Platonic THE in expressions like "THE B♭ in measure 12." I also challenged the word "IS" in statements like "THE harmony of measure 15 IS such-and-such."[10] The issue in greatest generality might be termed "Hidden prior restraints in common linguistic conventions."

Let me turn now to the subject of music theory as a source for analytic metaphors. When we describe the ways in which musical sound seems conceptually structured, categorically prior to any one specific piece, we nevertheless intend our conceptual sound-worlds to be rich in potential metaphors for analyzing specific pieces. At least most of us do. Marion Guck and others have been drawing our attention for some time now to metaphorical discourse for music analysis.[11] But I think it is not generally appreciated how deeply and necessarily metaphorical a music theory becomes, when it is used as the basis for an analysis. The accent is on "*necessarily*." It is not a question of our intending metaphorical discourse or not, when we bring a theory to an analysis. We cannot help it. A spectacular example, to my mind, is afforded by the opening of Milton Babbitt's *Philomel.*

Example 19.8a is an annotated short score and Example 19.8b provides a row-matrix, both courtesy of Richard Swift.[12] The tape voice, which returns again and again to the pitch class E, sings vocalise on the vowel eeeeeee. Looking at measure 1 of Example 19.8a, we see that the voice sings only the first note of row P_0; the accompaniment provides the other eleven notes. In measure 2, the voice sings F–E, the first two notes of row P_1; the accompaniment provides the other ten notes of P_1. In measure 3 the voice sings E♭–D–E, the first 3 notes of row P_{11}; the accompaniment provides the other nine notes of row P_{11}. And so forth.

Example 19.8b provides a theoretical construct that underlies the compositional procedure. The voice sings the first entry on the matrix, and the accompaniment finishes off the first row of the matrix. Then the voice sings the first two notes of the second matrix row, and the accompaniment finishes off the second row. Then the voice sings the first three notes of the third matrix row, and accompaniment finishes off the third row. And so forth.

Example 19.8b suggests a metaphor: the pitch-class structure of the piece is a loom, and the tape voice enters this structure in the act of beginning to weave a tapestry. The metaphor is suggestive and powerful, because weaving a tapestry is a paradigmatic act for the mythic Philomel.

10. David Lewin, "Music Theory, Phenomenology, and Modes of Perception," Chapter 4 in this volume.

11. Marion Guck's key article is "Musical Images as Musical Thoughts: The Contribution of Metaphor to Analysis," *In Theory Only* 5.5 (1981): 29–42.

12. Richard Swift, "Some Aspects of Aggregate Composition," *Perspectives of New Music* 14.2/15.1 (1976): 236–248. The score and matrix are on pages 242–243.

Example 19.8

In Ovid's story (*Metamorphoses,* Book VI), Philomel was raped by Tereus, the husband of her sister Procne. Tereus then cut out Philomel's tongue. But Philomel wove a tapestry depicting the outrage, and sent the tapestry to Procne. Procne understood the tapestry, killed the son she had borne to Tereus, and served the flesh to Tereus in a pie. The sisters fled through the woods of Thrace, pursued by Tereus. All three were magically transformed into various birds.

Example 19.8 cont.

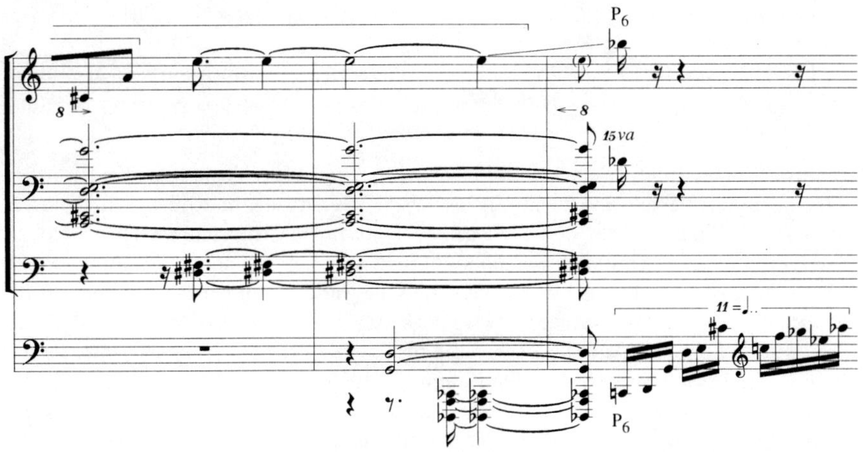

		I											
TAPE	P	0	11	1	9	4	6	3	2	7	8	5	10
TAPE	P	1	0	2	10	5	7	4	3	8	9	6	11
TAPE	voice	11	10	0	8	3	5	2	1	6	7	4	9
TAPE	voice	3	2	4	0	7	9	6	5	10	11	8	1
TAPE	voice	8	7	9	5	0	2	11	10	3	4	1	6
TAPE		6	5	7	3	10	0	9	8	1	2	11	4
		9	8	10	6	1	3	0	11	4	5	2	7
		10	9	11	7	2	4	1	0	5	6	3	8
		5	4	6	2	9	11	8	7	0	1	10	3
		4	3	5	1	8	10	7	6	11	0	9	2
		7	6	8	4	11	1	10	9	2	3	0	5
		2	1	3	11	6	8	5	4	9	10	7	0

E=0-diagonal

John Hollander's text for Babbitt's piece depicts only Philomel's transformation: the mute woman, rushing through the woods, becomes a nightingale. But Hollander writes that he had earlier had a particular interest in the weaving scenes for a possible opera. The tapestry was to be replaced by a wild expressionist painting, but the literary idea was the same.[13]

Hollander's special interest in the weaving scenes echoes the view of Karl Philip Moritz, an eighteenth-century art historian and aesthetician. Example 19.9 cites relevant material from Moritz; I shall put a few excerpts from my translation into the main text here.

13. John Hollander, *Vision and Resonance*, 2nd ed. (New Haven, Conn.: Yale University Press, 1985), 294–297.

Example 19.9

Karl Philip Moritz, *Schriften zur Ästhetik and Poetic,* ed. Flans Joachim Schrimpf (Tübingen: Max Niemayer Verlag, 1962).

DIE SIGNATUR DES SCHÖNEN / In wie fern Kunstweke beschrieben werden können? (1788; pp. 93–103). My thanks to Rienhold Brinkman for drawing this essay to my attention.

The double virgule (//) indicates a new paragraph.

Als *Philomele* ihrer Zunge beraubt war, webte die die Geschichte ihrer Keiden in ein Gewand, und schickte es ihrer Schwester, welche es aus einander hüllend, mit furchtbarem Stillschweigen, die gräßliche Erzahlung las. // Die stummen Charactere sprachen lauter als Töne, die das Ohr erschüttern, weil schon ihr bloßes *Daseyn* von dem schändlichen Frevel zeugte, der sie veranlaßt hatte. // Die Beschreibung war hier mit dem Beschriebenen eins geworden—die abgelöste Zunge sprach durch das redende Gewebe. // Jerder mühsam eingewürkte Zug schrie laut um Rache, und machte bey der mitbeleidigten Schwester das mütterliche Herz zum Stein. // Keine rührende Schilderung aus dem Munde irgen eines Lebendigen, konnte so, wie dieser stumme Zeuge, wirken. // Denn nichts lag ja dem Unglück der weinenden Unschuld *näher*, und war so innig damit verwandt, als eben dieß mühsame Werk ihrer Hände, wodurch sie allein ihr Daseyn kund thun, und ihre Leiden offenbaren konnte. // Eben darum konnte es seiner schrecklichen Wirkung nicht verfehlen. (p. 93)

[When Philomel was robbed of her tongue, she wove the story of her sufferings into a tapestry, and sent it to her sister, who, unrolling it, read the grisly tale in frightful silence. The mute characters spoke louder than sounds assailing the ear, since their very *existence* bore witness to the despicable outrage that had been the cause of their production. Description, here, became as one with the thing described—the severed tongue spoke through the eloquent web. Every painstakingly interwoven thread cried aloud for revenge, and hardened to stone the maternal heart of the concurrently offended sister. No moving description from the mouth of any living person could have produced the effect of this mute witness. For indeed nothing lay *closer* to the misfortune of the weeping innocent, nothing was so intimately connected with it, as just this laborious work of her hands. In that medium alone could she portray her being, and make known her sufferings. Exactly for that reason it could not fail to produce its horrible effect.)

Example 19.10

. . . unsre ganze Aufinerksamkeit mehr auf die Beschreibung selbst, als auf die beschrieben Sache gezogen wird, die wir durch die Beschreibung nicht sowohl kennen lemen, als vielmehr sie ihr *wieder erkennen* wollen. (Moritz, p. 99)

[. . . our entire attention is drawn more to the description itself, than to the things described. We do not so much come to know those things through their description; rather, through the description, we desire much more to apprehend the things [as if (? D.L.)] once more.]

As Moritz says of the tapestry, "the severed tongue spoke through the eloquent web. . . . nothing lay closer to the misfortune of the weeping innocent, nothing was so intimately connected with it, as just this laborious work of her hands. In that medium alone could she portray her being, and make known her sufferings." Just so, I claim, is Babbitt's Philomel speaking through the web of the serial matrix, through those painstakingly interwoven threads. Nothing lies closer to her than the laborious work of composing her piece, through Babbitt as a medium. In that manner alone can she portray her being, and make known her sufferings. To sing Babbitt's piece is to weave her tapestry.

Example 19.10 cites Moritz again, talking later on about the narrative power of visual art. The entire citation applies as well, I think, to Babbitt's serial loom.

The metaphor works both ways, emphasizing that Philomel's loom is a metaphorical matrix. An English dictionary entry, under "matrix," begins: "That which contains and gives shape or form to anything, Anat. the womb."[14] In literary classical Latin the word "matrix" means "mother" in the figurative sense, as a source or generator, as opposed to the literal sense used of the human female parent; however the anatomical sense of the word was increasing in medical and in vulgar usage, and was clearly in place by the time of the later Empire.[15] Philomel's loom, as matrix, gives birth to her tapestry, the fruit of her horrible union with Tereus. Procne, reading and understanding the tapestry, denies her human parenthood, murdering her own biological son. The metaphor of Babbitt's matrix thus brings us into the heart of a sexual relationship between the two sisters.

This approach to the piece opens up a host of suggestive critical questions. Does the live singer weave the piece, like Philomel, while the audience listens like Procne? And does the singer, as weaving Philomel, imagine how Procne will respond when she hears the piece? Or does the singer, like Procne, read an already-created piece? The roles of the two sisters seem to interpenetrate in the live singer, weaving in and out, both telling and reading the story. Is the tape Philomel a different psychological level of the singer? Or is Philomel-on-the-tape an analog for Philomel-in-the-tapestry? Both tape and tapestry unroll, to tell their stories. It seems clear to me that there are elements of all these ideas in the drama, and that is one thing which makes the piece so theatrical. Since the taped voice is always Bethany Beardslee's, the issues are very keen for those of us who first heard Beardslee as the live singer, and are now hearing other sopranos in that role.

Example 19.11a, to explore other theoretical metaphors, transcribes the main theme from the first movement of Schubert's G major quartet. Examples 19.11b through 19.11e provide my analysis using Schenkerian techniques and hence, Schenkerian metaphors. The analysis purports to show how the theme elaborates the structure of an underlying G major triad. The underlying triad is shown at level (e). The analytic method presumes that there IS such a phenomenon, and tells us how to go about constructing or reconstructing it. According to this presupposition, the G major at the end of the theme projects THE SAME (e)-level PHENOMENON as does the G major at the beginning of the theme. The end of the theme thereby metaphorically RETURNS to something from which it departed. More precisely, the end of the theme triggers a dialectic process whereby we can synthesize the ending and the beginning G majors into one higher level phenomenon, THE G major triad of level (e). Here, the term THE is perfectly correct. A special power of the system is that we can metaphorically identify the conceptual triad of level (e) with the acoustic signal that opens the quartet. An enormous structural

14. Funk & Wagnall's, *Standard Universal Dictionary* (New York: Garden City Publishing, 1946), 491.

15. J. N. Adams, *The Latin Sexual Vocabulary*, paperback ed. (Baltimore: The Johns Hopkins University Press, 1990), 105–108.

Example 19.11

significance can thereby be projected metaphorically by an almost instantaneous acoustic event.

Example 19.12 analyzes the theme as a journey on a map of chord or key relations promulgated by Hugo Riemann.[16] A step east on the map moves the root of the harmony a fifth up; a step south moves the root a major third down. Even in equal temperament, the different Gs on the map represent different conceptual places. Hence the theme, according to this theoretical metaphor, ends IN A DIFFERENT PLACE from where it began, rather than RETURNING to its beginning, or metaphorically projecting ONE higher-level phenomenon. We can even say that the theme MODULATES, from G-in-row-2 of the map, to G-in-row-3.

The modulation is carried out by a repeating harmonic progression at the opening of the theme, a progression represented by a strong visual motif on the map-journey. The motif comprises a step east and then a step southeast. It projects a threat

16. Hugo Riemann, *Grosse Kompositionslehre*, vol. 1 (Berlin and Stuttgart: W. Spemann, 1902), 479.

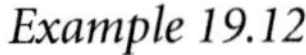

Example 19.12

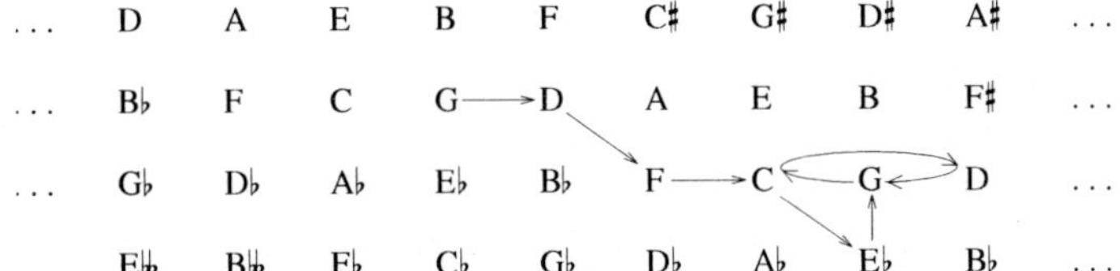

to wander off indefinitely east-by-southeast over the map, never centering around any tonic. Carl Dahlhaus feels the power of this metaphor when he writes that the progression from E♭ to G yanks the harmonic motif "forcefully back from its progression, or regression into the infinite."[17] Dahlhaus is apparently not sensitive to the metaphorical modulation on Example 19.12, when he hears the theme coming "back" to the final G on Example 19.12. I think he is mixing metaphors; the idea that there is only ONE Hegelian G-major triad associated with the theme is strongly present in Example 19.11, but just as strongly absent from Example 19.12.

Example 19.13

It would be the reverse sort of metaphor-mixing, to try to capture the Riemann motif on the Schenker sketch. Among other things, it would lead to excruciating contrapuntal fifths at the same level, as on Example 19.13. Compare Example 19.11b and c, where the structural upper voice descends in parallel sixths, not fifths, over the bass.

Early on, I spoke of music theory as describing "a conceptually structured sound-world that was categorically prior to any particular musical event, score, or experience." I should like now to show how immediately an abstract feature of the conceptual world can impinge on practical musical performing experience. Example 19.14 shows what Elizabeth West Marvin, in a strong and suggestive recent Spectrum article, calls a "dseg."[18] That is the numerical series <02113>.

Example 19.14

The dseg designates the class of all five-event durational series whose first event is shortest, whose third and fourth events, of equal duration, are longer, whose sec-

17. Carl Dahlhaus, "Sonata Form in Schubert," trans. Thilo Reinhard, in *Schubert, Critical and Analytical Studies*, ed. Walter Frisch (Lincoln: University of Nebraska Press, 1986), 10.

18. Elizabeth West Marvin, "The Perception of Rhythm in Non-Tonal Music," *Music Theory Spectrum* 13.1 (1991): 61–78.

ond event is longer yet, and whose fifth event is the longest. A specimen durational series belonging to the dseg class is also shown in Example 19.14.

Example 19.15

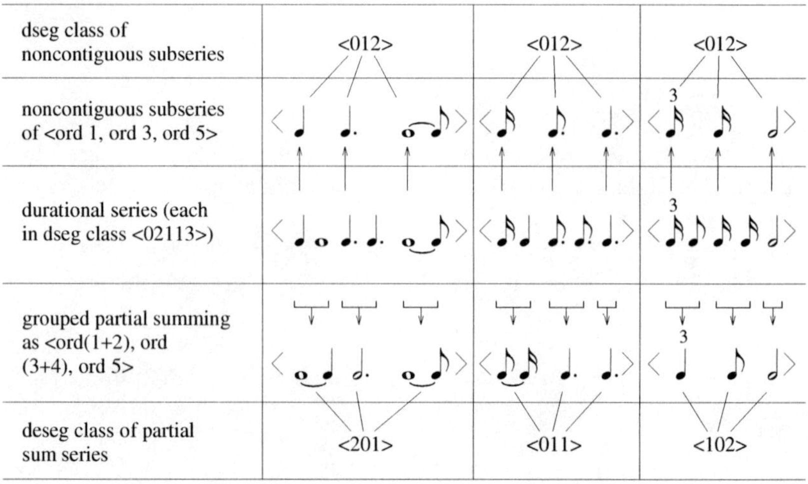

dseg class of noncontiguous subseries	<012>	<012>	<012>
noncontiguous subseries of <ord 1, ord 3, ord 5>			3
durational series (each in dseg class <02113>)			3
grouped partial summing as <ord(1+2), ord (3+4), ord 5>			3
deseg class of partial sum series	<201>	<011>	<102>

If the first, third, and fifth events are extracted from any durational series in this dseg class, clearly the first event will be shortest, the third event next shortest, and the fifth event longest. The three-event subseries will then necessarily belong to dseg class <012>. The top half of Example 19.15 shows such subseries for various durational series of dseg class <02113>; all the subseries are of class <012>, as they must be. Marvin, in her text, calls <012> here a "noncontiguous dsubseg" of <02113>, observing correctly that the notion is of very limited musical interest.

Marvin's pertinent musical example, however, confuses this notion with a notion of great musical interest, one I shall call a *grouped partial summing* from a given durational series. Given a five-note durational series, we can, for instance, construct one grouped partial summing by considering the sum of the first and second durations, then the sum of the third and fourth durations, and, finally, the fifth duration. The bottom half of Example 19.15 shows these grouped partial summings for the various durational series of the figure. Even though all three five-note series are of the same dseg class, the grouped summings belong to different dseg classes.

The bottom row of Example 19.15 thus *refines* the rhythmic contour description of the three five-event series. Indeed by means of the bottom row we can *distinguish* each series from the others. Even though all are in the same five-event dseg class, they are in distinct three-event dseg-classes as regards the partial sum series formed under the indicated grouping.

Similarly, the various three-event series of Example 19.16 can be distinguished, not by their overall dseg classes, which are all the same, but by the various dseg classes of their partial sum series formed under the indicated grouping. This can be a very practical aid to a performer, and not just a performer of recent music. Example 19.16 suggests that, to get the dotted figure of column B precise, you can

Example 19.16

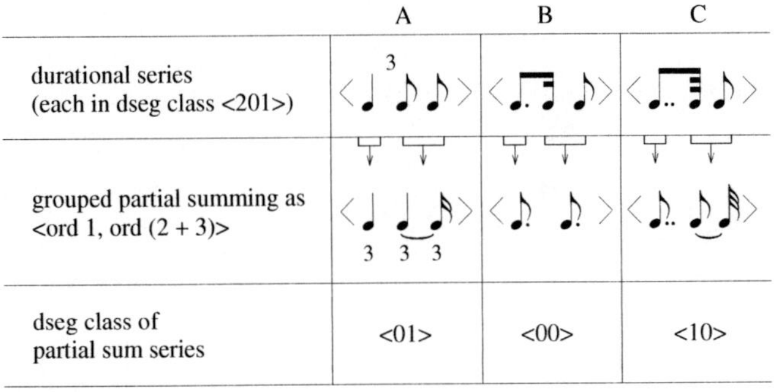

	A	B	C
durational series (each in dseg class <201>)	3		
grouped partial summing as <ord 1, ord (2 + 3)>	3 3 3		
dseg class of partial sum series	<01>	<00>	<10>

imagine it as if in 6/8 meter or Franconian third mode, and then check that the two parts of the gesture feel of equal duration. If the latter part of the gesture feels too long, you are erring in the direction of column A; lengthen your dot. If the latter part of the gesture feels too short, you are erring in the direction of column C; shorten your dot.[19]

Example 19.17 applies the theory to a very specific practical problem: that of performing the opening measure from Stockhausen's first piano piece. The music is given in Example 19.17a. Example 19.17b gives a pertinent mensural series, assigning a unit duration to the opening note of the music. Example 19.17c gives the dseg that pertains to Example 19.17b. 19.17c does not give us much help in preparing a performance.

But partial sum groupings do. Example 19.17d shows a grouping indicated by the composer's notation: the duration of the entire septuplet grouping is equal to the duration of the preceding low E♭ and F combined. Example 19.17e gives the mensural series <1,5,5> into which the measure is thereby articulated. Example 19.17f gives the dseg class of that gesture, <011>: something shorter is followed by two instances of something longer.

Example 19.17e projects a large rhythmic feeling for the measure but is too coarse; Example 19.17b is accurate but too fussy. A very useful intermediate grouping of partial sums can be found in Example 19.17g; the mensural series of sums i given by Example 19.17h. Example 19.17h renotates the sums for easier comparison. The fourth number of 17h′ is a bit more than the third; the fifth number is a bit less than the second. Example 19.17h″ tries to capture the idea by using the symbols alpha, beta, beta-plus, and alpha-minus; here alpha and beta sum to five; so do beta-plus and alpha-minus.

Example 19.17i gives a dseg for 19.17h, modified according to some ideas of Larry Polansky.[20] Here "1 plus" signifies that the fourth duration is about equal to the third, but just a bit longer. The modified dseg interprets the music as a short

19. The eighth-note duration of Example 19.14 is crucial here, not just the preceding long-short pattern. For that reason, Marvin's footnote 13 is not directly engaged, although it is interesting in this context.

20. Larry Polansky and Richard Bassein, "Possible and Impossible Melody: Some Formal Aspects of Contour," *Journal of Music Theory* 36.2 (1996): 259–284.

Example 19.17

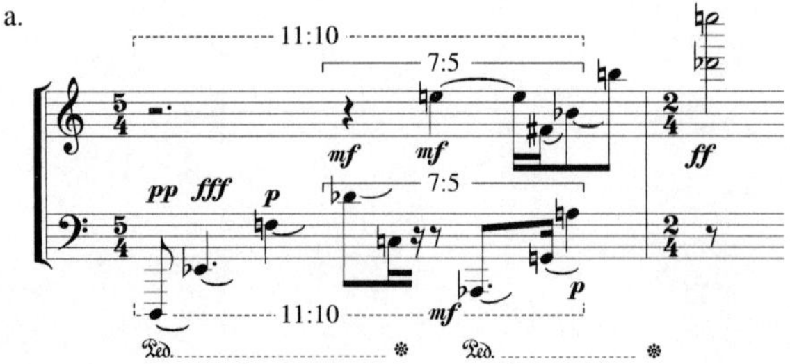

b. < 1 3 2 (5/7) (5/7) (5/7) (15/14) (5/14) (5/7) (5/7) >

c. <2541113011>

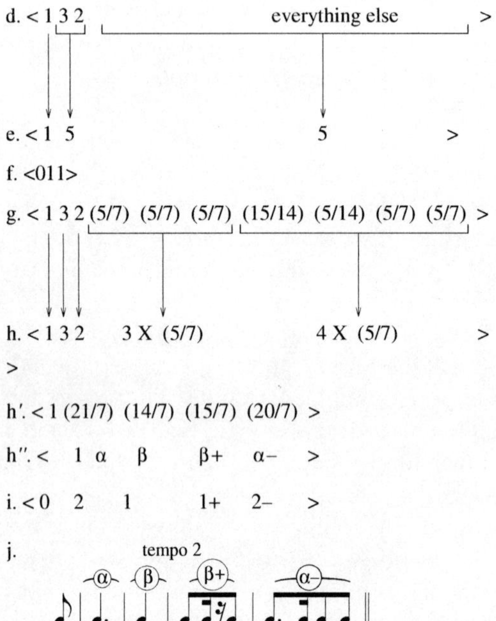

event, followed by a long event, followed by an event of middle length, followed by a slightly elongated middle-length event and a slightly abbreviated long event. Example 19.17j fleshes out the idea. Here, tempo 2 should be chosen so that beta-plus feels like a slightly *ritard*ed beta-span, while alpha-minus feels like a slightly accelerated alpha-span, as it were "going into" the bar line of measure 2. We can have those feelings even though written eighth equals written eighth throughout tempo 2.

Examples 19.17g through j explore only one grouped partial summing, one from among many theoretically available groupings. The particular grouping of 19.17j interacts strongly with the pedaling and with the hexachordal structure of measure 1, a structure that carries on into the piece as a whole.

So the apparently austere machinery of the conceptual a priori theory impinges upon this specific musical experience so as to engage notions of musical grouping, of feeling a bit shorter, of feeling slightly accelerated, going into the bar line, and so forth. And yet the partial sums were indeed, as my harmony student said, "just theory." We theorists know from experience how to tolerate the sarcasm of that remark, but we shall also feel some professional pride in the honor it implicitly confers upon us.

Appendix

After reading my essay, Babbitt sent me a letter approving my notion that weaving symbolism is enacted in the serial technique of *Philomel.* He specifically recalled his "unproduced Broadway musical 'Fabulous Voyage' . . . based on the *Odyssey*," for which "the central scene was that of Penelope at the loom, and the song 'Night Song' [had] the following initial words: 'As I undo what this day I have done.'"

INDEX

When an operatic character or work listed below is also the subject of an entire chapter, only page numbers excluding the chapter in question are given for that character or that work and its composer.

Chapter 1, "Figaro's Mistakes," originally appeared in *Current Musicology* 57 (1995): 45–60.

Chapter 2, "Musical Analysis as Stage Direction," is from *Music and Text: Critical Inquiries*, ed. Steven Paul Scher (Cambridge, England: Cambridge University Press, 1992). Reprinted with the permission of Cambridge University Press.

Chapter 4, "Music Theory, Phenomenology, and Modes of Perception," is from *Music Perception* 3.4 (1986): 327–392. © 1986 by the Regents of the University of California. Used with permission.

Chapter 5, "*Auf dem Flusse*: Image and Background in a Schubert Song," is reprinted from *Schubert: Critical and Analytical Studies*, edited by Walter Frisch, by permission of the University of Nebraska Press. © 1986 by the University of Nebraska Press.

Chapter 10, "Amfortas's Prayer to Titurel and the Role of D in *Parsifal*," is from *19th Century Music* 7.3 (1984): 336–349. © 1984 by the Regents of the University of California. Used with permission.

Chapter 11, "Some Notes on Analyzing Wagner: *The Ring* and *Parsifal*," is from *19th Century Music* 16.1 (1992): 49–58. © 1992 by the Regents of the University of California. Used with permission.

Chapter 14, "Women's Voices and the Fundamental Bass," is from *The Journal of Musicology* 10.4 (1992): 464–482. © 1992 by the Regents of the University of California. Used with permission.

Chapter 15, "Toward the Analysis of a Schoenberg Song (Op. 15, No. XI)," is from *Perspectives of New Music* 12.1 (1973–1974): 43–86.

Chapter 16, "A Way into Schoenberg's Opus 15, Number VII," is from *in theory only* 6.1 (1981): 3–24. © 1981 by the Michigan Music Theory Society. Used by permission of the Department of Music Theory, The University of Michigan.

Chapter 17, "Vocal Meter in Schoenberg's Atonal Music, with a Note on Serial Hauptstimme," is from *in theory only* 6.4 (1982): 12–36. © 1982 by the Michigan Music Theory Society. Used by permission of the Department of Music Theory, The University of Michigan.

Chapter 18, "*Moses und Aron*: Some General Remarks and Analytical Notes for Act I, Scene 1," is from *Perspectives of New Music* 6.1 (1967): 1–17.

Chapter 19, "Some Problems and Resources of Music Theory" is from *Journal of Music Theory Pedagogy* 5.2 (1991): 111–132. Article reprinted with permission of the *Journal of Music Theory Pedagogy*.